ELIHU BURRITT LIBRARY
CENTRAL CONNECTICUT STATE UNIVERSITY
NEW BRITAIN, CONNECTICUT 06050

TEST CRITIQUES: VOLUME V

Daniel J. Keyser, Ph.D.
Richard C. Sweetland, Ph.D.

General Editors

TEST CRITIQUES
Volume V

TEST CORPORATION OF AMERICA

Ref
BF176
T419
1984
V.5

© 1986 Test Corporation of America, a subsidiary of Westport Publishers, Inc., 330 W. 47th Street, Kansas City, Missouri, 64112. All rights reserved. No part of this publication may be reproduced, stored in a retrieval system, or transmitted in any form or by any means, electronic, mechanical, photocopying, recording, or otherwise, without the prior written permission of Test Corporation of America.

LC 84-26895

ISBN 0-9611286-6-6 (v. 1)
ISBN 0-9611286-7-4 (v. 2)
ISBN 0-9611286-8-2 (v. 3)
ISBN 0-933701-02-0 (v. 4)
ISBN 0-933701-04-7 (v. 5)

Printed in the United States of America

CONTENTS

ACKNOWLEDGEMENTS ix

INTRODUCTION xi

TEST CRITIQUES 1

Adolescent Multiphasic Personality Inventory   *Raymond H. Holden, Ed.D.*   3
Adult Neuropsychological Questionnaire   *Arlene I. Rattan, Ph.D., Gurmal Rattan, Ph.D., and Raymond S. Dean, Ph.D.*   6
Alcadd Test   *Susan D. Lonborg, Ph.D.*   9
Attitude to School Questionnaire   *Michael G. Jacobson, Ph.D.*   21
Basic Educational Skills Test   *Daniel W. Stuempfig, Ph.D.*   26
Blind Learning Aptitude Test   *David O. Herman, Ph.D.*   32
Botel Reading Inventory   *Timothy V. Rasinski, Ph.D.*   37
The Bzoch-League Receptive-Expressive Emergent Language Scale   *Jeanette M. Reuter, Ph.D.*   43
Canadian Cognitive Abilities Test   *Charles E. McInnis, Ph.D.*   48
The Child Abuse Potential Inventory   *Keith L. Kaufman, Ph.D. and C. Eugene Walker, Ph.D.*   55
The Children's Depression Inventory   *Lawrence J. Siegel, Ph.D.*   65
Comprehensive Test of Adaptive Behavior   *Jon D. Swartz, Ph.D.*   73
COPSystem Interest Inventory   *Robert H. Bauernfeind, Ph.D.*   76
Curtis Completion Form   *Raymond H. Holden, Ed.D.*   83
Daberon Screening for School Readiness   *Eilleen Kelble, Ed.D.*   86
Decision-Making Organizer   *Louis A. Quatrano, Ph.D.*   90
Detroit Tests of Learning Aptitude-Primary   *Thomas L. Layton, Ph.D.*   94
Developmental Activities Screening Inventory-II   *James E. Stahlecker, Ph.D.*   100
Devereux Elementary School Behavior Rating Scale II   *James L. Carroll, Ph.D.*   104
Dyslexia Determination Test   *Barry S. Anton, Ph.D. and Steven C. Parkison, Ph.D.*   109
Ego-Ideal and Conscience Development Test   *Carol H. Adams, Ph.D.*   113
Evaluating Communicative Competence: A Functional Pragmatic Procedure   *Luella Sude Smitheimer, Ph.D.*   118
Famous Sayings   *Frank J. Ofsanko, Ph.D.*   128
Flowers-Costello Tests of Central Auditory Abilities   *Ronald C. Pearlman, Ph.D.*   137
Fullerton Language Test for Adolescents (Experimental Edition)   *Sheldon L. Stick, Ph.D.*   141
General Aptitude Test Battery   *Jean Powell Kirnan, Ph.D. and Kurt F. Geisinger, Ph.D.*   150

v

vi *Table of Contents*

Geriatric Depression Scale   *Zoli Zlotogorski, Ph.D. and Liora Lurie, Ph.D.*   168
Goldman-Fristoe Test of Articulation   *Forrest G. Umberger, Ph.D.*   172
Gray Oral Reading Tests-Revised   *Lucille B. Strain, Ph.D.*   179
Group Embedded Figures Test   *Zita M. Cantwell, Ph.D.*   189
Hopelessness Scale   *Ronald R. Holden, Ph.D.*   198
The Houston Test for Language Development   *Dina Anselmi, Ph.D.*   203
Howell Prekindergarten Screening Test   *Gene Schwarting, Ph.D.*   209
Individual Phonics Criterion Test   *Danielle R. Zinna, Ph.D.*   212
Instrument Timbre Preference Test   *Richard Colwell, Ph.D.*   216
Interpersonal Language Skills Assessment: Final Edition   *Elizabeth Teas-Hester, Ph.D.*   221
Jesness Behavior Checklist   *Robert J. Drummond, Ph.D.*   226
Joseph Pre-School and Primary Self-Concept Screening Test   *Carol A. Gray, Ph.D.*   230
Learning Disability Rating Procedure   *Ellen Hedrick Bacon, Ph.D.*   237
Learning Efficiency Test   *Virginia E. Kennedy, Ph.D.*   244
Minnesota Infant Development Inventory   *Andrew S. Bradlyn, Ph.D.*   252
Minnesota Satisfaction Questionnaire   *Brian Bolton, Ph.D.*   255
Miskimins Self-Goal-Other Discrepancy Scale   *Diane Ganiere, Ph.D.*   266
Modern Language Aptitude Test   *Charles E. McInnis, Ph.D.*   271
Multilingual Aphasia Examination   *Michael D. Franzen, Ph.D.*   278
Neuroticism Scale Questionnaire   *Elizabeth Taleporos, Ph.D.*   283
Normative Adaptive Behavior Checklist   *Jon D. Swartz, Ph.D.*   287
The O'Brien Vocabulary Placement Test   *Jerry L. Johns, Ph.D.*   290
Offer Self-Image Questionnaire for Adolescents   *Gerald R. Adams, Ph.D.*   297
Partner Relationship Inventory: Research Edition   *Patrick J. Mason, Ph.D. and C. Eugene Walker, Ph.D.*   303
Peabody Developmental Motor Scales and Activity Cards   *John J. Venn, Ph.D.*   310
Perceptual Maze Test   *Mark Stone, Ed.D., ABPP*   314
The Personal Skills Map   *Roger D. Carlson, Ph.D.*   318
Politte Sentence Completion Test   *Elizabeth Taleporos, Ph.D.*   323
Position Analysis Questionnaire   *Glenn E. Snelbecker, Ph.D. and Michael J. Roszkowski, Ph.D.*   326
Preschool Behavior Questionnaire   *Alice G. Friedman, Ph.D. and C. Eugene Walker, Ph.D.*   341
Preschool Development Inventory   *Gene Schwarting, Ph.D.*   348
Primary Measures of Music Audiation   *Richard Colwell, Ph.D.*   351
The Pyramid Scales   *Dale Carpenter, Ed.D. and Ellen Hedrick Bacon, Ph.D.*   358
A Quick Screening Scale of Mental Development   *Theodore R. Cromack, Ed.D. and Jim C. Fortune, Ed.D.*   367
Revised Behavior Problem Checklist   *Tim Roberts, Ed.D.*   371
Riley Articulation and Language Test   *Donald Mowrer, Ph.D.*   378
Riley Motor Problems Inventory   *Russell H. Lord, Ed.D.*   382

Table of Contents **vii**

Rosenzweig Picture-Frustration Study   *Allan L. LaVoie, Ph.D.*   388
Ross Test of Higher Cognitive Processes   *Doris L. Redfield, Ph.D.*   396
School and College Ability Tests II & III   *Travis A. Carter, Ed.D.*   406
The Self-Conciousness Scale   *Timothy M. Osberg, Ph.D.*   412
The Self-Directed Search (1985 Revision)   *Jack L. Bodden, Ph.D.*   419
Shipley Institute of Living Scale   *Raymond G. Johnson, Ph.D.*   425
Somatic Inkblot Series   *Robert C. Reinehr, Ph.D.*   444
Stanford Hypnotic Clinical Scale for Children   *Leonard S. Milling, Ph.D.*   447
Stanton Survey   *Carl G. Willis, Ed.D.*   451
Structure of Intellect Learning Abilities Test-Form P (Primary)   *Alexinia Y. Baldwin, Ph.D.*   458
Test of Early Language Development   *Anne H. Widerstrom, Ph.D.*   464
Test of Early Reading Ability   *Anne H. Widerstrom, Ph.D.*   470
Test of Facial Recognition-Form SL   *Robert L. Heilbronner, Ph.D. and E. Wayne Holden, Ph.D.*   475
Test of Perceptual Organization   *Michael D. Franzen, Ph.D.*   483
Test of Written Spelling   *Connie K. Varnhagen, Ph.D.*   485
Tests of Adult Basic Education   *Robert H. Bauernfeind, Ph.D.*   494
Tests of Mental Function in the Elderly   *Jeanette N. Cleveland, Ph.D.*   499
Thinking Creatively in Action and Movement   *Ellis D. Evans, Ed.D.*   505
Three Minute Reasoning Test   *Roger D. Carlson, Ph.D.*   513
The 3-R's Test   *Jim C. Fortune, Ed.D. and Theodore R. Cromack, Ed.D.*   517
Time Perception Inventory   *Kenneth T. Wilburn, Ph.D.*   522
Time Problems Inventory   *John C. Daresh, Ph.D.*   524
Trait Evaluation Index   *Ardelina Albano Baldonado, R.N., Ph.D.*   529
Trites Neuropsychological Test Battery   *Michael D. Franzen, Ph.D.*   534
The Visual-Aural Digit Span Test   *Raymond E. Webster, Ph.D. and Theodore W. Whitley, Ph.D.*   537
Vocational Preference Inventory   *Robert J. Drummond, Ph.D.*   545
Wachs Analysis of Cognitive Structures   *Nu Viet Vu, Ph.D.*   549
Welsh Figure Preference Test   *G. Cynthia Fekken, Ph.D.*   556
Work Interest Index   *Linda Mezydlo Subich, Ph.D.*   565

INDEX OF TEST TITLES   571

INDEX OF TEST PUBLISHERS   581

INDEX OF TEST AUTHORS/REVIEWERS   588

SUBJECT INDEX   598

ABOUT THE EDITORS   609

ACKNOWLEDGEMENTS

The editors wish to acknowledge the special contributions of our test reviewers. They have done an outstanding job. Our thanks extend from our deep pleasure and gratitude over their participation and the quality of their work. We know many of the contributing reviewers were as "caught up" in this project as we, and are now writing additional reviews for subsequent volumes. And, thanks also go to the test publishers themselves who released information to the reviewers in an expeditious manner.

We also wish to express thanks to the staff members at Test Corporation of America who are involved in this project: Jane Doyle Guthrie, Steve Poole, Tom Johnson, Kelly Scanlon, Barbara St. George, and Marletta McCarty. Eugene Strauss and Leonard Strauss, directors of Westport Publishers, Inc., have given freely and generously their support, encouragement, and business advice. Our indebtedness to both gentlemen is legion.

Finally, we want to express our warmest thanks to our readers. It is their use of *Test Critiques* that gives a final validity to this project. It is our sincerest desire that *Test Critiques* will have a true application for them.

INTRODUCTION

Test Critiques is a fulfillment of a goal of the editors and a continuation of a task begun with the publication of *Tests: A Comprehensive Reference for Assessments in Psychology, Education and Business* (1983), its *Supplement* (1984), and *Tests: Second Edition* (1986). With the *Test Critiques* series, we believe that we have moved into the final phase of this project—to include those vital parts that were not appropriate for our directory. With *Tests: Second Edition* and the *Test Critiques* series, the reader will have a full spectrum of current test information.

When *Tests* was published, a decision was made to leave out important psychometric information relating to reliability, validity, and normative development. Normative data and questions of reliability and validity were considered simply too complex to be reduced to the "quick-scanning" desk reference format desired. It was also apparent to the editors that a fair treatment of these topics would unnecessarily burden less sophisticated readers. More learned readers were familiar with other source books where such information could be obtained. The editors were aware, however, that a fuller treatment of each test was needed. These complex issues, along with other equally important aspects of tests, deserved scholarly treatment compatible with our full range of readers.

The selections for each volume were in no way arbitrarily made by the editors. The editorial staff researched what were considered to be the most frequently used psychological, educational, and business tests. In addition, questionnaires were sent to members of various professional organizations and their views were solicited as to which tests should be critiqued. After careful study of the survey results, the staff selected what was felt to be a good balance for each of the several volumes of critiques and selection lists were prepared for invited reviewers. Each reviewer chose the area and test to be critiqued and as can be noted in each volume's table of contents, some reviewers suggested new tests that had not been treated to extensive reviews. As test specialists, some reviewers chose to review tests that they had extensively researched or were familiar with as users; some chose to review instruments that they were interested in but had never had the opportunity to explore. Needless to say, the availability of writers, their timetables, and the matching of tests and writers were significant variables.

Though the reviewers were on their own in making their judgments, we felt that their work should be straightforward and readable as well as comprehensive. Each test critique would follow a simple plan or outline. Technical terms when used would be explained, so that each critique would be meaningful to all readers—professors, clinicians, and students alike. Furthermore, not only would the questions of reliability and validity along with other aspects of test construction be handled in depth, but each critique would be written to provide practical, helpful information not contained in other reference works. *Test Critiques* would be useful both as a library reference tool containing the best of scholarship but also useful as a practical, field-oriented book, valued as a reference for the desks of all professionals involved in human assessments.

It might be helpful to review for the reader the outline design for each critique

xii *Introduction*

contained in this series. However, it must be stressed that we communicated with each critique writer and urged that scholarship and professional creativity not be sacrificed through total compliance to the proposed structure. To each reviewer we wrote, ". . . the test(s) which you are reviewing may in fact require small to major modifications of the outline. The important point for you to bear in mind is that your critique will appear in what may well become a standard reference book on human assessment; therefore, your judgment regarding the quality of your critique always supercedes the outline. Be mindful of the spirit of the project, which is to make the critique practical, straightforward, and of value to all users—graduate students, undergraduates, teachers, attorneys, professional psychologists, educators, and others."

The editors' outline for the critiques consisted of three major divisions and numerous subdivisions. The major divisions were Introduction, Practical Applications/Uses, and Technical Aspects, followed by the Critique section. In the Introduction the test is described in detail with relevant developmental background, to place the instrument in an historical context as well as to provide student users the opportunity to absorb the patterns and standards of test development. Practical Applications/Uses gives the reader information from a "user" standpoint—setting(s) in which the test is used, appropriate as well as inappropriate subjects, and administration, scoring, and interpretation guidelines. The section on Technical Aspects cites validity and reliability studies, test and retest situations, as well as what other experts have said about the test. Each review closes with an overall critique.

The reader may note in studying the various critiques in each volume that some authors departed from the suggested outline rather freely. In so doing they complied with their need for congruence and creativity—as was the editors' desire. Some tests, particularly brief and/or highly specialized instruments, simply did not lend themselves easily to our outline.

Instituted in Volume III, an updated cumulative subject index has been included in this volume. Each test has been given a primary classification within the focused assessment area under the main sections of psychology, education, and business. The subject index has been keyed to correspond with *Tests: Second Edition.*

It is the editors' hope that this series will prove to be a vital component within the available array of test review resources—*The Mental Measurements Yearbooks,* the online computer services for the Buros Institute database, *Psychological Abstracts,* professional measurement journals, etc. To summarize the goals of the current volume, the editors had in mind the production of a comprehensive, scholarly reference volume that would have varied but practical uses. *Test Critiques* in content and scholarship represents the best of efforts of the reviewers, the editors, and the Test Corporation of America staff.

TEST CRITIQUES

Raymond H. Holden, Ed.D.
Professor, Department of Psychology, Rhode Island College, Providence, Rhode Island.

ADOLESCENT MULTIPHASIC PERSONALITY INVENTORY
Bruce Duthie. Richland, Washington: Pacific Psychological.

Introduction

The Adolescent Multiphasic Personality Inventory (AMPI) is a personality inventory designed particularly for respondents aged 12 to 19. It is parallel in form to the widely renowned Minnesota Multiphasic Personality Inventory (MMPI), which has been used extensively in the past 25 years. Like the MMPI, the AMPI has three validity indicators (Lie, Fake, and Correction [KOR]) and 10 clinical scales: Hypochondriasis (HYP), Depression (DEP), Hysteria (HYS), Psychopathic deviate (PPD), Femininity (FEM), Paranoia (PAR), Psychasthenia (PAS), Schizophrenia (SCZ), Mania (MAN), and Social introversion (SIN). The two-page test booklet includes 133 items that can be answered "True" or "False" by the subject. Scoring can be completed by the examiner by using two paper scoring strips. Sums of the total true and false items are recorded on either the Male or Female scoring grid, and a profile is drawn by connecting the plotted points of the raw scores to obtain T-score equivalents, similar to the MMPI procedure. Interpretation of the AMPI profiles remains questionable, however, because the author advises against using the multi-point coding of the MMPI at present (Duthie, 1985).

Test author Bruce Duthie received his doctoral degree from Texas A & M University in 1976. He has been involved with adolescent alcohol and drug addicts for many years, and for the past five years he has been director of the Adolescent In-Patient Unit at the Mid-Columbia Psychiatric Hospital in Richland, Washington. He has considerable expertise with MMPI, having written the first computer program for this instrument, and he has interpreted over 10,000 MMPI records.

The AMPI was developed over a period of three years and was published in 1985. Duthie provides a rationale for the test's development, reporting that there are only three major tests presently used for the clinical evaluation of adolescents: the Millon Adolescent Personality Inventory (Millon et al., 1977), the Personality Inventory for Children (Wirt et al., 1982), and the MMPI (Dahlstrom et al., 1972). He then reviews the strengths and weaknesses of each of these tests. For example, the Millon Adolescent Personality Inventory is geared to the diagnostic categories of DSM-III, but has no available hand-scoring for quick scoring and interpretation. The Personality Inventory for Children extends into the primary grades, but requires that a person who knows the adolescent quite well complete the test. The advantages of the MMPI are well known, but its length, complexity, and high reading level are disadvantageous to some adolescents. The AMPI was developed to

4 Adolescent Multiphasic Personality Inventory

compensate for some of these weaknesses by its relatively short length, lower reading level, on-site scoring, and scales that are parallel to the MMPI.

Despite these scientific and realistic concerns, however, there is no mention in the manual of a theoretical rationale or closeness to contemporary personality theory. Nor is there any mention of the wide range of possible adolescent self-concepts or life-styles, such as depression, suicide, juvenile delinquency, alcohol or drug addiction, or social withdrawal.

Practical Applications/Uses

The AMPI must be considered in its early stages of development; the test requires much more work to make it a useful instrument for differential diagnosis in adolescents. Therefore, at the present time this instrument should only be used on a trial basis by psychologists who have relatively large subgroups of subjects (such as alcohol or drug addicts) where local norms can be developed. Individual item analysis is possible, although the task of analyzing all the items is rather tedious. Moreover, this test can be used for adolescents aged 10 to 20, but only from white, middle-class populations. This severely restricts its application in lower socioeconomic and minority groups of all kinds.

As noted, the test involves a two-page format of 133 true/false statements. The AMPI can be administered either individually or in groups (10-20 minutes testing time), and requires a psychologist or assistant to proctor. Vocabulary understanding is fortunately pegged at a fourth-grade reading level.

Scoring sheets are 4"x11" strips that appear fragile but are made of non-rip plastic (adopted after much experimentation). "True" items are counted and tallied for each scale, and then the same procedure is used for "false" items. The raw score tallies are graphed on the AMPI profile sheet, with male and female scores recorded on separate graphs. T-scores can then be read from the vertical axis. Time for scoring and graph plotting runs from 15 to 20 minutes per subject. A floppy disk is also provided for administration and scoring, but at present is compatible only with an IBM word processor. (An Apple version is currently under development.)

Although scoring itself is quite simple and quickly accomplished, interpretation of results is another matter. For this process, the examiner should be a clinical psychologist (or master's-level clinician) with a good background in the use and interpretation of the MMPI. Objective interpretation is not yet feasible; clinical judgment needs to be utilized for this task at present.

The AMPI has been the subject of two factor analytic studies, one with 40 high school students aged 16½ and another with 58 high school students also aged 16½. The majority were Caucasion, with an approximately equal mix of males and females. The two analyses produced four factors, of which two were replicated in both studies. Factor 1 is labeled the neurotic factor and includes the DEP, HYS and FEM scales. Factor 2 generally represents conduct disorders and/or antisocial personalities (PPD and MAN scales). To be considered "high" on either factor, the *average* of the scales composing the factor must be 65T or higher. Factor 3 is the validity factor (LIE and KOR). When this factor is high, it strongly indicates the adolescent is trying to place him- or herself in a favorable light. Factor 4 is the psychotic factor (PAR, PAS, SCZ and SIN). High scorers on this factor may be frankly psychotic or showing characteristics associated with borderline personality disorders.

Technical Aspects

The present normative data on the AMPI are inadequate. Only 53 males and 67 females from the Midwest were used, with a mean age of 16.5 years. No information is given as to the normality, psychopathology, or deviance of these subjects, only that they were mainly white and middle to upper-middle class. At present, 500 adolescents from the Midwest are being tested as a normative sample to remedy this serious problem. It is hoped that more complete demographic information will be provided for this sample and that the base will be widened for ethnic minorities and socioeconomic levels.

Test-retest reliabilities were computed using 58 members of the normative sample. A second test administration was given 10 days after the first administration. Pearson product-moment correlations ranged from a low of .63 on the HYS scale to a high of .86 on the PAS scale. The median r for all 13 scales is .76, which the author considers "generally acceptable" but which statisticians would generally consider somewhat on the low side.

Critique

One should regard the AMPI as primarily a research vehicle at present, with its findings considered only tentative, rather than a full-fledged addition to the clinician's armamentarium. However, work is progressing to remedy the test's faults. The skimpy 22-page manual needs considerable revision and enlargment to include results of present studies as they are completed. A codebook similar to the MMPI handbook is scheduled to be completed in the next two years and will include multiple code types (B. Duthie, personal communication, June, 1986).

The AMPI has a long way to go before it can even begin to enjoy the status and prestige of its parent, the MMPI. Nevertheless, there is the promising beginning of a "new boy on the block."

References

Dahlstrom, W. G., Walsh, G. S., & Dahlstrom, L. E. (1972). *An MMPI handbook: Vol. I*. Minneapolis: University of Minnesota Press.
Dahlstrom, W. G., Welsh, G. S., & Dahlstrom, L. E. (1975). *An MMPI handbook: Vol. II. Research applications*. Minneapolis: NCS Interpretive Scoring Services.
Duthie, B. (1985). *Manual for the Adolescent Multiphasic Personality Inventory*. Richland, WA: Pacific Psychological.
Millon, T., Green, C. J., & Meagher, R. B., Jr. (1977). *Millon Adolescent Personality Inventory*. Minneapolis: NCS Interpretive Scoring Services.
Wirt, R. D., Lachar, D., Klinedinst, J. E., Seat, P. D., & Broen, W. E., Jr. (1982). *The Personality Inventory for Children (PIC): Revised format*. Los Angeles: Western Psychological Services.

Arlene I. Rattan, Ph.D.
Research Fellow in Psychology, Ball State University, Muncie, Indiana.

Gurmal Rattan, Ph.D.
Associate Professor of Educational Psychology, Indiana University of Pennsylvania, Indiana, Pennsylvania.

Raymond S. Dean, Ph.D.
Professor of Psychology-Educational Psychology, Director of Doctoral Programs, Ball State University, Muncie, Indiana.

ADULT NEUROPSYCHOLOGICAL QUESTIONNAIRE

Fernando Melendez. Odessa, Florida: Psychological Assessment Resources, Inc.

Introduction

The Adult Neuropsychological Questionnaire (ANQ) is a 54-item semistructured interview designed "to inquire about complaints, symptoms and signs that may suggest underlying brain dysfunction or other organic conditions" (Melendez, 1978). The ANQ is not intended for use as a diagnostic instrument, but rather as an adjunct to a general interview for those referred for a psychological evaluation and/or treatment.

The ANQ was developed by Fernando Melendez as a method of outlining neuropsychological symptomatology. His work with students naïve to neuropsychological phenomenon "lead to the development of a series of questions related to establishing brain-behavior relationships" (Melendez, 1978). The logic behind the ANQ was to provide structure to the intake interview and ensure that all relevant information was collected for later interpretation. Melendez believes that this symptomatology endorsed by a patient can be verified by neuropsychological testing and can provide a basis for any subsequent referrals.

The current version of the questionnaire represents a "refinement of earlier items" (Melendez, 1978); however, no information is given to detail alterations in item content or explain the rationale for these changes. Indeed, no information is provided regarding the development, history, and later revisions of this questionnaire.

The ANQ consists of a manual and a record form comprised of 54 questions to which the subject responds in a yes/no fashion. While Melendez does not rule out self-administration, he strongly advocates administration by a "practitioner." The interviewer/practitioner is instructed to read aloud individual items of the ANQ and encourage the respondent to expand on those symptoms he or she ascribes. The author recommends inquiry into the frequency, intensity, and recency of the phenomenon being endorsed, but no structure is provided to guide the inquiry following most questions. Fortunately, however, there is some guidance, as noted on an item (Question #3) dealing with headaches ("Have you had headaches?"). Following an affirmative response to this question, the patient is asked to respond further with the type, location, and progression of the headache (i.e., "At what time of the day? Right side? Left side? Starting in back or front? What makes them better or worse?"). Unfortunately, this format is not expanded to other items. Although the ANQ was intended to assist the novice practitioner, with such an unstructured format the measure requires considerable knowledge of neuropsychology/neurology to glean necessary information (Dean, 1982).

The manual for the ANQ contains a one-page outline covering the purpose and development of the original questionnaire. The remaining nine pages are a restatement of the questions and the author's interpretation of what the symptoms may represent.

Practical Applications/Uses

Presenting symptomatology and history provide valuable information not often gleaned by formal psychometric measures of neuropsychological functioning. With technicians performing much of the formal testing in many neuropsychological laboratories, the value of a structured interview becomes apparent.

Melendez does not offer guidelines for the appropriate setting for the ANQ; however, because of its nature the measure would seem limited to neuropsychological laboratories. Although unstated, the questionnaire is apparently intended for use with subjects at least 17 years of age. A children's version of the Neuropsychological Questionnaire exists, but again the manual provides no guidelines as to its age appropriateness. The time required to administer the ANQ is not addressed in the manual, although 30 minutes would seem ample.

Interpretive guidelines for each item are included in the manual, with items classified as General Health, Substance Abuse, Psychiatric Problems, General Neurological, Right Hemisphere, Left Hemisphere, Subcortical/Cerebellar/Spinal, and Sensory/Perceptual. Melendez considers a number of items relevant in multiple categories. For example, the question concerning headaches applies to the General Health, Psychiatric Problems, and General Neurological categories. The manner in which responses are integrated into each category is not addressed, nor are references provided. Furthermore, no rationale is given for the choice of individual items included in the questionnaire; apparently, they are based on the author's clinical acumen and subjective judgment.

Although Melendez states that the ANQ was intended for use by students unsophisticated in neuropsychology, he adds a caveat that the user should have an adequate understanding of neuropsychology in order to fully appreciate this measure. Moreover, "the user should possess a fund of basic neuropsychological information in order to utilize this questionnaire to the fullest" (Melendez, 1978). This rationale, then, seems to defeat the purpose of developing such a questionnaire.

Technical Aspects

The ANQ was not designed as a psychometric instrument and does not address reliability and validity. Although the unstructured format would appear to be acceptable as an adjunct intake measure, the total lack of standardization causes one to question the value of this instrument. While the majority of items appear to relate to neuropsychological concerns, research regarding the choice of items or their relationship to neuropsychology would seem elementary for a measure offered for clinical use. With the abundance of available data concerning the relative incidence of neurological symptoms (e.g., Renfrew, 1967), it is disappointing that the author did not consult such data in developing the ANQ.

Critique

To date, no research has been reported using the ANQ. Moreover, a total lack of reliability and validity do little to instill the consumer's faith in this questionnaire. The current need for such a clinical measure is apparent. However, it is somewhat disconcerting that a review of the literature on neurological symptoms is not evident in the ANQ; this would have enhanced its utility. The consumer is therefore unaided in an attempt to interpret the questionnaire or determine its soundness. In sum, the total lack of background, psychometric information, and research makes the clinical utility of the ANQ highly questionable.

References

Dean, R. S. (1982). Test review: Neuropsychological Questionnaire. *Clinical Neuropsychology,* 4(3), 106-107.

Melendez, F. (1978). *Neuropsychological Questionnaire.* Odessa, FL: Psychological Assessment Resources, Inc.

Renfrew, S. (1967). *Diagnostic neurology.* London: E. & S. Livingston.

Susan D. Lonborg, Ph.D.
Assistant Professor of Psychology, Central Washington University, Ellensburg, Washington.

ALCADD TEST
Morse P. Manson. Los Angeles, California: Western Psychological Services.

Introduction

The Alcadd (alcoholic addiction) Test developed by Morse P. Manson is a 65-item test that was originally designed to "rapidly identify the alcoholic addict . . . and attempt the objective recognition of the characteristics of alcoholic addicts" (Manson, 1949, p. 200). The first version of the Alcadd Test, published by Manson in 1949, was actually a 60-item test used to compare alcoholics with nonalcoholics. It is important to note, however, that there is a discrepancy between the description of the test's purpose mentioned in the author's original research and the description provided in the Western Psychological Services publication catalog. Although Manson's intent was to develop a measure that would rapidly identify alcoholics and their characteristics, the publishers state that the Alcadd "is an objective paper-and-pencil test for assessment of the extent of alcoholic addiction. Not an instrument for *detecting* alcoholics, but for measuring areas of maladjustment" (Western Psychological Services, 1984, p. 3). The reason for this discrepancy is not known.

Manson was an active researcher in the area of alcoholism who had a particular interest in the measurement of alcoholic addiction and the behavioral characteristics of the alcoholic. He is also widely known for the development of another alcoholism measure, the Manson Evaluation, which was constructed to differentiate alcoholics from nonalcoholics. The 72 items contained in the test are at least remotely associated with drinking and represent one of seven scales: Anxiety, Depressive Fluctuations, Emotional Sensitivity, Resentfulness, Incompleteness, Aloneness, and Interpersonal Relations. The Manson Evaluation and the Alcadd Test were later combined to form one test, the Western Personality Inventory.

According to the manual, the purpose of the Alcadd Test is threefold: "1) to provide an objective measurement of alcoholic addiction in order to identify individuals whose behavior and personality structure indicated they were alcoholics or had serious alcohol problems; 2) to identify specific areas of maladjustment in alcoholics in order to facilitate therapeutic and recreational activities; and 3) to obtain better insight into the psychodynamics of alcoholic addiction" (Manson, 1965, p. 1).

The original version of the Alcadd was published by Manson in a report of his research on the development of the test. Using findings from clinical and experimental studies on alcoholics as well as his personal observations of alcoholics in hospitals, sanitariums, military services, government services, and Alcoholics

Anonymous meetings, Manson developed a questionnaire of 160 items. This questionnaire was then administered to groups of alcoholics and nonalcoholics that Manson reported to be reasonably comparable with regard to age, gender, intelligence, and socioeconomic status, and to be free from psychoses, illiteracy, or serious physical and mental deterioration. Upon receipt of the completed questionnaires, an item analysis was conducted, and from this 60 items were selected for the Alcadd Test.

These 60 items were then administered to 123 alcoholics (83 males, 40 females) and 159 nonalcoholics (78 males, 81 females). The nonalcoholic group was comprised of both abstainers and social drinkers. Manson's original article did not report how individuals were assigned to each of the two groups (alcoholic and nonalcoholic), though he did indicate that two thirds of the alcoholic subjects came from Alcoholics Anonymous groups and the rest were hospital patients. There was no mention of how the subjects in the nonalcoholic group were selected. All subjects in the original research using the Alcadd were "white, literate beyond the fourth grade level, free of mental deficiency, apparently free of serious deterioration, volunteers, and from Southern California" (Manson, 1949, p. 200).

Results of this study indicated highly significant statistical differences in mean scores on the Alcadd Test for alcoholics and nonalcoholics, with alcoholics receiving higher scores than nonalcoholics. Manson also reported data on the predictive validity of the Alcadd, noting that a cutoff score of 12 correctly identified 97.6% of male alcoholics, and a cutoff point of 14 successfully identified 97.5% of female alcoholics. Additionally, the Alcadd made approximately 97% correct predictions of alcoholics, 94% correct predictions for social drinkers, and 100% correct predictions for abstainers, using the cutoff scores developed by the author for this test. Reliability data provided by Manson (1949) found a Kuder-Richardson coefficient of reliability of .92 for male subjects and .96 for females.

As previously mentioned, one purpose of the Alcadd Test is to identify specific areas of maladjustment (emotional, social, behavioral, etc.) in alcoholics. To do so, Manson subjectively analyzed the original Alcadd data in order to identify five behavioral clusters or subscales that would provide further information about the alcoholic's situation. These clusters included: 1) Regularity of Drinking, 2) Preference for Drinking Over Other Activities, 3) Lack of Controlled Drinking, 4) Rationalization of Drinking, and 5) Excessive Emotionality.

A high score on the Regularity of Drinking scale generally indicates a pattern of steady drinking. The second scale, Preference for Drinking Over Other Activities, refers to exactly that—the alcoholic person often prefers to drink over other activities such as entertainment, dinners, concerts, and so on. One common characteristic of alcoholic persons is their inability to control their drinking; that is, in many cases in which an alcoholic begins drinking, he or she is unable to stop. A high score on the third scale, Lack of Controlled Drinking, indicates an individual's poor control over his or her drinking behavior. Rationalization of Drinking refers to the tendency of alcoholic persons to provide many "good" reasons, or excuses, for their drinking behavior. A high score on this scale indicates an individual's frequent lack of insight into the real reasons for his or her excessive or uncontrolled consumption of alcohol. The final scale, Excessive Emotionality, is based on the fact that alcoholics often experience numerous emotional difficulties, such as immature personality, hypersensitivity, depression, worry, or difficulties with emotional adjustment. High scores on this Alcadd scale typically indicate poor emotional control.

The Alcadd Test was apparently revised in 1965 with the addition of five "filler" items to the original test items. Four of these items appear at the beginning of the test, preceding the original 60 items, and appear unrelated to the use of alcohol. The fifth new item appears at the end of the test and contains information that is related to alcohol. None of the five new items are used in scoring the test. There is no mention in the manual of the reason for this addition to the original 60 developed by Manson, nor is there an explanation of the way in which these new test items were developed.

The Alcadd Test is designed to be self-administered, and as such may be administered either individually or in groups. The 65 test items are presented in a true/false format. The entire test booklet is worded very simply in language that is easy to understand. The directions to the examinee request the individual's cooperation and honesty and also indicate that there are no right or wrong answers to test items.

The Alcadd Test is presented in the form of a four-page, 8½"x11" booklet. The first page includes demographic questions (e.g., name, age, test date, occupation, marital status, education) and specific directions to the test-taker; the second and third pages contain the 65 test items as well as spaces for each of the individual's true or false answers; and the fourth page provides the Alcadd Psychograph, which is used for profiling the individual's total test and subscale scores.

Practical Applications and Uses

As mentioned previously, Manson originally developed the Alcadd Test as a screening device that could rapidly and easily identify the alcoholic as well as recognize the severity of maladjustment that accompanies the addiction. Given this purpose, the Alcadd could be utilized as an initial screening measure in agencies and institutions that serve large numbers of patients or clients. Manson proposed that state hospitals, Veterans' Administration hospitals and clinics, and inpatient alcoholism treatment centers might benefit from such an easily administered and scored alcoholism test. (To date, most of the research using the Alcadd Test has been conducted with patients in each of these facilities.) Additionally, physicians, psychologists, therapists, and social workers may find the information provided by the Alcadd Test useful in the assessment and treatment of individuals who are served by their agencies.

It is important to note however, that numerous concerns have been raised about the use of the Alcadd Test, specifically with regard to normative data, reliability and validity, and the method by which the test was constructed. (These concerns will be addressed later in this review.) Clinicians and researchers who choose to use the Alcadd with their patients or subjects should familiarize themselves with these methodological concerns.

In the test manual, Manson also suggests that the Alcadd might be useful to personnel executives in the identification of alcoholics prior to employment, training, or military service. Such a use of this test ought to be approached with utmost

12 Alcadd Test

caution, particularly in light of the instrument's limitations and the ethical considerations of the professional persons involved.

Clinicians may find this test useful in their assessment and treatment of individuals who seek out treatment for alcoholic addiction. In this context, the Alcadd may be helpful in identifying the severity of their drinking problems (e.g., regularity, lack of controlled drinking, etc.), as well as difficulties in emotional adjustment. Because of the transparent nature of the items on the Alcadd Test, it is quite easy for patients to falsify their responses. For example, if the Alcadd were to be used in deciding whether a patient needs inpatient alcoholism treatment, the patient who was resistant to such treatment could easily deny his or her alcohol problems in responding to items. In short, the Alcadd Test is probably more useful with patients who are willing to admit to their difficulties with alcohol and potentially much less informative when used with patients who are not yet willing to acknowledge alcohol problems should such problems exist.

The manual contains no reference to the age group for which the Alcadd is intended; however, research using the test has primarily focused on the adult population. Even though the language used in the test is relatively easy to understand and the reading ability required is that typically found in school children, there are at least two problems that arise when used with age groups other than adults is suggested. First, some of the test items focus on activities more commonly experienced by older adolescents and adults. More importantly, normative data is not available regarding the use of the Alcadd Test with populations other than adult males and females.

The test manual does not specifically identify ways in which the Alcadd Test can be adapted or changed in its administration. Conceivably, test items could be read aloud to those with visual or reading impairments. To date, the Alcadd has not been published in languages other than English.

Administration can be conducted by any individual (e.g., proctor, secretary, therapist, researcher, etc.) who is trained to do so; however, the interpretation of test results to patients ought to be provided by a clinician who is familiar with the assessment and treatment of alcoholism. The administration procedures outlined in the test manual are quite clear and easy to follow.

Initially, the role of the test examiner simply involves providing the examinee with the Alcadd materials. The manual indicates that the examiner may wish to read the directions to examinees in order to ensure their understanding and cooperation. Once the Alcadd has been completed, the test examiner can easily score it within 2 to 3 minutes by using the provided template. An individual's scores are then plotted on the Alcadd Psychograph, which allows for comparison of the individual examinee with data from the normative group. Although examinees are encouraged to work as quickly as they can, they are also informed that they will be given as much time as they need to complete the test. Typically, individuals can easily finish the test items within about 5 to 15 minutes.

The instructions for scoring the Alcadd Test are presented clearly in the test manual. Scoring procedures can be learned immediately and typically require about 10 minutes to read the manual and score the first test. After an individual has scored the first test, subsequent scoring takes no more than 2-3 minutes. To date, there are no machine-scoring services provided for the Alcadd. Given the speed with which the test can be hand scored, other scoring methods are likely to be found unnecessary.

Intrepretation of Alcadd Test results are based on objective scores that are compared with normative data provided on the Alcadd Psychograph. Examinees receive a total test score and separate scores for each of the five subscales measured by the test. Norms are provided separately for male and female examinees. Apart from providing normative data, there are no specific instructions in the manual regarding intrepretation of test data. Interpretation of test scores appears limited to providing examinees with information about how their test scores (total test and subscales) compare with the means for alcoholic and nonalcoholic persons. Also available is information about the critical, or cutoff, scores for male and female alcoholics.

Beyond these normative data, examinees may be provided with descriptive information regarding each of the five subscales. The clinician or researcher using the Alcadd Test for the first time may find the manual quite lacking in specific instructions for the interpretation of test results. Given this, the clinician who provides the test interpretation ought to have a good working knowledge of alcoholism and addiction in order to answer questions raised by examinees regarding their test results, particularly as such results pertain to larger questions regarding alcohol addiction.

Technical Aspects

Numerous reliability and validity studies have been performed with the Alcadd Test. Initial reliability data on the Alcadd will be examined here. Manson's (1949) original work reported Kuder-Richardson reliability coefficients of .92 and .96 for male and female examinees, respectively. The Kuder-Richardson formula provides a measure of internal consistency; in other words, the extent to which each test item correlates with every other item. Items that are highly correlated tend to sample from the same behavior domain. In light of this finding, Manson's reliability data indicate that in his particular sample of examinees, items on the Alcadd Test tend to be highly correlated with one another and as such tend to sample from the same behavior domain.

Other researchers have produced similar reliability coefficients (Barillas, cited in Jacobson, 1976; Dunlop, 1978; Murphy, 1956) that provide support for the internal consistency of items on the Alcadd Test. Data reported by Barillas suggest that, in one sample, reliability coefficients on the Alcadd were slightly higher for the alcoholics ($r = .89$) than for social drinkers ($r = .75$).

Results of numerous validity studies on the Alcadd Test are available for discussion here. Manson (1949) provided data to support the validity of the Alcadd in successfully discriminating alcoholic persons from nonalcoholics. His original research indicated that when a cutoff score of 12 on the Alcadd was used, only 2.4% of male alcoholics were *incorrectly* diagnosed as nonalcoholics; or conversely, 97.6% of male alcoholics were successfully identified as such. Similarly, only 6.6% of social drinkers were incorrectly identified as alcoholics on the basis of their Alcadd scores, while none of the abstainers included in the study were incorrectly diagnosed as alcoholic. Results for female examinees were quite similar. When a cutoff score of 14 on the Alcadd was used, 97.5% of female alcoholics were successfully identified; only 5.2% of female social drinkers were incorrectly identified as alcoholic, and none of the female abstainers were incorrectly identified.

One problem with Manson's methodology that has been consistently raised by other authors concerns the use of a sample of alcoholics predominatly comprised of Alcoholics Anonymous (A.A.) members. At least one researcher (Murphy, 1956) has provided data that suggest these subjects had significantly higher scores on the Alcadd test than did active alcoholics, a finding that supports other researchers' (Dunlop, 1978; Honzik, 1953; Hunsicker, 1953; Fowler & Bernard, 1965) hypotheses that Manson's choice of research subjects may have negatively skewed (increased the preponderance of high scores) the normative data on the Alcadd Test. Murphy (1956) suggested several reasons that A.A. members may have higher scores on the Alcadd: (a) their higher scores may be associated with a more accurate memory of drinking habits that those who have more recently been excessive in their consumption of alcohol; (b) there may be a tendency for A.A. members to maximize their previous difficulties with alcohol as a way of measuring progress, in contrast to recent addicts who may be more likely to minimize their drinking habits as a way of reducing guilt; (c) the A.A. members in Manson's particular sample may simply have had more deviant drinking habits than those of the active alcoholics who were tested in this study.

In an effort to provide additional data concerning the validity of the Alcadd Test, Barillas (cited in Jacobson, 1976) conducted a study with 135 male subjects; 52 were alcoholics, 54 were social drinkers, and 29 were total abstainers. The data indicated that all subjects were generally equal with regard to occupation, age, and level of education. Barillas concluded that the Alcadd Test is a valid instrument for the successful discrimination of alcoholics from social drinkers, alcoholics from total abstainers, and social drinkers from abstainers.

Murphy (1956) conducted an investigation that used female subjects in revalidating the Alcadd Test. The purpose was two-fold: 1) to provide further normative data on the use of the Alcadd with female examinees, and 2) to collect data on a broader continuum of severity of alcohol use, ranging from no use to obviously excessive use. Four groups of examinees were identified: active alcoholics, A.A. members who had maintained at least 6 months of continuous sobriety, social drinkers (whose alcohol use ranged from daily use to any time more than once a month), and abstainers (who never or rarely used alcohol). The A.A. members were asked to respond to the questionnaire based on their drinking habits prior to participation in A.A. groups. The results of this investigation demonstrated significantly different Alcadd test means for each of the four groups, and thus provided further support for the validity of the instrument with female examinees. Murphy, however, did acknowledge that because the Alcadd Test is quite transparent in its purpose, its use becomes somewhat limited in any testing situation in which subjects have some motivation to be evasive in their responses.

Because most of the previous research with the Alcadd had been conducted in inpatient settings or with A.A. members, Fowler and Bernard (1965) were primarily interested in the utility of this instrument in identifying alcoholics in an outpatient alcoholism treatment setting. In particular, they hypothesized that both

A.A. members and chronic hospital patients "are likely to be somewhat different from the undiscovered alcoholic with respect to awareness of and willingness to disclose the extent of pathological drinking" (Fowler & Bernard, 1965, p. 29). Their choice of alcoholics in an outpatient alcoholism clinic as research subjects was intended to yield "norms on alcoholics who would more nearly resemble the 'hidden alcoholic'" (p. 29).

Fowler and Bernard identified 297 male and 34 female alcoholics who were just becoming aware of the seriousness of their own alcohol problems. All were asked to complete the Alcadd Test, and test results were then compared with the normative data provided by Manson (1949). Interestingly, for the two groups of males (Manson's and Fowler and Bernard's), the differences in test score means were not significant; however, the test score means were quite different for the two groups of female examinees. The Fowler and Bernard research suggested that the test score means for outpatient women were significantly lower than the mean scores for Manson's female A.A. members and hospitalized alcoholics.

These researchers went on to suggest that in light of these differences, future Alcadd Test users might wish to consider lowering the cutoff score for females from 14 to 12. They indicated that application of Manson's cutoff scores of 12 for males and 14 for females would correctly identify 99% of the male alcoholics in their sample and 92% of the female alcoholics. Utilizing a cutoff score of 12 for females, rather than the 14 suggested by Manson, would subsequently improve the correct identification of female alcoholics to 96%. Additionally, the authors note that the distribution of scores for the outpatient sample of male and female alcoholics more nearly resembled that of a normal, bell-shaped curve and as such was less skewed than the distribution of scores in Manson's original normative sample.

An investigation by Ross (1973) examined the relationship between the severity of alcoholism, as measured by the Alcadd Test, and an individual's reported fears, worry, and anxiety. The subjects in this investigation were 38 male inpatients at a Veterans' Administration hospital that had expressed interest in participating in an alcoholism rehabilitation program. All of these subjects had been diagnosed as alcoholic. Ross found that the mean Alcadd score for these examinees was 44.89, a mean well above that demonstrated by Manson's (1949) male alcoholics. Additionally, significant positive correlations were found between the anxiety and depression measures and the severity of alcoholism indicated by the Alcadd Test scores. Ross suggested that "the average subject in the sample tested was not attempting to hide his difficulties, was generally quite anxious, and had high scores on the severity of alcoholism scale" (1973, p. 826). Generalizations based on Ross's research are quite limited, in part due to the very small sample size used in the study and because of the investigator's failure to screen subjects for other possible mental disorders besides the diagnosis of alcoholism.

A final study investigating the validity of the Alcadd Test was conducted by Dunlop (1978). The author's reported purpose was three-fold: 1) to examine possible demographic effects such as age and education on Alcadd scores; 2) to investigate the properties of the five Alcadd subscales; and 3) to develop a distribution of scores in a much larger sample of male alcoholics. The subjects were 917 Veterans' Administration inpatients who were voluntarily admitted to the alcoholism treatment program and diagnosed as alcoholic by professional staff members. Data for

16 Alcadd Test

this study was collected during an 11-year period. Once collection of the Alcadd test data was completed, several statistical analyses were performed.

Initially, correlations were calculated to determine relationships between the five subscales. All correlations were highly significant and indicated that the subscales were strongly related to one another as well as to the total test score. Next, the distribution of scores for subjects in the Dunlop study were compared with the distribution of scores reported by Manson (1949). Although the two distributions appeared to be quite similar, the distribution of data in the Dunlop study was slightly less skewed than that of the Manson research. Finally, age and education effects were analyzed. Dunlop's results suggested that the Alcadd test score means for those individuals in the youngest age group (20-29) were significantly greater than those of subjects in the three oldest groups (40-49, 50-59, 60-69). When education effects were examined, it appeared that those subjects who had at least some high school education reported greater Alcadd mean scores than those who had some college education. These differences were significant for all subscales except Preference for Drinking.

In summary, these findings indicate that, in this particular sample, subjects reported fewer alcoholic symptoms and behaviors as age and educational level increased. A particular strength of the Dunlop study is its use of a very large sample size; however, results of this investigation can only be generalized to Veterans' Administration hospital inpatients. The author did not indicate whether all subjects were male; however, given the small number of female veterans at the time period in which the data was collected, it is likely that the majority of the subjects, if not all, were male. If this is the case, then results regarding age and education effects are further limited to use of the Alcadd with male Veterans' Administration patients.

Two other research projects have investigated the utility of the Alcadd Test in measuring treatment effects. Lanyon, Primo, Terrell, and Wener (1972) used pre- and posttest means on the Alcadd to measure the effects of an inpatient alcoholism treatment program. Twenty-one male alcoholic patients in a state hospital were given one of three treatments involving aversion and desensitization activities or group discussion. All subjects were asked to complete the Alcadd prior to treatment, immediately following treatment, and again at a 6- to 9-month follow-up. Results demonstrated that five of the seven subjects who had participated in the aversion/desensitization treatment were abstinent from alcohol at the 6- to 9-month followup. Significantly more of the subjects in this condition remained abstinent than did subjects in either of the other two conditions. These changes in drinking behavior were clearly recorded in the Alcadd Test scores for each of the groups.

A second study by Ornstein (1978) investigated the utility of the Alcadd Test in predicting posthospital (posttreatment) drinking behavior. The subjects were 352 male participants in a 90-day alcoholism rehabilitation program at a Veterans' Administration hospital. All subjects participated in daily group counseling sessions, A.A. meetings, and other program activities. The subjects were asked to complete the Alcadd Test upon admission to the rehabilitation program and also upon discharge. Ornstein reported that the general characteristics of his sample were very similar to those reported by Manson (1949), except for the fact that 12.2%

of the subjects in the Ornstein study were black. At the 2-year follow-up after discharge, subjects were contacted by phone or through the mail and were asked about their drinking behavior since leaving the hospital. When possible, family members of the subjects were contacted in order to verify the subjects' self-reports. Following this procedure, the sample was divided into five categories: *Abstainers*—those with absolutely no posthospital drinking; *Improved*—those whose drinking was markedly below that of their prehospital behavior; *Unimproved*—those who had returned to same or similar patterns of drinking; *Unclassified*—those for whom there was insufficient or unverified information about posthospital drinking; and *Deceased*.

Ornstein then examined individuals' scores on the Alcadd completed upon admission to the program. He reported no significant pretest differences between the five groups who were identified on the basis of their 2-year follow-up reports, and he therefore concluded that the Alcadd *admission* scores were not useful in predicting posthospital drinking habits as measured within the first 2 years after discharge. On a more promising note, however, there were some significant differences in the mean *discharge* scores between the five groups. In particular, those individuals who were classified as Abstainers at the 2-year follow-up tended to have the lowest Alcadd scores at discharge. This was true not only for the total Alcadd score, but also for each of the five subscale scores. These research data appear to indicate that Alcadd Test scores gathered at discharge may be useful to clinicians in predicting posthospital drinking behavior or abstinence.

The Ornstein study also investigated the relationships between age of examinee and Alcadd scores and between length of hospital stay and Alcadd scores. These data confirm a finding discussed previously: younger subjects tend to report higher admission scores on the Alcadd. One possible explanation offered by Ornstein is that either younger patients may be more inclined to exaggerate their drinking behavior or perhaps they are more willing to acknowledge a drinking problem.

One of the issues that makes comparison of the numerous reliability, validity, and normative studies difficult is the fact that many of these studies sample very different populations. One of the investigations reviewed here used male and female patients at an outpatient alcoholism treatment facility as subjects (Fowler & Bernard, 1965). Other researchers have collected data from male subjects who are inpatients at Veterans' Administration hospitals (Dunlop, 1978; Ornstein, 1978; Ross, 1973). Still others have utilized volunteer subjects from Alcoholics Anonymous groups and/or inpatient alcoholism treatment centers (Lanyon et al., 1972; Manson, 1949; Murphy, 1956). An overwhelmingly large percentage of subjects in research on the Alcadd Test are male; only three studies have investigated its efficacy in identifying female alcoholics (Fowler & Bernard, 1965; Manson, 1949; Murphy, 1956). Only one study specifically identified the presence of black individuals (12.2%) in its sample (Ornstein, 1978). Another utilized patients who were involuntarily committed to a state mental institution (Canter, 1966). Finally, several investigations have indicated age effects on Alcadd scores, with younger subjects typically reporting higher Alcadd scores than older subjects (Barillas, cited in Jacobson, 1976; Dunlop, 1978; Ornstein, 1978). Additionally, Parker (1969) used the Alcadd Test in examining the relationship between sex-role disposition and drinking disposition in younger male subjects (mean age = 20.3), and presented mean

Alcadd scores for young adults in abstainer/moderate drinker, heavy drinker, and quasi-alcoholic categories. The wide range of populations sampled also interact with a diverse group of research methodologies in making systematic comparisons of the data nearly impossible. At the same time, each of these studies provides clinicians and researchers alike with clues about the efficacy of the Alcadd Test as well as ideas for future research, and several offer alternatives to the Alcadd norms provided by Manson (1949). Further research is clearly needed before the Alcadd Test user can place increased confidence in interpreting test results for members of special populations such as women, outpatients, individuals with dual diagnoses of alcoholism and other psychiatric disorders, ethnic and cultural minorities, and adolescents, to name a few.

Critique

Several issues relevant to the use of the Alcadd Test by clinicians and researchers include the following: the utility of the test manual, the developmental history of the test, its reliability and validity data, its normative data, and cautions to the consumer.

The Alcadd manual provides clear and concise information about the purposes of the test, descriptions of test scales, and instructions for administration and scoring. Examiners will generally find this information adequate in preparing them to administer and score the test. More serious difficulties arise in interpreting the test and in familiarizing oneself with the test's development as well as its reliability and validity data. The manual's brevity (two pages) may be the initial problem. The manual provides no specific instruction to the user regarding test interpretation; thus, the interpreter is left to his or her own creativity and expertise when explaining test results to the examinee. Three sections of the manual indirectly assist the user in this task: one section very briefly describes each of the five scales; a second provides a brief summary of Manson's reliability and validity data; and a third provides Manson's table of norms. It is important to note, however, that nowhere in the manual are there instructions about how this information should be used with the patient; therefore, presentation of test results should only be provided by a professional person qualified to interpret normative, reliability, and validity data.

A second serious omission in the manual is the lack of references regarding the reliability and validity of the test. In fact, there is no citation in the manual regarding Manson's (1949) study from which this section of the manual has been derived. Therefore, any user of the test must start from scratch in locating research studies that have investigated the efficacy of the Alcadd Test. From these two perspectives, the Alcadd Test manual is not particularly "user friendly."

In numerous ways, the developmental history of the Alcadd Test remains unclear. For example, Manson (1949) states that 160 questions were constructed and administered to a sample of alcoholics and nonalcoholics. He then states that "upon item analysis, 60 diagnostic items were selected for the final questionnaire" (p. 200). In what manner was this item analysis conducted? Secondly, though Manson has described very generally how the alcoholic sample was selected, there are no explanations regarding the method by which the nonalcoholic sample was selected. Furthermore, the author identified five basic behavioral clusters or subscales on the test, and yet apparently these five subscales were in some way subjectively derived. How? The test was revised in 1965, and five additional nonscorable items were added. The reasons for this revision are not identified.

As mentioned previously with regard to norms, numerous authors have raised questions about the use of a large number of Alcoholics Anonymous members in the original alcoholic sample, particularly in light of subsequent data that suggest that A.A. members may report significantly higher Alcadd scores and thus inflate the test's cutoff scores. Many researchers have indicated the need for new Alcadd norms for special populations, such as women, outpatients, ethnic minorities, adolescents, and others.

Further research on the reliability and validity of the Alcadd is warranted. Several studies have investigated the test's internal consistency, but there have been no reported investigations concerning test-retest reliability or stability of test scores over time. Some of the initial work on the utility of the Alcadd in treatment planning and in the evaluation of treatment effects has been promising and should be continued. As is the case with any research, replications of existing studies and any new research undertaken would greatly strengthen the usefulness of previous findings. A factor analytic study of the items contained in the Alcadd Test would provide one empirical method for testing Manson's subjective hypotheses about the existence of five subscales or behavioral domains. This factor analysis could provide more empirical information about factors underlying the 65 items on the test. Published research on the Alcadd Test has dropped off dramatically in the last decade, raising questions about its perceived utility and appeal to researchers.

Nonetheless, the Alcadd Test has enjoyed a history of both active research and clinical use. For this pattern to continue, more attention to the aforementioned issues is warranted. The Alcadd Test's strengths include the ease with which it is administered and scored, its potential utility as a rapid screening device, and its broad appeal to clinicians and researchers. However, in a thorough review of the research on the Alcadd Test, Jacobson (1976) remarked:

> We do believe that additional developmental work is needed, as is further research on validity and reliability, before the Alcadd can be considered a widely applicable diagnostic or assessment instrument. In the interim, consumers should be cautious in their application of the test in circumstances or populations differing from those of the original developmental studies, and diagnostic inferences should be guarded. (p. 42)

This reviewer wholeheartedly concurs. Despite nearly a 40-year history, research on the development and efficacy of this instrument is, in many ways, still in its infancy.

References

Canter, F. M. (1966). Personality factors related to participation in treatment by hospitalized male alcoholics. *Journal of Clinical Psychology, 22,* 114-116.

Dunlop, T. W. (1978). The Alcadd Test: An extension of norms. *American Journal of Drug and Alcohol Abuse, 5,* 211-220.

Fowler, R. D., & Bernard, J. L. (1965). Alternative norms for the Alcadd based on outpatient alcoholics. *Journal of Clinical Psychology, 21,* 29-33.

Honzik, C. H. (1953). Alcadd Test. In O.K. Buros (Ed.), *The fourth mental measurements yearbook,* (p. 74). Highland Park, NJ: Gryphon Press.

Hunsicker, A. L. (1953). Alcadd Test. In O.K. Buros (Ed.), *The fourth mental measurements yearbook* (pp. 74-75). Highland Park, NJ: Gryphon Press.

Jacobson, G. R. (1976). *The alcoholisms: Detection, diagnosis and assessment.* New York: Human Sciences Press, Inc.

Lanyon, R. I., Primo, R. V., Terrell, F., & Wener, A. (1972). An aversion-desensitization treatment for alcoholism. *Journal of Consulting and Clinical Psychology, 38,* 394-398.

Manson, M. P. (1949). A psychometric determination of alcoholic addiction. *American Journal of Psychiatry, 106,* 199-205.

Manson, M. P. (1965). *The Alcadd Test: Manual of directions and norms.* Los Angeles: Western Psychological Services.

Murphy, D. G. (1956). The revalidation of diagnostic tests for alcohol addiction. *Journal of Consulting Psychology, 20,* 301-304.

Ornstein, P. (1978). The Alcadd Test as a predictor of post-hospital drinking behavior. *Psychological Reports, 43,* 611-617.

Parker, F. B. (1969). Self-role strain and drinking disposition at a prealcoholic age level. *Journal of Social Psychology, 78,* 55-61.

Ross, S. M. (1973). Fear, reinforcing activities, and degree of alcoholism: A correlational analysis. *Quarterly Journal of Studies on Alcohol, 34,* 823-828.

Western Psychological Services. (1984). *1985-86 Catalog.* Los Angeles: Author.

Michael G. Jacobson, Ph.D.
Assistant Professor, Department of Elementary Education and Reading, Western Illinois University, Macomb, Illinois.

ATTITUDE TO SCHOOL QUESTIONNAIRE
G. P. Strickland, R. Hoepfner, and S. P. Klein. Hollywood, California: Monitor.

Introduction

The Attitude to School Questionnaire (ASQ), a group-administered measure for assessing attitudes toward school of children in kindergarten through second grade, was developed under the supervision of the UCLA Center for the Study of Evaluation (CSE). According to Strickland, Hoepfner, and Klein (1976), authors of the test manual, the ASQ was developed in response to the paucity of instruments available for measuring school-related attitudes in young children. They suggest that the failure of research studies to indicate a clear and consistent relationship between positive attitude toward school and academic achievement is instrument related.

The original ASQ was developed by Alpert and Klein (1969) from the Children's Attitudinal Range Indicator, which was used in the Westinghouse evaluation of the Headstart program (1969). The ASQ was revised by Strickland (1970) through factor analysis and item analysis to reduce the original 53-item scale to 28 items that assess three school-related attitudinal dimensions: attitude to school, attitude to school work, and attitude to school personnel. A study confirming the factor structure found by Strickland was conducted by Skager (1974), who further reduced the ASQ to 15 items. The final form of the questionnaire was applied in a California preschool evaluation study by Hoepfner and Fink (1974).

The ASQ contains 15 picture items, presented one per page in two forms: a boy's form featuring a boy as the main character, and a girl's form featuring pictures of a girl. Children are given oral descriptions of school-related situations while they observe a cartoon depiction of the situation. Children indicate their attitude by circling a drawing of a happy, neutral, or sad face. Therefore, the ASQ is not dependent on children's reading ability as no reading is required. The vocabulary used in the oral presentation of school-related situations corresponds to the Rinsland and Thorndike lists of most common words for first-graders. Colored pages are used to avoid dependence on children's number skills, and the use of second-person narration minimizes identification problems associated with third person narration. In developing the illustrations for the ASQ, the authors attempt to make characters racially universal so that all racial groups will be able to identify with the cartoon faces.

Practical Application/Uses

The ASQ has several applications for researchers, teachers, and counselors. The instrument is particularly useful in research situations that attempt to establish the nature and degree of the relationship between school-related attitudes and school achievement, IQ, SES, anxiety, creativity, and other variables in young children. Even if the ASQ were not able to demonstrate this relationship, it could be used to evaluate the affective outcomes of schooling. For example, it would be possible to use the ASQ to measure attitude changes resulting from school programs, innovative curricula, differing classroom management and instructional techniques, different teacher personalities, and the effects of political or sociological decisions externally imposed on schools (e.g., busing to achieve integration). Similarly, the ASQ could be used in cross-cultural studies in which differences in attitude toward educational programs and school organization are of importance.

Moderator variables such as demographics, the score on another test, interests, motivation, and attitudes make it possible to predict the predictability of different individuals with a given instrument (Anastasi, 1976). The ASQ may serve as a moderator variable to differentiate groups on the basis of attitude in order to facilitate other analysis.

The normative data presented in the ASQ test manual were derived from the kindergartners (N = 9,936), first- (N = 11,130), and second-graders (N = 10,229) included in the California State Preschool Program evaluation (Hoepfner & Fink, 1974). The majority of children participating in the study were economically disadvantaged. The manual presents item data including alternative response percentages, means, standard deviations, and item-to-total correlations. These analyses are reported by grade for girls and boys and for the total sample. Item-to-total correlations ranged from .29 to .61, and more than half the correlations were .50 or better. Standard deviations ranged between .49 to .86 for the total sample, indicating little variability in response. Although the manual also presents percentile norms for ASQ total scores for the three grade levels and for both sexes, a further description of the norming population in terms of socioeconomic status and racial composition would be helpful.

No special training or equipment is needed to administer the ASQ. The test can be administered by researchers and counselors as well as by teachers, for whom the administration procedures are detailed in the test manual. The ASQ is available in English only, although Hoepfner and Fink refer to the presentation of the oral text in both English and Spanish. The procedures for group administration include suggestions for the physical arrangement of the testing environment, special considerations for the age of the respondents, and a script that presents the school-related situations to evoke student attitude. The examiner is cautioned not to lead students into making a particular response by tone of voice or facial expression. The time required for testing is not specified in the manual. Strickland (1970) reports testing sessions for a longer version of the ASQ to be two sessions of approximately 20-25 minutes each. Promotional literature for the ASQ suggests that administration takes about 20 minutes.

The directions for scoring are discussed in the manual. Each happy face is awarded two points, a neutral face receives one point, as does an item for which there is no response, and an unhappy face receives no points. Total scores range from 0-30 points. Three or more consecutive omissions warrant the discontinuation of scoring. The higher the total score, the more positive the attitude toward school. Although normative data provided in the manual are extensive in terms of item statistics, the examiner's interpretation of test scores would be facilitated by a more detailed description of the sample population.

Technical Aspects

Strickland (1970) presents the results of a principal-axis factor analysis of the responses to the 53-item ASQ of 263 first-graders from a middle-class suburb. Of the eight first-order factors originally hypothesized, four (attitude to school, to school work, to teacher, and to principal) were found. In a second-order factor analysis of the original eight factors, three factors were obtained (attitude toward school, toward school work, and toward school personnel). Alpha coefficients for the second-order factors were .59, .69, and .77, respectively.

Skager (1974), in a study of 2,207 first-grade Los Angeles children responding to a 28-item version of the ASQ, found a factor structure similar to that of Strickland. Internal consistency (KR 20) was .92 for males, .91 for females, and .90 for the total sample. A test-retest coefficient of .13 was found for the 178 first-graders who took the test twice after an interval of 7 months.

Skager employed the same 28-item ASQ in a study of attitude change involving 91 first-graders and 89 second-graders. Internal consistency estimates (alpha) ranged from 0.70 to 0.77 (first-graders) to 0.65 to 0.73 (second-graders). Intercorrelations between the three ASQ factors were relatively high (0.45 to 0.67, first-graders; 0.44 to 0.57, second-graders) and supportive of the unidimensionality of attitude toward school in young children. Skager also found no significant difference in ASQ factors for those first-graders (N = 41) and second-graders (N = 53) tested a year later as second- and third-graders.

In an evaluation of the California State Preschool Program involving over 30,000 students in 148 elementary schools, the current 15-item ASQ was employed to assess motivation and attitude toward school (Hoepfner & Fink, 1974). Reported alpha coefficients were .81 for kindergarten (N = 9,936), .78 for first grade (N = 11,130), and .76 for second grade (N = 10,229). The ASQ was correlated with a measure of student's task orientation. Reported correlations ranged between –.11 to –.17, indicating a very modest relationship between the ASQ and task orientation.

According to most psychometric guidelines for discriminating among groups, the ASQ is reliable in terms of internal consistency. The relatively low stability coefficient (.13) found by Skager (1974) may reflect the dynamic nature of attitude toward school in young children (Ball, 1971). The validity information given for the ASQ is derived exclusively from factor analyses conducted by Strickland and by Skager, each reporting eight first-order and three second-order factors. The use of contrasting groups, common in attitude measurement, would offer additional construct validity data for ASQ. Correlating the ASQ with other measures purported to tap the same attitudes (such as teacher ratings of student attitude, rating children under simulated conditions, and non-reactive/unobtrusive measures) could be used to supplement the factor-analytic data available for the ASQ.

Critique

There are a variety of difficulties involved in the measurement of the attitudes of young children. In fact, the attitudes of any age group can only be assessed on the basis of observable behavior, certainly an indirect and inexact process. There are several methods that are useful in assessing the attitudes of young children. Few of them can be used with any degree of confidence, however, if one's objective is to make an assessment of the attitudes of a particular child. Rather, if measurements are carefully made, groups of children can be confidently assessed.

The ASQ is a carefully developed paper-and-pencil measure for assessing the attitudes of groups of children to school. Reliability data for the ASQ are more than adequate and reflect the care with which the test developers have considered the constraints in test construction dictated by the limited skill level of young children. Validity information is restricted to the results of factor analysis and should be supplemented by other measures.

A problem often encountered in the assessment of young children's attitude toward school is that youngsters are eager to please adults. They will say what they believe adults want them to say. This social desirability issue is particularly important with regard to the ASQ as the test manual calls for the instrument to be administered orally by the classroom teacher. Similarly, those studies that have contributed to the development of the ASQ suggest that young children's attitudes toward school are unidimensional and general in nature (Skager, 1974) rather than related to specific school subjects or a school's administrators or teachers. Strickland (1970, p. 15) suggests that to the young child, the school and the teacher are indistinguishable. Simply, the administrative procedures stipulated for the ASQ contribute to the charge of experimenter bias and may affect the degree of variability found in the test development studies. If the instrument is to be used in research, it must be administered by trained neutral examiners.

Constructing attitude tests for young children inevitably generates a number of compromises for the test developer. Certainly this is the case regarding the ASQ. Young children may be prone to rendering a set response when confronted with a perplexing situation such as those presented in the ASQ. A well-constructed test will try to overcome the problem by disguising the intent of the questions and varying the response format. Clearly, the ASQ developers must also consider the examinees (in this case kindergartners, first-, and second-graders) and their need for a test format that is easily understood and consistent. Therefore, response set is not controlled.

One of the standards by which an assessment instrument is judged is its frequency of use. Since its formal publication a decade ago, the ASQ does not appear in the educational research literature assessing young children's attitude toward school or assessments of the correlation between school-related attitudes and school achievement. Curiously, the UCLA Center for the Study of Evaluation, in its recommendations of instruments to measure young children's attitudes toward school, does not list the ASQ (Henerson, Morris, & Fitz-Gibbon, 1978).

Attitudes are often ignored in evaluations because of problems of instrumentation. The attitudes of young children toward school are extremely important and may forecast the quality of the future school-child relationship. Given the exercise of caution regarding administration procedures and the limitations of the norming population, the ASQ is nonetheless a valid and reliable general measure of young children's attitude toward school and offers perhaps the only alternative in a field in which there is indeed a paucity of available instrumentation.

References

Alpert, N., & Klein, S. P. (1969). *The Attitude To School Questionnaire*. Unpublished manuscript, University of California at Los Angeles, Center for the Study of Evaluation, Los Angeles.

Anastasi, A. (1976). *Psychological testing* (4th ed.). New York: Macmillan.

Ball, S. (1971). *Assessing the attitudes of young children toward school*. (ERIC Document Reproduction Service No. ED 056 086)

Henerson, M. E., Morris, L. L., & Fitz-Gibbon, C. T. (1978). *How to measure attitudes*. Beverly Hills: Sage.

Hoepfner, R., & Fink, A. (1974). *Evaluation study of the California State Preschool Program*. (ERIC Document Reproduction Service No. ED 043 919)

Skager, R. (1974). Evaluating educational alternatives. *New Directions for Education, 4*, 97-120.

Strickland, G. P. (1970). *Development of a school attitude questionnaire for young children*. (ERIC Document Reproduction Service No. ED 043 919)

Strickland, G. P., Hoepfner, R., & Klein, S. P. (1976). *Attitude To School Questionnaire manual*. Hollywood, CA: Monitor.

Westinghouse Learning Corporation. (1969). *The impact of Headstart* (Vol. 1). Athens, Ohio: Ohio University.

Daniel W. Stuempfig, Ph.D.
Associate Professor of Psychology, California State University, Chico, California.

BASIC EDUCATIONAL SKILLS TEST
Ruth C. Segel and Sandra H. Golding. East Aurora, New York: United Educational Services, Inc.

Introduction

The Basic Educational Skills Test (BEST) is an individually administered informal screening tool designed to help classroom teachers assess elemental academic skills and perceptual abilities of students from the end of the first through fifth grades. Assessment is conducted in the areas of reading, writing, and mathematics. Items are constructed to reveal the presence or absence of both a skill component in one of the three academic areas and the ability to process information through one or more of the following learning modes: auditory, haptic, visual, and speech. Students respond to items by answering questions verbally or performing very brief academic tasks. After carefully observing the child's response, the examiner judges whether an item was completed correctly and which processing ability appeared to be involved in any unsuccessful efforts. By examining patterns of skill and processing deficiencies associated with failed items, the teacher or parent presumably will find guidelines for how teaching might be conducted to meet the learning abilities of the student.

The co-authors of the BEST, Ruth Segel and Sandra Golding, are both experienced elementary school teachers. Segel has published several articles on assessment of learning and on intervention strategies, and Golding holds a master's degree in education from Boston University. At the time they developed the BEST they each had taught for 10 years or more and worked with children who had moderate special learning needs. They continue to work at the same elementary school near Boston, Massachusetts, where they function as language arts learning specialists.

In their role as learning specialists the authors developed informal tasks that they found useful in assessing children's learning needs. Following a central processing model of learning they analyzed the modalities through which children receive and respond to information. Through careful observation of students' performance of basic academic tasks they then related learning deficiencies to one or more of the learning modalities. Although this method of assessment was done informally, the need to document assessment results in writing was apparent. The authors were also impressed by the need for teachers to have useful clinical procedures that could be related directly to teaching methods. Their compilation and editing of those tasks they believed from their own experience to be most useful led to the development of the BEST items. Because the instrument was designed to be an informal clinical tool, no norms were established and no studies of reliability or validity were conducted.

The original screening procedure, first published in 1979 in a single form, is the only version of the BEST available, and it continues to be used by its authors and other teachers. No specific plans for revising the instrument have been made.

The items are contained in a 5½" x 8½" spiral-bound flip-book, with one item on each cardboard page. Each item consists of one or several written requests that direct the student to answer a question or perform a brief cognitive or psychomotor task. For some responses the child writes answers on paper.

The instrument is divided into three sections of reading, writing, and mathematics, each containing 25 items. Skill components assessed by items in each section have been identified in the manual as follows:

Reading: receptive and expressive language, eye coordination and eye span, figure-ground, visual-spatial order, vocabulary, general information, organization of thought, relation of symbol to sound, building words, understanding sentences, and reading interpretations. Typical questions from this section ask children to define, read, and form words and to read, construct, and tell the meaning of sentences.

Writing: ability to express oneself on paper, motor control, memory (auditory, visual, and haptic), integration (auditory-motor, visual-motor, and auditory-visual), and expression of original thoughts. Copying and drawing figures and letters, spelling complete words, and filling in letters that are missing from words are illustrative of tasks to be performed.

Mathematics: concept of time, space, size, volume, and zero, perception of shape, memory of symbols, number sense, operations, order and spatial organization, number facts, place value, visual-spatial ability, structure of numbers, left-right orientation, and logic. Representative items are questions about temporal or physical dimensions of common events and objects and simple story problems in arithmetic.

The skills just described presumably are mastered by most students by the fifth grade. Although the BEST is recommended for use with children as young as the end of the first grade, some items are clearly too difficult for a majority of these younger students to perform correctly.

The test administrator presents items one at a time and either reads them aloud or allows the student to read them to the extent that he or she is able. An examiner's major responsibility lies in his or her assessment of the skills exhibited and the learning processes employed in the child's performance at each task.

The form on which the examiner records the student's performance is a four-page booklet. Following the front page, on which background information and a performance summary can be written, are three pages for marking which items or parts of items in each section were completed successfully. The academic skill component and processing abilities associated with each item are also listed, and a small space is provided for remarks by the examiner.

In addition to an introduction to the instrument and brief instructions for administering items and marking responses, the manual contains four sample protocols and an analysis of the learning process as perceived by the authors. This analysis is applied to every item in each of the three sections.

28 Basic Educational Skills Test

Practical Applications/Uses

The BEST is designed to be a quickly administered diagnostic screening tool that "enables the teacher to analyze quickly and realistically the specific academic needs of each student and points out the modalities involved in each skill" (Segel & Golding, 1979, p. 7). By using this instrument the teacher is to be able to detect students who are "at risk" academically because of late development or neurological dysfunction.

The items themselves have been developed around an analysis of learning that stresses the functions of the basic systems, or modalities, whereby information is received, processed, and responded to. As mentioned, these modalities of learning are auditory, visual, haptic, and speech. Each item is also associated with a basic skill component that is required to achieve satisfactorily in one of the academic subjects. For example, in the reading section the item "a. How would you describe your favorite chair? b. How would you describe snow?" is related to the component "ability to verbalize ideas" of vocabulary skills. An incorrect response to the requests could be due to a possible deficiency in the speech modality. Likewise, the item "After reading sentences a and b, arrange words properly in sentences. a. The dog barks. b. The man hits the dog. c. angry dog man The bites the" is associated with the component "variation of meaning according to order of words" within the skill of understanding sentences. Failure at this task could involve problems in visual memory or in the ability to express ideas in the speech modality. Thus, what this device attempts to assess are absences of basic component skills in reading, writing, and mathematics and deficiencies in abilities to work with information in the four learning modalities.

The user should bear in mind that although the tasks require performance of components of an academic skill, they also contain components of other skills, such that failure at an item may not necessarily indicate lack of the particular academic component being assessed. For example, the task of copying shapes is related to perception of shapes in the manual, but lack of motor control could also result in failure at that item. In addition, a receptive language ability is involved in all the tasks, yet it is not listed as a possible problem for any of them. Likewise, in the attempt to detect disabilities in learning modalities, the modalities involved in failure to perform a task may be difficult to identify when any of several disabilities could result in deficient performance.

Once the attempt to identify academic learning problems has been completed, the information is supposed to be used to tailor appropriate teaching strategies. Unfortunately, the manual does not give any indication of how teachers who apply information from the instrument might alter their teaching. Examples of modifications that have lead to greater learning for the "at risk" student would be useful.

Because the BEST is designed to help diagnose basic learning problems in academic subjects, it is used almost exclusively in elementary schools. Usually a learning specialist would be in charge of a child's academic assessment and would be most likely to use this instrument. Use of this screening procedure or selected parts of it could also take place in the regular classroom as part of a quick informal assessment of learning difficulties.

As indicated previously, the examiner's manual indicates that students from the end of first through the fifth grades may be assessed with the BEST. Although the items students are required to perform are basic, there are a number of language and mathematics skill tasks that most normal younger children will not be able to perform correctly. Therefore, the instrument may be more appropriately used with children in the upper range of suggested grade levels. Low-functioning children above fifth grade could also be assessed for their lack of basic component skills. Regardless of the age of the student, however, the assessment is directed toward those who are suspected of having delays in development or other learning disabilities, not those who are emotionally handicapped.

The instrument is administered individually, and each section requires 15 to 20 minutes to complete. The three sections do not have to be given in any particular order, nor all on the same day. Normal nondistracting testing conditions should prevail.

No special training is required to learn to administer the BEST. As the critical part of the assessment lies in the careful observation of the way the child responds, the examiner should be well versed in the authors' analysis of the tasks to be performed and have considerable experience working with learning handicapped children. After studying the manual and test items, most learning specialists and some teachers would be qualified examiners.

Administration procedures are informal. The items may be read by the student or the examiner, or the student may be assisted in reading them. An exception to these options in administration are several items in the reading section that demand implicitly that the student read. Although elaborate instructions for administration are not necessary, more explicit directions on when paper and pencil are permitted would be helpful, as would a response sheet for items that require the children to use a pencil. No instructions about order of administration, degree of prompting permitted, or time limits are given; thus, the presentation of the instrument to children could differ widely from one examiner to another, and there is no indication given of the variation in results that could be expected to occur across different examiners.

Scoring is highly dependent on the observation skills and judgment of the examiner. He or she must determine both if the child has displayed the major skill demanded by the item and which learning modality is involved when the task is not performed correctly. To assist in assessing the quality of the child's response, a guide is provided with the copy of the item that the examiner reads when presenting it. The guide asks the examiner to consider whether the child's response demonstrates that he or she possesses certain skills or abilities. It may also state the correct answer, but it does not in all cases offer explicit criteria for scoring. For instance, one task in the writing section is to copy a sentence. The corresponding guide for the teacher is "Can the child complete the following tasks: a. Form letters correctly? . . . b. Space words properly? c. Copy words correctly?" Standards for correct formation and proper spacing are left to the judgment of the examiner.

Once the administrator has assessed the quality of the child's performance, he or she checks either the "yes" or "no" column alongside the number of each item or part of an item on the recording form. According to a note on this form "all facets of each question must be answered correctly to merit a 'yes' check." Although this direction is clear for most items, the criterion for a "yes" may leave a question in the minds of examiners on some items. In the sentence copying item previously mentioned, for example, a student could reverse one letter, crowd two words together, and perhaps omit one letter from a word. Because all aspects of the three tasks were not performed correctly, three "no" checks might be given, yet the examiner could be convinced that the child has demonstrated ability to do the same three tasks. Clear scoring standards for each item are needed to help achieve consistency in judging whether a skill has been attained.

If the examiner checks the "no" column for the task, he or she must use clinical judgment to determine which basic learning process was related to the difficulty. Because possible problem areas associated with each item are written on the recording form, the teacher needs only to circle the one or more areas identified. For example, in the aforementioned item the ability areas that might be circled include fine-motor control and spatial awareness under the haptic modality, and discrimination under the visual modality. The marking process can be done while the instrument is being administered.

After the protocol has been completed, scoring is a simple matter of taking a minute or two to total by hand the number of "no" checkmarks and the number of circled areas under each of the four learning modalities. There are no score transformations to perform. Provision is made on the front page of the recording form for displaying a summary of the totals.

There are two aspects to the interpretation of the results. One is the identification of children who are "at risk" academically because of learning disabilities. The other is a diagnostic/prescriptive interpretation that can be used to indicate appropriate teaching strategies to be used with the learner. According to both the manual and statements on the summary part of the recording form, the number of "no" checks on the protocol suggests different degrees of a child's need for help. Failure on approximately two-thirds, half, and one-third of the tasks indicates respectively, high and moderate probabilities of being "at risk" and a need for careful monitoring of the student. Further explanation of the meaning of high and moderate degrees of being "at risk" is not given, and no data are provided to demonstrate the basis on which the cutoff points for the different interpretations were determined. This lack of information, along with possible uncertainty in administration and scoring, dictate that extreme caution be exercised if one is using the interpretation guidelines for identifying "at risk" students. Teachers should adopt criteria based on their own experience with the BEST for judging students to be at risk.

The use of the results for the diagnostic/prescriptive function relies on the teacher's clinical judgment. Areas of deficiency in academic skills are determined by examination of specific responses. Weaknesses in use of one or more of the learning modalities are also determined on the basis of inspection of the pattern of deficiencies indicated on the protocol. Although no numerical guidelines are offered, the examiner is instructed to study the frequency with which abilities in each modality were involved in failure at items. On the basis of careful examination of patterns of deficiencies in academic skills and learning abilities, the teacher is to devise modifications in instruction to meet the identified needs of the student. However, guidelines for matching student needs with instructional content or teaching methods are not provided. Clearly, skill in interpreting areas of need is related to one's training and experience in working with learning disabled children and one's understanding of the learning model on which the BEST is constructed.

To make the most useful diagnostic/prescriptive interpretations, the teacher should have several years of elementary level teaching experience and instruction in the central processing model of learning.

Technical Aspects

This instrument is strictly an informal screening procedure and no normative data or information on its reliability or validity is available. To the knowledge of the authors, the test publisher, and this reviewer, there are no published studies concerning the BEST, although the test is listed in *Tests in Print III* (Mitchell, 1983).

Critique

Although the BEST is an informal instrument, potential users still must evaluate whether it accomplishes what it claims. Unfortunately, there is no evidence presented to support the assertions that the device detects children "at risk," identifies deficiencies in academic skills and learning abilities, or helps teachers choose appropriate teaching strategies. In order to allow for a meaningful interpretation of the results, satisfactory reliability in scoring should be demonstrated and cutoff scores for each of the three sections should be related to school performance characteristics of defined groups of students.

In spite of these drawbacks, the BEST may be of value to teachers and learning specialists. The items can be used as if they were criterion-referenced, and specific skills that a student does not perform can be identified. Results from the BEST may also help call attention to a clear weakness in one of the learning modalities. Further assessment of skill and processing deficiencies may then proceed with other tasks devised by the teacher. The teacher may also modify the items in order to "test the limits" (Sattler, 1974), a procedure that allows one to identify conditions under which a student may be able to complete a task successfully. To obtain the most value from the instrument, however, the teacher should develop his or her own standardization (Brown, 1983). After administering and scoring the BEST according to consistent standards, the teacher can compare the test performance of different types of students in the local school district and relate it to school achievement and response to different teaching strategies. In this way the specific validity and utility of the instrument for the user may be determined.

In conclusion, the value of the BEST as a screening and assessment tool depends primarily upon the skills and insight of the teacher. Therefore, any teacher who uses this tool needs to seek objective evidence for how effectively it assists in the assessment of the learning needs of his or her students.

References

Brown, F. G. (1983). *Principles of educational and psychological testing* (3rd ed.). New York: Holt, Rinehart and Winston.
Mitchell, J V. (1983). *Tests in print III*. Lincoln, NE: Buros Institute of Mental Measurements.
Sattler, J. M. (1974). *Assessment of children's intelligence*. Philadelphia: W. B. Saunders.
Segel, R. C., & Golding, S. H. (1979). *Basic Educational Skills Test*. East Aurora, NY: United Educational Services.

David O. Herman, Ph.D.
President, Measurement Research Services, Inc., Jackson Heights, New York.

BLIND LEARNING APTITUDE TEST
T. Ernest Newland. Champaign, Illinois: University of Illinois Press.

Introduction

The Blind Learning Aptitude Test (BLAT) is an individually administered test of "learning potential" for blind children aged 6 to 16 years. Other instruments have been used for this purpose in the past, such as the Verbal Scale of the Wechsler Intelligence Scale for Children or the Hayes adaptation of the Binet (Hayes, 1950), but as the author stresses, these instruments may be overly sensitive to the child's acculturation. While this may be true of many existing tests, the BLAT was especially constructed to minimize dependence on previous learning.

Young blind children are thought to enter school with a particularly wide range of acculturation. Some have been raised through their preschool years in a protected and restricted environment, while others have had broader experiences. To reduce as much as possible the test's cultural loading, the author has made use of several types of nonverbal items involving geometric shapes and their interrelationships. These are presented as raised dots and lines embossed on sturdy stock, and thus can be perceived by touch alone. The manual claims that practice in braille reading is not necessary to perceive the elements of the test items, although it is implied that some tactual discrimination training is helpful. The directions to the subject comprise the only overtly verbal aspect of the test, and the child indicates each chosen answer by pointing.

The items are cast in six different styles, all of them familiar from other nonverbal tests of reasoning. All involve perceiving similarities and differences and completing figure series and matrices. The items of a given style are presented in their own section of the test, and each section is introduced by two unscored training items.

Each item is presented on a single page, bound into a loose-leaf binder. The flexible pages appear to be of a heavy plastic material that will resist tearing and other kinds of wear. Although all items are cast in a multiple-choice format, the examiner's role is as active as with other individually administered intelligence tests. The BLAT manual gives specific directions for presenting the items that should be helpful to all examiners and most particularly to those who are inexperienced in testing the blind.

A separate response sheet is provided for recording the subject's answers, computing the total score, and recording incidental observations during the testing session.

Practical Applications/Uses

In the BLAT manual and two early articles (Newland, 1964a, 1964b), the author refers again and again to the importance of measuring the processes that make school achievement possible, rather than focusing on various aspects of achievement itself. The absence of curriculum-related content on the BLAT, the avoidance of verbal labels like "circle" or the names of letters in the directions to the child, and the use of pointing to indicate answer choices all reflect this orientation. Because the BLAT makes few demands on formal educational experiences, it should provide fair assessment to blind children from varied backgrounds.

The extremely detailed directions to the examiner are commendable in their coverage. Techniques for introducing the child to the task, guiding the child's fingers across the stimulus fields, presenting the training items that usher in each new item set, commenting on the child's performance, and handling special situations that may arise—all these are subtly different from procedures used with sighted subjects and are clearly presented in the manual. In spite of the breadth of detail here, this reviewer believes it will be generally unwise for examiners unused to working with blind subjects to attempt administration of the BLAT without advance practice, especially with young blind children who probably need considerable direct guidance from the examiner. This is in no way a criticism of the instructions in the manual, which clearly show the influence of extensive experience with the blind and concern for good assessment.

All 49 items are generally presented to all examinees, with the exception that the fourth group of items, of which there are 16, is discontinued after five consecutive failures. The test or portions of it may be discontinued if the child's test behavior is perseverative or inattentive, but the manual claims this is rarely necessary.

There are no formal time limits for the BLAT items, although the directions state that subjects usually respond to the items in less than two minutes. It seems likely that the 49 scored items and 12 training items could be presented within about an hour to most children. One notes that this is rather more time than sighted subjects would need to respond to similar items in a printed format; the long testing time may be tiring to some subjects.

All items are scored right or wrong, and the total raw score is the total number of correct answers. The process of scoring, however, is complicated by the poorly laid-out response sheet. The most serious design flaw is that answers to the unscored training items may easily be included by mistake when scoring an examinee's record. Even experienced scorers will need to be careful to avoid reporting inflated total scores.

Once the raw score is obtained, it is transformed to a "learning aptitude age equivalent," which is similar in meaning to a mental age, or to a "learning quotient," similar to a deviation IQ. The former score, called an LA, strikes this reviewer as lacking sufficient precision to make it useful. A single point of raw score can change the LA by about half a year between ages 6 and 13, and about three-quarters of a year between 13 and 16 years. Thus a change of a couple of points of raw score can make a substantial difference in the LA. (Knowing the standard error of measurement of BLAT scores would help gauge whether this is a real problem or not. As will be shown later, however, the standard errors of measurement given in the manual are uninterpretable in their present form.)

The learning quotient (LQ) is a within-age standard score with a mean of 100 and a standard deviation of 15. LQ equivalents of raw scores are presented at half-year intervals (except for three of the age groups, which encompass a full year of age). All of the normative information is based on the BLAT performance of 836 children aged 6 through 16 years. The sample is well described in demographic terms—age, sex, race, geographic region, and occupation of the family's major breadwinner—and according to enrollment in a residential versus a day school. Some of the children were classified as partially sighted, but those who used vision to any degree in solving the BLAT items were excluded from the sample.

It should be added that a portion of the standardization sample was tested in 1953-54 in connection with early item tryouts of a pool of 94 test items. The rest of the sample was gathered later, using the final set of 12 training and 49 test items. The total length of time over which the norms were gathered is not given.

As will be discussed later, the available evidence sheds dim light on what the BLAT measures. Logically, it would seem to get at some aspect of general ability similar to what is measured by nonverbal tests of abstract reasoning for the sighted, yet the empirical evidence is slender. Under these circumstances it seems prudent to regard the BLAT as supplementing traditional, more culturally loaded measures of intelligence that, after all, typically afford better prediction of educational outcomes than do tests of abstract reasoning. In effect, then, the BLAT can provide blind children with another opportunity to demonstrate their abilities, which may be especially important with young children from limited or restricted backgrounds.

Technical Aspects

The preceding paragraph alluded to the question of what the BLAT really measures. The manual does present coefficients of correlation of BLAT socres with scores on the Hayes-Binet and on the WISC Verbal Scale. These show that while the BLAT correlates reasonably well with the two other measures, the Hayes-Binet and WISC correlate better with each other. Other correlational data show that the BLAT correlates less well with various parts of the Stanford Achievement Test than do either the Hayes-Binet or the WISC Verbal Scale. Thus the BLAT measures something related to but different from what is shared by the Hayes-Binet and the verbal portions of the WISC. Even though these results are consistent with the author's premise that the BLAT taps the psychological processes as opposed to the contents of learning, other explanations of the data are possible. The user therefore is left with unanswered questions about what the BLAT does measure.

A factor analysis of the BLAT items has been carried out, and the rotated factor matrix of four factors is included in the manual. Unhappily, the reporting of details is grossly incomplete; there is no mention of the sample used or its size, or how the factors were extracted or rotated. In addition, the column of item communalities is incorrectly identified as loadings on a general factor. The factor loadings do indicate some tendency for the items to fall into groups that relate to the six different item styles used in the test. Nevertheless, it cannot be said that the information as presented helps one understand how the domain of the BLAT differs from that of other intelligence tests.

Reliability, too, is inadequately reported in the BLAT manual. A Kuder-Richardson 14 coefficient of .93 is reported, but for a sample of 961 subjects aged 6 through 20 years that includes the normative sample of 836 children. Reliability should, of course, be reported for separate age groups—generally the same groups for which the norms are presented. The .93 is almost certainly an overestimate of the within-age reliability because of the large score variance in wide-range age groups. Because not enough additional data are given in the manual to estimate the reliability by age, the internal consistency of the BLAT must be called unknown.

Stability of BLAT scores over a 7-month period is reported for two groups somewhat narrower in age span but still undesirably broad—6 through 10 years and 12 through 16 years. The retest coefficients were in the high .80s. Practice effects for this sample are given by individual years of age. The mean gain on retesting varies from 3 to 7 points, with younger children making the larger gains.

The table of age equivalents of BLAT raw scores also presents standard errors of measurement by age, but it is not clear how these were obtained. If the .93 overestimate of reliability was used in their computation, these standard errors are spuriously small. Furthermore, it is not clear whether they are expressed in terms of BLAT raw scores or in units of the age equivalents. These figures are not useful as now given.

In a closing section of the manual, the author presents some observations and speculations about the BLAT, many of which amount to researchable hypotheses for further study. The author's concern about young blind children and their education is reflected in these interesting questions, and it is hoped that they will be studied in the future. Research references on the BLAT are few, and much about the test remains to be explored.

Critique

The Blind Learning Aptitude Test represents an interesting attempt to measure the ability of blind children. The author recognizes that the BLAT is probably more appropriate for younger children than for older individuals, who have been more broadly exposed to formal education and to life experiences in general. For older children and for those with more schooling, the author suggests that adaptations of the Binet or Wechsler scales are generally more appropriate. In many circumstances it is probably a good idea to administer the BLAT together with, for instance, the Verbal Scale of the WISC-R, and to explore further any sizable differences between the two sets of results. (The Hayes-Binet dates back to 1950, and its norms and possibly its content are considerably out-of-date by now. It remains to be seen whether a special adaptation for the blind will be made available for the just-published revision of the Binet.) In connection with the recommendation that the BLAT be used with younger children, one wonders whether such subjects find the task repetitious and boring—a possible disadvantage of the test.

The BLAT manual does not meet contemporary standards of test publishing. Its discussion of validity is incomplete; reliability must be called undetermined; too many statistical tables lack important information like Ns, means, and standard deviations; and several of the tables seem to lead nowhere. This document should be reworked, perhaps at such time as the BLAT is restandardized.

The response sheet is crude and makes it too easy to compute inflated raw scores. It would take little effort to improve its design.

Nevertheless, the test has important strengths. It appears to have been carefully constructed, the directions for administration are remarkably thorough, the norms are based on a carefully designed sample of blind children (though these norms, too, are due for updating), and the test measures a domain somewhat different from that of other available intelligence tests for the blind. The BLAT is unique in its field.

References

Hayes, S. P. (1950). Measuring the intelligence of the blind. In P. A. Zahl (Ed.), *Blindness: Modern approaches to the unseen environment*. Princeton: Princeton University Press.

Newland, T. E. (1964a). Prediction and evaluation of academic learning by blind children, 1: Problems and procedures in prediction. *International Journal for the Education of the Blind*, 14, 1-7.

Newland, T. E. (1964b). Prediction and evaluation of academic learning by blind children, II: Problems and procedures in evaluation. *International Journal for the Education of the Blind*, 14, 42-51.

Timothy V. Rasinski, Ph.D.
Assistant Professor of Reading Education, The University of Georgia, Athens, Georgia.

BOTEL READING INVENTORY
Morton Botel. Cleveland, Ohio: Modern Curriculum Press.

Introduction

The Botel Reading Inventory (BRI) is primarily a survey instrument designed for placing students at appropriate levels of reading instruction and for checking progress and mastery of reading skills throughout the school year. Assigning students to instructional materials of appropriate difficulty is a crucial element of effective reading instruction. Through the use of four subtests that cover a range of related skills, the test identifies, by grade levels, the independent, instructional, and frustration reading levels of students. The test is most appropriate for students in Grades 1 through 6, although there are provisions for junior and senior high schools.

The author of the BRI, Morton Botel, is a well-known reading educator. Professor of education at the University of Pennsylvania, he serves as chairman and coordinator of the Language in Education program in the Graduate School of Education. Botel has served as president of the International Reading Association and has published texts in the areas of reading, spelling, English, and study skills.

The original version of the Botel Reading Inventory was published in 1961. This earlier version followed the same format and stated purpose of the current test. The lack of a spelling subtest in the original is the major difference between the two. In the original version of the Decoding subtest, students were required to write out the orthographic representation of sounds and letters produced orally by the examiner. This has been replaced in the current edition by a multiple-choice format in which students choose the correct response from a set of alternatives.

The current version of the BRI is made up of four subtests: Decoding, Spelling, Word Recognition, and Word Opposites. All subtests, except for Spelling, have their own individual answer forms available. Moreover, the Word Recognition and Word Opposites subtests have alternate forms. An administration manual completes the set of materials.

The Decoding subtest is made up of 12 subsections or levels and was designed to measure students' mastery of 12 decoding skills that are, ostensibly, required for proficient reading. The following subsections make up the subtest: 1) letter naming; 2) awareness of initial consonant sounds; 3) rhyming words; and 4-12) decoding words of various phonic and spelling patterns, such as consonant-vowel-consonant (CVC), CVC plus final *e*, CCVCC, CCVCC plus final *e*, multisyllable words, and so on. In the first three subsections, which contain 10 items each, the student responds to an oral stimulus produced by the examiner by choosing the appropriate letter or word from a set of alternatives. Each of the remaining subsections contain increasingly difficult lists of 10 words that the student pronounces. The examiner notes any mispronunciations, substitutions, or failures to respond. The examiner marks errors in subsections 4 through 9 on the student answer sheet. The student reads the word lists from the administration manual.

The second subtest is the Spelling placement test, the purpose of which is to give a graded estimate of students' spelling ability. This test consists of five lists of 20 words that are graded in difficulty from Grades 1-2 to Grade 6. The examiner pronounces each word twice and uses each in a sentence. The students write each word on a separate sheet.

The Word Recognition subtest consists of eight word lists graded in difficulty from pre-primer to the fourth-grade level. Each list contains 20 words that the student is required to pronounce. The examiner notes any mispronunciations, substitutions, or failures to respond on the individual student scoring sheet.

The Word Opposites subtest, a measure of students' reading comprehension ability, is made up of 10 ten-word subtests. As with the two previous subtests, the lists are graded in difficulty. In this case the grading ranges from first grade through senior high school. The students' task is to identify, from a set of three or four alternatives, the opposite of a word presented on the student answer form. This subtest may also be administered as a listening test, in which case the stimulus word and alternatives are presented orally by the examiner.

Two separate class summary sheets are provided by the publisher. One permits the examiner to record percentage or raw scores for up to 28 students on each of the subsections of the Decoding Subtest and the identified placement level on the Spelling subtest. The other summary sheet allows the examiner to record percentage scores for each level of the Word Recognition and Word Opposite (reading and listening) subtests for up to 20 students. It also allows the examiner to identify the highest instructional and potential reading levels for each student.

Practical Applications/Uses

The Botel Reading Inventory is designed to identify students' levels of reading achievement. The major purposes of the BRI are correct placement of students in instructional groups, the selection of materials of appropriate difficulty, and checking student progress in reading achievement. The test yields estimates of students' independent, instruction, and frustration reading levels. Knowledge of these levels is especially helpful in selecting appropriate materials and instructional methodologies for students.

The BRI measures a variety of decoding skills and general spelling ability. However, placement decisions are based solely on "general comprehension" (Word Opposites) and "oral reading fluency" (Word Recognition). These two tests, however, are in fact tests of students' knowledge of antonyms and their ability to read words in isolation.

The primary use for the BRI is any use for which an informal reading inventory is also appropriate. That is, testing situations for screening or placement purposes would be appropriate uses for the BRI. It should be noted that the Decoding and Spelling subtests may yield a limited amount of diagnostic information; thus, the test may have limited use in diagnosing certain deficiencies that a student may exhibit in word analysis skills.

The BRI can be used with a minimal amount of training or background in reading and/or testing. The test can easily be administered by a classroom teacher. However, given the amount of time necessary to administer the test and the fact that certain parts can only be administered individually, it is more likely to be a tool of reading specialists. The test may also be useful as a screening device for school psychologists.

The author does not indicate the specific populations for which the test is designed. However, as a general survey instrument, for screening and placement decisions and for evaluating achievement in reading, the BRI can be administered to students exhibiting a wide range of abilities. As previously mentioned, the Word Recognition and Word Opposites subtests have sections for junior and senior high school students. However, those areas are covered rather tersely. The test is most appropriate for students in Grades 1 through 6.

The first three subsections of the Decoding subtest of the BRI may be administered to groups; the remaining nine must be administered individually. The Spelling and Word Opposites subtests are group tests; Word Recognition, on the other hand, must be administered individually.

The administration manual presents fairly clear directions for both the group and individual tests. In the Spelling subtest, however, the manual does not provide the examiner with the sentences that should be used. This poses a problem in terms of the standardization of administration.

The manual recommends a testing program in which the Decoding and Spelling subtests are given near the beginning of the school year. The Word Recognition and Word Opposite subtests should be administered between the third and sixth weeks of the school year. However, the manual does note that any subtest of the BRI may be administered to students at any time of the year depending on the kinds of information desired.

The time required to administer the entire test depends on student ability. More proficient readers will be required to work through more levels of the various subtests, thus requiring larger amounts of time. In general, however, if given on an individual basis, the full test should take no more than 90 minutes to administer.

The instructions for scoring are clear and simple, and the procedure can be accomplished in minutes. Scoring requires the examiner to check whether the correct choice was made on the multiple-choice items (Word Decoding subsections 1 through 3 and Word Opposites), to determine whether the words pronounced by the student were done so correctly (Word Decoding subsections 4 through 12 and Word Recognition), and to check the spelling of words written by the students (Spelling).

Although the test interpretation is not difficult, it is cumbersome. The Decoding Subtest is, to a certain extent, diagnostic in nature. Each level or subsection of this subtest examines a specific decoding skill. Students who achieve less than 80% correct (fewer than eight of the 10 items per subsection correct) on any of the subsections could benefit from intensified instruction in those skills that the subsection measured.

The remaining three subtests are scored with the focus on grade level placement. Each subsection or word list on the Spelling, Word Recognition, and Word Opposites subtests corresponds to a grade level. Instructional level for the Spelling subtest is defined as the first level at which student scores below 80%. Instructional level for Word Recognition subtest is the level(s) at which the student reads 70-90% of the words correctly. In the Word Opposites Subtest, the instructional level is defined as the level(s) in which the student scores 70-80% correct.

Actual reading placement decisions are based only on analysis of the Word Recognition and Word Opposites subtests. The lower instructional level performance on the two subtests determines actual placement level. For example, a student having instructional levels of Grade 4 on the Word Recognition subtest and Grade 5 on Word Opposites should be placed at the fourth-grade level for reading instruction. Reading materials below the instructional level are identified as appropriate for free reading. Materials above the instructional level are considered frustration-inducing materials and should not be considered appropriate for the student.

The administration manual also allows for direct conversion of total raw scores on the Word Recognition and Word Opposites subtests to highest instructional levels. However, this method for obtaining instructional levels is recommended for researchers and not classroom teachers.

Technical Aspects

Information is provided in the BRI manual for content, criterion-related, and concurrent validity. With regard to content validity, the author argues that vocabulary words are a good indicator of reading proficiency. The work of Davis (1944, 1967) is used to support the argument. No rationale is provided for the inclusion of the Decoding or Spelling subtests in the BRI.

Criterion-related validity is established through the author's own work (Botel, 1969; Botel, Bradley, & Kashuba, 1970). In these studies, Botel investigated the ability of the BRI to place students at the correct reading level as identified by teacher and principal judgment as well as by other reading tests. The available information suggests that the BRI is a fairly good predictor of student reading placement. For example, correlations between .57 and .95 were found between scores on the BRI, and actual student placement in grade equivalents on a standardized reading test ranged from .51 to .92 for students in Grades 2 through 6. Interestingly, both sets of correlations tended to decline as grade level increased.

Concurrent validity was established by correlating the BRI with other reading tests. Botel (1969) found "fairly high" relationships between the BRI and other unspecified standardized reading tests. The correlations were high for Grades 2 and 3 (.80-.93), but were not as impressive for Grades 4 through 6 (.47-.74). In a study correlating the BRI with the Standard Reading Inventory (McCracken & Mullen, 1970), correlations ranging from .78 to .95 for Grades 1 through 6 were found.

Information regarding alternate form and internal consistency reliability is also reported in the manual. A significant omission is the noticeable lack of information regarding the stability of the test, or test-retest reliability. Without such information it is difficult to estimate the capriciousness of the scores from one administration to another. No information regarding standard error of measurement is reported.

The two forms of the BRI (Word Recognition and Word Opposites) seem to be equivalent for Grades 1, 2, and 3. Correlations between raw scores on Forms A and B range between .94 to .99 for Grades 1 through 6. Correlations between placement scores for the two forms, however, was significantly lower. For example, the correlation in placement scores for Grade 6 was .66. Placement correlations are high only for Grades 1 through 3.

Internal consistency was determined by correlating the Word Opposites and Word Recognition subtests of the BRI. For the three grades tested, Grades 1 through 3, the correlations ranged from .86 to .95. Although these correlations are high, correlations between subtests are not measures of consistency within the subtests themselves. A split-half measure would have been a more appropriate measure of internal consistency. Indeed, the high correlations between subtests suggest that those subtests are redundant.

Critique

Quite simply, given its intended purpose, the BRI is not an easy test to administer. The test is intended to be a quick and easily administered instrument for placing students in reading materials; in reality, the test is cumbersome in several respects.

First, the Spelling, Word Opposites, and parts of the Decoding subtests are intended for group administration, but the Word Recognition and other parts of the Decoding subtests must be given individually. Secondly, the BRI is *not* intended to be administered at one time or one set of times. It is recommended that the Decoding and Spelling subtests be given at the beginning of the school year, while the Word Recognition and Word Opposites subtests be administered after the third week of school. Next, in parts of the BRI the student marks his or her answers on the individual student response form while the administrator refers to the administration manual. In other parts of the test the student has the manual while the teacher marks the student response form. In addition, cutoff or critical scores for different subtests are not uniform. The critical score on the Decoding and Spelling subtests is 80%, 70% on two successive levels for the Word Recognition subtest, and 80% on two successive levels for the Word Opposites subtest. Further, the BRI is set up so that, within each subtest, individual scores for each level must be determined before permitting a student to go to the next level. This procedure can become awkward in group test situations. Finally, the class summary sheets are not uniform. The summary sheet for the Word Recognition and Word Opposites subtests can accommodate 20 students. The summary sheet for Decoding and Spelling have space for 28 students.

Each of these items may be minor. However, they point to a considerable lack of attention to test design and, taken as a whole, suggest strongly that the BRI can cause a great deal of difficulty and confusion in administration, especially for those teachers who are not highly familiar with the test. Teachers already burdened by other management chores will find the management of this test onerous. In current parlance, the BRI is not "user friendly."

Students taking this test are only asked to read words in isolation. One may ask if such a task is reflective of actual reading, at least the kind that probably will be required of students in school. Reading educators have argued against tasks that possess little ecological validity (cf. Goodman, 1981); that is, tasks that fail to reflect the kinds of reading done in schools are not valid measures of reading achievement or performance.

Moreover, the purpose of the BRI is similar to that of informal reading inventories; namely, to assign students to instructionally appropriate materials. Informal reading inventories have students read connected written discourse. By observing students reading real texts the teacher can garner information about the reader that the BRI simply cannot provide. The reader's use of context in word identification, quality of miscue (Goodman, 1969), reading rate (Samuels, 1979), reading fluency (Allington, 1983), student's use of prosody (Schreiber, 1980), and comprehension of the text are all important kinds of information that are denied the user of the BRI.

The Botel Reading Inventory appears to be a reasonably good reading placement instrument for the early elementary grades. However, given the possible procedural difficulties inherent in the BRI, the limited number of grade levels for which it is appropriate, and the limited and ecologically questionable kinds of information that the BRI affords, it is difficult to imagine how the BRI could serve reading placement purposes better than the administration of a widely recognized evaluation procedure, such as an informal reading inventory.

References

Allington, R. L. (1983). Fluency: The neglected goal. *The Reading Teacher, 36,* 556-561.

Botel, M. (1969). A comparative study of the validity of the Botel Reading Inventory and selected standardized tests. In J. A. Figurel (Ed.), *Reading and Realism* (pp. 721-727). Newark, DE: International Reading Association.

Botel, M., Bradley, J., & Kashuba, M. (1970, May), *Research design to test the validity of independent, instructional, and frustration levels.* Paper presented at the annual meeting of the International Reading Association, Anaheim, CA.

Davis, F. B. (1944). Fundamental factors of comprehension in reading. *Psychometrika, 9,* 185-187.

Davis, F. B. (1967). *Identification of fundamental reading skills of high school students* (Cooperative Research Project No. 3023). Washington, DC: U.S. Office of Education.

Goodman, K. S. (1969). Analysis of oral reading miscues: Applied psycholinguistics. *Reading Research Quarterly, 5,* 9-30.

Goodman, K. S. (1981). Response to Stanovich. *Reading Research Quarterly, 16,* 477-478.

McCracken, R. A., & Mullen, N. D. (1970, May). *The validation of speed, oral reading, errors, pronouncing vocabulary, and comprehension as measured by an IRI.* Paper presented at the annual meeting of the International Reading Association, Anaheim, CA.

Samuels, S. J. (1979). The method of repeated readings. *The Reading Teacher, 32,* 403-408.

Schreiber, P. A. (1980). On the acquisition of reading fluency. *Journal of Reading Behavior, 12,* 117-186.

Jeanette M. Reuter, Ph.D.
Professor of Psychology, Kent State University, Kent, Ohio.

THE BZOCH-LEAGUE RECEPTIVE-EXPRESSIVE EMERGENT LANGUAGE SCALE
Kenneth R. Bzoch and Richard League. Austin, Texas: PRO-ED.

Introduction

The Bzoch-League Receptive-Expressive Emergent Language Scale: For the Measurement of Language Skills in Infancy (REEL) measures receptive and expressive language abilities of children who are less than three years of age. The test items are graded language behaviors and are divided into two scales; expressive language and receptive language behaviors. The items of the test are administered to the child's caregiver by a professional, who converts the results of the interview to language developmental age scores and quotients from normative guides in the language development in infants and children. Eight guidelines are provided for interpreting the results of a REEL testing.

The manual, which is called "a handbook for the multidimensional analysis of emergent language," contains an introductory discussion of the stages and patterns of emergent language and a glossary of relevant terms. Because a REEL scoring can identify those language behaviors the tested child can be expected to develop next, the scale can be used for prescriptive planning with the parent of a child who is showing language development problems.

Dr. Bzoch received his Ph.D. from Northwestern University in 1956. In 1960 he went to the University of Florida-Gainesville, where in 1964 he became Chairman of the Department of Communicative Disorders. Currently Dr. Bzoch is a faculty member in the College of Health Related Professions at the J. Hillis Miller Health Center. Dr. League received his doctoral degree at the University of Florida-Gainesville in 1966 and is presently located in Orlando, Florida.

Drs. League and Bzoch began their work on the REEL project in 1964 at the University of Florida. Their purpose was to construct an instrument capable of measuring the various dimensions of emergent language. The authors had determined that none of the language tests available effectively measured emergent language skills in infants. Furthermore, most of the existing language tests contained a high percentage of visual, motor, and social behavior items not relevant to the measurement of emerging language skills. Finally, these tests usually required a high degree of professional training in order to administer them correctly.

> The authors state that their primary motivation was to fill the acknowledged need for an effective means of identifying very young children who may have

---

The contribution of Louis F. Reuter in the preparation of this review is gratefully acknowledged.

specific handicaps requiring early habilitative and educational intervention. . . . Much more can be done for the child who is developmentally deviant if the nature of the disorder is identified very early in infancy. . . . The most effective time for such a diagnosis is during the critical linguistic imprinting period—from birth until about three years of age. (Bzoch & League, 1971, pp. 12-13)

The test and manual were first printed in 1971. Additional printings followed, the latest in 1985. There have been no revisions, nor are there other forms of the test available at the time of this writing.

The REEL test materials consist of a 61-page manual ($14.00) and a 7-page test form (12 for $25.00). A summary page records demographic data on the child and his or her family. The test pages divide the language behavior items into receptive and expressive categories with a space to indicate "+" if the child regularly exhibits the behavior, "-" if not, and "+/-" whenever the behavior is "emergent or only partially exhibited." There are three receptive and three expressive language items for each of the first 12 months, followed by three each in the six two-month intervals in the second year and three in each of the four three-month intervals in the third year. These total 72 behavior items in the first year, 36 in the second, and 24 in the third, for a total of 132 items.

Practical Applications/Uses

The REEL is suitable for assessing the developmental language status of children from birth to the age of 36 months. Children more than 3 years old who have known language delays or who have come from "linguistically deprived" environments can also be assessed using the REEL. For example, Bzoch, Kemker, and Wood (1984) studied the language development of infants with cleft palates and Mahoney and Snow (1983) used the REEL to measure language development in infants with Down's syndrome.

The test consists of an interview with the child's mother or other caregiver, with the child present. This allows the examiner to observe the child's language behavior in a social context with its caregiver. The examiner is counseled to put the caregiver at ease with a "series of broad leading questions before going to the specific Scale items." The examiner is to "form a general impression of linguistic performance" and to try to "confirm all questionable items through direct observation or a supplemental interview with the informant" (Bzoch & League, 1971, p. 27).

The examiner starts the interview with the receptive items for the infant's chronological age interval. For example, initial questions for a child who was 13 months of age would be taken from the receptive items listed in the 12- to 14-month interval. If the child had two out of three "+" scorings in that interval, the examiner proceeds to the next age interval until the child misses two of three items. If the child misses two out of the three in the first age interval, the examiner starts going to lower age intervals until the child passes two out of the three items in an interval.

Scorings of "+/-" are counted as a "+" provided that the next highest age interval has at least 2 "+" scores. The receptive language age (RLA) is the highest age interval in which the child gets at least two "+" scores and it is recorded as the highest month of the age level (i.e., 22 months if the 20-22-month interval is the highest). The expressive language items are then presented, starting at the age level corresponding to the child's RLA. Exactly the same questioning process is repeated to determine the child's expressive language age (ELA).

The REEL provides four more expressions of the child's linguistic status. First the arithmetic average of the RLA and ELA is computed to give the Combined Language Age (CLA). Each of these is then divided by the child's chronological age and multiplied by 100 to give a Receptive Quotient (RQ), Expressive Quotient (EQ), and Language (Combined) Quotient (LQ). The Appendix contains two tables that can be used to calculate the CLA and the RQ, EQ, and LQ quotients.

The REEL can serve a screening function for language professionals who want to confirm and quantify early language delay. REEL Scale items that the child should have acquired (based on his or her chronological age), but had not, could be reviewed with the parent and suggestions given for supporting development of these behaviors. Thus the REEL gives the speech pathologist a menu of language items to use in developing habilitation plans with parents of language-delayed children.

Technical Aspects

The items on the REEL Scale were obtained in part from a search of the developmental literature covering research reports and existing developmental scales. Item age norms were established by the experience of the test authors. The normative sample for their longitudinal study consisted of 50 healthy infants who came from "enriched linguistic environments." The REEL is intended to represent the "full linguistic potential" possible in our culture rather than representing the average level of attainment.

The original 50 infants were given repeated monthly testings over a 2- to 3-year period. A second cross-sectional study was made on another 50 infants not identified as coming from "enriched linguistic environments," and the test results were similar to the original 50 infants. A third study with 27 "well babies," aged 6 months to 36 months, also gave similar test scores. Pilot studies varying gender and race showed normal REEL test scores. These normative studies are described in only very general terms in the test manual.

The manual for the REEL reports a test-retest and interjudge reliability study, with repeated testing after a three-week interval of 28 normal infants carried out by graduate students untrained in the administration of the REEL. Reliability criteria entailed test-retest agreement within plus or minus one age interval on the REEL Scale. ". . . Agreement between the different administrators for the infant population studied ranged from 90% to 100%." Test-retest results "yielded an overall Language Quotient (LQ) correlation value of $r = .71$" (Bzoch & League, 1971, pp. 19-20).

The validity criterion was whether the "normal" infants tested were found to have RLA, ELA, and CLA scores at or above their chronological ages. A longitudinal study of the 50 "normal" infants of the normative sample over a 2-3 year period showed *all* infants met this criterion. A second cross-sectional study (25 female, 25 male) had RLA, ELA, and CLA within "+/-" one age interval of their chronological age (CA). In three additional studies with different race and gender, REEL scores were equal to or above CAs.

Bzoch et al. (1984) compared the RLQ, ELQ, and CLQ of a sample (N = 43) of infants with cleft-palate disorders with REEL scores of his normative group. His patient population received RLQs, ELQs, and CLQs similar to the normative group. Differences between receptive and emergent language were not substantial between normal and cleft-palate children in this study.

McCauley and Swisher (1984) published a review of 30 language and articulation tests for preschool children, applying 1974 APA standards to develop 10 psychometric criteria; half met no more than two criteria and only three met more than four criteria. The REEL met only one: "Test administration procedures described in sufficient detail to enable the test user to duplicate the administration and scoring procedures."

Critique

Five journal reviews of the REEL were abstracted in *The Eighth Mental Measurements Yearbook* (Buros, 1978). Criticism focused on the inadequacy of the psychometric data available on the REEL and the use of the parent interview format. Ease and economy of administration were praised.

The REEL does not purport to be a formally normed and standardized test of infant language development. There is very little psychometric research available on this test. Rather, it is a structured interview for an experienced professional to administer to a caregiver. The norms for the judgment of performance are internalized, built out of the experience of the interviewer. Drs. Bzoch and League built the structured interview and their internalized age norms out of daily clinical practice. They shared the deposits of their experience with the REEL in the form of item age norms and a structured parent interview.

The assignment of specific language ages based on the REEL is not supported by normative data. The conservative way to use the REEL for this purpose would be to judge whether a given child's performance falls within or below that of normal children from enriched language environments.

In summary, the REEL is a useful clinical tool in the hands of a language development specialist. This is what it was designed for, and it has been widely used for this purpose in speech and language clinics throughout the country.

References

This list includes text citations and suggested additional reading.

Bannatyne, A. (1972). Review of the Bzoch-League Receptive-Expressive Emergent Language Scale. *Journal of Learning Disabilities, 5* (8), 512.

Bender, R. E. (1972). Review of the Bzoch-League Receptive-Expressive Emergent Language Scale. *Volta Review, 74* (8), 465.

Bzoch, K. R., Kemker, J. E., & Wood, V. L. (1984). The prevention of communicative disorders in cleft palate infants. *Speech and language: Advances in basic research and practice.* (Vol. 10), pp. 59-109. Orlando, FL: Academic Press, Inc.

Bzoch, K. R., & League, R. (1971). *Assessing language skills in infancy: A handbook for the multidimensional analysis of emergent language.* Baltimore: University Park Press.

Cripe, A. E. (1975). Review of Bzoch-League Receptive-Expressive Emergent Language Scale. In W. K. Frankenburg, & B. W. Camp (Eds.), *Pediatric screening tests* (pp. xii, 549). Springfield, IL: Charles C. Thomas.

Johnson, D. L. (1973). Review of the Bzoch-League Receptive-Expressive Language Scale. *Journal of Personality Assessment, 37* (6), 581-582.

Mahoney, G., & Snow, K. (1983). The relationship of sensorimotor functioning to children's response to early language training. *Mental Retardation, 21*(6), 248-254.

McCauley, R. J., & Swisher, L. (1984). Psychometric review of language and articulation tests for preschool children. *Journal of Speech and Hearing Disorders, 49*, 34-42.

Plotkin, W. H. (1973). Review of the Bzoch-League Receptive-Expressive Emergent Language Scale. *American Journal of Mental Deficiency, 78*(2), 226-227.

Charles E. McInnis, Ph.D.
Associate Professor of Psychology, University of Ottawa, Ottawa, Canada.

CANADIAN COGNITIVE ABILITIES TEST
R. Thorndike, E. Hagen, and E. Wright. Scarborough, Canada: Nelson Canada.

Introduction

The Canadian Cognitive Abilities Test (CCAT) is part of an integrated test series designed to assess the development of cognitive abilities related to verbal, quantitative, and nonverbal reasoning and problem solving. These are the abilities that are generally considered important in learning activities related to diverse school curricula. There is a Primary Battery (Level 1), which is appropriate for the second half of kindergarten through Grade 3, and a Multilevel Edition (Levels A–H), which is suitable for Grades 3–12. Level H can be used to test individuals in colleges, and it is also appropriate for testing adults who are college-educated. For other adult groups, one of the lower levels of the test would be preferable.

The overall goal of the CCAT, therefore, is to assess the development of generalized thinking skills. Specifically, the test assesses the ability to name and classify objects and the ability to deal with quantitative concepts. It is important to measure such skills in the educational milieu, because these are the skills required for the comprehension of diverse instructional content.

The Canadian Cognitive Abilities Test (CCAT) is based on the Cognitive Abilities Test (CAT) developed by Thorndike and Hagen (1978). In order to make the CCAT more relevant for a Canadian population, certain minor modifications in content were made under the direction of Wright. Canadian national norms were derived and are elaborated in the test manual (Thorndike, Hagen & Wright, 1982a). As a result of this adaptation, the tests maintain the quality of measurement found in the older edition (CAT), with the additional advantage of being more suitable for a Canadian population.

Robert L. Thorndike received his Ph.D. in Psychometrics from Columbia University in 1935 and was a professor at Columbia University from 1936 to 1976. In 1976, Thorndike was named Professor Emeritas in Educational Psychology. His special interests were in the fields of intellectual measurement and evaluation research.

Elizabeth Hagen is currently Professor Emerita in Educational Psychology at Columbia University. She received her Ph.D. from Columbia University in Educational Psychology in 1952, and her main field is psychometrics with a specialization in measurement and evaluation. She has been a member of the professoriate at Columbia since 1948.

The Canadian editor of the CCAT, Dr. Edgar N. Wright, is Chief Educational Research Officer of the Toronto Board of Education. Dr. Wright assumed the responsibility for designing the sampling specifications and selecting the sample. The actual standardization was a cooperative enterprise involving the publishers and authors of the CCAT, the Canadian Tests of Basic Skills, and a large number of Canadian schools (Thorndike, Hagen, & Wright, 1984).

Preliminary research on item selection for the original CAT was conducted to develop a single scale of difficulty for both the Primary Battery and the Multilevel Edition by estimating the distance in level of performance for consecutive grade groups. Each item was assigned a scale value derived from the percentage of success for the particular group for which it was most appropriate. An item was considered for inclusion in a test only if it showed satisfactory discrimination. In determining item validity or discrimination, biserial correlations were computed between the item (scored 1, 0) and the total subtest score (the continuous variable). Additional item analysis studies were conducted for the standardization sample.

The CCAT was constructed to measure a full range of individual differences; thus, items on the test range from easy to difficult. The major concern of the authors was to include tasks in each subtest that measure content that has already been learned by a particular age group. The examinee is then required to use familiar content in a novel manner. With this approach, the authors envisage the obtaining of reliable estimates of cognitive ability at different developmental stages, and also the provision of items of interest to examinees of diverse backgrounds.

In selecting the standardization sample and deriving representative norms, a number of principles were adhered to: precisely select, with respect to ability and achievement, an English-speaking school population; select a stratified random of schools, on the basis of province and size of school; select schools for K–3 and Grades 4–12 in order to provide longitudinal comparability of norms; and administer ability and achievement tests to the same pupils (Thorndike, Hagen, & Wright, 1984). The CCAT was normed jointly with the Canadian Tests of Basic Skills (CTBS), making possible subsequent comparisons of performance on achievement tests with performance on aptitude tests. Such comparisons facilitate the identification of levels of deviation in cognitive development with actual achievement of a student.

The Primary Battery is a single-score untimed nonreading group test of general cognitive skills, administered at a pace suitable for the group being tested. Reasonable average administrative time allotments vary from 12 to 16 minutes per subtest. By presenting the test item by item, the instructions for the tasks are reinforced; each pupil can be kept working, better control of the testing situation can be maintained, and the pace can be more readily adapted to the characteristics of the children being tested (Pullen & Somwaru, 1984).

The Primary Battery was constructed to appraise the full range of individual differences in the development of general cognitive skills among children in the primary grades. Test items vary from very easy to very difficult. Level 1 provides maximum discrimination among children and a maximum amount of information. Level 2 has a wide range of item difficulty and may be used for above-average Grade 1 or below, and average Grade 2 or 3 students in cognitive development.

The Primary Battery uses pictorial materials and oral instruction and is divided into four subtests: Rational Concepts, Object Classification, Quantitative Concepts, and Oral Vocabulary. Each subtest is based on content that children of this age are likely to have experienced; requires children to use familiar material in a novel manner; yields reliable assessments of cognitive development for children at different stages of development; emphasizes cognitive skills related to learning school tasks that children in Grades K through 3 are expected to master; and is of interest to children of various backgrounds (Thorndike, Hagen, & Wright, 1984).

It has generally been found that cognitive reasoning in adults and children involve the utilization of verbal, numerical, and geometric symbols. Levels of functioning in these areas provide some measure of individual competence. Because of individual differences, procedures have been devised to appraise levels of cognitive ability. The Multilevel Edition of the CCAT is a diagnostic instrument in that it provides a variety of tasks that use the three types of symbols; furthermore, it has selectively screened out irrelevant factors that influence performance (complexity of sentence structure and vocabulary for a particular age group). Basic elements of the tasks in each subtest have been kept relatively simple, clear, and familiar. An individual's score reflects the ability to discover relationships and demonstrate flexibility of thinking.

The term "multilevel" indicates a graded series of items for each subtest yielding eight distinct but overlapping scales. Each successive scale is somewhat more difficult than the preceding one, but the increase in degree of difficulty is small, the result being that there is a level that is of nearly optimum difficulty for any individual student or group. Eight levels of the Multilevel Edition provide one level for each grade in elementary school and for each two grades in secondary school (Thorndike, Hagen, & Wright, 1984).

The Multilevel Edition is organized into three separate batteries: Verbal (34 minutes); Quantitative (32 minutes); and Nonverbal (32 minutes). It is primarily a power test, and pupils should be able to attempt all items.

The four subtests of the Verbal Battery, Vocabulary, Sentence Completion, Verbal Classification, and Verbal Analogies, provide an accurate and useful measure of ability to deal with abstractions presented in verbal form and also yield a measure of scholastic aptitude. The subtests:

  a) appraise knowledge of different words and flexibility in identifying the specific meaning of the particular word being used;
  b) require the individual to have not only a sense of the structure of the English language but also a comprehension of the idea expressed in the sentence;
  c) require the individual to abstract the common element among three or four verbal stimuli; and
  d) assess the ability to discover the relationship between a pair of words and then, given a third word that is the first word of a second pair, complete the analogy (Thorndike, Hagen, & Wright, 1982a).

There are three subtests in the Quantitative Battery; Quantitative Relations, Number Series, and Equation Building, all of which provide an appraisal of general level of abstract reasoning. In the Quantitative Relations subtest, the individual is required to make judgments about relative size or amount of quantitative materials. In the Number Series subtest, the examinee is to discover the relationship among a series of numbers. In the Equation Building subtest, some knowledge of mathematical conventions is required. Performance is largely dependent on flexibility in using quantitative concepts.

Practical Applications/Uses

One suggested use of the CCAT is to assist in determining the rate of introduction of new material for group activities by looking at the average ability level for the group in question. The authors further suggest that scores on the CCAT can be used to identify students who require special attention. Through identification of weaknesses, the teacher may be in a better position to offer the individual student remedial work to improve the skills that he or she lacks. Furthermore, it is suggested that CCAT scores may be used by teachers to classify children into smaller and more homogeneous groups for specialized learning activities.

A teacher may also use the results of the CCAT in selecting curriculum materials and learning tasks. Moreover, the authors suggest that CCAT results for a particular child can be relayed to parents, provided that no specific scores are given (only relative standing such as "higher than" or "about the same as" should be used). This is to encourage parents to provide the child with "out-of-school" experiences to develop his or her cognitive ability. As a third use, CCAT scores may be of assistance in decision-making for proper grade placement of a child.

The CCAT Primary Battery is most appropriate for children in the second half of Kindergarten through Grade 2. (It can also be used for Grade 3 pupils if a nonreading test is required.) Because the test is administered item-by-item orally, it would be relatively simple to adapt this test in other languages.

The CCAT Multilevel Edition is appropriate for English-speaking pupils in Grade 4–12 (inclusive). It is necessary for the test user to be familiar with all levels of the Multilevel Edition so that he or she will be in a position to select the level most appropriate for the group identified for testing. When the test developer decides to adapt the tests in other languages or formats, it is particulary important to recognize that literal translation of items is no guarantee of equivalence with the original version.

The Primary Battery of the CCAT is a power rather than a speed test, and there are no time limits imposed. Reasonable average administration times vary from 12 to 16 minutes for each subtest. The items are administered one at a time, with adequate pacing by the test administrator and separate instructions for each item. According to the authors, "The pace should be made to fit the children; the children should not be forced to fit the pace" (Thorndike, Hagen, & Wright, 1982b).

The multilevel tests of the CCAT are administered with definite time limits; nevertheless, they are primarily power tests. Items are graded in difficulty, and most students have time to attempt all items. The actual working times for the three sections of the Multilevel Edition are as follows: Verbal Battery, 34 minutes; Quantitative Battery, 32 minutes; and a Nonverbal Battery, 32 minutes. There is ample time provided for distributing test materials, filling out the special answer sheet, giving directions, and administering the practice items.

The CCAT can be administered by a classroom teacher; however, the authors caution that the teacher must study the instructions and follow them carefully. It is also mandatory that the examiner be thoroughly familiar not only with the standardized directions, but also with the content of the CCAT. It is further suggested that the examiner read the directions a day or two prior to the administration, practice reading the instructions, emphasize key words, speak clearly, and pronounce final consonants distinctly, using a natural speech pattern.

The CCAT may be administered in two sessions, ideally on separate days. Examinees should be given a rest period between the subtests. Under no circumstances should more than two subtests be given in one session.

The CCAT can be scored either by hand or by machine. For hand scoring, pictorial strip keys are provided. Two types of scores must always be obtained for both the Primary Battery and the Multilevel Edition: raw score (total number of correct answers), and universal scale score (normalized standard score). Tables for conversion of raw scores to universal scale scores for age groups and grades are presented in the CCAT Examiner's Manual. Once the normalized standard scores are obtained, the examiner is then in a position to use and interpret additional score derivations such as standardized scores by age, percentiles by age, stanines by age, percentiles by grade, and stanines by grade. Grade norms enable comparisons of an individual's test performance to others of his or her grade group, while age norms permit comparisons of an individual's scores with his or her age group.

Scores on the CCAT provide information on the individual's ability to use and manipulate verbal, quantitative, and geometric symbols. These scores, together with other evidence on achievement, motivation, interest, and personality characteristics, provide information that is relevant for diverse educational decisions. Test results should be used constructively to enhance students' learning and to assist in their goal achievement.

CCAT scores provide for individualizing instruction by matching instructional materials and methods to the characteristics of the student. Both the "talented" and the "disadvantaged" pupils are identified, making possible for special provisions such as counseling.

The authors of the CCAT provide cautions that should be exercised in the use and interpretation of test results. No ability test measures solely the ability of the individual; scores can and do change after instruction and experiencing. All tests contain some degree of error, and a score should be looked upon in terms of a range rather than a particular point on a scale. It is for this reason that the use of stanines is quite useful, because they provide coarse grouping. Finally, it should be remembered that many additional factors can influence test scores: motivation, interest, family encouragement, physical health, and so on.

Technical Aspects

The standardization program in the fall of 1980 followed the model used in 1973, when the CAT and the CTBS were originally standardized. Once the program was completed, the proportion of pupils within each stratification category was determined. Adopting a "weighting procedure" to compensate for missing categories and higher proportions of pupils in specific categories, adjustments were made so that the weighted student distributions approximated quite closely population parameters. In evaluating the standardization procedure, the task was efficiently and competently executed.

Kuder Richardson Coefficients (Formula 20) were computed for each subtest separately. Then, the standard formula for the correlation of sums was used to estimate the reliability of the total test. Because the tests were power rather that speed tests, this was a correct procedure. For the Verbal Battery, the typical estimates were .92; for the Quantitative Battery, the estimates were about .89 and for the Nonverbal .90. The corresponding reliability estimates for the Primary Battery were somewhat lower, falling around .87. These reliability estimates suggest a high level of internal consistency (i.e., items within a particular subtest are highly intercorrelated). Data are not presently available to estimate stability over time because the CCAT was administered on only one occasion.

In terms of content validity, the authors, in preparing the CCAT, a priori defined certain characteristics that describe behavior. The test content incorporates tasks which require the examinee to deal with both abstract and general concepts; in most cases to interpret and use concepts; in large part, the deal with the relationships among concepts and symbols; and to demonstrate flexibility in organizing concepts and symbols.

A decision was made by the authors to organize the Multilevel Edition into separate Verbal, Nonverbal, and Quantitative Batteries. This was to ensure more homogeneity of content within each battery. It is observed, however, that the intercorrelations among these batteries range from .54 to .71, with over 85% of the values above .60. This would tend to suggest that the subtests measure a general ability factor for each grade.

For the Primary Battery, the test materials are presented orally to the examinee and one score is obtained. In terms of criterion-related validity, no data are presented for the Primary Battery.

In the case of the Multilevel Edition of the CCAT, evidence for criterion related validity is presented by comparing CCAT results with tests of educational achievement results (Canadian Tests of Basic Skills). All results were collected during the standardization testing; this procedure for establishing validity is what is labelled as concurrent validity. These data are presented in Table 6–1 of *Canadian Cognitive Abilities Test: Technical Notes*. Again, the intercorrelations among the CCAT and CTBS are moderately high: Verbal Tests, mid .80s; Nonverbal Tests, .60s; and the Quantitatives Tests, mid .70s.

Critique

The CCAT has been developed from the Cognitive Abilities Test. Except for minor changes or differences in certain spellings and systems of measurement, the test batteries are similar. This was acknowledged by the authors when they included data in the Canadian Technical Notes Manual from the U.S. edition. A Canadian standardization was required, however, and appropriate and representative norms were derived.

A detailed critique has been prepared for the CAT (Ansorge, 1985). Because evidence for test stability over time (test-retest) is lacking in the CCAT Technical Notes, data available on the CAT may be of relevance for test users. The same could be said for validity, because the only evidence in the CCAT Technical Notes is that for concurrent validity, which has limited utility. It is realized that the CCAT has only been recently standardized, which could account for the lack of published material in the research literature. Efforts to execute research on the CCAT should be continued so that its relevance can be established for use in Canadian Schools.

References

Ansorge, C. J. (1985). Cognitive Abilities Test, Form 3. In J. V. Mitchell (Ed.), *The ninth mental measurements yearbook* (pp. 351-352). Lincoln, NE: The Buros Institute of Mental Measurements.

Pullen, A., & Somwaru, J. P. (1984). *Canadian Cognitive Abilities Test*. (Report No. CAZ ON DE ON 00374). Toronto, Canada: Etobicoke Board of Education, Department of Research and Educational Measurement.

Thorndike, R. L., & Hagen, E. (1978). *The Cognitive Abilities Test*. Chicago, IL: Riverside.

Thorndike, R. L., Hagen, E., & Wright, E. N. (1982a). *Canadian Cognitive Abilities Test: Multilevel Edition: Test Manual*. Scarborough, Canada: Nelson Canada.

Thorndike, R. L., & Hagen, E., & Wright, E. N. (1982b). *Canadian Cognitive Abilities Test: Primary Battery: Examiner's Manual*. Scarborough, Canada: Nelson Canada.

Thorndike, R. L., Hagen, E., & Wright, E. N. (1984). *Canadian Cognitive Abilities Test: Technical Notes*. Scarborough, Canada: Nelson Canada.

Keith L. Kaufman, Ph.D.
Postdoctoral Fellow in Pediatric Psychology, The University of Oklahoma Health Sciences Center, Oklahoma City, Oklahoma.

C. Eugene Walker, Ph.D.
Professor and Director of Pediatric Psychology, The University of Oklahoma Health Sciences Center, Oklahoma City, Oklahoma.

THE CHILD ABUSE POTENTIAL INVENTORY
Joel Milner. Webster, North Carolina: Psytec, Inc.

Introduction

The Child Abuse Potential (CAP) Inventory was primarily designed as an initial screening device for protective service staff working with individuals suspected of child abuse. The CAP can also be used as a screening device to determine participation in prevention programs, for confirming treatment referral status, and as a pre/post program evaluation measure. The CAP is a self-report assessment instrument that includes separate measures of "Abuse," "Random Responding," "Inconsistency," and "Defensiveness" (Lie Scale). Personality traits associated with persons who have abused and/or neglected children were gleaned from the existing literature and are reflected in items on the Abuse Scale. The Lie Scale represents an attempt to identify individuals who purposely try to present themselves in a positive light ("fake-good"). The Random Responding and Inconsistency Scales were added to complement the Lie Scale by selecting individuals who invalidated their responses by carelessly completing the form, respondents who purposely mismarked the answer sheet, or individuals who were unable to read and understand the items. Distortion indexes ("fake-good," "fake-bad," and "random responding") serve to clarify validity scores further.

Dr. Joel Milner, creator of the Child Abuse Potential Inventory, is presently a professor of psychology at Western Carolina University. In 1976 Milner received a child-abuse-related grant and began intensive research in this area. For the past 10 years, he has continued to study and evaluate the CAP as a screening device.

The CAP was developed as a result of the author's recognition that protective service workers in the field needed a brief, self-administered screening device for assessing an individual's physical child abuse potential. Because many workers are relatively inexperienced and most caseloads allow only minimal time to investigate any particular report of abuse, a measurement instrument was required that would aid them in identifying the cases in need of additional investigation. A review of over 700 books and articles pertaining to child abuse and/or neglect served as the foundation for the initial item selection. The author reported that because some definitions of abuse include neglect, no attempt was made to differentiate characteristics particular to each. Rather, emphasis was placed on comprehensively sampling the domain, with the expectation that abuse-specific items would be empirically selected as a later step in test construction. The literature review suggested a number of predominant characteristics, including "unrealistic child-rearing attitudes and expectations, anxiety over a child's behavior, problems in interpersonal relationships, feelings of isolation and loneliness, depression, vulnerability, insecurity, inability to handle stress, rigid attitudes, impulsivity, dependency, immaturity, negative childhood experiences including abuse and neglect, and problems in parental relationships" (Milner, 1980). An average of 15-20 items were written to sample each personality characteristic. In some cases item themes were duplicated with slight variations in wording to account for possible effects of syntax differences. A total of 334 items written in an agree/disagree format comprised the preliminary version of the CAP Inventory.

In an effort to identify items that best discriminated abusive and nonabusive parents, an item analysis was completed by 19 abusive and 19 nonabusive (matched) parents. A chi-square analysis was performed on all 334 items to determine which ones significantly differentiated the two groups. Forty-three items were selected in this manner. An additional 117 were chosen, based on either significant phi-coefficients (where cell size was too small to perform a chi-square analysis) or average response probability of .5 (as suggested in the item analysis literature). This produced a version of the CAP containing 160 items. It should be noted that the author felt that adherence to a strict definition of physical abuse and extensive matching procedures (groups matched on location of residence, gender, age, ethnic background, education, marital status, number of children, age of children, and gender of children) superseded the benefits of utilizing a larger sample.

The importance of this approach is indicated by comparing two studies (J. Milner, personal communication, January, 1986) reported in Milner and Wimberley (1980). When unmatched college students (n=22) were compared to abusive parents (n=19), 38% of the original 334 items were found to discriminate significantly between the two groups. However, when carefully matched groups were employed, only 13% of the CAP items were found to discriminate between abusive and nonabusive parents (Milner & Wimberley, 1979). This suggests that some of the significant differences in the first study were most likely attributable to demographic differences. As a general approach to test development, the author expected to support the stability of test items with a series of subsequent studies utilizing larger samples from a variety of settings.

The 160-item revised CAP Inventory was administered to 65 abusive and 65 nonabusive (matched) parents in a second validity study conducted by Milner and Wimberley (1980). A chi-square analysis identified 77 items that significantly discriminated between the two groups. These items were included in a stepwise multiple regression analysis to determine appropriate beta-weights for development of a scoring key. Using these items Milner found that 96% of the parents were correctly classified into their respective groups. The five misclassifications all turned out to be false-negatives.

A factor analysis (principle factor with an oblique rotation) of the 77 significant items revealed an interpretable seven-factor solution. The factors consisted of distress, rigidity, child with problems, problems from family and others, unhappiness, loneliness, and negative concept of child and self.

In 1982, Milner reported on a series of studies to develop a Lie Scale as a means of reducing the number of misclassifications (predominantly false negatives). In the first study, 47 items were selected from an original pool of 59 (written specifically for this scale's development) and were administered to 51 male and 60 female undergraduates. As the intent of the scale was to eliminate individuals attempting to fake good, items were selected that were socially desirable and yet were not fully achieved by any individual (e.g., "I never lose my temper"). Items were selected for inclusion to approximate a 15% versus 85% split in agree versus disagree answers (with 15% reflecting the frequency of socially desirable responses). Thirty of the original 47 items were retained based on the criteria employed. In the second study, the 30 Lie Scale items were combined with 70 randomly chosen Abuse Scale items, which were administered to 15 males and 68 females who belonged to a Western North Carolina PTA group. Eighteen items were chosen based on the same criteria used in the first study. For these items, a mean of 16.3% and 83.7% was obtained for agree (socially desirable direction) and disagree responses respectively.

In subsequent studies, the 18 Lie Scale items were combined with 142 abuse items, 77 of which were found to discriminate between abusive and nonabusive subjects, and 65 items originally written for the Abuse Scale that failed to discriminate but were believed to have possible future utility, to form the final version of the CAP Inventory. This version was administered to 132 PTA parents in North Carolina. Findings indicated a mean score of 2.8 on the Lie Scale, with a score of seven or higher falling in the upper 5% of the distribution. Two additional studies established internal consistency estimates for the Lie Scale (with at-risk and control groups) and examined the correlation between the Abuse and Lie Scales (nonsignificant, low negative, and positive, depending on the target group).

Despite the CAP's third-grade readability level (Milner, 1980), a Random Response Scale (RR) was developed to identify respondents who "cannot or will not read items, . . . those who do not understand items and . . . those who answer randomly for other reasons (e.g., psychosis, drugs) "(Milner, 1986, p. 31). Items were selected for the RR Scale from a group of 65 inventory filler items, which were administered in conjunction with the CAP's 77 items (Milner & Robertson, 1985). Items were chosen for the scale if one alternative (i.e., agree or disagree) was selected by an overwhelmingly large proportion of the respondents and the item had a small correlation with the abuse scale. Furthermore, items were chosen to obtain an equal number of "agree" and "disagree" items on the final RR scale. Eighteen items were selected for the final version. When a cutoff score of 6 was used, less than 5% of the control subjects were misclassified in two separate studies.

Developed to compliment the RR scale, the Inconsistency (IC) Scale was intended to reduce false-positive random responders. A pool of item pairs was selected from the 160 CAP items that were either similar or dissimilar in content. A total of 10 similar and 10 dissimilar item pairs were chosen based on their consistent or inconsistent response patterns, respectively. On this scale one point is assigned each time a similar pair is endorsed in a dissimilar fashion and/or a dissimilar pair is answered in a similar fashion. Findings indicate that a cutoff of 6 resulted in a misclassification rate of less than 10%.

The distortion indexes were developed to clarify findings of the existing validity scales and, more specifically, to deal with difficulties associated with faking-good behavior, faking-bad behavior, and random responding. A faking-good profile is reflected by a Lie Scale score above its cutoff and a RR score below its cutoff. This assures that a socially desirable responding pattern does not simply reflect elevations due to a random responding. A faking-bad profile is composed of an elevated RR score and a nonelevated IC score. In the case of this index, infrequently endorsed items (RR scale) are chosen in a consistent pattern (low IC score). Finally, an elevated Random Response Index is indicative of elevations on both the RR and the IC scales. This twofold criterion reduces the number of false positives.

Normative data are presented reflecting 56 different studies of abusive, neglectful, failure to thrive, and control parents as well as college students. Normative data for a variety of control groups (N=836) are presented as well as data to support the use of an abuse cutoff of 215 points. Additional data are presented to support a less conservative cutoff score of 166 points based on the signal detection theory. In most cases, however, the 215-point cutoff score will be the criterion of choice.

Practical Applications/Uses

The CAP Inventory is a 160-item self-report measure that can be administered individually or in groups. There are no time limits for test completion, but most persons require 15-20 minutes to finish the inventory. As noted earlier, 77 of the inventory items comprise the Abuse Potential Scale (e.g., "I am sometimes very sad," "I am often lonely inside"), while an additional 65 items, which were written for the Abuse Scale but were not found to differentiate most groups, were also included because they might be useful in later scales. Finally, an additional 18 items that comprised the instrument's Lie Scale (e.g., "I sometimes act without thinking," "I am always a good person") were included, making a total of 160 items.

The CAP Inventory manual suggests that the instrument is appropriate for parents and adult primary caregivers of any age. Readability estimates suggest that the 160-item inventory has a readability level of Grade 3 (Fry, 1963), which makes the CAP a measure that can be used with virtually any sample.

Although initially designed as a research instrument, the CAP Inventory is one of the few measurement devices primarily intended to identify physically abusive parents/caretakers. Despite the need to be cautious in labeling persons "abusive," the CAP Inventory is a useful device for protective service workers screening cases to determine which ones require further investigation. Other applications include identifying parents "at risk" for abuse, who may then be selected to participate in prevention-oriented programs; evaluating the selection criteria for programs that treat abusers (Milner & Ayoub, 1980); and evaluating the effectiveness of treatment programs (Thomasson et al., 1981). The CAP Inventory may also prove useful in a variety of research applications. For example, the CAP could be utilized to prescreen study participants who might comprise abusive and nonabusive comparison groups. Using the CAP in this fashion ensures replicability in subject selection and the homogeneity of each group. It is likely that the CAP will be used in a diverse array of settings, including protective service units, hospitals, and child abuse treatment programs.

Instructions for administration are carefully described in the manual. The CAP is easily administered to either individuals or groups. The examinee is first asked to complete the demographic information on the first page of the test booklet, then to read the instructions at the top of the first page and complete the form as instructed. The examiner should be available to answer questions and should emphasize the need for the examinee to be "conscientious and candid" in responding (p. 8). Because it is not necessary for the examiner to be present while the respondent completes the inventory, the examiner can occupy his or her time with more productive endeavors. All in all, administration typically takes less than 5 minutes.

Scoring the CAP is also relatively simple. Directions for scoring are presented clearly and concisely in the manual. Plastic templates are available for scoring the Abuse Potential and Validity/Distortion Scales and the six descriptive factor scales. Scoring the Abuse Potential Scale entails summing the weighted scores (printed on the template) for each of the 77 items endorsed in the scorable direction by the respondent. Lie Scale items are given one point each if marked in the direction indicated on the template and are summed to get a total Lie Scale score. Additional templates are scored for the Random Responding and Inconsistency Scales. The Distortion Indexes (Fake-Good, Fake-Bad, and Random Responding) are derived from the three validity scale scores and do not require separate scoring.

Computer scoring programs for IBM and Apple computers are available from the author for $40. The author suggests the use of computer scoring to reduce the potential for clerical errors. The scoring program for the CAP is particularly well written. Each disc is accompanied by a brief instruction sheet describing how to get the program "up and running." While this is a nice addition, the simplicity of the program probably makes this unnecessary. The scoring program is totally menu driven, which means that there is little more for the user to do than choose options displayed on the screen. Data are entered easily and can be corrected either at the time of entry or after all the data have been entered. Page markers are indicated on the screen as a check that data have not been improperly entered, and the "key" describing symbols to be entered (e.g., "A" = Agree, "D" = Disagree) is also present on the screen.

Results are presented in a format that is clearly marked and easy to understand. When a profile is invalid, the program gives both an auditory and visual warning, thus ensuring recognition. A futher convenience is the fact that instructions in the manual include step-by-step directions and actual illustrations of the computer screen displays that present results. The only shortcoming of the program is that results cannot be printed out at this time. According to the author, such an option will be available in the near future. In the meantime, he will make summary sheets available (J. Milner, personal communication, January, 1986).

Interpretation of the CAP Inventory is a strictly objective process. Abuse Potential (weighted), Lie, Random Responding, and Inconsistency scores can be compared to the appropriate normative group scores presented in the manual. If the Abuse Potential score is greater than 215 (i.e., greater than 1.65 S.D. above the mean), the respondent would be considered at risk for abuse. It should be noted that a lower cutoff of 166 points has also been derived, based on signal detection theory. However, for most applications the more conservative cutoff of 215 points

60 Child Abuse Potential Inventory

will be preferred (see manual for further discussion). Cutoffs for the Lie Scale, Random Responding Scale, Inconsistency Scale, and Distortion Indexes are easily utilized and understood. A sophisticated knowledge of statistics or test construction is not necessary to comprehend CAP results. The only requirement is to understand that a score greater than 1.65 standard deviations above the mean has less than a 5% probability of occurrence by chance alone. Most professionals should have little difficulty comprehending test findings. Furthermore, normative data are extensive enough to allow researchers and clinicians to compare their data to that of a sample with similar characteristics.

Technical Aspects

The revised CAP manual includes reliability information on 2,610 control, at-risk, neglectful, and abusive subjects collected from a variety of sites in North Carolina and Oklahoma. Sites included medical clinics, a hospital, departments of social services, developmental evaluation centers, PTAs, and community organizations. Of these, 2,062 were controls, 178 were identified as "at risk" for maltreatment, 218 were neglectful, and 152 were physically abusive.

Split-half reliabilities for the abuse scale emerged as follows: controls = .96, at-risk group = .97, neglect group = .97, and abusive group = .98. Abuse scale reliabilities were fairly consistent across gender and education; however, lower reliabilities are reported for control subjects between the ages of 40-49 years and for at-risk blacks. The much shorter Lie Scale had consistently lower reliability estimates. Split-half reliability estimates were reported for controls .69, at-risk .63, neglectful .68, and abusive subjects, .73. Correction for attenuation resulted in significant improvements (controls = .82; at risk = .77; neglect = .81; abusive = .85). K-R 20 coefficients were again similar to estimates of split-half reliability (controls = .72; at risk = .63; neglectful = .71; abuse = .78). Split-half reliabilities for the Random Response Scale varied from .17 (controls) to .47 (at-risk) across subjects. It should be noted that reliabilities close to zero would be expected if responding were truly random. However, higher reliability estimates may reflect the inclusion of protocols that reflect patterns of random responding (e.g., a repeating "agree" then "disagree" pattern of responding). Reliabilities differed somewhat based upon subjects' gender, age, education, and ethnic background. Internal consistency estimates for the Inconsistency Scale range from .44 (abusive) to .64 (controls), which is not surprising given the length of the scale. Again, reliabilities were found to vary depending on subjects' demographic characteristics.

Test-retest reliabilities are reported for four nonclinical groups of subjects who were re-administered the CAP at one-day (N = 125), one-week (N = 162), one-month (N = 112), and three-month (N = 150) intervals (each interval represents a separate group of subjects). Abuse Scale coefficients vary between .91 for the one-day interval to .75 for the three-month interval (one week = .90; one month = .83). The test-retest reliabilities for the Lie Scale were .81 for one day, .84 for one week, .82 for one month, and .65 for three months. Test-retest coefficients are also provided for the Random Response Scale. These vary from .84 for one day to .55 for three months (one week = .74; one month = .54). Finally, Inconsistency Scale coefficients show a great deal of volatility over time (one day = .54; one week =

.71; one month = .57; three months = .70). The author suggests that part of the instability present in the re-administration of the CAP over a period of time may reflect the basic nature of the instrument (J. Milner, personal communication, January, 1986). Dr. Milner further states that the CAP is composed of trait- and state-oriented components. Correlational data presented in the manual, however, do not seem to strongly support the differential state and trait nature of the factors.

Estimates of the Standard Error of Measurement (SEM) are also provided for the CAP Inventory scales. As the author notes in the manual, "The SEM is an estimate of the standard deviation of obtained scores that would be calculated if a client was administered the CAP Inventory many times" (pg. 58). Estimates suggest that there is relatively little distortion across subject groups for CAP Abuse and Validity scales. Furthermore, less than a 4% variation in Abuse Scale scores over multiple testings would be expected given SEM estimates.

Evidence of criterion-related validity for the CAP is based on both predictive and concurrent studies. Milner, Gold, Ayoub, and Jacewitz (1984) followed 200 parents clinically (who were determined on the basis of CAP scores to be at risk for abuse or neglect) for 6 months after completion of the CAP. A significant relationship was found between the total abuse score and subsequent physical abuse ($p. < .0001$) and neglect ($p. < .05$). The .34 correlation between the abuse score and abuse reports was respectable, considering an upper limit of .67 (when a continuous and dichotomous variable are correlated). In two studies of concurrent validity, Milner and his associates (Ayoub, Jacewitz, Gold, & Milner, 1983; Milner & Ayoub, 1980) found that parents clinically determined to be at risk for abuse and/or neglect scored significantly higher on the Abuse Scale than subjects in the normative group. Finally, 44 subjects (nonclinical) were divided into two groups based upon high and low CAP scores (Pruitt & Erickson, 1985). Measures of heart rate and skin conductance were taken while subjects observed two tapes of an infant (one had a cooing segment and the other had a crying segment). Results indicated that, in contrast to the Low Abuse Potential group, the High Abuse Potential group was highly aroused and defensive regardless of the infant's behavioral state.

Support for the CAP's construct validity was provided with a variety of approaches. A number of authors have offered results of convergent and discriminant analyses to support the instrument's validity. Extensive validity studies have found that high abuse scores were found to be related to a number of variables, which include a history of abuse (Robertson, Milner, & Rogers, 1986; Chan & Perry, 1981); reported abuse sequelae (Robertson et al., 1986); external locus of control (Ellis & Milner, 1981; Stringer & LaGreca, 1985); poor self-esteem (Chan & Perry, 1981; Robitaille, Jones, Gold, Milner, & Robertson, 1985); less ego strength (Milner & Robertson, 1985); greater reactivity, emotional/personality problems, ineffective coping/problem-solving skills (Pruitt & Erickson, 1985); higher levels of apprehension, tension, anxiety, and lower levels of stability (Milner & Robertson, 1985); high life stress (Burge, 1982; Mee, 1983); and anxiety and anger in interactions with children (Aragona, 1983). The interested reader should see Milner, Gold, and Wimberley (1985) for a review of this literature, and the CAP manual (1986) for a more extensive discussion.

Other studies have demonstrated the CAP's ability to discriminate between subjects considered "at risk" and controls (Milner & Ayoub, 1980; Thomasson et al.,

1981). The scale has also been successful in differentiating controls from a mixed group of abusive/neglectful parents (Couron, 1981/1982), a group of known institutional abusers (Haddock & McQueen, 1983), and between groups thought to differ in their level of risk (Ayoub, Jacewitz, Gold, & Milner, 1981).

The CAP has also been utilized to evaluate treatment/intervention effectiveness. Significant pre- and post-treatment differences were reported by D'Agostino, Chapin, and Moore (1984) for a group of neglectful and abusive parents. Significant decreases in abuse scores were also noted when a group of high-risk parents in treatment were tested at pre-, post-, and follow-up sessions (Thomasson et al., 1981).

In a recent study, Milner, Gold, and Wimberley (1985) performed a factor analysis on the CAP with a large heterogeneous sample of abusive and nonabusive subjects (N=220). Results indicated the presence of six independent factors: Distress, Rigidity, Unhappiness, Problems from Others, Problems with Child and Self, and Problems with Family. A second factor analysis was performed on the 77 Abuse Scale items utilizing only valid abuse protocols. Results of the second factor analysis confirmed the utility of this solution. These findings were also quite similar to an earlier factor analysis performed on a smaller sample (Milner & Wimberley, 1980). The first five factors were found to differentiate significantly between abusive and nonabusive subjects (Factors 1-4, $p < .0001$; Factor 5, $p < .001$).

Critique

The CAP Inventory has been meticulously developed and extensively researched. The difficulty inherent in predicting a low base-rate, multidetermined act such as abuse in combination with the systematic research program carried out by the author probably accounts for much of the instrument's popularity. A closer examination reveals that confidence in this measurement device is well founded.

The author presents considerable evidence to support the internal consistency and temporal stability of the CAP Abuse and Validity Scales. While coefficients are somewhat lower for the Inconsistency Scale, this is not unexpected given the scale's length. Additional work is needed to clarify why the Random Response Scale's internal consistency coefficients are not closer to zero, as would be expected.

The breadth of available CAP norms represents a distinctive strength. Extensive data are provided to facilitate comparison of the CAP with appropriate norms in order to determine whether the target subjects' scores fall into the category of abusive, neglectful, or control. The variety of normative samples available will be of particular interest to empirical researchers using the CAP.

For a measure that first appeared in the literature just seven years ago, an amazing amount of validity research has been completed. Construct validity studies suggest convergent validity consistent with many dimensions previously associated with child abuse. Recent discriminant validity studies have quieted suggestions that the CAP measures only high levels of distress, and they support the notion that the instrument measures dimensions specific to abuse. Predictive studies reveal modest misclassification rates and a sensitivity to pre/post intervention differences.

The CAP's use is further augmented by detailed development of Validity and

Distortion Scales. Rather than simply discarding protocols as "invalid," scoring procedures allow the examiner to determine the response set associated with invalidation (whether that be "faking good," "faking bad," "random responding," or "inconsistency"). This will not only have clinical utility, but may facilitate research on how respondents with elevated abuse scores and valid protocols may differ from those with elevated abuse scores and invalid/distorted protocols.

The organization of the CAP manual itself merits mention. The manual is approximately 100 pages long and is written with great care and forethought. The organization follows the revised (1985) APA *Standards for Educational and Psychological Testing*. Each section includes a brief definition of the psychometric principle being evaluated (e.g., internal consistency, content validity) as well as a reference to the appropriate APA standard. In this way the manual can be easily utilized by laypersons as well as those interested in the finer points of test construction.

Despite the excellence of this instrument, a few cautions are in order. First, the author makes a point of suggesting that the CAP not be used as a clinical device. However, such use is inevitable and, with it, possible misuse. Clinicians should remain mindful of the fact that misclassification rates, while small, do exist and may increase as populations vary from the normative groups. Using the CAP as a *single* indicator of abuse seems inappropriate. Future clinical use of the measure probably will rely on its usefulness as part of a battery of assessment devices, or as a "first line" screening device to be followed by additional assessment devices where indicated. Second, the author stresses the fact that the use of extreme groups (ie., abusive, control) has minimized scores in the mid-range of the scale, resulting in a noninterval scale. Milner further cautions against use of scores *below* the abusive cutoff for decision making, yet this point is worth further punctuation. While there may be a temptation to group subjects with high scores below the "Abusive Cutoff" with those above the cutoff, this will result in erroneous conclusions and should be avoided. Finally, CAP items should not be manipulated in any way and shortened versions should not be used unless carefully validated with additional research. As with any other standardized instrument, even small changes will affect its psychometric properties, rendering normative data and cutoff scores useless.

In addition to these cautions, more work seems to be needed to explain some of the lower test-retest reliability coefficients. While the author suggests that these estimates reflect an underlying structure of state and trait dimensions, test-retest reliabilities for these descriptive factors do not seem to differentiate clearly state and trait dimensions. With the exception of the rigidity factor, most others have only moderate test-retest reliability over time.

References

Aragona, J. (1983). Physical child abuse: An interactional analysis (Doctoral dissertation, University of South Florida, 1983). *Dissertation Abstracts International, 44,* 1225B.

Ayoub, C., Jacewitz, M., Gold, R., & Milner, J. (1983). Assessment of a program's effectiveness in selecting individuals "at risk" for problems in parenting. *Journal of Clinical Psychology, 39,* 334-339.

Bunge, E. (1982). Child abusive attitudes and life changes in an overseas military environment (Doctoral dissertation, United States International University, 1982). *Dissertation Abstracts International, 43,* 562A.

Chan, D., & Perry, M. (1981). *Child abuse: Discriminating factors toward a positive outcome.* Paper presented at the biennial convention of the Society for Research in Child Development, Boston.

Couron, B. (1982). Assessing parental potentials for child abuse in contrast to nurturing (Doctoral dissertation, United States International University, 1981). *Dissertation Abstracts International, 43,* 3412B.

D'Agostino, P., Chapin, F., & Moore, J. (1984). *Rainbow Family Learning Center: Help for parents, haven for children.* Paper presented at the meeting of the Fifth International Congress on Child Abuse and Neglect, Montreal.

Ellis, R., & Milner, J. (1981). Child abuse and locus of control. *Psychological Reports, 48,* 507-510.

Fry, E. (1963). *Teaching faster reading.* London: Cambridge Press.

Haddock, M., & McQueen, W. (1983). Assessing employee potentials for abuse. *Journal of Clinical Psychology, 39,* 1021-1029.

Mee, J. (1983). *The relationship between stress and the potential for child abuse.* Unpublished master's thesis, Macquarie University, Australia.

Milner, J. (1980). *The Child Abuse Potential Inventory: Manual.* Webster, NC: Psytec Corporation.

Milner, J. (1986). *The Child Abuse Potential Inventory: Manual-revised.* Webster, NC: Psytec Corporation.

Milner, J., & Ayoub, C. (1980). Evaluation of "at risk" parents using the Child Abuse Potential Inventory. *Journal of Clinical Psychology, 36,* 945-948.

Milner, J., Gold, R., Ayoub, C., & Jacewitz, M. (1984). Predictive validity of the Child Abuse Potential Inventory. *Journal of Consulting and Clinical Psychology, 52,* 879-884.

Milner, J., Gold, R., & Wimberley, R. (1985). *Cross-validation of the Child Abuse Potential Inventory.* Paper presented at the meeting of the American Association for the Advancement of Science, Los Angeles.

Milner, J., & Robertson, K. (1985). Development of a random response scale for the Child Abuse Potential Inventory. *Journal of Clinical Psychology, 41,* 639-643.

Milner, J., & Wimberley, R. (1979). An inventory for the identification of child abusers. *Journal of Clinical Psychology, 35,* 95-100.

Milner, J., & Wimberley, R. (1980). Prediction and explanation of child abuse. *Journal of Clinical Psychology, 36,* 875-884.

Pruitt, D., & Erickson, M. (1985). The Child Abuse Potential Inventory: A study of concurrent validity. *Journal of Clinical Psychology, 41,* 104-111.

Robitaille, J., Jones, E., Gold, R., Robertson, K., & Milner, J. (1985). Child abuse potential and authoritarianism. *Journal of Clinical Psychology, 41,* 839-843.

Robertson, K., Milner, J., & Rogers, D. (1986). *History of childhood abuse and later abuse potential.* Paper presented at the meeting of the Southwestern Psychological Association, Fort Worth, TX.

Stringer, S., & LaGreca, A. (1985). Child abuse potential. *Journal of Abnormal Child Psychology, 13,* 217-226.

Thomasson, E., Berkovitz, T., Minor, S., Cassle, G., McCord, D., & Milner, J. (1981). Evaluation of a family life education program for rural "high risk" families. *Journal of Community Psychology, 9,* 246-249.

Lawrence J. Siegel, Ph.D.
Associate Professor, Department of Pediatrics, Division of Pediatric Psychology, University of Texas Medical Branch, Galveston, Texas.

THE CHILDREN'S DEPRESSION INVENTORY
Maria Kovacs. Pittsburgh, Pennsylvania: Maria Kovacs, Ph.D.

Introduction

The Children's Depression Inventory (CDI) is a 27-item self-rated symptom-oriented scale designed to assess depression in children ages 8 to 17 years. The inventory assesses commonly accepted symptoms of depression that the child has experienced in the two weeks prior to completing the evaluation.

The CDI was developed by Maria Kovacs, Ph.D., who is Associate Professor of Psychiatry at the Western Psychiatric Institute and Clinic of the University of Pittsburgh School of Medicine. Dr. Kovacs initially collaborated with Aaron Beck, M.D., the developer of the Beck Depression Inventory for adults. The Beck Depression Inventory served as a model for the development of the CDI (Kovacs & Beck, 1977). The CDI was intended as a research instrument, and it continues to undergo psychometric evaluations with various childhood populations.

A preliminary version of the CDI was released in 1975. A group of 10- to 15-year-old "normal" youths and a group of youths from inpatient psychiatric hospital units were asked to help word the items on the Beck Depression Inventory so that they could be understood by children their own age. In addition, the Beck item pertaining to sexual interest was replaced by an item on loneliness, and five additional items concerning school and peer functioning were added. In 1976, a revision was made regarding language and the numerical coding of responses. A new item on self-blame was also added. The final version of the CDI was published in 1977 following testing with a group of 8- to 13-year-olds seen at a child guidance clinic's full and partial hospitalization units, a comparison group of "normal" children with no psychiatric history, and a group of fifth and sixth grade public school children. Based on the findings from this phase of the testing, minor changes were made in four of the items, and the current version of the CDI was released. To date, the CDI has been translated into Hebrew and French.

Each of the 27 items that comprise the CDI describes a different symptom of childhood depression, including disturbances in mood and hedonic capacity, vegetative functions, self-evaluation, and interpersonal behaviors. Several items also evaluate the child's functioning in various contexts such as school. For each item, there are three sentences, and the child is required to choose the one that best describes him or her during the previous two weeks. Responses are scored on a 0 to 2 scale, with 2 representing a severe form of the depressive symptom and 0 representing the absence of that symptom. Thus, the CDI yields a potential score ranging from 0 to 54. Approximately half the items are arranged so that the first item reflects the greatest level of symptom severity, while the remainder are arranged in such a manner that the first item represents the absence of the symptom. An example of the item evaluating depressive mood is as follows:

> I am sad once in a while.
> I am sad many times.
> I am sad all the time.

The CDI was originally designed to be administered individually to a child. The examiner may read the items aloud while the child follows along on his or her own copy. For older children or children who do not have reading difficulties, the examiner may permit the child to complete the inventory on his or her own.

The CDI is considered suitable for use with children aged 8 to 17 years. The inventory was worded so that it could be read and understood by children as young as eight years old. A more formal analysis of the readability of the CDI suggests that it may be understood by children at the first grade level who are of at least average intelligence (Kazdin & Petti, 1982).

Practical Applications/Uses

At the present time, the CDI is used primarily as a clinical research instrument to identify the severity and nature of depressive symptoms in children and adolescents. It has been used as a criterion measure of depressed versus nondepressed children, as a comparison point in the validation of other methods for assessing depression, and more recently as a technique to assess treatment outcome. Because the various approaches to assessing depression in this population have appeared relatively recently and, therefore, are not yet well developed, no single instrument should be used to identify or diagnose depression. With this caveat in mind, the CDI can be used as a screening device to detect a major depressive syndrome in children when the diagnostic criteria for a Major Depressive Disorder from DSM-III (American Psychiatric Association, 1980) are used. The CDI assesses all the diagnostic criteria in DSM-III except psychomotor agitation or retardation. Because the CDI is easily administered and scored, it can be used along with a clinical interview and other assessment methods to provide a self-rated source of information about the child. The CDI can be used by school personnel or mental health practitioners who wish to evaluate the level of severity and particular constellation of depressive symptoms as perceived by the child.

The CDI has been used in research as a criterion measure of investigations of depressed versus nondepressed youth. It has also been used to discriminate between subjects with psychiatric diagnosis of Major Depressive Disorder from children with other psychiatric conditions.

This instrument has been used in numerous clinical and research settings including public and private schools, child inpatient and outpatient psychiatric facilities, and pediatric medical settings. The professional groups most frequently using this instrument are child psychologists, child psychiatrists, and school personnel such as counselors and teachers.

There are no specific skills or special training required of the examiner. The test booklet contains both the brief instructions to the child as well as the test items.

Therefore, the examiner only needs to read the instructions from the test booklet. The CDI is easily administered in approximately 10 to 20 minutes.

After rapport is established between subject and administrator, the child is given the test booklet and the examiner reads the brief instructions. The child is then asked to complete a sample item to ensure that the instructions are understood. Throughout the administration of the CDI, the examiner is asked to remind the child to answer about his or her feelings during the two weeks. If necessary, the test items can be repeated, but the examiner is not permitted to offer his or her own interpretation. Instead, the child is encouraged to indicate which of the three choices for a particular item best describes how he or she feels or thinks.

It should take no more than five minutes to score the CDI. The three alternatives from which the child selects the items most applicable to him or her are graded from 0 to 2 in the direction of increasing severity (0 = symptom is absent; 2 = symptom is severe and present all the time). The total CDI score for an individual child may range from 0 to 54, depending on the presence and severity of symptomology. Scoring is accomplished by adding the numerical values assigned to the item choices selected by the child. A scoring template is available.

At the present time, normative data pertaining to the scores yielded by the CDI and their relationship to depression in children are sparse. This is due in large part to the fact that clinicians and researchers have only recently reached a general consensus regarding the classification of childhood depression as an affective disorder. Furthermore, there has been only recent general agreement as to the diagnostic criteria for depression in this population.

Preliminary cutoff scores for degrees of severity of depression using the CDI have been reported based on various normative samples (Carlson & Cantwell, 1980; Kovacs, 1980/1981; Kovacs & Beck, 1977). In some instances, data on cutoff scores are based on earlier versions of the CDI or modifications of the current instrument.

Kovacs (1980/1981) initially reported that a total CDI score of 9 was an average score in nonpsychiatric samples. Based on preliminary data regarding the psychometric properties of the CDI, she suggested a cutoff score of 19 as appropriate for classifying children within the depressed range. A score of 19, based on the 54-point scale, was reported to represent the 90th percentile for normal children and adolescents. Using this method of classification, Mullins, Siegel, and Hodges (1985) found that approximately 13% of nonreferred grade school children were grouped within the depressed category. In a study by Kazdin, French, Unis, and Esveldt-Dawson (1983), children hospitalized on a psychiatric unit who met DSM-III criteria for depression obtained a mean CDI score of 15. Preliminary data from an ongoing study by Kovacs (1983) indicated that children who were diagnosed as having a Major Depressive Disorder, in accordance with DSM-III criteria, were also found to have a mean CDI score of approximately 14.

In the most recent unpublished manual for the CDI (Kovacs, 1983), the author provides a detailed discussion of empirically derived cutoff scores based on the scores of children with the diagnosis of Major Depressive Disorder. The adequacy of various scores for the purpose of screening subjects are evaluated against their "true positive" and "true negative" rates. The usefulness of three cutoff scores were evaluated. As a starting point, a score of 13 was selected because it was the mean CDI score of children diagnosed with Major Depressive Disorders. Based on the standard error of the test in this same group of children, two "lower-limit" cutoff scores (11 and 12) were also evaluated. Kovacs notes that in situations in which clinical evaluations are not used in conjunction with the CDI to select depressed subjects, a cutoff score of 13 is the most desirable. While a score of 13 misses approximately 49% of clinically depressed children, it yields the lowest number of false positive cases. If the CDI is used along with a clinical evaluation to permit the rejection of false positive cases, then a CDI cutoff score of 11 is suggested. A score of 11 would encompass approximately 67% of the children diagnosed as depressed.

Given the preliminary nature of the data regarding the diagnostic precision of various CDI scores, empirically derived cutoff scores should be interpreted cautiously when selecting subjects as depressed. At the present time, the CDI is best used along with a clinical interview to increase the diagnostic confidence of the CDI in selecting depressed cases.

Technical Aspects

Reliability of the CDI has been evaluated through internal consistency and test-retest reliability. Kovacs (1983) reports an acceptable internal consistency (coefficient alpha = .86) in a sample of children and adolescents with diverse psychiatric diagnoses. The scale's internal consistency in samples of pediatric medical outpatients and public school students was .71 and .87, respectively. Kazdin, French, and Unis (1983) also report a high internal consistency on the CDI in a group of children hospitalized in an inpatient psychiatric unit (coefficient alpha = .82). Similar alpha coefficients are reported by Saylor, Finch, Spirito, and Bennett (1984) for grade school children (.94) and children with heterogenous psychiatric diagnoses (.80). These same investigators also found split-half reliability coefficients of .61 for the even/odd split and .73 for the first half/second half split in the grade school sample. In the psychiatric group, the coefficient for the even/odd split was .74 and .57 for the first half/second half split.

Item-total score correlations for CDI have also been reported in three samples of children: psychiatric outpatients, newly diagnosed juvenile diabetics, and public school children (Kovacs, 1983). The coefficients are generally in the moderate but statistically significant range for the clinic and public school groups. In the diabetic sample, however, more than 50% of the items correlate less than .25 with the total score.

Relatively little data have been reported on test-retest reliability with the CDI. Kovacs (1983) reports a moderately high test-retest correlation coefficient of .82 over a one-month interval in a small sample of diabetic children. In a group of 90 public school children, a test-retest over a nine-week interval yielded a coefficient of .84. In a psychiatric population, a one-week test-retest reliability coefficient was found to be .87, but at 6 weeks the test-retest reliability dropped to .59 (Saylor, Finch, Spirito, & Bennett, 1984). These investigators also report a one-week test-retest reliability coefficient of only .38 for a sample of grade school children. Kazdin, French, Unis, and Esveldt-Dawson (1983) report a moderate test-retest reliability coefficient of .50 for children in a psychiatric inpatient unit.

The CDI has good content validity if the DSM-III diagnostic criteria for Major Depressive Disorder is used as the appropriate content domain to be assessed. All the diagnostic criteria are inquired about except for items pertaining to psychomotor agitation or retardation (Hodges & Siegel, 1985).

The majority of validity studies with the CDI examine concurrent validity by investigating the relationship between CDI scores and other measures that assess constructs relevant to depression. Kovacs (1983) reports a study in which the CDI scores of psychiatrically referred children were correlated with a measure of self-esteem (Coopersmith Self-Esteem Inventory) and a measure of trait anxiety (Revised Children's Manifest Anxiety Scale). There was a highly significant correlation between the severity of self-rated depressive symptoms and low self-esteem ($r = -.59$). In addition, there was a strong positive relationship between CDI scores and self-rated anxiety ($r = .65$).

In a sample of nonreferred grade school children, Mullins, Siegel, and Hodges (1985) found a strong positive relationship between external locus of control and level of depressive symptoms ($r = .57$). A moderate correlation of .47 was found between the CDI and negative life stress events. There was no consistent relationship between level of depressive symptomatology and cognitive interpersonal problem-solving ability.

Kazdin, Rodgers, and Colbus (1986) investigated the relationship between the CDI and a measure of hopelessness (i.e., negative expectations toward the future) in a sample of heterogeneously diagnosed children in an inpatient psychiatric facility. Children who reported higher levels of hopelessness were significantly more depressed. In a similar group of children in an inpatient unit (Kazdin, French, Unis, & Esveldt-Dawson, 1983), CDI scores correlated positively with hopelessness ($r = .51$) and negatively with self-esteem ($r = -.49$). Children diagnosed as depressed based on DSM-III criteria were also found to have higher scores on the CDI than nondepressed children.

Lefkowitz and Tesiny (1980) developed a sociometric measure to assess peer ratings of depression called the Peer Nomination Inventory of Depression (PNID). They reported a low but statistically significant correlation between the PNID and a modified version of the CDI ($r = .23$) in a sample of grade school children. This relatively weak relationship was attributed in part to the fact that the PNID is not oriented toward assessing psychopathology per se and it does not include items pertaining to somatic and vegetative symptoms (which are present in the CDI).

In a comprehensive investigation of the CDI, Saylor, Finch, Spirito, and Bennett (1984) examined the relationship between level of depression (as measured by the CDI) and a number of variables theoretically presumed to be associated with depression in children. The subjects were children with varying psychiatric diagnoses who were hospitalized on an inpatient psychiatric unit. Following a psychiatric interview, Achenbach's Child Behavior Checklist was completed and scores were obtained on the internality and externality of symptoms. Correlations between psychiatric ratings of depressive symptoms on the Checklist and scores on the CDI approached significance, but the CDI was not related to internality or externality scores. The CDI was significantly correlated, in the predicted direction, with a measure of self-concept ($r = -.64$) and a measure of attributional style that assessed children's patterns of attributions regarding the causes of good and bad events ($r = .46$). No relationship was found between the CDI and the Peer Nomination Inventory of Depression, a sociometric peer-rated scale of depression. Finally, the subjects were divided into high versus low depression groups based on their CDI scores. The relationship between these scores and three measures of anxiety, the Children's Manifest Anxiety Scale (CMAS), the State-Trait Anxiety Scale, and the Test Anxiety Scale for Children, and a measure of locus of control were also examined in this population of children. High versus low depression subjects did not differ on locus of control or on state anxiety. The high depression group did, however, report higher levels of anxiety on the CMAS, higher trait anxiety, and more test anxiety than the low depression group.

Saylor and his colleagues (Saylor, Finch, Baskin, Furrey, & Kelly, 1984), in another series of studies, compared the CDI scores of a group of variously diagnosed children on an inpatient psychiatric unit with ratings of depression from other sources. The findings indicated that the CDI failed to correlate significantly with several peer or staff ratings of depression.

Several studies have examined the criterion validity of the CDI. Using a short form of the CDI, Carlson and Cantwell (1979) found that children who met DSM-III criteria for affective disorders, whether as a primary or secondary diagnosis, rated themselves as significantly more depressed than children with other diagnoses. Similar findings are reported by Kazdin, French, Unis, and Esveldt-Dawson (1983) in a sample of newly admitted inpatients in a children's psychiatric unit.

Kovacs (1983) reports several studies with conflicting findings regarding the criterion validity of the CDI. Nearly identical mean CDI scores were found for a sample of heterogenously diagnosed outpatients at a psychiatric clinic (mean = 9.69) and a sample of public school youngsters (mean = 9.28). In addition, the correlation between CDI scores and independent clinical ratings of the severity of their condition was small and nonsignificant. On the other hand, Kovacs did find that children diagnosed as having a Major Depressive Disorder have significantly higher CDI scores than both children in partial remission from a depressive disorder and children in a public school sample. In addition, children with a major depressive disorder also reported significantly higher levels of depression on the CDI than children with a diagnosis of conduct or oppositional disorders.

Comparing the CDI scores of a heterogeneous group of hospitalized child psychiatric patients with a matched group of grade school children, Saylor, Finch, Spirito, and Bennett (1984) found mean CDI scores of 10.96 for the psychiatric sample and 6.29 for the school sample. This difference was statistically significant. These investigators also compared the CDI scores of depressed and nondepressed children in a psychiatric inpatient sample. Classification of depression was based on the combined ratings of the child's therapist, unit staff, and ratings by other children on the unit. The mean CDI for the depressed group was 12.8 and 8.5 for the nondepressed group. Although these differences between groups were in the predicted direction, they were not statistically significant. In addition, no significant differences were found between the CDI scores of a group of children in an inpatient psychiatric unit who met DSM-III criteria for depression and a sample of inpatient children with varying psychiatric diagnoses other than depression.

Finally, a multitrait-multimethod investigation by Saylor, Finch, Baskin, Furey, and Kelly (1984) examined the convergent and discriminant validity of several measures of depression (including the CDI) and anger in a group of 133 grade school children. Measures of these two constructs were completed by the child, classroom peers, and teachers. Overall, convergent and discriminant validity were statistically supported for each set of measures. Measures of the same construct tended to correlate more consistently with each other than with measures of the other construct. However, the method of measurement (i.e., self-report, teacher report) accounted for about twice as much variance as the trait being measured (depression versus anger). In addition, strong correlations were found among measures from the same source.

Critique

The CDI is currently the most frequently used self-report measure of depression in children. A major advantage of this instrument is that it is easily administered and scored. While available data regarding the psychometric properties of the CDI are promising, additional validation studies are clearly needed.

Generally, the CDI has good internal consistency of items for clinic and nonclinic samples. Test-retest reliability data, however, has been variable across different populations and time intervals. This variability may relfect the episodic nature of depressive symptoms in children (such as symptoms pertaining to mood), which are likely to fluctuate from day to day. Therefore, test-retest coefficients might not be expected to be high when time intervals between testing are over extended periods. Further research is needed to address this issue more thoroughly.

There is some evidence for criterion-related validity of the CDI. CDI scores have been shown to be related to a number of variables that are theoretically consistent with depression. The correlations between the CDI and these other factors have generally been in the low to moderate range. However, evidence for the discriminant validity of this instrument is insufficient. Available data suggests that the CDI measures a construct that is related to psychiatric disorders other than depression. For example, in both clinic and nonclinic populations, CDI scores have consistently shown significant correlations with various self-report measures of anxiety in children. Additional research within a multitrait-multimethod framework is needed to evaluate the convergent and discriminant validity of the CDI.

The effects of age, gender, and developmental factors such as cognitive development on the CDI needs to be evaluated. Few studies have systematically investigated these variables with the CDI. Data are needed regarding the extent to which self-reported symptoms vary as a function of age and cognitive development. The ability of children at different developmental levels to report affective symptoms on the CDI also warrants further study.

References

American Psychiatric Association. (1980). *Diagnostic and statistical manual of mental disorders.* (3rd ed.). Washington, DC: Author.

Carlson, G. A., & Cantwell, D. P. (1979). A survey of depressive symptoms in a child and adolescent psychiatric population: Interview data. *Journal of the American Academy of Child Psychiatry, 18,* 587-599.

Carlson, G. A., & Cantwell, D. P. (1980). A survey of depressive symptoms, syndrome and disorder in a child psychiatric population. *Journal of Child Psychology and Psychiatry, 21,* 19-25.

Hodges, K., & Siegel, L. J. (1985). Depression in children and adolescents. In E. E. Beckham & W. R. Leber (Eds.), *Depression: Treatment, assessment, and research.* Homewood, IL: Dow-Jones-Irwin.

Kazdin, A. E., French, N. H., & Unis, A. S. (1983). Child, mother, and father evaluations of depression in psychiatric inpatient children. *Journal of Abnormal Child Psychology, 11,* 167-180.

Kazdin, A. E., French, N. H., Unis, A. S., & Esveldt-Dawson, K. (1983). Assessment of childhood depression: Correspondence of child and parent ratings. *Journal of the American Academy of Child Psychiatry, 22,* 157-164.

Kazdin, A. E., & Petty, T. A. (1982). Self-report and interview measures of childhood and adolescent depression. *Journal of Child Psychology and Psychiatry, 23,* 437-457.

Kazdin, A. E., Rodgers, A., & Colbus, D. (1986). The Hopelessness Scale for Children: Psychometric characteristics and concurrent validity. *Journal of Consulting and Clinical Psychology, 54,* 241-245.

Kovacs, M. (1980/1981). Rating scales to assess depression in school-aged children. *Acta Paedopsychiatrica, 46,* 305-315.

Kovacs, M. (1983). *The Children's Depression Inventory: A self-rated depression scale for school-aged youngsters.* Unpublished manuscript.

Kovacs, M., & Beck, A. T. (1977). An empirical-clinical approach toward a definition of childhood depression. In J. Schulterbrandt & A. Raskin (Eds.), *Depression in childhood: Diagnosis, treatment, and conceptual models.* New York: Raven Press.

Lefkowitz, M., & Tesiny, E. P. (1980). Assessment of childhood depression. *Journal of Consulting and Clinical Psychology, 48,* 43-50.

Mullins, L. L., Siegel, L. J., & Hodges, K. (1985). Cognitive problem-solving and life event correlates of depressive symptoms in children. *Journal of Abnormal Child Psychology, 13,* 305-314.

Saylor, C. F., Finch, A. J., Baskin, C. H., Furey, W., & Kelly, M. M. (1984). Construct validity for measures of childhood depression: Application of multitrait-multimethod methodology. *Journal of Consulting and Clinical Psychology, 1984, 52,* 977-985.

Saylor, C. F., Finch, A. J., Spirito, A., & Bennett, B. (1984). The Children's Depression Inventory: A systematic evaluation of psychometric properties. *Journal of Consulting and Clinical Psychology, 53,* 955-967.

Saylor, C. F., Finch, A. J., Baskin, C. H., Furey, W., & Kelly, M. M. (1984). Construct validity for measures of childhood depression: Application of multitrait-multimethod methodology. *Journal of Consulting and Clinical Psychology, 52,* 977-985.

Jon D. Swartz, Ph.D.
Associate Dean and Professor of Education and Psychology, Southwestern University, Georgetown, Texas.

COMPREHENSIVE TEST OF ADAPTIVE BEHAVIOR

Gary Adams. Los Angeles, California: Western Psychological Services.

Introduction

The Comprehensive Test of Adaptive Behavior (CTAB) purports "to evaluate how well a retarded student is functioning independently in the environment" (Adams, 1984, p. 5). In contrast to Adams' Normative Adaptive Behavior Checklist (NABC), the CTAB was designed to provide *both* descriptive and prescriptive information for students from birth to adulthood.

The CTAB consists of the following materials: CTAB Record Form (12 pages), used in marking results and monitoring changes in test scores; the CTAB Test Manual (96 pages), containing a description of the test, how it can be used, and the individual test items with criteria and procedures; the Parent/Guardian Survey (16 pages), used for acquiring information from appropriate caregivers about behaviors not observed; and the CTAB/NABC Technical Manual, a 183-page document containing a description of adaptive behavior, the development of the CTAB and NABC, studies of reliability and validity, and so on. In addition to the hand-scored version of the CTAB Record Form, a computerized report of CTAB performance, using machine-scannable answer sheets, is available through Achievement-Oriented Systems, Inc.

"The CTAB was designed to help special educators, psychologists, and teachers quickly evaluate a student's performance even though the test contains a wide range of behaviors" (Adams, 1984, p. 5). In a school setting, the CTAB should be filled out by a teacher or psychologist who knows the student well. In other settings (e.g., an institution), the CTAB should be filled out by the person who knows the student best.

The CTAB was created by Gary L. Adams, Associate Professor in the Department of Exceptional Student Education at Florida Atlantic University. Development of the CTAB began in 1977, and it was published along with the NABC in 1984. Adams received his doctorate in special education in 1978 from the University of Oregon. He previously taught at the University of Nebraska-Lincoln.

Practical Applications/Uses

The CTAB is a 529-item individually administered paper-and-pencil rating scale that aids in the precise evaluation of handicapped students' adaptive abilities. It is

74 Comprehensive Test of Adaptive Behavior

not suitable for group use. The CTAB can be used for placement (to determine where an individual stands in relation to others of the same age or handicap) and for establishing the sequence/scope of training. The CTAB is inappropriate for normally developing individuals because skills are not sequenced in normal developmental order.

A more comprehensive version of the NABC, the CTAB contains 31 scores in six skill areas: self-help skills (toileting, grooming, dressing, eating); home living skills (living room, kitchen-cooking, kitchen-cleaning, bedroom, bath and utility, yard care); independent living skills (health, telephone, travel, time-telling, economics, vocational); social skills (self-awareness, interaction, leisure skills); sensory and motor skills (sensory awareness, motor); language and academic skills (language concepts, math skills, reading and writing); and a total score comprised of the sum of the six subscale scores.

Each test item is evaluated as "Yes" or "No." To help make correct decisions, each item has a test procedure. A ceiling rule (five consecutive "No" responses) is followed, but exceptions are allowed. Administration is untimed and could take several days as observations over a 10-day period may be necessary in order to score some test items.

Retarded children, adolescents, and adults (ranging in age from early childhood through old age) were sampled in both public school settings and in institutional or community-based training settings. In all, more than 6,000 retarded individuals were administered the entire CTAB standardization form. A total of over 4,500 retarded individuals were sampled from more than 20 different institutions and community-based programs around the nation. In addition, 15 different public school systems in Florida gave the CTAB to more than 2,000 retarded students in their programs. These two samples—school and nonschool—provided the basis for the CTAB retarded performance rankings. Tables in the Technical Manual report the numbers of examinees by age and sex across the school and nonschool samples; the nonschool sample summarized by region and sex; the nonschool sample by age and sex; and the school sample by age and sex. Within the school sample, 65.4% of the examinees were classified as educable retarded, 18.5% as trainable retarded, and 16.1% as severely/profoundly retarded.

Technical Aspects

The CTAB total score has been found to correlate .55 and .38 with the WISC-R (Wechsler, 1974) and the Stanford Binet Intelligence Scale (Terman & Merrill, 1973), two individual tests of intelligence; and .68 with the Vineland Social Maturity Scale (Doll, 1965), the original test of social competence/adaptive behavior. In addition, a study was carried out in which CTAB scores were correlated with rankings of 48 students by a staff member; the Pearson product-moment correlation between the two was .79. The only other validity study reported in the Technical Manual involved the correlation of the entire set of CTAB items with the NABC items; these correlations were very high (range: .87 to .995 for an N of 791; excluding total scores, median correlation of .97 for all scores across both sexes and two ages), as would be expected, because the two tests were developed concurrently.

Reliability is discussed in separate sections on interrater reliability, test-retest reliability, internal consistency, and the standard error of measurement. Interrater reliability coefficients for all CTAB categories, subcategories, and total test range from .89 to .99, with a median value of .98. (The kappa statistical analysis procedure, which adjusts for agreement based on chance, also revealed excellent reliability for the majority of items). Test-retest reliability coefficients reported range from .81 to .99, with a median value of .95 for 30 category, subcategory, and total test scores analyzed. Internal consistency correlations (coefficient alpha) at seven age intervals are given separately for males and females for each CTAB category; uniformly high, they range from .78 to .995, with a median correlation of .98. Standard errors of measurement for each CTAB category are reported separately for males and females for each of seven age levels (range: 5-6 years to 19-22 years) of school-retarded individuals, and for each of seven different age levels (range: 10-14 years to 60+ years) of nonschool-retarded individuals; these are generally low (range for school sample: 1.7 to 5.2; range for nonschool sample: 1.9 to 4.8).

Critique

The CTAB is a new, reasonably priced behavior checklist for evaluating how well a mentally retarded student is functioning in relation to others of the same age. It is a more comprehensive version of the NABC and consists of 529 test items organized into 31 scores in six skill categories. Like its companion test, the NABC, the CTAB is a promising new test of adaptive abilities. Despite its newness, the findings reported so far are very encouraging. As is the case with any new assessment instrument, however, further research with a variety of subject populations in different settings is needed.

References

Adams, G. L. (1984). *Test Manual: Comprehensive Test of Adaptive Behavior.* Columbus, OH: Charles E. Merrill Publishing Co.

Doll, E. A. (1965). *Vineland Social Maturity Scale:* Circle Pines, MN: American Guidance Service, Inc.

Terman, L. M., & Merrill, M. A. (1973). *Stanford-Binet Intelligence Scale.* Boston: Houghton Mifflin Co.

Wechsler, D. (1974). *Wechsler Intelligence Scale for Children-Revised.* Cleveland, OH: The Psychological Corporation.

Robert H. Bauernfeind, Ph.D.
Professor of Education, Northern Illinois University, DeKalb, Illinois.

COPSYSTEM INTEREST INVENTORY
Robert R. Knapp and Lila Knapp. San Diego, California: Educational and Industrial Testing Service.

Introduction

The COPSystem (Career Occupational Preference System) Interest Inventory (COPS) presents 168 job-activity items yielding 14 job-activity interest scores. The titles of the 14 scores are given below; detailed descriptions for each cluster are provided in the manual (Knapp & Knapp, 1984, p. 3).

SCIENCE, Professional . . . . (Emphasis on research)
SCIENCE, Skilled . . . . (Laboratory work)
TECHNOLOGY, Professional . . . . (Design work)
TECHNOLOGY, Skilled . . . . (Machines, repairs)
CONSUMER ECONOMICS . . . . (Shop work)
OUTDOOR . . . . (Farming, forestry)
BUSINESS, Professional . . . . (Management)
BUSINESS, Skilled . . . . (Sales work)
CLERICAL . . . . (Office work)
COMMUNICATION . . . . (Writing, advising)
ARTS, Professional . . . . (Creative arts)
ARTS, Skilled. . . . . (Artistic arrangements)
SERVICE, Professional . . . . ("Helping" careers)
SERVICE, Skilled. . . . . ("Helping" careers)

These titles seem to define their areas well, with one exception; the area called "Consumer Economics" mostly involves shop work and food preparation, and might better have been simply titled "Shop." The five paired titles are subdivided largely in terms of whether the job activities require 4 years (or more) of college training. Those that do are cited as "Professional." Thus, for example:

SERVICE, Professional . . . . Counselors, teachers, nurses
SERVICE, Skilled . . . . Flight attendants, hairdressers

As can be seen, high scores in the "Professional" areas would require the time, talent, and money to attend a 4-year college. Failing such resources, the client might consider career possibilities in the paired "Skilled" area, although, as will be noted later, the correlations among the COPS scores, including the paired scores, are not very high.

The COPS items present job activities (not job titles) written in straightforward English, each to be marked on a 4-point scale:

L—Like very much
l —like moderately

d—dislike moderately
D—Dislike very much

Thus, sample items look like this:

	L	l	d	D
11. Sell housewares door-to-door	∴	∴	∴	∴
22. Take and compare fingerprints	∴	∴	∴	∴
(SCORING)	(3)	(2)	(1)	(0)

The COPS was first published in 1966 as the California Occupational Preference Survey. Available for both hand and machine scoring, the hand-scoring edition remains a monument to sensitive design. Published in a cut-back paging arrangement, the four pages of item activities are recorded in four columns, with each row of answers devoted to one of the 14 scores. For example, for Science-Professional, there are three rows of item responses on the answer sheet. Hence, it is easy to calculate the raw score for those 12 items (four items in three rows), and it is also easy to note the actual items to which the client gave the most enthusiastic responses. Truly, this hand-scoring edition is a counselor's delight.

The current 1982 edition of the instrument continues the very attractive hand-scoring format. Several aspects distinguish the 1982 edition from the 1966 edition: 1) the 1966 edition provided for two levels of activities in the communications area; in the 1982 version these have been combined into a single Communication score, and the Consumer Economics (Shop) score has been added; 2) the authors have rewritten several items to reduce sex differences; 3) the authors have lowered the reading/vocabulary level of several items, claiming now that no words exceed a sixth-grade reading level; and 4) the authors have changed a few items to bring them more in line with actual job activities in the American world of work. However, the publishing format and the factorial structure of the scores, with the exceptions of Communication and Consumer Economics, remain much the same as they were in 1966.

The COPS is untimed, but most students finish marking their answers in less than 40 minutes. The publisher provides a Spanish edition of COPS. The identical English instrument is marketed in Canada, with interpretive information geared to the Canadian Classification and Dictionary of Occupations (CCDO). The publisher does not market a form for the visually impaired; however, the publisher does grant permission to reproduce to counseling agencies that deal with visually handicapped persons.

Practical Applications/Uses

The 14 COPS scores represent occupational clusters that can be used as entries to most occupational information systems. The authors write that

> the career guidance process begins by assisting individuals in defining areas for occupational investigation which are specific and appropriate to their personal interests. Investigation of a great many related occupations within a given area broadens the scope of career exploration. Through this process

individuals are more quickly and systematically introduced to those occupations in which they are likely to be occupied in years hence. (Knapp & Knapp, 1984, p. 1)

These are modest claims. It seems clear that the COPS instrument would be appropriate for use in junior high schools, senior high schools, and 2- and 4-year colleges, provided it is made clear that high scores represent career clusters to be *explored*, but not to be entered without exploration.

Technical Aspects

The authors of the COPS relied consistently on multiple-factor analysis studies to suggest appropriate scores and to guide their work in item selection and item revision. The initial studies, suggesting "Professional" item clusters separate from "Skilled" item clusters, were reported by Knapp (1967). Later studies, suggesting mutual independence of all 14 scores, have been reported by Knapp and Knapp (1984, pp. 33-35).

Although the present COPS manual shows data from these multiple-factor analysis studies, it does not show any complete 14x14 correlation matrices. However, the authors have provided this reviewer with several intercorrelation matrices, two of which are reproduced in Table 1. In Table 1, the upper right-hand section shows a 14x14 matrix for a national sample of high school girls (N = 500), and the lower left-hand section shows a 14x14 matrix for a national sample of high school boys (N = 500). The girls' matrix shows intercorrelations ranging from -.12 to .64, with a median of .24 (6% common variance). The boys' matrix shows intercorrelations ranging from -.13 to .65, with a median of .38 (14% to 15% common variance). The paired scores show correlations ranging from .44 to .64, with a median of .54 (29% common variance). All of these data would seem to justify the authors' treating all 14 scores, including the five paired scores, as reasonably unique. (As with any instrument having this type of response mode, we need to recall that the graduated response L-l-d-D item format allows enthusiastic people to mark items enthusiastically while low-energy people are marking items in a low-energy style.)

Of course, any intercorrelation findings are direct functions of the item data—that is, of the items as written. The 14 scores appear to be appropriate to the 168 items as written. If one believes that these items provide good samples of job activities performed by American workers, the 14 scores make sense. If one believes that these 168 items do not sample American job activities well, then the instrument should not be used. This reviewer believes that these items *do* provide a useful sampling of job activities and therefore endorses the 14 scores provided. A very attractive feature of the COPS items is that the activities cited are rather mundane, or "nonglamorous." Raw scores in each cluster can range from a high of 36 to a low of 0. The halfway score in each cluster would thus be 18. It is instructive that, of 112 means reported for eight norms groups, only 20 reached the midscore of 18.0 (Knapp & Knapp, 1984, p. 52). Many means languished around score values of 11, 12, or 13. Thus, we see that high-scoring students tend to "like" the routine chores associated with these 14 occupational clusters. As most jobs entail huge numbers of nonglamorous activities, these nonglamorous items appear to serve well as step-

CO P System Interest Inventory

Intercorrelations of the 14 COPS Scores (Upper-right—500 High School Girls; Lower-left—500 High School Boys)

	1 SCI-P	2 SCI-S	3 TEC-P	4 TEC-S	5 CONEC	6 OUTDR	7 BUS-P	8 BUS-S	9 CLERL	10 COM'N	11 ART-P	12 ART-S	13 SVC-P	14 SVC-S
1. SCIENCE-P		.64	.49	.23	.02	.36	.08	.01	-.10	.24	.09	-.03	.31	-.06
2. SCIENCE-Sk	.57		.38	.46	.32	.43	.06	.27	.25	.22	.00	.08	.40	.26
3. TECHNOLOGY-P	.50	.41		.58	.13	.28	.24	.20	-.04	.25	.32	.14	.10	-.01
4. TECHNOLOGY-Sk	.08	.45	.44		.36	.44	.02	.26	.16	.12	.16	.11	.08	.25
5. CONSUMER ECON	.14	.52	.23	.48		.46	-.11	.33	.44	.01	.11	.27	.26	.52
6. OUTDOOR	.23	.45	.15	.51	.54		-.09	.22	.14	.13	.09	.14	.24	.35
7. BUSINESS-P	.20	.21	.25	-.13	.06	-.08		.44	.36	.43	.09	.07	.22	-.05
8. BUSINESS-Sk	.12	.46	.20	.24	.43	.30	.54		.53	.40	.04	.33	.31	.48
9. CLERICAL	.09	.49	.14	.23	.55	.28	.49	.58		.09	-.12	.22	.30	.52
10. COMMUNICATION	.41	.47	.19	-.02	.28	.21	.53	.53	.41		.40	.43	.30	.15
11. ARTS-P	.30	.32	.47	.21	.29	.16	.14	.19	.20	.40		.58	.23	.12
12. ARTS-Sk	.26	.53	.28	.29	.53	.38	.22	.52	.50	.54	.53		.21	.44
13. SERVICE-P	.38	.54	.22	.18	.36	.31	.34	.42	.37	.52	.41	.44		.50
14. SERVICE-Sk	.17	.56	.18	.40	.65	.48	.14	.59	.59	.40	.28	.64	.52	

ping stones toward career-choice validity. (Intrigued by this COPS approach to predicting career satisfaction, a colleague of this reviewer suggested that people who like remedial teaching, reading papers, serving on unproductive committees, and battling with hostile bureaucrats are well on their way to enjoying work as college professors! Those are the job activities that consume most of our working hours.)

The 1984 COPS manual shows a variety of reliability studies of the 14 scores. The data include Cronbach alpha coefficients ranging from .86 to .91, parallel-forms coefficients ranging from .77 to .90, 1-week test-retest coefficients ranging from .80 to .91, and 1-year test-retest coefficients ranging from .62 to .80. These four sets of studies, based on students in junior and senior high schools, show median reliability coefficients of .885, .86, .87, and .70, respectively (Knapp & Knapp, 1984, p. 36).

This reviewer conducted an independent study of the internal consistency reliabilities for the two groups shown in Table 1. The raw-score means and standard deviations were treated as if they had been derived from tests consisting of 36 dichotomous items, and were analyzed using the relatively conservative KR-21 technique:

	Girls	Boys
Science, Professional	.91	.90
Science, Skilled	.85	.84
Technology, Professional	.86	.84
Technology, Skilled	.89	.89
Consumer Economics (Shop)	.83	.85
Outdoor	.87	.90
Business, Professional	.90	.89
Business, Skilled	.80	.81
Clerical	.89	.84
Communication	.86	.86
Arts, Professional	.83	.80
Arts, Skilled	.78	.81
Service, Professional	.86	.83
Service, Skilled	.85	.86

These coefficients, along with those reported by the COPS authors, appear to be quite satisfactory for a short graduated-response instrument of this type.

Authors of interest inventories (and personality inventories) move out in different directions, with differing rationales, differing styles of item writing, and differing item-response formats. The COPS instrument is no exception. Correlations between COPS scores and work-values (COPES) scores ranged from -.30 to a high of +.47 (Knapp & Knapp, 1979; summarized in the 1984 manual, pp. 45-46). Correlations between COPS scores and forced-choice (Kuder E) interest scores ranged from -.37 to a high of +.49 (Best & Knapp-Lee, 1982; summarized in the 1984 manual, p. 43). Correlations between COPS scores and Holland Hexagon (VPI) scores ranged from -.15 to a high of +.54 (Omizo & Michael, 1983; summarized in the 1984 manual, p. 45). But, as Kuder (1969) has noted, correlations of one interest inventory with other interest inventories have "little bearing on whether the inventory is accomplishing what it was intended" (p. 95). Thus, studies are needed relating COPS scores to current or projected "real life" activities.

COPS scores show positive relations with declared college majors (Knapp, Knapp, & Michael, 1979; summarized in the 1984 manual, pp. 46-47) and with areas of specialization in community colleges (Knapp & Knapp, 1984, pp. 47-48). There are positive relations between COPS scores in high school and actual job/college locations 1-3 years later (Knapp & Knapp, 1984, pp. 48-49), and college-bound students tend to score higher than other students on the five "professional" scales (Knapp & Knapp, 1984, p. 50). Lastly, students actually attending college tend to score higher than high school students on Science-Professional, Science-Skilled, Technology-Professional, Business-Professional (males only), Business-Skilled, Communication, Arts-Professional, Arts-Skilled, and Service-Professional (Knapp & Knapp, 1984, p. 52).

The presentation and write-up of the COPS norms groups are clearly the poorest part of the COPS package. They are also eminently correctible with more extensive samplings and more careful write-ups. National norms data for junior high groups, senior high groups, and community college groups are presented in the manual (Knapp & Knapp, 1984, pp. 51-52). The norms developments are presented in offhand and confusing ways (Wyoming is a Midwest state?); however, three conclusions are suggested by the data shown: 1) norms data for Grades 7-12 can be pooled into one set of norms for boys and another set of norms for girls; 2) community college groups tend to run higher raw scores (greater enthusiasm) than the Grades 7-12 groups; and 3) despite the efforts of the authors, norms for males are manifestly different from norms for females. These sex differences occur at each grade level studied.

This reviewer is inclined to trust those three findings, even as he wonders about the adequacy of the COPS general norms. In any event, it would seem prudent for users to develop local norms, based on the same people, for COPS and other tests. This reviewer would also urge COPS users to consider development of local norms for males separate from females.

Critique

The COPS instrument has received mixed reviews ever since it was first published in 1966:

L—Like very much (Bauernfeind, 1969)
l —like moderately (French, 1972)
d—dislike moderately (Bodden, 1972)
D—Dislike very much (Hansen, 1982)

As these are four different critics, no historical trends should be inferred from this presentation. As much as these four critics disagree with each other, there are a few areas of agreement, namely: 1) the job-activity items are well conceived and well written; 2) the graduated-response item format is attractive and comfortable; 3) the answer sheet layout will help busy counselors to see quickly the score pattern of individual students; and 4) the COPS manuals have, through the years, evidenced serious weaknesses, especially with regard to general norms and predictive validities.

It seems to this reviewer that every test package can be divided into two parts.

One is the instrument, on which the client makes pencil marks or whatever. The other is the manual, in which the authors report validity studies, norms studies, and the like. On a scale of 1 to 10, the COPS manual gets a 5 or 6. Some of the writing is confusing, and, as noted earlier, there is a great need for more norms studies and more predictive validity studies. But the questionnaire itself gets a 10. The items are well written and highly relevant to real-life job activities, the graduated-response format was developed with sensitivity, the pencil marks are easily scored, and most high school and college students seem to enjoy marking the COPS questionnaire.

If one must make a career choice soon, of course, the Strong-Campbell or the Kuder Occupational is to be preferred. If one has time to explore, though—to try part-time jobs, to read, to talk to people—the COPS stands out as an excellent instrument. This reviewer strongly endorses it as a propellant for career exploration.

References

Bauernfeind, R. H. (1969). Review of the California Occupational Preference Survey. *Journal of Educational Measurement, 6,* 56-58.

Best, S., & Knapp-Lee, L. (1982). Relationship of interest measurement derived from the COPSystem Interest Inventory and the Kuder General Interest Survey: Construct validation of two measures of occupational activity preferences. *Educational and Psychological Measurement, 42,* 1289-1293.

Bodden, J. L. (1972). The California Occupational Preference Survey. In O. K. Buros (Ed.), *The seventh mental measurements yearbook* (pp. 1403-1404). Highland Park, NJ: The Gryphon Press.

French, J. W. (1972). The California Occupational Preference Survey. In O. K. Buros (Ed.), *The seventh mental measurements yearbook* (pp. 1404-1405). Highland Park, NJ: The Gryphon Press.

Hansen, J. I. (1982). Review of the California Occupational Preference System. In J. T. Kapes & M. M. Mastie (Eds.), *A counselor's guide to vocational guidance instruments* (pp. 48-52). Alexandria, VA: National Vocational Guidance Association.

Knapp, R. R. (1967, November). *Classification of occupational interests into groups and levels.* Paper presented at the meeting of the Society of Multivariate Experimental Psychology, Berkeley, CA.

ests. *Measurement and Evaluation in Guidance, 12,* 71-76.

Knapp, R. R., & Knapp, L. (1984). *Manual: COPS Interest Inventory.* San Diego, CA: EdITS.

Knapp, R. R., Knapp, L., & Michael, W. B. (1979). The relationship of clustered interest measures and declared college major: Concurrent validity of the COPSystem Interest Inventory. *Educational and Psychological Measurement, 39,* 939-945.

Kuder, G. F. (1969). A note on the comparability of occupational scores from different interest inventories. *Measurement and Evaluation in Guidance, 2,* 94-100.

Omizo, M. M., & Michael, W. B. (1983). Relationship of COPSystem Interest Inventory scales to Vocational Preference Inventory (VPI) scales in a college sample: Construct validity of scales based on professed occupational interest. *Educational and Psychological Measurement, 43,* 595-601.

Raymond H. Holden, Ed.D.
Professor of Psychology, Rhode Island College, Providence, Rhode Island.

CURTIS COMPLETION FORM
James W. Curtis. Beverly Hills, California: Western Psychological Services.

Introduction

The Curtis Completion Form (CCF) is a sentence completion test designed to evaluate the emotional maturity and personal adjustment of adults and older adolescents. It consists of 50 incomplete sentences allowing free association and two structured items that elicit semistructured responses. Subjects are allowed to add extra comments in a final item. The test is printed in an expendable four-page booklet and is self-administering, either individually or in a group. There is no time limit, but most subjects complete the form in about 30 minutes.

James W. Curtis, the author of the CCF, has served as supervising psychologist for the Illinois Division of Vocational Rehabilitation and staff psychologist for the Memorial Hospital School of Nursing and has had extensive experience in clinical and consulting psychological positions.

The author's aim in developing the CCF was to combine favorable elements of both projective and objective methods of personality appraisal. Curtis had used sentence completion tests over a period of years and found the same dynamic factors consistently important in evaluating an individual's adjustment level, and these factors constitute the basis for the test's present scoring method (explained in detail later in this review).

Initially, several clinical psychologists and psychiatrists agreed to use and evaluate an experimental edition of the test. Their criticisms and suggestions were studied and the test modified accordingly. After two years of experimental use, the original 84 test items were reduced to the present 52.

The items themselves are short stems such as: "I wish that . . ."; "Father . . ."; "People I know . . ."; "I would like . . .". Sentence completions are scored as three group factors, either A, B, or C. Group A factors score two points each on any of the following contents: antagonism or hostility; suspiciousness; jealousy; self-pity or pessimism; insecurity or inadequacy; social inadequacy; environmental deprivation (social or personal); or severe conflict (suicidal or death wishes, sexual conflicts, withdrawal, or severe criticism of parents). Group B factors are ambiguous or incomplete sentences and are scored one point each. These include avoidance responses ("Doesn't apply to me"; "No comment") or endings with uncertain or unclear meaning ("To me, money is one of those things."). Group C factors include erasures, crossed-out material, or unnecessary quotation marks and are scored one point each.

A table is provided in the manual (Curtis, 1971, p. 4) to interpret the expectancy that a subject is normal, neurotic, or psychotic. For example, for total scores of less than 28, 98% of the population would be considered in the normal range. However, scores between 28 and 41 could be selected for counseling or therapy, and scores above 45 have a high probability of showing psychosis, with 100% probability for scores above 52.

Practical Applications/Uses

The CCF can be useful in any situation where it is important to evaluate emotional maturity and personal adjustment. It can be used in industrial selection to screen individuals whose emotional adjustment might make them poor employment risks. In educational and vocational counseling, the CCF can help identify students or employees who might benefit from counseling, psychotherapy, or psychiatric treatment. Clinicians would be able to use the CCF to screen clients for more detailed psychological assessment and in diagnosis as an aid to interpreting content dynamically or projectively. Besides the usual student or employee populations, Baranowski (1968) reported that the CCF could be used effectively with deaf patients who had the ability to read above a fourth-grade level.

Technical Aspects

Reliability of the CCF was estimated by the split-half technique in a sample of 133 adults ranging in age from 16 through 58 years; 50 were normal, 34 were neurotic, and 49 were psychotic. The estimated reliability of the entire form was .83 with a standard error of .027 (Curtis, 1971, p. 7). Reliability between scorers of three different professional disciplines ranged from .89 to .95, considered most satisfactory correlation coefficients.

A validity study was performed by the author utilizing 175 normal subjects who had no symptoms and no clinical history, 60 individuals who had emotional problems serious enough to require professional attention, and 100 severely disturbed individuals who were engaged in long-term psychotherapy. Their ages ranged from 17 to 55 years, and one-third of the sample was female. Mean scores on the CCF for each group (with standard deviations in parentheses) were as follows: normal, 22.6 (6.4); neurotic, 37.0 (4.8); and psychotic, 49.5 (10.5). No statistical significance between the groups is reported, but scores that are doubled between the extreme groups would appear to be quite significant, considering the sample size. Biserial r between the normal and the two non-normal groups was .98.

Critique

There have been three reviews of the CCF in the *Mental Measurements Yearbooks*, by Heilbrun (1959), Sarason (1965), and Shaffer (1965). There were no reviews in the seventh or eighth *Mental Measurements Yearbooks* (1972; 1978), probably reflecting a lack of interest in the instrument as well as a dearth of published studies utilizing the test. All three reviews were objective and moderate in praise of the CCF. Besides commenting favorably on the innovative scoring system, the reviewers recommended further studies of the test, concentrating particularly on further demonstrating its validity. My own comments are similar. However, it is doubtful that this test will rise like a phoenix and be recognized as a model of the projective sentence completion method, considering the wide range of the competition. The revised manual of 1971 cites only a handful of unpublished studies dated from the 1960s. Nevertheless, the Curtis Completion Form remains a suitable alternative to other sentence completion methods, particularly in the areas of educational and vocational assessment.

References

Baranowski, E. C. (1968, July). Brief report to James W. Curtis.

Curtis, J. W. (1971). *The Curtis Completion Form: Revised manual.* Los Angeles: Western Psychological Services.

Heilbrun, A. B. Jr. (1959). Curtis Completion Form. In O. K. Buros (Ed.), *The fifth mental measurements yearbook* (pp. 128-129). Highland Park, NJ: The Gryphon Press.

Sarason, I. G. (1965). Curtis Completion Form. In O. K. Buros (Ed.), *The sixth mental measurements yearbook* (pp. 207-208). Highland Park, NJ: The Gryphon Press.

Shaffer, L. F. (1965). Curtis Completion Form. In O. K. Buros, (Ed.), *The sixth mental measurements yearbook* (pp. 208-209). Highland Park, NJ: The Gryphon Press.

Eileen Stitt Kelble, Ed.D.
Coordinator of Early Childhood Education, The University of Tulsa,
Tulsa, Oklahoma.

DABERON SCREENING FOR SCHOOL READINESS
Virginia A. Danzer, Mary Frances Gerber, and Theresa Lyons. Portland, Oregon: ASIEP Education Company.

Introduction

The DABERON, an individually administered screening tool for 4-, 5-, and 6-year old children, is used to predict school readiness. The tool, by design, does not test children to their limits; therefore, it does not reflect the full extent of the child's capabilities. Accurate responses reflect readiness, whereas inaccurate responses may indicate "future problem areas, the need for further diagnostic and prognostic study, information that needs to be taught, and needed medical and/or psychological evaluations" (Danzer, Gerber, & Lyons, 1982, p. 6). In addition, the test can be used to establish a baseline for a continuing record of educational progress.

Virginia Danzer, Mary Frances Gerber, and Theresa Lyons, the authors of the DABERON, lend the test its name. All are educational specialists in Portland, Oregon schools.

The DABERON was developed in stages over a three-year period and originally field tested in Head Start centers and kindergartens in Portland, Oregon. The first design met with the approval of those largely interested in language evaluation of children entering Kindergarten and first grade. Classroom teachers, however, requested expansion of the original device. This was done based on the research reported by Gesell, Beery, Bangs, Piaget, Terman, Merrill, and other prominent people in the field of child development. Items were adjusted, added, and deleted in 1971 and 1972 to balance the level of differences.

The DABERON test kit includes a manual, screen forms, number concept cards, visual perception cards, picture cards for categorizing, 12 color slips, 20 one-inch cubes, a ball, a small box with a lid that is easy to remove, a small airplane, two identical small cars, a pencil, and four buttons or pennies. Teachers or skilled aides who have received adequate instruction can administer the test. Typically, the test is given by one person, but two or three examiners may divide the test format. Although the test is designed to be given in one session, it may be administered in more than one session. Estimated time for the total test will vary from 20 to 40 minutes depending on the child, the examination conditions, and the examiner.

The main body of the test consists of 122 items divided into the following categories: general knowledge, body parts, color concepts, number concepts, plurals, categorizing, prepositions, following directions, visual perception, and gross motor development. Scoring of the 122 items is accomplished by checking the child's responses on the screen sheet: "R" for a correct response, "W" for an incorrect response, "N" for no response, and "I" for an inappropriate response. ("Inappropriate" means the response is neither correct nor incorrect, but may be an echo of the question, unintelligible, or irrelevant.) The authors request that the person administering the test be as objective as possible when scoring. They stress that if a response is doubtful, it should be scored as incorrect.

The authors also recommend that the child experience as much success as possible. If the child fails to answer several items correctly or appears nervous or fearful, it is suggested that questions be asked that the examiner is sure the child can answer. If this does not work, testing should be stopped and resumed at a later date. To obtain a good baseline, it is also suggested that all items be tried, if possible.

The raw score for the test, which is the number of correct responses, is then converted to the DABERON Readiness Equivalency Age in years and months. In addition to the Equivalency Age, the DABERON allows for comments and observations of rotations, reversals, inversions, distortions, unusual language patterns, echoing behavior, and so on. The screen sheet provides a checklist to indicate areas in which help is needed.

For those children who are successful with the items on the DABERON and indicate school readiness, the authors suggest the use of additional readiness activities. These activities may include such things as asking the child to print his first name, count as high as he can, and name letters of the alphabet and numerals presented out of sequence.

Practical Applications/Uses

The final report, which may be shared with the parent, gives a good picture of the child's developmental status at the time of the testing. The DABERON is diagnostic and makes a sincere attempt to be objective. It does not require extensive training to give or score, which makes it superior to some of the leading readiness tests for the same age group.

As suggested by the authors, the DABERON provides a baseline of information for the young child early in his or her educational career. It can also become a tool by which the teacher can obtain the information necessary to individualize curricula.

The instructions for giving the test are easy to read and follow. The test provides a remarkably accurate picture of a child's physical and social capabilities. The recommendation that the test does not have to be given in one sitting has its merits for those children whose attention span has not reached the time span required to give the test. Most of the items hold the child's interest well, and the authors are flexible about the order in which the items are used. This means that if a child loses interest, a quick switch can be made to another area of the test to regain attention.

Technical Aspects

Sampling to standardize the DABERON on a national basis started in 1979. The population was defined as "normal children from the main stream of preschool and school-aged education" (Danzer, Gerber, & Lyons, 1982, p. 30). Normal children, in turn, were defined as "those children who were attending nursery schools, preschools, or elementary school programs and who appear to be functioning normally" (Danzer, Gerber, & Lyons, 1982, p. 30). Normal children, according to the authors, would not be considered handicapped as defined under Public Law 92-142. Slow learners, fast learners, physically handicapped children, and children with mild learning disabilities were included.

The sample involved 15 states and 1,849 cases ranging in age from 2 through 8 years. Chronological age was reported in years, months, and days and divided into 14 intervals. Only cases that had attempted every item on the test were used. Because the emphasis was on 4- and 5-year-old children, the 55- through 60-month age group had the largest "N" (548). The scattering of cases tailed out at both ends to an "N" of four for the 24- through 30-month age group and six for the 103- through 107-month age group. No significant difference was found between the United States Census Bureau figures for 1980 and the DABERON standardization population for grade distribution, sex, and ethnic background. No comparisons were made on income, but the income range is reported.

The raw mean score based on the number of correct answers increased gradually among the truncated chronological ages, which ranged from 2 through 8 years of age. The standard deviation decreased gradually. Analysis of the 122 test items and 19 subscales demonstrated a strong relationship between content and chronological age. Criterion-related validity was achieved through Pearson product-moment correlations. Significant r values were associated with 113 of the 122 test items and all 19 subscales. Bivariate linear regression between chronological age and raw total test scores established the DABERON Equivalency Age Scores, which are presented in chart form in the manual. Validity and reliability measures were adequate and positive.

Critique

A screening test for 4- to 6-year-old children should be short, easily scored, and measure all developmental aspects to give a complete picture of the status of the child. The DABERON is easy to score and measures physical and motor development, as well as some social, cognitive, and even emotional development. It is readily recognized that social and emotional developmental aspects are difficult to measure, and the definition of cognitive development is still being debated.

The DABERON is typical of many of the readiness tests designed for this age group. They are designed by well-meaning people who place great importance on physical, social, and emotional development as a requisite to entrance to the formal schooling process. They see Kindergarten as a place to socialize the child as well as a place to provide experience to increase emotional maturity and the time necessary for physical development to naturally unfold. Cognitive development is addressed, but at a very low level. Too frequently a test of this type is used to retain a child in Kindergarten because of poor motor and social development, without enough consideration given to the child's level of cognitive development. Our experience (research in progress) has been that children of the 1980s have developed more rapidly in the cognitive area than children did when the developmental research was done on which this and similar tests are based.

The value of the DABERON over similar tests is its ease of scoring and its relative objectivity. Although it does provide for interpretation, the single "Age Equivalency" score immediately labels the child and places him or her into an age category that largely reflects motor development but is frequently viewed by both parents and teachers as cognitive development. It is this age categorization that will influence attitudes towards the child despite all the cautions that we take. The authors stress that the test does not take the child to his or her full limits, but unfortunately the developmental aspect that is measured the least by the score is cognitive. On the other hand, the test purports to provide a baseline for a continuing record of the child and is recommended for use in the development of individualized educational plans for the child and for conferring with the parents. This is possibly where its failure to measure in the cognitive area more fully become the most dangerous.

Many things about the test are excellent, but more emphasis needs to be placed on the cognitive developmental level of the child through objective questions and scoring and less left to the subjective interpretation of a speech-language pathologist as recommended by the authors. A child can and frequently does mask his or her cognitive abilities behind overt behavior that may be labeled as immaturity. Too many of our bright young children are languishing in programs that simply do not challenge their full capabilities. As one teacher commented, "How many times can a child learn his numbers, letters, colors, and shapes?"

References

This list includes text citations and suggested additional reading.

Anderson, R. C., Hiebert, E. H., Scott, J. A., & Wilkinson, I. A. G. (1985). *Becoming a nation of readers.* Washington, DC: The National Institute of Education.

Charlesworth, R. (1983). *Understanding child development for adults who work with young children.* Albany, NY: Delmar Publishers.

Danzer, V. A., Gerber, M. F., & Lyons, T. M. (1982). *Manual: DABERON Screening for School Readiness.* Portland, OR: A.S.I.E.P. Education Company.

Elkind, D. (1981). *The hurried child.* Reading, MA: Addison Wesley.

Fitch, S. K. (1985). *The science of child development.* Homewood, IL: The Dorsey Press.

Fong, B. C., & Resnick, M. R. (1986). *The child: Developmemt through adolescence.* Palo Alto, CA: Mayfield.

Graves, D. H. (1983). *Writing: Teachers & children at work.* Portsmouth, NH: Heinemann Educational Books.

Hanson, R. (in press). *Report for U.S. Office of Education on follow-up study of children involved in the SWRL-Ginn 1972-73 early reading program.* Tulsa, OK: University of Tulsa.

Hanson, R., & Kelble, E. (in press). *Report to Tulsa Public Schools on a comparison of vocabularies of 1950 and 1983 kindergarten children.* Tulsa, OK: University of Tulsa.

Jewell, M. G., & Zintz, M. V. (1986). *Learning to read naturally.* Dubuque, IA: Kendall/Hunt.

Kagan, J. (1985). *The nature of the child.* NY: Basic.

Santrock, J. W., & Bartless, J. C. (1986). *Child development.* Dubuque, IA: William C. Brown.

Louis A. Quatrano, Ph.D.
Health Scientist Administrator, National Institute of Health, Bethesda, Maryland.

DECISION-MAKING ORGANIZER

Anna Miller-Tiedeman and Patricia Elenz-Martin. Bensenville, Illinois: Scholastic Testing Service, Inc.

Introduction

Theoretically, the Decision-Making Organizer views the world as rational; the authors suggest that people have a choice in their destiny and that by carefully planning and executing the designated plans an individual, within reason, can obtain what is planned. Thus, this self-monitoring instrument is designed to illuminate the context of decision making in relation to the activities in which respondents have or have not been participating during the college years. Specifically, the instrument is designed to solicit information from the respondent to clarify or stimulate his or her decision-making state in six areas: *self-understanding, education, work, barriers to decision making, time use,* and *designing employment.* In each of these areas the respondent is asked questions that are nested in the eight-stage/four-level Miller-Tiedeman pyramidal model of decision making (Elenz-Martin & Miller-Tiedeman, 1981; Tiedeman, 1961).

The Decision-Making Organizer was developed over a period of four years and was tested on students at several universities. The instrument is nine pages in length and contains the six primary sections previously listed. In addition, a secondary section refers to stages in the decision-making model described by Tiedeman. For example, the first section, *Self-understanding,* has the following secondary sections: exploration, crystalization, choice, clarification, and decision. Items under the secondary heading *Exploration* ask the respondent to clarify the problem (e.g., "I have been considering or am beginning to consider"). Items in the secondary category *Crystalization* query data-gathering activities related to the priorities set (e.g., "I have been gathering information by talking with persons working/living the occupation/lifestyle"). Checking which activities apply is the reader's task.

In *Choice,* another secondary section, respondents list preliminary alternatives identified for their life and provide narrative explaining the rationale for the path taken. In *Clarification* respondents list the advantages and disadvantages of selected occupations. In *Decision,* the final secondary section within the self-understanding section, respondents indicate what they have decided by checking an option. The options involve combinations of school and work. "Indecision" is also a response option. Depending upon their selection, "continue school," "return to school work," "work plus attend school" or "indecision," respondents are referred to another of the primary sections. In summary, the primary section *self-understanding* asks respondents if they have inventoried their strengths, weaknesses, preferences and what they would like to do as well as whether they have considered the potential consequences of their choices (e.g., I have decided to work). Depending upon their decision, they are directed to another section where they are asked to respond to additional items nested within the eight-stage/four-level model.

The Decision-Making Organizer is designed for college students, although a similar instrument is available for high school students. The instrument may be self-administered, used in an interview format, or group administered. The time required to complete the instrument may range from 10 to 60 minutes, depending upon the number of sections to be completed. There are no right or wrong answers, and the examinees record their responses in the booklet. Blank pages at the end of the booklet allow an individual additional room to complete descriptions or write responses. The completed instrument provides a record of decisions made and activities participated in and also provides a summary of the decision-making stages and levels in six distinct areas.

Practical Applications/Uses

The Decision-Making Organizer provides a vehicle to inventory current life status and prompt the decision-making process. Through this process (which is akin to the scientific process—identify the problem, assemble the resources, pursue alternative problem-solving strategies, and pose a solution), respondents complete an inventory analyzing their strengths and weaknesses. The inventory offers structured feedback about certain aspects of life and, in an academic sense, tells what stage of decision-making the respondent has reached. The Organizer helps the individual combine the six life choice activities into a manageable plan of action.

Administratively, information of this type could be combined to give counselors or instructors data on a group of students. This would permit them to show or discuss how students could manage their lives and plan for the future. The level of student decision making in the six areas could also be used to identify students who may need assistance.

In both instances, however, it appears that a debriefing, either individually or in a group, would facilitate student learning. Such a debriefing might provide role models about what particular choices were made in the six areas and what the positive or negative consequences of those actions were, and could potentially expose individuals to other perspectives within a structured framework.

Technical Aspects

The authors state that traditional test reliability issues do not apply because the Organizer is not a test, and it makes no assumption that a particular state has to exist for any length of time (Elenz-Martin & Miller-Tiedeman, 1981). The major issue is whether the respondent considers a state of his or her decision-making to be stable. The issue of stability is not clearly defined. The time period of activities explored and the decision process can be viewed as continuous processes, so taking a snapshot at one point in time may neither support nor refute the concept of stability. Apparently, the Organizer is intended to be a reflection of one point in time. If it is taken at another time the expectation is that some aspects will change because of the underlying theme. The discussion of reliability is incomplete.

The authors point out that the only major question of validity concerns whether the student understands the states. To determine whether this is so, the authors suggest discussing the Organizer's terms with the respondent. This activity may influence the validity of response. Obviously, predisposition of the respondent, predisposition of the discussant, and the process of the inquiry may introduce error into the process. Other factors such as social desirability of responses or acquiescence and deference on the part of the respondee may result in inaccurate information being collected. Therefore, the Organizer may be susceptible to further misunderstanding and self-deception.

Issues related to the predictive validity of the Organizer are not addressed. For example, if the respondent indicates that he or she is thinking about attending college, there is no way to confirm that this is occurring. No information is provided about the content validity of the instrument, and no discussion addresses the issue of representativeness of the collection of items that are used at each stage or at each level. Furthermore, the construction of item formats is open to criticism. Several items are fill-in-the-blank type, and the response patterns may vary. However, the Organizer appears to have face validity; that is, it "looks like" it measures what is is intended to measure.

The Organizer's construct validity is implied from the eight-stage/four-level model proposed, but how items relate to the model is not empirically displayed. Overall, the validity issues of the instrument are not fully addressed.

Critique

The authors purport that the Decision-Making Organizer "is a record of individual decisions and possibilities; it gives students a record of the decision-making stages and levels they have used and need to use in the six life-choice areas; and it provides research data necessary to build more adequate assistance programs for students" (Elenz-Martin & Miller-Tiedeman, 1981, p. 3). However, because of the openness of many of the questions and the potential for misunderstanding, the adequacy of the record is of concern. A debriefing in an individual or group session to explore responses and alternatives would be most beneficial.

The authors suggest that the instrument is a means of introducing the individual to a model of decision making through questions posed in six areas, which leads to "career decision making." In this respect the instrument tries to do several things simultaneously and may not be the best approach to them individually. For example, generic decision-making strategies, whether descriptive or prescriptive, may be taught through paper/pencil simulations or on microcomputers, in which the respondent is able to look at options, respond to a situation, and receive immediate feedback composed of information about error patterns, referral to resources, and so on. On the other hand, there are other theories of career decision making that utilize different decision making models (e.g., attribute matching, need reduction, probable gain, social structure, etc.) that may be useful to the individual (Mitchell, Jones, & Krumboltz, 1974; Roth, Hershenson, & Hilliard, 1970), but they will not be exposed to them in this instrument.

Finally, it is not clear how the research database can be used to build assistance programs. The subjective nature of the responses as well as the individual's readiness could provide broad variation in response patterns. Interpreting results should be done cautiously.

Despite these reservations, the organizer is a useful instrument. It is built on a reasonable model and is an attempt to help individuals use their interpretations to clarify where they are in a heirarchical decision-making model. With debriefing, the instrument could encourage individuals to take more initiative in certain areas of their lives.

References

Elenz-Martin, P., & Miller-Tiedeman, A. (1981). *The Decision-Making Organizer: The college years manual*. Bensenville, IL: Scholastic Testing Service, Inc.

Mitchell, A. M., Jones, G. B., & Krumboltz, J. D. (1974). *A social learning theory of career decision making*. Palo Alto, CA: American Institutes for Research.

Roth, R. M., Hershenson, D. B., & Hilliard, T. (1970). *The psychology of vocational development; readings in theory and research*. Boston: Allyn & Bacon, Inc.

Tiedeman, D. V. (1961). Decision and vocational development: A paradigm and its implications. *Personnel and Guidance Journal, 40,* 15-21.

Thomas L. Layton, Ph.D.
Associate Professor of Speech and Hearing Sciences, University of North Carolina, Chapel Hill, North Carolina.

DETROIT TESTS OF LEARNING APTITUDE-PRIMARY
Donald D. Hammill and Brian R. Bryant. Austin, Texas: PRO- ED.

Introduction

The Detroit Tests of Learning Aptitude-Primary (DTLA-P) is an adaptation of the Detroit Tests of Learning Aptitude-2 (Hammill, 1985) and the original Detroit Tests of Learning Aptitude (Baker & Leland, 1967). The DTLA-P is designed for use with children ages 3 through 9 and is intended to measure intellectual abilities in the same basic theoretical domains as the original battery (i.e., linguistics, cognition, attention, and motor), with two subtests measuring each of the four theoretical domains. However, rather than having a series of separate subtests with discrete test items like on the original DTLA, the DTLA-P contains 130 individual test items that each measures four different theoretical domains.

The specific skills measured by the eight domains were obtained from the general writings of Salvia and Ysseldyke (1985), Hammill, Brown, and Bryant (in press), McLoughlin and Lewis (1981), and Wallace and Larsen (1978). These skills include:

Articulation (5 items): imitation of the examiner's oral presentation;

Conceptual Matching (10 items): the child points to a picture at the bottom of the page that best goes with a picture at the top;

Design Reproduction (14 items): contains two types of items—Type I, in which the child copies the design while a stimulus figure is in full view, and Type II, in which the design is shown for 5 seconds then removed;

Digit Sequence (1 item): the child is asked to repeat the digit sequence, "1..9..7";

Draw-a-Person (13 items): after the child draws a picture of a boy or girl, points are earned for the inclusion of different body parts;

Letter Sequence (8 items): three types of items are used—Type I, in which the child points to the item that matches the stimulus set of letters found at the top of the page, Type II, in which the sequence letters are displayed for 5 seconds, then the child must select the appropriate response from a series, and Type III, in which a series of letters are displayed for 5 seconds, then the child is required to write the letters in sequence;

Motor Directions (11 items): the child is required to imitate motor patterns, such as pointing to body parts;

Object Sequence (9 items): contains three types of items—Type I items require the child merely to point to the response that matches the object-picture series at the top of the page; Type II items require the child to look at a picture for 5 seconds, then point to the response that matches the stimulus set, and Type III items require the child to look at a stimulus picture for 5 seconds, then select the appropriate picture; however, the response pictures are in a different sequence than the stimulus pictures, and the child is asked to write the numbers found below the pictures in the correct order;

Oral Directions (13 items): child is asked to complete simple or complex directions, such as "Draw a line inside the circle.";

Picture Fragments (5 items): child describes what a picture is, although only part of the picture is shown;

Picture Identification (5 items): child is shown a series of pictures and asked to label them;

Sentence Imitation (13 items): child hears sentences of varying length and is asked to repeat them;

Symbolic Relations (8 items): a series of geometric forms that are part of a pattern is shown with one form missing, and the child selects the response that completes the pattern;

Visual Discrimination (4 items): child points to response items—either letters or pictures—that match stimulus items at the top of the page;

Word Opposite (6 items): examiner says a word and the child responds with an opposite word;

Word Sequence (7 items): a series of unrelated words are spoken, and the child repeats them.

Each of these abilities, according to Hammill and Bryant (1986), contributes to the four overall theoretical domains of the test. The authors have subsequently divided each of the overall theoretical domains into two dichotomous areas so that diagnostic contrasts can be made. For example, in the linguistic domain the two dichotomous contrasts are *verbal aptitude* (i.e., items that measure knowledge of words and their use) and *nonverbal aptitude* (i.e., items that do not involve reading, writing, or verbalization). In the cognitive domain, *conceptual aptitude* (i.e., items that involve language, problem solving, abstraction and conceptualization) are contrasted with *structural aptitude* (i.e., items that involve knowledge of shapes, sequences, and patterns). The attentional domain is divided between *attention-enhanced aptitude* (i.e., items that require concentration and short-term memory) and *attention-reduced aptitude* (i.e., items that require long-term memory). Finally, the motoric domain is similarly divided between *motor-enhanced aptitude* (i.e., items that require complex manual dexterity) and *motor-reduced aptitude* (i.e., relatively motor-free items). The test items are combined to measure an overall aptitude, which the authors call General Intelligence (GI).

The DTLA-P was normed nationally on 1,676 children who represented the national population by sex (i.e., 51% males, 49% females), race (i.e., 85% white, 10% black, 5% other), and residence (i.e., 75% urban, 25% rural). At least 100 children were tested at each age level except at age 9 (in which only 89 children were tested). Also, a large number of children (40% of the total sample, or 677 children) fell within the 5- and 6-year age levels, which indicates that these children had a greater influence on the statistics of the test than did children at the other age levels.

Practical Applications/Uses

Hammill and Bryant (1986) suggest that examiners who administer the DTLA-P should have some formal training in test administration. Such training can be found, according to the authors, in departments of school psychology, special education, speech pathology, reading, and counseling. Any examiner who has completed such training should have little difficulty in giving, scoring, and interpreting the DTLA-P.

Three different scores can be obtained from administering the DTLA-P: raw scores, percentiles, and standard scores (quotients set at 100, with a standard deviation of 15). The raw scores provide little useful diagnostic information and are used merely to obtain standard score quotients. Percentiles are found by converting the standard scores to particular ranks. The standard score quotients are available for each of the eight basic aptitudes measures and for General Intelligence. According to Hammill and Bryant, "The best means of evaluating a person's specific strengths and weaknesses across the eight skill areas . . . is through the use of standard scores" (1986, p. 25). That is, in normal individuals the standard scores should cluster in size, while in atypical populations diverging quotients may occur that are more than one standard deviation apart.

The section on motor drawing minimally describes how to score the items. The authors provide some examples of what they term "minimal standards" for the items, but no descriptive data accompanied the standards. On the draw-a-person item, for example, the child is told to draw a boy or girl. For each specified body part drawn, the child receives one point; however, quality of the drawings is not considered in the scoring. The child only needs to include a specific body part in order to receive full credit.

The authors provide two practice test forms in the appendix to help the examiner learn to judge correct items. This information helps, but more examples are needed to allow for more accurate test protocols. A more detailed narrative describing the scoring of items would have been useful.

There is a computer software program available (Bryant, 1986) that provides a means of entering the test scores for a computer printout. The raw scores are converted by the program into standard scores and percentiles, and a printout of the data is done on a summary report that is suitable for inclusion in the child's IEP folder. There is, however, no mention whether the software program is applicable for an Apple, MacIntosh, IBM, or other computer.

Technical Aspects

Reliability scores are reported by the authors, but no other empirical studies are cited. Three different areas of reliability were reported, the first being internal consistency. Cronbach's alpha method, a version of Kuder and Richardson's K-R 20 test, was used to obtain split-half coefficients on 100 protocols at one-year intervals (3 through 9 years of age). These were randomly selected from the normative sample. The mean coefficients at or above the .89 level were indicative of good internal reliability.

The second measure of reliability was a test for stability; that is, test-retest reliability (Hammill & Bryant, 1986). Two separate studies are reported. In one study, 67 children (all white) ages 4 to 9 were tested on two separate occasions, one week apart. In the second study, 42 children (all black or Hispanic) from a Head Start program were tested twice, again one week apart. In both instances, reliability coefficients were computed on the raw scores, with coefficients ranging from .63 to .89. All the coefficient measures were significant at the .001 level, suggesting the DTLA-P is a stable instrument for different groups of children.

The third measure of reliability was reporting the test's standard error of measurements by age level (Hammill & Bryant, 1986). The SEM for the raw scores ranged from 2 to 3 points, while the SEM for the standard scores ranged from 4 to 5 points. The scores were all quite small and consistent across the different ages, suggesting the DTLA-P demonstrates confidence as a reliable instrument.

Besides the reliability measures, three measures of validity were reported on the DTLA-P: content, criterion-related, and construct. For content, the authors listed several popular models of intellect used in the selection of the test items (Guilford, 1956; Kaufman & Kaufman, 1983; Osgood, 1957; Salvia & Ysseldyke, 1985; Wechsler, 1974).

For criterion-related validity, Hammill and Bryant report concurrent correlations between the DTLA-P and other tests given to a subpopulation of the normative sample. This was done by asking the test examiners to report any other tests that had been given to these children. The number of children included in the validity sample varied across the criterion-related tests (with a range being from 28 to 81 children). Those individuals who were either enrolled in special education classes (i.e., classes for the mentally retarded or the learning disabled) or were being screened for special education placement constituted the majority of individuals in this validity study. The criterion-related tests tended to be either aptitude tests (e.g., Wechsler Intelligence Scale for Children-Revised, Detroit Tests of Learning Aptitude-2, Slosson Intelligence Test, or Peabody Picture Vocabulary Test-Revised) or achievement tests (e.g., SRA Achievement Series, California Achievement Tests, Metropolitan Readiness Test, or Wide Range Achievement Test).

There were 126 correlations computed between the DTLA-P and the criterion-related tests. The range of correlations was from .31 to .90, with a median coefficient of .74. These correlations were high enough to indicate the DTLA-P has good criterion-related validity. It should be pointed out, however, that the achievement tests tended to correlate consistently lower with the DTLA-P than did the aptitude tests. This indicates that the DTLA-P tends to be a better measure of aptitude than academic achievement—a finding that is not too surprising, because the DTLA-P was designed specifically to measure aptitude, not achievement.

The approach to measuring criterion-related validity on the DTLA-P has shortcomings that should be addressed. First, the children used in the criterion-related analysis were not well defined by age, race, sex, and concomitant handicaps. Because of this, future comparisons of the DTLA-P become problematic. It is possible that sampling error, for example, influenced the high correlations obtained during the analysis. That is, because age was not specified with the criterion-related sample, a group of older children combined with a group of younger children may have contributed to the high correlations obtained during the analysis.

Similarly, because several different examiners administered the criterion-related tests under different environments, interexaminer variability may have also affected the coefficient scores. Furthermore, the authors do not explain how many of the children were repeat subjects among the different criterion-related tests. This can be a confounding variable, especially if a particular subset of children with a strong impact on the results had been included among all of the reported tests, in which case the results would be consistent across their performance but would not represent a true sample. (For example, if the subset of children comprised lower functioning mentally retarded, this could cause all of their test scores to be low in comparison to a higher functioning group of children. The effect would be a spuriously high correlation between the various criterion-related tests and the DTLA-P, because a consistent low performance on one test would yield similarly low performances on the others.)

The third area of validity reported on the DTLA-P is construct validity. From all indications, the DTLA-P appears to have good construct validity. This was demonstrated by: 1) the increased scores on the DTLA-P across age levels, 2) the high intercorrelations between the subtests, 3) its significant relationship to school achievement, 4) its discriminative ability for distinguishing children with known deficient aptitude abilities from those with normal abilities, and 5) a strong relationship in item validity found during an item discrimination analysis.

Critique

The most obvious strength of the DTLA-P is its use with a younger age population than that of the original Detroit Tests of Learning Aptitude (Baker & Leland, 1967) and the revised edition. The clinical usefulness of the DTLA-P has not been established yet, because it is a new test and has not undergone a thorough examination in the field. Nevertheless, the measures of aptitude the DTLA-P assesses are relevant and important skills, especially to an examiner who wants to assess a child with learning difficulties. However, whether the aptitudes represented on the instrument will differentiate a child's abilities needs to be documented by the authors. If the instrument *can* discriminate a child's disabilities, are these disabilities consistent with clinical impressions of the child? Can the DTLA-P demonstrate changes in performance as a result of training on these disabilities? Additional research on these issues is needed before the utility of the DTLA-P can be fully assessed.

References

Baker, H. J., & Leland, B. (1967). *Detroit Tests of Learning Aptitude.* Indianapolis, IN: Bobbs-Merrill.

Guilford, J. P. (1956). The structure of intellect. *Psychological Bulletin, 53,* 267-293.

Hammill, D. (1985). *Detroit Tests of Learning Aptitude-2.* Austin, TX: PRO-ED.

Hammill, D., Brown, L., & Bryant, B. R. (in press). *A consumer's guide to tests in print.* Austin, TX: PRO-ED.

Hammill, D., & Bryant, B. R. (1986). *Detroit Tests of Learning Aptitude-Primary.* Austin, TX: PRO-ED.

Kaufman, A. S., & Kaufman, N. L. (1983). *Kaufman Assessment Battery for Children.* Circle Pines, MN: American Guidance Service.

McLoughlin, J., & Lewis, R. (1981). *Assessing special students: Strategies and procedures.* Columbus, OH: Charles E. Merrill.

Osgood, C. E. (1957). Motivational dynamics of language behavior. In M. Jones (Ed.), *Nebraska symposium on motivation* (pp. 348-424). Lincoln, NE: University of Nebraska Press.

Salvia, J., & Ysseldyke, J. E. (1985). *Assessment in special and remedial education.* Boston: Houghton Mifflin.

Wallace, G., & Larsen, S. (1978). *Educational assessment of learning problems.* Boston: Allyn & Bacon.

Wechsler, D. (1974). *Wechsler Intelligence Scale for Children-Revised.* San Antonio: The Psychological Corporation.

James E. Stahlecker, Ph.D.
Head of Psychological Services, Callier Center for Communication Disorders, University of Texas, Dallas, Texas.

DEVELOPMENTAL ACTIVITIES SCREENING INVENTORY-II
Rebecca Fewell and Mary Beth Langley. Austin, Texas: PRO-ED.

Introduction

The Developmental Activities Screening Inventory-II (DASI-II) is a revised and updated version of the Developmental Activities Screening Inventory (DASI). The DASI-II is intended to be used as a screening measure for children functioning in the developmental range of 0-60 months. The measure contains 67 items that are intended to tap the following 15 functions:

- Sensory Intactness
- Sensorimotor Organization
- Visual Pursuit/Object Permanence
- Means-end Relationships
- Causality
- Imitation
- Behaviors Relating to Objects
- Construction Objects in Space
- Memory
- Discrimination
- Association
- Quantitative Reasoning
- Seriation
- Spatial Relationships
- Reasoning

The 67 items are grouped across 11 developmental levels spanning the age range of 0-60 months (Level A: 1-2 months; Level B: 3-5 months; Level C: 6-11 months; Level D: 12-17 months; Level E: 18-23 months; Level F: 24-29 months; Level G: 30-35 months; Level H: 36-41 months; Level I: 42-47 months; Level J: 48-53 months; Level K: 54-60 months). Each developmental level, with the exception of the last, contains six items to be administered and scored according to the child's response; Level K contains seven items to be administered and scored.

Practical Applications/Uses

The DASI-II provides information that can be useful for instructional programming with children experiencing developmental delay. Instructional activities that might precede the attainment of individual test items are provided in considerable detail within the test manual (Fewell & Langley, 1984) and generally appear useful for program planning. The measure is appropriate for use with children who are hearing impaired and/or vision impaired, because the items do not require extensive expressive or receptive language skill.

DASI-II is an informal screening tool for the measurement of developmental functioning and can be administered by classroom teachers and others who are familiar with early childhood development. Minimal special training appears to be required, although familiarity with the various materials needed is essential for appropriate use of the instrument.

Because the DASI-II is intended to be used by teachers and others directly involved in the provision of educational service to young children, the kit does not contain many items commonly found in early intervention and early childhood program classrooms. Items less commonly in classroom use (picture, shape, word, and numeral cards), but used frequently in the assessment of early skills, are included with the test kit, whereas additional materials must be assembled by the examiner.

Instructions for the administration of the items within each developmental level are clearly specified, although no strict standard procedure for administration is suggested. The authors (Fewell & Langley, 1984) suggest that instructions to the child be communicated orally or manually (using signs, gestures or pantomime) in the case of hearing-impaired children. Specific adaptations in the administration of test items to visually impaired children are suggested for each item. These adaptations rely on greater tactile experience for the child and on the substitution of tactile exploration (size, shape, texture) for visual exploration (color, position in space).

It is suggested that testing begin one level below the examiner's estimate of the child's developmental level. The test basal is established when the child successfully accomplishes all items within a single developmental level. Testing continues upward until the child is unable to successfully accomplish any items within a single developmental level and a ceiling is established.

Fewell and Langley indicate that the test is designed to be individually administered, but that the items need not be administered in the sequence suggested by the test format. The DASI-II is not timed, and the length of time necessary for administration varies depending on the capabilities or limitations of the child being assessed.

Each item contains specific criteria for passable accomplishment of the task. Items are scored as passed (+) or failed (−), and all items below the established basal are scored as passed. The child receives one point for each item passed, and the total raw score is equal to the sum of all passed items.

Raw scores are converted to developmental age scores (in months) with the assistance of a table in the manual. Development quotients may be calculated by dividing the developmental age by the child's chronological age, and multiplying by 100. The manual also provides "a rough guide to interpretation" of the development quotient, which is consistent with most standard intelligence tests (above 140 = Superior; 121-140 = Above Average; 80-120 = Average; 60-79 = Below Average; Below 60 = Poor).

Individual analysis of DASI-II items, provided in the manual's appendix, is intended to "assist the evaluator in determining why a child performs as he does and to delineate performance strengths and weaknesses" (p. 93). The item analysis attempts to indicate the sensory and/or mental function tapped by each item across the 15 possible perceptual/conceptual functions.

Item analyses provided by the manual suggest that the DASI-II items most frequently tap behaviors requiring sensory intactness and sensorimotor organization, discrimination, association, imitation, and spatial relationship skill. The next most frequently tapped behaviors require the child's skill in memory, construction, reasoning, and seriation. Those skills least tapped include visual pursuit, quantitative reasoning, and understanding of means-end and causal relationships.

Technical Aspects

Although the DASI-II is not extensively documented in the research literature, the authors note their own work employing the DASI-II, which provides some indication that the instrument samples behaviors that relate closely to those commonly assessed in standard measures of cognitive development. Utilizing the DASI-II and either the Cattell Infant Intelligence Scale or the Merrill Palmer Scale, a group of 45 children with multiple disabilities was assessed. Significant correlations between the DASI-II and the other two measures (.91 in both cases) provided some evidence that DASI-II samples the same behavioral domain. Comparison of DASI-II test performance with that on the Denver Developmental Screening Test and the Preschool Attainment Record similarly yielded significantly correlated results (.95 and .97, respectively) when using both delayed and nondelayed children between the ages of 7-74 months (Fewell, Langley, & Roll, 1982). Similarly significant correlation (.98) was found between DASI-II and the Developmental Assessment of the Severely Handicapped in Dykes' (1980) study of severely and multiply handicapped children.

Interestingly, DASI-II has been found unrelated to language competence as assessed by the Receptive-Expressive Emergent Language Scale and by the Preschool Language Scale. This finding supports the authors' intent that the DASI-II assesses developmental functioning independent of speech and/or language competence.

Critique

The DASI-II is a well-organized and easy-to-administer instrument for the assessment of children in the developmental range of 0-60 months. The test kit does not contain all of the test items; however, items not provided should be easily obtained within the early childhood classroom. Organization of some test items (picture cards) is a bit awkward because loose cards are provided, which need to be presented in different organizational patterns at five different points during the testing. Minimal training is required for those wishing to use the DASI-II for developmental assessment, although familiarity with young children's development and behavior and with the test materials is necessary.

Although some research has provided evidence to suggest that the DASI-II samples a behavioral repertoire similar to that sampled by standard tests of cognitive development, the small number of items presented at each developmental level cannot provide the broad perspective of developmental functioning that a more formal developmental assessment might yield. The DASI-II should be considered a screening instrument and should be utilized neither as a formal test of developmental functioning nor as a test of intelligence because the behavioral repertoire sampled is, of necessity, rather narrow.

This instrument serves as an excellent prescriptive tool for classroom teachers' program planning. Specific activities that precede the attainment of each developmental accomplishment sampled by the test are provided in the manual. These activities could easily be integrated into the Individual Educational Plans written for children enrolled in special education programs and could provide the underpinning of an excellent program for children experiencing developmental delay.

References

Bzoch, K. R., & League, R. (1978). *Receptive-Expressive Emergent Language Scale*. Baltimore, MD: University Park Press.

Doll, E. A. (1966). *Preschool Attainment Record*. Circle Pines, MN: American Guidance Service.

Dykes, M. K. (1980). *Developmental Assessment for the Severely Handicapped*. Austin, TX: PRO-ED.

Fewell, R. R., & Langley, M. B. (1984). *Developmental Activities Screening Inventory (DASI-II)*. Austin, TX: PRO-ED.

Fewell, R. R., Langley, M. B., & Roll, A. (1982). Informant versus direct screening: A preliminary study. *Diagnostique, 7*(3), 163-167.

Frankenburg, W. K., Dodds, J. B., & Fandal, A. W. (1970). *Denver Developmental Screening Test*. Denver: Ladoca.

Stutsman, R. (1948). *Merrill-Palmer Scale*. Chicago: Stoelting.

Zimmerman, I. L., Steiner, V. G., & Pond, R. E. (1969). *Preschool Language Scale*. Columbus, OH: Charles E. Merrill.

James L. Carroll, Ph.D. *Associate Dean, College of Education, Arizona State University, Tempe, Arizona.*

DEVEREUX ELEMENTARY SCHOOL BEHAVIOR RATING SCALE II

Marshall Swift. Devon, Pennsylvania: The Devereux Foundation.

Introduction

The Devereux Elementary School Behavior Rating Scale II is used primarily for screening children in regular and special education programs, or for recording progress of these children with regard to school behavior and adjustment. The scale is also used in research on incidence of specific classroom behavior problems and in research on development of social competence.

The Devereux Elementary School Behavior Rating Scale II (DESB-II) is a form for collecting a teacher's ratings of the behavior of an elementary school child. For 30 of the 52 DESB-II items, a teacher indicates how often a child performs some particular response. For the remaining items the teacher reads a descriptive statement and then indicates the degree to which a child is similar to or different from the average child in a normal classroom with regard to the behavior described. The items included in the scale were selected because they describe achievement-related classroom behaviors. The DESB-II resembles the Devereux Elementary School Behavior Rating Scale (DESB) in form and contains many items from that scale (Spivack & Swift, 1967).

The author of the DESB-II, Dr. Marshall Swift, co-authored the DESB with Dr. George Spivack in 1966. Since 1966 Swift has published additional information on the DESB in several articles and a book (Swift & Spivack, 1975). Swift is currently a Professor in the Department of Mental Health Sciences at Hahnemann University. He received his Ph.D. in School Psychology from Syracuse University and is a Diplomate of the American Board of Examiners in Professional Psychology.

The DESB-II replicates and extends previous work on the DESB. The author believed it was time to revise the DESB within the current educational environment. Fifteen years of use and study had indicated ways in which the measure could more effectively relate to contemporary school environments and programs. In construction of the DESB-II, teachers again participated in selection of behaviors to be rated, and ratings of the selected behaviors were factor analyzed. Initial reliability and validity studies have been conducted.

Practical Applications/Uses

The DESB-II was developed to enable teachers to efficiently rate the classroom behavior of students. Items were developed and selected to focus on behaviors that affect academic achievement. The author's intent was to identify children with behavior problems early in elementary school so that special instruction of such students could begin as early as possible.

Teachers in regular and special education settings can use the DESB-II; teachers from both settings participated in the development and norming of the scales, and norms are available for students in special as well as regular education classrooms. These scales are intended for completion by teachers who are well acquainted with a student's classroom behavior, although classroom teacher aides may also be reliable raters. Neither parents nor professionals outside the child's classroom have the information needed to respond to DESB-II items.

The DESB-II is a four-page rating scale. The first page contains space for student information and instruction to raters. Pages 2 and 3 describe the rating scales and list the items. Page 4 again provides space for student information and contains a form for calculating behavior factor and behavior cluster scores and for recording estimates of achievement. A 38-page manual describes development of the test and provides administration guidelines.

A teacher needs approximately 10 minutes to complete the scale for each child. (More time may be required for the first several uses of the measure, until the teacher becomes acquainted with the instructions, scales, and items.) General instructions printed on the front of the rating form are clear and concise. Although two kinds of rating scales (i.e., frequency and degree) are used within the measure, each scale is printed above the items to which it applies, and directions are easily understood.

The rating for each item on the DESB-II is transferred to the DESB-II Profile by the rater. Items are grouped by behavior factor or behavior cluster and are summed within each factor or cluster. The total factor raw score can then be located on a standard score scale.

A teacher's ratings of frequency or degree for DESB-II items are subjective, although directions focus teachers' attention on recent and current behavior and specifically exclude use of information other than a teacher's own observation of the student. The author provides very specific interpretations for scores on each factor or cluster. For example, Peer Cooperation is a two-item behavior cluster. The two items are rated from 1 (not at all descriptive) to 7 (extremely descriptive). Swift (1982) indicates that "most children in the regular class score between 8 and 12 with special class children scoring more toward the lower end of the scale. A score of 7 or less is indicative of difficulties working with peers, difficulties which tend to interfere with learning" (p. 28). For some scales Swift's interpretation includes intervention specification. For the Work Organization factor score, the author suggests, "Such a score (of 12 or less) suggests the need for intervention and remediation specifically directed toward organization of work" (p. 11).

Technical Aspects

Research on and evaluation of the DESB provide a framework for examination of the development and standardization of the DESB-II. Although the format of the DESB-II matches the DESB, the items have been substantially reviewed and revised. The DESB-II includes 30 items for which raters make frequency observations, whereas the DESB included 26 such items. Of the 30 DESB-II items, 9 are exact duplicates of DESB items, 7 very closely match DESB items, and 14 are new. Moreover, the DESB-II includes 22 items for which raters make degree decisions; of those items 5 are exact matches, 4 are close approximations of previous items, and 13 are new.

Independent researchers have not reported much information about the DESB-II. The DESB, however, has been examined closely in a number of studies, and the issues raised by those researchers will be used to examine the data reported by Swift in the DESB-II manual. Past and current data support the internal consistency and test-retest stability of classroom behavior ratings by elementary school teachers. Support for Spivack and Swifts' (1973) claims for moderate to high test-retest and internal consistency reliabilities for the DESB has been provided by researchers in a variety of settings (Reynolds & Bernstein, 1982; Schaefer, Baker, & Zawel, 1975; Willis, Smithy, & Holliday, 1979). The DESB-II manual provides evidence of test-retest stability for children in special education classes. These data indicate quite satisfactory test-retest coefficients (for scales with so few items) (range .64 to .90, median r = .81).

Additionally, the DESB-II manual provides: grade, age, and I.Q. data for the regular class normative sample; behavior cluster means and standard deviations for males, females, and each grade level; and contrasts of means and standard deviations for regular and special education groups for each behavior factor and behavior cluster.

Given the care and precision with which researchers have raised a number of issues regarding the DESB, it is disappointing that the author does not provide a clear and detailed description of the factor analysis, a matrix of interfactor and intercluster correlation coefficients, or any acknowledgement of what a principal factor analysis yields in studies of the new measure. Until additional studies have been published, it seems reasonable to predict that the DESB-II, like the DESB, reduces to two or three factors that account for approximately 70% of the total variance. Interpretation of subscale scores for an individual should be approached with caution until data from factorial studies are available, and there is clarification of the extent to which subscales share variance. It may well be that factor scores can be constructed for a two or three factor solution and that concerns about interpreting 13 behavior factor and behavior cluster subtotals as discrete factors can be avoided.

Although means and standard deviations are presented for normative samples from regular and special education programs, additional description of the distributions is needed. Willis, Smithy, and Holliday (1979) indicated that "responses for 'normal' children tend to be skewed, with the item means falling near the positive end of the response continuum and with narrow standard deviations. Item means in the referred sample were closer to the center of the distribution and tended to have larger standard deviations" (p. 327). Data presented for the DESB-II indicate differences between the two samples in shapes of distributions as well as in means. Factor 1, for example, has an upper limit of 26 and, for children in regular classes, a mean of 17.35 and a standard deviation of 5.78. The skewness of this distribution can affect interpretation of scores. From data presented, it is not possible to determine how skewed the behavior factor distributions are, or if they are bimodal.

One of the primary claims for the DESB-II is that all scales relate to academic achievement as measured by California Achievement Test scores in reading and math, by I.Q. test scores, and by report card grades in reading and math. A table of correlations is provided, but no analyses are reported to indicate the total amount of variance in academic achievement accounted for by DESB-II factor and/or cluster scores. Test users need to know the extent to which the behavior factors in combination predict academic achievement. Analyses addressing that issue will also provide information regarding the amount of unique variance in academic achievement accounted for as each additional factor is entered.

Critique

Much work remains to be done in the statistical definition of the DESB-II, and that work is essential to accurate interpretation of ratings of individual students. Because the items accurately collect information on patterns of classroom behavior, and because observations relate (to some as-of-yet unspecified degree) to academic achievement, the scales have been found useful by professionals in education and by researchers in education and psychology (Elardo & Caldwell, 1979; Jorgenson, 1977; McKim, Weissberg, Cowen, Gesten, & Rapkin, 1982; Pellegrini, 1985). The clarity of instructions and ease of completion and scoring make the scales an appropriate tool for gathering teachers' observations of students' classroom behavior. However, interpretation of results must be made with cautious professional judgment and without assumption of the independence of factors or clusters.

References

This list includes text citations and suggested additional reading.

Elardo, P. T., & Caldwell, B. M. (1979). The effects of an experimental social development program on children in the middle childhood period. *Psychology in the Schools, 16,* 93-100.

Jorganson, G. W. (1977). Relationship of classroom behavior to the accuracy of the match between material difficulty and student ability. *Journal of Educational Psychology, 69,* 24-32.

McKim, B. J., Weissberg, R. P., Cowen, E. L., Gesten, E. L., & Rapkin, B. D. (1982). A comparison of the problem-solving ability and adjustment of suburban and urban third-grade children. *American Journal of Community Psychology, 10,* 155-169.

Pallegrini, D. S. (1985). Social cognition and competence in middle childhood. *Child Development, 56,* 253-264.

Reynolds, W. M., & Bernstein, S. M. (1982). Factorial validity and reliability of the Devereux Elementary School Behavior Rating Scale, *Journal of Abnormal Child Psychology, 10,* 113-122.

Schaefer, C., Baker, E., & Zawel, D. (1975). A factor analytic and reliability study of the Devereux Elementary School Behavior Rating Scale. *Psychology in the Schools, 12,* 295-300.

Spivack, G., & Swift, M. S. (1966). The Devereux Elementary School Behavior Rating Scales: A study of the nature and organization of achievement related disturbed classroom behavior. *Journal of Special Education, 1*(1), 71-91.

Spivack, G., & Swift, M. (1967). *Devereux Elementary School Behavior Rating Scale.* Devon, PA: The Devereux Foundation.

Spivack, G., & Swift, M. (1973). Classroom behavior of children: critical review of teacher-administered rating scales. *Journal of Special Education, 7,* 55-73.

Swift, M. (1982). *Devereux Elementary School Behavior Rating Scale II manual.* Devon, PA: The Devereux Foundation.

Swift, M., & Spivack, G. (1968). The assessment of achievement-related classroom behavior. *Journal of Special Education, 2*(2), 137-153.

Swift, M., & Spivack, G. (1975). *Alternative teaching strategies: A guide for teachers and psychologists.* Champaign, IL: Research Press.

Wallbrown, J. D., Wallbrown, F. H., & Blaha, J. (1976). The stability of teacher ratings on the Devereux Elementary School Behavior Rating Scale. *Journal of Experimental Education, 44*(4), 20-22.

Willis, J., Smithy, D., & Holliday, S. (1979). Item level validity of the Devereux Elementary School Behavior Rating Scale. *Journal of Abnormal Child Psychology, 7,* 327-335.

Barry S. Anton, Ph.D.
Professor of Psychology, University of Puget Sound, Tacoma, Washington.

Steven C. Parkison, Ph.D.
Psychologist, 97th General Hospital, Frankfurt, Germany.

DYSLEXIA DETERMINATION TEST

John R. Griffin and Howard N. Walton. Los Angeles, California: Instructional Materials & Equipment Distributors.

Introduction

The Dyslexia Determination Test (DDT) is designed to identify dyslexic patterns in children aged 7 to 18. The authors claim that the DDT will "differentiate the child who has dyslexia from the individual who is merely behind in reading, writing and spelling due to causes other than a dyslexic pattern as defined and determined by this testing procedure" (Griffin & Walton, 1981).

Dyslexia is defined in the DDT as "minimal brain dysfunction and/or differential brain function manifesting itself as a specific learning disability for language, i.e., reading (decoding), spelling (encoding) and writing (involving graphemes and nemkinesia)." Seven types of dyslexia are described. Three of these are considered to be basic types of dyslexia as determined by the DDT. Permutations of these three basic types generate seven subtypes:

1) *Dysnemkinesia:* a deficit in the ability to develop motor gestalts (engrams) for written symbols.
2) *Dysphonesia:* a deficit in symbol/sound (grapheme/phoneme integration, and the inability to develop phonetic word analysis synthesis skills.
3) *Dyseidesia:* a deficit in the ability to perceive whole words (total configuration) as visual gestalts and match them with auditory gestalts.
4) *Dysphoneidetic:* a deficit in grapheme/phoneme integration and in the ability to perceive whole words as visual gestalts and match them with auditory gestalts.
5) *Dysnemkinphonetic:* a deficit in the ability to develop motor gestalts for written symbols and in grapheme/phoneme integration.
6) *Dysnemkineidetic:* a deficit in the ability to develop motor gestalts for written symbols and in the ability to perceive whole words as visual gestalts and match them with auditory gestalts.
7) *Dysnemkinphoneidetic:* a deficit in the ability to develop motor gestalts for written symbols, grapheme/phoneme integration, and in perceiving whole words as visual gestalts and matching them with auditory gestalts.

The test authors, John R. Griffin and Howard N. Walton, are both optometrists who have interests in dyslexia and learning disabilities. A proposed book, *Therapy in Dyslexia and Reading Problems Related to Vision Perception and Motor Skills,* is being

110 Dyslexia Determination Test

written by them to assist reading instructors with an understanding of the visual aspects of reading.

The DDT is presented in a 42-page examiner's manual, with a 16-page supplement as well as an audiocassette "mini-seminar." There are two forms of the test, Form A and Form B. (Form B was designed for follow-up testing or as an alternate form.) Test materials consist of a booklet of Word Lists (Decoding Words Forms A & B), Decoding Patterns Checklist for Forms A & B, Interpretation Recording Forms, and the Examiner's Instructional Manual. Individual administration times range from 20 to 25 minutes.

Examinees are presented a series of tasks that assess three different abilities related to the deficit being examined. Thus, subtests that yield reversals of numbers and letters point to dysnemkinesia. Dysphonesia is suggested when phonetic reading ability is less than eidetic reading (in decoding) or when phonetic spelling is less than eidetic spelling (in encoding). Similarly, dyseidesia is likely when eidetic reading is inferior to phonetic reading (in decoding) and eidetic spelling is inferior to phonetic spelling (in encoding).

The decoding components of the DDT are directed at determining the examinee's eidetic ability; that is, the examinee's ability to recognize and correctly sight read words quickly at a particular grade level. The grade level is determined from the decoding of words in the Decoding Words List. The specific grade level is defined as the level at which the examinee can decode 5 of 10 words orally following a 2-second presentation of each word. These are defined as the Flash-Known words. Half of these 10 words are eidetic and half are phonetic. Thus, the 50% level defines the examinee's highest eidetic DDT grade level. Eleven word lists, ranging from preprimer words to college level words, comprise the test.

The second part of the decoding test is administered to determine if the examinee can decipher some of the words that were not recognizable during the initial 2-second presentation. During this phase of testing, the examinee is allowed 10 seconds per word to determine whether phonics, syllabication, and/or structural analysis may be of help in recognizing and reading the words orally.

Graded word lists for use in the decoding portion of the DDT were obtained from various sources, including words from the San Diego Quick Assessment Test (LaPray & Ross, 1969) and Boder (1973).

In the encoding procedure, the examiner repeats the Flash-Known words and the examinee writes them. Thus, this is a spelling test with no time limit. To assess eidetic encoding, previously recognized eidetic words are used. A table is then consulted to determine any evidence of dyseidesia. The encoding evaluation for dysphonesia is accomplished by having the examinee attempt to spell 10 unknown (unread) words. Correct spelling or phonetic equivalents are considered acceptable. Another table is consulted to determine the presence or severity of dysphonesia.

Practical Applications/Uses

The purpose of diagnostic testing in an area such as learning disabilities is to help guide instruction by determining strengths and weaknesses. The DDT, therefore, would be of primary interest to those who regularly teach elementary and junior high school students experiencing difficulty in learning to read. Specifically, this would include reading specialists, reading clinicians, special education teachers, basic skills teachers, school psychologists, and other professionals. To a lesser extent, educational researchers may want to consider this test if defining populations of dyslexic readers is of interest to them.

Interpreting the results of the DDT requires making inferences based on understanding the relationship among the subtests. The manual accompanying the DDT contains descriptions of these relationships, but this information may seem overly simplistic.

A related concern is the level of skill necessary to administer and score the tests. Procedures for the first tests for dysnemkinesia are straightforward: the examinee is required to print either all upper- or lowercase letters of the alphabet and numbers from 1 to 10. However, when the examiner administers the decoding section of the dysphonesia and dyseidesia test sections, he or she is required to simultaneously time 2-second trials and determine whether the spoken response is correct. There is no pronunciation guide in the manual. In addition, there is nothing to prevent the examinee from looking at upcoming words while proceeding down the list. Caution should be exercised in using this test with children who speak a nonstandard dialect or with those for whom English is not the dominant language. Lucas and Singer (1976) have shown that Spanish language experience was related to syntactic ability in English, which in turn was significantly correlated with oral reading achievement.

Technical Aspects

The authors state that the DDT is a clinically validated test based on their many years of clinical experience. They say that the DDT is consistently corroborated by case histories, parent/teacher observations, and by real and theoretical information relative to brain anatomy and physiology. However, the manual contains no test development information. The same is true with respect to validity and reliability. No studies of any kind could be found in the literature addressing these important criteria. Before any test can be properly used, good reliability and validity evidence should be included in the test manual.

Another concern is the lack of criteria for what constitutes a good phonetic equivalent in the encoding section of the DDT. There are no guidelines for the examiner to use in determining whether a response offered by an examinee is a good phonetic equivalent or not.

The authors provide several tables in the manual, which the examiner is to use to classify scores in terms of the severity of dyslexia. However, there are no norms. Descriptive terms such as *borderline normal, mild, moderate,* and *marked* are used with no external referent.

Critique

The DDT does not include criteria for scoring, normative information, reliability, or validity data. The word-list approach for classifying readers into groups has a long history as a technique for distinguishing normal from dyslexic reading patterns. However, this instrument does not meet the needs for screening reading disability and diagnosis of subtypes of developmental dyslexia solely through reading and spelling performance. While the test delineates criteria for different subtypes of dyslexia, the severity scales associated with these subcategories are not useful because of deficiencies in standardization.

Touted as a practical and easily administered test that can be administered by various professionals, the procedures are not easily understood. There is a complex set of instructions, timing requirements, and contingencies that may leave the examiner with many questions about procedure. Mastering this test appears to require a great deal of clinical or teaching experience in the area of reading disabilities.

The test's strengths include a qualitative analysis of reading and spelling as interdependent functions. The conceptual underpinnings draw heavily from current research in neuropsychology and cognitive psychology. The two cognitive processes of gestalt versus analytic are basic to the two standard methods of teaching reading (whole word vs. phonetic). Recent efforts to refine this procedure to provide a valid technique have been more successful (Boder, 1983). The DDT, while showing early promise in this regard, does not go far enough and thus would be of limited use to the experienced examiner.

References

Boder, E. (1973). Developmental dyslexia: A diagnostic approach based on three atypical reading-spelling patterns. *Developmental Medicine and Child Neurology, 15* (5), 663-687.

Boder, E., & Jarrico, S. (1982). *The Boder Test of Reading-Spelling Patterns*. New York: Grune & Stratton, Inc.

Griffin, J. R., & Walton, H. N. (1981). *Dyslexia Determination Test*. Los Angeles: Instructional Materials & Equipment Distributors.

LaPray, M., & Ross, R. (1969). Quick Gauge of Reading Ability. *The Journal of Reading, 12,* 305-307.

Lucas, M. S., & Singer, H. L. (1976). Dialect in relation to oral reading achievement: Recoding, encoding, or merely a code? In H. Singer & R. B. Ruddell (Eds.), *Theoretical models and processes of reading* (pp. 429-439). Newark, DE: International Reading Association.

Carol H. Adams, Ph.D.
Clinical Director, Indian Rivers Mental Health Center, Tuscaloosa, Alabama.

EGO-IDEAL AND CONSCIENCE DEVELOPMENT TEST
R. N. Cassel. Hollywood, California: Monitor.

Introduction

The Ego-Ideal and Conscience Development Test (EICDT) is an objective personality inventory designed to assess the similarity between one's values (i.e., one's ego-ideal or conscience) and those of mainstream American society. It was developed by R. N. Cassel, a clinical psychologist with over 30 years of experience with adolescents and young adults in a variety of personnel, clinical, and research settings.

The EICDT is based on Freudian personality theory, which conceives of the conscience as the internalized standards of society. This inner "voice" keeps a person in line by causing him or her to feel guilty for violating or, sometimes, even *thinking* about violating, society's rules. Working in conjunction with the conscience is the ego-ideal, which provides pleasure and a sense of satisfaction when one avoids temptation and does the right thing. Collectively, the conscience and the ego-ideal are referred to as the superego.

Dr. Cassel approaches the problem of delinquency through assessment of conscience and ego-ideal development. Considering the finding that many delinquents are unaware of how mainstream society expects people to solve social and interpersonal conflicts (Carstensen, 1970; Cassel & Blum, 1969; Chiu, 1969; Reise, 1969), how, he asks, can they be expected to behave appropriately? Cassel assumes that by providing young people with information about the areas in which their behavior departs from mainstream society, progress can be made toward preventing and treating delinquency.

Toward this end, the Computer Assist Counseling Program was also developed by Dr. Cassel and his graduate students (Carstensen, 1970; Chiu, 1969). Similar in content to the EICDT, the Computer Assist Counseling Program detects aspects of a youth's value system that are at odds with predominant societal values and provides "meaningful guidance."

The first edition of the EICDT was published in 1967 and was followed in 1969 by the current edition. The test construction sample consisted of 2,785 individuals selected to represent a cross-section of mainstream society in the United States; age range of this sample was 12 to 60 years, approximately equal numbers of males and females were included, and all races were represented. The manual states that 25 different groups contributed to this subject pool, but the nature of these groups was not specified. Respondents were presented with 80 items assessing, in the experience of Dr. Cassel, typical social problems faced by 12- to 18-year olds.

Respondents selected what they judged to be the ideal solution to each problem from five alternatives. The alternatives ranged from highly conforming solutions to highly nonconforming ones, with fairly neutral options in the middle. The most frequently selected alternative for each of the 80 items became the keyed response used to score subsequent protocols. The normative sample contained 6,199 persons who similarly represented mainstream society.

Eight areas of conscience and ego-ideal are represented by the EICDT, with 10 items per area. The eight categories are as follows: Home and Family, Inner Development, Community Development, Rules and Law, School and Education, Romance and Psychosocial, Economic Sufficiency, and Self-Actualization.

Practical Applications/Uses

The Ego-Ideal and Conscience Development Test is most suitable for adolescents and young adults. It has been used in the classroom, in counseling and psychotherapy situations, and in correctional institutions with delinquents.

Nonprofessional persons can readily handle both administration and scoring. A verbatum orientation to the test is provided in the manual and may be particularly useful for group administration. The test is virtually self-administering for responsible subjects whose reading comprehension is at or beyond the 6th-grade level, and a sample test item is provided in the test booklet for practice. Additional proctoring, which might include reading the test aloud, is suggested for those with reading or motivational problems. The EICDT can be completed in an hour and hand-scored in 10 minutes through the use of a stencil key. (Scoring can also be accomplished by machine.) Parallel forms (Forms A and B) are available to permit retesting.

Raw score totals for each of the eight areas are computed by counting the number of concurrences with those solutions chosen most frequently by the test construction sample. The total score is simply the sum of the eight area scores. These nine scores (total score plus eight area scores) are plotted on interpretation forms included in the test packet and displayed as T scores. The area and total scores are also represented as deviation scores, which provide a rough indication (in standard deviation units) of the extent of an individual's discrepancy from mainstream society in the United States.

Interpretive paragraphs are provided for each of the five categories of deviation scores. For example, + + represents individuals whose total score is 70 T or better, or 2 standard deviations above the mean. Persons who fall in this category are described as "extremely sensitive" to the expectations of mainstream society in the United States. The four other categories are: +, 0, –, and – –. The simplicity of this scoring and interpretive system makes the EICDT useful for those with limited psychometric background, such as teachers, guidance counselors, and probation officers.

Technical Aspects

Parallel forms of the EICDT were administered concurrently to several large samples of people, including college students, junior and senior high students, delinquents, and a mixed society group to establish test reliability (Cassel, 1969). When total scores were considered, fairly good agreement between forms was found. Pearson r's, a statistic designed to quantify the degree of similarity between two sets of scores, ranged from .77 to .94 across samples. Reliability estimates for the eight area scores were considerably lower, as would be expected with only 10 items per scale; Pearson r's for these categories were in the middle .40's.

Reliability was also assessed by measuring the degree of internal consistency among items on the same form (Cassel, 1969). Several different statistical techniques were employed: K-R Formula 20, Cronbach Alpha, and Horst Pearson r. Varied samples were studied: college students, junior and senior high students, parents involved in PTA, society mainstream, and delinquents. Pooling across statistical methods, total score reliability estimates ranged from a low of .687 (with the delinquent sample) to .910 (with an upper-division college sample). When area scores were considered, lower estimates were obtained, again around the middle .40's.

Taken together, these studies suggest moderately high reliability for the total score of the EICDT (middle to high .80's, on the average). However, the total score does not appear to be sufficiently stable to recommend its use singly (i.e., without additional clinical or test data) in making significant decisions about a respondent's life. Reliability of area scores is too low to make meaningful comparisons among individuals and should be interpreted very cautiously, if at all.

Three types of validity studies are described in the test manual. The content validity of the EICDT rests on the extent to which its author adequately represented the areas of the conscience and ego-ideal by the eight categories he chose, and the extent to which the 10 items in each area represent those categories. In developing the EICDT, Dr. Cassel relied solely on his judgment to select categories and items. A sounder procedure involves submitting proposed items and categories to a panel of judges with some expertise in the area. Items can be retained or deleted on the basis of their judged relevance. In relying on only one expert's opinion, the possibility of bias cannot be ignored.

The second type of validity, predictive validity, involves the extent to which a test is capable of predicting some relevant criterion, such as parole or probation readiness. Dr. Cassel stated in the test manual that these studies were planned but had not yet been undertaken. Encouragingly, the manual cites several studies in which expected differences on total and area scores have been found when delinquent and nondelinquent populations were compared (Cassel, 1969). While the strength of the relationships between EICDT scores and group membership is not provided, these results suggest that the test may have predictive validity in terms of predicting group membership (delinquent versus nondelinquent).

The test manual also indicates that many of the studies attempting to establish the EICDT's construct validity suffer from small sample size as well as variable results within samples. The author's assurance of a "clear trend in the findings" leaves much to be desired in terms of rigor.

A deviant test-taking attitude by the respondent can also be a threat to the validity of a test. Even a highly reliable and valid test can produce meaningless, misleading results if the respondent fails to respond honestly to its items. No assessment is contained within the EICDT of the examinee's attitude; anyone wishing to fake a socially desirable protocol could readily do so. From a practical standpoint, it becomes essential to base any major decisions about the examinee on data from a variety of sources, such as a clinical interview or other test scores. From a theoretical standpoint, the extent to which the total score on the EICDT correlates with a measure of social desirability, such as the Crowne-Marlowe Social Desirability Scale (Crowne & Marlowe, 1960), would be important to assess.

Critique

The Ego-Ideal and Conscience Development Test represents a creative effort to assess superego development and to pinpoint specific areas of departure from mainstream American society. It has applications in the classroom (as an aid to values clarification), in individual counseling and psychotherapy settings, and it may prove useful when used with other indexes to assess probation readiness.

It has been shown to be a reasonably good instrument psychometrically. I have to take issue, however, with its content validity. I think the test overemphasizes the cognitive aspect of the superego, thereby reducing inadequate superego development to a matter of ignorance. This cognitive bias is apparent when Cassel moves beyond assessment to treatment of deficiencies in conscience and in ego-ideal development. While few theoreticians would argue with the premise that inadequate superego development is responsible for some of the crime in our society, I do not think that many psychotherapists would agree with Cassel that information alone would be particularly effective in dealing with antisocial personalities. From the psychoanalytic perspective, conscience development is basically complete at age 6. Efforts after that age to instill a true appreciation of the rights of others would not be expected to be successful. While Cassel bases the EICDT on Freudian personality theory, Cassel erroneously assumes that after the phallic stage, remediation through provision of information is possible.

One would hope that those who use the EICDT do not categorically equate conformity to mainstream society with morality (as Cassel does at one point in the manual). History provides us with vivid examples of nonconformists who, in the larger perspective of time, were shown to be highly evolved morally—Abraham Lincoln, Susan B. Anthony, Gandhi, and Martin Luther King, to name but a few.

Finally, caution should be exercised in interpreting the results of the EICDT for subgroups within American society that differ markedly from the mainstream. Although many of the characteristics of the normative sample are specified, there is no indication that the important variable, socioeconomic status, is controlled. One should also make allowances for the changes in our society that have occurred in the 17 years since the EICDT was published.

References

Carstensen, D. (1970). *Ego-ideal development by computer assist counseling for delinquency prevention among high school youth.* Unpublished master's thesis, University of Wisconsin-Milwaukee.
Cassel, R. N., (1969). *The Ego-Ideal and Conscience Development Test.* Hollywood, CA: Monitor.
Cassel, R. N., & Blum, L. P. (1969). Computer assist counseling (COASCON) for the preven-

tion of delinquent behavior among teenagers and youth. *Sociology and Social Research, 54,* 72-79.

Chiu, A. (1969). *A preliminary evaluation of a computer assisted counseling program for delinquent youth.* Unpublished master's thesis, University of Wisconsin-Milwaukee.

Crowne, D. T., & Marlowe, D. A. (1960). A new scale of social desirability independent of psychopathology. *Journal of Consulting Psychology, 24,* 349-354.

Reise, M. (1969). *A comparison between delinquent youth and typical individuals on the Ego-Ideal and Conscience Development Test.* Unpublished master's thesis, University of Wisconsin-Milwaukee.

Luella Sude Smitheimer, Ph.D.
Speech and Language Pathologist, Port Washington Speech, Language and Hearing Center, Port Washington, New York.

EVALUATING COMMUNICATIVE COMPETENCE: A FUNCTIONAL PRAGMATIC PROCEDURE

Charlann S. Simon. Tucson, Arizona: Communication Skill Builders, Inc.

Introduction

The Evaluating Communicative Competence (ECC) instrument was developed to analyze an individual's communicative skills through a series of 21 informal tasks. These tasks serve as probes of the subject's auditory and expressive skills. The major objective of the tool is to place emphasis on the observation and description of competent versus incompetent communicative behaviors. The ECC is not a test but a series of probes designed to provide observational data. The procedure gives the user an opportunity to observe the auditory processing, cognitive-linguistic, pragmatic, and stylistic behaviors of subjects between the ages of 9 and 17 years.

The ECC was developed by Charlann S. Simon, a speech/language pathologist who holds an M.A. in speech/language pathology from the University of Kentucky (1969) and the certificate of clinical competence in Speech and Language Pathology from the American Speech-Language-Hearing Association (ASHA). In addition to part-time employment for the Tempe (Arizona) elementary school district as a speech/language pathologist servicing a junior high school, Simon is a consultant, author, and adjunct professor in the department of Speech and Hearing Sciences at Arizona State University. She has specialized in servicing learning-disabled and emotionally handicapped children in addition to serving as a consultant/instructor in a variety of situations. In conjunction with Communication Skill Builders, Inc., Simon has published a monograph, *Communicative Competence: A Functional-Pragmatic Approach to Language Therapy* (1979), and a set of materials to augment her treatment approach. "Communicative Competence: A Functional-Pragmatic Language Program" (1980).

According to Simon, her ECC procedure was developed to solve two dilemmas that she faced during her experience as a practicing speech and language pathologist working with public school students. The first dilemma emphasized the author's recognition of the value of oral language elicitation procedures as used by clinicians in the field of speech and language pathology. She felt that nonstandardized methods to the assessment of language should play a major role. She reviewed approximately 50 language samples over a three-year period to determine whether "role-playing" probes were a more efficient method of evaluation than the short responses found on typical standardized tools. Simon determined that the quality of information gained through tasks that focused primarily on language was far more valuable than scores achieved on standardized instruments.

The second dilemma concerned Simon's discontentment with available standardized tests used to assess a student's ability to process auditory information. She stated that she had read enough journal articles criticizing tests of auditory processing abilities to encourage her to develop informal tasks that would permit observation of specific auditory processing skills.

A preliminary format for the ECC procedure was presented as a mini-seminar at the 1979 convention of the American Speech-Language-Hearing Association. The first published form of the procedure appeared in *Language, Speech and Hearing Services in Schools* (April, 1984). The first edition of the ECC was published in 1984. The revised edition consists of the same tasks provided in the 1984 publication, but the instrument has been reorganized to clarify essential procedures. In addition, the revised edition includes an administration booklet that had not been given in the 1984 format.

The ECC procedure contains 21 informal probes or tasks. In the revised format, each task lists a description of the task and the materials needed, a rationale for using the task, a clinician directive outlining exactly what to say during task performance, and an analysis procedure. The use of two standardized tests or subtests is encouraged. Simon suggests the use of the "Grammatic Closure" subtest of the Illinois Test of Psycholinguistic Abilities (ITPA; Kirk, McCarthy, & Kirk, 1968) or the Peabody Picture Vocabulary Test, Revised Edition (PPVT; Dunn, 1980) for the first norm-referenced measure to be used, and the Auditory Association subtest from the ITPA for the second measure.

The procedure is separated into two parts. The first part, Auditory Tasks, consists of the following:

Task 1, Step 1: The Interview. During the interview, the student is asked questions that require (a) personal factual information, and (b) appropriate answers to a variety of Wh questions.

Task 1, Step 2: Administration of the two standardized tests or subtests. Upon completion of Step 1, the two norm-referenced measures are given. Simon uses the Grammatic Closure subtest for students under age 10 and the PPVT for those over 10. As indicated previously, the Auditory Association subtest of the ITPA is suggested as the second measure. The author stresses that the tests indicated are suggestions only and clinicians could select from available options.

Task 2: Identification of Absurdities in Sentences. The student is required to listen to the clinician or examiner read six nonsense sentences (e.g., "I eat ice cream with a shovel."). The student is asked to identify the absurdity and tell why it is absurd.

Task 3: Identification of Absurdities in Long Sentences and Paragraphs. When contrasted to Task 2 given above, the absurdities in this task are more subtle. The child is required to detect a semantically absurd element in each item and explain why it is absurd. For each of six items, the student must hold information in short term memory, integrate the details, and perform a logical estimate of why the statement could not be true. (e.g., "Some of my favorite fruits are apples, pears, green beans, and oranges.")

Task 4: Integration of Facts to Solve a Riddle. This probe consists of seven riddles. Each one contains three pieces of information (e.g., "I am very soft. I have sharp claws and drink milk. I like to play with string. What am I?"). The student is required to solve the riddle. Usually each item can be answered correctly with a single word response.

Task 5: Comprehension and Memory for Facts. Here the student must listen to eight separate items, and each item is composed of two to four sentences. Then the student is asked comprehension questions that tax short term memory for facts presented. For the eight listening items, there are a total of 21 comprehension questions. For example, "Tom's teacher made popcorn yesterday for her class. What was made? Who made it?"

Task 6: Comprehension of a Paragraph. The student is requested to listen to two short paragraph-length stories. The first story (Story A) is a 97-word passage at high second-grade reading level. After the reading, five comprehension questions are asked about the story. The second story (Story B) is a 106-word passage at fourth-grade reading level. Five comprehension questions again are asked. The second story, unlike the first, assesses the student's ability to make inferences and predictions.

Task 7: Comprehension of Directions. Finally, the student is requested to follow directions using three blocks (e.g., "Touch the yellow block with the green block.") There are ten directions for the student to follow.

The second section, Expressive Tasks, contains the following 14 probes:

Task 8: Sequential Picture Storytelling. The subject is requested to look at two sequential picture stories, each containing four frames. The student's first task is to tell the story. Then, the student is requested to paraphrase a story told by the examiner about the pictures. The pictures are included in the procedural kit.

Task 9: Maintenance of Past Tense in Storytelling. The examiner provides an introduction to a sequential picture story. The introductory phrase is designed to set the time frame for past tense oral performance. Then, the student is asked to tell the story. In this probe, the student's ability to use the verb system is examined. According to the rationale found in the manual, it is primarily through the English verb system that a listener knows when an event has occurred. If the speaker does not maintain a consistent tense reference throughout a story, it adversely affects the clarity of the content.

Task 10: Maintenance of Present Tense in Storytelling. The examiner gives the student an introduction to a sequential picture story that sets the time frame in the present tense. The student then is asked to tell the story.

Task 11. Tense Shifts Based on Introductory Adverbial Phrase. The student is to complete a sentence in a tense consistent with the adverbial phrase. A choice of stimulus photos is offered. The student may choose any one of six photos as the basis of a creative, descriptive sentence to be stated in the tense designated by the introductory adverbial phrase. In this probe, the student is required to complete sentences that use the past, present, progressive, and future tenses. The adverbial phrases used are "each day," "tomorrow," "yesterday," "last summer," "in a little while," "right now," "at this moment," and "every morning."

Task 12. Semantically Appropriate Use of Clausal Connectors. In this task, the student is given a clausal connector and asked to use that word during the formulation of a sentence about one of six pictures used in Task 11. The author emphasizes, however, that this task is to be used with students above age 11 because research (cited in the manual) has indicated that fluent use of clausal connectors is a later developing skill. The clausal connectors are "instead," "while," "although," "because," "until," "since," "unless," "however," "so," and "except for."

Task 13. Stating Similarities and Differences Between Two Stimuli. This task evaluates the student's ability to analyze two stimuli in order to discover the similarities and differences between them. For example, the student is requested to look at a photo of two objects (a stapler and a paper clip) and tell how the two objects are alike and how they differ.

Task 14: Sequential Directions for Using a Pay Telephone. The student is asked to role-play a situation that requires the speaker to provide sequential directions to an individual who had never seen or used a pay telephone. The student takes the role of the speaker, and the examiner the naive listener.

Task 15: Description of Clothing and a Person. The student is asked to describe three photos showing (a) a single article of clothing, (b) an outfit, and (c) a person.

Task 16: Explanation of the Relationship between Two Forms. The student is required to look at four photographs showing a pair of stimuii; and then role play. The situation to be played is one in which the teacher has asked for the student's help in teaching kindergarten children. The student is to take the role of the teacher and is to explain the relationship between each of four sets of items. For example, when shown a photo of a hanger and a coat, the student would have to explain why the two items go together.

Task 17: Creative Storytelling. The student is asked to create a story either from an oral story-starter (e.g., "It was a dark and gloomy night.") or a picture provided by the examiner. The subject chooses the stimulus. If the student chooses to use a picture, four stimulus pictures are presented and the student chooses one as the basis for the story. If the student decides to use a story-starter, the examiner reads a list of available choices.

Task 18: Situational Analysis and Description. The student is required to view an object (a pencil) in four contexts, and to decide how the object would be described in each context. In the example, the student first is asked to look at photos of pencils placed among various office supplies. However, in subsequent tasks, more and more pencils are introduced. The student must decide how to describe the stimulus pencil in each context so that the listener would be able to give the object requested.

Task 19: Expression and Justification of an Opinion. Here, the student is asked to view four photographs that serve as stimuli for expressing and justifying an opinion on four issues. The first issue concerns the student. The student is asked about feelings related to doing chores at home. The second issue deals with hitchhiking. The third issue concerns pets, and the final issue deals with men doing household chores.

Task 20: Twenty Questions. The student is required to gather information in a systematic way through the familiar game, "Twenty Questions." A major difference for this probe, however, is that the student is able to view the "mystery item" before the game begins. A bag of objects is emptied on the desk and the student is asked to view them for about ten seconds, then turn his or her head while the examiner removes one item. When told to view the remaining items, the student must ask a series of questions to determine which item was removed. Because objects are not included in the procedural kit, the examiner must obtain 20 items. Suggestions are given in the manual for the type of material to collect.

Task 21: Barrier Games. This task consists of three sections: (a) speaker in block arrangement, (b) listener in block arrangement, and (c) speaker in barrier card game. In (a) speaker in block arrangement, the student and examiner take a set of three blocks. A barrier is placed between the participants to separate the field of vision. The student is required to arrange the blocks and give the examiner directions so that the examiner can duplicate the pattern. In (b) listener in block arrangement, the examiner gives the student directions for arranging the blocks but the directions are incomplete. As a result of insufficient information, it is necessary for the student to ask clarification questions to complete the pattern. In (c) speaker in barrier card game, the student and examiner each have a set of clown pictures but the details within the pictures vary only slightly. The student is to describe the picture with sufficient detail so that the examiner can locate it.

Practical Applications/Uses

This instrument has been designed to obtain important pragmatic information about an individual's ability to communicate. The probes used attempt to take into account many pragmatic areas. One such area concerns the situational needs of speaker/listener roles. For example, in some of the expressive tasks, the speaker must take into account the listener's informational needs. If unwarranted assumptions are made about shared speaker-listener knowledge or experience, the message content can be unproductive. Another pragmatic area measured is that of organization. There should be a coherent statement of a series of events permitting the listener to follow the chronology of details. Structurally, the speaker must have enough control over the linguistic code so that the content is given in a coherent manner; that is, the speaker should have sufficient control of the syntax (grammar) of language to express thoughts, feelings, or complex relationships, thereby enabling the listener to follow the chronology of details.

The ECC was developed also to gain pragmatic information about a student's ability to understand the linguistic code of the English language. According to Simon, her theoretic base in designing the procedure is the result of a synthesis of research on the nature of communication and communication deficits. She gives five receptive considerations for the reader's perusal. One consideration, for example, concerns the fact that the meaning of words, inflections, and relationships among words need to be assimilated by the listener for comprehension to occur. A second consideration deals with the fact that we do not communicate in isolated sentences. Instead, we produce a series of sentences with related meanings in order to present a complete description, narrative, or discourse. The burden of responsibility is on the listener, who must retain in memory and integrate the segments of information in order to decipher the ideas being expressed. It is Simon's belief that an evaluative procedure that provides descriptive data about a student's skills in both listener and speaker roles is far more valuable than test scores obtained on standardized instruments. Simon indicates that classroom teachers, for example, need to have information about whether their students can integrate information within and among sentences, engage in verbal reasoning, and evaluate the truthfulness and completeness of a message.

The ECC procedure was developed by a speech/language pathologist for use by public school speech/language pathologists who see students from the middle elementary grade levels through high school. The informal procedure is designed to observe the strengths and weaknesses of the language performances of students in 4th through 12th grade. Students with suspected speech and language problems may be referred to school speech and language pathologists by classroom teachers. Generally, standardized instruments are administered to such students. Simon considers the ECC procedure to be a supplement to standardized tools and necessary to determine real communication problems. She also sees it as a valuable means for determining a student's strengths, which can be tapped for further improvement.

The manual includes a section for data organization and presentation. The purpose is to help the speech/language pathologist organize the results, present the data at staff conferences, and to use the results for writing individualized educational prescriptions (IEP). From the manual, then, it would seem that Simon designed this procedure for the exclusive use of school speech/language pathologists. But if professionals from other disciplines (special educators, learning disability specialists, resource room specialists, remedial reading specialists, and psychologists) were to administer the probes, important descriptive observations might be available. The ECC procedure may be used, also, by private school speech/language pathologists as well as those in clinical settings, hospital speech and hearing centers, and by speech/language pathologists in private practice.

The ECC procedure was designed to evaluate school children between 9 and 17 years of age. The objective is to obtain descriptive data that would provide information about a student's flexibility in various speaker and listener roles. It is meant to augment findings from standardized tests (mandated by PL 94-142) by providing opportunities for students to demonstrate their skills as they perform in listener and speaker roles. The procedure was developed for use with children diagnosed as having communication disorders, learning disabilities, and emotional handicaps. It can be used with the blind or deaf. It can be used, also, with bilingual students who demonstrate academic deficits and difficulty with the English language. The principle focus of the ECC is to observe how well the individual can manipulate the English language. Although not specifically designed for an adult population, the ECC might be adapted for use with adults with communication disorders. The 21 probes (or even a shorter version) might provide valuable information about the language use of adults with head trauma due to accident or those recovering from stroke. The ECC probes might also be used to learn more about the communication difficulties of the geriatric population.

The procedure should be administered by an examiner experienced with the multiple probes included in the kit. It should be given on a one-to-one basis in a private, quiet setting. All responses from both parts (auditory and expressive) should be audiotaped for future analysis. The rationale that contains the theoretical underpinnings of the procedure can be found in the manual. The administration time for the procedure, including two short subtests from standardized measures, is approximately one hour. However, the amount of time can be reduced by omitting some probes. The author accommodates 45-minute class periods at the junior high level by administering two subtests from standardized tests and then the following probes: all seven auditory tasks, then nine of the expressive; that is, tasks 8, 9, 12, 14, 15b, 16, 17, 19, 21a, and 21b. The sequence of the probes also may be altered. The probes, for the most part, are simple to administer and no special skills are required. The author does present a warning, however, about the rate of speech used during the administration of the ECC. She stresses that it is necessary to speak at a slower rate—about 120 words per minute, because language/learning-disabled students have rate-specific auditory processing problems. She indicated that most adults generally average 140-160 words per minute while speaking.

Another problem concerns the amount of material presented in the manual. The author acknowledges that the amount of material may seem overwhelming. She suggests that examiners think of the manual as a workshop or college course on this method of evaluation.

An Administration and Recording Form accompanies the manual. This form serves two purposes: (1) it is the examiner's script for presenting the ECC probes, and (2) the student's responses and behavioral notations are to be recorded. A back page of the form, Performance Summary, is to be used to summarize the examiner's observations, while the front cover is to be used to obtain a Performance Profile. The profile is formatted so that the data can be organized according to the following categories: (1) general notation such as development of syntax and morphology, articulation of speech sounds, cognitive organization, verbal fluency, (2) auditory processing skills, (3) oral language expression skills, and (4) metalinguistic skills such as maintenance of past and present tenses or composing sentences with clausal connectors. Each task is to be judged as Good, Adequate, Marginally Adequate, Present but Inadequate, or Not Present.

The criterion for adequate performance is the answer to the question, "Has the student addressed the nature of the task?" Immediately after the question and under the subheading titled Criterion there is the following statement: "With a few exceptions, normal-functioning students in third or fourth grade will perform within 80% to 90% accuracy on the 21 tasks" (Simon, 1986, p. 10). There is, however, no support given for this statement.

Recording the results requires two forms. One form is to use behavioral notations with some tasks and verbatim transcriptions of oral performances from audiotape recordings. The second form of recording is that of reporting percentages based on fractions (i.e., +5/6 = 83%). Verbatim transcriptions, rather than behavioral notions, are recommended by the author for six of the probes (8, 12, 14, 15b, 16 and 17). If, however, the examiner is extremely limited in time, only tasks 8 and 17 should be transcribed. Information obtained from transcriptions of oral language performance gives the examiner the opportunity to assess objectively the complexity of oral language structure and to derive a mean length of utterance (MLU) score from the language corpus. Potential users of the ECC will find a sample case of a 13-year-old 7th-grade boy in the Appendix. The completed Administration and Recording Form shows the student's percentage scores as well as behavioral notations or verbatim transcriptions for each of the tasks.

The simple percentage scores are easy to obtain. But verbatim transcriptions of oral language samples do take a great deal of time. As suggested above, language sample analyses provide a wonderful opportunity for examiners to assess the complexity of the language used by the students. However, the amount of time required and the skills needed to transcribe correctly could present major difficulty for examiners with time limitations and/or unfamiliarity with procedures required for valid transcriptions of audiotaped oral language. Recognizing the possibility that examiners who lack such knowledge might be potential users and scorers, the author added a section to the Appendix that includes information on how to segment language samples.

Unfortunately, this reviewer found some technical errors printed in the Administration and Recording Forms received with the Revised Edition of the ECC Manual. The Scoring forms showed errors with respect to ECC Task Number and Description of Task on the Performance Summary Sheets. The errors concerned five of the probes. A technical printing error was noted, also, within the 16-page booklet while attempting to record responses for Task 6b. This printing error would have an effect on the calculation of percentages based on fractions.

To aid the ECC user in the review and organization of the resultant material obtained during the administration of the 21 probes, the author has included a section aptly called Data Organization and Presentation. This section is designed to help the clinician organize the information, present it at staff conferences, and write educational objectives based on the data. This section seems to be designed to ease the user's handling of the data. As previously mentioned, the examiner is to calculate fractional scores and a percentage of accuracy for each task. In addition, verbal transcriptions and behavioral notations are to be used to analyze the adequacy of performance on all auditory and expressive tasks. Upon completion of the Performance Profile, the examiner should obtain a descriptive profile of the student's general communication, auditory, metalinguistic, and functional language skills. By virtue of the nature of the methods used to evaluate a student's communication profile, interpretation of the data is not based on objective scores but on internal clinical judgment. Accurate clinical judgment, then, would require a high level of clinical sophistication and linguistic training.

Technical Aspects

According to the manual, the ECC is a criterion-referenced procedure. As a result, reliability and validity concepts are not applicable. Because reliable and valid measures have been mandated by PL 94-142, the ECC should not be used instead of, but either as a support or a supplement to, standardized instruments. Criterion-referenced measures have been used to gain information about an individual's ability to perform specific language functions or tasks. The purpose of criterion-referenced measures is not to compare a student's behavior with the behavior of other students. Instead, it is to determine how well a particular language behavior is established based on pre-established behavior. Speech and language clinicians frequently set a criterion measure for various communicative behaviors. One frequently used procedure that is criterion-referenced is oral language sampling (Newhoff & Leonard, 1983). The ECC, which incorporates an oral language sampling technique, provides information about the nature of a student's language system relative to certain specified tasks. It is to be used systematically to gather descriptive data about the language characteristics of a particular student. This data would lead to a student's profile of linguistic competence and might provide the basis for designing an individualized educational program for students with communication disorders.

Critique

Because the revised edition of the ECC is comparatively new, other reviews of this edition are not available at the time of this publication. Having had experience with both editions of the procedure, this reviewer finds the revised edition to be better organized than the first, and the administration and recording form a welcome addition to the format. Of course, as previously mentioned, technical printing errors were found with the new scoring forms. Undoubtedly the publisher will rectify these errors quickly. The 21 probes of the ECC were administered, by the reviewer, to three language/learning disabled students, ages 9.1, 11.10, and 16.8. The data obtained provided new insights about the linguistic capabilities of each student. Thus, this reviewer found the ECC useful and recognized that it has excellent potential in spite of its limitations. The strength of this criterion-referenced tool is that analysis of the semantic, syntactic, and pragmatic components of language is possible and this information, in turn, could lead to a therapeutic program. Weaknesses of this type of criterion-referenced procedure are that it can be time-consuming and requires a high degree of clinical skill.

The reviewer agrees with Simon's suggestion that research be developed through the use of the ECC probes. She suggests two research designs: (1) To note ECC task performance differences between achieving and nonachieving students at various grade levels, and (2) to obtain comparative data for students of various ages and socioeconomic backgrounds. She offered, further, the opinion that such data would provide useful information for determining the severity of problems revealed through the ECC procedure. After using the ECC probes with the three students mentioned earlier, this reviewer supported Simon's view because it was difficult to ascertain if certain marginal behaviors should be considered inappropriate for a particular age level. Although the author provides sample responses to the ECC probes for 25 students (grades 3-8) selected as "good communicators," the performance examples varied considerably from the responses given by the reviewer's language/learning-disabled students.

Another problem occurred when the reviewer attempted to determine the skill levels of the subjects. After recording the fractions and percentage scores for each task (behavioral notations were included) within the Administration and Recording Form, the reviewer tried to transfer this information from the Performance Summary Sheet to the Performance Profile Sheet. After studying Simon's definition for each descriptive term: Good, Adequate, Marginally Adequate, Present but Inadequate, and Not Present, the reviewer determined that the definitions were inappropriate when applied to the three subjects. For example, the reviewer could not differentiate between the terms Good ("performance needs little, if any, modification and is commensurate with the quality of performance observed in peers") and Adequate ("performance reflects the student's general intellectual, emotional, and academic performance as described by related test scores and staff comments").

As a result, judgmental changes were made that were considered necessary to complete the student's performance profile. It was determined that the 16.8 female subject's scores were Good if the percentiles achieved were 85% and above, Marginally Adequate if the scores ranged between 77% and 50%, and finally, Present but Inadequate if her scores fell below the 50th percentile. Indeed, this student did achieve scores ranging from 42% to 8% on four of the ECC tasks. With a second male subject, aged 11.10, however, it was decided that his scores were Good if they ranged from 80% to 100%. Thus, for two subjects two columns, Adequate and Not Present were excluded for the final analysis.

More work is necessary to assess the usefulness of this procedure. Research data would provide helpful information for identifying high risk students as well as those with communication disorders and would increase clinical knowledge about the normal development of communication skills by middle school and adolescent youth.

References

Dunn, L. M., & Dunn, L. M. (1980). Peabody Picture Vocabulary Test (rev. ed.). Circle Pines, MN: American Guidance Service.

Kirk, S. A., McCarthy, J. J., & Kirk, W. D. (1968). The Illinois Test of Psycholinguistic Abilities. Urbana: University of Illinois Press.

Newhoff, M., & Leonard, L. B. (1983). Diagnosis of developmental language disorders. In I. J. Meitus, & B. Weinberger (Eds.), *Diagnosis in speech-language pathology*. Baltimore: University Park Press.

Simon, C. S. (1979). *Communicative competence: A functional-pragmatic approach to language therapy*. Tucson, AZ: Communication Skill Builders.

Simon, C. S. (1980). Communicative competence: A functional-pragmatic language program (Monograph). Tucson, AZ: Communication Skill Builders.

Simon, C. S. (1986). Communicative competence: A functional pragmatic procedure (rev. ed.). Tucson, AZ: Communication Skill Builders.

Frank J. Ofsanko, Ph.D.
Human Resources Research Consultant, Southern California Edison Company, Rosemead, California.

FAMOUS SAYINGS
Bernard M. Bass. Missoula, Montana: Psychological Test Specialists.

Introduction

Famous Sayings (FS) is a personality test that yields scores on four dimensions: conventional mores (CM), hostility (HO), fear of failure (FF), and social acquiescence (SA). It is intended primarily for use in industrial and professional screening and classification.

The examinee indicates general agreement, disagreement, or uncertainty of agreement with 131 one-sentence proverbs, axioms, maxims, adages, and aphorisms, such as "Don't cry over spilt milk" or "A fool and his money are soon parted." The majority are not well-known, but each examinee will recognize a few of them. Because of their wide-ranging, pithy, analogous nature, they make for interesting and engaging reading. By expressing agreement with the sayings, the examinee indirectly reveals the dimensions measured by the test. Thus, Famous Sayings is a disguised personality test that uses a structured format and task, allowing examinees to project dimensions of which they are relatively unaware.

This test was developed by Bernard M. Bass in the late 1950s when he was teaching at Louisiana State University. Bass earned an M.A. and Ph.D. in I-O psychology at Ohio State University and is currently a Diplomate and Distinguished Professor of Management at the State University of New York at Binghamton. He has held offices in the International Association of Applied Psychology, served on many APA and APA Division committees, and written numerous books and articles in the I-O field. He has done a scrupulous job of presenting both the positive and negative features of this test.

Bass set out to develop a test measuring personality dimensions that are important for occupational success. Noting that clinicians used proverbs for assessment purposes, he compiled lists of 20 proverbs related to each of 13 personality needs specified by H. A. Murray in his classic *Explorations in Personality* (1938). These needs include achievement, affiliation, deference, autonomy, aggression, abasement, and more. Bass culled the proverbs from existing lists in *Explorations in Personality*, Bartlett's *Familiar Quotations*, Richmond's *Modern Quotations*, and private lists of black proverbs. (For consistency with the test title, these proverbs will henceforth be referred to as "sayings.")

Forty additional sayings were added to the lists and an initial 300-item questionnaire was assembled. This questionnaire was administered to a diverse sample of approximately 2,000 cases; 400 cases representing American job applicants for professional, managerial, and technical jobs were than extracted from the larger sample and their results factor-analyzed. Conventional Mores (CM), Hostility (HO), and Fear of Failure (FF) factors emerged from the analysis.

Using a new sample of 200 cases drawn from the original 2,000, item-analysis techniques were used to select the most discriminating items for measurement of the three factors. The 30 best items were selected for CM, the 30 best for HO, and the 20 best for FF.

A new sample of 100 cases was drawn and used to compute intercorrelations among the three new scales, the intercorrelations running .45 to .54. In the manual (Bass, 1958), the same sample was used to compute corrected split-half reliabilities for the scales (CM .83, HO .72, FF .69). Ten additional items were written and added to the FF scale, making a total of 90 test items.

During the 1950s there was professional interest in the examinee's social acquiescence (the tendency to agree with *any* general statements concerning human behavior). Bass set about developing a Social Acquiescence (SA) scale for the test. A sample of 200 college students took the original 300-item questionnaire. Item analysis identified 56 items that best separated the students who agreed with the most number of sayings (regardless of their content) from the students who agreed with the least number. The 56-item scale correlated .95 with a tendency to accept or reject each of the total 300 items. A new sample of 100 yielded a corrected split-half reliability of .92 for the new SA scale.

Fifteen of the 56 SA items overlapped the 90 items already selected for the test. The other 41 SA items were added to the 90 items to constitute the complete new test. There have been no revisions or alternate forms of the test developed.

Normative studies showed various significant differences on the scales among 20 sample groups. For example, salesmen scored significantly higher on CM and FF and lower on HO than non-salesmen. Distinguishing differences also were found for other occupational groups, penitentiary inmates, high school versus college students, and for geographic regions.

The Famous Sayings test is four pages, printed back-to-back in a 7"x8½" booklet. Printing is black on white. Design and clarity are good. Paper quality is sturdy and slick. The print is quite small and might be a strain for some examinees to read.

The first page is the instruction page. At the top of the page are two lines for computing scores, with the lines including the two-letter abbreviations of the four scales. The first things the examinee sees are these lines and abbreviations, which may prompt questions as to their meaning. Because of the disguised nature of the test, this could be troublesome. Examinee identification demographics requested on the page include age, sex, last school grade completed, and marital status. These could be troublesome in today's equal employment opportunity legal climate unless the items are specified as optional or required for EEO purposes.

The directions state that the test measures attitudes towards famous sayings. This is consistent with the disguised nature of the test. However, examinees may raise questions about the meaning and face validity of agreeing with abstract sayings. The directions ask the examinee to respond by marking "yes," "no," or "?" for each saying according to whether he or she agrees, disagrees, or is uncertain about agreement with the saying. This is confounded by a later statement that uncertainties might be resolved by marking "yes" or "no" according to whether the statement is usually true or usually false. The frequency with which behavior is observed may not correspond with agreement with the behavior.

Pages 2 through 4 list the sayings one by one. The sayings are heterogeneous in sequence, not being clustered by content or subparts. Each of the three pages has three columns of answer boxes in the order of "yes," "?," and "no." Answers are marked in the booklet. The boxes are in the right margin for page 2 and in the left margin for pages 3 and 4. This change of format facilitates scoring somewhat, but could be a bit disorienting to the examinee. The two-letter scale abbreviations also appear on the second page in two conspicuous places. The test ends with an informal "That's all!"

The Famous Sayings test is essentially self-administering; administrators are necessary only to answer questions and maintain control. The manual's administration instructions are clear. A competent, trained clerk should suffice as an administrator. The test may be administered individually or to groups, and is appropriate for examinees of high school age and upward. Vocabulary is normal high school level, although individuals may have difficulty with words such as "subdue," "tyranny," and so on. The test is untimed, taking 15-30 minutes. Because the last page has only SA scale items, eliminating that page yields a shortened version of the test with only CM, HO, and FF scores.

Scoring instructions are clear, and the test is scored easily by lining up a punched-out stencil over the answers. The stencil must be aligned separately for each scale. The stencil is sturdy, but the one used by this reviewer had the punches considerably out of alignment. On CM, HO, and FF, each "yes" answer counts 2 points and each "?" answer counts 1 point. On SA, "yes" answers count 1 point. Hence, credit is given only for "yes" or "?" answers on the test. The scoring formulas are printed on the front page. There are no total or composite scores. The blanks for filling in the numbers of "yes" and "?" answers are too small. A blank is omitted for the SA score. It takes approximately two minutes to score the test, and it could be readily adapted for machine scoring.

Practical Applications/Uses

The Famous Sayings test attempts to measure four personality dimensions as an aid to job applicant screening and classification. High CM scores indicate agreement with statements supporting the following: helping others, being generous, forgiving others, obeying one's conscience, being virtuous, forming and maintaining friendships, being humble, being conventional, and maintaining faith. Later work suggests that CM is an indirect measure of conservatism, conscientiousness, rigidity, and sociability (Vidulich & Bass, 1960).

High HO scores indicate agreement with statements that people enjoy being hostile and aggressive, and that it's best to do things alone—to be alert for false friends, to ignore people of low ability, to avoid joining organizations, and to avoid being indebted to others. Later work suggests that HO measures dogmatic, aggressive, suspicious, and immature tendencies, as well as tendencies to be disagreeable and to lack objectivity (Vidulich & Bass, 1960).

High FF scores indicate agreement with statements supporting ambition, fame, achievement, industriousness, and the fear of carelessness.

High SA scores indicate agreement with any generalization about human behavior. The test manual indicates that high scoring SA people tend to be non-intellectual, socially insensitive, socially uncritical, and socially conforming.

In addition to these scale interpretations, the manual provides norms for seven samples: salesmen, factory supervisors, school teachers, student nurses, penitentiary inmates, and college and high school students. Sample sizes range from 36-520. An eighth sample of 369 sales applicants is offered for the SA scale. Manual norms are presented in T-scores and percentiles. There are no explanations or definitions for these terms, nor of "standard deviation" and other technical terms used in the manual. (The manual is a monograph supplement.) Hence, interpretation and proper use of the test require considerable professional knowledge and background, preferably at the master's level in tests and statistics. The monograph and the test publisher flyer very leniently state that personnel managers who have studied statistics qualify as test interpreters.

For job applicant screening purposes, Famous Sayings may have some merit for specific occupations. A validity study for the specific job of interest would first have to be performed to determine whether the test had value. Famous Sayings may also be useful as a classification aid. The manual reports occupational norms for supervisors, salesmen, school teachers, and student nurses. Normative information also has been reported in the literature for student beauticians (Darbes & Platt, 1968) and nurses and physicians (Walsh, 1966). However, some of the norms are based on small samples, and all of the norms are old and require updating.

The test also could be used in vocational counseling. Again, occupational profiles and norms would require updating. The test does not appear useful in predicting academic success. There is little reported use of the test for selection, college admissions, classification, or vocational counseling.

Famous Sayings may help clinicians, who have long used understanding and explaining proverbs as indicators of verbal comprehension, thought processes, and abstract verbal functioning. Individual sayings on the test could be used as interview discussion questions to probe the four test dimensions as well as other feelings, attitudes, values, and clinical characteristics (e.g., Baumgarten, 1952). In some counseling situations scale results could be used as feedback to the client. Results may even be useful to monitor change, such as in therapy. These uses would have to be informal and judgmental, as the lack of empirical foundation precludes rigorous use of test results. The test may be useful in clinical diagnosis. Other proverbs tests have differentiated normals from schizophrenics (Gorham, 1956). In one study, FF correlated -.285 with ego development level (Smith, 1982). However, there is little published background to justify its immediate use for diagnosis.

This test also may serve as a research tool. The publisher's flyer for the test suggests research in job satisfaction, leadership potential, productivity, and worker compatibility. The test has been used to measure time orientation (Platt, et al., 1971), and goodness of fit between campers and camp counselors (Sweeney, 1981). Because of the factored nature of the three scales, the test may be useful in exploring, developing, and studying the relationships among personality variables and traits. Several correlations between the scales and other personality tests are reported in the test manual and in the professional literature (e.g., Joubert, 1977; Vidulich & Bass, 1960).

Technical Aspects

The multiple centroid factor analysis of the original test questionnaire results is straightforward and commendable. The factor loadings of the needs clustering in the CM, HO, and FF factors are high and their clustering is not unreasonable in their meaning. The variances accounted for by the factors are not given.

The item analysis for the scales selected items that (a) best discriminated between the upper and lower quarters of the group scored on the need scale with the highest loading on the factor (two pooled needs were used for CM) and (b) were relatively independent of performance on the other two scales.

Looking more closely at the individual scales, the CM factor loaded the highest on the need for nurturance (.85), superego strength (.77), and the needs for affiliation (.70), abasement (.68), and deference (.66). The CM scale correlated .43 with sociability and .31 with cooperativeness on the Guilford-Zimmerman Temperament Survey (GZTS; Bass, 1958); .31 with nurturance, .29 with aggression, and .25 with affiliation on the Edwards Personal Preference Schedule (EPPS); .27 with conscientiousness, .26 with sociability, and .26 with rigidity on the 16PF; .40 with conservatism; and .30 with dogmatism (Vidulich & Bass, 1960). The correlations reported in this and the following two paragraphs are most of the highest ones reported, but do not represent all of the correlations.

The HO factor loaded the highest on the needs for aggression (.76), autonomy (.65), and rejection (.64). HO correlated -.30 with responsibility on the Gordon Personal Profile (GPP; Bass, 1958); .578 with neuroticism on the Eysenck Personality Inventory (EPI; Joubert, 1977); .29 with aggression on the EPPS; .34 with suspicion-jealousy, -.24 with maturity, -.26 with agreeableness, and -.34 with objectivity on the 16PF; and .49 with dogmatism (Vidulich & Bass, 1960).

Highest loadings on the FF factor were the needs for achievement (.84) and harmavoidance (.62). These agree with McClelland's finding that motivation stems from a need to achieve or a fear of failure. FF correlated .48 with dogmatism (Vidulich & Bass, 1960).

The manual points out that intercorrelations of the three scales vary with the homogeneity of the samples. The intercorrelations reported in the manual approximate .50 in a heterogeneous sample, but drop to negative ranges for college sophomores and penitentiary inmates. Intercorrelations vary considerably in other studies, averaging about .40 (Eisenman & Platt, 1970; Joubert, 1977; Vidulich & Bass, 1960).

Corrected split-half reliabilities were .83 (CM), .72 (HO), and .69 (FF) for the heterogeneous sample. The reliabilities are quite high for this type and length of scale, but are marginal for individual prediction purposes.

After the factor analysis, item analysis, intercorrelations, and reliability estimates, 10 new FF items were written and added to the test. This totaled three scales of 30 items each. The additional items naturally affect the preceding statistics involving the FF scale.

Evidence of validity offered in the manual for CM, HO, and FF include mean differences between educational and occupational groups on each scale. F-tests indicated significant variation on each scale for 20 samples ranging in sample size from 34 to 361. T-tests were run between means of selected samples, showing significant differences in the directions expected by Bass. For example, salesmen were significantly higher than non-salesmen in CM and FF and lower in HO. High school students scored significantly higher than college students on all three scales. Southerners scored significantly higher than non-Southerners on CM and HO. Six occupational groups were ranked on each scale, falling into the approximate order expected by Bass. Bass's expectations about mean differences and rankings appear intuitive rather than as hypotheses developed and tested.

The test manual reports predictive validity studies of the three scales. Merit ratings of 53 factory supervisors two years after the testing were used as criteria. Validity coefficients were -.14 (CM), -.12 (HO), and -.26 (FF), with -.27 needed for the 5% level of significance. Another study used ratings of success as criteria for six groups of grocery products salesmen and sales supervisors three to six months after testing. Only the FF scale coefficient reached significance (-.33) for one group of 62 salesmen. The other 17 correlations were pretty evenly distributed in positive and negative directions. The only pattern among them was a weak negative relationship for CM for four groups of salesmen (validities -.10 to -.17). Although these studies suggest possible occupation validity, they do not demonstrate it statistically. There are no other known published criterion-related validity studies using these scales.

Turning to the SA scale, the SA factor did not emerge from factor analysis but was simply assumed to exist as a general or second order factor. Its corrected split-half reliability was .92. This high reliability, strengthened by its scale length, is sufficiently high for individual decisions.

SA also is distinguished from the other three scales by containing 15 items that overlap the other scales. No correlations between SA and the other three scales, with or without the overlapping items, are given in the manual. Of the 15 overlapping items this reviewer found nine of them overlapped CM, five overlapped FF, and one overlapped HO. Therefore, the resulting correlation between CM and SA is particularly spurious, as reflected in the .67 correlation found by both Vidulich and Bass (1960) and Eisenman and Platt (1970). These same two studies reported correlations of .40 and .15 between SA and HO, and .49 and .38 between SA and FF.

If desired, it is simple enough to obtain nonoverlapping scale scores. The 15 overlapping items are on pages 2 and 3, and page 4 is devoted exclusively to the remaining 41 SA items. By scoring only the SA items on page 4, one can obtain independent scale scores, albeit the SA score would be truncated. This truncated score obviously would not have the same statistical characteristics as the full scale.

SA was found to correlate with the F scale (authoritarianism) and with tendencies to agree with small group decisions and other group members (Bass, 1958). Bass reviewed the SA means and standard deviations of 15 samples of occupational groups, student groups, and residents. He also inspected the product moment correlations of SA with GPA, years of education, peer nominations, leaderless discussion scores, and 13 other ability and personality tests. Among the stronger correlations found were .27 with sociability, .25 with cooperativeness, and -.25 with introversion on the GZTS; .34 with sociability on the GPP; .45 with peer nominations of "likes to help," .42 with "thinks well of most," and -.29 with "rugged individualist"; .34 with an empathy test; and .32 with initiative in leaderless discussions. From this information Bass inferred that high scores indicate a Babbitt type social conformity (from the Sinclair Lewis novel, *Babbitt*). This inference is offered for investigation, rather than demonstrated or proved. Among the SA test correlations found in the subsequent literature are .506 with neuroticism on the EPI (Joubert, 1977); -.25 with objectivity on the 16PF; and .40 with dogmatism (Vidulich & Bass, 1960).

The manual reports two predictive validity studies of SA on grocery product salesmen and oil refinery supervisors. Results failed to reach significance (validities .03 and -.11). No other published criterion-related validity studies using this scale are known.

Regarding the test's fakability, Bass reports a study in which college students retook the SA scale while imagining themselves as job applicants (Bass, 1958) and raised their SA scores significantly (1% level). Braun and Dube (1963) had 21 students take the test a second time as applicants attempting to appear favorable to the employer. All scale mean scores on the retest were significantly different from the original administration mean scores (except for CM, which fell just short of significance). Correlations of scale scores between the two administrations were significant only for SA (.54). This reviewer retook the test in an applicant set, changing all of his scale scores and practically doubling his FF score. There is no correction for faking offered for the test and the pattern of faking may be expected to vary by the specific job under consideration.

Critique

The high, spurious correlation of .67 between CM and SA raises questions regarding the meaning of the scale dimensions. SA did not emerge from the factor analysis; is it a higher order factor, response set, personality characteristic, or some combination of all three? The intervening years since the test was developed have not found social acquiescence a very fruitful concept.

Aside from item overlaps, any SA tendency should affect all scale scores. Because response sets increase as items become ambiguous, and because several of the famous sayings are ambiguous (at least in part), item ambiguity also should affect scale scores. There is the nagging problem that all scales are scored for positive (or "?") answers, and one overlapping scale specifically measures a yea-saying tendency, but there are no methods offered for dealing with or interpreting these interrelationships.

Although the correlations of SA with the three other scales is spuriously high because of overlapping items, the intercorrelations of the other three scales are similarly substantial (around .50). Although derived from factor analysis, the factors are not as independent as one might expect. The scale correlations with other tests also tend to blur the distinctions among the factors. Several tests each correlate highly with several of the four scales. The overlapping nature of the factors and their relationships does not provide a good nomological network to support scale construct validity. This overlap of factors may not be a problem if the test is used properly, but it should be kept in mind.

Nor are there significant criterion-related validity studies demonstrating the test's usefulness in industrial selection, one of the test's primary intended purposes. Its validity support rests upon its factorial derivation and its ability to show significant mean differences between occupational, educational, and regional groups. However, the norms in the manual and in the literature are outdated. Societal values and jobs have changed; occupational profiles and differences may have changed as well.

The test's vulnerability to faking is another critical aspect related to its primary intended use. Unless faking detection or correction scales are developed, applicant scores are apt to be seriously distorted.

This is not to say that the test has no value. The a priori selection of the sayings, the factor analysis results, the item analyses, the suggestive validity results, and the generally reasonable significant differences found between occupations, educational levels, and geographic regions all argue for the viability of the three scales. This is boosted by reasonable correlations of the scales with such familiar tests as the GZTS, GPP, and 16PF. Despite this evidence, however, today's use of the test for industrial screening would require several actions and considerations.

First, a validity study meeting today's professional and governmental standards would have to be done. Because of the test's vulnerability to faking, validation samples should be actual job applicants. Some means should be developed to deal with the overlapping SA test items and/or correcting all the scales for the SA tendency. New test norms would have to be gathered. Because sex, ethnic, and age differences may appear, the user should be concerned with the impact of these differences on selection and with performing the required test fairness studies. Although the disguised nature of the test may be an advantage, the test user should consider its lack of face validity to job applicants and how the test can be rationalized to them.

Assuming all these were successfully accomplished, the test user would then need to develop a more complete selection battery. Because of the marginal reliabilities of three of the four scales, the limited number of scale dimensions, and the low predictive validity usually demonstrated for this type of test (if any), the test could only be used for rough screening.

Most of the previous comments also generally apply to use of the test in classification. In clinical use, the test may tap dimensions of interest in diagnosis, counseling, and/or therapy. HO scores may act as crude indicators of sociopathy, for example. FF scores may indicate motivational characteristics and all scales may relate to interpersonal characteristics. The disguised nature of the test would be a distinct advantage in working with examinees who are defensive, manipulative, malingering, and so on. But test faking would still be a problem.

Use of the individual sayings to evaluate thought processes, abstract verbal ability, and ego functioning can continue to be of assessment value when used in the context of a fuller assessment. Besides helping diagnosticians and clinicians in their work, test results also may provide useful feedback in certain kinds of counseling. However, the scale reliabilities, the meager and outdated norms, and the lack of a track record for the test indicate that it could only serve as an adjunct or support for more extensive assessments. It certainly offers speed and convenience of use, compared to most projective techniques.

The Famous Sayings test is interesting and may well warrant further research and refinement. However, it would need substantial work to utilize it for its intended purposes. The potential user should consider whether this test's potential benefits warrant the preparation required for its proper use. Though for other purposes the test can frequently serve as a crude indicator, it is doubtful whether it could ever be used as a sole decision maker.

References

Bass, B. M. (1955). Authoritarianism or acquiescence? *Journal of Abnormal and Social Psychology, 51,* 616-623.

Bass, B. M. (1956a). Development and evaluation of a scale for measuring social acquiescence. *Journal of Abnormal and Social Psychology, 53,* 296-299.

Bass, B. M. (1956b). Development of a structured disguised personality test. *Journal of Applied Psychology, 40,* 393-397.

Bass, B. M. (1957). Validity studies of a proverbs personality test. *Journal of Applied Psychology, 41,* 158-160.

Bass, B. M. (1958). Famous Sayings Test: General manual [Monograph]. *Psychological Reports, 4,* 479-497.

Braun, J. R., & Dube, C. S. (1963). Note on a faking study with the Famous Sayings Test. *Psychological Reports, 13,* 878.

Darbes, A., & Platt, J. J. (1968). Notes on the Famous Sayings Test for student beauticians. *Psychological Reports, 23,* 244.

Eisenman, R., & Platt, J. J. (1970). Authoritarianism, creativity, and other correlates of the Famous Sayings Test. *Psychological Reports, 21,* 267-271.

Gaier, E. L., & Bass, B. M. (1959). Regional differences in interrelations among authoritarianism, acquiescence, and ethnocentrism. *Journal of Social Psychology, 49,* 47-51.

Gorham, D. R. (1956). *Clinical manual for the proverbs test.* Louisville, KY: Psychological Test Specialists.

Joubert, C. E. (1977). Some correlations between Famous Sayings Test and Eysenck Personality Inventory variables. *Psychological Reports, 40,* 697-698.

Vidulich, R. N. & Bass, B. M. (1960). Relation of selected personality and attitude scales to the Famous Sayings Test. *Psychological Reports, 7,* 259-260.

Smith. C. A. (1982). A study of the relationship between the use of proverbs and ego development levels. *Dissertation Abstracts International, 43,* 4310A.

Sweeney, D. P. (1981). An examination of counselor effectiveness and return as a function of goodness of fit. *Dissertation Abstracts International, 42,* 4202B.

Walsh, T. M. (1966). Responses on the Famous Sayings Test of professional and non-professional personnel in a medical population. *Psychological Reports, 18,* 151-157.

Ronald C. Pearlman, Ph.D.
Graduate Associate Professor of Audiology, School of Communication, Howard University, Washington, D.C.

FLOWERS-COSTELLO TESTS OF CENTRAL AUDITORY ABILITIES

Arthur Flowers and Mary Rose Costello. Dearborn, Michigan: Perceptual Learning Systems.

Introduction

The Flowers-Costello Tests of Central Auditory Abilities are tests for possible learning disabilities in the area of reading skills for children in grades one through six. The tests are based on the ability of the subject's central auditory system to process information.

Learning is a complex process involving audition, sight, motor skills, smell, experience, and so on. Most of the information a child receives in the classroom is through the auditory sense. While a child may have an intact auditory sense organ, interpretation of information at the central nervous system (brain and spinal cord) level may be impaired. Such a child is at risk for information processing and therefore learning.

The Flowers-Costello tests are but one method of attempting to test the auditory system under stress in order to determine the extent of function and relate current auditory function to future learning. A pure tone audiometric screening test is incapable of stressing the central auditory system enough to determine the processing skills of the brain; consequently, special auditory tests must be administered.

Arthur Flowers is Executive Director of the Central Auditory Abilities Research Institute. Mr. Flowers was Associate Professor of Audiology at the State University of New York at Albany. He has been involved in central auditory processing for over 25 years. Dr. Mary Rose Costello is a Speech Pathologist at the Henry Ford Hospital in Detroit, Michigan. The test manual was written with the help of Dr. Victor Small. The Flowers-Costello Tests were developed in 1964 when information about central auditory processing was gathered from the "Grand Blanc Longitudinal Study" (sponsored in part by the Office of Education). Five subtests were administered to 287 normal Kindergarten subjects. Along with the auditory tests, a Peabody Picture Vocabulary Test, a Gates Advanced Primary Reading Test, and a Stanford Achievement Test were also administered. Elimination of children from the study with incomplete data resulted in a sample of 189 subjects (90 boys, 99 girls). From the information obtained from the original research group, the Flowers-Costello Tests were revised to consist of only two subtests: The Low Pass Filtered Speech test and the Competing Message test. The revised test was again administered to a Kindergarten population of the Grand Blanc School in 1967. Subjects were measured with the Test of Primary Mental Abilities, yielding a mean IQ of 99.7 with a standard deviation of 16.1. Later, data for grades one through four were obtained for other school systems. Groups were divided by gender, age, and paternal occupation. Knowledge of gender, age, and paternal occupation were not found to be significant enough for producing separate norms on the tests.

Teachers were asked to select 42 students of high, low, and average achievement at each grade level. The data was used to compute the Kuder-Richardson estimate of internal consistency and reliability and to establish percentile rank scores for each grade level. Scores were converted to stanine measurements and compared to a Reading Expectancy Chart devised by the researchers.

The tests consist of a magnetic recording tape, test record forms, the instruction manual, and two test picture books that contain three pictures on each page. The subject is to point to one of three pictures that completes a sentence the child hears. Sentences are presented to the subject by magnetic recording tape. Either reel-to-reel (7½ I.P.S.) or cassette tapes are available, but the authors recommend the reel-to-reel version of the test for optimum fidelity. Test record forms are double-sided, with the Competing Message test on one side and the Low Pass Filtered Speech test on the other. Practice and test items are listed on the form and are easily scored by marking an "X" next to each incorrect answer. Some versions come with Koss Pro-4A headphones, which provide great fidelity and help to provide a barrier to some unwanted noise. An Electronic Intensity Calibration System (E.I.C.S.), which is a VU meter, plugs into a tape recorder (not supplied with the test) in order to set the volume at a standard level ("0" dB on the VU meter when a 15-second calibration tone is played on the tape). Other versions of the test come without headphones/VU meter. If a clinical audiometer is to be used with TDH-39 earphones in MX-41 cushions, the presentation level is 65 dB HL. Without audiological equipment and test room facilities, the E.I.C.S. kit would seem very advantageous.

Practical Applications/Uses

Directions for taking the test are given on the tape. Once the practice items are completed, the test is continued through the last item as long as the child continues to point to a picture after an auditory stimulus. The subject need only point to the correct picture in the test book and the examiner or child turns the page after the answer is given or after an audible "beep" is sounded 4 seconds after the stimulus on the test tape.

For each of the Low Pass Filtered Speech and Competing Message tests there are nine practice items. Practice items increase in difficulty with each successive item. For example, the first practice item on the Low Pass Filtered Speech test is not filtered at all. Filtering continues from items two through nine until the filter reaches the maximum filtering of 960 Hz. In the Low Pass Filtered Speech test as well as the Competing Message test, the test questions are sentence stems that must be correctly completed by choosing from among several pictures. On the Competing Message test the intensity of the children's story continues to increase on the practice items until the test item and competing story are of the same intensity, both mixed and presented to each ear. The child is told to listen only to the sentences.

According to the authors, the Low Pass Filtered Speech test represents the auditory perceptual factor of resistance to distortion. It measures the child's ability to resist distortion within the auditory perceptual system. The Competing Message test, on the other hand, is supposed to represent the auditory perceptual factor of selective listening.

Flowers and Costello have normed their test to reflect a prognosis for future difficulty in the area of reading. The test should not be used for any other purpose unless new research justifies other uses. The authors do encourage the tester to produce norms for his own test population—a good suggestion for any widespread test use, especially for those serving non-mainstream populations. There is no "cutoff" point at which a score indicates difficulty with central auditory processing. However, a very poor score on the test with an attentive subject should be cause for more advanced and/or collaborative audiological tests such as the Phonemic Synthesis Test, the Kindergarten Auditory Screening Test, The Jerger Pediatric Speech Intelligibility Test (PSI), the Willeford CST and IC-CS Test Battery, or others. The examiner may compare his test results with the original Flowers-Costello sample. Table 8 in the manual gives the confidence interval that the obtained test score is within a "useful" test score range; for example, if the examiner obtained a test score of 32, the table indicates that the true test score has 99 in 100 chances of falling between 25 and 39. Table 3 will then yield the approximate percentile score and mean for the child's grade level. It is up to the examiner to determine how well or poor the child did in comparison to the research sample. Again, there is no "pass" or "fail" score, only an indication of how well the child did on a continuum.

Although space-filling lesions (e.g., tumors of the brain) are relatively uncommon in children who have not had traumatic injury, very poor test results on the Flowers-Costello tests along with other unusual neurological signs (e.g., headache, vomiting, blurred vision, abnormal gait, etc.) should alert the examiner to seek neurological, otological and/or audiological evaluations. The construction of the tests does parallel other tests that are sensitive to brainstem dysfunction, such as the Synthetic Sentence Index with Ipsilateral Competing Message (Willeford, 1985).

Research on the use of the Flowers-Costello tests with special populations is not prolific, so the test should continue to be used as a screening test for "normal" children in Kindergarten to sixth grade at this time. Anderson and Novina (1973) compared 20 ethnic minority children (17 Mexican-American and 3 black subjects) on the Illinois Test of Psycholinguistic Abilities (ITPA) auditory subtests with the Flowers-Costello. The Flowers-Costello was found to correlate with three of the five ITPA auditory tests (reception, association, and sound blending). The memory and closure subtests were not correlated. Anderson and Novina suggest that norms be developed for the two subtests of the Flowers-Costello rather than using a single raw score for the total test because, they believe, the subtests are measuring two separate processing functions. Complexity of the total auditory mechanism is underlined by the different measurements obtained when trying to access the same central auditory system. Test results sometimes do not correlate even though the tests are purported to measure the same central auditory function.

Technical Aspects

Internal consistency and reliability of the revised 1970 Flowers-Costello tests were calculated for 42 subjects in Kindergarten to sixth grade using the Kuder-Richardson Formula 20. Reliability of the revised battery decreased from a high of .87 in Kindergarten to .70 for grades one and two, to a low of .60 and .37 for grades three and four. Grades five and six were below .30. The lower the grade level, the greater the internal consistency and reliability of the tests. Analyses of the Peabody Picture Vocabulary Test tends to indicate the children of the Grand Blanc Schools, on which the Flowers-Costello tests were based, are representative of the total Grand Blanc School population. Test results of clear, undistorted test items produced median scores of 45, while the Low Pass Filtered and Competing Message subtests produced scores of 28. These lower test scores tend to indicate significant test condition effects.

Critique

From an audiological point of view, the Flowers-Costello tests lend little to the diagnosis of central auditory dysfunction. First, there is little or no information on how the test relates to children officially diagnosed as having a central auditory impairment. Without test data relating specifically to this disorder, no conclusions are reliable. Only extreme scores can indirectly point to a central auditory disorder. The Flowers-Costello tests should only be used to predict possible learning difficulty in the area of reading, probably due to a central auditory learning disorder. This correlation seems to be mystical at times in that several assumptions tend to be skipped, even though the final conclusion is probably accurate. As a screening procedure with other central auditory tests for follow-up evaluation, the Flowers-Costello is ideal. For students having a normal pure tone auditory examination, who nonetheless give the impression they are in their own special world and do not hear you, the Flowers-Costello Tests of Central Auditory Abilities are an important next step in the evaluation.

References

Anderson, A., & Novina, J. (1973). A study of the relationship of the tests of central auditory abilities and the Illinois Test of Psycholinguistic Abilities. *Journal of Learning Disabilities, 6,* 167–169.

Willeford, J. (1985). Sentence tests of central auditory dysfunction. In J. Katz (Ed.), *Handbook of clinical audiology* (3rd ed.). (pp. 404–420). Baltimore: Williams & Wilkins.

Sheldon L. Stick, Ph.D.
*Professor of Special Education and Communication Disorders,
University of Nebraska-Lincoln, Lincoln, Nebraska.*

FULLERTON LANGUAGE TEST FOR ADOLESCENTS (EXPERIMENTAL EDITION)
Arden R. Thorum. Palo Alto, California: Consulting Psychologists Press, Inc.

Introduction

Initial efforts at developing an instrument to distinguish language-impaired from normal children between the ages of 11 and 18 were started in 1975. Existing instruments were considered inadequate for application with adolescents suspected of having language problems because appropriate normative data was not available. To some extent, the lacuna was circular, because research on adolescent language was handicapped by a lack of appropriate instrumentation; however, the appropriate instrumentation was not developed because of the lack of systematic collection of data on adolescent subjects. In 1975 a collaborative grant was awarded to the Fullerton Union High School District and the California State University at Fullerton by the California State Department of Education. The project was to be funded for five years, during which time the grantees were to develop a model program for serving adolescents with speech and language impairments. Additionally, one of the project's early objectives was the development of an instrument that could be used to determine the extent of linguistic and language deficiencies among adolescents.

In 1977 the field-study edition of the Fullerton Language Assessment Test for Adolescents was administered to ten individuals at each year level between ages 11 and 18, (N=180). Reportedly that version of the test contained more than a sufficient number of items for each of eight subtests predetermined as sampling different aspects of language. The subsequent item analysis and interpretation of the results from the field testing allowed for refining the instrument into its present experimental edition form, which consists of two receptive language subtests (oral commands and syllabication) and six expressive subtests (auditory synthesis, morphology competency, convergent production, divergent production, grammatic competency, and idioms). All items initially included were selected on the basis of existing language assessment tools containing similar tasks, and an apparently empirical investigation into the processes and skills presumed to be associated with the acquisition and development of language. Further input into the development and subsequent experimental edition selection of items was based upon input from individuals reported to be experts in the field of language pathology and learning disability as well as classroom teachers and psychologists who commented upon the learning behaviors of children between 11 and 18 years of age.

Collection of the normative data was accomplished by using graduate students majoring in communicative disorders at the California State University at Fullerton and professional speech and language specialists from the Fullerton Union High School district and other districts within Orange and Los Angeles counties. All participants received an eight-hour in-service training session on the purpose, administration, and scoring of the test. Similar in-service training on test administration and scoring was provided to a number of additional speech and language specialists from San Diego, Sacramento, and parts of Oregon, who also assisted in the data collection for the field-study edition. Between October, 1978, and April, 1979, the experimental edition of the Fullerton was standardized on a sample of 11- to 18-year-olds drawn from urban and rural areas of California and Oregon. All subjects attended regular public school classrooms and were considered representative of students in the mainstream of the educational process. However, it was noted that a few of the sample subjects were identified as presenting undetected learning disabilities. Data from those subjects apparently was not excluded from the standardization process of the Fullerton. The 762 subjects who comprised the standardization sample for the experimental edition were tested individually by approximately 45 professional speech and language specialists and by graduate students majoring in communication disorders. A demographic analysis of the sample subjects revealed that protocols were included from only 727 of the tested 762 subjects. The difference was attributed to the fact that missing information was identified on 35 of the protocol forms. The sex ratios were comparable with 362 males versus 365 females. Caucasions comprised 78.6% of the total sample, blacks were 7.0%, Spanish surname comprised 11.2%, and 3.2% were identified as "other". At the time of this review the experimental edition protocol was available in one English language form.

The Fullerton Language Test for Adolescents is an individually administered test that requires about 45 minutes to complete. Examiners should have a thorough understanding of the test objectives and how to administer and score the various subtests. The accumulative raw scores for each of the eight subcomponents to the Fullerton are interpreted by comparison to means and standard deviations for each of the respective subtests. Testing is done by an examiner presenting items verbally to a subject who makes verbal and/or nonverbal responses that are evaluated in terms of adequacy for that particular test item. Examiners are expected to follow the standard manner of item presentation, which is facilitated by having the directions for the examinees printed in italics. There is no prescribed sequence for subtest presentation, which provides an examiner with a notable degree of flexibility and the option of completing the entire test in more than one testing period.

Subtest one is entitled Auditory Synthesis. Its objective is to obtain information on an individual's ability to synthesize phonemic sounds/sound units comprising actual or nonsense words. There are two parts to this subtest. In part A the number of phonemic elements varies between two and seven. In part B, the phonemic units are syllables varying between two and seven. Subjects are required to blend the various sounds. The maximum raw score is 20, with ten points being assigned to Part A and to Part B. The rationale offered for including an auditory synthesis subtest was that language-impaired individuals may have difficulty performing such a task, and references were made to a number of commercially available tests that sample such sound blending abilities (Roswell & Chall, Auditory Blending Test, 1963; Oliphant Auditory Synthesizing Test, 1971; Illinois Test of Psycholinguistic Abilities, 1968; Woodcock & Johnson, Psychoeducational Battery, 1977; Stanford Diagnostic Reading Test, 1966).

Morphology competency is the second subtest. Its objective is to provide information on an individual's ability to analyze the morphological elements of words and then to demonstrate competency in using them correctly. Each of the twenty words included in this subtest is presented individually by an examiner who asks a subject to utilize that particular word in a phrase or sentence. Part A contains 15 root words plus a variety of suffixes. Part B has five root words with a number of prefixes. It was stated that this particular subtest was similar to the procedure used in a number of other assessment instruments such as the Test of Language Development (Hammill & Newcomer, 1977), the Bankson Language Screening Test (Bankson, 1976), the Berry-Talbot Development Guide to Comprehension of Grammar (Berry, 1977), and the Illinois Test of Psycholinguistic Abilities (Kirk, McCarthy, & Kirk, 1968). However, on the Fullerton morphology competency subtest each word is presented to a subject instead of using a closed procedure for sentence completion.

Oral Commands is the third subtest and the only one to require use of stimuli that come with the test kit. The objective is to determine an individual's ability to perform a number of different tasks presented verbally that vary in length of utterance and in syntactical complexity. Responses must be in a prescribed manner. The procedure followed for this subtest is reported to be similar to activities from the Token Test for Children (1979), the Neurosensory Center Comprehensive Examination for Aphasia (1969), the Muma Assessment Program (1979), and the Clinical Evaluation of Language Functions (1980). Each of the twenty items assesses specifically linguistic elements that reportedly are sensitive to the identification of semantic/cognitive impairments generally not tapped by other tasks.

The fourth subtest is entitled Convergent Production. Subjects are presented with a series of words that sound alike but have different meanings (homonyms or homographs), and are required to either give an example using the word correctly or define the actual word. The intent is to obtain information on an individual's ability to call up words and definitions from long term memory, which is viewed as a reflection of vocabulary power. The 17 key words can be defined according to four main syntactic categories (noun, verb, adjective, and adverb) and a category designated as "other." Accumulatively there are 75 possible definitions or uses for the 17 key words, which vary from concrete to highly abstract. It was reported that the measurement approach used for this subtest was similar to that followed in the Illinois Test of Psycholinguistic Abilities (1968) and the Detroit Test of Learning Aptitude (1959).

The fifth subtest is entitled Divergent Production. The tasks presented to a subject presumably provide information on ability to produce a variety of words and concepts in response to five different concept classes: parts of the body; types of transportation; types of grocery store items; types of sports; and subjects offered in school. Examinees are allowed 20 seconds to respond to each category class. The approach is reported to be similar to tasks on the McCarthy Scales of Children's Abilities (1970), the Boston Diagnostic Aphasia Examination (1972), and the Detroit Tests of Learning Aptitude (1959).

Subtest six is entitled Syllabication. Each of the 20 items, varying from single words to eight-word sentences with between 1 and 11 syllables, are to be presented in a cadence resembling normal speech production. The individual's task is to blend the sound sequences and tell the examiner the actual word(s). The rationale for inclusion of this task was the speculation that having the ability to blend syllables may facilitate word and sentence recall. Support for inclusion of this was based on the fact that it was similar to tasks on the Stanford Diagnostic Reading Test (1966) and the Gates-McKilliop Reading Diagnostic Tests (1962).

The seventh subtest is entitled Grammatic Competency. Its purpose is to determine an individual's ability to correctly identify grammatical from ungrammatical sentences and to present the correct syntactic constructions for sentences of the latter type. The 20 sentences mainly sample the concepts of time, space, action/agent, quantity, and quality. An individual's ability to make judgments regarding correctness of grammatical constructions was considered to be dependent upon knowledge of the rules for a community's language and an individual's intuitive knowledge about such a language. Other tests cited as having similar components were the Carrow Elicited Language Inventory (1974), the Assessment of Children's Language Comprehension (1972), the Language/Structured Auditory Retention Span Test (1973), the Northwestern Syntax Screening Test (1969), the Bankson Screening Test (1977), and the Clinical Evaluation of Language Functions (1980).

Subtest eight, Idioms, samples an individual's ability to define the figurative meaning of utterances that also have a literal interpretation. Recognition of the duality in language is an activity commonly displayed by children of 11 years of age. However, the manual reports that little information is available reporting the relative role of idioms in conversational interactions, and that there are no comparable tasks commercially available when sampling language ability of individual's presumably having language impairments. This subtest is viewed as the most nontraditional of the eight components in the Fullerton, but might be viewed as an index of a subject's ability to be flexible in using and understanding language as well as a subject's exposure to language in a variety of contexts. The 20 idioms included in the experimental edition of the Fullerton were those generally known by at least 30% of the subjects in the field test. They were adapted from *Raining Cats and Dogs* (Auslin, 1978) and *Language Remediation and Expansion* (Bush, 1979).

There are no prescribed basal or cutoff points during the administration of the Fullerton Language Test for Adolescents. Instead, each subtest is presented in its entirety. Items vary in their apparent level of difficulty throughout each of the eight subtests, and it is possible for several of the earlier items to be missed and the later items to be given correct responses. The test manual (including bibliography) is only 28 pages long, and the scoring form and profile is an eight-page document. The items required with subtest three fit into a small plastic bag, and the entire package can be carried conveniently. An interesting dimension to this test is that it does not presume to identify a specific level at which an individual is functioning; instead, each of the eight subtests are profiled according to one of three levels, based upon the raw score points earned. The competence level is viewed as the point wherein a person tested has adequate skills and abilities for the processes involved on a particular subtest. The instruction level is viewed as a time when an individual is in a period of transition. Such an individual presumably would have most of the prerequisite processes required for performing acceptably on a given subtest (task), but additional instruction or practice is required for the individual to demonstrate competence consistently. The frustration level is considered the point where an individual does not have prerequisite skills/abilities to perform appropriately on a given subtest. Performance at this level reflects a lack of readiness skills, and instruction is required beginning at an elementary level. Overall, the three levels (competence, instruction, and frustration) allow an examiner to identify relative strengths and weaknesses in an individual and provides directions for prescriptive intervention. Furthermore, the raw scores can be viewed in terms of comparison to a mean score on each of the subtests, and standard deviations are provided to reflect the extent to which a given raw score is either above or below the average for a particular subtest.

Practical Applications/Uses

Forty-five minutes of testing time, which is what the Fullerton Language Test for Adolescents generally requires, is not an excessively long period of time to spend gathering data samples from eight different areas of language behavior. Allowing for the fact that an examiner using this instrument should be sophisticated in the area of language acquisition (from the perspectives of processes and contents), the instrument should serve its stated purpose of distinguishing language-impaired adolescents from individuals whose language has been developing normally. Decision-making difficulties perhaps would occur when confronted with adolescents displaying marginal competence levels of performance or presenting a profile with several subtests rated at the instructional level. In such instances, it would be incumbent upon an examiner to utilize clinical judgment in terms of the subject's age and other factors that might contribute to a decision in terms of additional testing, a period of trial treatment, a decision not to provide treatment but to retest at a later date, and so on. The obvious advantage to using an instrument such as the Fullerton is that an examiner has specific pieces of information that can be analyzed from a variety of perspectives. In the hands of an unsophisticated examiner the potential benefits of using an instrument such as the Fullerton can become limited and possibly negated.

Speech-language pathologists serving an adolescent population (ages 11-18 years) probably would view the Fullerton as a welcome asset to their repertoire of procedures and tests that can be used with older school-aged children. However, as with most instruments, caution should be exercised in placing too great a reliance upon the data obtained from the test. The flexibility provided to the examiner in terms of variability in subtest presentation, completion of the total test in more than one testing period, conversion of raw scores into means and standard deviations in addition to the three performance levels, and the implications for pursuing directions for treatment make this a highly attractive instrument, even for usage with subjects displaying moderate language abilities. When considering the nature of the tasks involved in the subtests, it becomes apparent that the Fullerton has potential applicability with populations other than adolescents having suspected language impairments. For example, the Fullerton could be used with adults (closed head injury and/or suspected degenerative conditions) and with adolescents whose apparent language difficulties might be attributed to a variety of possible etiologies (i.e., behavioral impairment/emotional disturbance and/or cerebral dysfunction with soft or hard sides present). The ease with which a trained examiner can administer the test makes it conducive to being used in less than optimal testing environments, which commonly are found in public school settings.

It is likely that well-trained professionals from disciplines allied to speech-language pathology will be tempted to utilize the Fullerton Language Test for Adolescents. Sophisticated examiners most likely would be able to administer the test, but it is questionable whether they would be able to do more than a straight data interpretation. The real benefit to the Fullerton seems to be in utilizing the information it provides in terms of pursuing other lines for data collection and planning treatment. In fact, the manual does provide suggestions for subtest interpretation and planning of intervention programs. When coupled with more extensive knowledge of phonological, syntactic, semantic, and pragmatic development, the ideas suggested can be valuable tools for working with adolescents presenting language impairments.

Technical Aspects

Because the objective of the Fullerton Language Test for Adolescents was to provide professional speech and language pathologists with an instrument for differentiating language-impaired from normal adolescents, items were included in the eight subtests on the basis that most 12-year-olds would demonstrate a ceiling effect on a number of the tasks. That expectation was realized with the standardization sample. Therefore, items included were not rank-ordered in terms of any degree of apparent difficulty. Instead, they were included in the various subtests on the basis of how well they discriminated between language-impaired adolescents and those who ostensibly had normal language development. Furthermore, the dispersement of easy items throughout the various subtests was viewed as a positive factor in helping to sustain motivation and a relative feeling of achievement among all subjects tested. The issue of sustaining motivation and apparent fatigue reportedly was not a negative factor based on the fact that the last three items on five of the subtests were responded to correctly at least 85% of the time by all of the subjects in the standardization sample. With the exception of the divergent production subtest, the mean item difficulty ranged from .47 to .92. The divergent production subtest was an open-ended activity that did not lend itself to evaluation in terms of absolute ranking. Seventy-five subjects from the standardization sample were selected randomly and retested within a month of the original testing. The test-retest reliability coefficients by subtest ranged from a low of .84 (conversion production) to a high of .96 (morphology competency and idioms). The Pearson product-moment correlations were statistically significant beyond the .01 level of competence. Kuder-Richardson split-half reliability coefficients for the eight subtests ranged from a low of .71 (convergent production) to a high of .85

(idioms), which indicated that the items within each subtest were measuring essentially the same skills or processes.

Content and item validity for the eight subtests were determined on the basis of two criteria. The first was that there was existing theoretical support, based on available literature, that the activities required by a given subtest were deemed to be aspects of language development. The second criterion for inclusion was that similar activities were included in existing commercially available instruments assessing language. Except for the idioms subtest, there were at least four commercially available tests containing such activities. It should be noted that no correlations were reported between the Fullerton subtests and any of the commercially available items used as justification for content and item validity. Therefore, it would seem that the type of validity being reported was really face validity.

A second type of validity reported was diagnostic validity. For this analysis a t-test was applied to the data from two groups of adolescents, one consisting of 489 students functioning within a regular public school program, the second consisting of 73 public school students identified as having some academic difficulties and receiving a variety of special education services. Scores on the Fullerton did differentiate between the two groups beyond the .001 level of confidence, which can be interpreted as meaning the Fullerton is able to differentiate adolescents with academic problems from those who have ostensibly normal language development and no apparent academic difficulties. It was noteworthy that the 73 students receiving special education and services included individuals identified as learning-disabled, language-impaired, having reading difficulties, and requiring special resource services. Additional technical information reported included means of standard deviations for every item in each one of the eight subtests, and a table that presented mean scores of standard deviations for each of the eight subtests according to six-month intervals, beginning at 11.0-11.5 years and extending up to 18.0-18.5 years.

Critique

The experimental edition of the Fullerton Language Test for Adolescents likely will prove to be increasingly attractive to speech-language pathologists faced with obtaining language data on adolescents and adult subjects. The eight subtests clearly provide information that can be used when planning treatment programs, and analysis can be made of the responses given to the individual items on the various subtests. In fact, the test provides standards against which subject responses can be compared. The test is "user friendly." Professionals with a good background in language should find that the test provides them with specific pieces of valuable information that customarily might be overlooked during efforts to obtain language samples or other indices of language performance. When the Fullerton subtest data is used in conjunction with language samples that are evaluated on the basis of rule application to phonology and syntax and the semantic-pragmatic expression of differing concepts in varying contexts, there should be little question about the direction of an intervention program because the entire communicative process would have been sampled. It is noteworthy that a language sample can be elicited from a subject by utilizing aspects of the Fullerton.

148   Fullerton Language Test for Adolescents

Despite the positive features of this test, there are some points that users should recognize as limitations. For example, in Figure 12 of the manual the demographic features of the experimental edition sample show that the number of subjects (male and female) for each year level vary from a low of 40 (18-year level) to a high of 111 (11-year level). Subject selection seems to have been made on the basis of students available in different locales instead of systematically setting out to obtain a predetermined number of subjects at given age levels. Another concern with the presentation of demographic information occurs when Figure 11 information (demographic features of the sample) is compared to Table 9 (number of subjects, means, and standard deviations at 6-month intervals). The data from Figure 11 present the numbers of males and females tested at each age level. Table 9, which shows the 6-month interval central tendency data by subtest, presents information that appears to indicate only one sex was tested at each six-month interval. For example, Figure 11 shows that 54 males and 57 females were tested at age 11. Table 9 (the 6 month interval between 11.0-11.5 months) reports 54 subjects. The succeeding 6 month interval (11.6-11.11) shows 57 subjects. A similar pattern was noted for each of the next eight 6-month intervals. At the 16-year age level, Figure 11 shows 40 males and 61 females were tested; however Table 9 shows that between 16.0-16.5 months there were 61 subjects tested, and at the 16.6-16.11 6-month interval there were a total of 50 subjects. Additionally, Figure 11 shows that at the 17-year level there were 42 males and 37 females tested (N = 79), but Table 9 indicates there were 52 subjects tested at the 17.0-17.5 interval and another 52 subjects at the 17.6-17.11 interval (n = 104). In all likelihood, the apparent confusion between Figure 11 and Table 9 is due to typographical errors. But that raises a question about how carefully the other data were edited in terms of the central tendency data and the statistical interpretations. Another point worthy of noting is that in Figure 11 there is an asterisk beside the total number of subjects from the eight age levels. The figure presented as the total number of subjects from the eight age levels. The figure presented as the total is 727, and it is mentioned that 35 of the test forms had information that was missing; consequently, there were not included. Yet throughout the remainder of the test manual, reference is made to the fact there were 762 subjects in the experimental edition sample.

Another point that is somewhat bothersome stems from the consistent reference to using tasks commonly found in other commercially available language assessment tests. It seems that constitutes a form of face validity, yet in the section of the manual reporting on research and technical data reference is made to content validity. It is not clear how content validity was determined, and there is no indication that concurrent validity was attempted with some of the commercially available tests. Despite the questions about the presentation of some of the data and types of validity reported, the test is attractive as a tool for assisting in differentiating adolescents with apparent language-impairments. Obviously an examiner should be cautious about interpretations made on the basis of data obtained, and efforts should be made to substantiate impressions with other test data and/or observations or reports from other professionals. The manual reports that the Fullerton has met selected (undefined) criteria that make it worthy of being presented to the public as an experimental version of a test that purports to sample selected aspects of language. With that statement in mind, the test is viewed as a welcome addition. However, it seems appropriate to urge that a revised edition be made available in the immediate future, and that efforts be made to clarify the validity issues and apparent typographical errors in presentation of data in the experimental edition.

References

This list includes text citations and suggested additional reading.

Auslin, M. (1978). *Raining cats and dogs*. Beaverton, OR: Dormac, Inc.
Baker, H., & Leland, B. (1959). *Detroit Tests of Learning Aptitude*. Indianapolis: Bobbs-Merrill Company.
Bankson, N. (1977). *Bankson Language Screening Test*. Baltimore: University Park Press.
Berry, M. (1977). *Berry-Talbot developing guide to comprehension and grammar*. (Available from Mildred F. Berry, 4332 Pine Crest Road, Rockford, IL, 61107)
Bush, C. (1979). *Language remediation and expansion: 100 Skill Building Reference Lists*. Tucson, AZ: Communication Skill Builders, Inc.
Carlsen, B., Madden, R., & Gardner, E. (1966). *Stanford Diagnostic Reading Test*. New York: Psychological Corporation.
Carlsen, L. (1973). *Language-Structured Auditory Retention Span Test*. Novato, CA: Academic Therapy Publications.
Carrow-Woolfolk, E. (1974). *Carrow Elicited Language Inventory*. Boston: Teaching Resources Corp.
DiSimoni, F. (1979). *The Token Test for Children*. Boston: Teaching Resources Corp.
Foster, R., Gidden, J., & Stark, J. (1972). *Assessment of children's language comprehension*. Palo Alto, CA: Consulting Psychologists Press.
Gates, A., & McKilliop, A. (1962). *Gates-McKilliop Reading Diagnostic Tests*. New York: Teachers College Press.
Goodglass, H., & Kaplan, E. (1972). *Boston Diagnostic Aphasia Examination*. Philadelphia: Lea and Febrieger.
Hammill, D., & Newcomer, P. (1977). *Test of Language Development*. Austin, TX: PRO-ED.
Kirk, S., McCarthy, J., & Kirk, W. (1968). *Illinois Test of Psycholinguistic Abilities*. Urbana: University of Illinois Press.
Lee, L. (1969). *Northwestern Syntax Screening Test*. Evanston, IL: Northwestern University Press.
McCarthy, D. (1970). *McCarthy Scales of Children's Abilities*. New York: Psychological Corporation.
Muma, J., & Muma, D. (1979). *Muma Assessment Program*. Lubbock, TX: Natural Child Publishing Company.
Oliphant, G. (1971). *Oliphant Auditory Synthesizing Test*. Cambridge, MA: Educators Publishing Service, Inc.
Roswell, F., & Chall, J. (1963). *Roswell-Chall Auditory Blending Test*. New York: Essay Press.
Semel, E., & Wiig, E. (1980). *Clinical evaluation of language functions*. Columbus, OH: Charles E. Merrill Publishing Company.
Speen, O., & Benton, A. (1969). *Neurosensory Center Comprehensive Examination for Aphasia*. Victoria, British Columbia, Canada: University of Victoria.
Woodcock, R., & Johnson, M. (1977). *Woodcock-Johnson Psychoeducational Battery*. Boston, MA: Teaching Resources Corporation.

Jean Powell Kirnan, Ph.D.
Assistant Professor of Psychology, Trenton State College, Trenton, New Jersey.

Kurt F. Geisinger, Ph.D.
Associate Professor and Chairperson of Psychology, Fordham University, Bronx, New York.

GENERAL APTITUDE TEST BATTERY

U.S. Employment Service. Washington, D.C.: United States Department of Labor.

Introduction

The General Aptitude Test Battery (GATB) was developed by the United States Employment Service (USES) in response to the growing need for a comprehensive instrument for use in occupational counseling. Utilizing tests that measure a variety of basic aptitudes, the GATB evaluates an applicant's ability to perform successfully in a wide variety of occupations. As such, its introduction in 1947 was welcomed by job counseling and selection professionals faced with the task of placing the growing labor market of the post-World War II era.

Since its inception in 1947, the GATB has undergone continuous revision and modification. Its development spans a 50-year period as today it continues to be the object of considerable research. The groundwork for the GATB was laid in the mid-1930s when the development of tests of aptitudes and skills was widespread among psychologists and others. Tests that could quickly and accurately match applicant abilities with job requirements were greatly needed both during World War II and in the years following. Both the Minnesota Stabilization Research Institute and the Occupational Research Program in the USES pioneered this research. By the 1940s, over 100 aptitude tests had been developed for use in placing workers. However, this growing number of tests made the task of efficient and accurate placement almost impossible for general counseling purposes. In order to be counseled for more than one occupation, individuals seeking vocational guidance would have to be administered several tests. Researchers recognized that similarities existed in the factors being measured by the varying tests as well as the basic aptitudes required by different occupations. Factor-analytic techniques then were used to identify basic aptitudes and to reduce the number of tests needed to measure them.

The factor analysis performed by USES was conducted during the period 1942 to 1944 and employed several experimental groups, totalling 2,156 individuals. Each of these individuals had taken some combination of 59 tests—54 of which were Employment Service tests representative of the 100 tests then in use by the Service. While all subjects were male and applicants for or incumbents in defense training courses, the sample was otherwise representative of the Employment Service's counselees in terms of age, education, and experience.

The analysis identified ten factors: Intelligence, Verbal Aptitude, Numerical Aptitude, Spatial Aptitude, Form Perception, Clerical Perception, Aiming, Motor Speed, Finger Dexterity, and Manual Dexterity. The tests to measure these factors were selected on the basis of internal or factorial validity (magnitude of the factor loading) as well as external or practical validity (based on a review of previously conducted criterion-related validity studies in the occupations). It must be noted, however, that the criteria of occupational success are not provided in the manual. It is also not reported whether the studies were concurrent or predictive in nature. The resulting 11 paper-and-pencil tests and four apparatus or performance tests comprised the first form of the GATB, B-1001. Thus, from over 100 available tests, 15 were chosen that in a single administration could measure the basic aptitudes required of most of the jobs for which USES employed ability tests. The aptitudes and the tests that measure them are provided in Table 1.

A second version of the instrument, B-1002 Form A, was introduced in 1952. Several enhancements were made in this revision: B-1002 provided examinees with a separate answer sheet (for this reason, items in B-1001 that were not in multiple choice format were revised accordingly), new experimental items were added, provision was made for an alternate form (Form B), and new time limits were set to accommodate the new items as well as the use of a separate answer sheet. The new items allowed for the replacement of current B-1001 items that were no longer effective as well as the construction of the alternate form. In order to accomplish all the above, an experimental test consisting of the revised B-1001 items, new items, and a separate answer sheet was administered under untimed conditions to 10 samples of approximately 200 subjects each. The tests were administered in an untimed fashion to help establish new time limits and to facilitate the subsequent item analysis by ensuring that each examinee had the opportunity to attempt every item.

The final items for the B-1002 forms were selected on the basis of item difficulty and discriminability. Alternate forms were made as equivalent as possible. Several easy items were included in the beginning of each test to allow the examinee to "warm-up," and all items were arranged in order of increasing difficulty. Efforts were made to reduce testing time by eliminating tests that were redundant. Three tests—Two-Dimensional Space, H Markings, and Speed—were dropped from the original B-1001. These were eliminated for one of two reasons; either they were not weighted heavily in determining an aptitude score, or ongoing validity studies had shown that they did provide incremental validity. The revision also resulted in the elimination of one aptitude, Eye/Hand Coordination, which was found to be highly correlated with and thus redundant of another aptitude, Motor Speed. With this change, Motor Speed was renamed Motor Coordination.

Thus, the current version of the GATB assesses nine aptitudes through the use of 12 tests, as listed in Table 2.

Numerous variations on the answer sheet were to follow the revision to B-1002. Typically, these were minor changes to allow for machine scoring on different optical scanning equipment. In every case, comparability studies were conducted to ensure the new answer sheets did not affect applicants' scores.

No information on the development of Forms C and D, the most recent versions of the battery, were included in the development manual (Section III) provided by USES. It certainly must be hoped that similar comparative studies were conducted

Table 1

Original Version of the GATB

Aptitude	Test
Intelligence	Three-Dimensional Space Vocabulary Arithmetic Reasoning
Verbal Aptitude	Vocabulary
Numerical Aptitude	Computation Arithmetic Reasoning
Spatial Aptitude	Two-Dimensional Space Three-Dimensional Space
Form Perception	Tool Matching Form Matching
Clerical Perception	Name Comparison
Aiming or Eye/Hand Coordination	H Markings Mark Making
Motor Speed	Speed Mark Making
Finger Dexterity	Assemble and Dissassemble
Manual Dexterity	Place and Turn

to equate these new versions with Forms A and B. A subsequent research report (Kolberg, 1977) states that Forms C and D had been developed as alternates in response to a liberal retesting policy in local Employment Service offices.

Initially, norms were established based on test results of 519 employed workers who took the GATB. However, it was necessary to update these data because the sample of 519 did not include an adequate sampling of occupations. In 1952, a special stratified sample of 4,000 cases was extracted from 8,000 records of job incumbents tested while they were working in a wide variety of occupations. These were selected in a stratified procedure to be representative of the 1940 U.S. census data of the working population. The primary variable in the stratification was Occupation. Sex, age, and geographic location were also considered as factors. Because of the changing role of women in the work force—both during World War II and in the years following—it was arbitrarily decided that the sample be half male and half female. The geographic distribution of the 4,000 cases was found to differ significantly from the U.S. census data; the North Central region was overrepresented because there was a high degree of diversification of occupations as well as many

Table 2

Current Version of the GATB

Aptitude	Test
Intelligence	Three-Dimensional Space
	Vocabulary
	Arithmetic Reasoning
Verbal Aptitude	Vocabulary
Numerical Aptitude	Computation
	Arithmetic Reasoning
Spatial Aptitude	Three-Dimensional Space
Form Perception	Tool Matching
	Form Matching
Clerical Perception	Name Comparison
Motor Coordination	Mark Making
Finger Dexterity	Assemble and Dissassemble
Manual Dexterity	Place and Turn

large centralized industries in that region. The authors, however, did not consider these to be of sufficient magnitude to threaten the usefulness of the data.

Thus, norms for the GATB version B-1001 were calculated on the sample of 4,000. When B-1002 Form A was introduced, new conversion tables were needed. The formulae for these tables were derived from a study of 585 high school and junior college students tested in three different states. Form B of B-1002 also has separate conversion tables; again, these were derived from a study of 412 high school juniors and seniors in two states. In 1966, an analysis of data collected in a variety of studies (1950-1966) reaffirmed the stability of these norms.

Only 2 of the 10 aptitudes in B-1001 were based on a single test score. The other eight were derived via weighted linear combinations of scores. The justification for combining these measures was obtained from the earlier factor analysis conducted on the sample of 2,156 examinees, as well as the initial normative sample of 519. Factor loadings and intercorrelations among the tests were used to determine how these tests would be weighted additively to arrive at a single aptitude score. Data from the normative sample were also used to aid in standardizing these scores so that each of the resulting GATB aptitudes had a mean of 100 and a standard deviation of 20.

Similarly, conversion tables were needed to convert raw scores to aptitude scores for the subsequent versions of the GATB. Normative data from high school comparability studies cited above were used to derive equivalent aptitude scores for B-1002 Forms A and B.

Not all aptitudes are required in every occupation. Therefore, the identification of those aptitudes necessary for a given occupation and the determination of the predicted levels of competency was required. Groups of aptitudes essential for a given occupation were combined and called Specific Aptitude Test Batteries or SATBs. A total of more than 450 SATBs have been developed, each composed of two, three, or four GATB aptitudes.

Aptitudes were evaluated as being important to job performance (and thus selected for a SATB) on the basis of job analysis information and statistical data described below. When possible, predictive validity studies were used. When this type of design was not feasible, the concurrent approach was employed. The data for these analyses were collected at various state employment offices and consolidated for analysis at the national office. The statistical data considered in addition to the job analysis information were: 1) the three aptitude tests yielding the highest mean scores within an occupation, 2) aptitude tests with low standard deviations (evidence of relative homogeneity), and 3) aptitudes demonstrating significant correlations ($p < .05$) with the criterion (job or training performance).

Once selected, the aptitudes were used to arrive at "trial norms," which were evaluated in the sample for their ability to discriminate "successful" and "unsuccessful" workers. The resulting norms were subsequently cross-validated on new occupational samples.

To calculate all SATBs for any one applicant would be extremely time-consuming; on the other hand, computation of a select few would be too specific for general counseling purposes. For this reason, families of jobs called Occupational Aptitude Patterns or OAPs were constructed. By grouping occupations into families and assessing each candidate on all the job families, the OAPs make maximum use of the data gathered by the GATB. The OAPs are especially useful in counseling because most applicants are being counseled for a large number of occupations.

The initial decision as to which occupations would comprise an OAP was determined by grouping the SATBs according to the aptitudes that they had in common. These trial OAPs were then evaluated and finalized based on their correlation with job success. The cut scores for the OAPs were determined from the cut scores of the SATBs that comprise them. The OAPs have been revised on a number of occasions and currently there are 66 OAPs.

A major criticism of the SATB development is that a number of different aptitude combinations were equally effective in predicting success. This lack of stability further affects the OAPs, which rely heavily on SATB validity information for their development. For this reason, the development of the OAPs has shifted from a heavy reliance on the SATB validity studies to an emphasis of job analytic data because these data are considered to be more reliable.

This new emphasis on job analysis in OAP development corresponds with an overall effort to integrate the GATB and its associated measures with the *Dictionary of Occupational Titles* (DOT) (U.S. Department of Labor, 1977). The DOT provides a detailed description of the 12,000 occupations in the U.S. economy. The usefulness of the GATB can be maximized by coordinating the job descriptions and required aptitudes with those described in the DOT.

More recently, a comprehensive system for job counseling called the Counselee Assessment/Occupational Exploration System has been introduced. The most recent edition of the *Dictionary of Occupational Titles* (4th edition) serves as the core of this system. The primary components of the system are: 1) the Guide for Occupational Exploration, 2) measures of occupational interest (USES Interest Inventory and the Interest Check List), and 3) measures of the necessary aptitudes (the GATB). The guide classifies the occupations in the DOT into 12 Interest Areas and 66 Work Groups. As stated previously, the OAPs have been developed to correspond to these work groups and cover 97% of the non-supervisory occupations listed in the DOT. Thus, applicants can be measured on interests as well as aptitudes.

Much concern has been raised over the use of tests requiring reading and arithmetic calculations with educationally and culturally disadvantaged persons. In 1965, the USES introduced the Nonreading Aptitude Test Battery (NATB) as an alternative to the GATB for use with educationally deficient individuals. Designed for those with low levels of literacy skill, the NATB utilizes 14 tests to arrive at measures of the same nine aptitudes as the GATB.

The GATB was relied on heavily in the development of this new instrument. The rationale for this dependence was that the GATB measures the most important aptitudes for the occupations under consideration, and it had already been validated. Thus, the GATB norms could be used cautiously for the NATB. In fact, correlation with the GATB was one of the criteria used in the selection of the 14 NATB tests. The strategy of high correlation with an existing, validated, in-use instrument is an acceptable and common means of initially demonstrating validity. However, the fact that the NATB was specifically designed for individuals for whom the GATB was not a valid measure raises concern over the use of this technique in the NATB's development. USES recognizes this shortcoming and refers to it as "indirect" validity.

Tests 8 through 12 of the GATB—Mark Making and the Finger and Manual Dexterity measures—are included in the NATB. The nine other tests that comprise the NATB are: Picture Word Matching, Oral Vocabulary, Coin Matching, Matrices, Tool Matching, Three-Dimensional Space, Form Matching, Coin Series, and Name Comparison.

However, a relatively recent report (Angrisani, 1982) indicates that the NATB has undergone at least one revision. In a description of the NATB, this report, like other articles, states that 14 tests are used to measure the 9 aptitudes. However, when giving an in-depth description of the NATB, only 11 tests were listed and these were referred to as the 1982 edition. No indication was given as to how or why three tests were dropped from the original version.

In conjunction with the NATB, USES designed a screening procedure to identify disadvantaged individuals. Using this procedure, a counselor can determine in about five minutes if an applicant will be able to understand the instructions and test items on the GATB. It is suggested that those who do not pass the exercises should probably be tested with the NATB. However, because the screening test has not been validated, it is advised that it be used only as an aid and not as the sole basis for such a testing decision.

The documentation on the prescreening instrument is confusing. It is referred to as the Wide Range Scale, the BOLT Wide Range Scale, and the GATB-NATB Screening Device. It is assumed that all these names refer to the same instrument,

156   General Aptitude Test Battery

which consists of eight vocabulary and eight arithmetic items. The use of this prescreening device appears to be twofold: 1) to determine whether the GATB or the NATB should be administered; and 2) to determine what level of the Basic Occupational Literacy Test (BOLT) should be given. The BOLT was designed by USES as a measure of the applicant's literacy skills and relates these to literacy requirements of jobs. It is recommended that the BOLT be given to anyone who takes the NATB. The use of the prescreening device with BOLT may explain this variation on its name.

Additional aids to disadvantaged applicants are the Pretesting Orientation Techniques. These procedures were designed to orient and provide test-taking practice for disadvantaged individuals through the use of booklets and sample items available in: "Doing Your Best on Aptitude Tests," "Group Pretesting Orientation on the Purpose of Testing," "Doing Your Best on Reading and Arithmetic Tests," and "Pretesting Orientation Exercises."

A Spanish version of the GATB, the Bateria de Examenes de Aptitud General (BEAG), has been available since 1978. Two of the Prescreening Orientation Techniques—"Doing Your Best on Aptitude Tests" and "Group Pretesting Orientation on the Purpose of Testing"—are also available in Spanish.

A number of modifications to the GATB have recently been made in an effort to accommodate handicapped applicants better. These include special administration methods for the testing of deaf applicants and special norms for the manual dexterity tests administered to seated applicants (those confined to wheelchairs or otherwise unable to stand for extended periods of time).

The GATB consists of 12 tests (eight paper-and-pencil and four performance tests) that yield measures of nine aptitudes. The paper-and-pencil tests are presented to the applicant in one of two booklets, and responses are recorded on a separate answer sheet. Book 1 contains the first four paper-and-pencil tests; Book 2 contains tests 5-7. Test 8, Mark Making, requires a separate response sheet, and the performance tasks in tests 9-12 require special materials. Descriptions of the 12 tests and some sample items follow. (Actual items from the GATB are not presented for reasons of confidentiality. Rather, a representative item from each of the four tests was chosen and then modified for inclusion.)

1. *Name Comparison*—determining if name pairs are similar or different.

Example: H. W. Longfellow & Co.——H. W. Longfellow, Co.
(*Answer:* different)

2. *Computation*—arithmetic exercises utilizing addition, subtraction, multiplication, and division.

Example: MULTIPLY (X)   A   3822
                              B   3972
              427   C   3843
                9   D   3783
              ___   E   none of these

(*Answer:* C)

3. *Three-Dimensional Space*—selecting the proper three-dimensional representation of a flat, two-dimensional drawing. Lines appear on the two-dimensional stimulus figure indicating where it is to be folded or bent.

4. *Vocabulary*—from four words, select a word pair that constitutes either a synonym or an antonym.

Example: a. kind   b. empathetic   c. cruel   d. good
(*Answer:* a and c)

5. *Tool Matching*—identifying the exact likeness of a stimulus tool from four drawings that differ only slightly from each other.

6. *Arithmetic Reasoning*—solving of mathematical word problems.

Example: John can run 1/5 as far as Bill. Bill runs 12 miles. How far can John run?

A   2.4 miles
B   2 miles
C   3 miles
D   1 mile
E   none of these
(*Answer:* A)

7. *Form Matching*—matching similar shapes and forms in two different groups.

8. *Mark Making*—require making specified marks in a series of squares preprinted on a special response sheet.

The four performance tests, 9 through 12, are conducted using boards and are designed as measures of manual and finger dexterity. Tests 9 and 10 are referred to as *Place* and *Turn*, respectively. A rectangular pegboard divided into two sections, each containing 48 holes, is used for both tests. The examinee is required to move pegs from one side of the pegboard to the other for "Place." For "Turn," examinees must pick up each peg and turn it, or invert it, before returning it to the same hole in the pegboard. Test 9, Place, is performed three times, and then Test 10, Turn, is performed three times. The final score for each test is the number of pegs attempted summed across the three timed trials.

Tests 11 and 12, the measures of finger dexterity, are referred to as *Assemble* and *Disassemble*, respectively. The apparatus differs slightly, depending on the form of the test. For all forms, the major work part is a rectangular board containing 50 holes. What varies across forms is the location of the washers and rivets, which the individual is required to either assemble or disassemble. For Forms A, B, and D, the rivets are to be picked up (Assemble) or returned to (Disassemble) the upper portion of the board, where 50 additional holes are located. The rivets are to be taken from or returned to a vertical rod located at the mid-line of the board. However, for Form C, both washers and rivets are taken from and returned to two shallow cups built into the top of the board. No documentation was provided as to why this difference exists between the forms. Regardless of form, the basic tasks were the same. On the Assemble test, examinees place one washer and one rivet into each hole in the pegboard. On the Disassemble test, they remove the washers and rivets and return them to their original locations. Unlike Place and Turn, there is only one trial for Assemble and Disassemble.

158 General Aptitude Test Battery

While the administration of the battery does not require professional expertise, the role of the examiner is an active one. In addition to the normal administration duties of reading instructions, timing the tests, answering questions, and reporting any unusual conditions, the examiner must also demonstrate examples, set up equipment for performance tests, and score the performance tests.

Practical Applications/Uses

Tests developed by USES are intended for use by the public employment system in occupational counseling. Thus, they are available to the United States Employment Service as well as all State Employment Services. However, it is recognized that these instruments may prove useful to other counselors in both employment and educational settings. Use by other organizations requires prior approval from the State Employment Service. While the GATB could be used for any applicant to a State Employment Service, the usual age range of such applicants is 18 to 54, and most of the subjects in the standardization and validation samples fell into this age range.

The Administration and Scoring manual reports that only the earlier Forms, A and B, are available for release to other agencies. Form D is the primary test for use in government agencies, with Form C as the first retest. Forms A and B are also used as subsequent retests by government users.

In addition to its ability to predict job success, the GATB has been examined for its usefulness in predicting college success, especially for those occupations that require college training. In this capacity the GATB might help those who counsel high school students unsure of whether or not they should attend college. Because of time and cost considerations, most of the studies of the GATB with college students were restricted to using academic performance in college (e.g., grades) as the criterion of success rather than subsequent job performance. A consistent result was that Intelligence, Verbal Aptitude, and Numerical Aptitude were most frequently found to have significant correlations with this form of success. Because Intelligence correlates most highly, a minimum cutoff score for this aptitude was developed for use in counseling. In fact, three different cutoffs for this aptitude were derived for use with different types of colleges: junior colleges, four-year colleges, and four-year professional colleges (defined as colleges offering highly specialized professional courses, such as medicine, dentistry, and engineering). However, if the counselor requires information regarding a specific occupation or field of study, the GATB norms developed for that occupational area should be used.

Consideration was given to the use of the GATB with younger high school students. Studies of grades 9-12 revealed substantial maturational increases in aptitude scores. Additionally, the rate of maturation was quite varied for the individual subjects. For this reason, separate norms were derived for students enrolled in 9th and 10th grades. Reliability studies showed a good deal of instability and thus special bands were established. The purpose of these bands is to identify marginal scorers (marginal in the sense of qualifying for an OAP). If a student was a marginal scorer on an OAP, no interpretation was given for that particular occupational group. If the purpose of the GATB is to direct students to occupational groups for which they are qualified, it would seem that the entire battery would be invalidated if one OAP could not be interpreted. Four aptitudes—Intelligence, Verbal Aptitude, Numerical Aptitude, and Clerical Perception—were most predictive of success in six different high school subject areas: science, English, math, social studies, foreign language, and communication. In terms of validity, however, when used to predict college success, none of the aptitudes was as effective as a measure of academic standing in high school. Thus, because the OAPs are not reliable for this age group and academic standing in high school is superior in validity, there seems no reason to use or promote the use of the GATB for 9th and 10th graders.

Instructions for the administration of the GATB are clear and comprehensive. The administrator is advised as to materials needed, proper test environment, and preparation tips. The manual includes highlighted verbatim instructions, examples of common misunderstandings on the part of examinees, and suggestions for the testing of handicapped individuals. The instructions are so thorough that they provide a model for the administration of any standardized instrument. However, the booklet is lengthy, and the danger lies in the fact that many administrators may not have the time or inclination to read it thoroughly.

The aptitude battery requires approximately two-and-one-half hours for its administration. However, actual working time is only 48 minutes. The additional time is required for instruction, distribution of materials, and scoring of the performance tests. All tests are timed and provide for practice exercises in Tests 1-7, examples for Test 8, and demonstrated examples for Tests 9-12.

The test is most efficient if administered to groups. The manual provides suggested ratios of examiners to examinees. These ratios are: 1 to 10 for Tests 1-8 and 1 to 5 for the performance tests, Tests 9-12.

Normally, the 12 subtests are administered in numerical order. However, some deviations are acceptable. These are provided in the Administration manual. No indication is given as to whether the test may be given in two different administrations.

Scoring services are provided by Intran Corporation (INTRAN) and National Computer Systems (NCS), or the examiner may elect to hand-score the battery. Stencils are available to facilitate hand-scoring. Two interesting points are raised in the scoring section of the manual. The manual suggests, to those who hand-score the test, that if parts of the GATB are administered for specific batteries, only the appropriate parts of the battery should be scored instead of scoring the entire test. This statement is the only reference in the manual to the administration of specific parts of the GATB rather than the entire battery. Its placement in the hand-scoring section of the Administration and Scoring Manual is obscure at best. There are no clear instructions as to when this type of administration would be appropriate or how it should be undertaken.

Additionally, the hand-scoring instructions alert the examiner to unusually low scores. When such scores appear, the examiner is instructed to determine if the examinee made an error in recording his or her responses on the answer sheet. This often occurs if the examinee skips a question. When this appears to have happened, the examiner is instructed to give credit for correct answers that are recorded incorrectly. However, the manual does not indicate if low scores are given the same special consideration when the tests are machine scored.

160 General Aptitude Test Battery

For each examinee the scoring services provide a special report containing actual aptitude scores, aptitude scores plus one standard error of measurement, and a rating of H, M, or L (assumed to mean High, Medium, or Low) for each of the 66 OAPs. For hand-scoring, the Test Record Card is provided as an easy method of recording aptitude scores and evaluating the candidate on the OAPs. The examiner begins by recording raw scores on this card. A table (referred to as a "conversion table") is used to translate the raw scores into converted scores. Each of the 12 tests has its own conversion table, and separate tables are provided for each form of the GATB—A, B, C, and D. Additionally, simple linear equations are provided to convert the raw scores for users whose raw data have been computerized. These converted scores are then added together (where more than one test contributes to the measure of an aptitude) to arrive at the nine aptitude scores.

These aptitude scores are then compared to the cut scores established for each of the 66 OAPs. Three norm tables are available for this evaluation—9th grade, 10th grade, and adult. The examinee receives a rating of H, M, or L for each OAP. An H indicates a high probability that the individual will do well in that particular occupational group (OAP). An H is assigned if scores meet or exceed the cut scores for all the aptitudes associated with that particular OAP.

A rating of M indicates that the individual's score is similar to the scores obtained by workers judged as satisfactory in job performance. These individuals will do well on the job but probably not as well as someone judged to be an H. The M is assigned if the individual's scores plus one standard error of measurement meet or exceed the appropriate cut scores.

An L is assigned if an individual's scores are more than one standard error of measurement below the cut scores for the aptitudes identified as essential. This rating indicates that the probability of satisfactory performance on the job is very low. Other occupations should be considered, and counselors should suggest other possible avenues to explore.

Thus, through machine scoring or hand-scoring, a rating of H, M, or L is assigned for each of the 66 OAPs. The same procedure can be followed for determining the applicant's qualifications on the SATBs. However, these determinations must always be made by the examiner, as the machine scoring services do not provide this information. It is recommended that an applicant be evaluated on a SATB only if the individual is applying for a specific job opening. The SATBs, therefore, are used selectively, while every applicant is evaluated on all the OAPs. One of the reasons for this selectivity is that there are over 450 SATBs. Thus, evaluation on all SATBs would be rather cumbersome and overwhelming for the counselee.

In Section II of the manual, Occupational Aptitude Pattern Structure, over 2,500 occupations are listed within their respective OAP categories. These are a subset of the over 10,000 occupations listed in the Guide for Occupational Exploration. Counselors are instructed to refer to this Guide for occupations not listed in the GATB manual. It should be recalled that the OAPs apply only to nonsupervisory occupations.

While the instructions for hand-scoring are clear and easy to follow, the process is quite time-consuming, particularly if one were evaluating several candidates. Additionally, the sample record presented in Section I, Administration and Scoring, of the manual is incorrect. The sample indicates that the applicant took Form D of the GATB when in fact the raw score conversions are based on those for Form B, a quite confusing problem for an examiner engaged in hand-scoring, especially if he or she does not have access to both the Form B and Form D conversion tables.

Some of the advantages of the GATB are that the battery enables the counselor to evaluate the candidate on a large number of occupations through the use of one exam. Also, only those aptitudes essential for successful performance on the job are utilized. The use of multiple cutoffs prevents any one aptitude from compensating for the lack of another, a practice that may be beneficial or detrimental.

The test authors caution against the use of the GATB alone and stress that counselors should use other information at their disposal such as school records, the interview, background data, and other standardized tests. Specifically mentioned are interests, leisure activities, physical capacity, personal traits, social and economic factors, acquired skills, and education and training.

Two instruments have been developed by USES to assess an applicant's occupational interests. It is suggested that the Interest Check List and the USES Interest Inventory be used in conjunction with the GATB. However, the manual provides very little direction for the measure of these other variables or how they should be incorporated into either counseling or selection decisions. Other USES reports make reference to the previously mentioned Guide for Occupational Exploration. Descriptions of the Guide refer to it as useful to counselors in coordinating the interests and aptitudes of applicants.

Technical Aspects

The reliability of the GATB was assessed using the test-retest method. Time periods between testing administrations ranged from 1 day to 3 years. Retest studies have been conducted using the same test as well as an alternate form. Reliability coefficients for the aptitudes typically ranged from .80 to .90. A practice effect, common in most retesting situations, is typically observed on the GATB. The manual is confusing in its treatment of retests; counselors are warned to be cognizant of the practice effect in a retest situation, but statistical corrections are not provided. On the other hand, the manual suggests that because of the high reliability observed over several years, there is no need for retesting unless the applicant has experienced significant training. Additional evidence against retesting is found in a subsequent discussion in the manual in which training on the job did not increase aptitude scores. However, a research report states the reason behind the development of Forms C and D was to provide alternate forms for retesting situations. Thus, it is rather confusing when retesting is warranted, and it is not clear how a counselor should view the scores of a retest.

The reliabilities for Finger and Manual Dexterity tests were lower than for the other aptitudes, an expected finding in that performance tasks typically show greater contamination from retests than do paper-and-pencil tests.

Numerous studies have been conducted in a variety of State Employment offices over a period of time. Several studies examined males and females separately and found consistently significant reliability coefficients for both groups. Subjects included high school and college students, local office applicants, and current employees.

162 General Aptitude Test Battery

The validation research of the GATB has been, and continues to be, ongoing. Most notably, this research has resulted in the development of the Specific Aptitude Test Batteries (SATB) and the Occupational Aptitude Profiles (OAP) discussed earlier. The validation of the SATBs and OAPs was not conducted in a single time or place; studies were carried out at the various State Employment offices over a period of time. The manual reports the results of these studies in table form and cites a few in detail as examples. For this reason, discussion of the validation can only be carried out on a general level.

The effectiveness of the GATB as a selection tool is continually being measured by follow-up studies of job success for applicants tested with the GATB. Results of these studies indicated that those individuals who met the norms of an OAP or SATB were more successful as evidenced by lower turnover rates, lower training costs, lower make-up costs, and higher productivity (the manual does not define what "make-up" costs entail). Additionally, from the counselee's perspective, some studies showed that individuals who followed counseling advice based on GATB results were more satisfied with their occupations than those who did not follow the counselor's recommendations. Only one study was cited that reported no differences in job success for those who met OAP norms as compared to individuals who did not meet the norms. The manual mentions problems with the sample and criteria but is not specific.

A number of studies have been conducted on both the correlation of the GATB with other tests as well as the intercorrelations of the GATB subtests. In general, the GATB aptitudes correlate highly with other measures of similar aptitudes. Additionally, relatively high intercorrelations were found among the measures of cognitive abilities, and lower intercorrelations were found between measures of cognitive and motor abilities.

The manual provides a wealth of statistical data on the specific occupations for both counseling and research needs. Some limited research results are also presented on a variety of topics, such as training effects and GATB differences for sex, age, minority, and disabled groups. More research is clearly needed in these areas.

A series of research studies were recently conducted by John Hunter for the USES. These provide up-to-date information on a variety of topics including validity, utility, fairness, and the replacement of the SATB cutoff scores with a regression model. This line of research has primarily addressed two critical issues: 1) expanding the use of the GATB to other occupations; and 2) increasing its utility by replacing the ratings of H, M, and L with percentile rankings. The first step in this process was the application of the validity generalization model to over 500 validity studies already conducted on the GATB. This research effort demonstrated that the GATB is valid and that this validity can be generalized to the over 12,000 occupations listed in the *Dictionary of Occupational Titles*. Additionally, the findings suggested the use of an alternative scoring method, which utilizes general aptitudes specifically keyed to a job family structure based on the job complexity levels listed in the DOT.

Such a method involved the reduction, using factor analysis, of the nine aptitudes to three general abilities similar to Fleishman and Quaintance's (1984) formulations. Each of the three general abilities is composed of three specific abilities, as shown in Table 3.

Table 3

Abilities Tested by the GATB

General	Specific
Cognitive	General Intelligence
	Verbal
	Numerical
Perception	Spatial
	Form Perception
	Clerical Perception
Psychomotor	Motor Coordination
	Finger Dexterity
	Manual Dexterity

The use of different multiple regression equations, each utilizing a different combination of abilities, would enable researchers to maximize high validity for a large number of occupations. For example, high complexity jobs were better predicted by cognitive abilities, while low complexity jobs were more accurately predicted by psychomotor abilities. Hunter provides five different regression equations for use with the three general abilities of the GATB.

The equations were designed for use with the DOT. As previously described, the DOT is part of a job analysis system that provides job descriptions for 12,000 occupations. Each of the occupations is rated for complexity on a scale of one to five. The five regression equations correspond to the five complexity levels. Thus, given the level of complexity of the job, a measure of predictive job performance could be obtained using the appropriate equation. (Five separate regression equations are also provided to predict training success in the different complexity levels).

The proposed regression model is contradictory to the multiple cutoff technique currently used to arrive at the ratings of H, M, and L. The USES manual specifically states that the relationship between aptitudes and job success is nonlinear and cites this finding as a major reason behind the use of multiple cutoff scores. However, this claim of nonlinearity has not been substantiated by other researchers. Hunter cites studies of Employment Service data and employment industry data as a whole that contradict the USES claim by providing support for the existence of a linear relationship between test scores and job performance.

If one accepts Hunter's findings and assumes the relationship between test scores and job performance to be in fact linear (or at least well-represented by a linear relationship), then the designation of individuals as H, M, or L would not prove optimal. That is, when trying to select the best applicants, an employer is unable to differentiate between a high H and a low H and thus selects randomly within a given category. Similarly, in a tight labor market, an employer is unable to identify the high M or high L for employment.

Substantial losses in productivity using the multiple cutoff method have been documented by Hunter through utility analysis. The importance of this loss is especially great when one considers the application of the GATB on a national level. Hunter anticipates increases in worker productivity through the introduction of the multiple regression model at 50 to 100 billion dollars a year.

Hunter calls for the use of optimal selection to maximize the utility of the GATB. Optimal selection is defined as using the most predictive ability test for a given job and selecting the top scorers on that test(s). He cites benefits for the employer such as increased productivity, increased promotional pool, and a competitive edge. Additionally, there may be psychological and economic benefits to applicants who are properly placed in jobs.

However, optimal selection usually results in adverse impact and the subsequent failure to meet Affirmative Action goals because ethnic minority groups historically average lower scores on cognitive ability tests. This finding is also true of the GATB and raises concern over its fairness. However, evidence provided by Hunter indicates that these lower average scores on the GATB correspond to lower average job performance. In fact, Hunter provides evidence of a slight tendency for overprediction of minority job performance by the GATB. For this reason, the GATB may be considered a fair instrument when used properly. To substantiate this finding, a validity generalization study by Hunter of over 51 validity studies found no evidence of either differential validity (a significant difference between the correlations obtained for two ethnic groups) or single group validity (a statistically significant correlation for one ethnic group but not for the other). The problem then becomes one of maximizing utility while still hiring representative numbers of minorities. Hunter suggest the use of optimal selection within each protected group as a possible solution.

Interestingly, minorities score higher on the measures of psychomotor abilities. As a major battery measuring psychomotor abilities, the GATB may be a fairer and more valid predictor of occupations that require such skills. As stated earlier, lower complexity jobs are frequently more accurately predicted by tests of psychomotor ability. Thus, for these occupations, use of the GATB would result not only in better qualified hires but also in a more racially balanced workforce.

Critique

The GATB is a comprehensive test battery designed to meet the occupational counseling needs of a specific time period. It has been the object of much research, and a wealth of data has been collected on this instrument. Despite its extensive use and research, the GATB does have some psychometric shortcomings.

Perhaps the two gravest criticisms are directed at the development of the SATBs and the use of multiple cutoff scores. First, the factor analysis that identified the aptitudes, the tests used to measure them, and the weights used for this purpose were based in part on a normative sample of only 519. The reader will recall that no women were included in this sample, and all examinees were either trainees or applicants for training courses. Additionally, this was the same sample referred to subsequently as nonrepresentative of the working population because it did not include a wide range of occupations. In fact, this was the reason that the second normative sample of 4,000 was analyzed. Thus, the sample that was inadequate for general working norms was somehow adequate for factor analysis.

Humphreys (1985) was among a number of critics who pointed out that the 59 tests used in the factor analysis did not include measures of a number of traits found by other researchers to be effective, such as measures of mechanical information and comprehension. Fleishman and Quaintance's (1984) current model of abilities includes 52 different abilities for example. One must wonder also, with computerization and other technological advances in the workplace, if skills necessary for new occupations, as well as redefined existing jobs, are not being overlooked. In conjunction with this, Weiss (1972) points out that the original occupations were overwhelmingly blue collar while today jobs are predominantly of a white collar nature.

Several critics have commented on the high intercorrelations among the aptitudes, particularly Intelligence, which is composed of three measures that are used in estimating other aptitudes as well (Keesling, 1985). Perhaps most disconcerting is the high intercorrelations among the factors that comprise the SATBs. Keesling notes that because of these high correlations a variety of "aptitude-cutting score" combinations exist that would be equally valid to those finally decided upon. This instability in the SATBs is recognized in the manual. The heavy reliance of the OAP development on the SATBs serves to carry these errors into other aspects of the GATB.

As stated earlier, multiple cutoffs were defended in part on the nonlinear relationship of the criterion and the predictor. However, this logic contradicts the statistical procedures employed in the construction of the GATB, many of which assume or imply that a linear relationship exists between the test and the criterion. Such a relationship is implied in the use of high mean score and low standard deviation as two of the criteria considered in determining which aptitudes would constitute a SATB (Weiss, 1972).

Additionally, the validity studies usually reported a phi correlation measuring the relationship between the dichotmized variables of predictor—exceeded or met the norm or failed to meet the norm, and criterion—successful on the job or not successful. It is unclear whether "met the norm" refers to applicants rated as H or as both H and M.

The continual reliance on high school samples for major statistical work is questionable. For example, the conversion of B-1001 to B-1002, Form A, was based on a study of high school students in only four states. Similarly, the conversion study of B-1002, Form A, to Form B was based on a sample of high school students in three states.

There were three major reasons cited in the manual for the use of multiple cutoff scores: 1) ease in computation for clerical staff in local state offices; 2) (apparent) benefits of a noncompensatory model; and 3) the lack of a linear or "straightline" relationship between aptitudes and job success. Prior to 1945, a total weighted score was in use, a method that was abandoned because the norms did not demonstrate a "straightline" relationship with job success.

In addressing the first rationale above, this benefit would hardly seem to be an issue today in light of technological advancements. The machine scoring services provided by NCS and INTRAN could easily be programmed to provide predictors based on multiple regression equations. Many offices now have personal computers, so that even if hand-scoring was elected, the data could easily be run through a program to calculate predicted scores.

Several critics have referred to the other two reasons as "pseudo-problems." Claims of nonlinearity and the need for a noncompensatory model are not supported empirically and are actually contrary to the assumptions in the test's construction cited earlier (Weiss, 1972). The regression model suggested by Hunter responds to the criticisms aimed at the multiple cutoff score. Additionally, it bypasses the errors inherent in the instability of the SATBs and their subsequent effect on the OAPs. In fact, by utilizing three general aptitudes, the regression model agrees with the basic assumptions underlying the initial development of the GATB: the existence of certain basic aptitudes common to many occupations.

However, the introduction of such a model would probably change the way in which the GATB is used. This model provides five regression equations, each designed to predict job performance for the five different job complexity levels identified in the *Dictionary of Occupational Titles*. As such, an applicant can be evaluated for any occupation by referring to the job complexity level listed in the DOT. The developmental history of the GATB suggests that its primary use is for general occupational counseling and not specific job placement. The new model would be useful on a general level only as a means of indicating to which job complexity levels an applicant should be directed. Whether complexity level alone is adequate for differentiating occupations remains to be seen, but this seems unlikely to the current authors.

Overall, the manuals are comprehensive but overwhelming to the layperson and the professional alike. The manual on test development in particular is confusing because of numerous references to all the different versions and forms of the GATB. Instead of presenting the history of the instrument in a chronological manner, it is presented chronologically within subsections such as item analysis, factor analysis, validity, and so on. It is often unclear as to which sample and what version is being used in a particular analysis.

USES should be commended for its noble efforts in providing assessment techniques sensitive to the special needs of the educationally and economically disadvantaged applicants. The NATB, BEAG, BOLT, and Prescreening Techniques are all evidence of USES' commitment to fairness and equal opportunity. However, the heavy reliance in the NATB's development on the GATB and the lack of separate validation studies for the NATB leave too many unanswered questions to warrant recommendation of its use.

The GATB has proven useful in its application and, relative to other tests, its technical development is good. However, USES should certainly correct the shortcomings cited by researchers over the years. The more recent research efforts in validity generalization, fairness, and regression-based scoring are a first step in addressing these concerns.

References

This list includes text citations and suggested additional reading.

Angrisani, A. (1982). *U.S. Employment Service tests and assessment techniques* (USES Test Research Report No. 32). Washington, DC: U.S. Employment Service, U.S. Department of Labor.

Droege, R. C., Ferral, M., & Hawk, J. (1977). *The U.S. Employment Service occupational test development program* (U.S. Employment Service Test Research Report No. 31). Washington, DC: U.S. Employment Service, U.S. Department of Labor.

Fleishman, E. A., & Quaintance, M. K. (1984). *Taxonomies of human performance.* Orlando, FL: Orlando Academic Press.

Humphreys, L. G. (1959). General Aptitude Test Battery. In O. K. Buros (Ed.), *The fifth mental measurements yearbook* (pp. 698-700). Highland Park, NJ: Gryphon Press.

Hunter, J. E. (1983a). *The dimensionality of the General Aptitude Test Battery (GATB) and the dominance of general factors over specific factors in the prediction of job performance* (USES Test Research Report No. 44). Washington, DC: U.S. Employment Service, U.S. Department of Labor.

Hunter, J. E. (1983b). *Fairness of the General Aptitude Test Battery: Ability differences and their impact on minority hiring rates* (USES Test Research Report No. 46). Washington, DC: U.S. Employment Service, U.S. Department of Labor.

Hunter, J. E. (1983c). *Overview of validity generalization* (USES Test Research Report No. 43). Washington, DC: U.S. Employment Service, U.S. Department of Labor.

Hunter, J. E. (1983d). *Test validation for 12,000 jobs: An application of job classification and validity generalization analysis to the General Aptitude Test Battery* (USES Test Research Report No. 45). Washington, DC: U.S. Employment Service, U.S. Department of Labor.

Keesling, J. W. (1985). General Aptitude Test Battery. In J. V. Mitchell, Jr. (Ed.), *The ninth mental measurements yearbook* (pp. 1645-1647). Highland Park, NJ: Gryphon Press.

U.S. Department of Labor. (1977). *Dictionary of occupational titles* (4th ed.). Washington, DC: U.S. Government Printing Office.

U.S. Department of Labor. (1970). *Manual for USES General Aptitude Test Battery, Section III: Development.* Washington, DC: Government Printing Office.

U.S. Department of Labor. (1979). *Manual for the General Aptitude Test Battery, Section II: Occupational Aptitude Pattern Structure.* Washington, DC: Government Printing Office.

U.S. Department of Labor. (1980). *Manual for the General Aptitude Test Battery, Section II-A: Development of the Occupational Aptitude Pattern Structure.* Washington, DC: Government Printing Office.

U.S. Department of Labor. (1982). *Manual for the General Aptitude Test Battery, Section I: Administration and Scoring (Forms A and B).* Minneapolis, MN: Intran Corporation.

U.S. Department of Labor. (1983). *Manual for the General Aptitude Test Battery, Section I: Administration and Scoring (Forms C and D).* Salt Lake City, UT: Utah Department of Employment Security.

Weiss, D. J. (1972). General Aptitude Test Battery. In O. K. Buros (Ed.), *The seventh mental measurements yearbook* (pp. 1058-1061). Highland Park, NJ: Gryphon Press.

Zoli Zlotogorski, Ph.D.
Professor of Psychology, The Hebrew University of Jerusalem, Mount Scopus, and Chief Neuropsychologist, Department of Psychiatry, Shaare Zedek Medical Center, Jerusalem, Israel.

Liora Lurie, Ph.D.
Neuropsychologist, Shaare Zedek Medical Center, Jerusalem, Israel.

GERIATRIC DEPRESSION SCALE
T. L. Brink. San Carlos, California: T. L. Brink.

Introduction

The Geriatric Depression Scale (GDS) is an easily administered self-rating scale that, as opposed to other instruments designed to assess depression, was developed to measure depression specifically in the aged and was validated within this population. Given that the elderly comprise a significant and increasing proportion of the population and that depression is a major public health problem, the development of such an instrument is long overdue. Furthermore, the need for a reliable and valid geriatric depression scale stems from the unique pathology and phenomenology that may be characteristic of this segment of the population.

The present 30-item GDS scale evolved from a wider pool of 100 varied yes/no questions, which were evaluated for their potential utility in distinguishing normals from depressives in an elderly population. Brink and his colleagues (1982) administered the 100-item self-rating form to 47 subjects. Subjects were either male or female members of the community or elderly persons hospitalized for depression. Although all subjects were over 55 years of age, the authors fail to provide more precise data for mean age and range of ages. The final pool of 30 items was selected on the basis of highest correlation with total score based on the rationale of prima facie validity for the entire scale. The median correlation among those items was .675 (range = .47 to .83).

It is interesting to note that 12 of the original items assessed classic somatic complaints normally associated with depression; however, none of these items achieved the empirical criterion for inclusion. It would seem therefore that the somatic symptoms that are usually central to a diagnosis of depression in the young are less useful in the elderly. In addition, Brink and his colleagues (1982, 1984) argue that the elderly are more resistant to psychiatric evaluation than younger patients. Consequently, the GDS is designed to fit this population. Questions about sexuality, suicidal intent, and guilt are avoided, and the scale is relatively simple and easily understood.

In the initial study, the GDS was administered to a group of normal elderly persons ($N = 20$) and to a group of geriatric patients ($N = 51$) receiving treatment for depression. Each subject was also rated on the Hamilton Rating Scale for Depression (HRS-D; Hamilton, 1960) and the Zung Self-rating Depression Scale (SDS; Zung, 1965). Brink et al. (1982) report that all three scales were able to distinguish between the depressed aged and the control group. In addition, they report a superior tradeoff of sensitivity (84%) and specificity (95%) for the GDS.

In the follow-up validation study (Yesavage & Brink, 1983), the 30-item GDS was administered to two groups of geriatric subjects. Forty normal elderly subjects recruited from the community served as the control group. The experimental group was comprised of 60 elderly subjects under treatment for depression. These subjects were both inpatients and outpatients in a variety of public and private institutions. The depressed subjects were further subdivided into mild and severe depression groups using the Research Diagnostic Criteria for major affective disorders. Thus the final sample of subjects consisted of normal elderly ($N = 40$), mild depressives ($N = 26$), and severe depressives ($N = 34$). Subjects in all groups were given a clinical interview that was used to assess the HRS-D, the SDS, and the GDS. Again, each scale successfully distinguished normals, mild, and severely depressed subjects.

Practical Applications/Uses

The 30 GDS items, each of which is a brief question answered "yes" or "no," comprise mood quality, level of energy and motivation, hopelessness, social initiative, and subjective evaluation of various cognitive abilities and functions. In 20 of the 30 items, the answer "yes" indicates depression; in the remaining 10 the answer "no" indicates depression. The individual's total GDS score consists of the sum of all items. A score of 0-10 indicates no depression, 11-20 indicates mild depression, and a score of 21-30 indicates moderate/severe depression.

The GDS is an assessment instrument that seems especially sensitive to various aspects of depression experienced by the elderly. In a recent study, Gallagher, Slife, and Yesavage (1983) found that the GDS differentiated depressed and nondepressed elderly arthritics. The GDS was also successful in categorizing depression among subjects who were undergoing cognitive treatment for senile dementia (Yesavage, Rose, & Lapp, 1981). In other words, the GDS may have potential for application as an assessment tool with the physically ill as well as the cognitively impaired elderly.

The GDS test authors point out that ease of administration and economy of time are among the desirable features of the instrument. In order to minimize the difficulties imposed by short attention span, fatigue, or poor concentration sometimes found in elderly subjects, Sheik and Yesavage (1986) have developed a 15-item version of the GDS. Eighteen normal elderly subjects and 17 elderly depressed patients were administered both the long and short versions of the GDS. Both forms successfully differentiated between the groups and the authors report a high correlation ($r = .84$, $p < .001$) between the two versions. Thus the alternate short form may prove useful as a screening instrument with cognitively impaired or physically ill elderly patients.

Technical Aspects

The reliability of the GDS was studied by comparing 40 normal elderly to 60 depressed elderly patients selected from a variety of clinical settings (Yesavage &

Brink, 1983). The depressed subjects included 26 "mild" and 34 "severe" depressives as assessed by the Research Diagnostic Criteria (RDC). Several indices of internal consistency were calculated on the GDS scores. Both the Cronbach alpha and the split-half reliability coefficient were .94. The median correlation between the items was .56 (range = .32 to .83) while the mean interitem correlation was .36. These reliability measures were found to be comparable to the HRS-D and better than Zung's SDS. Test-retest reliability coefficients were reported to be .85 over a span of one week (Yesavage & Brink, 1983) and .86 after a 5-minute delay (Brink et al., 1985).

Several validity studies regarding the GDS were carried out. Yesavage & Brink (1983) found that the GDS scores of nondepressed, mildly depressed, and severely depressed subjects were significantly different. In addition, the GDS showed concurrent validity (r = .82) with the measure used to classify the level of depression (RDC). The GDS also had high convergent validity with the HRS-D (r = .83) and with the SDS (r = .84).

The validity of the GDS in comparison to other depression scales includes studies with the Beck Depression Inventory (BDI), the Depression Adjective Check List (DACL), and the Center for Epidemiological Studies Depression Scale (CES-D). Hyer and Blount (1984) found that the GDS and BDI scores were highly correlated (r = .73) in a group of male psychiatric inpatients. In fact, the GDS was reported to be superior to the BDI in discriminant validity in this elderly psychiatric population. Best and his colleagues (1984) compared the GDS to the HRS-D, the DACL, and the CES-D. Again the GDS and the HRS-D were found to be superior to the others in discriminating depression from nondepression in the elderly.

Thus, the studies of validity for the GDS suggest that this scale can identify depressed from nondepressed elderly persons as well as the HRS-D and better than several commonly used depression scales. This finding has special practical implications, because the GDS is easier to administer than the HRS-D and does not require a lengthy clinical interview.

Critique

The GDS appears to be a reliable and valid screening test for depression in the general elderly population. However, at this point it is still not clear if the GDS adequately addresses a few specific issues relevant to the elderly. These issues center on the diagnostic utility of the GDS with cognitively impaired elderly and the atypical depressions of the elderly (pseudodementia and masked depression).

In psychiatric inpatient samples there is some indication that the GDS over-includes nondepressives in the mild depression category, due to the overlap of symptoms between the GDS and other psychiatric entities (Hyer & Blount, 1984). In other words, the GDS may tap more than depression. Therefore, research with heterogeneous psychiatric nosologies is needed.

In the cognitively impaired elderly, Yesavage, Rose, and Lapp (1981) found that the GDS was useful in identifying depression. However, Brink (1984) suggests that when deeper dementia is involved the GDS loses some validity. Thus, the GDS does not fulfill the assessment needs with a substantial portion of the cognitively impaired elderly. Finally, Weiss, Nagel, and Aronson (1986) point out that most research on the elderly uses subjects in their 50s, while the typical problems of old age probably begin later in life. Weiss et al. (1986) describe the presentation of depression in people over 75 as having special features of masked depression (i.e., a depression in which lack of energy, apathy, and hopelessness are the central features rather than guilt or dysphoric mood). The GDS does not seem to address this type of depression adequately. Thus, further validation for the over-75 population and for the idiosyncratic ways in which depression manifests itself in this group is needed. Despite these limitations, the GDS represents a significant step towards the reliable and valid assessment of depression in the elderly.

References

Best, D. L., Davis, S., Morton, K., & Romeis, J. (1984, October). *Measuring depression in the elderly: Psychometric and psychosocial issues*. Paper presented at the annual meeting of the American Gerontological Association, Houston.

Brink, T. L. (1984). Limitations of the GDS in cases of pseudodementia. *Clinical Gerontology, 2*(3), 60-61.

Brink, T. L., Yesavage, J. A., Owen, L., Heersema, P. H., Adey, M., & Rose, T. L. (1982). Screening tests for geriatric depression. *Clinical Gerontology, 1*(1), 37-43.

Brink, T. L., Curran, P., Dorr, M. L., Janson, E., McNulty, U., & Messina, M. (1985). Geriatric Depression Scale reliability: Order, examiner and reminiscence effects. *Clinical Gerontology, 3*(4), 57-59.

Gallagher, D., Slife, B., & Yesavage, J. (1983). *Impact of physical health status on Hamilton Rating Scale Depression scores*. Unpublished manuscript.

Hamilton, M. (1960). A rating scale for depression. *Journal of Neurology, Neurosurgery and Psychiatry, 23*, 56-62.

Hyer, L., & Blount, J. (1984). Concurrent and discriminant validities of the GDS with older psychiatric patients. *Psychological Reports, 54*, 611-616.

Sheik, J. I., & Yesavage, J. A. (1986). Geriatric Depression Scale (GDS): Recent evidence and development of a shorter version. In T. L. Brink (Ed.), *Clinical gerontology: A guide to assessment and practice* (pp. 165-173). New York: Haworth.

Yesavage, J., Rose, T. L., & Lapp, D. (1981). *Validity of the Geriatric Depression Scale in subjects with senile dementia*. Palo Alto, CA: Clinical Diagnostic and Rehabilitation Unit, Palo Alto Veterans Administration Medical Clinic.

Yesavage, J., & Brink, T. L. (1983). Development and validation of a geriatric depression screening scale: A preliminary report. *Journal of Psychiatric Research, 17*, 37-49.

Weiss, I. K., Nagel, C. L., & Aronson, M. K. (1986). Applicability of depression scales to the old-old person. *Journal of the American Geriatrics Society, 34*, 215-218.

Zung, W. W. K. (1965). A self-rating depression scale. *Archives of General Psychiatry, 12*, 63-70.

Forrest G. Umberger, Ph.D.
Associate Professor and Director of Speech Pathology Program, Department of Special Education, Georgia State University, Atlanta, Georgia.

GOLDMAN-FRISTOE TEST OF ARTICULATION
Ronald Goldman and Macalyne Fristoe. Circle Pines, Minnesota: American Guidance Service.

Introduction

The Goldman-Fristoe Test of Articulation is an individually administered speech articulation test designed for assessing an individual's articulation of the consonant sounds. The instrument contains three subtests that provide descriptive information about the examinee's speech articulation skills. The subtests employ both spontaneous and imitative production of consonants in single word and conversational speech.

The developers of the Goldman-Fristoe Test of Articulation are Ronald Goldman and Macalyne Fristoe. Dr. Goldman is the training director of the Sparks Center and professor in the Department of Biocommunication at the University of Alabama. Dr. Fristoe is a professor in both the Audiology and Speech Sciences and the Psychological Sciences departments at Purdue University.

The Goldman-Fristoe Test of Articulation was developed after a period of four years of revision and research. Test procedures were developed that would:

1. examine all the necessary phonemes;
2. obtain an adequate and accurate sample of the subject's speech production under several conditions, ranging from imitative to conversational speech;
3. be presented in a form that would be easy to administer, eliminating loose cards or objects as stimulus material;
4. be colorful and interesting to the subject;
5. be conducive to the minimizing of distractions and to the focusing of the subject's attention on the stimulus materials;
6. provide a form for recording responses that is easy to use and that facilitates a comparative evaluation of the subject's pattern of errors under the various test conditions. (Goldman & Fristoe, 1986).

An optional filmstrip version of the test is available for children who respond better to this type of presentation.

The normative data for the test are based on a stratified national sample of students in grades 1 through 12 (ages 6 to 16+), which were tested on the National Speech and Hearing Survey in 1971. Norms for the Sounds-in-Words Subtest for ages 2 through 5 are based on the standardization of the Khan-Lewis Phonological Analysis in 1984.

The materials used in the test include an easel that contains the test plates, a package of response forms, and an examiner's manual with complete instructions for administering, scoring, and interpreting the results.

When closed, the easel is the size of an 8½x11 notebook. It contains 35 pictures for the Sounds-in-Words Subtest and nine pictures for the Sounds-in-Sentences Subtest. The Stimulability Subtest materials are presented on two cards following the Sounds-in-Sentences Subtest. The easel also contains Appendix B: Percentile Rank Norms.

Each Response Form provides a means for recording an individual's speech responses for all three subtests. The responses for all three subtests can be compared side-by-side by folding over the Sounds-in-Sentences Response Matrix.

The examiner must face the subject in a manner allowing him and the subject access to the easel. The plate facing the examiner contains the dialogue or presentation stimulus to be used as well as the intended response. The target sounds to be evaluated are identified for the examiner. For example, the subject's side of the easel may contain a picture of a telephone. The examiner's side of the easel would contain the eliciting stimulus, "What is this?" The intended response is also on the examiner's plate, "*tele*p*h*one" with the /t/ and /ph/ identified as the sounds to evaluate.

The test is not difficult and can be administered to preschool children because no reading is required. Norms for the Sounds-in-Words Subtest extend from 2 to 16 + years of age.

The Sounds-in-Words Subtest consists of 35 pictures depicting objects and activities. These pictures contain material familiar to children. A total of 44 responses is elicited when the subject names the pictures or answers questions about the pictures. More than one sound may be elicited and evaluated when the subject names a given picture. This subtest permits the examiner to test the subject's spontaneous production of all but one of the English consonant sounds in their most common positions, as well as 11 consonant blends.

The Sound-in-Sentences Subtest provides a method of eliciting content-controlled, conversational-type speech, formulated by the subject. It consists of two stories read aloud by the examiner, and illustrated by sets of four and five pictures. The subject recounts each story, using the pictures as memory aids. The subtest has the potential for assessing most of the consonant sounds, but is usually limited to those consonants more likely to be produced inadequately.

The Stimulability Subtest enables the examiner to evaluate the subject's ability to produce a previously misarticulated phoneme correctly when given maximum stimulation, both visual and oral. Information from this subtest gives the clinician an idea of the sounds that may respond most readily to speech therapy and those that will probably require a greater length of time to correct.

Each Response Form provides matrices for recording the subject's speech responses from the Sounds-in-Words, Sounds-in-Sentences, and Stimulability Subtests. Sounds-in-Words and Stimulability Subtest matrices are located on one side of the form, and the Sounds-in-Sentences matrix is on the other side. The sounds being evaluated are recorded as they occur on the appropriate response matrix. The responses for all three subtests can be compared side-by-side by folding over the Sounds-in-Sentences Response Matrix.

Although norms are provided, the test is based on the assumption that the criterion for comparison for each sound should be correct production. When considering the remediation program, knowledge of which sounds an individual produces incorrectly and the type of misproduction is of more value than a normative score.

Practical Applications/Uses

While the Goldman-Fristoe Test of Articulation would ordinarily be used by a speech pathologist, it can also be used by education personnel (i.e., classroom teachers). A classroom teacher would find the test useful to evaluate speech sound production for the presence of error. Such information would be useful in making a decision whether to refer a child for therapy or not. In contrast the speech pathologist would judge speech sound production for type of error. This type of judgment would require basic training in phonetics and in the nature of articulation disorders. The instrument, therefore, is useful for making judgments about the presence and/or type of speech sound production error in which an individual's speech performance would interfere in any way with his or her ability to benefit or participate in any social, educational, or communicative setting.

According to Goldman and Fristoe (1986), the primary purpose of this test is to provide a method of assessing an individual's articulation of consonant sounds. The test is not designed specifically to study vowel and diphthong production, but these sounds are present in the Sound-in-Words Subtest and can be monitored for deviations.

The test also allows comparison of articulation at increasing levels of complexity. A comparison of articulation at the single word level can be compared to articulation occurring in contextual speech. Such comparisons are useful for identifying those areas of greatest difficulty as well as checking the stability of articulation production of various sounds. Deviations in the subject's vocabulary and syntax can be noted when the subject retells the stories in the Sounds-in-Sentences Subtest. Moreover, repeated recordings over time of the subject's performance on the Sounds-in-Sentences Subtest can supply the speech pathologist with a means of evaluating change over time.

When the test is used to determine the presence of a production error the classroom teacher can use this information in referring a child for therapy.

The test can be administered in settings in which speech therapy services may be rendered or referrals for speech therapy are available. These settings may include schools, hospitals, speech clinics, and private practices. The professionals most likely to use this test would be speech pathologists in the aforementioned settings or teachers who may be interested in determining the presence of speech sound production errors to aid them in referral decisions.

The Goldman-Fristoe Test of Articulation is an individually administered test. The best setting is a quiet room that is adequately lighted and furnished with a table and two chairs. The examiner should be able to see the subject's face and the back of the easel. This can be accomplished if the examiner sits to the right or left of the subject, across the corner of the table.

The qualifications of the examiner are dependent on the level of the evaluation to be attempted. The authors identify two levels. The first level is for simply determining the presence of error in each sound production. For this level the examiner must be able to retain an auditory image of the subject's response long enough to determine if an error is present. The second level is for determining the type of error in each sound production. This level requires the examiner to have had basic training in the nature of articulation disorders and knowledge of phonetics. Therefore, the individual administering the test on the second level would most likely be a speech pathologist, while examinations focusing on the first could be administered by another professional such as a classroom teacher.

The instructions in the test manual are clear, and sufficient examples are given. The subtests can be used alone (with the exception of the Stimulability Test, which is seldom used alone) or in various sequences, depending on the type of information the examiner is seeking. For example, the manual suggests that the Sounds-in-Sentences Subtest may be used alone to identify children with mild problems, such as those apparent only at the conversational level.

The test is not difficult to administer once the manual has been read and the examiner has had an opportunity to become familiar with the materials. Test administration for all three subtests usually takes approximately 30 minutes, but the examination time may vary depending on the number of error sounds that the examiner evaluates in the Stimulability Subtest.

Instructions for scoring the test are explicit, with illustrated examples for both Level One and Level Two administration. Learning to score the test should be accomplished after one or two trial runs with the manual as a guide. Scoring for Level One is simply a matter of entering one of two symbols in the matrix, indicating the sound was produced incorrectly or not produced at all. The cell in the matrix is left blank for correct productions of the sound. For Level Two scoring, the examiner must become familiar with a number of symbols that are used to indicate the type of speech error produced. Notations include substitutions, omissions, sound plus additional sound, and distortions ranked either 2 (for a mild distortion) or 3 (for a severe distortion). Additional symbols are illustrated to identify glottal stops and nasalized and dentalized productions. Similar symbols and instructions are provided for the Stimulability Subtest. The test must be scored by hand due to the clinical judgments that must be made throughout the test.

The interpretation, according to the manual, is based on the assumption that the criterion for comparison for each sound should be correct production. Normative data, therefore, are not as valuable in setting up a program of therapy as knowledge of which sounds an individual produces incorrectly and the type of misproduction.

The manual lists eight dimensions upon which observed articulation patterns may be observed:

1. Positions in which misarticulations most frequently occur—initial, medial, or final;
2. Types of error observed most frequently—substitutions, distortions, omissions, and so on;
3. Consistency of error as complexity increases;
4. Tendency for errors to appear on the more frequently occurring sounds such as /t/, /s/, /r/, or on the less frequently occurring sounds such as /ʃ/, /θ/, /ʤ/;

5. Tendency for errors to occur on one type of consonant—nasal, plosive, or fricative;
6. Tendency to misarticulate sounds requiring similar placement of articulators such as "tongue-tip sounds," labila sounds, linguavelar sounds, and so on;
7. Errors in voicing such as /b/ used for /p/, /d/ used for /t/, /v/ used for /f/;
8. Occurrence of misarticulation only on sounds that are likely to appear late in speech development as opposed to occurrence on sounds at many different developmental levels.

Further information can be obtained from the Stimulability Subtest, which reveals how easily a subject can produce error sounds correctly with auditory and visual stimulation. This information may provide some estimate on prognosis and sounds that will require greater efforts to correct.

By folding back the Sounds-in-Sentences Response Matrix the subject's responses on all three subtests can be compared simultaneously. These subtests, with the exception of the Stimulability Subtest, provide information on the subject's patterns of articulation in simple and complex speech activities.

Technical Aspects

Normative interpretation information was obtained from the National Speech and Hearing Survey (Hull, Meilke, Timmons, & Willeford, 1971, 1972). The front of the Response Form contains space for recording the number of errors and percentile rank for Sounds-in-Words and Syllable Stimulability. The authors recommend that percentile ranks be used in communicating to teachers and other professionals a child's standing in relation to the child's peer group.

Reliability of the Goldman-Fristoe Test of Articulation was assessed for test-retest reliability, interrater reliability, and intrarater reliability. For purposes of this test, the manual defines reliability as the consistency with which the same response is recorded for each sound in each position. This is a better measure of reliability than using the *total* number of sound errors recorded on each test because, as the manual points out, even though the total number of error sounds may be the same on the two tests, the error sounds could be completely different from one test to the other. The number of agreements on the type of sound produced or on the presence of an error was determined for each cell in the subtest matrices in determining the reliability. The possible number of agreements for a particular cell are compared with the number of agreements found for each cell to determine the percentage of agreement.

Test-retest reliability was obtained by testing 37 articulatory defective children between the ages of 4 and 8. They were tested by eight experienced speech pathologists, each of whom held the Certificate of Clinical Competence issued by the American Speech and Hearing Association. Each examiner administered each subtest twice, with one week intervening between tests. Comparisons were made between test and retest results, noting the presence or absence of error in production of each speech sound. The Sounds-in-Words Subtest had a median agreement of 95 percent, while the Sounds-in-Sentences Subtest median agreement was 94 percent. Similar comparisons were made of the specific type of speech sound production recorded—distortion, substitution, omission, addition, or correct production. Median agreement for the Sounds-in-Words Subtest was 89 percent, while median agreement for Sounds-in-Sentences Subtest was 86 percent.

To obtain inter-judge reliability, six judges evaluated recorded test responses of four subjects whose articulation problems were rated mild (11% errors) to severe (72% errors). The judges were chosen for demonstrating sufficient experience with the Goldman-Fristoe Test of Articulation as well as other tests of articulation. The median percentage of agreement on type of production was 88.

The interrater reliability of the Sounds-in-Sentences Subtest has not been obtained for this edition.

Clinicians meeting the same criterion previously mentioned were used in intrarater reliability for the Sounds-in-Words Subtest. The median percentage of agreement was 91 percent for presence or absence of error and 91 percent for type of production.

The manual does not have intrareliability information on the Sounds-in-Sentences Subtest.

The authors of the Goldman-Fristoe Test of Articulation employed "logical methods of test construction and a representative collection of items" (Goldman & Fristoe, 1986). The authors assure the test's content validity through the collections of items used to assess speech sound production. All but one of the consonants in English are sampled in the Sounds-in-Words Subtest. The Sounds-in-Sentences Subtest taps those phonemes most likely to be misarticulated, and the Stimulability Subtest evaluates the sounds known to be misarticulated.

Validity was further evaluated by comparing the Sounds-in-Words Subtest results with the Sounds-in-Sentences results. Because these subtests assess somewhat different skills, a comparison would be expected to reveal less correspondence between the subtest results. The two subtests were compared for agreement on the presence or absence of error (86% agreement) and for agreement on the type of speech sound production (72% agreement). Neither of these values exceeded the lowest found for any test-retest value. These results, therefore, indicate that the two subtests are indeed measuring different aspects of articulatory development.

Critique

The Goldman-Fristoe Test of Articulation is widely used by speech pathologists in both public schools and various clinical settings. For assessing the speech articulation of children, the test is valuable for a number of reasons. First, it is economical in terms of time because it assesses more than one phoneme per stimulus presentation, thus cutting down on administration time and reducing the possibility of subject fatigue. Second, it does not require the subject to read; therefore, it can be used with younger children and older subjects who cannot read. Third, the test can be utilized by a number of professions for determining the presence of error and is therefore a valuable tool for making referral decisions. Fourth, administration at both Level One and Level Two can be mastered within a short period of time, and scoring can be mastered readily with the aid of the manual. Moreover, the subtests can be administered individually or in various combinations, therefore allowing the examiner to observe a specific area of production without having to administer the entire test. Finally, the physical management of the test is convenient due to the absence of multiple materials and cards. The easel offers optimum viewing for both the subject and examiner.

References

This list includes text citations and suggested additional reading.

Fristoe, M., & Goldman, R. (1968). Comparison of traditional and condensed articulation tests examining the same number of sounds. *Journal of Speech and Hearing Research, 11*, 583-589.

Goldman, R., & Fristoe, M. (1967). The development of the filmstrip articulation test. *Journal of Speech and Hearing Disorders 32*, 257-262.

Goldman, R., & Fristoe, M. (1986). *Goldman-Fristoe Test of Articulation*. Circle Pines, MN: American Guidance Service.

Hull, F. M., Meilke, P. W., Timmons, R. J., & Willeford, J. A. (1971). The National Speech and Hearing Survey: Preliminary results. *Asha, 13*(9), 501-509.

Hull, F. M., Meilke, P. W., Timmons, R. J., & Willeford, J. A. (1972). *The National Speech and Hearing Survey: Analysis and interpretation*. Final report for USOE Project No. 152222, Grant No. OE-32-15-0050-5010 (607).

Irwin, R. B., & Musselman, B. W. (1962). A compact picture articulation test. *Journal of Speech and Hearing Disorders, 27*, 36-39.

Keenan, J. S. (1961). What is medial position? *Journal of Speech and Hearing Disorders, 26*, 171-174.

Khan, L. M. L., & Lewis, N. P. (1986). *Kahn-Lewis Phonological Analysis*. Circle Pines, MN: American Guidance Service.

Milisen, R. (1954). A rationale for articulation disorders [Monograph]. *Journal of Speech and Hearing Disorders, 4*, 6-17.

Lucille B. Strain, Ph.D.
Professor of Education, Bowie State College, Bowie, Maryland.

GRAY ORAL READING TESTS-REVISED
J. Lee Wiederholt and Brian R. Bryant. Austin, Texas: PRO-ED.

Introduction

The 1986 revision of the Gray Oral Reading Tests (GORT-R) comprises individually administered standardized tests designed to measure several aspects of oral reading ability. The tests yield information regarding oral reading speed and accuracy, oral reading comprehension, total oral reading ability, and oral reading miscues. Results of the tests are reported as Passage Scores, Comprehension Scores, and Oral Reading Quotients. Provisions are made for recording five types of oral reading miscues: meaning similarity, function similarity, graphic/phonemic similarity, multiple sources, and self-correction.

For nearly three-quarters of this century, the Gray Oral Reading Tests have been preeminent among the relatively few widely used tests designed to measure oral reading ability. Developed by educator, scholar, researcher, and writer Dr. William S. Gray, the tests were originally published in 1915 as the Standard Oral Reading Paragraphs (SORP). Revised in 1963 by Dr. Helen M. Robinson, editions of the Gray Oral Reading Tests (GORT) were published in 1963 and again in 1967.

Dr. William S. Gray, to whom a tribute is paid by J. Lee Wiederholt and Brian R. Bryant, authors of the current GORT-R, was eminently qualified by education and experience for establishing a prototype for the measurement of oral reading ability. Dr. Gray's educational career spanned many years and included many levels of education. His teaching career, which began in the rural schools of Adams County, Illinois, in 1904-1905, subsequently included several years of teaching and research at the University of Chicago. His educational administration career included service as director of the Training School at Illinois State Normal University and dean of the College of Education at the University of Chicago. A proponent of the eclectic method of reading instruction and an innovator, Dr. Gray initiated the first course in reading education at the University of Chicago and the annual reviews of the literature of reading research. He was originator of the first annual reading conference at the University of Chicago. Not only was he one of the founders of the International Reading Association, but he was also its first president in 1956.

Prolific in writing and research, Dr. Gray authored approximately 500 books, articles, and research reports. These included the monographs *Studies of Elementary School Reading through Standardized Tests* and *Remedial Cases in Reading: Their Diagnosis and Treatment*. Known widely as the "father of the Dick and Jane books," he was co-author of the Scott-Foresman Basic Reader Series and the Elson-Gray readers. During the years 1925, 1937, and 1948, respectively, Dr. Gray served as chairman of the Yearbook Committees of the National Society for the Study of Education (NSSE). The Standard Oral Reading Paragraphs was among the then-available standardized tests described in the 1925 NSSE Yearbook.

Available in one form and consisting of only four pages, the SORP contained a series of independent paragraphs designed to measure oral reading ability from first through eighth grade. The test combined oral reading rate and oral reading accuracy in order to arrive at what was called a "B" score, similar to a grade-equivalent score. The limited purpose of the "B" score was to determine whether a student should be promoted to the next school grade. Materials accompanying the paragraphs were directions and a form for recording test results.

The 1963-1967 Gray Oral Reading Test (GORT) appeared in four equivalent forms designed for student use. Each form contained 13 independent paragraphs of ascending levels of difficulty. Each paragraph was followed by four questions for assessing literal comprehension. The first paragraph in each form was preceded by a picture. Three measures were recorded for each passage: errors, time, and comprehension performance. A grade-equivalent score was determined by the amount of time required for reading a passage along with the number of errors made. Passage Scores were converted to tentative grade norms for boys and girls, respectively. Oral reading errors included words aided, gross and partial mispronunciations, omissions, insertions, substitutions, repetitions, and reversals. Other observations for which provisions were made included word-by-word reading, poor phrasing, lack of expression, monotonous tone, overuse of phonics, loss of place, and the like. Materials accompanying the GORT included a *Manual of Directions for Administering, Scoring and Interpretation, Revised* and an *Examiner's Record Booklet* for each of the forms of the tests.

Two estimates of reliability were reported in the manual for the GORT: Coefficients of Equivalence and the Standard Error of Measurement. Validity was based solely on the nature of procedures used in construction of the tests. The GORT was normed on a sample of 502 subjects from public schools in two districts in Florida and in several schools in metropolitan and suburban Chicago. Sex of the students was the demographic factor emphasized, and attempts were made to include only "average" students at each grade level.

The GORT-R is available in two alternate, equivalent forms: Form A and Form B. Both Form A and Form B are included in a single, spiral-bound book identified as the Student Book. Each of the forms contains 13 independent paragraphs of progressively ascending levels of difficulty. Each paragraph is followed by five multiple-choice test items designed to measure a variety of types and levels of comprehension.

The Passage Score of the GORT-R measures a student's ability to read a paragraph with speed and accuracy. The score results from determination of the amount of time required for reading the paragraph and the number of deviations made from the print. A Conversion Matrix, appropriate for the particular passage, is then used to determine the applicable Passage Score. Each conversion matrix provides a vertical axis for Deviations from Print (an index of accuracy) and a horizontal axis for Rate (an index of speed). The point at which these two indexes intersect for a student's performance yields a Passage Score somewhere within the range from 0-9. A Passage Score is generated for each paragraph read and the number of these is summed after testing is completed.

The GORT-R Comprehension Score is derived from a student's responses to the five multiple-choice test items following each paragraph. The questions are designed to assess comprehension at literal, inferential, and critical levels and to focus variously on cognitive and affective outcomes. The sum of all questions answered correctly provides this raw score. A combination of the Passage Score and the Comprehension Score produces an Oral Reading Quotient (ORQ), which provides an overall index of the student's total ability to read orally.

The quantitative data produced by the GORT-R are interpreted as standard scores and percentiles. Thus, provisions are made for comparing GORT-R scores with test scores resultant from administration of other tests. Ease of communication and understanding is facilitated by the use of percentiles.

In addition to the quantitative data generated by the GORT-R, provisions are made for analyzing and recording five types of oral reading miscues: (a) meaning similarity, (b) function similarity, (c) graphic-phonemic similarity, (d) multiple sources, and (e) self-correction. Analysis of miscues related to meaning similarity (replacing a printed word with another word similar in meaning) permits assessment of a student's use of comprehension strategies. Analysis of function similarity (substitution of a printed word with a word of similar syntactic function) permits assessment of a student's use of appropriate grammatical forms in reading. Analysis of graphic-phonemic similarities (occurring when printed words are replaced with words similar in appearance or sound) permits assessment of a student's use of word-attack strategies. Analysis of multiple sources permits an examiner to determine the nature of the miscues made by a reader that fit several categories at the same time. Analysis of self-correction miscues sensitizes an examiner to the self-correction strategies used by a student during oral reading.

In addition to the five categories of miscues for which special provisions are made in the GORT-R, attention can be given to the miscues of omissions, additions, dialects, and reversals (at the option of the examiner).

The 54-page GORT-R manual contains information pertaining to test administration, scoring procedures, interpretation, uses of test results, and development of the tests. In the overview of the manual, a comparison is made between the earlier versions of the GORT and the GORT-R. Emphasis is placed on the new normative, reliability, and validity data supporting the GORT-R, the new comprehension questions, development of the paragraphs, and modifications of the scoring criteria and analysis of miscues.

According to directions given in the manual, administering, scoring, and interpreting the results of the GORT-R are relatively simple procedures. The tests are designed for students between the ages of 6 years, 6 months and 17 years, 11 months. The time required for administration of each form of the GORT-R ranges from 15 to 30 minutes. Although it is recommended that the tests should be administered in one session, suggestions are also given for modifying testing time if essential. An explanation is given of the uses of basals and ceilings and their influence on reduction of testing time. Instructions are given for interpreting results of the tests, for completing the Profile/Examiner Record Form, and for pursuing additional assessment and instructional strategies.

Appendix 1 of the GORT-R manual contains standard scores and percentiles for Passage Scores and Comprehension Scores for both forms and a table for conversion of standard scores to quotients and percentiles. Appendix 2 contains four Passage-Score Conversion Matrices for paragraphs 1 through 13, useful with either of the test forms. Appendix 3 presents samples of student performance on the tests, and Appendix 4 is a reproducible Examiner's Worksheet for analyzing and recording oral reading miscues.

The Profile/Examiner Record Form is used for recording and summarizing a student's oral reading performance on either Form A or Form B. The record form is designed for specifying pertinent information about the examiner and the student, recording the GORT-R scores, noting the results of other tests, profiling the student's scores, summarizing oral reading miscues, and making comments and recommendations. The form is used also for recording the rate for each paragraph read and for scoring the comprehension items.

All of the paragraphs contained in Form A and Form B are reproduced in the Profile/Examiner Record Form. Each paragraph in the Profile/Record Form is preceded by a "prompt," a statement to be read by the examiner to the student prior to the reading of the paragraph. The prompt serves to provide the student with an immediate purpose for reading the paragraph. Each paragraph is followed by blanks for scoring pertinent aspects of the student's performance.

Practical Applications/Uses

The purposes served by the GORT-R are such that the practical applications and uses of the tests serve a wide range of practitioner needs in a variety of professional settings. The tests are useful to teachers at all levels of schooling, to counselors of various types, to graduate students and other researchers, and to administrators in educational and other settings.

Specific purposes for which the tests are designed are stated in the GORT-R manual: (a) to help identify those students who are significantly below their peers in oral reading proficiency and who may profit from supplemental help, (b) to aid in determining the particular kinds of reading strengths and weaknesses that individual students possess, (c) to document students' progress in reading as a consequence of special intervention programs, and (d) to serve as a measurement device in investigations in which researchers are studying the reading abilities of school-age children.

All the purposes for which the GORT-R is designed are, at various times, of interest to teachers both at the elementary-school level and at the level of secondary education. In elementary-school classrooms, identification of students who need special help in reading either in the classroom or in clinical settings is frequently a concern. The classroom teacher who expects to use effective and efficient techniques of corrective reading needs easily acquired data for making as precise a diagnosis of a student's reading difficulties as possible. In addition, dependable data are needed by classroom teachers who wish to identify those students whose reading difficulties are severe enough to merit recommendation for further diagnosis and remediation in a clinical setting. The ease with which the GORT-R can be administered and the relatively short time required for its administration make it especially useful for gathering initial data for corrective reading or for making referrals of students for remedial reading by reading specialists.

In secondary schools, in which the major concerns for reading regard content areas such as mathematics, natural or social sciences, and the like, a short time spent by a teacher administering the GORT-R to an individual can lead to the use of those instructional strategies of most value in achieving objectives of a content area. Although oral reading and silent reading are not entirely synonymous, they require enough of the same types of abilities that knowledge of an individual's capabilities in one mode of reading can offer some insights into the other. Oral reading assessment can help in the identification of some of the most debilitating problems that may be hampering the reading of a student. As in the case of the classroom teacher at the level of elementary education, a teacher at the secondary level needs data to substantiate referrals of students to sources for particular assistance.

Because of the nature of the GORT-R, a student's specific reading difficulties can be identified. Not only do the results of the GORT-R yield information regarding the relative standing of a student in comparison with pertinent peers, but the precise nature of the student's difficulties can be identified.

Reading specialists in clinical settings need baseline or initial data prior to engaging in more detailed diagnostic procedures or to implementing a remedial reading program for a student. Results of the GORT-R can suggest direction for subsequent diagnostic procedures needed for acquiring in-depth understanding of a student's reading problems. The results of the GORT-R are also useful for determining the types of remediation approaches that may be effective initially for a student. Because it can produce baseline data as a result of pretesting and subsequent data through posttesting, the GORT-R is a convenient instrument through which the effectiveness of any intervention program can be determined.

The GORT-R is particularly suitable for types of action research frequently implemented by teachers and administrators in classroom or school settings. Because of its two equivalent forms, the GORT-R can be used for assessment purposes before and after the use of instructional materials or procedures. Similarly, the tests are useful to graduate students and other researchers interested in experimental research in reading.

For reading diagnosticians seeking to determine patterns of a student's reading behaviors, the GORT-R is useful as an instrument by which results of other types of assessment measures can be compared. Results of informal assessment techniques such as informal reading inventories and cloze procedures can be compared with results of the GORT-R for a more certain evaluation of a student's needs in oral reading instruction. Because of its standard scores, results of the GORT-R can be compared to results of standardized measures of reading behaviors other than those required for oral reading.

Uses of the GORT-R, however, are not confined to educational settings. The tests can be used in any setting in which there may be a need to gain some insight into the reading ability of individuals of the relevant ages served by the tests.

Technical Aspects

Information regarding the technical development of the GORT-R is available in the test manual. Detailed accounts are given about the construction of the paragraphs and test items, standardization procedures, and studies related to reliability and validity of the tests.

Both text structure and content of the paragraphs were given careful attention and subjected to a number of criteria to determine suitability for inclusion in the GORT-R tests. The organization and complexity of the text as well as the interrelationship of ideas in a passage were taken into account. Text content was selected according to difficulty level of the vocabulary and interest level of the topic.

Prepared by a professional writer, the paragraphs in the GORT-R were subjected to some of the same criteria used to determine difficulty and suitability for the various levels of the 1967 GORT. In light of newer research results, however, less reliance was placed on use of readability formulas for determining difficulty levels in the GORT-R. While paragraphs and test questions in the GORT-R were subjected to analysis by appropriate readability formulas (Flesch, Fry, Dale-Chall, Farr-Jenkinson-Patterson, and Danielson-Bryan), concerns were broadened to include attention to several other factors. These factors included sentence structure, logical connections between sentences and clauses, and the coherence of topics. Three word lists comprising words to which students are exposed during the school years were used as primary sources for controlling the vocabulary in GORT-R paragraphs.

Some of the paragraphs in the GORT-R are modifications of content used in the 1967 GORT while others are based on fables, current events, unusual situations, or satirical social interactions. In accordance with the intent of the GORT-R to assess general reading ability and skills, general content rather than content emphasizing specific academic subjects was utilized in the paragraphs.

Unlike the 1963-67 GORT, in which comprehension questions were limited to literal comprehension, the GORT-R utilizes comprehension questions representing all levels of comprehension. For example, questions that assess comprehension at inferential and critical levels are also included. In addition to focusing on cognitive concerns, affective questions requiring personal and emotional reactions to the text are also taken into consideration. Most of the questions are passage-dependent because comprehension of particular paragraphs is being tested. Questions were avoided that could be answered through recall of similar text features, such as matching shapes or sounds of words in the questions with those in the paragraphs. In addition, care was taken to ascertain that the vocabulary used in the questions was not more difficult than that used in the paragraph on which the questions were based.

Unlike the open-ended questions posed in the 1963-67 GORT in which students were asked to make free responses, the GORT-R utilizes multiple-choice test items to assess oral reading comprehension. In the GORT-R, the student selects the response choice that best completes the idea expressed by the stem. Examiners are no longer required to judge the correctness of answers on the basis of suggested answers given in the record booklet.

Statistical criteria related to item discrimination (or discriminative power of the test items) are presented in the GORT-R manual. Item discrimination was interpreted as "the degree to which an item discriminates correctly among examinees in the behavior that the test is designed to measure" (Anastasi, 1982, cited in the GORT-R manual, p. 29). The point-biserial correlation technique, in which each item is correlated with the total test score, was used to determine the discriminative power of the test items. It is reported that, in view of lack of guidance in the literature concerning the magnitude of acceptable coefficients for item discrimination, the conventions governing interpretations of validity coefficients were utilized. On this basis and on the average, test items were found to be satisfactory in terms of discriminative power.

The GORT-R was standardized on a sample involving 1,401 students representing 15 states: Alabama, California, Iowa, Kansas, Louisiana, Maine, Massachusetts, Mississippi, Montana, New Mexico, New York, Texas, Virginia, Washington, and Wisconsin. The states represented four regions of the United States: Northeast, North Central, South, and West. Other demographic characteristics of the standardization sample included sex, type of residence (i.e., urban or rural), race, ethnicity, and age. Sample percentages for each of the characteristics were representative of percentages reported in the *Statistical Abstract of the United States* (1965) and were considered nationally representative.

Studies were undertaken during development of the GORT-R to determine its reliability with respect to three types of reliability: internal consistency, alternate forms, and standard error of measurement.

Internal consistency pertains to the degree to which individual items of a test intercorrelate and measure the same construct. In the case of the GORT-R, the construct under question was reading comprehension. Coefficient alpha, a statistical technique that shows how well scores obtained under just one condition represent universe (true) scores (Cronbach, 1970), was used to estimate the internal consistency reliability of each of the two GORT-R test forms. Using 25 protocols selected at random from the normative sample representing each one-year interval between 7 and 17 years of age, coefficients alpha were developed for Passage Scores and Comprehension Scores for each test form. Coefficients reported in Table 4 of the manual range from .83 to .98 for Passage Scores and Comprehension Scores across all levels of both forms. Guilford's (1978) formula for computing internal consistency coefficients for composites was used in calculations for the Oral Reading Quotients. All coefficients obtained across both forms of the GORT-R range from .92 to .95, indicative of a satisfactory degree of internal consistency.

Assessment of alternate-form reliability of the two forms of the GORT-R produced satisfactory results. To investigate the alternate-form reliability, correlation coefficients were computed across both forms to determine the degree to which each test related to its counterpart. Calculations on the means of the scores of 100 protocols selected across ages from the normative sample yielded the following coefficients: Passage Scores, .80; Comprehension Scores, .81; and Oral Reading Quotients, .83. All three coefficients were found to be significant at the .001 level. Results of the analysis of student-performance means were all within one standard error of measurement of each other.

The standard error of measurement for the GORT-R tests was calculated with reliability coefficients from the internal consistency research and is reported both for raw scores and standard scores in the GORT-R manual. Thus, the examiner can determine the probability of the range of scores within which the true score of an individual may lie.

The GORT-R was subjected to validity studies to assess the degree to which the tests are indeed measures of oral reading ability. Content, criterion-related, and construct validity were investigated.

For content validity, the paragraphs and test items were systematically examined to determine whether the content and skills required covered a representative sampling of behaviors involved in oral reading ability. This examination, along with the care used in construction of the paragraphs and test items, indicated appropriate content validity according to the purposes of the tests.

The GORT-R was examined for criterion-related validity by using concurrent measures as the relevant criterion. Results of the GORT-R were compared to the results of achievement tests related to reading performance and with ratings by teachers of students' overall reading ability. Specifically, GORT-R scores of 100 students (Grades 9-12) of the norming sample were correlated with the students' scores on the Iowa Tests of Educational Development (ITED). This process resulted in coefficients of .28 (Comprehension Scores), .47 (Passage Scores), and .38 (Oral Reading Quotients). For some of the students from the norming sample, scores on Form C of the Formal Reading Inventory (FRI) by Wiederholt (1986) were correlated with the scores for Form A and Form B of the GORT-R. The resultant coefficients were Form A—CS = .66, PS = .44, ORQ = .54; Form B—CS = .59, PS = .59, and ORQ = .48. For 98 of the students, scores from the GORT-R were also correlated with the ITED Total Reading Scores, resulting in the following coefficients: CS = .37, PS = .38, and ORQ = .39. Correlations made between the scores of 74 students of the sample (Grades 3 and 4) on the Comprehensive Test of Basic Skills (CTBS) and their scores for Form A of the GORT-R yielded the following coefficients: CS = .49, PS = .40, and ORQ = .47.

Additionally, ratings by three elementary teachers (Grades 3, 4, and 5) of 37 of their students' overall reading ability using a Likert-type rating scale (1-poor to 5-excellent) were correlated with the GORT-R scores of the students with the resultant coefficients: Form A: CS = .72, PS = .47, ORQ = .63; Form B: CS = .78, PS = .67, ORQ = .74.

Construct validity was examined according to certain traits generally recognized as related to reading ability. These included age, language abilities, total school achievement, and intelligence factors. With respect to age, investigation showed an increase of the GORT-R scores with increase in age, as expected. Furthermore, it was shown that the difficulty level of successive paragraphs in the GORT-R increased. Investigation of the relationship between the GORT-R scores and language ability of a group selected from the norming sample produced coefficients indicative of the construct validity of the GORT-R scores. Support for the construct validity of the GORT-R scores was also found in correlations involving the GORT-R scores of 206 students in the normative sample and their total school achievement. The results of two analyses run to investigate the relationship between the GORT-R scores and results of intelligence measures supported the construct validity of the GORT-R scores. Other evidence of construct validity of the GORT-R scores was apparent in the degree to which the scores discriminated between groups of readers and in the degree of discriminative power of the test items.

Critique

The Gray Oral Reading tests, for many years popular and highly satisfactory for their intended purposes, promise even greater effectiveness as a result of the 1986 revision by J. Lee Wiederholt and Brian R. Bryant. Available from PRO-ED publishers under the new title GORT-R (Gray Oral Reading Tests-Revised), the tests represent a continuation of the best features of previous editions and improvement in the aspects in which changes were desirable.

The GORT-R continues use of the traditional format of 13 paragraphs of difficulty ascending levels. Continued as well is the practice of presenting one paragraph per page in the examinee's book. The revised questions for assessing comprehension of the paragraphs are characterized by significant changes in both form and role. Rate and accuracy continue to play important parts in evaluation of oral reading ability, but these are only aspects of a wide complex of behaviors examined by the GORT-R.

Several positive changes are apparent in the physical properties of the GORT-R. For example, by shortening the manual and the Profile/Examiner Record Form by one inch, materials for this text can now be stored in files and notecovers of conventional sizes. In addition, deleting the picture preceding the initial paragraphs of the two forms will enhance the quality of testing and prevent early "datedness" of the tests. Finally, the "prompts" provided for the examiner to use prior to having a student read a paragraph is in keeping with what is known about the importance of establishing a purpose for reading.

The expansion of purposes increases uses for which the GORT-R is suitable. The content of the paragraphs is in keeping with events and ideas timely in terms of student's experiences and interests. Use of multiple-choice test items with specific correct answers improves objectivity in assessing comprehension of the paragraphs. Questions pertaining to a particular paragraph are placed on the reverse side of the page on which the paragraph appears, which keeps the questions immediately available to the examiner and makes it easy for the student to read along as the questions are read. Rather than testing literal comprehension solely, the GORT-R questions utilize a variety of comprehension forms; testing, then, of oral reading comprehension is more closely related to the nature of comprehension as it is conceived for silent reading or for listening. Because the raw scores achieved from the comprehension tests are converted to standard scores and percentiles using normative data, several types of comparisons are therefore possible.

The GORT-R reflects excellent technical preparation. Many of the criticisms levelled at the previous editions have been taken into consideration and used to improve technical aspects of development. Appropriate norms, no longer "tentative," are available in the manual. Normative scores are presented as standard scores and percentiles for Comprehension Scores, Passage Scores, and Oral Reading Quotients for Form A and Form B. The norming sample of 1,401 students, representing a variety of demographic characteristics, was to a large extent a nationally representative group of students in the United States. The tests will be appropriate for an expanded population of users. It should be noted that the tests continue to be focused on students of average abilities. Modifications are recommended for use of the tests by individuals who are outside the ranges of the ages or other specific characteristics of the norming sample.

Basic testing procedures of the GORT-R are simple, easy to understand, and easy to follow even by examiners who may lack experience in testing. Steps in administration and scoring are clearly explained in the manual. Testing time of 15 to 30 minutes is relatively short for an individually administered test. Ages of students served by the GORT-R are inclusive of students throughout the elementary and secondary levels of school. In some cases, the tests will be appropriate for college-level students, including those who require some type of reading remediation or those who may serve as subjects in research projects related to improvement of reading ability or instruction.

The GORT-R is designed for measurement of oral reading ability. It makes no claims for measurement of silent reading ability or for interpretation of its results in terms of other aspects of reading ability. Developers of the GORT-R express recognition of the contradictory results of research investigating relationships between oral and silent reading. In view of these results, they recommend administration of silent reading tests when warranted. They also offer the suggestion that further testing may not be essential when a student's silent reading comprehension is satisfactory for his or her age and ability.

The GORT-R thus is an essential and timely addition to the relatively few tests available for measuring oral reading ability. Not only is it important as a measurement device, but it focuses attention on—and offers insights regarding—the importance of oral reading instruction per se.

References

This list includes text citations and suggested additional reading.

Allington, R. I., Chodos, L., Domaracki, G., & Truex, P. (1977). Passage dependency: Four diagnostic reading tests. *The Reading Teacher, 30,* 369-375.

Anastasi, A. (1982). *Psychological testing* (5th ed.). NY: Macmillan.

Buros, O. K. (Ed.). (1965). *The sixth mental measurements yearbook.* Highland Park, NJ: The Gryphon Press.

Cook, R. C. (Ed.). (1941-1942). *Who's who in american education* (4th Ed., Vol. 10). Nashville, TN: Who's Who in American Education, Inc.

Cronbach, L. J. (1970). *Essentials of educational testing.* NY: Harper & Row.

D'Angelo, K., & Mahlios, M. (1983). Insertion and omission miscues of good and poor readers. *The Reading Teacher, 36,* 778-782.

Durkin, D. (1978-1979). What classroom observations reveal about reading comprehension instruction. *Reading Research Quarterly, 14,* 482-533.

Goodman, K. S. (1969). Analysis of oral reading miscues: Applied psycholinguistics. *Reading Research Quarterly, 5,* 9-30.

Gray, W. S. (1967). *Gray Oral Reading Tests.* Austin, TX: PRO-ED.

Guilford, J. P. and Fruchter, B. (1978). *Fundamental Statistics in Psychology and Education.* NY: McGraw-Hill.

Wiederholt, J. L., & Bryant, B. R. (1986). *GORT-R (Gray Oral Reading Tests-Revised) manual,* Austin, TX: PRO-ED.

Zita M. Cantwell, Ph.D.
Professor of Educational Psychology, Brooklyn College of the City University of New York, Brooklyn, New York.

GROUP EMBEDDED FIGURES TEST
Philip K. Oltman, Evelyn Raskin, and Herman A. Witkin. Palo Alto, California: Consulting Psychologists Press, Inc.

Introduction

The Group Embedded Figures Test (GEFT) was designed as an adaptation of the Embedded Figures Test (EFT), an individual measure of perceptual disembedding, to be used in situations in which group as opposed to individual testing is practical (e.g., screening on field-dependence/field-independence dimension or large scale correlational studies of personality attributes). The contents of the GEFT are modelled closely on those of the EFT; the former includes 18 scored complex figures, of which 17 have been taken from the EFT (Witkin, Oltman, Raskin, & Karp, 1971).

Cognitive styles are habitual modes that individuals use to process information. While cognitive styles color human behavior over a broad spectrum of activities, they cannot be identified as abilities. However, cognitive styles do affect the development of patterns of abilities and, therefore, have important implications for research and practice related to behavior. Kogan (1971) describes nine cognitive styles that have been identified from the research literature. The field-dependence/field-independence approach of Witkin is among the most widely researched and most familiar of the group (Witkin, 1978; Witkin & Goodenough, 1981; Witkin, Moore, Goodenough, & Cox, 1977).

The field-dependence/field-independence construct has been defined from the theory of psychological differentiation—the latter concerned largely with the complexity of structure of a psychological system (Witkin, Dyk, Faterson, Goodenough, & Karp, 1962). Psychological differentiation is manifested in cognition by global versus analytical cognitive structuring; in perception, by field dependence/field independence. The GEFT is concerned with assessing functioning on a narrow type of perceptual task; namely, tasks requiring disembedding. The examinee is asked to identify a simple form within a complex one (Witkin, Oltman, Raskin, & Karp, 1971). The field-dependent individual will have a difficult time doing this task, preferring to take the perceptual organization of a complex figure as given and finding breaking it up a difficult and not too congenial task. On the other hand, the field-independent individual can restructure the perceptual field—break the complex figure into component parts—with relative ease and find the simple figure. Field-dependent individuals tend to rely on external sources of information in perception and problem-solving; field-independent individuals, on internal sources of information (Oltman, 1982).

Witkin (1978) notes that evidence points toward field-dependent individuals having a pronounced interpersonal orientation when compared to field-independent individuals. The former seek both physical and emotional closeness to others, pay selective attention to social cues, are social and interested in people, and are effective in interpersonal situations. On the other hand, field-independent individuals show greater competence in cognitive restructuring; for example, tasks requiring disembedding, speed of closure, and "perspectivism" or Piaget's decentration (i.e., the ability to recognize and adopt another individual's perspective). Field-independent individuals also are active hypothesis testers.

Five characteristics distinguish the cognitive style qualities of the field-dependence/field-independence continuum (Witkin, 1978; Witkin & Goodenough, 1981). First, the two are process variables (i.e., they represent techniques for moving toward goals rather than the goals themselves). Second, they are pervasive dimensions of individual functioning that are expressed across personal domains, as for example body concept, sense of separate identity, nature of defenses, perceptual and cognitive functioning (but only on cognitive tasks requiring restructuring). Furthermore, an individual's position on the field-dependence/field-independence continuum shows a trend toward consistency over time, especially in the 8- to 18-year age range (Witkin, Goodenough, & Karp, 1967). This leads to the next characteristic—namely, the bipolarity of the field-dependence/field-independence cognitive style. Field dependence/field independence represent a continuum. Each individual has a place somewhere on that continuum, either at or between the two extremes. Finally, this cognitive style is value-neutral. Tending toward field dependence or field independence is neither good nor bad; it refers to an individual's way of structuring reality and, therefore, can provide information about how that individual might be expected to respond to particular perceptual or problem-solving tasks.

Oltman (1982) reports that 32 trial complex forms (24 from the EFT and eight new but similar items) made up the preliminary version of the GEFT. Two 16-item tests were constructed. Items or complex forms were arranged in four different orders. One of the two tests plus the Rod and Frame Test (RFT) and the EFT were administered to individual members of the sample. From the original 32, 20 complex forms were selected based on an item's pass/fail ratio and correlation with the RFT and the EFT. Further testing yielded the final version of the GEFT: 18 complex forms organized in two subtests of nine forms each, plus an introductory subtest of seven practice forms. The two subtests do not stand alone; performances on both are combined for the total score of the GEFT. One point is assigned to each correct response; the total score can range from 0 to 18. The last page of the booklet contains eight simple forms. For each item, the examinee is asked to find and outline in pencil one of these eight simple forms in the complex form. The complete simple form must be outlined; no partial credit is given. Each of the subtests is timed at 5 minutes. Reference can be made to the simple forms during the testing time as often as is needed.

Practical Applications/Uses

The GEFT test has accumulated a large research bibliography; a published bibliography of studies through 1981 lists upwards of 2,800. A review of the research literature for the past 10 years in which the GEFT has been used as either the dependent or independent variable measure yielded numerous studies covering a broad field of topics ranging from hypothesis testing on topics of cognitive processing in a research laboratory to applied research on aspects of human behavior in natural environmental settings. Study samples included subjects from early elementary grades through old age and from various cultural, socioeconomic, and racial backgrounds. The aims of many of the studies have been to determine whether relationships exist between field dependence/field independence and selected variables or whether performances on the variables studied differ according to positions on the field-dependence/field-independence continuum, frequently considered in conjunction with other personal variables. In addition, there have been studies on psychometric characteristics of the GEFT. A selection of the categories of topics and studies is presented in the following paragraphs to give some idea of the scope of the applications of the GEFT.

1. *Cognitive processing.* GEFT has been used in studies of memory, such as working memory in relation to field articulation (Robinson & Bennick, 1977) and interaction between field dependence/independence and pictorial recognition memory (Berry, 1984); spatial reasoning among hearing-impaired and deaf subjects (Hauptman, 1980); metacognition (Larson et al., 1985); cooperative learning and transfer (McDonald, Larson, Dansereau, & Spurlin, 1985); discourse processing (Spiro & Tirre, 1980); lateral eye movement as an indicator of cognitive ability and style (Owens & Limber, 1983); and relationship to overall cognitive performances (Riding & Dyer, 1983).

2. *Thought processes.* GEFT has been used in studies of formal operational thought (Flexer & Roberge, 1983); proportional reasoning (Nummedal & Collea, 1981); creative thinking (Noppe & Gallagher, 1977); concept learning (Park, 1984); relationship of perceptual disembedding, as measured by GEFT, and verbal processing (Longoni & Pizzamiglio, 1981); and syntactic complexity (Kagan, 1980).

3. *Instructional strategies, materials, student assessment.* GEFT has been used in a wide variety of studies dealing with instruction and learning, such as text style and text processing (Brooks, Dansereau, Spurlin, & Holley, 1983); small group instructional techniques (McLeod & Adams, 1979; science curriculum materials (Pringle & Morgan, 1978); personalized systems of instruction (PSI; Jacobs & Gedeon, 1982); the effectiveness of various study techniques (Annis, 1979); the matching of instructional tasks to cognitive style (Frank & Davis, 1982); and response of students to classroom environments designed to enhance school motivation (Bolocofsky, 1980).

4. *School achievement.* GEFT has been used in studies of school achievement in a wide variety of subject areas and with samples ranging from elementary school groups through adults: overall college achievement (McDonald, 1984); mathematics (Gordon, 1977; Frerichs & Eldersveld, 1981; Weiner & Robinson, 1983); art appreciation (Copeland, 1984); engineering graphics (Wilson & Davis, 1985); information science (Johnson & White, 1981); prose composition (Adejumo, 1983); reading research (Roberge & Flexer, 1984); and complex motor skills (Swinnen, 1984).

5. *Instructor and student cognitive style match.* GEFT has been used in studies to determine whether students fare better and instructors manage the learning environment more effectively when there are matches between the cognitive styles of instructors and students (Renninger & Snyder, 1983; Mahlios, 1981, 1982). The

test has also been used to study the effects of client/counselor cognitive style match on the outcome of counseling (Fry & Charron, 1980).

6. *Personal attributes.* GEFT has been used in studies of personal characteristics, such as motivation (Samers, 1982); personality variables in old age (Panek, 1982); leadership (Hoffman, 1978; obesity (Pine, 1984); egocentricity (McIlvried, 1980); body boundaries (Del Miglio, 1984); self-consciousness (Davies, 1984); extraversion/introversion (Mwamwenda, Dionne, & Mwamwenda, 1985); locus of control (Owie, 1983); and development of moral judgment (Guthrie, 1985).

7. *Socialization factors.* The GEFT has been used in studies of socialization and acculturation across multiethnic groups as well as within groups (Ghuman, 1980; Shade, 1981).

In the majority of these and other studies, the GEFT has been used to describe behavior of groups of subjects. This use is in keeping with the stated purpose for the construction of the test; namely, large scale screening or correlational studies.

The GEFT is comprised of two sets of nine complex forms each. The examinee is asked to identify one of the eight simple forms printed on the last page of the booklet in each of the complex forms. The outline of the complete simple form is to be drawn in the complex figure. The test is printed in blue ink so that the pencil outlines are easy to discern. The simple form must be completely traced to be scored "correct"; no partial scores are given. The range of scores is from 0 to 18. Seven practice forms are included; they are worked through under timed conditions (2 minutes) before the two sets of nine. Directions indicate that 5 minutes are to be allowed for completion of each of the sets of nine. The GEFT is very easy to administer; directions are clear and to the point and the test format is not complex. If time limits given in the manual are adhered to, the administration can be completed comfortably within 20 or 30 minutes. GEFT is easy to score, but must be scored by hand. If the sample is large, such a task can be time-consuming.

A microcomputer version of the GEFT has been developed (Burroway, 1984).

Technical Aspects

A very good theoretical rationale for the construct validity of the GEFT is provided in the test manual. The additional statistical data on reliability and validity supplied in the manual are based on a small sample of men and women from "an eastern liberal arts college" (Witkin, Oltman, Raskin, & Karp, 1971, p. 28). These are limited data. Certainly the same time frames cannot be applied realistically to high school and elementary students and, perhaps, adults. In addition, reliability and validity data cannot be extrapolated to populations with differing characteristics.

The research literature provides more information about technical aspects of the GEFT. Initial studies showing that the test measures a single factor have been confirmed in some studies (see, for example, Denson, 1976, 1977; Loo, 1982). Some researchers hypothesize that the GEFT is a measure of general intelligence (Cooperman, 1980); others have studied the covariation of intelligence and field dependence/field independence (Roberge & Flexer, 1981). Psychometric data on reliability and validity have been published, for example, for college students (Carter & Loo, 1980), deaf individuals (Dowaliby, Burke, & McKee, 1980), adolescents (Leino, 1980; O'Leary, Calsyn, & Fauria, 1980), a cross-sectional sample of late adolescent through middle-aged subjects (test-retest reliability; Kepner & Neimark, 1984), and elementary school students (Thompson, Pitts, & Gipe, 1983). Adult samples with specific characteristics, such as mineworkers (Sims, Graves, & Simpson, 1983), have tended to perform differently than the "norming" sample.

While these studies of the psychometric characteristics of the GEFT support the quality of the instrument, they indicate that, when administered to different populations, the instrument discriminates differently across these groups. For example, Panek, Funk, and Nelson (1980), studying the performances of 17- to 72-year-old female subjects, found the internal consistency of the GEFT stable across the age range, but the construct validity did not hold for all age subgroups. Thompson, Pitts, and Gipe (1983) found that the GEFT discriminated generally well among the fourth- to sixth-grade subjects in their study. However, response patterns for two of the complex figures—items 7 and 13—deviated significantly from those expected. The GEFT yielded a satisfactory test-retest reliability for a sample of undergraduates 18 to 51 years, even though the mean scores on the retests increased significantly (Kepner & Neimark, 1984).

Further studies have indicated the presence of a practice effect of the first scored subtest on the second (Lusk & Wright, 1981a), as well as a speed effect (Denson, 1976). This latter factor becomes important given the fact that the only time limits provided in the test manual are based on performances of a small, single sample of college students. For example, Mahlios & D'Angelo (1983) determined norms for an elementary-school-age sample that differed significantly from those appropriate for the college sample presented in the manual, while DiNuovo (1984) found that performances of young adult males and females varied significantly when administration times for the GEFT were altered. Findings with regard to sex have been varied somewhat, depending largely on developmental age. For the most part, the GEFT does not appear to discriminate differently between males and females (Bergum & Bergum, 1981; Lusk & Wright, 1981b; Mahlios & D'Angelo, 1983). However, one study has indicated that these differences may be masked by the characteristics of sample selected (De Sanctis & Dunikoski, 1983).

These and other data on the technical aspects of the GEFT presented in the literature need to be incorporated into a preliminary technical manual designed to inform users of the current status of psychometric characteristics of the instrument.

Critique

The GEFT can be a powerful tool for assessing the perceptual visualization dimension of disembedding that appears to interact with other personal attributes (e.g., in areas of cognition, socialization, personality). The cognitive style of field dependence/field independence measured by the GEFT, while not an ability, affects the development of abilities. The instrument can yield data that provide insights for those engaged in cognitive style research. Field dependence/field independence appears to have a strong chance of being relatively stable from approximately age 8 at least into young adulthood, and probably beyond. The GEFT has been developed for group screening and large scale studies. In its present state of development, it is neither ready nor intended for individual use. More adequate technical data should be provided in the test manual, especially with regard to validity, reliability, and norms for different age groups. The question of the appropriate time limits for different ages needs to be studied, as does the practice effect of performance on the first subtest on performance on the second and the appropriateness of the 18 complex forms (plus practice forms) for different age groups and for different adult groups.

References

Adejumo, D. (1983). Effect of cognitive style on strategies for comprehension of prose. *Perceptual and Motor Skills, 56,* 859-863.
Annis, L. (1979). Effect of cognitive style and learning passage organization on study technique effectiveness. *Journal of Educational Psychology, 71,* 620-626.
Bergum, J. E., & Bergum, B. O. (1981, April). *Field dependence, perceptual instability, and sex differences.* Paper presented at the Annual Convention of the Southwestern Psychological Association, Oklahoma City. (ERIC Document Reproduction Service No. 195 888)
Berry, L. (1984, January). *The role of cognitive style in processing color information: A signal detection analysis.* Paper presented at the annual meeting of Association for Educational Communication & Technology, Dallas. (ERIC Document Reproduction Service No. 243 414)
Bolocofsky, D. N. (1980). Motivational effects of classroom competition as a function of field dependence. *Journal of Educational Research, 73,* 213-217.
Brooks, L. W., Dansereau, D. F., Spurlin, J. E., & Holley, C. D. (1983). Effects of headings on text processing. *Journal of Educational Psychology, 75,* 292-302.
Burroway, R. L. (1984, January). *Testing and measurement potentials of microcomputers for cognitive style research and individualized instruction.* Paper presented at the annual meeting of Association for Educational Communication & Technology, Dallas. (ERIC Document Reproduction Service No. 243 415)
Carter, H., & Loo, R. (1980). Group Embedded Figures Test: Psychometric data. *Perceptual and Motor Skills, 50,* 32-34.
Cooperman, E. W. (1980). Field differentiation and intelligence. *Journal of Psychology, 105,* 29-34.
Copeland, B. D. (1984). The relationship of cognitive style to academic achievement of university art appreciation students. *College Student Journal, 17,* 157-162.
Davies, M. F. (1984). Conceptual and empirical comparisons between self-consciousness and field dependence-independence. *Perceptual and Motor Skills, 58,* 543-549.
Del Miglio, C. M. (1984). Body boundaries and field dependence of adolescent girls. *Perceptual and Motor Skills, 58,* 883-886.
Denson, T. A. (1977, April). *Three measures of cognitive style: Characteristics, factor structure, and implications for research.* Paper presented at the annual meeting of American Educational Research Association, New York. (ERIC Document Reproduction Service No. ED 137 344)
Denson, T. A. (1976, May). *Three tests of cognitive style: Item analyses and characteristics.* Paper presented at the annual conference of New England Educational Research Organization, Provincetown, MA. (ERIC Document Reproduction Service No. ED 132 175)
De Sanctis, G., & Dunikoski, R. (1983). Group Embedded-Figures Test: Psychometric data for a sample of business students. *Perceptual and Motor Skills, 56,* 707-710.
Di Nuovo, S. (1984). Administration times for Witkin's Group Embedded Figures Test. *Perceptual and Motor Skills, 58,* 134.
Dowaliby, F. J., Burke, N. E., & McKee, B. G. (1980, April). *Validity and reliability of a learning style inventory for postsecondary deaf individuals.* Paper presented at annual meeting of American Educational Research Association, Boston. (ERIC Document Reproduction Service No. ED 189 808)

Flexer, B. K., & Roberge, J. J. (1983). A longitudinal investigation of field dependence-independence and the development of formal operational thought. *British Journal of Educational Psychology, 53*, 195-204.

Frank, B. M., & Davis, J. K. (1982). Effect of field-independence match or mismatch on a communication task. *Journal of Educational Psychology, 74*, 23-31.

Frerichs, A. H., & Eldersveld, P. J. (1981, April). *Predicting successful and unsuccessful developmental mathematics students in community colleges.* Paper presented at the annual meeting of American Educational Research Association, San Francisco. (ERIC Document Reproduction Service No. ED 202 507)

Fry, P. S., & Charron, P. A. (1980). Effects of cognitive style and counselor-client compatibility on client growth. *Journal of Counseling Psychology, 27*, 529-538.

Ghuman, P. A. (1980). A comparative study of cognitive styles in three ethnic groups. *International Review of Applied Psychology, 29*, 75-87.

Gordon, M. (1977). Mathematics presentation as a function of cognitive/personality variables. *Journal for Research in Mathematics Education, 8*, 205-210.

Guthrie, K. H. (1985). Locus of control and field independence-dependence as factors in the development of moral judgment. *Journal of Genetic Psychology, 146*, 13-18.

Hauptman, A. R. (1980, April). *An investigation of the visual and tactile spatial reasoning abilities of the hearing impaired/deaf student.* Paper presented at the annual meeting of American Educational Research Association, Boston. (ERIC Document Reproduction Service No. ED 195 101)

Hoffman, D. A. (1978). Field independence and intelligence: Their relation to leadership and self-concept in sixth-grade boys. *Journal of Educational Psychology, 70*, 827-832.

Jacobs, R. L., & Gedeon, D. V. (1982). Proctor/student interactions and achievement in a PSI technology course. *Journal of Industrial Teacher Education, 19*, 18-26.

Johnson, K. A., & White, M. D. (1981). The field dependence/field independence of information professional students. *Library Research, 3*, 355-369.

Kagan, D. M. (1980). Syntactic complexity and cognitive style. *Applied Psycholinguistics, 1*, 111-122.

Kepner, M. D., & Neimark, E. D. (1984). Test-retest reliability and differential patterns of score change on the Group Embedded Figures Test. *Journal of Personality and Social Psychology, 46*, 1405-1413.

Kogan, N. (1971). Educational implications of cognitive styles. In G. S. Lesser (Ed.), *Learning, cognition, and educational practice* (pp. 242-292). Glenview, IL: Scott-Foresman.

Larson, C. O., Dansereau, D. F., O'Donnell, A. M., Hythecker, V. I., Lambiotte, J. G., & Rocklin, T. R. (1985). Effects of metacognitive and elaborative activity on cooperative learning and transfer. *Contemporary Educational Psychology, 10*, 342-348.

Leino, A. L. (1980). *Learning process in terms of styles and strategies: Theoretical background and pilot study* (Research Bulletin No. 54). Helsinki, Finland: Helsinki University Institute of Education. (ERIC Document Reproduction Service No. ED 201 604)

Longoni, A. M., & Pizzamiglio, L. (1981). Aspects of verbal processing in relation to perceptual disembedding. *Journal of Psycholinguistic Research, 10*, 199-208.

Loo, R. (1982). Cluster and principal components analysis of the Group Embedded Figures Test. *Perceptual and Motor Skills, 54*, 331-336.

Lusk, E. J., & Wright, H. (1981a). Note on learning the Group Embedded Figures Test. *Perceptual and Motor Skills, 53*, 370.

Lusk, E. J., & Wright, H. (1981b). Differences in sex and curricula on learning the Group Embedded Figures Test. *Perceptual and Motor Skills, 53*, 8-10.

McDonald, B. A., Larson, C. A., Dansereau, D. F., & Spurlin, J. E. (1985). Cooperative dyads: Impact on text learning and transfer. *Contemporary Educational Psychology, 10*, 369-377.

McDonald, E. R. (1984). The relationship of student and faculty field dependence/independence congruence to student academic achievement. *Educational and Psychological Measurement, 44,* 725-731.

McIlvried, E. J. (1980, August). *Egocentric behavior and psychological differentiation in the aged.* Paper presented at the Annual Convention of American Psychological Association, Montreal, Quebec. (ERIC Document Reproduction Service No. ED 198 412)

McLeod, D. B., & Adams, V. M. (1979). The interaction of field independence with small-group instruction in mathematics. *Journal of Experimental Education, 48,* 118-124.

Mahlios, M. C. (1982). Effects of pair formation on the performance of student teachers. *Action in Teacher Education, 4,* 65-70.

Mahlios, M. C. (1981). Effects of teacher-student cognitive style on patterns of dyadic classroom interaction. *Journal of Experimental Education, 49,* 147-157.

Mahlios, M. C., & D'Angelo, K. (1983). Group Embedded Figures Test: Psychometric data on children. *Perceptual and Motor Skills, 56,* 423-426.

Mwamwenda, T. S., Dionne, J. P., & Mwamwenda, B. B. (1985). Theoretical and empirical link between psychological differentiation and extraversion. *Psychological Reports, 56,* 147-154.

Noppe, L. D., & Gallagher, J. M. (1977). Cognitive style approach to creative thought. *Journal of Personality Assessment, 41,* 85-90.

Nummedal, S. G., & Collea, F. P. (1981). Field independence, task ambiguity, and performance on a proportional reasoning task. *Journal of Research in Science Teaching, 18,* 255-260.

O'Leary, M. R., Calsyn, D. A., & Fauria, T. (1980). The Group Embedded Figures Test: A measure of cognitive style or cognitive impairment. *Journal of Personality Assessment, 44,* 532-537.

Oltman, P. K. (1982). Development of the Group Embedded Figures Test. In National Association of Secondary School Principals (Ed.), *Student learning styles and brain behavior: Programs, instrumentation, research* (pp. 58-60). Washington, DC: Author.

Owens, W., & Limber, J. (1983). Lateral eye movement as a measure of cognitive ability and style. *Perceptual and Motor Skills, 56,* 711-719.

Owie, I. (1983). Locus of control, instructional mode, and students' achievement. *Instructional Science, 12,* 383-388.

Panek, P. E. (1982). Relationship between field-dependence/independence and personality in older adults. *Perceptual and Motor Skills, 54,* 811-814.

Panek, P. E., Funk, L. G., & Nelson, P. K. (1980). Reliability and validity of the Group Embedded Figures Test across the life span. *Perceptual and Motor Skills, 50,* 1171-1174.

Park, O. C. (1984). Example comparison strategy versus attribute identification strategy in concept learning. *American Educational Research Journal, 21,* 145-162.

Pine, C. J. (1984). Field-dependence factors in American Indian and Caucasian obesity. *Journal of Clinical Psychology, 40,* 205-209.

Pringle, R. G., & Morgan, A. G. (1978). The effects of laboratory-oriented experiences in SCIS on the stability of cognitive style of teachers. *Journal of Research in Science Teaching, 15,* 47-51.

Renninger, K. A., & Snyder, S. S. (1983). Effects of cognitive style on perceived satisfaction and performance among students and teachers. *Journal of Educational Psychology, 75,* 668-676.

Riding, R. J., & Dyer, V. A. (1983). The nature of learning styles and their relationship to cognitive performance in children. *Educational Psychology, 3,* 275-287.

Roberge, J. J., & Flexer, B. K. (1984). Cognitive style, operativity, and reading achievement. *American Educational Research Journal, 21,* 227-236.

Roberge, J. J., & Flexer, B. K. (1981). Examination of the covariation of field independence, intelligence, and achievement. *British Journal of Educational Psychology, 51,* 235-236.

Robinson, J. A., & Bennick, C. D. (1977). *Field articulation and working memory.* Lexington, KY: University of Kentucky. (ERIC Document Reproduction Service No. ED 174 032)

Samers, B. N. (1982). *Cognitive style and motivation in continuing education.* Stamford, CT: Cooper & Co. (NSF Sponsorship) (ERIC Document Reproduction Service No. ED 218 135)

Shade, B. J. (1981). Racial variation in perceptual differentiation. *Perceptual and Motor Skills, 52,* 243-248.

Sims, M. T., Graves, R. J., & Simpson, G. C. (1983). Mineworkers scores on the Group Embedded Figures Test. *Journal of Occupational Psychology, 56,* 335-337.

Spiro, R. J., & Tirre, W. C. (1980). Individual differences in scheme utilization during discourse processing. *Journal of Educational Psychology, 72,* 204-208.

Swinnen, S. (1984). Field dependence as a factor in learning complex motor skills and underlying sex differences. *International Journal of Sport Psychology, 15,* 236-249.

Thompson, B., Pitts, M. M., & Gipe, J. P. (1983). Use of the Group Embedded Figures Test with children. *Perceptual and Motor Skills, 57,* 199-203.

Weiner, N. C., & Robinson, S. E. (1983, November). *Cognitive abilities, personality, and gender differences in math achievement of gifted adolescents.* Paper presented at the annual midyear conference of the American Educational Research Association Research on Women and Education Special Interest Group, Tempe, AZ. (ERIC Document Reproduction Service No. ED 242 648)

Witkin, H. A. (1978). *Cognitive style in personal and cultural adaptation* (The 1977 Heinz Werner Lectures). Worcester, MA: Clark University Press.

Witkin, H. A., Dyk, R., Faterson, H. F., Goodenough, D. R., & Karp, S. A. (1962). *Psychological differentiation.* New York: Wiley.

Witkin, H. A., & Goodenough, D. R. (1981). Cognitive styles: Essences and origins. *Psychological Issues* (Monograph #51). New York: International Universities Press. (N.B. A new edition is announced by the publisher for 1986.)

Witkin, H. A., Moore, C. A., Goodenough, D. R., & Cox, P. W. (1977). Field-dependent and field-independent cognitive styles and their educational implications. *Review of Educational Research, 47,* 1-64.

Witkin, H. A., Goodenough, D. R., & Karp, S. A. (1967). Stability of cognitive style from childhood to young adulthood. *Journal of Personality and Social Psychology, 7,* 291-300.

Witkin, H. A., Oltman, P. K., Raskin, E., & Karp, S. A. (1971). *Manual: Embedded Figures Test, Children's Embedded Figures Test, Group Embedded Figures Test.* Palo Alto, CA: Consulting Psychologists Press.

Wilson, R. C., & Davis, P. D. (1985). The prediction of success in engineering graphics using the Group Embedded Figures Test and the Hidden Figures Test. *Journal of Studies in Technical Careers, 7,* 65-72.

Ronald R. Holden, Ph.D.
Assistant Professor of Psychology, Queen's University, Kingston, Canada.

HOPELESSNESS SCALE
Aaron T. Beck, Arlene Weissman, David Lester, and Larry Trexler. Washington D.C.: American Psychological Association.

Introduction

The Hopelessness Scale is a structured self-report, 20-item, true/false psychological inventory designed to assess pessimistic expectations in adults. Hopelessness has been implicated as an important variable in depression, suicide, schizophrenia, alcoholism, sociopathy, and physical illness. Thus, the Hopelessness Scale potentially offers relevant, objective data on a dimension that is pertinent to a variety of serious psychological dysfunctions.

Dr. Aaron T. Beck of the University of Pennsylvania and the Philadelphia General Hospital developed this scale with his associates, Arlene Weissman, David Lester, and Larry Trexler in order to quantify objectively an individual's negative expectations about the self and the future. Previously, hopelessness had been viewed as an important component of depression (e.g., Beck, Ward, Mendelson, Mock, & Erbaugh, 1961); however, the supposed nebulosity of the concept had deterred the development of specific, objective measures of the hopelessness domain. Nevertheless, based on clinical observation (e.g., Minkoff, Bergman, Beck, & Beck, 1973) and empirical evidence that linked pessimism to self-harm (e.g., Cropley & Weckowicz, 1966), Beck and his colleagues have attempted to define and measure the characteristic of hopelessness.

Construction of the Hopelessness Scale emphasized theoretical, clinical, and rational considerations. Initial test item development was based both on a previous inventory of attitudes about the future and on pessimistic statements made by patients who had been evaluated by clinicians as hopeless; from this, 20 test items were generated. Revisions based on depressed patients' ratings of relevance and clarity, and clinicians' evaluations of face validity and comprehensibility were then made. The resultant version of the Hopelessness Scale is a 20-item, true/false, self-report inventory. Eleven items are keyed true, nine items false. Item responses are scored 0 or 1 and scores on all items are summed to yield a scale score, which may range from 0 to 20. Based on a factor analysis of the responses of 294 psychiatric inpatients who had made recent suicide attempts, the authors have also identified three facets to the Hopelessness Scale: an affective factor (Feelings About the Future), a motivational component (Loss of Motivation), and a cognitive dimension (Future Expectations). This then represents the current adult version of the Hopelessness Scale. A distinct version for children, constructed by Kazdin and his colleagues (Kazdin, French, Unis, Esveldt-Dawson, & Sherick, 1983), has recently been developed.

At present, the Hopelessness Scale exists as an inventory published in a journal article. Because of the objective, self-report nature of the scale, the test examiner's participation in the testing process is minimal. The Hopelessness Scale was devised for use with adults and does not require a high level of reading ability. Currently, no regular question booklet, answer sheet, profile form, standard normative data, or manual are available for the Hopelessness Scale.

Practical Applications/Uses

The Hopelessness Scale was formulated to provide a standardized, objective quantification of pessimistic cognitions associated with various psychological problems. In particular, professionals working in the areas of depression and suicide (e.g., psychiatrists, psychologists, program evaluators) may find the Hopelessness Scale an important component of a larger assessment battery (e.g., Shaw, Vallis, & McCabe, 1985, p. 398). Furthermore, because there are no historical items on the scale, the inventory would appear to be responsive to changes as a result of therapeutic intervention, time, or other factors. Thus, the Hopelessness Scale is potentially useful as an initial status measure, a sign of ongoing change, or an outcome indicator.

The Hopelessness Scale requires approximately 5 to 10 minutes to be completed. Test administration requires minimal instruction and any responsible individual should be capable of adequately supervising the testing procedure. Hand scoring of the Hopelessness Scale is straightforward and readily learned, with an answer key published in the original journal article. Two to five minutes would seem to be the approximate amount of time needed for scoring the test. Because of the simplicity of the basic scoring system, no readily available computerized scoring is offered.

Involvement of a professional with training in testing and a knowledge of psychometrics appears *mandatory* for interpretation of Hopelessness Scale results. Particularly when dealing with issues of predicting suicidal risk, interpretation must consider the consequences of misclassification (both false positives and false negatives), base rates, other relevant assessment information, and past clinical experience. In this regard, expertise in clinical testing and basic psychometric theory are necessities. Furthermore, no standard norms or interpretative manual are available. Consequently, inferences from test scores must be made with extreme caution.

Technical Aspects

No standard norms exist for the Hopelessness Scale. Table 1 presents means and standard deviations obtained from various samples. Although Greene (1981) suggests little need for establishing separate norms for various demographic subgroups, the discrepancy between the mean obtained on her sample of 396 Irish adults and the mean associated with Durham's (1982) 197 American college students would suggest otherwise. Thus, scale score interpretation with respect to any currently available data must be made guardedly.

Indices of reliability that are relevant for an objective test include parallel forms

Table 1

Hopelessness Scale Means and Standard Deviations for Various Samples

Source	Sample	M	SD
Beck et al. (1975)	384 suicide attempters	9.00	6.10
Beck et al. (1984)	20 female alcoholics	7.30	5.30
	20 female heroin addicts	8.30	5.25
Durham (1982)	99 forensic psychiatric patients	6.62	4.88
	118 general psychiatric patients	6.04	4.67
	197 college students	2.32	2.25
Greene (1981)	396 "normal" adults	4.45	3.09
Lester & Beck (1976)	102 neurotic suicide attempters	9.00	5.80
	84 psychotic suicide attempters	8.10	6.20
Mendonca et al. (1983)	27 psychiatric controls	7.15	4.55
	41 suicide ideators	11.29	5.58
	10 suicide attempters	10.20	6.34
Nekanda-Trepka et al. (1983)	140 depressive outpatients	13.05	5.17
	20 depressives	11.10	6.15
Wetzel et al. (1980)	73 psychiatric inpatients	6.30	5.60

reliability, internal consistency, (e.g., KR-20) and stability (e.g., test-retest reliability). Given that only one form of the Hopelessness Scale exists, parallel forms reliability may not be calculated. The internal consistency of the Hopelessness Scale is high. The authors calculated a KR-20 of .93 for a sample of 294 recent suicide attempters; Mendonca, Holden, Mazmanian, and Dolan (1983) found a KR-20 of .91 for a sample of 78 psychiatric patients in crisis; and Durham (1982) reports KR-20s of .86, .83, and .65 for groups of forensic psychiatric patients, general psychiatric patients, and college students, respectively. (It should be noted that the lower internal consistency estimate for the nonpsychiatric sample is undoubtedly a function of restriction of range.) Test-retest reliability information on the Hopelessness Scale is almost nonexistent. Zamble, Porporino, and Kalotay (1984), studying Canadian prison inmates, report a one year test-retest reliability of .61 (N = 100).

With respect to validity, a number of investigations are particularly relevant. Using 23 outpatients in general medical practice, the authors report a correlation of .74 between the Hopelessness Scale and clinical ratings of hopelessness. They also found a correlation of .62 between the Hopelessness Scale and similar clinical ratings for a sample of 62 recent suicide attempters. Studying a sample of 384 suicide attempters, Beck, Kovacs, & Weissman (1975) found the Hopelessness Scale to correlate .66 with independent clinical ratings of hopelessness. Other clinical criteria have also been employed. Dyer and Kreitman (1984) found that the Hopelessness Scale correlated .50 with indices of suicide intent, a finding that remained significant after statistically removing the influence of depression. Similar findings with predicting suicide intent have been reported elsewhere (e.g., Wetzel, Margulies, Davis, & Karam, 1980) and are summarized by Dyer and Kreitman (1984). Using clinical evaluations of suicide ideation as criteria, the Hopelessness Scale has been found to correlate at levels of .47 (Beck, Kovacs, & Weissman, 1979) and .28 (Holden, Mendonca, & Mazmanian, 1985) for samples of hospitalized suicide ideators (N = 90 and 50, respectively).

From a factor-analytic perspective, results appear equivocal. The authors, using an eigenvalue-one criterion, reported a three-component solution for the Hopelessness Scale items. Nekanda-Trepka, Bishop, and Blackburn (1983), again based on eigenvalues greater than unity, found a five-factor solution. Finally, Mendonca et al. (1983), although also finding five eigenvalues exceeding unity, have argued that the Hopelessness Scale is essentially unidimensional.

Critique

The development of the Hopelessness Scale represents significant theoretical and practical advancement for the understanding and prediction of suicidality. Theoretically, hopelessness appears as a promising candidate in the prediction of future suicidal behavior (Petrie & Chamberlain, 1985). Practically, the Hopelessness Scale also appears related to suicidal behavior; however, current information regarding the instrument has yet to be fully developed.

On the negative side, normative data for all relevant diagnostic groups need to be collected and consolidated, demographic effects should be further explored, and the scale's factor structure requires more study. In addition, the influence of response styles (e.g., social desirability) on the scale needs to be clarified (Holden & Mendonca, 1984). Ideally, prospective studies with the scale should also be undertaken.

On the positive side, the Hopelessness Scale has a great deal of merit. It shows high internal consistency and demonstrates convergence with relevant clinical ratings. Furthermore, scale scores are associated with important aspects of depression and suicidal behavior. Thus, although users of the scale must integrate other relevant data, the Hopelessness Scale appears to have a great deal of research and clinical utility.

References

Beck, A. T., Kovacs, M., & Weissman, A. (1975). Hopelessness and suicidal behavior: An overview. *Journal of the American Medical Association, 234,* 1146-1149.

Beck, A. T., Kovacs, M., & Weissman, A. (1979). Assessment of suicidal intention: The Scale for Suicide Ideation. *Journal of Consulting and Clinical Psychology, 47,* 343-352.

Beck, A. T., Steer, R. A., & Shaw, B. F. (1984). Hopelessness in alcohol- and heroin-dependent women. *Journal of Clinical Psychology, 40,* 602-606.

Beck, A. T., Ward, C. H., Mendelson, M., Mock, J., & Erbaugh, J. (1961). An inventory for measuring depression. *Archives of General Psychiatry, 4,* 561-571.

Beck, A. T., Weissman, A., Lester, D., & Trexler, L. (1974). The measurement of pessimism: The Hopelessness Scale. *Journal of Consulting and Clinical Psychology, 42,* 861-865.

Cropley, A. J., & Weckowicz, T. E. (1966). The dimensionality of clinical depression. *Australian Journal of Psychology, 18*, 18-25.
Durham, T. W. (1982). Norms, reliability, and item analysis of the Hopelessness Scale in general psychiatric, forensic psychiatric, and college populations. *Journal of Clinical Psychology, 38*, 597-600.
Dyer, J. A. T., & Kreitman, N. (1984). Hopelessness, depression and suicidal intent in parasuicide. *British Journal of Psychiatry, 144*, 127-133.
Greene, S. M. (1981). Levels of measured hopelessness in the general population. *British Journal of Clinical Psychology, 20*, 11-14.
Holden, R. R., & Mendonca, J. D. (1984). Hopelessness, social desirability, and suicidal behavior: A need for conceptual and empirical disentanglement. *Journal of Clinical Psychology, 40*, 1342-1345.
Holden, R. R., Mendonca, J. D., & Mazmanian, D. (1985). Relation of response set to observed suicide intent. *Canadian Journal of Behavioural Science, 17*, 359-368.
Kazdin, A. E., French, N. H., Unis, A. S., Esveldt-Dawson, K., & Sherick, R. B. (1983). Hopelessness, depression, and suicidal intent among psychiatrically disturbed inpatient children. *Journal of Consulting and Clinical Psychology, 51*, 504-510.
Mendonca, J. D., Holden, R. R., Mazmanian, D., & Dolan, J. (1983). The influence of response style on the Beck Hopelessness Scale. *Canadian Journal of Behavioural Science, 15*, 237-247.
Minkoff, K., Bergman, E., Beck, A. T., & Beck, R. (1973). Hopelessness, depression, and attempted suicide. *American Journal of Psychiatry, 130*, 455-459.
Nekanda-Trepka, C. J. S., Bishop, S., & Blackburn, I. M. (1983). Hopelessness and depression. *British Journal of Clinical Psychology, 22*, 49-60.
Petrie, K., & Chamberlain, K. (1985). The predictive validity of the Zung Index of Potential Suicide. *Journal of Personality Assessment, 49*, 100-102.
Shaw, B. F., Vallis, T. M., & McCabe, S. B. (1985). The assessment of the severity and symptom patterns in depression. In E. E. Beckham & W. R. Leber (Eds.), *Handbook of depression: Treatment, assessment, and research* (pp. 372-407). Homewood, IL: Dorsey Press.
Wetzel, R. D., Margulies, T., Davis, R., & Karam, E. (1980). Hopelessness, depression, and suicide intent. *Journal of Clinical Psychiatry, 41*, 159-160.
Zamble, E., Porporino, F., & Kalotay, J. (1984). *An analysis of coping behaviour in prison inmates* (Programs Branch User Report 1984-77). Ottawa, Canada: Ministry of the Solicitor General of Canada.

Dina Anselmi, Ph.D.
Assistant Professor of Psychology, Trinity College, Hartford, Connecticut.

THE HOUSTON TEST FOR LANGUAGE DEVELOPMENT
Margaret C. Crabtree. Chicago, Illinois: Stoelting Company.

Introduction

The revised Houston Test for Language Development (HTLD) assesses communicative development in infants and young children. The test serves as a general measure of linguistic performance, measuring various prelinguistic (e.g., babbling, gestures) and linguistic (e.g., vocabulary, syntax) skills as well as more general cognitive abilities (e.g., counting, geometric design). A child's score is based on both direct observation and the elicitation of specific behaviors. The HTLD evaluates language functioning on four categories: Self-Talk, Auditory Comprehension, Nonverbal Communication, and Oral Communication. Clinical assessment of specific language problems such as hyperactivity, echolalia, and perseveration are possible from observing a child's performance on the various test items.

The HTLD was devised by Margaret Crabtree in two parts (Crabtree, 1957, 1958, 1963). The first part, published in 1958, was designed to evaluate the language development of children between the ages of 6 months and 3 years. It was one of the earliest tests developed to measure the communication skills of preverbal children. The second part, published in 1963, focused on children between the ages of 3-6 and contained measures of linguistic and cognitive ability such as vocabulary, drawing, and counting. The 1978 revised edition combines the items from Parts 1 and 2. The age ranges were modified to reflect different stages of language development. The revised version contains an Infant Test to evaluate communicative ability between birth and 18 months and a Preschool Test to assess language development from ages 2 to 6. Overlapping questions from the previous forms were deleted and new questions were added to reflect the different ages tested in the two scales.

The Infant Scale is divided into three age-grouped behaviors. For children 0-6 months of age, nine behaviors are tested: smiling, cooing, babbling, listening, blowing bubbles, laughing, volume control, squealing, and grunting. In the 6-12 month category, nine different behaviors are evaluated: the holding out of arms, vocalizing syllables, repeating syllables, imitating sounds, using reflexive jargon, clapping, waving, using at least two words, and following a command. At the 12-18 month level, six additional behaviors are assessed: using conversational jargon, pointing, using at least 10 words, identifying at least three parts of the body, naming at least one picture, and naming and pointing to at least five pictures.

For the measurement of certain behaviors, the examiner (or a familiar adult) may elicit the specific response. In other cases, the child is observed during the entire session and the appropriate spontaneous expression is scored. The examiner chooses items at the 6-month age range that appear appropriate for the child's developmental level. If the child fails certain items, the examiner is instructed to go to the preceding age level.

The 2-6 Year Test consists of 18 subtests, each of which measures a different aspect of linguistic/cognitive functioning. The first subtest evaluates children's ability to answer specific questions about themselves in terms of their name, sex, and age. The second section measures vocabulary knowledge of objects, actions, feelings, and colors. Responses to questions about various parts of the body make up the third subtest. Subtests four and five assess nonverbal and verbal comprehension. In the next five tests the child's spontaneous conversation in a toy-playing situation is evaluated for instances of story construction, sentence length, temporal context, syntax, and prepositions. The ability to recall numbers serially and to count a specific number of objects is measured in the next two subtests. The thirteenth, fourteenth, and fifteenth tests involve imitation of linguistic structure, prosodic patterning, and geometric designs. The final three evaluate the communication of an idea in a graphic medium (i.e., drawing), the verbal conversation that occurs during the process, and whether the child can name, describe, and imagine what he or she has drawn.

The 24 items of the Infant Scale and the 18 subtests of the Preschool Scale are also grouped into four categories to provide a more sensitive measure of a child's linguistic strengths and weaknesses. The Self Talk Category focuses on communication that is self-initiated rather than directed at others. The Auditory Comprehension Category involves the ability to process information that comes primarily from the auditory system. The Nonverbal Communication Category is related to the use of movement, gesture, or drawing to express ideas or feelings. The final category, Oral Communication, is associated with more traditional measures of linguistic ability such as vocabulary, syntax, and sentence length.

There are separate forms for scoring and recording responses for the Infant and the Preschool Scales. These forms and the necessary test materials (vocabulary cards, miniature toys, crayons, and drawing paper) are available in the test kit.

Practical Applications/Uses

The HTLD is useful in providing an assessment of general linguistic functioning for children of a wide age range. The general language behavior of a child can be compared with normative peer data (Bloom & Lahey, 1978; Young, 1984). Moynihan and Mehrabian (1978) classify the HTLD as a general measure of intellectual functioning rather than as a test of linguistic ability because it includes questions that relate to cognitive functioning.

As a diagnostic technique, the HTLD is more limited. While a child's score, especially on the four Categories of Linguistic Functioning, can be used to detect certain general language impairments, more sensitive measures and clinical expertise would be necessary to pinpoint a specific problem. The test has research value and has been used in several studies as a screening device for identifying samples of language-impaired (Warren, McQuarter, & Rogers-Warren, 1984;

Leonard, Bolders, & Miller, 1976) or mentally retarded (Perozzi, 1973) children.

According to the manual, the examiner does not need special training to administer the HTLD. The manual does recommend, however, that the scales be administered by an individual who has a basic knowledge of testing procedures and familiarity with the behaviors of young children as well as a thorough understanding of all the test items. This latter point is particularly important because the test requires the examiner to make a number of subjective judgments in determining how to elicit specific test responses from a child. The manual must be read very carefully in order to comprehend all the different testing procedures. In addition, any valid interpretation of the clinical observations would need to be conducted by a trained specialist, as many language disorders are difficult to diagnose.

The physical test arrangements will vary depending on the age of the child. For younger infants, a baby bed or playpen may be necessary for testing, whereas for older infants and preschool children, size-appropriate furniture or the floor can be used. The test must be administered individually, and the time required depends on the skill of the examiner and the cooperation and age of the child. The Infant Scale should take 20-30 minutes and the Preschool Scale 30-40 minutes to administer.

The revised manual includes information on scoring and interpretation. For some items, scoring is relatively simple. However, many of the items involve some degree of subjective evaluation, which is not necessarily clear from the scoring instructions presented in the manual. For example, in the Gesture subtest of the Preschool Scale it is difficult to know how to score the different actions that the child must perform. Several measures ask the child to give a verbal response that could be easily misinterpreted if he or she does not articulate or share the same dialect or speech style as the examiner. This issue is especially relevant for assessing items on the Preschool Scale, which are based on a child's spontaneous discourse. Samples of young children's conversations are often quite difficult to record in a test situation. (The use of a tape recorder could alleviate this problem.) There is also no method for establishing examiner reliability, particularly on the items that involve judgments of a subjective nature.

For each test (Infant and Preschool), a score for Communication Age and Level of Functioning is obtained. Clinical observations based on test performance can also be recorded, although the manual does not give specific guidelines for what information to use in forming clinical judgments.

Communication Age for the Infant Scale is calculated by summing the correct responses for each age level. These numbers are multiplied by the item value to determine the score in months at each age. An infant's Communication Age represents all the scores totaled together. An infant's level of functioning is determined by the scores from the Infant Scale according to their category type. A score three months above age level is considered a strength, while a score three months below may be cause for concern.

Communication Age for the Preschool Scale is determined by the number of items passed at each age level multiplied by the appropriate item value. Each value is totaled to form a score that indicates a child's Communication Age in years and months. Scores on the Level of Functioning categories are determined by calculating the number of items passed at the appropriate age norms for each category type. An area of strength or weakness is defined as one in which 50% or more of the items are passed above or below the norm average.

The only information given about norms in the revised edition is that the sample used consisted of 370 Standard-American-English-speaking children residing in both rural and urban areas. Norm placement on any item was calculated by the differences in the percentage of children passing at a specific age level, a year below, and a year above.

Scores from the Infant Scale (at least up to 12 months) may be considered relatively culture free, as many of the items evaluate preverbal rather than verbal skills. A child's failure on most of these items could indicate a problem that would exist apart from any specific language. Scores from the Preschool Scale should not be considered culture free, as the norms were based only on Standard-English-speaking children. Therefore, extreme caution must be observed when interpreting the test results of any child whose language environment is different. This is especially true for the subtest items that relate to the spontaneous connected discourse.

In interpreting scores, the manual notes that the subtest scores show greater variation than the total score. A more meaningful analysis of a child's linguistic ability may be obtained from interpreting the categories of Self Talk, Auditory Comprehension, Nonverbal Communication, and Oral Communication. In determining the nature of a specific language problem, the case studies presented in the manual would be only minimally useful even for a trained language specialist.

Technical Aspects

Virtually no validity data are available for the HTLD. The only validity study reported was conducted by Battin (1965), who administered the HTLD and the Verbal Language Development Scale to 21 children and did not find a significant difference between the scores of the two tests. However, this measure of concurrent validity is not particularly useful without a specific estimate of the correlation between the two measures. No other validity measures were reported in either the manual or the research literature.

Reliability for the HTLD was established using a test-retest procedure on 25 children between the ages of 6 months and 6 years. The HTLD was given to these children twice within a one-week interval. The correlational coefficient between the test scores was .98, with a standard error of 2 and a standard deviation of 10 (Crabtree, 1978). The problem with this measure of reliability is that it fails to provide specific information about the correlation coefficient for each specific age range. Without those values, one cannot judge whether the test is reliable for different ages, especially for infants who traditionally are quite variable in responding across different time points.

Critique

The HTLD is primarily a measure of linguistic performance that has the potential for providing a language specialist with general age-appropriate information about certain language problems. It consists of items that assess a variety of language skills ranging from vocabulary, sentence length, syntax, and verbal comprehension. The scales are relatively easy to administer if the manual is read carefully. The time required to conduct the test is reasonable for the attention span of infants and young children.

However, the problems associated with using the HTLD in its present form are numerous. Many of the technical problems of administration and interpretation have already been mentioned. The most serious problem is the lack of validity data. There is no way of determining if the items being tested are the best measures of linguistic functioning or impairment. Although many of the items used on the Preschool Scale are similar to those used in other language tests, this does not guarantee that the specific ways these skills are measured in the HTLD are appropriate. An even more significant problem exists with the Infant Scale. It is not obvious from a review of the test why the different prelinguistic or nonlinguistic items (e.g., grunting, waving, or even smiling) should be considered measures that relate to language development. In fact, the precise relationship between prelinguistic and linguistic behaviors is a current issue of debate in the language development literature. Without specific estimates of predictive, construct, and concurrent validity, the supporting case for the HTLD is weak.

As no information on subtest variability is presented, it is impossible to decide how to use the subtest scores. While the Level of Functioning Categories provide a more detailed composite view, the HTLD does not permit the differentiation of expressive and receptive language skills. This distinction can be quite important in determining an appropriate intervention program if a language problem is suspected. More specific norms, as given in the Bayley Scales of Infant Development, and clearer reliability estimates on a larger age sample are necessary.

In its present state, the HTLD is of limited value in assessing a child's level of language processing. Some of the weaknesses are endemic to general language development measures (e.g., difficulty in precisely pinpointing a complex language impairment). Other problems are specific to the HTLD (e.g., lack of sufficient validity, reliability, and normative data) and need to be corrected in order for the test to be considered a viable measure of young children's communicative functioning.

References

Battin, R. (1965). A comparison of three tests of language development in the USA. *De Therapia Vocis et Loquelae*, Vol. 1, Vienna.

Bayley, N. (1969). *Bayley Scales of Infant Development*. San Antonio: The Psychological Corporation.

Bloom, L., & Lahey, M. (1978). *Language development and language disorders*. New York: John Wiley & Sons.

Crabtree, M. C. (1957). *The construction and trial study of a language development test for children*. Unpublished doctoral dissertation, University of Houston.

Crabtree, M. C. (1958). *The Houston Test for Language Development*. Houston: The Houston Test Company.

Crabtree, M. C. (1963). *The Houston Test for Language Development, Part II*. Houston: The Houston Test Company.

Crabtree, M. C. (1978). *The Houston Test for Language Development, Revised Edition*. Chicago: Stoelting Co.

Leonard, L. B., Bolders, J. G., & Miller, J. A. (1978). Examination of semantic relations reflected in language usage of normal and language-disordered children. *Journal of Speech and Hearing Research, 19,* 371-392.

Moynihan, C., & Mehrabian, A. (1978). Measures of language skills for 2-year-old to 7-year-old children. *Genetic Psychology Monographs, 98,* 3-49.

Perozzi, J. A. (1973). Services provided for mentally retarded by school clinicians—Preliminary survey. *Journal of Communication Disorders, 6,* 213-218.

Warren, S. F., McQuarter, R. J., & Rogers-Warren, A. K. (1984). The effects of mands and models on the speech of unresponsive language-delayed preschool children. *Journal of Speech and Hearing Disorders, 49,* 43-52.

Young, E. C. (1984). A review of general language performance tests for pre-school children. *Topics in Early Childhood Special Education. 4(2),* 100-111.

Gene Schwarting, Ph.D.
Project Director, Preschool Handicapped Program, Omaha Public Schools, Omaha, Nebraska.

HOWELL PREKINDERGARTEN SCREENING TEST
Howell Township Schools. North Bergen, New Jersey: Book-Lab.

Introduction

The Howell Prekindergarten Screening Test (HPST) is designed for children entering kindergarten, to identify which would benefit from regular classroom placement, remedial/special education placement, or gifted/talented programs. The instrument is administered directly to the child examinees, using expendable test booklets, and may be used in a group setting.

The HPST was not developed by an individual, but rather is a product of a school system. It was sponsored by the Howell Township Schools of Howell, New Jersey, following the directive of the Board of Education. A pilot version of 100 items was developed, administered, and modified to obtain the final version of 73 items, which was administered in 1981, 1982, and 1983 within the school district.

This screening test consists of a 20-page booklet for each child and a 50-page examiner's manual (Ryan & Mead, 1984). Other materials required for administration include primary pencils, tape, oak tag strips to be used as markers, and a box of crayons for each child. The test is to be administered in four sittings of approximately 30 minutes each over a two-day period prior to kindergarten entrance. Administration requires reading aloud very basic instructions as well as the questions for each item. The test contains 21 short subtests of from one to six items. Many of these tasks involve selecting the correct picture response to an auditory stimulus. The selections measure such skills as letter and number recognition, auditory comprehension and memory, visual discrimination, vocabulary, math concepts, and so on.

Practical Applications/Uses

The HPST would appear to be fairly restricted in its usage and therefore primarily of interest to school districts in their kindergarten screening programs. However, it also would be of use to preschools and Head Start programs as a posttest, as an aid to parents in school-entrance decisions, and as a screening instrument for psychologists. As specified, it is appropriate for children of kindergarten entrance age. The age range is not specified, but would appear to be 4½ to 6 years. Due to the instrument's design, it would be inappropriate for children with visual, auditory, or physical handicaps as well as those with receptive language delays.

Administration and scoring do not appear to be difficult. Due to the population involved, it is assumed that teachers would for the most part perform these duties, although parents, volunteers, and paraprofessionals could perform these tasks. Directions for administration are very general and indicate that examiners are to rely on their own judgment in answering questions and responding to children who are not adjusting to a formal test situation (as many 4-year-olds may not). Examiner judgment is also required in deciding how to score if two responses are marked for the same item or if a mark is placed between two responses. Sample or "warm-up" items are not presented, and due to the ages of the children involved, skill in taking tests as well as the ability to use pencils and crayons will be a factor. Neither scoring templates nor computer scoring are available, requiring that the 18 pages of the booklet be scored by hand for each child. Scoring criteria are sometimes quite subjective, such as in the evaluation of drawings.

A total of 73 points are possible on the HPST (draw-a-person, which has no scoring criteria presented, is not included), with only the total number of correct responses being recorded. Scores of 52 or above are considered "very high" and the children may require challenging material in kindergarten; scores of 31-51 are considered "regular" and the children are considered prepared for kindergarten; scores of 30 or below are within the "critical region," suggesting children possibly in need of remedial services. Subtest scores are to be interpreted with caution, as cutoffs are not provided.

Technical Aspects

The norm group for the HPST consisted of 631 children from Howell Township Schools. The community is described as middle-income, suburban-rural in nature, with a heterogeneous school population. Data regarding the age, sex, and race of the children as well as parental income or occupation are not presented. Split-half reliability, using KR-21, is .88.

The manual presents statistical information on criterion-related and predictive validity. The criterion-related study involved examining the test scores of children who at the end of the kindergarten year were divided into four groups by their teachers, from those requiring special remedial programs to the "gifted." The mean HPST scores for children so categorized were significantly different, with approximately nine raw score points separating each group. However, with an interval of a school year between the two measures this should be considered a measure of predictive validity. A similar procedure was also utilized with the original pilot version of the instrument, with data also presented in the manual; however the information is of limited applicability unless the pilot version of the test is being used.

Evidence of predictive validity involves a comparison with the California Achievement Test (edition not specified—Form X, Level Y). Relationships between the HPST and the California Achievement Test with a one-year interval were .71 for reading and .68 for mathematics. With a two-year interval, the relationships were .64 for reading and .72 for mathematics.

Critique

The concept of a screening instrument for kindergarten entrance is a popular one, with many school districts performing such screening. The use of a paper-

and-pencil instrument with such a population, however, is a cause for concern. Such an instrument might work well in Howell Township, in which the mean first-grade California Achievement Test is at the mid-second-grade level, but may not be appropriate for other districts containing educationally disadvantaged children with more limited preparation for school. The impact of a lack of test-taking skills, the test's emphasis on receptive language (such as understanding "same"), the absence of practice exercises, and the minimal directions provided for the examiner exacerbate this concern. Reliability and validity appear adequate, but an explanation of the drop in N from 196 to 138 between kindergarten screening and first-grade completion would be welcome for the 1982-83 study. Also, information as to age of the children, number of subjects with preschool experience, number of kindergarten retentions, and information on parents would be appropriate. Based upon these concerns, consideration of adoption of this instrument should be thorough.

References

Ryan, J. P., & Mead, R. J. (1984). *Howell Prekindergarten Screening Test examiners manual*. North Bergen, NJ: Book-Lab.

Tiegs, E. W., & Willis, W. C. (1970). *California Achievement Test*. Monterey, CA: CTB McGraw-Hill.

Danielle R. Zinna, Ph.D.
Assistant Professor of Education, Department of Education and Counseling, Trinity College, Washington, D.C.

INDIVIDUAL PHONICS CRITERION TEST
Edward Fry. Providence, Rhode Island: Jamestown Publishers.

Introduction

The Individual Phonics Criterion Test is an individually administered, criterion-referenced survey test. This measure is designed to assist teachers in identifying those grapheme-phoneme, or letter-sound, correspondences known by their students, thus enabling the teacher to locate specific areas of phonics that need further review. Rather than present individual letters and letter combinations in isolation, graphemes are always presented in a nonsense word context. The student is required to provide a pronunciation for a listing of printed nonsense words.

The Individual Phonics Criterion Test was developed by Edward Fry, Ph.D., Professor of Education and director of the Reading Center at Rutgers University in New Brunswick, New Jersey. Dr. Fry has published numerous articles, texts, and student drill books on such topics as programmed learning, teaching machines, and methods of reading instruction, among others. Dr. Fry's specific interest in phonics is further supported by publications on the use of a diacritical marking system and the initial teaching alphabet in early reading instruction (Fry, 1965) and the development of phonics charts (Fry, 1971).

Although the individual Phonics Criterion Test was developed for use as a criterion-referenced measure, the technical information reports that students obtaining a score of approximately 6.0 on the California Achievement Test vocabulary measure score at a near-perfect level on the Individual Phonics Criterion Test. Therefore, the author maintains that useful information can be obtained from administration of this measure to any individual scoring less than 6.0 on a standardized reading vocabulary test. Test norms, which appear in a graph format, are provided. This information allows a teacher to compare performance and progress of a class or an individual student with what can be considered "typical" performance as based on performance on the California Achievement Test vocabulary measure and the Individual Phonics Criterion Test.

Because this measure has been available for only two years, revisions have not been made. Although alternate forms for non-native English speakers are not provided, the tasks included in the Individual Phonics Criterion Test could be utilized to examine knowledge of English grapheme-phoneme correspondences among non-native English speakers.

The actual test materials utilized during evaluation consist of two double-sided pages that include the student test copy, the examiner record, and the test instructions. A sheet containing documentation of technical information about test range, reliability, validity, and norming is included with the test materials.

Individual Phonics Criterion Test

The test is divided into 14 categories of grapheme-phoneme correspondences. For example, easy consonants are embedded in a nonsense word set (e.g., *tob, nud*), consonant diagraphs in another (e.g., *tham, whev*), and short vowels in a third (e.g., *fid, bot*). This framework allows the examiner to select those sounds that are in need of review. Significantly, letters are not presented in isolation, but rather in the nonsense-word context; thus, the examiner is able to evaluate the student's knowledge of letter-sound correspondences as specific letters appear in a word structure. The technique of embedding the vowels provides a much more natural task than that provided by asking the student for the short or long pronunciation of an isolated vowel grapheme.

The examiner plays an active role in the testing process by explaining the task and offering encouragement to the student as he or she attempts to sound out each nonsense word. The student is given two attempts at each word, and the test directions caution against the examiner's provision of correct pronunciation as the measure can be used in a posttest situation. Scoring of a student's responses is made on a sheet identical to the listing provided for the student. For a response to be considered correct, it is only necessary that the child provide the correct pronunciation of the target letter, not the correct pronunciation of the entire word.

Practical Applications/Uses

Any professional involved in the teaching of reading or in evaluation of the reading area will find the Individual Phonics Criterion Test useful. Notes accompanying the test indicate that it can yield useful information when administered to students scoring lower than the sixth-grade level on vocabulary subtests of group achievement tests such as the California Achievement Test. Clearly, the measure would have limited utility with young readers inexperienced with printed words. Although the test author does not provide specific reports of the test's use with visually impaired individuals, the measure could be adapted for administration in braille.

The Individual Phonics Criterion Test is an individually administered measure. The administration procedures are clear, and the examiner is provided with specific questions to clarify responses when necessary. In addition, an examiner with limited knowledge of phonic principles will find the notes about letter pronunciation to be very helpful. The actual testing time is difficult to determine. The author suggests that an individual be tested on only one or two sections per session, and it is assumed that an individual with well-developed phonic skills could complete the entire measure in less than half an hour. A student with reading difficulty would be best assessed with one or two subtests per session, however. Specific categories are easily administered apart from the total test in order to gain specific information about the student's knowledge in a particular area.

The scoring of the measure is completed quickly by hand. Each response is immediately recorded as correct or incorrect. Obtaining the raw score is easily accomplished by counting correct responses. Although the total phonics score can be utilized to provide a general idea of an individual's performance in relation to students in various grades, the most useful application of this measure is in identifying strengths and weaknesses among a group of students or within an individual. The Individual Phonics Criterion Test is a valuable source of information for the planning of future lessons and for periodic checks of a specific skill.

Technical Aspects

Because the Individual Phonics Criterion Test is best used as a criterion-referenced measure, the studies typically conducted for the determination of reliability and validity may not be required (Meskauskas, 1976). However, some limited reliability information is reported. In an administration of the Individual Phonics Criterion Test to an unspecified group of 63 first- through fourth-graders, a reliability coefficient of .94 was obtained using the Kuder-Richardson formula 21. Theoretically, the KR-21 only approximates reliability and is designed to be used only when test items are of equal difficulty (Guilford, 1956), a criterion which has not been met on the Individual Phonics Criterion Test.

Much of the validity of this test relies on its content validity. The author reports that the selection of items for inclusion on the Individual Phonics Criterion Test was based on frequency counts of phoneme-grapheme correspondences (Moore, 1951; Fry, 1964, 1977). As a result of this study, the measure was developed to include all of the common correspondences. In an attempt to establish concurrent validity, studies were conducted to examine the correlation between the total score of the Individual Phonics Criterion Test and the California Achievement Test vocabulary measure for the sample utilized in the reliability studies. The correlation between the two measures was .57.

Critique

The Individual Phonics Criterion Test provides a professional involved in the teaching or evaluation of reading with a means to identify a child's knowledge of grapheme-phoneme correspondences as they appear in nonsense words. The need for a teacher or diagnostician to have such information is certainly warranted, given results of research indicating that training in letter-sound relationships results in better decoding ability and reading achievement (Jeffrey & Samuels, 1967).

Instruction in code-breaking can employ explicit training, such as that used in the study conducted by Jeffrey and Samuels (1967), in which children were taught letter sounds in isolation. Alternatively, implicit training can be provided by presenting the phoneme-grapheme correspondences in word contexts. The implicit procedures are useful if students are presented with large numbers of words containing the target structure. The use of such procedures is further supported by research that has implicated the use of an analogy strategy in determining the pronunciation of unfamiliar words (Baron & Strawson, 1976; Glushko, 1979; Zinna, Liberman, & Shankweiler, in press).

The format of the Individual Phonics Criterion Test appears to be designed to examine a student's implicit knowledge of phoneme-grapheme correspondences. A close examination of the words included in the test reveals that several of the nonsense word items violate orthographic constraints. For example, the grapheme *v* appears in the final position of nonsense word items, but is not followed by *e* as identified in the orthographic standard documented by Venezky (1967). On other items, the letter *f* appears as a single letter in the final position, rather than as a double consonant, as in the words *cuff* and *sniff*. As a final example, the consonant combination *gh* is identified as a silent blend, yet does not appear in a context that would have been encountered by the student during experiences with printed text.

Despite these weaknesses, the Individual Phonics Criterion Test can serve as a valuable tool in determining a student's status and progress in recognizing the relationships between graphemes and phonemes. The measure is complete and examines a wide variety of grapheme-phoneme correspondences as these structures appear in nonsense word contexts.

References

Baron, J., & Strawson, C. (1976). Use of orthographic and word-specific knowledge in reading words aloud. *Journal of Experimental Psychology: Human Perception and Performance, 2,* 386-393.

Fry, E. (1964). A frequency approach to phonics. *Elementary English, 41,* 759-765.

Fry, E. (1965). *First-grade reading instruction using a diacritical marking system, the initial teaching alphabet and a basic reading system.* Unpublished manuscript, Rutgers University, New Brunswick, NJ.

Fry, E. (1971). *Ninety-nine phonics charts.* Highland Park, NJ: Dreier Educational Systems.

Fry, E. (1977). *Elementary reading instruction.* New York: McGraw-Hill.

Fry, E. (1984). *The Individual Phonics Criterion Test.* Providence, RI: Jamestown Publishers.

Glushko, R. J. (1979). The organization and activation of orthographic knowledge in reading aloud. *Journal of Experimental Psychology: Human Perception and Performance, 5,* 674-691.

Guilford, J. (1956). *Fundamental statistics in psychology and education.* New York: McGraw-Hill.

Jeffrey, W. E., & Samuels, S. J. (1967). The effect of method of reading training on initial learning and transfer. *Journal of Verbal Learning and Verbal Behavior, 6,* 354-358.

Meskauskas, J. A. (1976). Evaluation models for criterion-referenced testing: Views regarding mastery and standard testing. *Review of Educational Research, 46,* 133-158.

Moore, J. T. (1951). *Phonetic elements appearing in a 3000 word spelling vocabulary.* Unpublished doctoral dissertation, Stanford University, Palo Alto, CA.

Venezky, R. L. (1967). English orthography: Its graphical structure and its relation to sound. *Reading Research Quarterly, 2,* 75-105.

Zinna, D. R., Liberman, I. Y., & Shankweiler, D. (in press). Children's sensitivity to factors influencing vowel reading. *Reading Research Quarterly.*

Richard Colwell, Ph.D.
Professor of Music and Education, University of Illinois at Urbana-Champaign, Urbana, Illinois.

INSTRUMENT TIMBRE PREFERENCE TEST
Edwin E. Gordon. Chicago, Illinois: G.I.A. Publications.

Introduction

Edwin Gordon's Instrument Timbre Preference Test is designed to provide information to teachers, students, and parents that will be helpful in selecting a musical instrument for the student. The data from the test are to be used in aiding the teacher in the prediction of successful performance on a wind instrument by beginning music students.

The task for the examinee is to indicate the preferred timbre when two different timbres are sounded by a Moog synthesizer. Seven different timbres are used in the test, which is administered via tape. Each of the seven is paired twice with every other timbre, with each being heard once as the first item of a pair and once as the second item. Forty-two items constitute the test. The duration of the tape is 22 minutes; thus, administering the test takes about 30 minutes.

The timbres generated by the synthesizer match the timbres of musical instruments only in a general way. Gordon's rationale was to construct a test where the cultural association a student has with a particular instrument or performer is minimized. The timbres are intended to be close to those of the wind instruments of the band and orchestra. Timbre 1 is purported to be similar to that of a flute; timbre 2, the clarinet; timbre 3, the Sousaphone and French horn; timbre 4, the oboe, English horn, and bassoon; timbre 5, the trumpet and cornet; timbre 6, the trombone, baritone, and French horn; and timbre 7, the tuba and Sousaphone. No explanation is given for considering French horn timbre similar to both timbres 3 and 6.

The philosophy behind this test is that a student will be more successful on an instrument that emits a timbre pleasing to him or her. The argument is founded on the belief that the student will be more successful—not that he or she will practice more, have more fun, or show increased interest in participating in school music programs.

Edwin Gordon has had a career-long fascination with music aptitude and the prediction of success in instrumental music. The publishing of the Instrument Timbre Preference Test in 1984 represents one additional effort on his part to reduce the unknowns in instrumental music education. Gordon's Musical Aptitude Profile represented a 7-year effort to develop a music aptitude test that would provide important information to teachers, curriculum developers, parents, and students. The criterion for construct validity of the Musical Aptitude Profile was the degree of success in instrumental music after 3 years of study. Gordon believes that high scores on the profile account for about 56% of the reason for success in the study of instrumental music. He believes that intelligence might account for as little as 4%. The Instrument Timbre Preference Test was developed to further reduce the unknown variance, and the author believes that the test accounts for an additional 10% of the reasons for success in instrumental music. The test consists of one cassette tape recording, one 50-page test manual, 100 student answer sheets, which can be scored on ScanTron or by hand, seven scoring masks, and one class record sheet.

Practical Applications/Uses

As the purpose of the Instrument Timbre Preference Test is to assist teachers and parents in the selection of an instrument, there is little reason to give the test as a part of a general music program. Gordon is concerned that many students who have considerable talent are not afforded the opportunity to study an instrument in school, and he likely would argue that any testing that identified talent and any test that could provide further guidance of how one might capitalize upon that talent is fully justified in a general music program.

The data to answer questions satisfactorily about the practical use of the test, unfortunately, do not exist. For example, we have no data on the educational issues involved with encouraging nonvolunteers to enroll in instrumental music whether on appropriate or inappropriate instruments. Of practical importance to teachers is the ability to provide feedback to all students following testing. After scoring the test seven times, data for only the extreme high-scoring students and extreme low-scoring students are the only useful data from administering the test.

Gordon's data, gathered at the time the test was developed, indicate that students who were aided in the selection of their instrument by the results of this test actually attained a higher level of skill in the performance of technical exercises. The causal relationship is unclear because these same students were less interested in participating in school ensembles. The test, of course, is designed as a supplement to a music aptitude test and has limited value as a "stand alone" item. If the test results contribute 10% to the variance in performance success, Gordon's inference is that this 10% is related to a "factor" of preference for timbre and is not simply an additional part of general musical aptitude. If his inference is true, the test would be valuable in its own right and should provide information, given whatever talent the student has, that he or she would be better advised to select an instrument with the preferred timbre.

The teacher should listen to the test before administering it and be ready to answer typical student questions for a timed, aural test. The teacher reads two paragraphs of specific directions prior to playing the cassette; no other special arrangements need to be made for administering the test. With no right and wrong answers and only the need to indicate a preference for one of two tones, fourth-, fifth-, and sixth-grade students can easily complete the test; even younger students should have few problems.

The test is to be given at whatever age instrumental music instruction is begun. The author suggests this to be fourth, fifth, or sixth grade. Test data are of three types. Scores of 10, 11, and 12 for a particular timbre are favorable scores, and the student scoring 10 and above should be encouraged to select an instrument with similar timbre. Scores of 3 and above and 9 or less are ignored, as the student has no strong preference one way or the other. Scores of 0, 1, and 2 toward a timbre indicate a dislike for that sound, and thus the instrument should not be selected. One practical consideration is that the test is cumbersome to score. Having to score each test sheet seven times, using seven different templates, is time-consuming. Presumably, some test scorers will become confused and mistakenly use the same template twice.

Interpreting the test is also somewhat more complicated than tests the average teacher may be accustomed to using. For some students there will be results indicating a range of timbres to avoid and timbres to encourage. For others in the same class there will be only one indicator (a timbre to avoid or a timbre to encourage), or no useful data, as certain examinees may neither like nor dislike a particular timbre.

Technical Aspects

The technical data in the manual that are of value to the user are found in the reported test-retest reliability. After one week, reliability is reported to be about .70. Of importance, however, is the reliability of individual timbres, especially those rated high by a student and/or those rated low. The rationale of the test is based on the concept of reliability: the student must respond consistently throughout the seven parts of the test in order to score high enough or low enough for a preferred timbre to be determined. The reliability data of interest are the data from the students whose scores are to be used (2 and below and 10 and above).

Of interest is the change that occurs between grade/age levels. The data from one school cited in the manual give mean scores for each of the seven timbres for students in Grades 3 through 8. Preference in this sample appears to be age related, not reassuring information for the parent or teacher who hopes that a student will select an instrument and stick with it for a sufficient period of time to develop some useful skills.

Content validity is based on the fact that older students and music teachers can consistently relate synthesized sound to the sound of a real instrument. The experienced individual is not likely to confuse a tuba and a flute; thus, whatever value this exercise has for validity is primarily one of the ability to identify middle-range instruments with the synthetic timbre. Grouping (a) saxophone and French horn, (b) oboe, English horn, and bassoon, and (c) trombone, baritone, and French horn reduces the difficulty of the task.

Gordon is a careful worker; the development of the Instrument Timbre Preference Test took several years. To establish criterion-related validity, which is the relationship with success in instrumental music, Gordon developed and administered the test, allowed the students at least one school year to learn an instrument, and assessed their achievement in relationship to their initial timbre test scores. Results showed that students playing appropriate instruments (i.e., the preferred timbre) received consistently higher ratings on the tone quality dimension of the assessment. Dropout rate for nonvolunteers playing appropriate instruments was 80%, compared to 8% for volunteers playing appropriate instruments and 17% for volunteers playing inappropriate instruments.

The same degree of thoroughness exhibited by Gordon in the development of the Musical Aptitude Profile is not evident in the developmental steps of the Instrument Timbre Preference Test, but the test still was thought through carefully in comparison with most other music tests.

Criterion-related validity is provided by combining the scores attained by performing three etudes and comparing these combined scores of an experimental group (N = 33) and a control group (N = 47). Performance ratings on the etudes were based on the tonal, rhythm, tone quality, and expressive aspects of the students' performance with each of the three exercises sight read. A score of 120 was possible for all three exercises; the mean scores were 46.4 and 37.4, both with rather large standard deviations (20.1 and 17.1 respectively).

With no right or wrong answers the test is neither a criterion- nor a norm-referenced test. Traditional technical considerations in test construction are often not appropriate and more sophisticated techniques appropriate for this test have not been employed as of this writing.

Critique

This reviewer administered the Instrument Timbre Preference Test to a sample of the same size as that used by the test author in obtaining his initial data. This reviewer did not, however, wait a year to ascertain the attainment of the students, but rather administered the test and collected data 3 months later with respect to the instrument actually selected by the student.

Of 77 students who began instrumental music study (in one of two school systems used), only 8 selected the instrument recommended by the timbre test's results. Four students selected instruments that, by their timbre, should have been avoided. Of the eight "matches," five were for flute timbre. Possibly these students were starting on the wrong instrument, but the teachers interviewed indicated that they would rather have the student begin on a student-selected instrument (presumably an instrument the student will play in band or orchestra) than to have the benefit of a slightly higher score on a performance examination. Admittedly, many of the students used by this reviewer may drop out of the school music program, but Gordon also does not have definitive long-term drop-out data on his sample. Fifty-two percent of Gordon's experimental group discontinued study after 1 year. Precise data are not available, but a 52% drop-out rate in the first year would seem to equal or slightly exceed the norm. A 55% drop-out rate of wind players and 80% for strings during the entire public school years is thought to be about average.

Several nagging questions arose during this reviewer's investigation. Race, for example, seemed to be a factor in determining preference for the artificial sounds generated in the preference test. Blacks in this sample did not like the tuba sound and seldom preferred the other brass instruments. Teachers and college music majors taking the test never selected their major instrument, and 50% of our sample indicated a dislike for the timbre of their major.

The test manual is more a research report on the relationship of the preference test to other Gordon publications and research than it is a useful test manual. Considerable space is given over to the reporting of mean scores—something of interest to the test developer but perhaps of limited value to the classroom user. One table provides data on correlations between preference scores and scores on Gordon's Musical Aptitude Profile, and another reports the relationship of scores with the Otis-Lennon Mental Ability Test. Use of the mean score for each of the seven timbres allowed this reviewer to compute the relationships between preference and aptitude, preference and intelligence, and preference and other demographic data. Because the mean score has no meaning, the correlations presented have no meaning for the user. Gordon seems arbitrarily to have established the cutoff points of 10, 11, or 12 for preference and 0, 1, or 2 for nonpreference, the two data units of value to the test user.

In this test, as with Gordon's other work, there is little available evidence that he attempts several iterations in the development of a test; rather, his tests are constructed and research is conducted justifying their value. For example, Gordon initially selected seven timbres and did not experiment with either number or type of timbres in the pilot and subsequent testing. This is consistent with his approach to the construction of the (earlier) PMMA, where emphasis on content validity led him to retain items with low discrimination value.

The primary contribution of Edwin Gordon in constructing the Instrument Timbre Preference Test is to raise substantive questions. If long-term preference and motivation to practice an instrument are not being measured, what is? To what extent is a synthesized timbre transferable to the timbre of an instrument performed by a professional? Data exist that preferences are present and necessary when comparing a poor clarinet sound with a good one or comparing good sounds in an instrument's extreme low register with sounds characteristic of extreme high-register pitches. These preferences appear to be more important for success on an instrument than the preferences measured in this test. Presently, the results obtained from use of the Instrument Timbre Preference Test will contribute more to knowledge within the research community than to teachers, students, or parents.

References

Gordon, Edwin E. (1986). *Instrument Timbre Preference Test*. Chicago, IL: G.I.A. Publications.

Elizabeth Teas-Hester, Ph.D.
Neuropsychiatric Institute, University of California, Los Angeles, California.

INTERPERSONAL LANGUAGE SKILLS ASSESSMENT
Carolyn M. Blagden and Nancy L. McConnell. Moline, Illinois: LinguiSystems, Inc.

Introduction

The Interpersonal Language Skills Assessment (ILSA) is a test of the pragmatic behaviors of 8-to-14 year-old children while interacting with peers in a natural context. The authors suggest that the ILSA is "appropriate for any youngster experiencing difficulty with peer acceptance or with social situations requiring verbal communication" (Blagden & McConnell, 1985, p. 8). The authors add, however, that the child must meet the following prerequisites: 1) adequate hearing for normal conversation, 2) adequate vision for typical table games, 3) oral language comprehension at or above the simple sentence level, and 4) oral language production skills at or above a simple sentence level.

The test was developed by Carolyn M. Blagden, M.S., C.C.C., and Nancy L. McConnell, M.S., C.C.C. Both authors have worked with language- and learning-disordered children in public school settings. Ms. Blagden is currently the editorial manager of LinguiSystems, Inc., and Ms. McConnell is a speech-language specialist in the San Mateo City School District.

The authors created the ILSA format in an attempt "to address the need for a system which accounts for language form and complexity as well as pragmatic functioning" (Blagden & McConnell, 1985, p. 48). It was originally administered to a group of 34 normal youngsters aged 8 to 14. Eight language-disordered youngsters provided comparison information. Following this pilot study, normative data were collected based on a random sample from a large metropolitan area. The standardization sample contained 528 subjects (264 male and 264 female) at yearly age levels from 8 to 13. An attempt was made to ensure adequate representation of minority populations.

Test materials include a manual and protocols. The ILSA is meant to provide standardized information regarding specific, observable communication behaviors during the playing of a standard table game such as "SORRY." The players' conversation is recorded on tape, and the behaviors of the subject are tallied and categorized by the examiner on the ILSA test form. The eight categories—Advising/Predicting, Commending, Commenting, Criticizing, Informing, Justifying, Requesting, and Supporting—are then analyzed for "significant patterns of linguistic behaviors which may place an unnecessary burden on the listener" (Blagden & McConnell, 1985, p. 8). These patterns may be compared to the norms that represent guidelines of behavioral patterns rather than correct or incorrect behaviors.

Differentiating tallies are used to indicate Straightforward Comments (✓); Circle-Check Comments (Ⓒ) containing sarcasm, double-meaning or name-calling; Negation (⊁); or (Ⓝ) for comments under each category. Each tally is classified as a Non-Errored Comment or as an Error. Errors are further analyzed as to type: Production, Efficiency, Grammar, Semantic, or Unfinished Comment. Examples and explicit instructions are provided to aid the examiner in assigning the proper category and error types.

A summary chart on the test protocol provides information on each of the eight categories, negations, circle-checks, and errored comments for 1) number of comments, 2) percentage of total comments, 3) mean percentage of total comments, 4) percentile rank, and 5) standard score. The chart also yields a Mean Total Comments Summary Figure. Error types are also summarized for 1) number, 2) percentage of total, 3) mean of total, and 4) total of all error types. These scores can be plotted on two profiles, also found on the protocol. One profile indicates percentile rank, and the other indicates the standard score. Standard scores for this test have a mean of 50 and a standard deviation of 10.

These profiles are meant to provide a means for observing patterns of interaction that may be "in need of refinement or change in order to enable a youngster to convey his thoughts, intentions, or suggestions without alienating himself from his peers" (Blagden & McConnell, 1985, p. 75). The authors believe that behaviors observed during the ILSA are a reflection of a child's behavior in other contexts with peers.

Interpretation of profiles using a profile similarity index (Cattell, 1949) and Kendall tau values for category rank order for normal and language-disordered subjects is discussed. The language-learning-disordered subjects were identified as: 1) at least of average intelligence; 2) diagnosed as language disordered by a school speech-language pathologist or resource specialist; and 3) receiving language intervention in a public school setting. There were 64 subjects in this group, but no information is provided by the authors about their ages or sex.

Practical Applications/Uses

Although deficits in the social use of language by adolescents has been acknowledged previously (Gallagher & Darnton, 1978; Skarakis & Greenfield, 1982), until now few attempts have been made to identify or systematically characterize these deficits. The ILSA provides a framework for the identification and classification of language behaviors in a social setting.

The ILSA is unlike traditional tests in that it does not have a standard set of items to be administered by an examiner. It is an instrument for the systematic observation of language behaviors during the spontaneous interaction of adolescents. It is an open-ended test, limited not by a finite set of items, but by the "individual language habit patterns of the individual" (Blagden & McConnell, 1985, p. 43).

Reliability studies for the ILSA used speech pathologists as observers and raters. Speech pathologists might find this a useful instrument not only in the public schools but in mental health and hospital settings as well. Other requirements for using the test include:

1) audio recording plus direct observation;
2) a board game such as "SORRY"; and
3) group selection
   a) 3 or 4 players
   b) players should know each other
   c) players must be same sex
   d) players must be of similar overall levels of functioning, such as grade level, language ability, cultural background, and experience with playing board games.

The test should be administered in an environment in which the players will not be distracted.

Observation time of 15 minutes is thought by the authors to provide a representative cross section of the student's interpersonal language skills. It is not stated when the sample should be taken during the playing time. Information from the ILSA could be used to increase the knowledge and sensitivity of families and other professionals to the adolescent's language use and communicative style.

Technical Aspects

The nontraditional, open-ended nature of the ILSA poses special problems when reliability and validity issues are raised. The authors chose to follow statistical solutions proposed by Bales (1951) and Flanders (1966) for some analysis of the ILSA.

The normative data for the ILSA were based on a random sample of 528 subjects, and all subjects came from the same metropolitan area. No attempt was made by the authors to obtain a representative national sample. Subjects were placed in one of six age groups from 8 through 13. There was a total of 264 males and 264 females. An attempt was made to ensure that minority populations were adequately represented. No description is provided about whether these subjects were screened for language-learning disabilities, about their intelligence, or about their primary language.

The authors determined that the percent of time of category use was more important than the actual number of times a category was used. Mean percents and standard deviations by Category, Negations, Circle-Checks, and Errored Comments were computed. Also computed were the means and standard deviations for the total comments per age group. Scores are reported as percentiles and as standard scores. Standard scores have a mean of 50 and a standard deviation of 10.

The only reliability testing done for the ILSA was interrater reliability for scoring a language sample that had been transcribed and previously tallied by the authors. The raters were given special in-service sessions covering the "language model on which the ILSA is based" (Blagden & McConnell, 1985, p. 47), category definitions, tallying rules, and practice tallying. No information regarding the language model is provided in the current ILSA manual. Reliability using Scott's method (1955) was established for interrater agreement for tallying. No reliability was obtained for observing and transcribing the language sample, a variable that could affect the application of the tallies themselves.

Additionally, no attempt was made by the authors to determine test-retest reliability. It is not known whether a child's profile for language use would remain relatively constant from one time to the next, given the same partners and same board game. If the ILSA is to be a reliable tool for determining change in a social language use, minimal testing of reliability would appear to be necessary. At present, no evidence has been presented by the authors to indicate that the ILSA accurately and consistently provides a true profile of social language use.

The validity of the ILSA was tested by "comparing the language performances of a randomly selected group of subjects from the normative population with that of a group of 64 subjects previously diagnosed as having language-learning disorders" (Blagden & McConnell, 1985, p. 49). T-test comparisons yielded significant differences between groups.

Comparisons were also made of the profiles of normal and LLD subjects using Cattell's (1949) profile similarity index and Kendall's tau statistic (1948).

A larger, unanswered issue still remains about the content and construct validity of the ILSA.

Critique

Ms. Blagden and Ms. McConnell are to be commended for their efforts to develop an instrument to measure the use of language in a social context. The ILSA's strength is that it allows the user to quantify categories of pragmatic use during game-playing and to reveal a profile of pragmatic style. This descriptive information should be helpful to speech language pathologists in developing treatment strategies and goals. In addition, it should make the professional more aware of the pragmatic style the child employs in other social contexts.

The pragmatics of game-playing are not the same as those employed when asking someone for a date, requesting an increase in allowance, or just talking with a friend. Each of these situations requires a different pragmatic awareness and language use, and therein lies one limitation of the present instrument.

The ILSA has obvious potential value as a tool to evaluate pragmatic style. The authors should be encouraged to expand the normative sample to include a wider geographic area and to probe cultural differences more extensively. More rigorous reliability and validity studies should also be undertaken.

References

Bales, R. F. (1951). Some statistical problems in small group research. *Journal of the American Statistical Association, 46,* 311-322.

Blagden, C., & McConnell, N. (1985). *Interpersonal Language Skills Assessment manual.* Moline, IL: LinguiSystems, Inc.

Cattell, R. B. (1949). r_p and other coefficients of pattern similarity. *Psychometrika, 14,* 279-298.

Flanders, N. (1966). *Interaction analysis in the classroom.* Ann Arbor: University of Michigan Press.

Gallagher, T., & Darnton, B. (1978). Conversational aspects of the speech of language-disordered children: Revision behaviors. *Journal of Speech and Hearing Research, 21,* 118-135.

Kendall, M. G. (1948). *Rank correlation methods.* London: Griffin.

Scott, W. A. (1955). Reliability of content analysis: The case of nominal scale coding. *The Public Opinion Quarterly, 19*(3), 321-325.

Skarakis, E., & Greenfield, P. (1982). The role of new and old information in the verbal expression of language-disabled children. *Journal of Speech and Hearing Research, 25*(3), 462-467.

Robert J. Drummond, Ph.D.
Program Leader for Counselor Education, University of North Florida, Jacksonville, Florida.

JESNESS BEHAVIOR CHECKLIST
Carl F. Jesness. Palo Alto, California: Consulting Psycholgists Press, Inc.

Introduction

The Jesness Behavior Checklist (JBC) is a behavioral checklist used to assess dimensions of noncognitive and nonintellectual social behavior. There are two forms, an Observer Form and a Self-Appraisal Form. The scale was originally developed for use with delinquents in an institutional setting, but has been modified to be used with individuals across different age levels and settings.

Carl F. Jesness, author of the JBC, is the research manager for the Department of Youth Authority for the California Youth and Adult Correction Agency. The JBC was initially developed in 1960 as a part of a study of institutionalized delinquents. The scale was designed to be used to rate the behavior of youth by teachers and youth counselors. The items were developed using the critical incident technique. Two hundred twenty-seven items were written from 15,000 descriptions of behavior incidents; cluster analysis and factor analytic techniques refined their placement. The 40 items with the greatest predictive and discriminating power were selected. Another 40 items were added based on the literature identifying behavior postulated as (a) necessary for success of delinquents when they were on parole or (b) important for job-seeking or job-keeping skills. The Self-Appraisal Form was written to enable the JBC to be used in helping youth plan and contract for behavior change.

The JBC contains 80 items and measures 14 bipolar factors. Eleven scales are based on the factor and cluster analyses that have been performed on the test. The fourteen scales follow:

1. Unobtrusiveness vs. Obtrusiveness (8 items)
2. Friendliness vs. Hostility (5 items)
3. Responsibility vs. Irresponsibility (9 items)
4. Considerateness vs. Inconsiderateness (7 items)
5. Independence vs. Dependence (5 items)
6. Rapport vs. Alienation (5 items)
7. Enthusiasm vs. Depression (5 items)
8. Sociability vs. Poor Peer Relations (4 items)
9. Conformity vs. Non-Conformity (7 items)
10. Calmness vs. Anxiousness (6 items)
11. Effective Communication vs. Inarticulateness (5 items)
12. Insight vs. Unawareness and Indecisiveness (6 items)
13. Social Control vs. Attention Seeking (4 items)
14. Anger Control vs. Hypersensitivity (4 items)

The Conformity scale was based on a priori considerations. The first and second factor were split on the basis of item content into four scales. The Unobtrusive and Friendliness items were generated from factor 1, the Responsibility and Considerateness items from factor 2.

As mentioned, there are two forms. The blue Observer Form is for an observer to rate the behavior of a person on a 5-point scale, ranging from "very often" to "almost never." The rater is asked to evaluate 80 behaviors. The four-page booklet provides instructions and required demographic information on the first page and the items, arranged in double columns, on the second and third pages. The Self-Appraisal Form is orange and contains the same items, rewritten to read usually "I get . . . I look . . . I make" and so on. This form has the same format as the Observer Form.

The ratings are recorded in the test booklet rather than on special answer sheets. A profile sheet is available to translate the raw scores into T-scores and percentile ranks, so a graphic depiction of the scores can be made.

Practical Applications/Uses

Psychologists and counselors can use the JBC as a systematic way of recording their observations of the social behavior of their clients or students. The data of observer and client can be compared for discrepancies. The form can be a starting point for initiating behavior contracts or plans for behavior change. The instrument also has value as a research tool.

The checklist is easy to administer and does not require any special training. However, the raters must have had the opportunity to observe the person being rated over time and in different contexts in order for the observations to be meaningful. Verbal interaction with the client is essential for the rater to check the items on Factor 12 (Insight). Jesness states: "Depending upon the frequency of contacts, the number of subjects, and the number of hours during which the observer has had a chance to observe the subject, from one to four weeks of time will usually be needed before a valid rating can be provided" (1984, p. 10). The JBC can be completed by a rater in 10 to 20 minutes and the self-appraisal form can be completed in 20-25 minutes.

There are hand-scoring templates available for the JBC as well as computer scoring services. The computer program can be used to score the Self-Appraisal and Observer forms and superimpose them on the same profile, as well as give additional scores on five scales: 1) Self-Observer Distance (an index indicating the distance between the subject's self-ratings and those of the observer); 2) Self-Observer Correlation (the degree of similarity in the shape of the self-rated and observer-rated profiles); 3) Self-Observer Relative Position (the extent to which the subject's overall self-appraisal is more positive or more negative than that of the observer's); 4) Observer Rating (the average observer ratings of the 14 factors); and 5) the overall Self-Rating (the subject's average on the 14 scales).

Interpretation is based on objective scores. The JBC norms are based on a delinquent population of 1,879 males and 235 females. (Norms are not provided for any other type of group.) The scales are discussed, but very little information is included in the manual on using and interpreting the scale. There are no case studies or illustrative profiles provided. Whereas a wide variety of individuals could complete the ratings on an individual, it would take a trained counselor or psychologist to interpret the results.

Technical Aspects

Validity of the JBC is examined by comparing the correlations between different raters across the 14 factors. The raters' observations are also compared with subjects' self-appraisal. The correlation between self-ratings and observer ratings range from a low of .10 on Independence to a high of .45 on Responsibility. Jesness also reports studies of the predictive validity of the instrument. He found scores on Anger Control, Unobtrusiveness, and Conformity to be related to subsequent arrests.

Jesness reports the coefficients of stability and test-retest reliability for 66 youths after an average of seven months. The composite observer scores range from a low of .09 on Insight to a high of .51 on Conformity. The median coefficient was .41. Stability coefficients for the Self-Appraisal Form range from −.05 for Insight to .58 for Considerateness.

The author also presents the interreliability of the scale based on the ratings obtained by 48 raters of 122 youth. The coefficients range from a low of .63 on Conformity to a high of .80 on Responsibility. Butt (1978), in her review of the JBC, questions the "heteromethod-heterotrait" technique of assessing validity of the scale, in which each observer rating or observer and self-rating can be considered a different method. She feels this is poor evidence of the convergent-discriminant validation. Butt concludes that the checklist has potential but needs more work. The JBC she feels, has too many ill-defined scales with too few items.

Megargee (1978) feels that there should be more evidence of the validity of the scale, especially of the criterion-referenced type. He suggested that Anger Control and Social Control could be correlated with the number of times a youth was seen fighting or making hostile remarks to others in class or therapeutic environments. Megargee concludes that the Jesness Behavior Check List is designed to fill an important gap in the array of assessment devices, but considerable additional work needs to be done on the standardizing of the instrument and determining its reliability and validity (1978, p. 594).

Critique

This reviewer has used the JBC with juvenile offenders and correctional workers when evaluating a correctional environment utilizing Reality Therapy as a treatment modality. Although the staff felt they wanted the information contained in the JBC to help them assess the youths, they disliked using the scale because of the number of ratings they had to make and the number of youths they had to rate. Although Jesness states that the behaviors are observable and do not involve inference, not all the items are of this type. The scale also uses sex-biased language ("his" rather than "his or her"). Youths also had low tolerance and sometimes poor reading comprehension and reacted negatively to the large pool of items. The JBC vocabulary needs to be simplified and the verbal complexity reduced.

This reviewer feels that anyone adapting the instrument to a setting other than correctional facilities would need to be very cautious about using and interpreting the results, and questions whether the items primarily generated from critical incidents and literature on delinquents would be generalizable to other groups. A test should show evidence that it is valid and reliable in the contexts in which it is to be used. The JBC may be of value to skilled clinicians, for it presents a frame of reference for the client to study different perceptions of his or her social behavior and thus facilitates planning. However, there needs to be additional developmental work done on the instrument even if it is used only to assess delinquents.

References

Jesness, C. F. (1984). *Jesness Behavior Check List*. Palo Alto, CA: Consulting Psychologists Press.

Butt, D. S. (1978). Review of Jesness Behavior Check List. In O. K. Buros (Ed.), *The eighth mental measurements yearbook* (pp. 874-875). Highland Park, NJ: The Gryphon Press.

Megargee, E. I. (1978). Review of Jesness Behavior Check List. In O. K. Buros (Ed.). *The eighth mental measurements yearbook* (pp. 875-876). Highland Park, NJ: The Gryphon Press.

Carol A. Gray, Ph.D.
Associate Professor of Educational Psychology, University of Washington, Seattle, Washington.

JOSEPH PRE-SCHOOL AND PRIMARY SELF-CONCEPT SCREENING TEST
Jack Joseph. Chicago, Illinois: Stoelting Company.

Introduction

The Joseph Pre-School and Primary Self-Concept Screening Test (JPPSST) was originally developed to meet the needs of a psychoeducational screening program aimed at identifying high-risk preschoolers. Joseph believes that self-concept information is critical to a predictive outcome model, yet traditional screening batteries provide little adequate information for the psychologist/educator. In particular, he implicates self-concept as a key factor in how well a youngster copes with complex cognitive as well as social demands of school. He defines self-concept as "the way an individual perceives himself, his behaviors, how others view him, and the feelings of personal worth and satisfaction that are attached to these perceptions" (Joseph, 1979, p. 1). The JPPSST measures two primary and three secondary dimensions of self-concept in the preschool and primary age child. In its present form it is suitable for use with both boys and girls from 3.6 to 9.11 years of age.

Jack Joseph has an extensive background in education, having received his undergraduate degree from Northern Illinois University in mathematics and an M.S. from Western Illinois University in school psychology. At present he is working on his doctorate in educational psychology at Loyola University in Chicago. Joseph is currently Director of Special Education with the Skokie (Illinois) Schools, having previously worked as a school psychologist. His interest in early assessment has continued, and he reports that his most recent work has focused on examining the predictive validity of the JPPSST.

In the introductory comments in the manual, Joseph emphasizes that the JPPSST was developed from a theoretical conceptualization drawing heavily upon the work of Rogers (1951) and Coopersmith (1959, 1967). The author reports that the actual test items were selected on the basis of rational face validity, reflecting his previously mentioned five self-concept dimensions. Item selection was also constrained by the test-taking limits of very young children, their restricted expressive language ability, and their short attention spans, which set practical limits on the type of questions and responses that are reasonable in the target age range.

The first step in test development was to decide how best to elicit responses that were reflective of a child's self-concept. Joseph identified a number of situations that could theoretically be used to evoke self-concept reports. In order to get a sense of how young children would pictorially represent some of these situations (e.g., a "bad" girl or boy and a "good" girl or boy), 1,120 drawings were collected from first and second graders, along with teachers' transcripts of the children's interpretations. The final result is a grouping of 15 situations/items, with accompanying pictures representing the self-concept dimensions under study. The drawings used for the test itself are simple black-and-white line sketches that are said to capture the flavor of the samples done by the children. Because the test uses pictorial representations with a minimum of verbal instructions and asks the child to do no more than draw and point, it can be used with children of limited language capabilities.

As mentioned, the JPPSST is built on a five-dimension model of self-concept. The five dimensions represented in the final version of the test are described as follows:

1. *Significance*—our perception of how others value us;
2. *Competence*—the extent to which we feel able to master the challenges we face day by day;
3. *Power*—our perception of the extent to which we are in control of events surrounding us;
4. *General Evaluative Contentment*—satisfaction with our world as it exists;
5. *Virtue*—our perception of the extent to which we are "moral" people.

Joseph points out that these dimensions are not independent of one another, nor should they be weighted equally in evaluating a child's self-concept. This caveat has some serious implications for scoring and interpretation, which will be discussed in later sections of this review.

The test itself comes in a sturdy cardboard box and includes a manual, a packet of stimulus drawings (including both a boys' and a girls' set), a set of Identity Reference Drawing (IRD) forms for both boys and girls, and a package of Individual Record Forms. In addition, the examiner should have a clipboard and some sort of a bookstand. The stimulus drawings are plasticized and should hold up pretty well, even with sticky little fingers.

The JPPSST is an individually administered test; according to the manual, it should take from 5 to 7 minutes per child under normal conditions. The first part of the test exercise, the IRD form, is a line drawing of a gender-appropriate figure with a blank face. The child is asked to draw his or her own face in the blank, the purpose being to remind the child that the questions are about himself or herself. The balance of the test session is based on the 15 self-concept items. For each of the items there is a pair of pictures (there are gender-appropriate picture sets), one picture representing a negative self-concept situation and the other representing a positive self-concept situation. The child is first shown the pair of pictures and then is asked by the examiner to indicate, by pointing, which is the most like him- or herself. For example, one pair shows a picture of a clean boy or girl on one card and a dirty boy or girl on the other. The examiner asks the child to point to the picture that "is most like you." (Three items are exceptions to this procedure, either changing the referent or using no stimulus card.) After the child has pointed to one of the cards, the examiner can record the response directly on the Individual Record Form.

Practical Applications/Uses

The JPPSST manual claims that there are five potential uses for the test:

1. Quick screening to identify high risk for learning and/or adjustment problems;

2. A diagnostic tool yielding social-emotional information, as well as identifying possible cognitive, experiential, or receptive language deficits;
3. An evaluation instrument for assessing the outcomes of educational programs in the target age range;
4. A method of conducting personality assessments;
5. A research instrument (Joseph, 1979, p. 9).

This is an instrument that can be used as part of a general screening battery. There are few, if any, existing tests that yield information about the self-concept of the preschool or primary-aged child (Hughes, 1985), thus making this a one-of-a-kind instrument. However, there is no sound evidence to support using the JPPSST diagnostically or as a method of personality assessment. But as part of a screening battery, the speed and ease of administration of the JPPSST is a real advantage.

If scoring is held to a straightforward, quantitative computation of the Global Self-Concept Score, then both administration and scoring can be completed by a trained paraprofessional. Any applications beyond this should be limited to professionals with adequate training and experience to understand the qualitative aspects of the instrument (e.g., psychologists, psychiatrists, counselors). There is far too great a potential for abuse if it is used as a quick personality assessment by inadequately trained individuals.

The JPPSST manual suggests that it can be used for children from 3.6 years to 9.11 years of age. At the youngest age range it is likely that some of the children will not understand the instructions or the expectations of the examiner, and the examiner should be alert to this possibility. At the upper age range—children nearing 10 years of age—the materials and questions may prove to be overly simplistic and, as the author points out, social desirability begins to play a significant role. From a practical point of view, this test is most useful with the prekindergarten through early elementary-aged child.

There are limitations to the usefulness of the JPPSST with some special populations. Obviously, children with visual deficits cannot respond to the stimulus materials. A subtler, but equally limiting, factor is the choice of situations depicted on the cards. There are some that are transparently culturally biased. The content of the pictures and the norming of the responses were based on two groups (N = 112 & N = 1245) of predominantly white children (91%).

Even though there is attention paid to the urban/rural distinction, the test items were developed based on data from children from only one state (Illinois) and a somewhat limited range of racial and cultural groups. The test items appear to represent conventional, white, middle-class values, and this fact should be considered before using the test with any other cultural groups (e.g., Native American, Hispanic, Asian, or children from chronically economically disadvantaged homes).

Scoring is done using the Individual Record Form provided in the test materials. Each of the 15 items is scored from zero to two points as follows: Positive Self-Concept = 2 points; Ambivalent or Don't Know = 1 point; and Negative Self-Concept = 0 points. The scores from the 15 items are summed, and the resulting Global Self-Concept Score (GSC) can range from 0 to 30 points. The interpretation of the GSC is based on both the total points and the chronological age of the child.

Joseph Pre-school and Primary Self-Concept Screening Test   233

There are five self-concept classifications: (a) high-risk negative, (b) poor, (c) watch list, (d) moderately positive, and (e) high positive. The range of scores for each of these classifications is based on the age of the child when the child was tested. The ages are blocked into three groups—3.6 to 4.6, 4.7 to 5.11, and 6.0 to 9.11. For example, a GSC score of 22 would fall in the "moderately positive" classification for a four-year-old, the "poor" classification for a five-year-old, and the "high-risk negative" classification for an eight-year-old (Joseph, 1979, p. 20). There is an additional scoring option for recording confusions; that is, the child's inability to discriminate between the two pictures in a set. The manual indicates that the total number of confusions (up to 12) should be recorded in the summative score.

Finally, the manual provides what is called an "item dimension chart," which is to be used to diagnostically assess the child's self-concept based on the five-dimension model. It is recommended for use with any scores falling into the two lowest classifications ("high-risk negative" or "poor"). Each item on the test that received a score less than 2 is noted, and the self-concept dimension associated with the item (e.g., Significance, Virtue, General Evaluative Contentment, Competence, or Power) is recorded. The total number of items scoring 2 or less in each dimension is recorded, the resulting scores representing a key to specific areas of deficit in the child's self-concept. Because of the serious problems of nonindependence among the dimensions and overlapping items, the dimension analysis is seriously flawed and does not appear to be a useful exercise in its present form.

In both administration and scoring, the examiner is given a good deal of latitude in deciding whether to probe for information. For example, the instructions state that if the examiner feels the child is guessing, he or she can ask the child to confirm the response either by pointing or by giving a verbal reply for clarification.

Joseph offers a number of suggestions for test interpretation throughout the manual; however, Chapter 5 is devoted solely to interpretation. There appears to be at least three different ways to approach interpretation. The first is an item-by-item look at the "meaning" of different responses. The second is the classification scheme based on the Global Self-Concept Score, and the final is the qualitative assessment of the Identity Reference Drawings. These three approaches are probably best understood when taken one at a time, although they are certainly not independent of one another.

As a guide to item analysis, Joseph has offered summaries of his clinical views on the meaning of each of the items. He points out that in his view negative responses to certain items can be considered clinical red flags, while others are far less significant. There is some evidence of a marked developmental trend in the way the items are answered and, in fact, some of the items may be less valid at some ages than at other ages. This is not at all surprising in view of the evidence that is emerging about the developmental nature of self-concept (Parke & Asher, 1983; Shavelson & Bolus, 1982). There are no factor analytic data to support Joseph's interpretations; rather, they seem to be mainly based on intuitive appeal and clinical experience.

The second aspect of interpretation is based on the Global Self-Concept Score. According to the author, the GSC "is relatively meaningless unless it is translated into a functional descriptive category" (Joseph, 1979, p. 20). Basically, the Self-

Concept by Classification table on the record form is supposed to do this job. The manual does comment on the clinical implications of a child being in each of the five self-concept categories. Unfortunately, the recommendations for interpreting the resulting classifications suggest that the GSC can only truly be understood in the light of subjective and qualitative data available from the IRD, parent or teacher reports, and so forth. It does not seem that the GSC score is viewed as having much credibility on its own merits.

Finally, there is a lengthy section on the qualitative interpretation of the IRD, with sample drawings illustrating the scoring criteria. This scoring approach draws heavily on Koppitz (1968) and Machover (1949). The projective analysis of the child's personality characteristics based on these interpretations is a questionable practice; in fact, there is virtually no evidence in the literature to suggest that such interpretations have any validity. It is too bad that the author saw fit to include this section in the manual, because it greatly increases the likelihood that the test will be used inappropriately.

The intermingling of objective and subjective scoring rules has created something of a problem in terms of setting standards for examiner qualifications and training. If the test had been limited to a quantitative approach (as with the item scores), then it could be administered and interpreted by counselors, nurses, and classroom teachers. However, the inclusion of the qualitative or clinical judgment aspect (as well as suggesting its use as a projective personality assessment) dictates that the JPPSST should only be used and interpreted by a psychologist or similarly trained person. These limitations have not been specified in the manual.

Technical Aspects

Several reliability estimates are reported in the test manual. For example, test-retest reliability for 18 preschoolers with a 4-week interval between administrations is .87. Kuder-Richardson (K-R 20) estimates of internal consistency ranged from .59 to .81, with a median of .73. Finally, item discrimination coefficients (point-biserials) ranged from .30 to .70 (Joseph, 1979, p. 36).

Construct validity is reported based on the correlation (r = .41) obtained between the JPPSST and a teacher perception of student self-concept measure, using scores from 25 preschoolers (median age 4.10). Three correlations are reported with a 10-item teacher report form described as associated with self-esteem. The correlation for the aforementioned 25 preschoolers is .65; a second group of 44 kindergarteners and first graders (median age 6.6) produced a correlation of .52, while a third group (n = 57, median age 5.4) yielded a correlation of .31 (Joseph, 1979, p. 57). The author also reports results from a correlation between the teacher rating scale and the JPPSST scores for two samples of children (median age 4.6 and 5.5 respectively), whom he describes as all residents of an affluent upper-middle-class suburban community. These results are disappointing in that the median correlation is .03.

The author claims that the test has predictive validity for later academic achievement. The evidence is inconclusive because the correlations reported are concurrent rather than longitudinal. The author states that concurrent validity is necessary for predictive validity, and one assumes that he also believes concurrent validity is sufficient to infer predictive validity. This is not the case, and the argument for the use of the JPPSST as a predictive test would be strengthened by some longitudinal data. However, there is evidence of a significant effect of IQ (r = .66), language ability (r = .63), and visual motor skills (r = .69) on the Global Self-Concept Score. These data suggest that roughly one-third of the variance in the self-concept scores could be accounted for by other than self-concept factors as defined in the JPPSST.

Critique

The Joseph Pre-School and Primary Self-Concept Screening test is, at present, one of the best—and, in fact, only—tests of its kind on the market. Although there has been a remarkable increase in interest in self-concept as a social emotional factor in early childhood development, there has been a serious lag in the assessment materials. The greatest strength of the JPPSST is the fact that Joseph has made an admirable effort to present a rational theoretical framework in support of the test. The manual is thoughtful and, although some of the theoretical aspects are now a bit dated, the author's intentions remain sound.

The test materials are relatively inexpensive, and the test is easily and quickly administered, thus lending itself to a screening program. The techniques used in administration are well suited for use with preschool-aged children and will likely capture and hold their attention.

However, there are some significant problems with the JPPSST that should not go without comment. First is the lack of factor-analytic evidence to support the diagnostic dimensional evaluation. The user should not use the test results in planning interventions as suggested in the manual. There is no foundation in data for such an application beyond the intuition and clinical experience of the author.

A second area of weakness is the use of the Identity Reference Drawings as a quick personality screening device. As previously indicated, there is no evidence in the literature to suggest that such an analysis is justified. Having these suggestions and guidelines appear in the manual only serves as a temptation to the armchair psychologist.

Finally, the list of potential uses for this test is misleading. APA measurement guidelines call for data to support all claims for screening, diagnostic, or evaluation outcomes, and there are not data to support any of the claims listed on page 9 of the manual, such as diagnosis of cognitive deficits, program evaluation or personality assessment. It would have been much better if the author had acknowledged the limitations of the instrument. Until something better comes along, this instrument will in all probability continue to be widely used; however, it is hoped that potential test users will consider the limitations suggested in this review in their evaluations of the Joseph Pre-School and Primary Self-Concept Screening Test.

References

Coopersmith, S. (1959). A method for determining types of self-esteem. *Journal of Abnormal and Social Psychology, 59,* 87-94.
Coopersmith, S. (1967). *The antecedents of self-esteem.* San Francisco: W. H. Freeman.

Hughes, H. (1984). Measures of self-concept and self-esteem for children ages 3-12 years: A review and recommendations. *Clinical Psychology Review, 4,* 657-692.

Joseph, J. (1979). *Joseph Pre-School and Primary Self-Concept Screening Test.* Chicago: Stoelting Company.

Koppitz, E. (1968). *Psychological evaluation of children's human figure drawing.* New York: Grune & Stratton.

Machover, K. (1949). *Personality projection in the drawing of the human figure: A method of personality investigation.* Springfield, IL: Charles Thomas.

Parke, R. D. & Asher, S. R. (1983). Social and personality development. *Annual Review of Psychology, 34,* 465-509.

Rogers, C. (1951). *Client-centered therapy.* Boston: Houghton Mifflin.

Shavelson, R. J. & Bolus, R. (1982). Self-concept: The interplay of theory and methods. *Journal of Educational Psychology, 73,* 3-17.

Ellen Hedrick Bacon, Ph.D.
Assistant Professor of Special Education, Western Carolina University,
Cullowhee, North Carolina.

LEARNING DISABILITY RATING PROCEDURE

Gerald J. Spadafore and Sharon J. Spadafore. Novato, California: Academic Therapy Publications.

Introduction

The Learning Disability Rating Procedure (LDRP) provides a format for summarizing information on students being considered for placement in a learning disabilities class. Designed for use by regular classroom teachers, special education teachers, psychologists, and guidance counselors, it purports to provide a method for facilitating the group decision-making process on placement of elementary and secondary students into learning disability programs. The LDRP is not a psychometric test; rather, it is an instrument used to structure evaluations of behavior in the school setting by members of the diagnostic team on 10 indicators deemed critical by the authors.

The LDRP was developed by Gerald J. Spadafore and Sharon J. Spadafore. Dr. Gerald Spadafore is a professor in the department of counselor education and special education and director of the school psychology program at Idaho State University. Sharon Spadafore is a resource-room teacher who works with learning disabled (LD) students.

The authors present very little information on the development of this rating procedure. Ten critical indicators of a learning disability are presented, along with a brief rationale for each. These indicators are IQ Score, Reading Decoding, Listening Comprehension, Comprehension Variance, Socially Inappropriate Behavior, Expressive Verbal Language Development, Learning Motivation, Expressive Writing Development, Independent Work Level/Distractibility, and Severe Learning Discrepancy. There is no evidence presented that these indicators were selected or verified on the basis of any investigations or studies that would demonstrate their combined ability to predict or diagnose a learning disability. According to the authors, "These indicators were extrapolated from the P.L. 94-142 definition of learning disabilities and selected because of their frequent use during both formal and informal student evaluations" (Spadafore & Spadafore, 1981, p. 11).

The authors determined norms for the procedure by having a panel of experts rate each of the indicators in a manner they felt would be representative of a typical LD student, although no age was specified for the student. The panel consisted of seven school psychologists, 10 regular classroom teachers, and 29 resource-room teachers. In the Spadafores' opinion, this panel of experts was considered attitudinally representative of those who govern learning disability placement. These rankings by the panel of experts were used to develop the categories indicating whether a student would be an excellent candidate, a good candidate, a fair candidate, or a poor candidate for learning disability placement.

The LDRP is designed to be used at a school-based placement meeting for either elementary or secondary students. It is assumed that those in attendance would include the principal, the diagnostic evaluator, the teacher, the parents, and the child (when appropriate). The instrument should be distributed and reviewed before the meeting, but the rankings should be done by each participant separately after presentation of information and discussion.

When participants at the school placement meetings rate students on the 10 indicators, they need three types of information: 1) previously administered IQ and achievement tests, 2) previously administered teacher-constructed measures of reading decoding skills and listening comprehension, and 3) information from observing the child in the regular classroom. Five of the indicators (5-9) are based totally on teacher judgment. The manual instructs the evaluation team to consider the regular classroom teacher as the best source of information regarding the students' performance in the classroom. No further instructions are available to guide observations or judgments in rating these five items.

The LDRP consists of a manual and a rating form. The 4-page rating form contains descriptions of the 10 indicators and spaces for ranking the student on a scale of 1 to 4 for each. These indicators and the assumptions about expected performance of an LD student are given as follows:

1. *IQ Score.* The LDRP states that LD students are likely to have average or above-average intelligence. Students with IQs measured at 116 or above are given a 4, the highest ranking (i.e., a characteristic most like LD students).

2. *Reading Decoding.* The manual states there is a positive relationship between low reading scores and learning disabilities. Low scores on Reading Decoding (50% correct or less on an informal reading measure of 100 words) would receive a ranking of 4.

3. *Listening Comprehension.* The authors base this indicator on the belief that students with learning disabilities are likely to have sufficient cognitive development to comprehend reading material at grade level when the material is read to them (Spadafore & Spadafore, 1981). Therefore, students who score better than 90% correct on an informal listening comprehension measure receive 4 points.

4. *Comprehension Variance.* Learning disabled students are assumed to demonstrate better developed skills in listening comprehension than in decoding. Students whose listening comprehension is 30% higher than their decoding score are given 4 points.

5. *Socially Inappropriate Behavior.* LD students, according to the LDRP, are more likely to exhibit socially appropriate behavior than inappropriate behavior. Students who are judged to have well-developed social skills receive the highest ranking of 4. Students with "excessive episodes of socially inappropriate behavior" receive a 1.

6. *Expressive Verbal Language Development.* The LDRP states that learning disabled students frequently have better developed verbal language skills than academic skills. Therefore, well-developed language skills receive the highest ranking and severe language problems are given 1 point.

7. *Learning Motivation.* LD students are assumed by the Spadafores to be more

motivated to succeed in class than are emotionally handicapped or retarded students. Having an excellent attitude toward school and learning would earn the student the highest ranking of 4. Having a negative attitude would receive a 1.

8. *Expressive Writing Development.* Learning-disabled students are assumed to manifest developmental lags in expressive writing skills; therefore, severe limitations in expressive writing skills receive the rank of 4.

9. *Independent Work Level/Distractibility.* LD students are assumed to be off-task during a significant portion of classroom time. Students who are judged to be on-task 25% of the time or less receive the highest ranking of 4. Those on-task 75% or more are given a rating of 1.

10. *Severe Learning Discrepancy.* Learning-disabled students are likely to show a significant gap between potential and actual achievement level. The formula used is C.A. (IQ/300 + 0.17) − 2.5 = Severe Discrepancy Level. (This is the controversial formula presented in the Federal Register [1976, p. 52405] that is seldom used, having been discarded as being unnecessarily cumbersome.) A student whose severe discrepancy level is more than one year above his or her achievement score would receive the highest rank.

The scores from the rankings on these 10 factors are totaled and used to assist in placement decisions for students being considered for a learning disability program.

Practical Applications/Uses

As mentioned, the Learning Disability Rating Procedure purports to be a systematic method for summarizing and interpreting information regarding a child's placement in LD classes. However, individual states have stringent guidelines for such placements. The authors may be assuming that states may adopt the LDRP as a placement procedure; otherwise, it could be used only as a supplemental technique. The LDRP is intended to identify only those LD students who have strengths in expressive and receptive language and appropriate social skills with deficits in reading, writing, and on-task behaviors. It is inaccurate and inappropriate to assume all variations of learning disabilities fall into the authors' hypothetical profile of a typical LD student.

The procedure is intended for use with either elementary or secondary students, but no data are provided that substantiate its appropriateness for use with either. The manual states that primary consideration should be given to the rankings or opinions of the regular classroom teacher because the rankings of the student's behavior should reflect his or her behavior in the regular classroom (Spadafore & Spadafore, 1981). However, a specific procedure for weighting rankings is not provided. It should be noted that the recommendation regarding the relative importance of teacher rankings/opinions was not reflected in the composition of the panel of experts who ranked the "typical learning-disabled student" (there were 29 resource-room teachers compared to 10 regular classroom teachers).

Although the LDRP is not a test, two informal measures of achievement are necessary in order to rank a student on Reading Decoding and Listening Comprehension. The instructions for assessing reading decoding ability require the examiner to ask the student to read aloud a passage of approximately 100 words from a selection chosen by the examiner as appropriate for the student's grade. The number of words correctly pronounced are counted and the percentage of words read correctly is determined. On the basis of this the student receives a ranking on item #2. A similar technique is used for assessing listening comprehension (item #3). A second passage of comparable difficulty is selected and read to the student. The manual states the examiner should construct and ask five or more comprehension questions and determine the percentage answered correctly. No guidelines are presented for choosing the passage or constructing the questions. Item #3 is ranked on the basis of this score. The difference between item #2 and item #3 is the basis for the ranking of the next item (#4—Comprehension Variance).

According to the manual, scoring the LDRP should take approximately 10 minutes. Five items require the rater to make a clinical evaluation of the student with minimal guidelines for making such judgments. Examiners are asked to rank students subjectively on Socially Inappropriate Behavior, Expressive Language Development, Learning Motivation, and Expressive Writing Development. Raters are asked to distinguish between an adequate attitude toward school and learning and an excellent attitude toward school and learning. No further information is provided to help the rater distinguish between the two categories. These poorly defined items make the instrument difficult to score with confidence (Illback, 1985).

After all 10 indicators are ranked, a total is obtained. When being used by a group, the average score is found. This score is used to place the student in one of four categories: 33-40, excellent candidate for learning disability placement; 30-32, good candidate; 27-29, fair candidate; and 10-26, poor candidate. The total score on the rating scale combines objective test scores (e.g., IQ scores) with poorly defined subjective rankings. The authors then suggest using the total score as an objective score with predictive validity. The inclusion of subjective rankings with poor reliability and validity in the final total means that the final total is likely to be subject to the same measurement errors. Therefore, any interpretation of the total score on the LDRP would be difficult because of the combination of objective measures and clinical judgments.

Technical Aspects

Interrater reliability was examined by having four raters assess five students who were being considered for placement in a resource room. The four raters discussed each part of the indicators as they scored the Learning Disability Rating Procedure. Although the manual states that 82% agreement was obtained across the 10 indicators (Spadafore & Spadafore, 1981, p. 23), the reader is not told whether the 82% agreement was found for each of the 10 items, or whether the figure represents agreement on the total test score.

Interrater reliability and reliability of ratings over time are critical measures for a subjective rating scale. However, the only evidence of reliability presented is based on only four raters and five students. In addition, the raters discussed each item before ranking the students. This type of cooperative rating on so few students should not be construed to be a measure of reliability (Aiken, 1985).

Validity measures of a test should indicate whether it can be used for its stated purpose. The authors show some confusion on the actual purpose of the LDRP. The stated purpose of the procedure, as given in the manual's introductory descriptions, is to provide "those involved in the assignment of special education services with a systematic framework which will enhance their ability to make consistent and reliable decisions when considering the assignment of the learning disability label to elementary and secondary students" (Spadafore & Spadafore, 1981, p. 5). This statement certainly implies that the procedure would aid in discriminating learning-disabled students from underachievers, slow learners, or learning problems of a temporary or environmental nature. The authors claim the LDRP should assist in determining which students should be assigned to special education and which ones should not be taken out of the regular classroom. In spite of these claims, in the only validity study cited in the manual the purpose is narrowed to distinguishing LD students from mentally retarded and emotionally disturbed students. Those who have dealt with the vagaries of assessment will realize that the first purpose is a great deal more difficult to achieve than the second.

The validity study involved 30 students who had been evaluated as learning disabled, mentally retarded, or emotionally disturbed (Spadafore & Spadafore, 1981, p. 23). Five students from the elementary grades and five from secondary grades were evaluated for each handicapped group. A two-way analysis of variance showed the LDRP significantly discriminated the three groups. No information is provided as to how the students were chosen, who the raters were, or how the raters were selected. The manual does not state whether the raters worked separately or collectively. Means and standard deviations of the groups are not provided. However, even if the methodology had been adequate, the study does not indicate that the stated purpose of the LDRP is valid; it only indicates that the LDRP can discriminate between students already diagnosed and placed as mentally retarded, emotionally disturbed, or learning disabled.

The authors report a study using the LDRP in which they hoped to determine norms. They used the panel of experts convened for the development of the test to rank 183 students on the LDRP. These students had already been diagnosed as learning disabled through traditional methods. The average score for these LD students was 27.08, which would place them at the lower end of the "fair candidate" category for learning disability placement. In other words, when the panel of experts ranked students already diagnosed as learning disabled, their scores fell 1 standard deviation below the mean that the authors had predicted for learning-disabled students. Although not described as such by the authors, this appears to be a validity study indicating that the procedure does not predict which students should be placed in learning disability classes. Surprisingly, the authors conclude that the error lies with the inconsistent manner in which students are now placed in the learning disability classes. The authors appear to be saying that if the LDRP does not predict accurately, the learning disability placement of the student was incorrect. This argument does not add merit to the case for the validity of the instrument.

The LDRP is not a test but a framework for summarizing and interpreting information. However, informal measures and ratings on the LDRP lack adequate assurances of reliability and validity. Technical data as presented are minimal and difficult to interpret. The studies do not present evidence that the LDRP could be scored consistently or reliably or that the procedure does what it purportedly can do.

Critique

When a team of professionals meet to make a decision about diagnosis or placement of a learning-disabled student, they may take into consideration a number of factors, such as the discrepancy between the student's potential and achievement as measured by standardized tests, information from informal educational tests, personal-social assessment measures, and the child's motivation, work habits, and attention. The Spadafores have attempted to quantify these factors into 10 indicators that can be added up to make a diagnosis or placement. "The Learning Disability Rating Procedure consists of ten indicators which allow those involved in the assignment of special education services to summarize the elementary or secondary student's behavior and to determine whether or not the assignment of the learning disability label is appropriate" (Spadafore & Spadafore, 1981, p. 11). In doing so, they have made assumptions about learning disabilities which have no foundation other than unsupported assumptions about how LD students act.

1. The Spadafores state that LD students are likely "to exhibit socially appropriate behavior" in spite of considerable research evidence to the contrary (Bryan, 1974, 1976; Garrett & Crump, 1980; Schumaker, Hazel, Sherman, & Sheldon, 1982).

2. Students who have well developed language skills are ranked as being most likely to have a learning disability although some theorists argue that a learning disability is primarily a language disability (Vellutino, 1977).

3. Learning-disabled students are assumed to have an excellent attitude toward school and learning. The Spadafores state that "Frequently, learning disabled students are motivated to succeed in class, whereas emotionally impaired or retarded students display a negative or indifferent attitude towards school and learning" (Spadafore & Spadafore, 1981). Users of the LDRP should review the research on the motivational difficulties of LD students before accepting this assumption (Adelman & Taylor, 1983; Licht, Kistner, Ozkaragoz, Shapiro, & Clausen, 1985; Thomas, 1979).

4. The LDRP states that learning-disabled students will be off-task during a significant portion of classroom time. Ratings of 3 are given to students on-task 25% to 50% of the time, and ratings of 4 are given to those on-task 25% or less of classroom time. No rationale is provided to substantiate these figures except that LD students are known to be inattentive.

5. Students are given the highest LD rating if they have IQs in the above average range. Recent data collected on students diagnosed as learning disabled do not validate the assumption that LD students have above average intelligence (Kirk & Elkins, 1975; Norman & Zigmond, 1980; Warner, Schumaker, Alley, & Deshler, 1980).

These unwarranted assumptions about learning disabilities comprise five of the 10 items. Three other subtests, which are nonstandardized informal measures of reading decoding, listening comprehension, and the discrepancy between the two, are inadequate; these items are ranked on the basis of arbitrary measures that have no pretense of standardization, but function entirely at the discretion of the examiner as to what reading and listening selections are appropriate for the student's grade and what comprehension questions are asked. Although these types of informal measures may be suitable for a teacher who wants to understand his or her students' strengths and weaknesses, it would be unethical to use these as major indicators for placement in a class for handicapped students.

In the opinion of this reviewer, the LDRP is an inadequate rating scale that should never be used in its current form for diagnosing a learning disability or determining placement of a student. Without further research, reliability and validity measures will remain virtually nonexistent. Guidelines for ranking students on the 10 indicators need substantial revision, as presently they are vague and poorly conceived. Thus, in summary, this reviewer cannot recommend any valid use for this procedure at the present time.

References

Adelman, H. S., & Taylor, L. (1983). *Learning disabilities in perspective.* Glenview, IL: Scott Foresman & Co.

Aiken, L. R. (1985). Three coefficients for analyzing the reliability and validity of ratings. *Educational and Psychological Measurement, 45,* 131-142.

Bryan, T. H. (1974). Peer popularity of learning disabled children. *Journal of Learning Disabilities, 7,* 621-625.

Bryan, T. (1976). Peer popularity of learning disabled children: A replication. *Journal of Learning Disabilities, 9,* 307-311.

Federal Register. (1976, November 29). pp. 52404-52407. Washington, D.C.: U.S. Office of the Federal Register.

Garrett, M. K., & Crump, W. D. (1980). Peer acceptance, teacher preferences, and self-appraisal of social status among learning disabled students. *Learning Disability Quarterly, 3,* 42-48.

Illback, R. J. (1985). Learning Disability Rating Procedure. In J. V. Mitchell, Jr. (Ed.), *The ninth mental measurements yearbook* (pp. 830-831). Lincoln, NE: The Buros Institute of Mental Measurements.

Kirk, S., & Elkins, J. (1975). Characteristics of children enrolled in the Child Service Demonstration Centers. *Journal of Learning Disabilities, 47,* 496-510.

Licht, B. G., Kistner, J. A., Ozkaragoz, T., Shapiro, S., & Clausen, L. (1985). Causal attributions of learning disabled children: Individual differences and their implications for persistence. *Journal of Educational Psychology, 77,* 208-216.

Norman, C. A., & Zigmond, N. (1980). Characteristics of children labeled and served as learning disabled in school systems affiliated with Child Service Demonstration Centers. *Journal of Learning Disabilities, 13,* 542-547.

Schumaker, J. B., Hazel, J. S., Sherman, J. A., & Sheldon, J. (1982). Social skill performances of learning disabled, non-learning disabled, and delinquent adolescents. *Learning Disability Quarterly, 5,* 409-414.

Spadafore, G. J., & Spadafore, S. J. (1981). *Learning Disability Rating Procedure manual.* Novato, CA: Academic Therapy Publications.

Thomas, A. (1979). Learned helplessness and expectancy factors: Implications for research in learning disabilities. *Review of Educational Research, 49,* 208-211.

Vellutino, F. R. (1977). Alternative conceptualizations of dyslexia: Evidence in support of a verbal-deficit hypothesis. *Harvard Educational Review, 47,* 334-351.

Warner, M. M., Schumaker, J. B., Alley, G. R., & Deshler, D. D. (1980). Learning disabled adolescents in the public schools: Are they any different from other low achievers? *Exceptional Education Quarterly, 1,* 27-36.

Virginia E. Kennedy, Ph.D.
Adjunct Lecturer, Special Education, Graduate School of Education, University of California, Los Angeles, Los Angeles, California.

LEARNING EFFICIENCY TEST

Raymond E. Webster. Novato, California: Academic Therapy Publications.

Introduction

The Learning Efficiency Test (LET) is designed to measure visual and auditory memory abilities in persons aged six through adult. The test assesses ordered and unordered recall under the conditions of immediate recall, short-term recall, and long-term recall. The memory task entails a series of nonrhyming consonants, presented either visually or verbally in strings of two to nine letters. Responses are indicated verbally.

Immediate recall refers to the amount of information a person can store and retrieve from short-term memory in the absence of extraneous verbal interference and without benefit of drill or repetition. The short-term recall condition measures the effects of irrelevant verbal material introduced after the string is presented and the immediate recall is assessed. During the short-term recall condition, the serial string is held in short-term memory while the student counts aloud, thus providing interference by preventing the student from rehearsing the string. The score on this task indicates the amount of material lost from short-term memory when verbal interference is presented. The third condition, long-term recall, introduces additional verbal interference while requiring the student to transfer the initially presented letters from short-term to long-term memory. The verbal interference takes the form of a meaningless sentence that the student must repeat. After the sentence is repeated, long-term recall is assessed by asking the student to state the letter string again.

The LET consists of two subtests, Visual Memory and Auditory Memory, each measuring the three recall conditions. Within each condition is also provided a measure of the examinee's ordered recall (the number of items correctly recalled in the proper sequence) and unordered recall (the number of items correctly recalled without reference to correct sequential order). Thus, for each subtest, six scores are obtained (three recall conditions, ordered and unordered recall within each condition).

As stated, the test items are comprised of series of nonrhyming consonants. Each series was constructed by randomly selecting letters from the following list: F, H, J, L, M, P, Q, R, S, X, and Y. No letter is used more than once in any serial string. The serial strings range in length from two to nine letters. Nine letters were set as the maximum number in a string based on research which shows that the average adult remembers about seven items, plus or minus two, in short-term memory (Miller, 1956).

The test's author, Raymond E. Webster, is Assistant Professor of Psychology at East Carolina University in Greenville, North Carolina. He is the author of professional articles and co-author of two textbooks about learning handicapped students.

A unique contribution of the LET to the testing field is its attention to transfer of information from short-term memory to long-term memory. Webster believes this transfer to be a vital aspect of the learning process and one that is not addressed in other memory tests. The Learning Efficiency Test was developed to fill a perceived need for a memory test that approximated the conditions in an actual classroom situation. The author states that most tests of memory require recall of ordered items in a setting with no verbal interference. This test attempts to overcome the disparity between this condition and memory requirements in classrooms by accompanying the memory items with controlled verbal interference.

The theoretical basis for the development of the test rests on two models influential in the assessment of students with learning problems: 1) the modality model, which posits that some individuals learn and remember information better through one sensory modality—auditory, visual or kinesthetic—than another (discovering this preference in a particular student may lead to more effective teaching approaches); and 2) the two-store model of memory (Atkinson & Shiffrin, 1968). According to this model, information can be retained in one of two stores: short-term memory, which has a limited capacity, and long-term memory, which has a much larger storage capacity. Memory deficits have been associated with the academic difficulties of learning disabled students.

The LET was standardized on a total of 575 public school students between the ages of 5 years, 0 months and 18 years, 11 months. Students with a general IQ score of less than 85, organically or physically based learning problems, or serious behavioral or emotional problems were excluded from the normative group. A total of 21% of the students resided in large cities, 32% in medium-sized or small cities, 35% in suburban communities, and 12% in rural areas of the northeastern United States. Sixty-two percent were white, 31% black, and 7% Hispanic. As a comparison of the performance of males and females on the LET failed to show statistically significant differences between the two groups, only one set of norms is provided for both sexes.

The mean and standard deviation for each of the 12 raw score categories (6 visual, 6 auditory) of the LET were obtained for each age group. Ages were grouped in one-year intervals from age 6 through 16 and age 17 and above for the adult group. Using these means and standard deviations, a z score was defined for each possible raw score value within +3 or −3 standard deviations from the mean for each age group; z scores were then transformed to a standard score scale with a mean of 10 and a standard deviation of 3. Percentile ranks that correspond to the standard score distribution for each age group are also provided.

The LET materials consist of a set of stimulus cards, record forms, and the test manual. The stimulus cards are a ring-bound set of cardboard cards, 5"x3", with a large uppercase letter on each. (Blank cards are included to demarcate the ends of serial strings.) The cards are used for the Visual Memory portion of the test. No materials are needed for the Auditory Memory portion except the Record Form, which is used to record examinees' answers, to enter total raw scores and standard scores, and to display percentiles on a profile chart. The profile chart is designed to show a student's percentile ranks in ordered versus unordered recall in the three recall conditions for both Visual and Auditory Memory. A separate four-page form is completed for each examinee. The back page is designed for the examiner to note other test results, comments, and recommendations.

Practical Applications/Uses

The Learning Efficiency Test yields information about a student's ability to remember auditory and visual letter sequences when immediately asked to recall them, and after interferences are interjected. Its structure is similar to memory tasks used in experimental research and in traditional cognitive tests (i.e., the use of strings of digits or letters to be memorized); therefore, the test would be of use to an educator concerned with the mnemonic abilities of certain students. Because it is individually administered, it would not be practical to give the LET to all students in a class; instead, the test should only be given to those for whom memory could be an area of difficulty. The LET would be of greatest value as part of a battery of tests given to a student to determine areas of strengths and weaknesses in reading, spelling, and mathematics and their underlying skills.

The purpose of the Learning Efficiency Test is to measure how efficiently and effectively a person processes and retains information presented through either auditory or visual modalities. The test is norm-referenced; therefore, an individual's test results can be compared to the scores obtained by others in his or her age group. The LET is intended to be used as a diagnostic instrument when assessing individuals with suspected learning problems. It is designed to yield information about the functioning of several different aspects of memory—in particular, memory skills required in everyday classroom learning. This approximation of "real-life" settings is accomplished by introducing verbal interference into the memory task and by specifically including a measure of a student's ability to transfer data from short-term memory to long-term memory.

This test is useful in all educational settings and in any other setting in which knowledge of an individual's memory abilities is needed. The professionals most likely to use the LET are special education teachers, reading specialists, learning disabilities specialists, educational/school psychologists, and educational therapists. Language disorder specialists might also find it helpful, particularly because auditory memory may be examined separately from and in contrast to visual memory. A potential new application of this test is its use in memory research studies when investigators need norms for different age groups in order to make comparisons.

The LET is used appropriately for subjects within the age groups of the norming sample. Although the IQ cutoff was 85 in the norming sample, students with IQ scores down to approximately 70 could be administered this test and useful results obtained, as long as those interpreting the results realize these students were omitted when the norms were established. The test's content and administration is relatively free of any cultural bias, but the examinees must understand and speak English. As no physical movements other than looking and speaking are required, students with physical disabilities involving the limbs or trunk would not have any undue difficulty. The auditory section of the test may be administered to blind or visually impaired students without any adaptations.

The LET must be administered individually and in a quiet setting with a minimum of distractions. A desk or table should be available. Teachers and psychologists would be the most likely examiners. No training is required for the examiner, although the manual must be read carefully and the test administered in several practice sessions before it is given for the purpose of reporting the results.

The administration of the test is composed of two main sets of instructions, one each for the Visual Memory and Auditory Memory subtests. Before these subtests are presented, the examiner must pretest the examinee on the alphabet to determine whether he or she can identify the letters to be used as test items. The first card in the stimulus book contains all the letters in the test. The examiner directs the student to identify each letter, and if any difficulty is encountered, the test is discontinued.

Following this, the Visual Memory subtest and then the Auditory Memory subtest are administered. For both subtests, the sequence is to test immediate memory, then short-term memory, and finally long-term memory. For the Visual Memory subtest, each item in a stimulus string is shown to the examinee for two seconds before moving on to the next item. For the Auditory Memory subtest, the items are read from the Record Form with a one-second pause between each item. After a string is presented, immediate recall is tested by asking the student to recall the letters in the order presented or, if this cannot be done, to recall as many letters as possible. Short-term recall is then tested by having the student count aloud (instructions are on the Record Form) and then state the letters presented earlier in correct order or in any order if he or she cannot recall them in their correct order. Finally, long-term recall is tested by asking the student to repeat a nonsense sentence indicated on the Record Form and then again to recall as many of the original letters as possible, either in the correct order or in any order. Testing for each subtest is discontinued when two consecutive errors are made in immediate recall.

The administration of the LET is easy and is clearly explained in the manual. Alterations in the instructions to the examinee or in the sequence of the test would not be advisable as these are integral to the test's purpose of examining different types or stages of memory. The test generally requires only 10 minutes to administer.

The directions for recording responses are clearly presented and illustrated in the test manual, although the actual method advocated could be difficult. Examiners new to the LET would probably need to record all responses as made and then return to them after the completion of the test to compare them to the order of the actual strings rather than to analyze them as they are made, as directed by the manual. Only one to two hours should be necessary to learn and practice the recording and scoring. Once learned, the test should require about five minutes to score.

Scoring the LET is not difficult. Separate scores are obtained for ordered and unordered recall. The ordered recall scores are based on the responses to the last string recalled in its correct order during immediate recall. The number of items recalled in their correct order in each of the three recall conditions for that string constitutes the scores for each condition.

The unordered recall scores are based on responses to the string with the most letters recalled during immediate recall, without respect to correct sequence. One point is given for each letter recalled in each recall condition.

Interpretation of test results is based both on the obtained scores and on clinical judgment. The manual contains explanations of methods for analyzing actual scores, patterns of responses, and behaviors exhibited during test administration.

Score analysis is accomplished by converting all raw scores to standard scores, comparing the student's results to those of others of the same age in the norm group, and then examining the student's profile of scores to determine relative strengths and weaknesses. Thus, both external and internal comparisons can be made.

The test's author suggests that additional information about the student's learning style can be gained from analyzing patterns of responses, either those observed during test administration or those determined by examining the test protocol afterwards. Observable behaviors such as lip movements to indicate use of a rehearsal strategy or chunking items into pairs or triads when repeating them can be noted as clues to the student's processing style and ability. Perseverations, short-term versus long-term memory as the locus of difficulty, and problems in sequencing might be detected by analyzing the test protocol.

The third type of interpretation suggested is behavior analysis. Noting behaviors that indicate the student's cooperation, motivation to do well, responses to success and failure, quickness of response, length of attention span, and any unusual verbal or physical problems may be helpful in diagnosing the child's learning problems.

For an examiner to interpret the LET adequately and properly, he or she should be trained in the interpretation of numerical results. Also necessary, however, is knowledge in the area of memory so that the examiner can recognize patterns of responses and testing behaviors as they occur and know how to plan effective interventions based on them. A further caution about interpretation concerns the nature of the LET's memory tasks and their relationship to acutal memory demands in the classroom. The LET items are discrete units of information that are symbolic (alphabet letters) but carry little meaning. Much of the information to be remembered in school requires recognition and manipulation of meaningful items (i.e., categorization, associations). In addition, it has recently been shown that at least for learning disabled students, their memory performance approximates that of average students if the material is highly meaningful (Krupski, 1985). Statements about a student's memory capacities based on this test should acknowledge this limitation.

The manual contains a chapter on remediation, which suggests specific remedial techniques for different memory problems. Most of these problems would be detected as a result of careful observation of behaviors during testing rather than from an analysis of results.

Technical Aspects

Reliability of the LET was assessed by the test-retest method. The subjects were 40 secondary students with learning and behavior problems, but with measured

IQ scores of 90 or higher. High test-retest reliability was found for both Visual and Auditory Memory subtests, with coefficients ranging from .81 to .97 and a median of .94. Therefore, performance appears to be consistent over a short period of time (the test-retest interval ranged from one week to six weeks). However, no conclusions about the permanence of the memory abilities tested on the LET can be drawn from this study.

In contrast, the performance of emotionally disturbed and learning disabled students was more inconsistent across modalities. Although this might be expected for learning disabled students (uneven performance across different skills is characteristic of these students), no explanation for the inconsistent performance of emotionally disturbed students is given. Since the performance of emotionally disturbed students is even more inconsistent than that of learning disabled students on unordered visual and auditory recall, the usefulness of this test for differential diagnosis of specific learning handicaps is questionable.

Patterns of information lost from one recall condition to the next were also studied. The average and emotionally disturbed students retained about the same amount of information as they moved through the recall conditions. Although the immediate recall of the learning disabled group was almost at the same level as the average group, subsequent verbal interference produced far more information loss for the former group. The educable mentally retarded group had a lower immediate recall score than the other groups and lost a great deal of information after verbal interference, including more loss at the long-term memory stage on most subtests than all other groups (including learning disabled students).

Although these analyses are provocative in their implications, no link is made by the author between these findings and their value in diagnosis.

Three types of LET validity were assessed: content, diagnostic, and predictive validity. The author states (Webster, 1981) that content validity was established by the use of nonrhyming letters as test items, which provides a large number of choices; by the use of serial strings ranging from two to nine letters, which allows for an examination of a full range of memory; and by using a methodology that tests memory at three stages of recall. By including these features, the LET is constructed to test a spectrum of memory abilities with a minimum of confounding with other cognitive abilities.

Diagnostic validity was evidenced by examining the pattern of intercorrelations of the Visual Memory and Auditory Memory subtests for different groups of students. A randomly selected sample of average students from the standardization sample and groups of learning handicapped students identified as either emotionally disturbed, learning disabled, or educable mentally retarded were the groups under study. The characteristics of the four groups are displayed in Table 1.

As can be seen, the Full Scale WISC-R IQ scores for the emotionally disturbed and learning disabled groups were 14 points below that of the average group, although all were in the average range. Of the four groups studied, average and educable mentally retarded students showed the greatest consistency in their performance on both kinds of subtypes, although the performance of the educable mentally retarded students was consistently low in relation to the other groups.

The third type of validity studied, predictive validity, is an important feature of the LET, because the test is designed to define a student's memory abilities in order

Table 1

Characteristics of Learning Groups Used in Validity Studies*

Learning Group	N	Mean Chronological Age	Verbal	Mean WISC-R IQs Performance	Full Scale
Average	202	10.81 (4.95)	109.45 (19.51)	108.33 (16.21)	109.81 (18.18)
ED	79	13.64 (6.31)	94.80 (11.92)	97.86 (14.06)	95.82 (11.80)
LD	145	10.53 (23.23)	94.33 (14.28)	97.17 (14.34)	95.29 (13.24)
EMR	36	11.74 (3.26)	64.81 (7.48)	64.13 (11.30)	61.88 (9.26)

*from the *Learning Efficiency Test*. Reproduced by permission of Academic Therapy Publications © 1981.

to develop an appropriate instructional program. Predictive validity was examined by correlating reading and math achievement levels with LET raw scores.

As can be seen in Table 2, the multiple correlation coefficients for the average group were only .50 (reading) and .49 (math). However, the correlations for the

Table 2

Validity of the LET and the LET and WISC-R in Predicting Academic Achievement

Learning Group	Predictor Variables	Multiple Correlation with Reading	Multiple Correlation with Math
Average	LET only	.50	.49
	LET, WISC-R	.50	.50
LD	LET only	.62	.59
	LET, WISC-R	.64	.60
ED	LET only	.74	.69
	LET, WISC-R	.74	.69
EMR	LET only	.92	.93
	LET, WISC-R	.93	.93

*from the *Learning Efficiency Test*. Reproduced by permission of Academic Therapy Publications © 1981.

learning handicapped groups were higher, ranging from .62 (reading) and .59 (math) for learning disabled students to .92 (reading) and .93 (math) for educable mentally retarded students. Therefore, the LET is relatively nonpredictive of academic performance in average students, but more predictive for learning handicapped students. The author points out, however, that the higher correlations for learning handicapped students may reflect more accurate assessments of achievement level in these students than in average students who typically do not receive an individualized program; this explanation has merit since achievement levels were determined by teachers' statements of the grade level of the texts used by each student rather than any objective measure; grade levels had most likely previously been pinpointed by testing of learning handicapped students.

Critique

The LET appears to be most useful for learning more about the failure of certain students in school subjects. The predictive validity for LD subjects was low; however, this is not surprising in light of the acknowledged heterogeneity of children given this label. For students in this group whose learning problems appear to involve memory deficits, the LET could be a valuable diagnostic tool. The results of this test could also be helpful in instructional planning for and differential diagnosis of other students with learning problems (emotionally disturbed and mildly retarded students).

Although the stated purpose of the test is to define and relate learning styles to classroom functioning, no analysis was performed of the relationship between different learning styles (relative strength in visual vs. auditory memory) and school achievement. Therefore, it is not possible to attribute academic deficiencies to the weaker modality, although if this information is considered with data from other forms of assessment, it would contribute to a total picture of a student's functioning.

In summary, the Learning Efficiency Test can be a worthwhile instrument as part of a battery of tests to diagnose learning problems.

References

This list includes text citations and suggested additional reading.

Atkinson, R., & Shiffrin, R. (1968). Human memory: A proposed system and its control processes. In K. Spence & J. Spence (Eds.), *The psychology of learning and motivation: Advances in research and theory* (Vol. 2, pp. 89-195). New York: Academic Press.

Farnham-Diggory, S., & Gregg, L. (1974). Short-term memory function in young readers. *Journal of Experimental Child Psychology, 19*, 279-298.

Krupski, A. (1985). Variations in attention as a function of classroom task demands in learning handicapped and CA-matched non-handicapped children. *Exceptional Children, 52*, 52-56.

Miller, G. (1956). The magical number seven, plus or minus two: Some limits on our capacity to process information. *Psychological Review, 63*, 81-97.

Torgesen, J. (1977). Memorization processes in reading-disabled children. *Journal of Educational Psychology, 69*, 571-578.

Webster, R. E. (1981). *Learning Efficiency Test.* Novato, CA: Academic Therapy Publications.

Andrew S. Bradlyn, Ph.D.
Associate Professor, Department of Behavioral Medicine and Psychiatry, West Virginia University Medical School, Morgantown, West Virginia.

MINNESOTA INFANT DEVELOPMENT INVENTORY

Harold Ireton and Edward Thwing. Minneapolis, Minnesota: Behavior Science Systems, Inc.

Introduction

The Minnesota Infant Development Inventory (MIDI) is a 75-item parent-completed checklist of developmental behaviors. The parent is asked to respond ("Yes"/"No") to questions concerning the infant's development in five areas: Gross Motor, Fine Motor, Language, Comprehension, and Personal-Social. The infant's reported functioning within each area is then compared to established developmental age norms. The purpose of the inventory is to provide professionals and parents with information useful in reviewing the developmental status of infants from birth through age 15 months.

Harold Ireton, the primary author of the MIDI, earned his doctoral degree in clinical psychology from the University of Minnesota in 1963 and is presently a faculty member at the University of Minnesota Health Sciences Center, where he specializes in clinical child and developmental psychology. The authors have developed two additional developmental scales, the Minnesota Child Development Inventory (MCDI) and the Minnesota Preschool Inventory (MPI).

Many of the items contained in the inventory were drawn from previous research focusing on the development and validation of the Minnesota Child Development Inventory; thus, there are known developmental age norms supporting their inclusion. The authors provide no information regarding the availability of forms for special populations.

The Minnesota Infant Development Inventory is comprised of two pieces of material: a booklet containing the 75 items to be completed by the parent and a set of interpretation guidelines to be used by the professional administering the inventory. The items included are similar to those commonly found on developmental screening inventories such as the Denver Developmental Screening Test (Frankenburg et al., 1975) or on more standardized infant evaluation measures such as the 1969 Bayley Scales of Infant Development (Mental and Motor). Other than a one-page overview, there is no manual as such.

The authors suggest using this inventory in one of two ways. The MIDI may be completed by the parent and then reviewed by the professional prior to examination of the infant, or the structure of the inventory may be used as a standardized format for interviewing the parent and observing the child. The adult respondent (either the parent or the professional) simply fills in the circle in front of each item that is true of the infant. There is neither a separate answer sheet nor a separate profile; however, the professional is instructed to use the item form to label the levels at which items endorsed/not endorsed would be considered above/below age expectations.

Practical Applications/Uses

This inventory is most useful for those professionals who are concerned with the developmental status of infants. Thus, pediatricians, nurses, psychologists, and developmental clinic personnel would be considered prime targets. Although the authors state that the test has not been validated for screening or classification purposes, the MIDI is potentially useful for reviewing the acquisition of developmental skills with parents and perhaps assisting in decisions regarding the need for further evaluation of the infant's functioning. The MIDI also provides a format and structure in which professional users can obtain relatively standard information about the infant's development in a consistent fashion, allowing for more accurate tracking than informal, idiosyncratically administered interviews and observation. Finally, the practitioner may find the MIDI useful in "anticipatory guidance" with the parents; that is, reviewing the status of the infant's development with the parents and then advising them both on emerging skills and on strategies that may enhance development.

The items in the MIDI were taken from the Minnesota Child Development Inventory, and thus have empirical support for their inclusion. The MCDI was validated on 796 suburban Caucasian children from Minnesota without severe sensory or neurological/organic handicaps. Therefore, it is not clear how or if the MIDI should be employed with handicapped infants; if a practitioner does elect to use this inventory with such children, caution should be exercised in interpreting the results. The authors do recommend an age-correction procedure when examining premature infants with the MIDI.

Administration appears to be relatively straightforward and can be adapted to the requirements of the situation. The MIDI can be administered easily in a clinic or office setting, as well as in the home. Review of the materials would suggest that little formal training in its administration would be necessary; an examiner who is experienced in child development and interviewing parents would most likely be an appropriate person to employ this inventory. The administration time is not specified in the inventory's instructions; most likely it is a function of whether the inventory is completed by the parent alone or in interview format with the professional also observing the child. Overall, the administration can be characterized by its flexible nature.

Given the nature of the inventory and its intended use, there are no resulting scores. Instead, the practitioner is encouraged to examine the infant's functioning with regard to age expectations across the five domains.

Interpretation of the MIDI is accomplished by comparing the behaviors that have been endorsed to established age norms. The authors provide guidelines for identifying those behaviors that are "advanced" for an infant of a specific chronological age and those that fall below age expectation. The authors caution that these interpretations should be based on both the parent's responses to the inventory and the practitioner's observations of the infant.

Technical Aspects

Because the MIDI is not being promoted as a test per se, there are no data available on its psychometric properties. The authors explicitly state that the inventory has not been validated for screening or assessment purposes.

Critique

The MIDI represents a useful instrument that can be relatively easily incorporated into the examination of infants. Its use may offer several benefits to health care professionals, be they psychologists or pediatricians, and parents. For example, a periodic, consistently administered review of an infant's developmental status can alert the primary-care physician to any cause for concern. Given the generally accepted position that intervention, as early as possible, is desirable, the MIDI provides the structure for gathering initial data in the chain of decision-making. Obviously, for the parents of the infant, the MIDI can assist them in attending to their child's development by suggesting specific observable behaviors.

It is important to note that the MIDI has not been validated as a screening/diagnostic instrument and that its use with handicapped children may not be appropriate. Overall, however, the MIDI does present the opportunity for a variety of practitioners involved with infants to conduct developmental reviews.

References

Frankenburg, W. K., Dodds, J. B., Fandal, A. W., Kazuk, E., & Cohrs, M. (1975). *Denver Developmental Screening Test* (rev. ed.). Denver, Colorado: Ladoca.

Bayley, N. (1969). *Bayley Scales of Infant Development.* San Antonio, Texas: The Psychological Corporation.

Brian Bolton, Ph.D.
Professor, Research and Training Center in Vocational Rehabilitation, University of Arkansas, Fayetteville, Arkansas.

MINNESOTA SATISFACTION QUESTIONNAIRE
Work Adjustment Project. Minneapolis, Minnesota: Vocational Psychology Research, University of Minnesota.

Introduction

The Minnesota Satisfaction Questionnaire (MSQ) was designed to measure an individual's satisfaction with 20 different aspects of the work environment. Job satisfaction is the worker's appraisal of the extent to which the work environment fulfills his or her vocational needs or preferences for reinforcers. Each item in the instrument refers to a need reinforcer in the work setting. Respondents indicate how satisfied they are with each reinforcer on their present jobs. The MSQ requires minimal time to administer, has a low reading level, and possesses good technical characteristics.

The MSQ was constructed in conjunction with the Work Adjustment Project, which was initiated in 1957 at the University of Minnesota. The theory of vocational adjustment that resulted, the Minnesota Theory of Work Adjustment (MTWA), has been fully described in a book by Dawis and Lofquist (1984) and is summarized in a recent chapter by Dawis (1986). The principal developers of the MTWA, Rene V. Dawis, Lloyd H. Lofquist, and David J. Weiss, are professors of psychology at the University of Minnesota. They have authored more than 100 monographs, journal articles, and research reports concerned with various aspects of the MTWA.

Briefly, the MTWA postulates that an employee's job satisfaction is a function of the correspondence between the individual's vocational needs (similar to work values) and the need reinforcers available from the job. In an analogous fashion, the employee's work satisfactoriness is postulated to be a function of the correspondence between the individual's occupationally relevant abilities and the ability requirements of the job in which the individual is employed. The ultimate criterion of the MTWA, the individual's vocational adjustment (which is operationalized as job tenure), is hypothesized to be a function of the employee's levels of satisfaction and satisfactoriness.

The MSQ is predicated on the following theoretical rationale: a) employees have a set of *expectations* concerning their work environments that derive from their work histories, abilities, and interests; b) employees have a set of *work attitudes* that emerge from the fulfillment or nonfulfillment of their expectations; and c) these attitudes constitute employees' *evaluations* of their work environments. The MSQ was designed to measure employees' evaluations of their work environments (i.e., their job satisfaction).

The long-form MSQ consists of 100 items, each specifying a need reinforcer in the work setting. Twenty different aspects of the work environment (or 20 classes of job reinforcers) are each measured by five items (5 job reinforcers x 20 scales = 100 items). Respondents indicate their degree of satisfaction with their present jobs using five alternatives: very satisfied (VS), satisfied (S), neither satisfied nor dissatisfied (N), dissatisfied (D), and very dissatisfied (VD).

The 20 MSQ scales, each illustrated by the satisfaction item with the highest item-scale correlation, are as follows:

1. *Ability utilization.* The chance to do something that makes use of my abilities.
2. *Achievement.* The feeling of accomplishment I get from the job.
3. *Activity.* Being able to keep busy all the time.
4. *Advancement.* The chance for advancement on this job.
5. *Authority.* The chance to tell other people what to do.
6. *Company policies and practices.* The way company policies are put into practice.
7. *Compensation.* My pay and the amount of work I do.
8. *Co-workers.* The way my co-workers get along with each other.
9. *Creativity.* The chance to try my own methods of doing the job.
10. *Independence.* The chance to work alone on the job.
11. *Moral values.* Being able to do things that don't go against my conscience.
12. *Recognition.* The praise I get for doing a good job.
13. *Responsibility.* The freedom to use my own judgment.
14. *Security.* The way my job provides for steady employment.
15. *Social service.* The chance to do things for other people.
16. *Social status.* The chance to be "somebody" in the community.
17. *Supervision—human relations.* The way my boss handles his or her employees.
18. *Supervision—technical.* The competence of my supervisor.
19. *Variety.* The chance to do different things from time to time.
20. *Work conditions.* The working conditions.

In addition to the 20 scale scores, a general satisfaction score can be calculated by summing the responses to the 20 "best" items (those having the highest item-scale correlation; listed above). This subset of 20 job reinforcers, when administered alone, comprises the short-form MSQ, which uses the same response format as the long form but is scored on only three scales; intrinsic satisfaction, extrinsic satisfaction, and general satisfaction.

Practical Applications/Uses

The MSQ is essentially self-administering and requires only a fifth-grade reading level. For individuals with poor reading skills or those with visual limitations, the MSQ could be administered easily via audiocassette. The time required for completion of the long-form MSQ is typically 15 to 20 minutes, while the short form takes about 5 minutes.

Because unit scoring weights are used, raw scores can be readily generated using the scoring keys in the manual (Weiss, Dawis, England, and Lofquist, 1967). For some counseling applications, the raw scores for the 20 scales of the long-form MSQ can be simply rank ordered from high to low, providing a profile of job reinforcers ranked from most to least satisfying for the individual. Raw scores can also be converted to percentile scores using the extensive normative data presented in the manual. A computer-scoring service is provided by the publisher.

Minnesota Satisfaction Questionnaire 257

For the long-form MSQ, 25 occupational norm groups in five categories are available: Professional (e.g., accountants, engineers, social workers), Clerical (e.g., bookkeepers, secretaries), Service (e.g., housekeeping aides), Benchwork (e.g., assemblers), and Miscellaneous (e.g., laborers, truck drivers). Seven occupational norm groups ranging from engineers to janitors are provided for the short-form MSQ. The presentation of norm group data in the manual is excellent, including detailed demographic descriptions of the samples, thorough summary statistics on the MSQ, and conversion tables.

The MSQ is especially appropriate for use in individual employment counseling situations and in industrial personnel programs aimed at improving the work environment. Several strategies may be followed in employment counseling applications. The most straightforward is to examine the employee's MSQ profile for sources of job satisfaction and dissatisfaction, using the review of the profile as a basis for discussion of work problems. To establish a reference point for the discussion, it would be helpful for the employee to complete the Minnesota Importance Questionnaire (MIQ; Rounds, Henly, Dawis, Lofquist, and Weiss, 1981), which measures the individual's general vocational needs (i.e., preferred job reinforcers).

Because the MIQ is scored on the same 20 scales as the MSQ, a comparison of the results of the two instruments provides a framework for the analysis of discrepancies between the employee's preferred reinforcers and the *actual* reinforcement derived from the current job. This counseling strategy is an application of Locke's (1976) value theory, which posits that the *importance* of job reinforcers to the individual must be considered in assessing job satisfaction. Schaffer (1953) and other theorists have also proposed explanatory models of job satisfaction that focus on the importance of needs or potential reinforcers to the individual. Furthermore, the use of the MIQ and the MSQ together in diagnosing job problems is consistent with the MTWA's hypothesis that job satisfaction (MSQ) is determined by the extent of correspondence between preferred job reinforcers (MIQ) and objectively measured occupational reinforcers.

Personnel specialists concerned with enhancing the morale of a work force might use aggregate MSQ data as the basis for identifying areas that require attention, on the assumption that dissatisfaction with available reinforcers indicates that workplace reforms are needed. It would be naïve, however, to believe that increased job satisfaction will result in enhanced productivity because evidence suggests that there is no simple causal relationship between the two variables.

Since the publication of Hoppock's (1935) now-classic *Job Satisfaction* half a century ago, more than 4,000 studies on the topic have been published. Numerous reviews of various segments of the job satisfaction literature have been reported, but there are very few handy overviews of the results of these efforts. Lofquist and Dawis (1984, pp. 224-229) prepared a useful summary of the main findings concerning job satisfaction and work adjustment:

1. Job satisfaction is negatively related to job turnover (or positively related to job tenure).
2. Job satisfaction is negatively related to withdrawal behaviors such as absenteeism and lateness.

3. Job satisfaction is positively related to job involvement.
4. Job satisfaction and worker alienation are negatively correlated.
5. Job satisfaction is positively related to work group morale.
6. Job satisfaction is only minimally correlated with job performance and productivity [see Iaffaldano and Muchinsky (1985) for a quantitative review of the evidence].
7. Job satisfaction is positively related to overall life satisfaction and is an important predictor of longevity.

The reason that these conclusions are stated only as "relationships" is that the direction of causal influence is not clear in most situations; causality is probably bidirectional and interactive in most cases, depending on other critical variables. For some relationships, the direction of causal influence is counterintuitive and contrary to early thinking in industrial/organizational (I/O) research. For example, in the 1930s, research on job satisfaction proceeded on the assumption that increased satisfaction would result in greater productivity. It is now generally accepted that just the opposite is true (i.e., successful job performance is one principal determinant of satisfaction with work). For thoughtful discussions of the nature of the aforementioned relationships, see Dawis (1984, pp. 286-291), Landy (1985, pp. 406-415), and clarifying comments by Lofquist and Dawis (1984, pp. 224-229).

Technical Aspects

After reviewing the existing literature on job satisfaction, Scott, Dawis, England, and Lofquist (1960) concluded that available research justified inclusion of job satisfaction measures among the major indicators of work adjustment. Further, they concluded that two types of measures were warranted: overall job satisfaction and satisfaction with specific job-related factors. The latter included pay, co-workers, supervision, type of work, working conditions, identification with the company, security, management, and opportunity for advancement.

Carlson, Dawis, England, and Lofquist (1962) administered the Industrial Relations Center's Employee Attitude Scale (54 items), Hoppock's Job Satisfaction Blank (4 items), and 22 experimental job-attitude items to a heterogeneous sample of employed persons. Cluster analyses of the 80 items separately for groups at different occupational levels produced six replicated scales: General Satisfaction, Working Conditions, Supervision, Cooperation, Co-workers, and Sensitivity. Although scale reliabilities were in the .80s and interscale correlations were in the .90s, factor analysis indicated that there was just one underlying satisfaction factor.

The authors concluded that the 80-item job satisfaction instrument was too cumbersome to score (it involved different item response weights for different occupational groups) and it was disproportionately concerned with environmental or extrinsic satisfaction (such as working conditions and supervision), while neglecting intrinsic reinforcers such as achievement and ability utilization. (The importance of the latter deficiency is made clear in the recent study by Mottaz [1985], which found that intrinsic rewards are the primary determinant of overall job satisfaction at all occupational levels.) The decision was made to construct a new job satisfaction instrument using the same 20 reinforcement dimensions that had previously been identified in the development of the MIQ. The scales were drawn from three sources (Weiss, Dawis, England, and Lofquist, 1964b): a) 12 dimensions postulated by Schaffer (1953), b) the results of the preliminary job satisfaction study, and c) the authors' "general knowledge of occupational reinforcers" (Weiss et al., 1964a, p. 20).

In fact, the MSQ items were simply rewritten from MIQ items to stress satisfaction with current job (Weiss, Dawis, England, & Lofquist, 1964a). The conceptual distinction between the two instruments is that the MIQ measures *potential* satisfaction with a reinforcer (i.e., its general "importance" to the individual), while the MSQ measures *actual* satisfaction with a reinforcer in a particular job (i.e., it presumes employment). For the development sample of 1,800 employees, internal consistency reliabilities for the 20 scales ranged from .81 to .94, with a median of .88. The subscale intercorrelations ranged from .21 (between Compensation and Authority) to .86 (between the two supervision scales). Factor analysis of the 20 scales identified two factors: intrinsic satisfaction (Responsibility, Achievement, Ability utilization, Creativity, Social service) and extrinsic satisfaction (Supervision—human relations, Supervision—technical, Company policies, Recognition). The median communality for the 20 scales was .54. When compared to the median reliability of .88, this indicates that more than 30% of the reliable variance is specific to each scale, suggesting that considerable useful information is contained in the profile of 20 job reinforcers.

Additional reliability data and some validity evidence is reported in the manual (Weiss et al., 1967). The median internal consistency reliabilities for 21 satisfaction scales (20 reinforcer scales plus general satisfaction) calculated separately for 25 occupational groups ranged from .78 to .93, with a median of .86. Retest reliability coefficients with a one-week interval for a heterogeneous sample of employees ranged from .66 to .91 for the 20 reinforcer scales, with a median of .83. For general satisfaction the retest reliability was .89. Retest stability coefficients with a one-year interval for a heterogeneous sample ranged from .35 to .71 for the 20 reinforcer scales, with a median of .61. For general satisfaction the one-year stability coefficient was .70.

Validity evidence for the MSQ that is presented in the manual is limited and derives in good part from early tests of various propositions of the MTWA. Subsequent investigations of the MTWA have supported further the construct validity of the MSQ (i.e., the MSQ measures job satisfaction in accordance with theoretical expectations). For example, studies by Carlson, Dawis, and Weiss (1969) and Dawis, Weiss, Lofquist, and Betz (1967) demonstrated that job satisfaction (as measured by the MSQ) moderates the prediction of satisfactoriness from ability test scores (i.e., prediction is more accurate for satisfied employees than for dissatisfied employees).

Additional results of studies of MTWA propositions that support the construct validity of the MSQ are:

1. Multivariate relationships between job satisfaction and satisfactoriness are minimal, indicating the essential independence of the two constructs.
2. Job satisfaction is predictable from the correspondence of vocational needs and reinforcers present in the job.
3. Employment tenure is predictable from satisfactoriness for satisfied workers but not for dissatisfied employees. (For details about all three conclusions, see Dawis and Lofquist, 1984, pp. 74-91).

In the 20 years that have elapsed since publication of the manual, dozens of studies using the MSQ have provided additional indirect evidence of its validity.

Evidence for the concurrent validity of the MSQ can be inferred from differences among occupational groups in average job satisfaction. Comparisons among the 25 MSQ occupational norm groups on the 20 reinforcer scales and general satisfaction produced highly significant differences in every analysis. Furthermore, the differences were consistent with the existing literature in that professional groups (e.g., managers and teachers) reported the highest job satisfaction while unskilled groups (e.g., housekeeping aides and laborers) reported the lowest satisfaction with their jobs. The finding that persons in higher-level occupations are more satisfied with their jobs is not surprising, but it should be stressed that differences among employees within occupations far exceed average differences in job satisfaction among occupational groups.

To investigate the internal structure of the long-form MSQ, factor analyses were carried out for 14 occupational norm groups consisting of at least 100 employees. Results of these analyses indicated that about half of the variance common to the 20 reinforcer scales could be subsumed by an *extrinsic* satisfaction factor, defined primarily by the two Supervision scales, Company policies, Working conditions, Advancement, Compensation, and Security. The other half of the common variance was accounted for by one or more *intrinsic* satisfaction factors, these being dependent on the particular occupational group. Thus, the structural organization of job satisfaction varies somewhat among occupational groups.

The short-form MSQ was developed for the express purpose of economical administration and data collection (Weiss, Dawis, Lofquist, & England, 1966, pp. 41-51). The short-form MSQ is composed of the 20 items that correlated highest with the 20 reinforcer scales in the original MSQ developmental sample. For a heterogeneous sample of 1,460 men employed in six occupations (engineers, salesmen, clerks, machinists, assemblers, and janitors), the following results were obtained: a) correlations among the 20 items ranged from .16 to .73, with a median of .32, and b) factor analysis produced two factors, intrinsic (IS) and extrinsic (ES) satisfaction.

Unit-weighted factor scores were developed for the short-form MSQ by assigning items to IS and ES scales based on factor loadings. Twelve items compose IS, six items compose ES, and all 20 items are summed for a general satisfaction (GS) score. Internal consistency reliabilities calculated separately for the six occupational groups ranged from .83 to .91 for IS, .78 to .82 for ES, and .87 to .93 for GS, with median coefficients of .86, .80, and .90, respectively. Correlations between IS and ES for the six groups ranged from .52 to .68. One-week retest reliability and one-year stability can be extrapolated from results for the long-form general satisfaction scale (the items are identical), which are .89 and .70, respectively. The six occupational groups differed significantly in the expected directions on IS, ES, and GS, supporting the concurrent validity of the short-form MSQ.

Critique

One indication of the quality of a psychometric instrument is the extent of its usage in published research. Although it is difficult to enumerate all studies in the literature that included the MSQ, a fairly accurate estimate can be obtained by collating the citations from several sources. Using bibliographies from three sources, a computer search of the *Psychological Abstracts* database, the last three editions of the *Mental Measurements Yearbook*, and a list compiled by Vocational Psychology Research at the University of Minnesota, it can be conservatively estimated that the MSQ has been used in at least 75 investigations reported in journals, 100 Ph.D. dissertation projects, and 20 other research studies. The primary research applications of the MSQ have been in vocational psychology, organizational behavior, and personnel management. Although the range of journals is substantial, the *Journal of Vocational Behavior*, the *Journal of Applied Psychology*, and recently the *Academy of Management Journal* have been the main outlets for research using the MSQ.

In a survey of studies published in five I/O journals between 1973 and 1978 that measured job satisfaction, O'Connor, Peters, and Gordon (1978) found that almost half of the studies used an instrument that was not used in any other study. These personalized or nonreplicated measures were typically constructed or adapted for the particular investigation. The Job Descriptive Index (JDI; Smith, Kendall, and Hulin, 1969) was by far the most frequently employed measure of job satisfaction during the period, being used in slightly more than one quarter of all studies. Although the MSQ ranked second in popularity, it was used in only 5% of the applications. Ten other instruments, including Hoppock's Job Satisfaction Blank (JSB), were employed in more than one study.

O'Connor et al. (1978) argued reasonably that the use of such a diversity of job satisfaction measures complicates the search for stable, lawful relationships in I/O psychology. Of course, the converse argument is that the generalizability of any consistent findings would be enhanced. But the evidence suggests that the various operationalizations of job satisfaction are not interchangeable, especially facet satisfaction instruments and overall measures. The net result of unstandardized job satisfaction measurement may well be to preclude the incremental building of knowledge across studies. The authors recommend that researchers employ multiple measures of job satisfaction when feasible, or at least select a commonly used instrument, but they advocate strongly a long-range strategy of programmatic construct validation research on extant job satisfaction instruments.

It is apparent that the two most popular instruments for measuring job satisfaction, the JDI and the MSQ, have been used extensively in I/O research. A direct comparison between the JDI and MSQ reported by Gillet and Schwab (1975) found evidence of convergent validity for four pairs of scales (with correlations in parentheses): Compensation (.56), advancement (.57), supervision (.70/.68), and coworkers (.49). Guion (1978) subsequently factor-analyzed the entire MSQ-JDI correlation matrix published in Gillet and Schwab (1975, p. 315). The five first-order oblique factors did not align with the JDI scales, but the two second-order factors were clearly the intrinsic and extrinsic categories of the MSQ.

It has been known since the 1950s that job satisfaction measures that sum the respondent's satisfaction with a series of job facets are not equivalent to global measures of job satisfaction. In concrete terms, facet satisfaction instruments such as the MSQ do not correlate as highly as would be expected with global measures like Hoppock's JSB, if the two types of instruments were measuring the same underlying construct. One hypothesized explanation of the discrepancy is that facet instruments neglect several critical components that are implicitly evaluated by respondents to global satisfaction measures.

The sum-of-job facets approach to measuring job satisfaction entails two assumptions:

1. Comprehensive sampling of job facets (i.e., the job facets included in the instrument represent all major reinforcers available in the work environment).
2. Additivity of job facets (i.e., the simple, unweighted sum of facet scores translates into overall job satisfaction).

The validity of the first assumption for the MSQ is addressed below. Various attempts to weight job facets by their importance to the individual in summing to overall satisfaction have not generally been successful, so there is no substantial evidence to contradict the additivity assumption.

A recent investigation by Scarpello and Campbell (1983) addressed the hypothesis that the MSQ omits one or more important job facets. In addition to administering the short-form MSQ and two single-item global job satisfaction instruments, individual interviews were conducted with 185 employees. Analysis of the MSQ facets, the resulting interview-based facets and the global satisfaction measures supported two conclusions:

1. Facet instruments neglect major determinants of job satisfaction. Specifically, the MSQ does not measure (at least) five facets: flexibility in scheduling work, tools and equipment, work space, co-workers as facilitators of work, and pleasantness of interactions with people at work.
2. The "whole" of job satisfaction is more complex than the sum of the parts. The clear implication is that the sum of a set of facet satisfactions should not be used as a measure of overall job satisfaction.

Interestingly, the Minnesota investigators realized 20 years ago that the MSQ did not cover all relevant aspects of job satisfaction, and subsequently constructed 10 experimental scales to measure work challenge, company image, organization control, feedback, physical facilities, work references, company prestige, company goals, closure, and compensation II. Twenty-three additional facet scales specifically oriented to scientific personnel were also developed for preliminary study. None of these experimental satisfaction scales were deemed sufficiently valuable to warrant their inclusion in the MSQ.

One possible problem with both the long-form and short-form versions of the MSQ is the "ceiling effect" associated with many of the scale scores. In general, score distributions on MSQ scales are centered around the "satisfied" anchor point, which is fourth on the 5-point response format. This means that discrimination among employees who are satisfied with their jobs is limited with the MSQ. Very few respondents ever use the "dissatisfied" and "very dissatisfied" designations. For all practical purposes, then, the effective response format entails a 3-point range.

It is important to emphasize that this characteristic of the MSQ is entirely consistent with the results of job satisfaction research. Hoppock's (1935) studies found that the vast majority of American workers were satisfied in varying degrees with their jobs and that few (less than 15%) were actually dissatisfied. This finding has been repeatedly confirmed during the past 50 years.

Still, because of the restricted variability on the original MSQ scales, the Minnesota investigators developed a modified response format consisting of one category of job dissatisfaction ("not satisfied") and four degrees of satisfaction ("only slightly satisfied," "satisfied," "very satisfied," and "extremely satisfied"). Research indicated that the modified format produces score distributions that are centered on the middle anchor ("satisfied") and are symmetrical in form. However, because there are no norm groups available for use with the modified MSQ format, it should be used only for research purposes.

A recent book by Cook, Hepworth, Wall, and Warr (1981) provides researchers and practitioners easy access to the instruments currently available for measuring job satisfaction. The volume includes standardized overviews of 17 measures of overall job satisfaction and 29 facet measures of job satisfaction. (The authors located 249 measures of work-related attitudes!) For each instrument, the following information is presented: description and background, descriptive statistics, scale reliability and validity, scale usage, and scale items and response format. The last two sections summarize research results published between 1974 and 1980 and list the actual items composing the instrument, respectively. For reasons that are not clear, only the short-form MSQ is reviewed by Cook et al. (1980, pp. 21-25), although it is apparent that they were fully acquainted with the long-form or facet version of the MSQ.

In summary, the Minnesota Satisfaction Questionnaire is a self-report measure of the extent to which the employee's vocational needs and expectations are satisfied by the work environment. Phrased in terms of the MTWA's hypothesis concerning the principal determinant of job satisfaction, the MSQ is an internal (i.e., within the individual) indicator of the correspondence between the employee's preferred reinforcers and the reinforcers present in the job. It is recognized that the antecedents of job satisfaction are in the individual's personal work history, which includes acquired needs, values, and expectations.

The MSQ long-form is a facet satisfaction instrument that generates a multidimensional profile across 20 aspects of the job, while also providing a general satisfaction score. However, the MSQ general satisfaction scale is not interchangeable with similarly-named scales that are based on an employee's global evaluation of job satisfaction. The strengths and advantages of the MSQ are:

1. It is based on an explicit theoretical formulation that is consistent with research findings and mainstream thinking in the I/O literature.
2. It has an excellent psychometric foundation and is the product of a series of carefully designed developmental studies, and its validity is supported by a variety of construct validation investigations.
3. It has an excellent set of occupational norms that are probably unparalleled in instruments of this type.
4. It consists of an extensive (although not comprehensive) set of satisfaction facets that are especially useful in diagnostic applications.

Favorable published evaluations by Guion (1978), Cook et al. (1981), and numerous authors of journal articles attest to the psychometric quality and practical utility of the MSQ. The single most serious problem is that the manual is almost 20 years old. It should be revised to incorporate validity evidence that has accumulated in the period since original publication. Some type of check on selected norm groups to see if they may be out of date would be a good idea. For practitioners and researchers, it is recommended that Hoppock's Job Satisfaction Blank or some other global measure of job satisfaction be administered concurrently with either form of the MSQ.

References

Carlson, R. E., Dawis, R. V., England, G. W., and Lofquist, L. H. (1962). *The measurement of employment satisfaction* (Minnesota Studies in Vocational Rehabilitation: 13). Minneapolis: Vocational Psychology Research, University of Minnesota.

Carlson, R. E., Dawis, R. V., & Weiss, D. J. (1969). The effect of satisfaction on the relationship between abilities and satisfactoriness. *Occupational Psychology, 43,* 39-46.

Cook, J. D., Hepworth, S. J., Wall, T. D., & Warr, P. B. (1981). *The experience of work.* New York: Academic Press.

Dawis, R. V. (1984). Job satisfaction: Worker aspirations, attitudes, and behavior. In N. C. Gysbers & Associates (Eds.), *Designing careers: Counseling to enhance education, work, and leisure* (pp. 275-301). San Francisco: Jossey-Bass.

Dawis, R. V. (1986). The Minnesota Theory of Work Adjustment. In B. Bolton (Ed.), *Handbook of measurement and evaluation in rehabilitation* (2nd ed.). (pp. 203-217). Baltimore: Paul Brookes.

Dawis, R. V., & Lofquist, L. H. (1984). *A psychological theory of work adjustment.* Minneapolis: University of Minnesota Press.

Dawis, R. V., Weiss, D. J., Lofquist, L. H., & Betz, E. (1967). Satisfaction as a moderator in the prediction of satisfactoriness. *Proceedings of the 75th Annual Convention of the American Psychological Association, 2,* 269-270.

Gillet, B., & Schwab, D. P. (1975). Convergent and discriminant validities of corresponding Job Descriptive Index and Minnesota Satisfaction Questionnaire scales. *Journal of Applied Psychology, 60,* 313-317.

Guion, R. M. (1978). Minnesota Satisfaction Questionnaire. In O. K. Buros (Ed.), *The eighth mental measurements yearbook* (pp. 1679-1680). Highland Park, NJ: The Gryphon Press.

Hoppock, R. (1935). *Job satisfaction.* New York: Harper & Row.

Iaffaldano, M. T., & Muchinsky, P. M. (1985). Job satisfaction and job performance: A meta-analysis. *Psychological Bulletin, 97,* 251-273.

Landy, F. J. (1985). *Psychology of work behavior* (3rd ed.). Homewood, IL: Dorsey Press.

Locke, E. A. (1976). The nature and causes of job satisfaction. In M. D. Dunnette (Ed.), *Handbook of industrial and organizational psychology* (pp. 1297-1349). Chicago: Rand McNally.

Lofquist, L. H., & Dawis, R. V. (1984). Research on work adjustment and satisfaction: Implications for career counseling. In S. D. Brown & R. W. Lent (Eds.), *Handbook of counseling psychology* (pp. 216-237). New York: John Wiley & Sons.

Mottaz, C. J. (1985). The relative importance of intrinsic and extrinsic rewards as determinants of work satisfaction. *The Social Quarterly, 26,* 365-385.

O'Connor, E. J., Peters, L. H., & Gordon, S. M. (1978). The measurement of job satisfaction: Current practices and future considerations. *Journal of Management, 4* (2), 17-26.

Rounds, J. B., Jr., Henly, G. A., Dawis, R. V., Lofquist, L. H., & Weiss, D. J. (1981). *Manual for the Minnesota Importance Questionnaire.* Minneapolis: Vocational Psychology Research, University of Minnesota.

Scarpello, V., & Campbell, J. P. (1983). Job satisfaction: Are all the parts there? *Personnel Psychology, 36,* 577-600.

Schaffer, R. H. (1953). Job satisfaction as related to need satisfaction in work. *Psychological Monographs*, No. 364.

Scott, T. B., Dawis, R. V., England, G. W., & Lofquist, L. H. (1960). *A definition of work adjustment* (Minnesota Studies in Vocational Rehabilitation: 10). Minneapolis: Vocational Psychology Research, University of Minnesota.

Smith, P. C., Kendall, L. M., & Hulin, C. L. (1969). *The measurement of satisfaction in work and retirement*. Chicago: Rand McNally.

Weiss, D. J., Dawis, R. V., England, G. W., & Lofquist, L. H. (1964a). *Construct validation studies of the Minnesota Importance Questionnaire* (Minnesota Studies in Vocational Rehabilitation: 18). Minneapolis: Vocational Psychology Research, University of Minnesota.

Weiss, D. J., Dawis, R. V., England, G. W., & Lofquist, L. H. (1964b). *The measurement of vocational needs* (Minnesota Studies in Vocational Rehabilitation: 16). Minneapolis: Vocational Psychology Research, University of Minnesota.

Weiss, D. J., Dawis, R. V., England, G. W., & Lofquist, L. H. (1967). *Manual for the Minnesota Satisfaction Questionnaire* (Minnesota Studies in Vocational Rehabilitation: 22). Minneapolis: Vocational Psychology Research, University of Minnesota.

Weiss, D. J., Dawis, R. V., Lofquist, L. H., & England, G. W. (1966). *Instrumentation for the theory of work adjustment* (Minnesota Studies in Vocational Rehabilitation: 21). Minneapolis: Vocational Psychology Research, University of Minnesota.

Diane Ganiere, Ph.D.
Assistant Professor of Psychology, Mary Baldwin College, Staunton, Virginia.

MISKIMINS SELF-GOAL-OTHER DISCREPANCY SCALE

R. W. Miskimins. Ft. Collins, Colorado: Rocky Mountain Behavioral Science Institute, Inc.

Introduction

The Miskimins Self-Goal-Other Discrepancy Scale (MSGO) is a personality test in which one rates oneself relative to 15 prescribed qualities (for example, "hardworking" vs. "lazy") on a Likert-type scale, the purpose of which is to measure any discrepancy between one's evaluation of self, one's goals, and perception of others' evaluation of oneself. There are also five blanks provided (in the same format) in which one places other bipolar qualities of importance. These blanks may also be filled with other adjectives of interest to a researcher. The measure can be scored with or without these last five items.

The MSGO is based on the assumption that the discrepancies between a person's self-perception, goals, and perceptions of others' evaluations will create certain tensions and determine the person's behavior. An understanding of these discrepancies will contribute then to an understanding of the behavior.

In 1961 R. W. Miskimins, Ph.D., constructed a test to meet the demand created by the aforementioned theoretical framework, to help distinguish "abnormals" and "normals," to discern certain types of pathological patterns, and to serve as a clinical tool in treatment. The constructs were decided upon with the help of graduate students in clinical psychology, who listed and sorted relevant adjectives until, from about 100 original items, the 18 most meaningful were selected and placed into categories related to states of general, social, and emotional well-being. The test was refined by administering it, in a series of studies, to undergraduates and patients under psychiatric care, along with the Taylor Manifest Anxiety Scale (Taylor, 1953) and the MMPI.

An MSGO-II was designed for use with certain individuals and small groups, in which high rapport and personal attention from an examiner is required to ensure full understanding. Examples of such groups include children, adolescents, mental retardates, deteriorated psychiatric patients, certain physically handicapped persons, the elderly, and the educationally disadvantaged. The MSGO-II is slightly shorter and uses simplified vocabulary. For example, "physically attractive" versus "physically unattractive" was changed to "good looking" versus "ugly" for this supplemental test. The format was also simplified, with larger spaces provided for responses.

Practical Applications/Uses

The MSGO differentiates emotionally disturbed patients from so-called "normals," and differentiates various subcategories within the emotionally disturbed group. It may also be used as a clinical tool to describe one individual for the purpose of diagnosis and treatment, in which case it is suggested that the MSGO be treated as one aspect of a larger number of observations relative to the self. The test would be of use to anyone who subscribes to the ideas that 1) a person's self-concept is important, 2) the degree to which a person's goals match the real, or the realistic, will contribute to the anxiety or tension experienced by that person, and 3) a person's impression of how others perceive him or her will also be associated with varying amounts of comfort and discomfort. The test could provide helpful data and a springboard for use with a counselee to whom the results had been explained. It might also be of use with clients who have more serious problems by confirming the results of other tests, such as the Minnesota Multiphasic Personality Inventory (MMPI).

The MSGO involves placing checks indicating ratings from one through nine, describing oneself relative to 15 prescribed bipolar attributes and five self-scribed bipolar attributes. The format is simple and can be administered to a wide range of research or clinical populations. One page of the MSGO-I is devoted to personal data blanks (name, etc.), directions, and examples. The remaining two pages contain the rating scales themselves.

In the MSGO-II, explicit verbal directions are included in the examiner's manual, and the rating scales fill three pages. A hand-scoring summary sheet and a profile sheet are included with each test, although computer scoring is available. The profile sheet includes eight dimensions, which can be used to assist in the clinical evaluation of discrepancy scores with the use of the normative data provided in the manual.

Instructions for scoring are clear and only two pages long, but complicated in practice. The user should be prepared to spend a number of hours examining the test's inner relationships and the meanings of the scores and subscores. Although computer scoring is available and recommended for large group use, it will be meaningless without a thorough knowledge of the sources and implications.

The test yields numerical scores, and the manual is replete with profiles of various types of populations; for instance, previous test results include an average college population of 122 males and females and groups of 5-55 mental health center patients covering a number of personality disorders from neuroses to schizophrenia. There are commentaries on certain atypical profiles, but the manual warns against using these interpretations with a "cookbook" approach. Once I became thoroughly familiar with the test, this reviewer estimated that it would take between 15 and 30 minutes to administer to a normal person or group, and an hour to score and interpret each test.

Technical Aspects

The MSGO was first refined by administering it, along with the Taylor Manifest Anxiety Scale (MAS), to 71 undergraduate students. The total of discrepancies correlated significantly with the TMAS ($r = .54$, $p < .001$), along with the discrepancy between self-concept and goal self-concept ($r = .25$, $p < .05$). To measure internal reliability, each item was correlated with the total discrepancy score and afforded positive correlations ranging from .20 to .78, with all but three above .45. The three below were dropped from the test.

To validate the improved test, another study was done by the author and reported in the manual (Miskimins, 1979) using 63 college students from the University of Colorado. The correlations of two subtotals with the TMAS were .63 and .713. The same students were also given the MMPI. Virtually all of the MSGO values correlated positively with the MMPI F (validity) scale, the highest correlation being .56 for the positive discrepancy scores between self-concept and goal self-concept (based on the category of adjectives termed "general"). These positive discrepancy scores between self-concept and goal self-concept, when based on the category of adjectives termed "emotional," also correlated with the MMPI Psychopathic Deviate scale (.43). Discrepancies between one's self-concept and one's goals, when based on emotional values, correlated .60 with the Schizophrenia scale. (This value was also the highest predictor of anxiety in the TMAS.) The total of all deviance scores also correlated with the Psychopathic Deviate scale of the MMPI at .40. When scores indicated that one was choosing atypical goals, such as preferring to be unsuccessful, sad, or socially awkward, this correlated only with the Psychopathic Deviance scale. Scores indicating that one perceives other people as regarding one poorly correlated positively with Psychasthenia. Twenty-one MSGO values correlated above .5 with the Social Introversion scale. As would be expected, seven MSGO values correlated significantly and negatively with the Lie scale, and many correlated negatively with the K scale. The values that reflect that others view one rather negatively correlated significantly and positively with the MMPI Hypochondriasis scale. In summary, MSGO-I reflects to some degree the psychopathology as measured by the MMPI, especially depression, psychasthenia, schizophrenia, and social introversion.

Another validity study (Miskimins, 1979) matched 29 controls with no history of psychiatric treatment and 29 Ss undergoing psychiatric treatment. Without exception, all comparisons produced differences in the predicted directions. Of the variables employed, 19 were found to differentiate between the groups at statistically significant levels. In this case, the discrepancies between one's self-concept and oneself as perceived by others provided the most critical discrimination.

Another study was done by the author (Miskimins, 1979) to examine the efficacy of the MSGO for differentiating various degrees of psychopathology. Forty-seven matched pairs of Ss from a mental health center were placed either in a "moderate" pathology group or a "severe" group, based on their ratings on six items of the *Mental Status Summary* used by the center. Although virtually all differences were as predicted, only four reached statistical significance. Again, these were based on the discrepancy between one's self-concept and how one thinks one is perceived by others. The only absolute sum distinguishing between the groups was goal self-concept, the more severely disturbed having goals which were much "higher" and difficult to attain.

Another study (Miskimins, 1979) was done comparing patients in a more operational-behavioral manner—considering length of stay and form of discharge. Differences were in the predicted directions for the grand total of discrepancy scores and for the self-concept-goal/self-concept total scores, but differences were not statistically significant when subjected to analysis of variance.

For studying the internal structure of the MSGO-I, all possible intercorrelations were obtained using the previously mentioned 63 student protocols. The two major subtotals correlate at .98. These are the values most completely reflecting all aspects of the self. These totals represent the summing of all incongruities on all items and, theoretically, emotional disturbance is related to the total amount of discrepancy in the self-system. Other correlations of minor items ranged from .33 to .89. Factor analysis revealed that the scale was internally sound and suited to logical interpretation, with the positive and negative discrepancy scores between "self-concept and self-concept goal" and "self-concept and self as perceived by others" being most easily interpretable.

Test stability was observed in the scores of 51 university students who took the test with two weeks intervening, the *r* of the total subscores being .80 and .87, with the *r*s of minor items ranging from .28 to .86. This may indicate that total amount of "tension" remains stable, although its sources may fluctuate to some degree.

Validity of the MSGO-II is closely related to that of the MSGO-I. In a study by the author involving 118 Ss who were administered both tests in a counterbalanced design (including two groups who took the same form of the same test twice), the correlations of the total scores of the MSGO-I followed by the MSGO-II, and the MSGO-II followed by the MSGO-I, averaged .77. The correlations of the minor items ranged from .43 to .78, with all but one above .62.

According to the manual, Miskimins studied the instrument to see if different types of psychopathology would be evidenced in different patterns of discrepancies presented. He observed that psychoneurotics show a higher positive discrepancy between the self-concept and goal self-concept, while psychotics showed a greater negative discrepancy between self-concept and self as perceived by others. Depressive neurotics displayed a discrepancy between self-evaluation and professed goals, as well as overvaluing others, as would be expected. More complete and inclusive descriptions of the relationships between the data and the disorder are included in the manual, but these should be used with caution, as the manual advises.

Critique

This test has involved the use of 379 subjects in the validation and reliability studies just described. Forty pages of the 72-page manual are devoted to the technical display and analyses of these findings. Another 13 pages are devoted to the interpretation of different profiles. While the MSGO is newer (c. 1979) and has been researched on a smaller scale than some of the more commonly used personality tests such as the MMPI, it is admirably thorough in its development. Its greatest contribution is that it measures self-concept, the discrepancies between self-concept and goals, and self-concept and one's perceptions of others' views of self in a relatively straightforward, short, numerically scorable test. It will be welcomed by mental health care workers who find these concepts useful in counseling or therapy and who want to confirm or broaden the data base on their clients with this type of information.

References

Miskimins, R. W. (1979). *Manual: MSGO (Miskimins Self-Goal-Other Discrepancy Scale)*. Fort Collins, CO: Rocky Mountain Behavioral Science Institute, Inc.

Charles E. McInnis, Ph.D.
Associate Professor, School of Psychology, University of Ottawa, Ottawa, Canada.

MODERN LANGUAGE APTITUDE TEST
John B. Carroll and Stanley M. Sapon. San Antonio, Texas: The Psychological Corporation.

Introduction

The Modern Language Aptitude Test (MLAT), developed by Carroll and Sapon (1959), was designed to predict an individual's probable degree of success in learning a foreign language. The mastery of a foreign language is not simply restricted to "speaking" and "understanding," but also to "reading," "writing," and "translating" the language. Although it is recognized at the outset that the psychometric properties of the battery have been well researched and the predictive validity of the MLAT was based on well-documented and acceptable psychometric procedures, it was considered a challenge to this consultant to administer the MLAT individually to a number of acknowledged professionals in such abstract areas as mathematics, music, and literature. It was expected that their reactions to the types of abilities measured by the subtests would be in close agreement with the descriptions in the test manual. Additionally, this consultant had considerable experience with the MLAT, as it was one of the main instruments used in research assessing the potential of candidates for success in intensive French language courses in the Canadian Public Service (McInnis, 1973).

Brief descriptions of the MLAT subtests follow: Part I—*Number Learning.* Via tape recording the examinee is taught a simple artificial system of number expression utilizing nonsense syllables to represent the digits 0, 1, 2, 3, and 4. The examinee is then required to identify the arabic numerals from a list of two- and three-digit numbers in the artificial system (Lutz, 1967). This subscale seems to measure one aspect of the memory component of foreign language aptitude, but the part also has a fairly large specific variance, which one might label a special "auditory alertness" factor. Such a factor should play a role in the auditory comprehension of a foreign language (Carroll & Sapon, 1959). Normally, examinees can be expected to complete this subtest in five minutes.

Part II—*Phonetic Script.* The examinee learns a series of phonetic symbols for some of the phonemes of English by listening to taped pronunciations of syllables following their printed representations in phonetic symbols on the test paper. After every five items, the examinee is tested on the material just learned. After the learning period, there is a 30-item test in which the examinee must indicate, for each item, which of four phonemically provided syllables is pronounced on the tape. All phonemes used on the test occur in English, and no fine phonetic discrimination is required (Lutz, 1967). This subscale purports to measure "sound-symbol association ability"; that is, the ability to learn correspondences between speech sounds and orthographic symbols. It may also measure a sort of "memory for speech sounds," and it tends to correlate highly with the ability to mimic speech sounds and sound combinations in foreign languages (Carroll & Sapon, 1959). This subtest continues on the tape for about 13 minutes.

Part III—*Spelling Clues*. This is an objectively scored adaptation of the Turse Phonetic Association Test. The subtest consists of 50 items, which must be completed within 5 minutes. The examinee chooses which of five words has the same meaning as the word represented in abbreviated form. Lutz (1967), in reference to Carroll's (1962) study, suggests that this subtest is most closely related to the ability to produce phonemes accurately and to mimic basic sentences. Scores depend on students' English vocabulary knowledge. It measures sound-symbol association ability (as does Phonetic Script), but to a lesser extent. This subtest is highly speeded and is to be completed in 5 minutes.

Part IV—*Words in Sentences*. Each of the 45 items in this subtest consists of a key sentence with a word or phrase underlined and a second sentence or set of sentences with five words or phrases underlined. The examinee's task is to choose the one underlined word or phrase in the second sentence that serves the same function as the underlined word or phrase in the key sentence. This subtest should seem to measure sensitivity to grammatical structure and is hypothesized to have particular relevance to the student's ability to cope with the grammatical aspects of a foreign language. No grammatical terminology is involved; therefore, scores do not depend on specific memory for grammatical terminology. Examinees have exactly 15 minutes to work on this subtest.

Part V—*Paired Associates*. The examinee is given 2 minutes to learn the definitions of 24 Kurdish words. The examinee is then presented a Kurdish word and five English words and is required to choose the English equivalent (for all 24 Kurdish words). An exact time limit of 4 minutes is given, and the examinee is not permitted to look back at either the previous information or the practice exercise sheet (Gliksman, Gardner, & Smythe, 1979). This subtest purports to measure the rote memory aspect of the learning of foreign languages.

The principal author of the MLAT, John B. Carroll, was Professor of Educational Psychology at Harvard University from 1957-66. He was a senior research psychologist at the Educational Testing Service (ETS) from 1967-74. Carroll was subsequently Kenan Professor Emeritus of Psychology and director of the L.L. Thurstone Psychometric Laboratory at Chapel Hill, North Carolina, from 1974 to the present. Dr. Carroll received his Ph.D. in general psychology from the University of Minnesota in 1941 and has established an international reputation as one of North America's best-known and leading psychometricians. The second author of the MLAT, Stanley Sapon, received his Ph.D. in psychology from Columbia University in 1949 and has been a researcher in the Verbal Behavioral Laboratory at the University of Rochester in New York.

The Modern Language Aptitude Test (MLAT) is a synthesis of a 5-year research study by Carroll and Sapon at Harvard University from 1953-1958. Since the early 1950s, extensive research has led to the development of several commercial test batteries for the prediction of success in language learning for children, adolescents, and adults. Test development procedures involved the initial use of diverse measures hypothesized to be useful predictors of success in a variety of foreign language instructional situations. Criteria for evaluation of success generally included teachers' ratings of student performance, grades, success in language courses, and proficiency test scores subsequent to varying periods of language training (Wesche, Edwards, & Wells, 1982). Earlier efforts to develop foreign language aptitude tests resulted generally in two types of tests: 1) tests of ability and achievement in the English language, and 2) work-sample tests involving short lessons or problems either in the language to be studied or in an artificial language. Tests developed initially presented essentially intellectual tasks to be solved by analytical procedures. These tests were generally unsatisfactory because they correlated highly with general intelligence measures that were not previously found to be highly predictive of success in learning a foreign language. Moreover, many of these earlier tests involved knowledge of grammatical terminology and morphological processes, such as *prefining* and *suffining*, and were incompatible with changing objectives that emphasized more the development of oral language abilities than the specific development of skills in writing a foreign language.

In the subsequent process of development of language aptitude tests, Carroll has continued research in the area of language achievement and has elaborated a coherent theory of the nature of foreign language aptitude. The impetus for foreign language aptitude testing originally resulted from the recognized need for selection devices, not only to screen prospective students but also to assign students to appropriate levels of language study (Lutz, 1967).

In the process of constructing the MLAT, 30 experimental tests were administered to about 5,000 persons: 1,200 high school students, 2,500 college students, and 1,300 individuals in various foreign language courses conducted under military or government auspices (Carroll & Sapon, 1959). From the correlational and factor analytic study of the 30 experimental tests, as well as through subsequent studies with the MLAT battery, Carroll identified four relatively independent components of language aptitude. Three of these components are purported to be measured explicitly by the MLAT and have been labelled as "phonetic coding ability," "grammatical sensitivity," and "rote memory for foreign language materials." A fourth ability, "inductive language learning ability," which according to Carroll is an important component of language aptitude, is not strongly represented in the MLAT (Wesche, Edwards, & Wells, 1982).

The MLAT provides an indication of an individual's probable degree of success in learning a foreign language: speaking and understanding, reading, writing, and translating the "modern" spoken languages such as Latin and Greek. It has been validated primarily for literate subjects in Grades 9 and above who possess English with either native or near-native fluency (Lutz, 1967).

In addition to the MLAT-English version, a French version has been adapted and validated for use in the Canadian public service (Sarrazin, Wells, & Wesche, 1979). No published studies are yet available on this revision; however, a detailed study of the manual would suggest that the standardization and validation process was competently executed.

The MLAT has been standardized for Grades 9 to adult. In the administration of the test, a tape recorder is required to present the test instructions. The entire test can be administered in a 60- to 70-minute time period. For the shorter form of the MLAT (Parts III, IV, and V), a tape recorder is not required, and these subtests can be administered in 30 minutes. In administering either the total test or the shorter form, a reusable test booklet, a double-faced answer sheet, and an electrographic pencil are required. The test can either be scored manually or by machine, using a correct scoring key that is provided.

In addition to the standardization of the MLAT on average populations, Gajar et al. (1983) reviewed the literature on foreign language and written expression in the learning disabled. The abilities purported to be measured by subtests of the MLAT (e.g., memory, auditory discrimination, and grammatical sensitivity) are cited in the literature as potential areas of deficit in learning-disabled populations. For instance, learning-disabled children often demonstrate particular deficiencies in the processing of syntax as well as in auditory discrimination and memory.

Gardner and Lambert (1965) reported research that attempted to modify the MLAT for blind students. Modifications were made usually without recourse to braille; dot-answer sheets were used for responses and the test items were used auditoriaIy. The Cooperative Vocabulary Test (Form 9) was substituted for Spelling Clues, and a Phonetic Discrimination Test was substituted for Phonetic Script. It was hypothesized by Gardner that, because of the instructions necessary with blind students, validity would be improved by the increased reliance of the modified tests on memory skills. Gardner obtained consistent predictive power with the MLAT Words in Sentences subtest and positive correlation with the MLAT Number Learning, MLAT Spelling Clues, and Vocabulary subtests.

The five MLAT subtests provide a profile on each examinee. In the MLAT manual, expectancy tables facilitate decisions in selecting students for foreign language courses. A minimum scale (cutting score) is established, and scores below the cutting score suggest low ability (Carroll & Sapon, 1959).

Practical Applications/Uses

Scores on the MLAT can be used by counselors to estimate an individual's probability of success in studying a foreign language, assuming that motivation and interest are sufficient. The MLAT does not provide differential predictions for different languages.

Low scores on different parts of the MLAT suggest learning difficulties in various areas. For instance, low scores on the Phonetic Script subtest indicate difficulties in learning the phonology (sound system) of a foreign language and also difficulties in mimicking spoken sentences accurately; low scores on the Words in Sentences subtest suggest a difficulty in learning the grammar and structure of a foreign language; and low scores on the Paired Associates subtest show difficulty in the rote memory aspect of learning a foreign language.

It has been generally observed that individuals who choose difficult foreign languages (e.g., Russian) have higher MLAT scores than individuals who choose easy languages (e.g., Spanish); therefore, some self-selection of language occurs according to language aptitude (Carroll & Sapon, 1959). In fact, individuals' ratings of their own language aptitude tend to correlate with their MLAT score, and candidates can and do select foreign languages according to their perceptions of their language aptitude. In the upper grade levels, the norms in the test manual show sex differences in MLAT scores. Girls tend to score higher than boys on the MLAT and also obtain higher academic grades on foreign language tests (Carroll & Sapon, 1959).

The complete MLAT yields a more comprehensive appraisal of foreign language aptitude than the three subtests comprising the shorter version. As mentioned previously, the administration of the complete MLAT takes about 60 to 70 minutes and requires the use of a pre-recorded magnetic tape. The usual precautions for group test administration should be observed, and the examiner should adhere strictly to the instructions outlined in the manual and/or tape. The maximum scores for each subtest and for the complete test follow:

	Side A of answer sheet	
Part I—Number Learning	43	
Part II—Phonetic Script	30	
		73
	Side B of answer sheet	
Part III—Spelling Clues	50	
Part IV—Words in Sentences	45	
Part V—Paired Associates	24	
		119
Total score, complete test		192

The "Right Key" is used to count the number of correct responses for both hand and machine scoring. The total correct responses are converted to percentiles.

Reading and writing superiority in a foreign language tend to be predicted mainly by the Words in Sentences subtest of the MLAT. Active performance in the foreign language (speaking) is predictable by relatively lower scores on the Spelling Clues subtest (Markessinis, 1968).

Technical Aspects

The validity of the MLAT is the degree to which scores on the battery can be used to predict success in foreign language training. The expectancy tables in the MLAT manual are a useful way of interpreting the predictive validity of the tests. These are actuarial tables that give the probabilities of success in foreign language courses for persons with specific MLAT scores. Measures of performance in foreign language learning are termed *criterion measurements* and are actually what the MLAT was designed to predict. The generally high validities reported in the test manual and other research sources suggest that the MLAT measures basic abilities essential to facilitate foreign language learning. Scores on the MLAT generally have been found highly predictive of success in foreign language study, particularly in intensive language training (Carroll, 1962).

The Research Division of the U.S. Peace Corps has either conducted or sponsored numerous studies showing satisfactory validity of the MLAT in predicting success in Peace Corps language training programs (Krug, 1962). Hobbs (1963) further points out that the MLAT has been found to predict success not only in various training programs but also in the operational setting. This later finding could suggest the existence of some general ability-to-learn factor.

Indeed, several parts of the MLAT are explicitly learning tasks, particularly subtests I, II and V. The MLAT, therefore, appears to have satisfactory predictive validity.

The MLAT battery has also been shown to have reasonable internal consistency reliability. The odd-even reliability estimates for the various subscales for students in Grades 9, 10, and 11 range from .55 to .89, with the majority of the reliability coefficients (65%) exceeding .80. Gliksman, Gardner, and Smythe (1979) also provide evidence of satisfactory test-retest reliability for the different subtests of the MLAT. The short form of the MLAT was administered to students in Grades 7-11 to investigate the reliability of the subtests at each grade level and also the effects of repeated use of the test on students of various ages. Gliksman et al. conclude that the short form of the MLAT seems to be more appropriate for use with students in Grades 10 and 11 than with younger students, in that test-retest reliability coefficients reach acceptable levels for the older and more advanced students. At the earlier grade levels (7 and 8), the tests were generally found to be unreliable over time, and factors such as education and motivation seem to influence scores differentially on the various subtests.

Critique

An overall study of the MLAT as reviewed from the MLAT manual and the research literature would tend to support its predictive validity. The reader who researches the published literature is impressed with the care taken in developing the test battery, the extremely large samples that have been administered the battery, and the continuing research.

Gardner and Lambert (1965) factor analyzed 24 variables in order to determine the factorial structure of a battery of tests designed to measure various language skills. It was hypothesized that such a factorial structure would clarify the relationship of intelligence to language aptitude and second language achievement, and also delineate the specific language skills associated with learning a second language. According to Lutz (1967), it would appear that the two main factors of success in second language acquisition are verbal intelligence and motivation.

When examinees take the MLAT or another language aptitude test, they usually do so for a particular purpose (placement, training, etc.). Although motivation is not specifically assessed by the MLAT, motivation must be an integral part of language aptitude and ability, which would be necessarily reflected in MLAT scores. Therefore, motivation should be considered an important factor contributing to high scores. There is a need for more coordination of research in this latter area.

This reviewer would tend to support Carroll's (1962) view that facility in learning to speak and understand a foreign language is a fairly specialized talent (or group of talents), relatively independent of those traits included under "intelligence," and that a relatively small fraction of the general population have sufficient talent to be assigned to the rigorous, intensive, expensive foreign language training programs (Lutz, 1967). Carroll's view of language aptitude as a collection of abilities that together form a multifactor construct has considerable promise. The MLAT would seem to measure this collective set of abilities.

References

This list includes text citations and suggested additional reading.

Carroll, J. B. (1958). A factor analysis of two foreign language batteries. *Journal of General Psychology, 59,* 3-19.
Carroll, J. B. (1962). The prediction of success in intensive language training. In R. Glaser (Ed.), *Training Research and Education* (pp. 87-136). Pittsburgh: University of Pittsburgh Press.
Carroll, J. B., & Sapon, S. M. (1959). *Modern Language Aptitude Test (MLAT): Manual.* New York: The Psychological Corporation.
Eisenstein, M. (1977). *Childhood bilingualism and adult language learning aptitude* (CUNY Forum, No. 3). New York City University of New York, Graduate School and University Center Program. (ERIC Document Reproduction Service No. MFED 163 814)
Fiks, A. I. (1968). *The Modern Language Aptitude Test in a Peace Corps content: Validity, expectancies, and implications for further research.* (ERIC Document Reproduction Service No. MFED 050 136)
Gajar, A., Murphy, T., Raymond, M., Pelco, L., & Baird, N. (1983). *The learning disabled university student: A synopsis of applied research.* (ERIC Document Reproduction Service No. MFED 235 598)
Gardner, R. C., & Lambert, W. E. (1965). Language aptitude, intelligence, and second-language achievement. *Journal of Educational Psychology, 56,* 191-199.
Gliksman, L., Gardner, R., & Smythe, P. C. (1979). An investigation of the test-retest reliability of the subscales of the Modern Language Aptitude Test (MLAT). *Canadian Modern Language Review, 25*(2), 204-210.
Hobbs, N. A. (1963). A psychologist in the Peace Corps. *American Psychologist, 18*(1), 47-55.
Krug, R. E. (1962). *An analysis of eighteen Peace Corps projects.* Pittsburgh, PA: American Institute for Research.
Lutz, M. (1967). *The development of foreign language aptitude tests: A review of the literature.* Princeton, NJ: Educational Testing Service. (ERIC Document Reproduction Service No. MFED 119 487)
Markessinis, J. (1968). *Summary of Dr. John B. Carroll's "The Foreign Language Attainments of Language Majors in the Senior Year."* Washington, DC: Peace Corp. (ERIC Document Reproduction Service No. MFED 131 697)
McInnis, C. E. (1973, April). *Does either a moderator model, or a multiplicative model improve prediction over the usual multiple regression model in the context of an intensive French language training program?* Paper presented at the Annual Meeting of the Canadian Psychological Association, Victoria, British Columbia.
Politzer, R. L., & Weiss, L. (1969). *An experiment in improving achievement in foreign language through learning of selected skills associated with language aptitude (Final Report).* Stanford, CA: Stanford University, California School of Education. (ERIC Document Reproduction Service No. MFED 046 261)
Sarrazin, G., Wells, W., & Wesche, M. (1979). *Test d'aptitude aux langues vivantes.* Montreal: Institut de recherches psychologiques.
Wesche, M., Edwards, H., & Wells, W. (1982). Foreign language aptitude and intelligence. *Applied Psycholinguistics, 3*(2), 127-140.

Michael D. Franzen, Ph.D.
Director of Neuropsychology, West Virginia University Medical Center, Assistant Professor of Behavioral Medicine and Psychiatry, School of Medicine, and Assistant Professor of Psychology, West Virginia University, Morgantown, West Virginia.

MULTILINGUAL APHASIA EXAMINATION
Arthur L. Benton and Kerry deS. Hamsher. Odessa, Florida: Psychological Assessment Resources, Inc.

Introduction

The Multilingual Aphasia Examination (MAE) is a collection of short tests that were designed to determine the presence, degree, and type of language disorder in a subject. There are nine separate procedures (although eleven measures are taken, because there is a rating of articulation and a rating of the praxic features of writing conducted on data taken from earlier procedures).

According to test co-author Arthur Benton, the purpose of the MAE is to "provide a relatively brief (hence, clinically practicable) assessment which is more informative than the usual brief screening battery but which, at the same time, does not provide the more elaborate and detailed assessments of longer test batteries" (A. Benton, personal communication, April 14, 1986). Benton is well known as the founder of the Iowa school of clinical neuropsychological assessment and as one of the first psychologists to bring laboratory methods of measurement and evaluation into the neurological clinic. Dr. Kerry deS. Hamsher, co-author of the MAE, is a student of Benton's and a well-known neuropsychologist in his own right.

In an early paper, Benton outlined what must have been one of the first incarnations of what was to become the MAE (Benton, 1967). He discussed some of the guides by which a test of language function was to be optimally developed. These guides include a careful selection of items, an evaluation of the reliability and validity of the test scales, acquisition of normative data, an evaluation of the effects of age, sex, and education on performance with subsequent separate norms, an evaluation of the effects of prior exposure or practice on performance, and the derivation of standard scores so as to allow comparison among subtest scores in the same individual and comparison of scores among subjects.

In the same paper, Benton discussed some of the goals in developing a test for aphasia. These goals included the provision of a comprehensive examination of the clinically relevant aspects of language, the provision of in-depth assessments of each area of function covered by the test, and the inclusion of specific tests to evaluate the existence of different types of aphasic disorders as well as to document recovery in each area. Additionally, the optimal test battery was to include tests of functions that were related to aphasic disorders but that were not primarily linguistic in nature.

Not all of the goals seem to have remained consistent in the eventual product, and the description of tests in the 1967 paper are sometimes different from those that appeared in the MAE. The differences undoubtedly reflect progress in knowledge regarding language functions as well as changes in the authors' conceptualization of the assessment of language functions.

For example, in the original version (published in 1978), the Object Naming Test consisted of 60 items. On the basis of preliminary data, 40 of these items were retained and formed into four groups of ten objects each. For reasons of practicality, the final version of the Object Naming Test consists of individually presented line drawings of the objects rather than the objects themselves.

Practical Applications/Uses

The first MAE subtest is the Visual Naming Test, which includes ten line drawings that serve as stimulus items. The examiner points to a picture and asks the subject to name the object. The examiner then points to a detail of the picture and asks the subject to name the detail. There are 30 required responses in this test. A scoring sheet allows the examiner to record responses verbatim, allowing an eventual scoring for mistakes in articulation as well as for the time until response. In order to score correctly, the subject must give the proper name of the object within 10 seconds. The manual presents a list of acceptable responses for each item. Scores are corrected for age and education, then compared to tables of normative data from control subjects and from aphasic subjects. The raw scores can be translated into percentile scores.

The second subtest is the Sentence Repetition Test, and it consists of 14 sentences of increasing difficulty. There are two forms of this subtest. Comparison of the performance of two groups of 85 patients each resulted in nonsignificant differences, indicating the approximate equivalency of the two forms. The record sheet for this subtest includes the stimulus sentences and space for recording the obtained scores. Scores for this subtest are corrected for age and education and can be compared to tables of normative performance.

The third subtest, Controlled Oral Word Association, requires the subject to produce words that begin with a certain letter of the alphabet. There are again two forms of this subtest, each with three letters to be used as stimuli. The subject is told that a letter will be given and that he or she is to give as many words beginning with that letter as possible, deleting proper names and different forms of the same word (such as verbs in different tenses). The subject is allowed one minute to complete the task, and the score is the number of allowable words produced in that time. Forms A and B of this subtest have not been separately normed. When the two forms were given to the same 54 subjects in counterbalanced order, a correlation coefficient of .82 was obtained, and the difference in mean scores for the two forms was not significant.

The next three subtests are the Oral Spelling Test, the Written Spelling Test, and the Block Spelling Test. There are three lists of words, and the manual states that any of the three can be used with any of the three forms of spelling (p. 15). In the

Oral Spelling Test, the subject is required to spell the word aloud. In the Written Spelling Test, the subject is required to write the words on a sheet of unruled paper. For the Block Spelling Test, the subject is required to spell the words using a group of plastic letters provided in the test equipment. The three forms of the tests were normed on a sample of 350 medical inpatients. Scores are corrected for age and education and may be converted to percentile scores. Additionally, the manual presents a table of the relative frequency of differences obtained among the three forms of administration.

The next subtest is a Token Test, which contains 22 items. It is an abbreviated and somewhat changed form of the Token Test designed by De Renzi and Vignolo (1962). The plastic tokens are in five colors, two sizes, and two shapes (circles and squares). The items are arranged in order of increasing linguistic complexity. The scoring and record sheet for this test also contains the instructions for each item. There are no age or education corrections for this test. There are two forms, which the manual states are equivalent. Although there are no formal data presented regarding the empirical equivalency of the two forms, an inspection of the items in each form indicates that respective items contain the same instructions and level of grammatical and linguistic complexity. The differences between the two forms are changes in either the shape or the color referred to in the instructions (e.g., "point to a yellow circle" rather than "point to a black circle"). As with the other tests, interpretation is by reference to two tables, one with values and percentiles for normal control subjects and one with values and percentiles for aphasic patients.

The next subtest, Aural Comprehension of Words and Phrases, requires 18 responses. The stimulus booklet for this subtest has six pages, with four pictures per page. The subject is shown each page and asked to point to the picture that best illustrates what the examiner is saying. The stimulus items range from simple nouns ("buckle") to simple phrases ("cat on a chair"). Scores are interpreted with reference to two tables of obtained values for the same two samples used in the tables for other subtests. However, subjects with less than an eighth-grade education were excluded from the sample. The only adjustment for age is to add one point to the scores of individuals who achieved less than a high school diploma.

The ninth subtest, Reading Comprehension, was designed to be the counterpart of the preceding test. In this subtest the subject is shown a series of 18 words and short phrases and is asked to read the words aloud and to point to the picture that best illustrates each item. The score is recorded in terms of the number of correct responses, although instances of misarticulation and paraphrasia are noted as well. As with the previous subtest, the normative sample for this subtest consisted of the original normative sample minus those subjects who had less than an eighth-grade education and those subjects who had a history suggestive of reading disability. Score adjustments are made for level of education and are compared against the distribution of control subjects and of aphasic patients.

The manual also describes a method for rating the articulation of responses (p. 28). The rating system consists of a nine-point categorical scale. The manual reports that interrater agreement is satisfactory; however, empirical data regarding this point are not reported. There is also a nine-point categorical rating scale for praxic aspects of the subjects' writing. Again, the manual reports good interrater agreement but no explicit empirical data are provided (p. 30). Finally, there is a summary sheet for recording the results of each of the subtests, including the raw score, the percentile compared to aphasic patients, and the percentile compared to control subjects.

The MAE is intended to operate as a screening device for the presence of aphasic disorders. The manual further states that it is useful in the assessment of subjects with dementia and in the assessment of subjects who are demonstrating an apparent decline in linguistic ability (p. 4). The MAE is most useful in settings similar to that in which it was developed—namely, an inpatient medical center. There are many medical disorders that affect the language functioning of patients. Because of its two sets of norms, the MAE can be used both with those patients who have distinct aphasic disorders and those whose linguistic functions are only mildly impaired. The two sets of norms also make the MAE potentially useful for detecting the early signs of linguistic impairment in progressively dementing disorders (such as Alzheimer's disease), which have specific patterns of language deficits. One study (Rosen, 1980) substantiates the utility of the Controlled Oral Word Association subtest in assessing dementia, but while no significant differences were found among groups of normal control subjects, mildly senile subjects, and severely senile subjects on the number of words produced in response to a single letter stimulus, there were significant decrements in the ability of the senile subjects to associate words to a category stimulus.

The MAE is administered in a one-to-one situation because of the interactive nature of the test procedures. The manual does not address the issue of the level of training needed to administer this battery reliably. The administration and scoring procedures appear to be objective enough to allow administration by a supervised, experienced neuropsychological testing technician. The interpretation guides presented in the manual are rudimentary and refer mainly to descriptions of levels of skill in the various language area assessed by each subtest. A qualified clinical neuropsychologist with experience in aphasic disorders is likely to be able to use the instrument to gather information regarding the differential diagnosis or etiology of various aphasic disorders, but clinicians without that level of expertise should restrict their interpretations to simple descriptions of the results.

Technical Aspects

The battery of MAE tests, with the exception of the spelling test and the last two rating scales, was standardized on a sample of 360 patients who did not demonstrate signs of brain disease. These subjects ranged in age from 16 to 69 years of age and had English as a native language. The spelling tests were standardized on a second sample of 350 control patients. Other norms are available for older populations for the Controlled Oral Word Association subtest. These norms are based on a sample of 28 subjects between 65 and 69 years of age, 62 subjects between 70 and 74 years of age, 35 subjects between 75 and 79 years of age, and 37 subjects between 80 and 84 years of age (Benton, Eslinger, & Damasio, 1981). The manual states that translations of the MAE were made into French, Spanish, Italian, and German (Benton & Hamsher, 1983), but only the English version was standardized for clinical use (p. 1).

The interrater reliability of the Sentence Repetition and the Controlled Oral

Word Association subtests was evaluated in the normative sample noted previously. Other forms of reliability and validity have not been formally evaluated. This is due mainly to the philosophy of the test designer, Arthur Benton, who explained that empirical and quantitative reliability and validity estimates have not been calculated "because their validity in the sense of their power to discriminate between aphasic and control patients is so clear that one can assume that they possess a satisfactory degree of reliability" (personal communication, May 14, 1986). This reflects an attitude that has been widely held in clinical neuropsychological assessment: reliability has usually been assumed when the discriminative validity of the instrument could be demonstrated. Such an attitude was appropriate when the main task of clinical neuropsychological assessment was to provide the diagnosis or to localize the lesion. However, as clinical neuropsychologists have become more interested in rehabilitation and as these same clinicians have been asked to provide serial assessments in cases of decline or recovery, the estimate of test-retest reliability has become an important component in the evaluation of an assessment instrument.

Critique

The clinical utility of the MAE could be increased by conducting research into other forms of its reliability, research into its construct validity and factorial structure, and research into its applicability in special populations. The most promising feature of the MAE, its translation into other languages, provides potential for cross-cultural research regarding language impairment. For the present, the MAE remains useful as a quick screen of language functions in inpatient medical populations.

References

Benton, A. L. (1967). Problems of test construction in the field of aphasia. *Cortex, 3,* 32-58.
Benton, A. L., Eslinger, P. J., & Damasio, A. R. (1981). Normative observations on neuropsychological test performance in old age. *Journal of Clinical Neuropsychology, 3,* 33-42.
Benton, A. L., & Hamsher, K. deS. (1983). *Multilingual Aphasia Examination.* Iowa City, IA: AJA Associates, Inc.
DeRenzi, E., & Vignolo, L. A. (1962). The Token Test: A sensitive test to detect receptive disturbances in aphasics. *Brain, 85,* 665-678.
Rosen, W. G. (1980). Verbal fluency in aging and dementia. *Journal of Clinical Neuropsychology, 2,* 135-146.

Elizabeth Taleporos, Ph.D.
Associate Professor of Psychology, Long Island University, Brooklyn, New York.

NEUROTICISM SCALE QUESTIONNAIRE
Raymond B. Cattell and Ivan H. Scheier. Champaign, Illinois: Institute for Personality and Ability Testing, Inc.

Introduction

In the Neuroticism Scale Questionnaire (NSQ), respondents are asked to read 40 short statements containing descriptions of opinions, attitudes, or preferences and then to indicate whether the statement accurately describes them. Patterns of agreement and disagreement with these self-descriptions are thought to reflect certain basic personality traits, specifically those associated with the characteristic of neuroticism.

Drs. Ivan Scheier and Raymond Cattell developed the NSQ to be a brief but accurate method of assessing neurotic trends. They take issue with previous definitions of neurosis as being based on clinical diagnosis, but do not provide a satisfying general, conceptual definition to replace it. The authors define the trait by referring to the factors that emerge from analyses of responses to the NSQ, namely:

1. Overprotection (vs. Tough-Mindedness)
2. Depressiveness (vs. Cheerfulness)
3. Submissiveness (vs. Dominance)
4. Worry and Guilt (vs. Assured Self-Confidence)
5. Ergic Tension from Frustration (vs. Calm Relaxation)
6. Ego Weakness (vs. Ego Strength).

In their interpretive comments, the authors describe each of these traits in a more conceptual way, putting some construct "meat" around the empirical factors. However, these descriptions are drawn from empirical research findings that were derived from an extensive set of research studies. They are also somewhat unsatisfactory in that they define the construct in terms of the validation findings, rather than the reverse (having the research findings validate the conceptual definitions of the constructs).

The lack of a theoretical base is disappointing. In fact, the major theoretical reference here is to Freud's statement concerning the central role of anxiety in neurosis. To deal with this and to make the NSQ stand apart from the measurement of anxiety per se, Scheier and Cattell are careful to weight the scores that emerge from these factors to reduce the relative dominance of the role of anxiety. They develop their total NSQ scores to combine the last three factors into a second-order measure of anxiety, thus counting it as only ¼ of the total score (rather than ½, as would have resulted from the equal weighting of the last three out of the six that emerged).

NSQ items were developed from a pool that was originally designed to help measure the more broadly defined personality traits on the 16PF. The authors state that the items were selected from the pool for a variety of reasons, the main ones being that they: 1) provide maximum discrimination between normals and people classified clinically as neurotic; 2) provide maximum discrimination of degrees of the neurotic trend in normal individuals; 3) are correlated with only one of the four factors that are derived; 4) are relatively easy to read and comprehend for people whose educational level is as low as sixth or seventh grade; and 5) are not obvious and do not lend themselves to deliberate falsification.

Practical Applications/Uses

The NSQ items are presented in a four-page booklet. Each item is followed by three possible response boxes. For statements of belief or opinion, the responses are marked either "Yes," "No," or "Undecided." For items of preference, the boxes indicate which activity or object is preferred or indicate that the respondent is in-between the choices given, not having strong preference for one or the other. For items requesting degree of self-descriptiveness of the statement or frequency with which the behavior described is typical of the respondent's behavior, the three boxes provided offer the possibility of three levels of self-descriptiveness or degrees of frequency. Items are balanced in their presentation so that those scored positively for neuroticism have equal numbers of middle, right-, and left-sided responses keyed.

The NSQ can be administered individually or in a group setting. Adequate provision must be made for good testing conditions so that the examinee can concentrate on the items. The test is administered without time limits and is designed for adolescents and adults.

NSQ test items are presented in a booklet that can be hand-scored using a template. The back cover of the test booklet serves as a record form. Space is provided to include name, age, and sex of examinee, and there is room to indicate raw scores, derived sten scores, and a graphic representation of the individual's profile for the four factors comprising the subscales of neuroticisms (as defined by the factor analyses). Space is also provided in the record form for examiner's comments and recommendations.

The raw scores for each of the four factors and a total raw score can be interpreted through the use of derived sten scores developed for males and females separately, and for both sexes combined. The norming group consisted of 1,068 persons, 675 men and 393 women. The sample was drawn from 15 geographical locations with a range in age from 15 to 60 (the average being 32 years of age). Educational level of the sample also varied, with the average being 12 years of school completed.

As previously described, norms are provided for NSQ component scores and for total scores in the form of a conversion table, allowing the examiner to transform raw scores into standard sten scores and their equivalents in standard deviation units. This table also provides a range of percentiles corresponding to each sten score interval and a percentile value corresponding to the center of the sten interval. For example, a raw score of 32 on Total NSQ converts to a sten score of 3, using the table for males and females combined. This sten score is equivalent to a score that is from 1 to 1.5 standard deviations below the mean. The percentile range corresponding to this sten interval is 6.69 to 15.88, with a central percentile value being 10.6. In general usage, one assumes that a person with a raw score of 32 has scored lower than 11% of the norming group.

The norms tables are followed by an extensive descriptive interpretation of the four NSQ component scores. The descriptions summarize information gathered in a variety of research studies conducted over a 20-year period. Persons with extreme scores on each of the component dimensions are described qualitatively in clinical case summaries. In some cases, the etiology of each of the component extremes is suggested.

Technical Aspects

The test authors report moderate levels of internal consistency reliability for each of the NSQ component scores. They are, however, surprisingly high given the small number of items involved. Most of the validity information centers on group research studies, and the instrument is clearly most appropriate for use in relation to group findings. The authors are careful to describe their instrument as primarily relevant to group data collection, with hypotheses suggested by examining individual scores appropriately followed-up with more extensive individual testing.

The performance of the various subgroups in the research studies cited provides much of the validity evidence. For various clinical groups, the patterns of statistically significant differences between the subgroup and the population as a whole are interesting. For example, citing some of the findings for the relatively large N subgroups, male homosexuals' scores reflect a greater degree of tender mindedness than is found in the normal population; on Depressive component scores, convicts, alcoholics, and narcotics users score higher than the normal population; on Submissiveness, juvenile delinquents score lower than the normal population; and on Anxiety, almost all subgroups scored higher than the normal population (reflecting factors of Worry and Guilt, Ergic Tension, and Ego Weakness). In examining psychotic groups, the only differences in neuroticism between members of subgroups and the normal population were found for manic-depressives, who scored higher than the normal population on Depressiveness and Anxiety. No differences were found for schizophrenics, regardless of type or degree of chronicity.

Additional validity information can be seen in the pattern of NSQ scores for various occupational groups. For example, higher neuroticism scores are evident for housewives and psychiatric technicians; lower NSQ scores are found for athletes of various sorts, underwater demolition-team members, airmen, and city policemen.

Of course, the factor integrity of the scale also supports the construct validity of the component scores. While empirically selected to satisfy this criterion, the items included in each of the factor scores apparently measure given components of the construct, and can be seen to operate relatively independently of each other. This is especially important in the case of anxiety, a trait that is central to the construct and that might overshadow other aspects of more general trait.

Critique

In general, the impression the NSQ gives is one of a brief and attractive opportunity to measure a personality trait or characteristic in a way that will enhance research. The instrument clearly offers a valuable addition to the field and should provide methodology that can expand understanding of normal human personality structure and its relation to a variety of other interpersonal and social psychological variables. Few people would take its evidence further, and indeed the authors go to great lengths to ensure that their scale is not misused by overzealous clinicians.

The NSQ stands relatively unchallenged by other such personality assessments and appears to provide more technical evidence for its usefulness than its major contender, the Neuroticism Score of the Eysenck Personality Questionnaire (EPQ; Eysenck & Eysenck, 1976). In addition to the impressive body of research evidence and validation work done on the NSQ (in contrast to the scarcity available for the EPQ), attention to details of scale construction such as the attempt to minimize social desirability and item halo effects is evident in the NSQ (also contrasting the EPQ, in which all items appear to be easily "faked good" and are all keyed in the direction of the "yes" response).

The NSQ has the potential to be a valuable aid to researchers in psychology and related fields. Although not without limitations, it appears to be the best and most thoroughly investigated measure of the general trait of neuroticism that could be found by this reviewer.

References

Cattell, R. B. & Scheier, I. H. (1961). *Neuroticism Scale Questionnaire manual.* Champaign, IL: Institute for Personality and Ability Testing.

Eysenck, H. J. & Eysenck, S. B. G. (1976). *Eysenck Personality Questionnaire manual.* San Diego, CA: Educational and Industrial Testing Service.

Jon D. Swartz, Ph.D.
Associate Dean and Professor of Education and Psychology, Southwestern University, Georgetown, Texas.

NORMATIVE ADAPTIVE BEHAVIOR CHECKLIST

Gary L. Adams. San Antonio, Texas: The Psychological Corporation.

Introduction

The Normative Adaptive Behavior Checklist (NABC) is a 120-item paper-and-pencil checklist of adaptive behavior skills, "designed to fill the need for a valid, descriptive test of adaptive behavior that could be administered in a relatively short amount of time" (Adams, 1985, p. 2). Developed concurrently with the Comprehensive Test of Adaptive Behavior (CTAB) and employing items from the same item pool used to construct the final form of the CTAB, the NABC was normed on 6,130 individuals from infancy through age 21 (as part of the CTAB standardization, all items also were administered to an additional 6,000 individuals with mental and physical handicaps).

The NABC was created by Gary L. Adams. Development began in 1977, and the test was published in 1984. Adams received his doctorate in special education in 1978 from the University of Oregon. Formerly at the University of Nebraska-Lincoln, he is currently an associate professor in the Department of Exceptional Student Education at Florida Atlantic University, where he has been since 1980. In addition to the NABC, Adams is the author of the Comprehensive Test of Adaptive Behavior (CTAB). At present he is engaged in research on the computerized assessment of adaptive behavior (G. L. Adams, personal communication, March 7, 1986).

The NABC consists of a 12-page checklist containing the test items and a 12-page examiner's manual, which provides guidelines for administration, scoring, and interpretation. The 120 test items all are answered "Yes" or "No" (pass/no pass) and were selected to determine quickly an individual's performance in six behavior domains: Self-Help, Home Living, Independent Living, Social Skills, Sensory/Motor, and Language Concepts/Academic Skills. A Yes response means the individual being assessed independently performs the behavior and usually does so, while a No response means the behavior is not independently performed. To assist a respondent in answering Yes or No to the behavior described, almost all of the items are defined in more detail in an "Explanation" column on the record form. This column allows the respondent to imagine the subject in the situation described. The respondent also may check the individual's actual behavior by following the directions in the explanation. No discontinue rule, or ceiling, has been established for the NABC for a variety of reasons (Adams, 1984b, p. 19).

Practical Applications/Uses

The NABC is intended as a screening device for deciding the developmental level of an individual and is designed to be filled out by "the person who knows the child best" (Adams, 1985, p. 2). The respondent usually is a parent or guardian, but may be someone else who knows the subject very well. If results indicate the individual is below the normal range, other follow-up testing is indicated. The checklist is an individually administered rating scale that can be completed in approximately 20 minutes by an informed respondent; it is not suitable for group use.

Scoring is straightforward; when the checklist has been completed, the number of Yes responses are counted to obtain the raw score for each of the categories. The total score is computed by adding all the category subtotals. With this total raw score, and knowing the subject's sex and age, a standard score (mean of 100, standard deviation of 15) and a percentile rank can be obtained that will yield an age equivalent, both in months and in years and months. In addition, the behaviors measured by each of the six categories sampled can be rated as low, low average, average, high average, or high. NABC performance also can be compared to that of retarded students of the same sex in both school and nonschool settings for the following age intervals: 5-6, 7-8, 9-10, 11-12, 13-14, 15-18, 19-22 (school sample); and 10-14, 15-19, 20-29, 30-39, 40-49, 50-59, and 60+ (nonschool sample).

Technical Aspects

In the manual's section on validity (Adams, 1984b, pp. 31-33), the NABC is discussed in relation to the CTAB, the test with which it was developed (much more space is given to the latter instrument). In the only section on validity devoted exclusively to the NABC, it is stated that, because of the intended use of the checklist as a screening device, its predictive validity "is perhaps its most important property . . ." (p. 33). The reader is then informed, however, that the only predictive study carried out so far is the correlation of NABC items with the entire set of CTAB items! Not surprisingly, these correlations are very high (range: .87 to .995 for an N of 791; excluding total scores, median correlation of .97 for all scores across both sexes and two ages). When the NABC items are eliminated from the scoring, the correlations still are quite high (a median correlation of .93, excluding total scores). While the CTAB is the recommended instrument when prescriptive data on specific behaviors are needed, it is concluded that "the NABC total score is a near-perfect predictor of the CTAB total score" (p. 33).

Reliability is discussed in separate sections on interrater reliability, intrarater reliability, test-retest reliability, internal consistency, and the standard error of measurement. Interrater reliability coefficients for Self-Help Total, Home Living Total, Independent Living Total, Social Skills Total, Sensory/Motor Total, Language Concepts/Academic Total, and Total Score are .98, .96, .97, .98, .97, .99, and .98, respectively. For intrarater reliability, the "percentage agreement" statistic (the same rater responding to the same item placed in different locations within a 100-item test) range from .82 to .99 (median correlation: .96). Test-retest reliability coefficients reported are .99, .91, .79, .97, .98, .99, and .99 for the categories of Self-Help Total, Home Living Total, Independent Living Total, Social Skills Total, Sensory/Motor

Total, Language Concepts/Academic Total, and Total Score, respectively. Internal consistency correlations (coefficient alpha) at seven age intervals are given for each NABC category and for the total test, separately for males and females. They are uniformly high, with a median correlation of .985 for the 14 NABC Total Scores. Standard errors of measurement for each NABC category and total test for the seven age intervals also are given separately for males and females; these are generally quite low (2.1 or less for the sub-categories, 4.9 or less for the total scores).

In summary, the data reported in the manual on validity and reliability are quite impressive. Of course, much of the statistical evidence presented in support of the NABC is derived from still another new test, the CTAB.

Critique

The NABC is a new, reasonably priced checklist for quickly identifying individuals who exhibit subnormal adaptive behavior. Painstakingly constructed, easy to administer and score, with normative data on more than 12,000 normal and mentally retarded individuals, the NABC is a very promising test. As with any new assessment instrument, however, more research in a variety of settings and with a variety of subject populations is needed.

References

Adams, G. L. (1984a). *Normative Adaptive Behavior Checklist*. Columbus, OH: Charles E. Merrill Publishing Co.

Adams, G. L. (1984b). *Technical manual: CTAB/NABC*. Columbus, OH: Charles E. Merrill Publishing Co.

Adams, G. L. (1985). *NABC examiner's manual*. Columbus, OH: Charles E. Merrill Publishing Co.

Jerry L. Johns, Ph.D.
Professor of Reading, Northern Illinois University, Reading Clinic, DeKalb, Illinois.

THE O'BRIEN VOCABULARY PLACEMENT TEST
Janet O'Brien. Freeport, New York: Educational Activities, Inc.

Introduction

The computer-based O'Brien Vocabulary Placement Test is a graduated list of vocabulary words presented in a multiple-choice format. This "word opposites" test is used to determine a student's independent reading level and to estimate his or her instructional reading level. Designed to assess reading levels from the beginning (readiness) stage of reading through the sixth-grade level, the test was developed to provide teachers with a quick and easy way to place students in reading materials in which they will be successful.

First used in 1975, The O'Brien Vocabulary Placement Test is composed of a six-page manual or program guide (copyrighted in 1983) and a diskette (copyrighted in 1980 and 1982). The diskette contains the test and has provisions for storing test results and corresponding independent reading levels for up to 50 students. Diskettes or cassette tapes are available for Apple II, TRS-80 (Models III and IV), Atari (800 and 800XL), Commodore 64, and PET. If the test is used with a computer that uses information from a cassette tape, the student information file will be retained in memory only until the power to the computer is switched off.

The author, Janet O'Brien, is an elementary school guidance counselor in Deerfield Beach, Florida. She has been associated with the Broward County Title and Chapter 1 Reading and Mathematics Program for over 9 years. O'Brien earned her M.S. degree from Hofstra University. Her certification in Reading, Guidance, and Administration was awarded by Florida Atlantic University. In addition, O'Brien created several educational games.

This review is based on an analysis of the Apple II diskette used with the Apple IIe computer and Imagewriter printer. The diskette contains directions, an example of the type of test items, and the actual items. After the student's name is entered into the computer and the examples are given, testing begins. All students begin with the first item.

The O'Brien Vocabulary Placement Test is composed of six subsections, not apparent to the user, which correspond to grade levels one through six. Each subsection contains ten vocabulary words, set up in the following format:

What is the opposite of short?
1) table
2) tale

3) tall
4) took

Type in the number of your choice, then press the RETURN key.

Test items appear on the screen until the student misses 5 out of the 10 items in any one subsection; the computer program is designed to stop at this point. Testing usually requires 2 to 10 minutes, depending on a student's age and reading ability.

Once testing is completed, the computer program determines a total score for all sections the student completed. This score is then automatically converted into an independent level ranging from readiness through the sixth-grade. The scores may also be printed on paper, as illustrated by Figure 1.

Although the manual does not specify an age group for the test, it appears to be intended for students reading at the beginning stages of reading through the sixth-grade level. These students may be in typical classrooms, special education programs, or remedial reading (Chapter 1) programs.

Figure 1.

EDUCATIONAL ACTIVITIES, INC.

O'BRIEN VOCABULARY TEST

STUDENT'S SCORES

STUDENT: TOM JONES

SCORE	LEVEL
40	FOURTH GRADE

STUDENT: BETH SCHANTZ

SCORE	LEVEL
60	SIXTH OR ABOVE

*** END OF LIST ***

Practical Applications/Uses

The O'Brien Vocabulary Placement Test requires no special training to use. Once students understand the basic format of the test, little or no teacher involvement is necessary. Because this is a computer-based placement test, a wide variety of professionals and lay volunteers could use the instrument with a diverse group of students.

The test is primarily designed to find the student's independent level in less than 10 minutes. The independent level is defined as knowledge of 99% of the words in a story or selection with comprehension of at least 90%, which is consistent with similar definitions quoted in the field of reading (Harris & Hodges, 1981). The test may also be used to help identify students with reading deficiencies. In addition, it can be used to place students in appropriate reading and content area texts, such as English and social studies. The manual claims that the test is in a format that will meet the needs of special education students; however, no further clarification of this point is presented in the manual.

The directions are given on the computer screen. There is no mention that the CAPS LOCK key on the keyboard must be down for the test to receive input. Students, especially those in the beginning stages of reading, may require assistance from the test administrator to understand the basic testing format because words such as "opposite," "inversed," "choices," and "number" are used. Such assistance should easily remedy this potential problem.

Once the testing begins, the student is presented with a stimulus word and asked to type the number (1, 2, 3, or 4) beside the response word that is the opposite of each stimulus word. When the student responds and presses RETURN, the next item is automatically presented. No provisions for changing responses are stated in the manual or on the computer screen. This reviewer found that using the left arrow key on the Apple computer permitted changes to be made. It would have been helpful to have this information readily available for both teachers and students.

Legibility of print in the test is generally adequate. One notable exception is the letter *m*, which generally connects with other letters. Less-proficient readers may have their performances affected by this kind of print. Overall, the size of type and leading (space inserted between successive lines of print) seem adequate.

The computer program automatically stops the test when the student misses 5 out of 10 items in any one of six subsections of the test; it then determines the student's score and independent reading level. These items are retained on a management system that only the teacher should know how to access.

The management system or student information file is adequately explained in the manual. Provisions in the program permit the teacher to view the scores for a single student or for an entire file. Scores can be displayed or sent to a printer to produce a hard copy. Provisions are available to purge a single student's record from the file or to erase the entire file. There is a monitoring device in the program that alerts the teacher to any student who tries to repeat the test. This feature may be helpful to professionals who inadvertently assign the same student to the test a second time.

Use of this test requires one of five computers for which a program has been prepared. Most schools with computers should be able to use one of the available programs.

Technical Aspects

There is no specific mention of the terms validity or reliability in the test manual. There is, however, a brief presentation of supporting data for The O'Brien Vocabulary Placement Test. In 1974, the test was first used with approximately 500 students enrolled in a Title I (remedial reading) program in Florida. The following year, it was used with 1,500 students. In 1975, more than 5,000 students from grades one through ten used the test. No data regarding the findings from these tryouts are included in the manual; however, correspondence with the author revealed the following additional information.

During 1974, O'Brien kept data analysis, by reading level, on the percentage of correct responses for each word. She then selected three words that were found to be easy for that level, three words that were found to be difficult for that level, and four words that fell into the average range.

In the second year of tryouts (1975), when the revised test was administered to 1,500 students, O'Brien recorded the correct responses for each word in each level. She then made vocabulary adjustments, choosing words from graded word lists by recognized reading authorities and basal publishers. Through data analysis, O'Brien found that it was fairly common for students to "guess" three or four correct answers from each subsection of ten words. To help correct this guessing, no credit is given in a subsection unless the student scores at least five correct answers.

In May, 1977, the manual reports that 38 Title I (remedial reading) teachers were surveyed to compare the effectiveness of the test with results obtained from an Informal Reading Inventory (an individually administered test comprised of a series of graded word lists and reading passages). After testing over 6,000 students, each of the 38 teachers reported that none of the reading levels obtained from The O'Brien Vocabulary Placement Test were higher than those achieved from Informal Reading Inventories. The percent of agreement or accuracy reported in the manual ranged from 70% to 90%. For example, 11 teachers reported 90% accuracy in testing 2,070 students. While the meaning of these results is not clear, they seem to indicate that, for this sample, the reading levels indicated by The O'Brien Vocabulary Placement Test agreed with the reading levels students achieved on the Informal Reading Inventory 90% of the time. There is no clear indication whether this agreement is with independent levels, instructional levels, or both. Based on information in the manual, it appears that when there was not agreement between the two tests, The O'Brien Vocabulary Placement Test score was a more conservative (lower) estimate of reading level than the Informal Reading Inventory.

The test is designed so that the correct answer must be selected from words beginning with the same letter or letters. Such a provision minimizes the possibility of a student guessing correctly by using only initial consonant sounds. There are no data regarding the sources for the 60 vocabulary words and the possible answers that comprise the test. The absence of stated word sources may reduce the confidence that can be placed in the results, especially in light of the limited technical data presented. Because the test was used with over 6,000 students prior to publication, considerable data were available and could have been analyzed and reported.

Critique

The O'Brien Vocabulary Placement Test is, in essence, an alternative to administering an Informal Reading Inventory (IRI). The author claims that few teachers are trained to administer IRIs; however, prospective elementary teachers commonly enroll in undergraduate reading courses in which they learn to administer IRIs (Masztal & Smith, 1984). Perhaps the larger question concerns the quality of the training and the time required to administer most IRIs. 30 to 45 minutes would not be uncommon for the administration of an IRI.

While the definition used for the independent level is consistent with similar definitions, O'Brien's definitions of the instructional and frustration levels (see Table 1) are different from the traditional criteria proposed by Betts (1954).

According to the Betts criteria, word recognition should be 95% at the instructional level and 90% at the frustration level. The O'Brien Vocabulary Placement Test, however, uses 90% and 80% respectively. Percentages for comprehension also differ. The Betts criteria are 75% for the instructional level and 50% for frustration level, with a gray area between 50% and 75%. Even though The O'Brien Vocabulary Placement Test uses the same criteria as Betts for the instructional level, 70% or below is used for the frustration level. Although there is not total agreement on the criteria for determining the three reading levels (independent, instructional, and frustration), the Betts criteria have been widely used.

A review of articles and research studies relating to Informal Reading Inventories (Johns, Garton, Schoenfelder, & Skriba, 1977) indicated that most studies reported word recognition criteria for the instructional level at or above 95%. More recent studies (Leslie and Osol, 1978; Hoffman, O'Neal, Kastler, Clements, Segel, & Nash, 1984) also seem to support the 95% criteria. In no study was the criteria for *frustration* level placed at 80% as used by The O'Brien Vocabulary Placement Test.

A disturbing statement in the manual indicates that the *instructional* level is assumed to be 6 months to 1 year above the independent level. Although this statement may be generally true, professionals familiar with Informal Reading Inventories have seen students achieve instructional levels that can sometimes span two or more grade levels. The manual suggests that students should first be placed at their independent level. Teacher judgment should then be used to determine how rapidly a student moves to instructional level materials. Given the questionable generalization about the instructional level in relation to the independent level, the author's suggestion to delay placement at the instructional level is a good one. It should be routinely followed by users of this test.

Matching students with reading materials that they can comprehend successfully is an important instructional goal. Standardized reading survey tests are widely *misused* for this purpose. Because the vast majority of standardized tests are not designed for this purpose, other devices are needed. The O'Brien Vocabulary Placement Test is one instrument that attempts to help achieve the accurate place-

Table 1

Criteria for Word Recognition and Comprehension at the Instructional and Frustration Levels

	WORD RECOGNITION		COMPREHENSION	
AUTHOR	*Instructional*	*Frustration*	*Instructional*	*Frustration*
BETTS	95	90	75	50
O'BRIEN	90	80	75	70

ment of students in reading materials. The brevity of the test is an asset, as is computer administration and scoring. Whether a word-opposites test like The O'Brien Vocabulary Placement Test is the best way to determine the student's independent level is questionable. On the surface, comprehension and vocabulary seem to be natural partners. In fact, Harris and Sipay (1985), in a review of studies on the relationship between vocabulary knowledge and reading comprehension, report that vocabulary knowledge accounts for substantial proportions of the variance of reading comprehension. There are moderate to high correlations (.71 to .93) between vocabulary and reading comprehension. Knowledge of vocabulary seems to be a necessary condition for comprehension. Anderson and Freebody (1981), however, note that vocabulary scores may not primarily reflect background knowledge that is crucial for reading comprehension. It appears, therefore, that vocabulary knowledge is not a sufficient condition for comprehension of textual materials.

The O'Brien Vocabulary Placement Test represents one way to determine a student's independent reading level. The test is quick and easy to administer. Although specific data related to the choice of test items, validity, and reliability are lacking, professionals may find the test useful as one way to gather information that will help place students in reading materials. A toll-free number is available for users of the program living outside of New York state who need assistance with the test. Used in conjunction with other student achievement data, The O'Brien Vocabulary Placement Test should be helpful to busy classroom teachers and specialists who provide reading instruction or remediation.

References

Anderson, R. C., & Freebody, P. (1981). Vocabulary knowledge. In J. T. Guthrie (Ed.), *Comprehension and teaching: Research reviews*. Newark, DE: International Reading Association.
Betts, E. A. (1957). *Foundations of reading instruction*. New York: American Book.
Harris, A. J., & Sipay, E. R. (1985). *How to increase reading ability* (8th ed.). New York: Longman.
Harris, T. L., & Hodges, R. E. (Eds.). (1981). *A dictionary of reading and related terms*. Newark, DE: International Reading Association.
Hoffman, J. V., O'Neal, S. F., Kastler, L. A., Clements, R. O., Segel, K. W., & Nash, M. F. (1984). Guided oral reading and miscue focused feedback in second-grade classrooms. *Reading Research Quarterly, 19,* 367-384.

Johns, J. L., Garton, S., Schoenfelder, P., & Skriba, P. (1977). *Assessing reading behavior: Informal Reading Inventories.* Newark, DE: International Reading Association.

Leslie, L., & Osol, P. (1978). Changes in oral reading strategies as a function of quantities of miscues. *Journal of Reading Behavior, 10,* 442-445.

Masztal, N. B., & Smith, L. L. (1984). Do teachers really administer IRIs? *Reading World, 24,* 80-83.

Gerald R. Adams, Ph.D.
Professor of Family and Human Development and Psychology, Program Director, Laboratory for Research on Adolescence, Utah State University, Logan, Utah.

OFFER SELF-IMAGE QUESTIONNAIRE FOR ADOLESCENTS

Daniel Offer, Eric Ostrov, and Kenneth I. Howard. Chicago, Illinois: Institute for Psychosomatic and Psychiatric Research and Training, Michael Reese Hospital.

Introduction

The Offer Self-Image Questionnaire for Adolescents (OSIQ) is a broadly used self-report measure of personality that assesses self-esteem and adjustment of adolescents. The instrument evolves from the authors' interests in the developmental psychology of adolescence with the underpinning belief that "it is essential to have a baseline of the phenomenology of normal adolescents before anyone can appreciate the psychology of deviant adolescents" (Offer, Ostrov, & Howard, 1981, p. 6). Based on the perspective that empathy provides the foundation on which one comes to acquire knowledge about the private meaning of behavior, the OSIQ is presented as a measure that provides a self-report *empathetic knowing* about the adolescent's self-perceptions of the self. More specifically, the OSIQ measures differences in adolescent self-images between adolescents (inter-group comparisons) and within various self-image domains (intra-individual comparisons) inside the individual adolescent. The instrument is designed to be utilized as an assessment that has the power to differentiate normal, aberrant, or deviant self-images using a normative baseline for comparison. Given considerable over-estimations of self-image disturbances by psychiatric and clinical professionals for adolescent populations (e.g., see Offer, Ostrov, & Howard, 1984b), the OSIQ has a particular strength in helping professionals to delineate disturbance from normality in self-images during adolescence.

The primary authors of the OSIQ include Daniel Offer (M.D.), Chairman of the Department of Psychiatry at Michael Reese Hospital, and his colleagues Eric Ostrov (J.D., Ph.D.), Director of Forensic Psychology at Michael Reese, and Kenneth Howard (Ph.D.), Professor of Psychology at Northwestern University. This interdisciplinary team includes a physician/psychiatrist, lawyer/forensic psychologist, and clinical psychologist/research consultant. The historical foundation for the development of this instrument rests on the leadership of Daniel Offer and his longstanding interest in the study of normality and adolescent behavior (e.g., see Offer, 1969; Offer & Offer, 1975; Offer & Sabshin, 1984). The OSIQ items were originally constructed in 1962 with reliability and validity data reported in several publications. The most useful written summaries of scale development are to be found in Offer, Ostrov, and Howard (1981; 1984). Particular strengths in the development of the scales are the comparative data in the norming process between males and females (e.g., see Offer, Ostrov & Howard, 1984b), between younger and older adolescents, or between normal American, Australian, Irish, Israeli, or Hungarian youths (Offer, Ostrov, & Howard, 1981; Kertesz, Offer, Ostrov, & Howard, 1986), as well as normal, disturbed, and physically ill adolescents (Offer, Ostrov, & Howard, 1986, 1984a&b; Ostrov, Offer, & Howard, 1982a&b).

The first version of the OSIQ consists of 130 items that assess 11 content areas that were originally derived from reviews of published research, theory of the self, and clinical experience. The 11 content areas include subscales measuring the psychological, social, sexual, family, and coping self. The description for each of these areas and their subscales are as follows:

1. *Psychological Self:* concerns, feelings, wishes and fantasies.
    A. Impulse Control: the degree to which the adolescent is strong enough to ward off various pressures.
    B. Emotional Tone: the degree of affective harmony and the extent to which there are reported emotional fluctuations.
    C. Body and Self-Image: the degree to which the adolescent is adjusted to or feels awkward about his or her own body.
2. *Social Self:* perceptions of interpersonal relationships.
    A. Social Relationships: a self-assessment of object relationships and friendship patterns.
    B. Morals: the extent to which the superego has developed.
    C. Vocational-Educational Goals: the degree to which the adolescent is learning and planning such tasks for a vocational future.
3. *Sexual Self:* the degree to which there is integration of an emerging sexual drive into the psychosocial life of the adolescent.
    A. Sexual Attitudes: feelings, attitudes, and behaviors toward the opposite sex.
4. *Familial Self:* attitudes toward the family.
    A. Family Relationships: feelings toward parents and the emotional atmosphere in the home.
5. *Coping Self:* coping or adaptation strengths of the individual.
    A. Mastery of the External World: the degree to which the adolescent adapts to the environment.
    B. Psychopathology: identification of overt symptomatology of psychopathology.
    C. Superior Adjustment: a measure of coping with self, others, and the world as reflected through ego strength.

In the second edition of the OSIQ six additional items are provided to measure *idealism*. This new scale is to be considered an experimental scale only.

Over the total history of scale development these scales have been given to more than 10,000 adolescents. The assumption has been that adolescents can be functioning well on one or more of the various measures of *self* while not mastering others. Likewise, it has been assumed that adolescents are sensitive enough to accurately describe their own inner states. During the early development of the and the various scales, a variety of measurement techniques were utilized to build the subscales. These techniques include Q-sort strategies, content analysis, pilot studies to determine discriminant validity, replacement and/or rewriting of items, and checks on meaningfulness and clarity with adolescent groups.

The OSIQ is presented in a test booklet format with 22 items provided per page. At the top of each page the six response choices are provided as a reminder: 1) Describes me very well; 2) Describes me well; 3) Describes me fairly well; 4) Does not quite describe me; 5) Does not really describe me; 6) Does not describe me at all. A separate answer sheet is used where adolescents circle their choice for each item. Space is provided for the student to list his or her name, sex, age, and father's and mother's occupation.

Practical Applications/Uses

The OSIQ has strong utility in assessing the self-image and self-reported adjustment of adolescents between the ages of 13 and 19 years. The instrument can be utilized to assess the relative strengths and weaknesses in self-images of adolescents. It has practical utility in assessing self-images of adolescents. It has practical utility in assessing self-image disturbances that are markedly different from normal perturbations or variances for the typical adolescent, and excellent utility for research and evaluation efforts where the professional is interested in a multidimensional assessment of self-concept or self-image. The instrument can be charted to show a profile analysis similar to that provided in the format of the Minnesota Multiphasic Personality Inventory. Not only can it be used to compare males and females and disturbed and normal groups, it also can be used to compare younger and older adolescents between cultures. Thus, it would be an excellent cross-cultural measure of self-image. It is unclear to what degree this measure is useful, however, for comparisons between ethnic (e.g., Native Americans versus Hispanics) or minority/majority (e.g., black versus white) group youths in the United States. However, given its strong comparative findings in cross-cultural contexts, it would appear to be an acceptable tool for consideration for minority youth research within this country.

The OSIQ is designed for group administration under the direction of an adult—teacher, counselor, school psychologist, and so on. Each teenager is provided with a test booklet, answer sheet, and simple instructions on how to proceed. Respondents can either complete the instrument by themselves or the administrator can read the items aloud. For the younger adolescents or individuals with less than a 9th-grade reading level, it might be wise to read the items aloud. All items are to be completed independent of the prior responses with the test taking approximately 40 minutes to complete. Given the length of the test, hyperactive, disturbed, or acting-out youths may need a break about halfway through the testing. Likewise, smaller groups or individual administration may be desirable for such adolescents to ensure serious consideration of each item.

Scoring and interpretation of the OSIQ is supported by several test package options. A sample kit is available for $17.00 and provides all of the general necessary information to become acquainted with the test. The 1982 OSIQ Manual costs $15.00 each. Male and female OSIQ booklets cost $1.00 each, with answer sheets costing 15 cents apiece. Scoring can be requested from the Adolescent Research Center, which includes a printout of raw data, standard deviations for each subject, subgroup means and standard deviations for each scale (with subanalyses for sex and age), and a distribution score for each item for the sample and the norming group. The cost includes a $10.00 base fee plus $2.00 per subject. A formal profile for each subject costs $5.00 per subject. Other resources such as special analyses, a scoring program code and scoring diskette, data provided on a tape, and so on can be purchased or arranged through the Adolescent Research Center at Michael Reese Hospital.

The directions for the OSIQ instruct the adolescent to respond to each item on a six response choice format. So that items are read carefully, approximately half the items were written in a positive and half in a negative direction. The scoring process must take into consideration the direction of the item with appropriate reverse weighting procedures applied. For all scales a low score reflects positive adjustment or self-image. Raw scores are converted into a standard score using sex- and age- appropriate norms. The age norms include two norming groups: 13-15 and 16-19 year olds. Standardized T scores with a mean of 50 and a standard deviation of 15 are used. For handscoring, the manual provides conversion tables that provide the raw score, standard score, and corresponding percentile for each of the 11 scales. A high standard score implies positive adjustment in all content areas. This is important to note. In that low raw scores imply positive adjustment but through the conversion process a high standard score implies positive adjustment and self-image. The manual provides excellent graphic displays of different profile types and other useful descriptive statistics. Profile analysis provides a multidimensional examination of the relative degree of self-esteem or self-image across 11 content subscales using a normative standard of 50 for each subscale and a standard deviation of 15.

The interpretation of the test requires a working knowledge of standard scores and the concept of standard deviation. Scoring is based on an objective version of self-report information using these concepts. Little clinical judgment or inference is used given that the scoring is based on an age criterion of normality. Cross comparisons of domains ideally require a certain degree of clinical insight and a working knowledge of various theories of self development.

Technical Aspects

Self-concept or self-esteem measures as assessments of self-knowledge are generally constructed around two indices of reliability (test-retest and internal consistency) and at least three measures of validity (face, predictive or concurrent, and construct). Likewise, evidence of the degree to which scores are effected by response bias (e.g., social desirability, halo or extreme response biases) are generally provided.

Reliability indices are reasonable. Offer, Ostrov, and Howard (1982b) report stability coefficients ranging between .48 to .84 for subscales and .73 for the total score over a six-month period. Other reports of strong stability or test-retest reliability are provided elsewhere (e.g., Offer, 1969; Offer & Offer, 1975). Likewise, internal consistency appears acceptable based on several estimates using Cronbach alphas. For example, a recent report by Kertesz, Offer, Ostrov, and Howard (1986) indicates alphas ranging from .48 to .85 for young and older male and female Hungarian adolescents. Table II in the Offer et al. (1982b) test manual reports a range of .40 to .88 with a mean alph of .63.

Face and content validity have been established through a process of identifying appropriate domains and the preparation of items that are understood and readable to teenagers. Predictive validity has been established by showing that various adolescent groups (e.g., disturbed versus normal adolescents) report differences that are consistent with expectations (e.g., see Ostrov, Offer, & Howard, 1982b). Likewise, several studies have shown conceptually appropriate correlations with other personality scales such as the Bell Inventory, the Minnesota Multiphasic Personality Inventory, and other instruments (see Offer, 1969; Coche & Taylor, 1974). Likewise, Offer, Ostrov, and Howard (1982b) report data from an unpublished doctoral dissertation that shows concurrent validity between the OSIQ and another self-image test. Regarding construct validity, Offer, Ostrov, and Howard (1982a&b) report good to strong interitem correlations within subscales and with the total score. However, this reviewer was unable to find a factor analytic study on the OSIQ that provides a broader evidence base for the subscales and their internal item structure.

The OSIQ Manual provides no summary of item correlations with a measure of social desirability. Therefore, it is uncertain to what degree a social desirability bias is operating in the measurement of self-images. However, careful analyses of the distribution of responses to each and every item suggests the items have no particular halo or response bias in their distribution across the six choice format.

Critique

The OSIQ has considerable strengths and should be given consideration when selecting an appropriate measure for assessing self-image and adjustment of adolescents. Individuals wanting a multidimensional measure of self-image will find this instrument of considerable appeal. The evidence of good reliability is particularly noteworthy. Broad-based norming efforts with younger and older adolescents, males and females, cross-cultural groups, and normal and disturbed groups make this assessment a widely usable measure. Likewise, the focus on the normative base for determining disturbance or deviance in self-images is a strong and positive factor.

Limitations to the OSIQ include incomplete evidence on the concurrent validity with other widely used self-concept and self-esteem measures, less than rigorous efforts at establishing construct or factorial validity, and limited information regarding the predictive validity of the OSIQ for observed behaviors in social, academic, or familial contexts. Nonetheless, this reviewer judges this instrument as being the most promising measure of self-image currently emerging today. It is easy to administer, provides a strong profile of self-images, has initial evidence of acceptable psychometric properties, and has an excellent support package that can be purchased as needed.

This reviewer remains cautious in using the instrument in clinical settings in which major decisions are being made regarding an adolescent until more work is completed on criterion-related validity based on direct behavioral observations and stronger evidence of construct validity. However, as a research or experimental clinical measurement tool, I believe it is superior to any other measure currently available. Given the study of adolescence includes distinctions of early adolescence, adolescence proper, and late adolescence, it would be useful if the authors would also norm the instrument on a college-aged population. Also, more information is needed on the usefulness of the instrument for assessment with minority groups such as blacks, Native Americans, and Hispanic youths.

References

Coche, E., & Taylor, S. (1974). Correlations between the Offer Self-Image Questionnaire for Adolescents and the Minnesota Multiphasic Personality Inventory in a psychiatric hospital population. *Journal of Youth and Adolescence, 3,* 145-152.

Kertesz, M., Offer, D., Ostrov, E., & Howard, K. I. (1986). Hungarian adolescents' self-concept. *Journal of Youth and Adolescence, 15,* 273-284.

Offer, D. (1969). *The psychological world of the teenager: A study of normal adolescent boys.* New York: Basic Books.

Offer, D., & Offer, J. (1975). *From teenage to young manhood: A psychological study.* New York: Basic Books.

Offer, D., Ostrov, E., & Howard, K. I. (1981). *The adolescent: A psychological self-protrait.* New York: Basic Books.

Offer, D., Ostrov, E., & Howard, K. I. (1982a). Family perceptions of adolescent self-image. *Journal of Youth and Adolescence, 11,* 281-291.

Offer, D., Ostrov, E., & Howard, K. I. (1982b). The Offer Self-Image Questionnaire for Adolescents. Chicago: Institute for Psychosomatic and Psychiatric Research and Training, Michael Reese Hospital.

Offer, D., Ostrov, E., & Howard, K. I. (1984a). Body image, self-perception, and chronic illness in adolescence. In R. Blume (Ed.), *Chronic illness and disabilities in childhood and adolescence.* New York: Grune & Stratton.

Offer, D., Ostrov, E., & Howard, K. I. (1984b). Patterns of adolescent self-image. In D. Offer, E. Ostrov, & K. I. Howard (Eds.), *New Directions for Mental Health Services.* (Monograph No. 22). San Francisco: Jossey-Bass.

Offer, D., Ostrov, E., & Howard, K. I. (1986). Self-image, delinquency, and help-seeking behavior among normal adolescents. In S. C. Feinstein (Ed.), *Adolescent psychiatry: Developmental and clinical studies: Vol. 13* (pp. 121-138). Chicago: University of Chicago Press.

Offer, D., Sabshin, M. (1984). *Normality and the life cycle.* New York: Basic Books.

Ostrov, E., Offer, D., & Hartlage, S. (1984). The quietly disturbed adolescent. In D. Offer, E. Ostrov, & K. I. Howard (Eds.), Patterns of adolescent self-image. *New directions for metal health services.* (Monograph No. 22). San Francisco: Jossey-Bass.

Ostrov, E., Offer, D., & Howard, K. I. (1982). Values and self-conceptions held by normal and delinquent adolescent males. *Journal of Psychiatric Treatment and Evaluation, 4,* 503-509.

Patrick J. Mason, Ph.D.
Postdoctoral Fellow, Pediatric Psychology, Department of Psychiatry and the Behavioral Sciences, University of Oklahoma Health Sciences Center, Oklahoma City, Oklahoma.

C. Eugene Walker, Ph.D.
Professor, Pediatric Psychology, Department of Psychiatry and the Behavioral Sciences, University of Oklahoma Health Sciences Center, Oklahoma City, Oklahoma.

PARTNER RELATIONSHIP INVENTORY: RESEARCH EDITION

Carol N. Hoskins. Palo Alto, California: Consulting Psychologists Press, Inc.

Introduction

The Partner Relationship Inventory (PRI)* is an 80-item self-report inventory designed to measure perceptions of how well a marital partner's emotional and interactional needs are being met by his or her spouse. The purpose of the PRI is to provide researchers and counselors with a quick index of marital partners' level of marriage satisfaction. The instrument was developed on the assumption that the best predictor of marital satisfaction is the absence of conflict over emotional and interactional needs.

The PRI was developed by Drs. Carol N. Hoskins and Phillip Merrifield and continues to be revised by Dr. Hoskins. The most recent version available is a "research edition" of what was called the Interpersonal Conflict Scale. The PRI manual, scheduled for publication in February, 1987, is also called a research edition. Dr. Hoskins developed the scale as part of her doctoral dissertation at New York University. From 1978 to the present, Dr. Hoskins has been conducting research in the area of chronobiology. Using a variation of time series analyses, she has investigated possible existing relationships between biological rhythms and emotional states. She continues to work in this area as well as in the area of psychometrics as Associate Professor and Chairperson in the Program in Research and Theory Development in Nursing Science at New York University.

---

*At the time this critique was written, the only existing published version of this inventory was called the Interpersonal Conflict Scale (ICS; Hoskins & Merrifield, 1981). The editors of Consulting Psychologists Press have announced that they intend to publish a revised form of this inventory and title it Partner Relationship Inventory. This review is based on the galley proofs of the upcoming publication (Hoskins, in press) as well as the existing Interpersonal Conflict Scale manual.

304 Partner Relationship Inventory

The Interpersonal Conflict Scale (ICS) emerged from the authors' desire to develop an instrument that would provide a highly sensitive measure of marital conflict over time. The theoretical basis for the ICS was borrowed from researchers and clinicians in family therapy and interpersonal conflict (Ackerman, 1958; Locke & Wallace, 1959; Matthews & Mihanovich, 1963; Smith, 1970; Taylor, 1967). More specifically, the ICS was developed from 50 items from the Burgess and Wallin Marital Adjustment Scale (Burgess & Wallin, 1953). Matthews and Mihanovich (1963) found that these 50 items discriminated between "happy" and "unhappy" marital partners. The items were classified first in either an "emotional need" category or an "interactional need" category, then further classified by the authors into nine subcategories: agreement in thinking, communication, disagreement in behavior, perception of other's feelings, companionship and sharing, emotional satisfaction, security, recognition, and perception of behavior. Eventually, new items were written to obtain 10 items for each subcategory.

The resulting 90 items were used to develop statements, each followed by four response categories: "Definitely Feel," "Feel Slightly," "Does Not Apply/Cannot Decide," and "Definitely Do Not Feel." A typical item reads "My partner and I think alike on most things," followed by the four response categories.

The PRI research edition contains the following materials: PRI research edition manual, Long Form Inventory, Form I Inventory, and Form II Inventory. The Long Form is essentially an 80-item genderless edition of the Interpersonal Conflict Scale. (One of the nine subcategories, Perception of Behavior, was dropped from the PRI during the scale development.) Form I contains alternate forms A and B and each consists of 40 items taken from the Long Form. Form II contains six alternate forms of 33 items. Form II differs from the Long Form and Form I in that each alternate form includes six items designed to assess sexual needs. In addition, Form II collapses the emotional and interactional needs into a single scale called the Interactional/Emotional Needs. It is not clear whether additional interactional and emotional needs items were constructed to develop Form II; if not, then the six alternate forms for Form II must contain many duplicate items. Form II is provided in an appendix of the PRI manual and may be photocopied (if permission is first obtained from the author).

Practical Applications/Uses

The administration of the PRI is simple and demands very little of the administrator's time. Instructions, found on the faces of the test forms, are easy to follow. The Long Form takes approximately 30 minutes to complete. Each variation of Form I takes approximately half that time. Subjects are asked to respond to the items based on how they "feel at that moment."

Scoring is also simple. Scoring keys are provided that involve summing the values determined for each item. The scoring key yields scale scores for emotional and interactional needs factors. Identification of items for each subcategory are not provided on the scoring key but can be obtained from information in the manual. Interestingly, there are no scoring operations that actually measure the discrepancy between the couple's responses.

To date, the PRI has been used in very few published research articles. Hoskins

(Hoskins, 1979; Hoskins & Halberg, 1983) has examined the relationship between the PRI and subjective and objective indices of activation (e.g., body temperature and self-report data). In a study using 16 married couples, Hoskins (1979) failed to find significant correlations between the degree of the couples' differences in the activation indices and their scores on the PRI.

In a single case study (Hoskins & Halberg, 1983), one married couple completed activation checklists, activation-deactivation checklists, and Form II of the PRI six times daily during each of 35 consecutive days. Body temperature was continuously monitored using a rectal probe, and readings were taken every two minutes during this 35-day series. The probe was connected to a portable recording device worn by subjects and was only removed prior to bowel movements and bathing. The authors were attempting to investigate patterns of differences of the couple for activation and interpersonal conflict. Three activation-factor scores (Interactional Need, Emotional Need, and Sexual Needs) and three conflict-factor scores (General Activation, Deactivation, and High Activation) were used in rhythmometric and correlational analyses.

Rhythmometric analyses indicated that a pattern of circadian rhythm was detected for the Emotional Need factor for the man only. Pearson product-moment correlation coefficients were calculated for the man and woman across six daily time periods for the three activation and three conflict scores. Of the resulting 108 correlation coefficients, statistically significant correlations were only reported for the male partner in the early morning time period between the interaction conflict scores and two of the activation scores. The female partner in the midday time period had a statistically significant correlation between her emotional conflict score and one of the activation scores. The probability of these three correlation coefficients being significant, given the number of correlation coefficients that were calculated, was not addressed. The error rate of significant correlations for 108 correlations at $p = .05$ is 5.4. The three coefficients reported by Hoskins fall within this error rate.

The PRI has also been used as an index of marital satisfaction (Moore, 1983). A comparison between a Lamaze childbirth class and a hospital-based childbirth class was made using 70 couples from the Lamaze class and 35 couples from the hospital-based class. Subjects were self-selected and a short form (45 items) of the Interpersonal Conflict Scale was used. The author reports that there were no significant differences in the female partners' scores at three measurement times: 24 to 28 weeks of pregnancy, 36 to 38 weeks of pregnancy, and 3 to 21 days postpartum. The author reports that the male "total score" revealed a significant difference between the Lamaze and hospital-based programs: the males who participated in the Lamaze class reported lower levels of conflict.

Technical Aspects

The initial forms of the Interpersonal Conflict Scale were administered to 52 white, middle-class married couples with a mean length of marriage of 10.5 years (Hoskins & Merrifield, 1981). This 90-item inventory later evolved into 80 items after 10 items from the Perception of Behavior category were deleted. This standardization sample was administered the male and female forms of the Interpersonal

Conflict Scale. (The PRI Long Form does not have reference to gender.) The couples in this sample population lived in the suburbs near a large metropolitan area. Hoskins (1981) stated that the couples were randomly selected, but the means of solicitation of subjects was unclear in the article. However, in a personal communication (July 22, 1986) with Hoskins, she stated that the 52 couples were a "convenience sample" from community organizations and graduate school classes. The men in the sample worked as professionals or skilled laborers and most of the women did not work outside the home. Children in the home ranged in age from 6 to 12 years. The couples completed the 90-item versions of the Interpersonal Conflict Scale in the morning and in the late day or early evening.

Form I of the PRI was standardized by Haber in an unpublished doctoral dissertation at New York University (cited in Hoskins, in press). Haber's sample consisted of 168 married couples with a mean length of marriage of 8.5 years. These couples had an average of one child per family and were classified in the middle socioeconomic range. Means in standard deviations for Form I are presented in the PRI manual.

In a further development of the PRI, a "Sexual Needs" category was added, "based on evaluation of the scale by potential publishers and subjects" (Hoskins, 1983, p. 76). This further development represents the first attempt at piloting Form II of the PRI. Form II has since been revised to contain 33 items for each of six alternate forms. The standardization sample, however, is based on the 111-item version.

This revised inventory, consisting of 80 items from the Long Form and 31 "Sexual Need" items that were developed by Hoskins, was administered to 212 married subjects. The characteristics of this sample population include a mean age of 35.9 years, approximately half had completed college, and 36% had received graduate-level education. It is not reported how many of the subjects were a partner to another subject or the number of males and females in the study. The manual does not provide the results from this sample. Hoskins states that adequate norms have not yet been obtained.

Reliability of the PRI Long Form was investigated using a test-retest strategy. This was performed using the 90-item version of the ICS (before the Perception of Behavior subcategory was dropped) with the standardization sample of 52 married couples. The couples were instructed to complete the 90-item ICS at early morning and later that same day. Pearson product-moment correlations between the morning and evening tests were calculated and then applied to the Spearman-Brown prophecy formula. The PRI manual indicates Spearman-Brown correlations for the subcategories between .69 and .92. The original ICS manual (Hoskins & Merrifield, 1981) reported Spearman-Brown coefficients for what appears to be the same data ranging from .78 to .95. Furthermore, two articles by Hoskins report apparently these same coefficients to range from .78 to .98 (Hoskins, 1979; Hoskins et al., 1979). The Spearman-Brown prophecy formula typically is used to estimate reliability of an instrument when the number of items are increased or decreased. It is unclear why this formula was used or what the resultant coefficients might mean. Interestingly, two subcategories had significantly greater means for the evening testing: Perception of Feelings and Recognition of Needs.

Alternate forms of Form I of the PRI were constructed by dividing the ten items from each subcategory into two groups, using the serpentine method on the data collected from the aforementioned sample of 52 couples. The serpentine method, attributed to Merrifield through personal communication with Hoskins (Merrifield was the second author of the Interpersonal Conflict Scale), involves assigning items to alternate groups based on the mean values of each item. The correlations between Form IA and Form IB for the Interactional and Emotional Needs scales were .94 and .93, respectively. Correlations between Form IA and Form IB appear to have comparable and adequate levels of reliability.

When a factor analysis was performed on the nine subcategories from the ICS, two factors emerged. Factor I was called Interactional Needs and included the following subcategories and their loadings: Agreement in Thinking (.73), Communication (.91), Disagreement in Behavior (.69), Perception of Other's Feelings (.71), and Companionship and Sharing (.63). Factor II was called Emotional Needs and included these subcategories: Emotional Satisfaction (.77), Security (.72), and Recognition (.87). The loadings of the subcategories on all of the factors are not provided. Further, the criteria for including a subcategory in a factor is not described.

The results of the initial factor analysis have been challenged by the results from Hoskins' further development of the scale (Hoskins, 1983). Hoskins administered the same 80-item ICS along with 31 additional items related to sexual needs to 212 married subjects. A factor analysis of the original eight subcategories along with two sexual needs subcategories failed to replicate the emergence of separate emotional needs and interactional needs factors. It was decided that the Interactional Need factor and the Emotional Need factor should be collapsed and called an Interactional/Emotional Need conflict score.

The items selected for inclusion in the PRI were scrutinized by an educational psychologist and a marriage counselor for content validity. The items included in the PRI Long Form and Form I were those agreed upon by these two experts. Further, the items were compared to the content of Bienvenu's (1968) Marital Communication Inventory.

Construct validity was approached by comparing the ICS scores of the aforementioned 52 couples with their scores on the short form of the Locke-Wallace Marital Adjustment Scale (Locke & Wallace, 1959). Subjects completed the Locke-Wallace scale apparently on the same day that they completed the ICS forms. Pearson product-moment correlation coefficients were computed between the scores on the Locke-Wallace and each of the eight subcategories of the ICS. Resultant coefficients ranged from -.40 to -.75. The negative correlations reflect an inverse relationship between marital adjustment (Locke-Wallace) and marital conflict (ICS). Thus, of the variance associated with the ICS (a measure of conflict) and the Locke-Wallace (a measure of adjustment), the amount of variance shared by these two instruments is between 16% and 56%. The correlation between the total scores on the ICS and the Locke-Wallace is not reported.

Critique

Although test construction appears to be adequate for the Partner Relationship Inventory Long Form and for Form I, test development and studies of the utility of the PRI are lacking. The major issue warranting consideration involves the use of a

4-point scale ranging from "Definitely Feel" to "Definitely Do Not Feel" in the initial construction of the PRI. This scale appears to be confounded by the presence of the "Cannot Decide" response category in the third position. The author of the PRI recognizes this problem and states that the PRI is not a "true scale." Hoskins' justification for its inclusion, however, is not convincing:

> The option of "Cannot Decide" was viewed as a viable response possibility indicative of a feeling that is negative, absent, or conflicted, but not to the degree of "Definitely Do Not Feel." In fact, the overuse of "Cannot Decide" is indicative of a negative feeling or repressed ambiguity that indicates a need for conflict resolution. (Hoskins, in press, p. 9)

The response category "Cannot Decide" does not appear to fit logically on a continuum of "Definitely Feel" to "Definitely Do Not Feel." The writers of this critique understand "feelings" to be associated with emotions; because the items on the PRI are declarative statements, the only emotion we would expect a respondent to have upon reading these statements would be that of acceptance or lack of acceptance. The "Cannot Decide" response category could have been better used as an *alternative* to scaling. In any case, the "scale" of the PRI does not appear to be logically correct.

There are a number of issues about the use and interpretation of the PRI that demand attention. These concerns are based on the limited norms available and the lack of studies using clinical populations. The PRI manual provides the reader with quartile scores for the standardization sample of the Long Form and Form I. The manual states that individuals whose scores fall above the 70th percentile of the norms "would be candidates for counseling" (Hoskins, in press, p. 5). There are no data reported in the PRI manual or found in the literature that support this statement. Studies attempting to differentiate between "normal" couples and those in need of counseling are sorely needed. Until such studies are conducted, the use of the PRI Long Form and/or Form I should be strictly limited to experimental settings.

The PRI was originally designed from a need to assess subtle day-to-day and even hour-by-hour changes in perceptions of fulfillment of interactional and emotional needs by a partner. To this end the author has been somewhat successful with the use of rhythmometric (time series) analyses for identifying time-of-day patterns of the degree of perceived fulfillment. Attempts at linking these findings to patterns of autonomic arousal and general activity have met with virtually no success. Further research in this area is needed. Forms IA and IB have been demonstrated to be comparable and may provide a useful and brief tool for assessing perceptions of fulfillment in interactional and emotional needs, though adequate validity studies are lacking.

Finally, the manner in which the construct "conflict" is addressed is of concern. Hoskins (in press) defines conflict as "a discrepancy between partners in specific perceptions that results in a lack of fulfillment of particular needs" (p. 1). However, the scoring system does not yield differences between partners on items, subcategories, or the interaction-emotional scales. Thus, "discrepancies between partners" is never assessed. Perhaps this explains why the scale's name was changed from the Interpersonal Conflict Scale to Partner Relationship Inventory. This does not, however, resolve the problems encountered in the manner in which conflict was operationalized.

Form II of the PRI was not extensively discussed in this critique because the scale is still in the developmental stages. No reliability or validity data are reported. Hoskins welcomes fellow researchers to request copies of Form II so that the collection of a data base may begin.

References

Ackerman, N. W. (1958). *The psychodynamics of family life.* New York: Basic Books.
Bienvenu, M. J. (1968). *A Marital Communication Inventory.* Saluda, NC: Family Life Publications.
Burgess, E. W., & Wallin, P. (1953). *Engagement and marriage.* Chicago: Lippincott.
Hoskins, C. N. (1979). Level of activation, body temperature, and interpersonal conflict in family relationships. *Nursing Research, 28,* 154-160.
Hoskins C. N. (1981). Psychometrics in nursing research: Construction of an interpersonal conflict scale. *Research in Nursing and Health, 4,* 243-249.
Hoskins, C. N. (1983). Psychometrics in nursing—Further development of the Interpersonal Conflict Scale. *Research in Nursing and Health, 6,* 75-83.
Hoskins, C. N. (in press). *A manual for the Partner Relationship Inventory.* Palo Alto, CA: Consulting Psychologists Press.
Hoskins, C., & Halberg, F. (1983). Circadian relations among levels of activation, conflict, and body temperature assessed by chronobiologic serial section. *Psychological Reports, 52,* 867-876.
Hoskins, C. N., Halberg, F., Merrifield, P. R., & Hillman, D. C. (1979). Chronobiology: Circadian activation rhythms of married couples. *Psychological Reports, 45,* 607-614.
Hoskins, C. N., & Merrifield, P. (1981). *Teachers and counselors guide to Interpersonal Conflict Scale (Experimental Edition).* Saluda, NC: Family Life Publications.
Locke, H. J., & Wallace, K. M. (1959). Short marital adjustment and prediction tests: Their reliability and validity. *Marriage and Family Living, 21,* 251-255.
Matthews, V. D., & Mihanovich, C. S. (1963). New orientations on marital adjustment. *Marriage and Family Living, 25,* 300-304.
Moore, D. (1983). Prepared childbirth and marital satisfaction during the antepartum and postpartum periods. *Nursing Research, 32,* 73-79.
Smith, J. R. (1970). Perception of self and other (mate) as motivation for marriage counseling: An interactionist approach. *Sociology and Social Research, 54,* 466-475.
Taylor, A. B. (1967). Role perception, empathy, and marriage adjustment. *Sociology and Social Research, 52,* 22-32.

John J. Venn, Ph.D.
Associate Professor of Special Education, University of North Florida, Jacksonville, Florida.

PEABODY DEVELOPMENTAL MOTOR SCALES AND ACTIVITY CARDS

M. Rhonda Folio and Rebecca R. Fewell. Allen, Texas: DLM Teaching Resources.

Introduction

The Peabody Developmental Motor Scales and Activity Cards (PDMS) is a comprehensive program that includes an individually administered developmental test and an instructional packet. The standardized test measures the fine- and gross-motor skills of children from birth to 7 years of age. The instructional packet consists of activity cards that suggest appropriate interventions for each of the test items. The Fine-Motor Scale has 112 items and the Gross-Motor Scale has 170 items. The large number of items makes the PDMS useful for conducting in-depth diagnostic prescriptive programming in a variety of settings with handicapped and nonhandicapped children.

Rhonda Folio and Rebecca Fewell developed the PDMS while Dr. Folio was a doctoral student and a member of Dr. Fewell's multidisciplinary evaluation team for severely imparied/multiply handicapped children at Peabody College. Dr. Folio earned her Ed.S. and Ed.D. in physical education for the handicapped from George Peabody College for Teachers. She has extensive experience and expertise in all areas of motor development. Dr. Fewell served as director of the Multiple Handicapped Project at the Peabody College Child Study Center when the PDMS was initially developed. She has published extensively, especially in the area of assessment in special education.

Originally published as a criterion-referenced test in 1973, the PDMS was revised in 1974 when it was published by the Institute on Mental Retardation and Intellectual Development at Peabody College. Some initial reliability and validity studies were conducted in 1974. The test was further revised in the late 1970s, resulting in the preparation of the Field Test Edition in 1979. The Field Test Edition was used in the standardization process in 1981 and 1982, resulting in the current edition.

The PDMS materials are contained in kit form inside a carrying case and consist of a lengthy and well-written manual, a set of response/scoring booklets, an indexed file of activity cards for both the fine- and gross-motor scales, and many of the materials needed to administer the fine-motor tasks. The PDMS kit is well designed, organized, and neatly packaged.

The examiner is directly involved in the testing process when using the PDMS. Each item is administered and scored by the examiner following specific criteria, and no scoring is done by interview or report of a primary caregiver. Individuals with experience in giving developmental tests to young children will find the PDMS easy to administer.

The PDMS is intended for use with nonhandicapped and handicapped children from birth to 7 years of age and for handicapped children over 7 whose motor development falls within a birth-to-7 developmental age range. The Fine-Motor Scale's 112 items are grouped into four skill clusters: grasping, hand use, eye/hand coordination, and manual dexterity. The 170 items of the Gross-Motor Scale are grouped into five skill clusters: reflexes, balance, nonlocomotor, locomotor, and receipt and propulsion. Norms are available for the overall scales as well as for each skill cluster.

The 12-page response/scoring booklet contains a summary sheet, a motor development profile form, and a detailed response form for each scale. The profile is arranged to illustrate a child's motor performance across each of the skill clusters and the total scales.

Practical Applications/Uses

The PDMS is designed to provide an assessment of both overall motor development and specific motor skill development. In addition, the activity cards provide a practical way to design individualized motor intervention programs. Although the test was originally designed for use with severely/multiply handicapped children in a diagnostic center, other uses have evolved. These include preschool developmental programs, special education classrooms, home intervention programs, and as a guide for parents. The PDMS has been widely used by diagnosticians, classroom teachers, psychologists, occupational therapists, physical therapists, and physical education teachers.

The scales and activities are particularly appropriate for use with children who have motor impairments or delays. Because of the large number of items, the test is also appropriate for use with severely and profoundly handicapped children who may perform few if any motor skills at their chronological age level. The test can be easily adapted for use with children who have sensory impairments including deafness, blindness, or both. Special adaptions should be noted on the response/scoring booklets, specifying that the scales were not administered according to the standardized procedures.

It is preferable to administer the PDMS in settings that have the materials commonly found in programs for infant, preschool, and primary children because some of these are necessary in giving the test. If this is not possible, then some materials will need to be brought to the testing site.

Examiner qualifications include a complete knowledge of the manual and the test as well as practice in administering and scoring the test. Professionals should find the administration procedures easy to follow. A minimum of 45-60 minutes is required to administer the PDMS. The administration instructions are clear and the method of altering the sequence of presentation of items to meet the needs of the child is well described.

A number of standardized scores can be obtained from the PDMS, including age equivalents, percentiles, and developmental motor quotients. These scores are available for overall motor development, total fine- and gross-motor development, and for each skill cluster. The scoring instructions are clearly presented and, on the average, it takes less than 30 minutes to learn how to score the PDMS. After the procedure is mastered, scoring takes approximately 10 minutes. The response/scoring booklet is well designed and easy to use. Of particular merit is the provision of adequate space on the response form to make notations and comments about the child's performance on specific items.

Interpretation of the results is not difficult and is based on objective scores. The results are compiled in a manner that makes it easy to identify strengths and weaknesses, gaps in development, and intervention priorities. Three criteria are used for scoring each item rather than a simple pass/fail scoring system. The three-point scoring system helps in identifying emerging skills and in measuring the progress of children who are learning new motor skills very slowly. Specific guidelines for interpretation are provided, including detailed case studies that illustrate how to use and interpret the PDMS. The case studies are well written and clearly show how to use the PDMS to measure motor skill development and how to carry out instructional programs, including IEP development.

Technical Aspects

The PDMS was standardized on a sample of 617 infants and children. The sample was representative in terms of geographical region, race, sex, and other demographic factors. As part of the standardization process, two types of reliability studies were performed: test-retest and interrater. Test-retest reliability was determined by retesting 38 children in the norm sample. The results indicated the PDMS has adequate test-retest reliability (.99 and .95 for the Gross-Motor Scale and .95 and .80 for the Fine-Motor Scale). The interrater reliability coefficients were .99 for both scales.

Validity studies with the PDMS have included construct and criterion-related validity. The construct validity research included comparison of performance between adjacent ages and regression analysis age-score correlation. The criterion-related validity investigations included correlating the PDMS with the Bayley Scales of Infant Development (Bayley, 1969) and the West Haverstraw Motor Development Test (1964). The correlations for the PDMS Fine-Motor Scale were .36 with the Bayley Motor Scale and .62 with the West Haverstraw. These correlations provide some initial evidence concerning the criterion-related validity of the PDMS.

Overall, the PDMS has demonstrated adequate initial reliability and validity. Additional study is needed to confirm the results of these investigations.

Critique

The PDMS is a well-designed assessment instrument and programming guide in the area of developmental motor skills. From its initial publication in 1973, the PDMS has been continually developed and expanded. The current standardized edition offers important improvements compared to the earlier criterion-referenced editions. The PDMS has several unique features. First, it contains a very useful set of activity cards for programming purposes. It is appropriate with nonhandicapped, mildly handicapped, and severely handicapped children. Further, unlike many other developmental scales, it has been standardized and norms are available from a national sample. Finally, the PDMS provides a comprehensive evaluation and programming system that can be used to develop an in-depth diagnostic prescriptive program for children who need intensive intervention in motor skill development.

References

Bayley, N. A. (1969). *Bayley Scales of Infant Development.* New York: The Psychological Corporation. *West Haverstraw Motor Development Test.* (1964). West Haverstraw, NY: New York State Rehabilitation Hospital.

Folio, M. R. & Fewell, R. R. (1983). *Peabody developmental motor scales and activity cards manual.* Allen, Texas: DLM Teaching Resources.

Mark Stone, Ed.D., ABPP
Professor of Psychology, Forest Institute of Professional Psychology, Des Plaines, Illinois.

PERCEPTUAL MAZE TEST
Janice Smith, David Jones, and Alick Elithorn. London, England: Medical Research Council.

Introduction

The Perceptual Maze Test (PMT) occupies a unique place in the psychometric history of mazes for evaluating mental processes. The most well known of the mazes is that of Porteus. However, the design of the PMT is ingeniously different.

The nature of the PMT is common to all the test forms available from the authors. The background for each maze is either a rectangular or triangular lattice network. Target dots are located at various intersections on this lattice background. The task of the subject is to draw a path through this lattice, passing through the greatest number of target dots. The procedure requires the subject to remain on the path. Also, at each intersection the traversed path must continue in a forward direction. (The choice is left or right, but the subject must move ahead and not double back.)

In the arrangement of target dots, there is frequently more than one "best" pathway. Success is achieved whenever the subject succeeds in tracing one of these paths. The item is considered passed when the subject successfully chooses a pathway with the greatest number of dots. The score for the test is the number of perceptual mazes passed. In one form of the test, the correct number of dots is indicated on the page below the lattice for the examinee to see and use as a guide to a correct solution. Another form of the test has this information removed.

The PMT occurs in a number of forms. The basic set of the PMT consists of the VC series. Each of these versions consists of 18 test items preceded by three demonstration patterns. The sets are considered equal in difficulty. Two parallel versions of the PMT, identified as Neuropsychiatric Sets NP1 and NP2, consist of 12 test items preceded by practice sets. A children's version is available with 16 items preceded by three demonstration patterns. There is a short form consisting of 15 designs. For the researcher, earlier versions of the PMT consisting of the 72 mazes and original items used in the development of this test are made available by the authors upon request.

Test times are given as 10 minutes for all regular forms. This reviewer's use of the PMT suggests that these times are minimal. Thirty to forty-five minutes is more common for the standard forms. An automated version of the PMT is available for operation on the Apple II and NorthStar Horizon microcomputer. The authors indicate that programs for other microcomputers are available on request.

The current version of the PMT makes use of a triangular lattice network. Earlier versions of the test used a rectangular maze. In addition, mirror versions of all mazes are possible due to the unique construction of the maze itself. An alternate form of every item is easily developed by producing a mirror image of the original.

The test itself and the accompanying manual are produced in an experimental form. The manual itself is described as "an interim report which is for private circulation only." This interim report provides sufficient material to administer the test and gain insight into the development of the PMT. Some studies are reported, and a bibliography is included. The manual itself is truly an interim report with insufficient information to allow for widespread use. The test materials themselves consist of individual pages stapled together containing one maze on each. Therefore, the current availability of the test is in the most meager form. Appropriate use of the PMT at the present time is for research only.

Practical Applications/Uses

The test has been utilized in several studies as the major instrument for the measurement of localized brain damage. Studies by Elithorn report success using the PMT in distinguishing between groups of subjects with small lesions in the temporal region, and the PMT is considered to be particularly sensitive to frontal lobe damage. In a study of 200 subjects among 27 other tests, the PMT was found to be one of the most sensitive in identifying brain damage (Benton, 1963). And another study utilizing the PMT reported its sensitivity to cerebral damage (Colonna and Faglioni, 1966).

Technical Aspects

The PMT cannot be considered ready for general use. There are no norms for the PMT given in the accompanying manual. Reference is made in the manual to Davies (1965), who has provided norms on a sample of 540 subjects, 50 men and 40 women in each of six age groups: 20-29, 30-39, 40-49, 50-59, 60-69 and 70-79. Several additional normative studies are cited in the manual, but the authors have provided no normative information in the present manual.

The reliability of the test appears to be good. A test-retest reliability coefficient of .89 is reported in the test manual. An alternate form coefficient of .81 demonstrates the general equivalence of test forms. It is clear, however, that further published research on the validity and the reliability of this instrument is required.

In studies cited in the manual, the PMT is shown to correlate .74 with the Block Design subtest of the Wechsler Scale. It correlated .62 for men and .54 for women with the Raven Progressive Matrices.

The PMT, according to the authors, requires a perceptual scanning strategy for successful performance, depending upon the size of the unit scanned and the rate of scanning. Subjects reported that the solution is achieved by a rapid and irregular perceptual scanning of the items, in which they first identify areas with high target dot density and attempt to link these dots to a correct solution. The task requires the subject to make some analysis of the grouping of dots and their relationship to one another. An important factor is deciding how the dots can be linked to form this correct solution. The arrangement of specific dot configurations constitutes the item difficulty index according to three specific parameters: the size of the background lattice, the number of target dots on the lattice, and the arrangement of those dots in a pattern. Hence, the difficulty level of each maze can be empirically determined and subsequently evaluated in conjunction with psychological constructs.

A particularly ingenious application of the PMT is its availability in a form for computer construction, administration, and scoring. In this format, the construction of items can be empirically determined by the parameters mentioned above. There is in effect an infinite number of items that can be created given the constraints of the three parameters contributing to item difficulty. Thus, a program to develop any pattern of any size is not difficult.

Critique

It is clear from the provided test materials that the PMT is not yet ready for general distribution. The instrument is basically a research instrument whose usefulness seems considerable. However, given the dates of its initial development, it appears that the instrument is slow in reaching a state of readiness. The test materials are meager; the items are provided as designs printed on odd-sized paper and stapled together. While these materials are sufficient for use and in no way impair the utility of the instrument, it is clear that a finished product has not been achieved. Users must be wary of its application in any other area than research until further documentation is provided by the authors.

On the positive side, the PMT represents a quantum leap forward in the use of mazes as instruments for measuring ability. The test is ingenious and attracts a subject's attention. Its application and simple binary solution for computer programs makes the PMT particularly well-suited to computerized construction, administration, recording, and analysis. The conceptual framework of the PMT clearly identifies it as appropriate for the identification of focal brain lesions and useful in development of studies dealing with problem-solving abilities. In addition, many other applications await use of the PMT.

References

Benton, A. L., Elithorn, A., Fogel, M. L., & Kerr, M. (1963). A perceptual maze test sensitive to brain damage. *Journal of Neurology, Neurosurgery and Psychiatry, 26*(6), 540-544.
Buckingham, R. A., Elithorn, A., Lee, D. N., & Nixon, W. L. B. (1963). A mathematical model of a perceptual maze test. *Nature, 199,* 676-678.
Colonna, A., & Faglioni, P. (1966). The performance of hemisphere-damaged patients on spatial intelligence tests. *Cortex, 2,* 293-307.
Davies, A. D. M. (1965). The perceptual maze in a normal population. *Perception and Motor Skills, 20,* 287-293.
Davies, A. D. M., & Davies, M. G. (1965). The difficulty and graded scoring of Elithorn's perceptual maze test. *British Journal of Psychology, 56,* 295-302.
Davies, M. G., & Davies, A. D. M. (1965). Some analytical properties of Elithorn's perceptual maze. *Journal of Mathematical Psychology, 2*(2), 371-380.
Elithorn, A. (1964). Intelligence perceptual integration and the minor hemisphere syndrome. *Neuropsychologia, 2,* 327-332.
Elithorn, A. (1965). Psychological tests: An objective approach to problems of task difficulty [Monograph]. *Acta Psychiatrica Scandinavica, 47,* 661-667.

Elithorn, A., Jones, D., & Kerr, M. O. (1963). A binary perceptual maze. *American Journal of Psychology, 76*(3), 506-508.

Elithorn, A., Jones, D., Kerr, M. O., & Lee, D. N. (1964). The effects of the variation of two physical parameters on empirical difficulty in a perceptual maze test. *British Journal of Psychology, 55*(1), 31-37.

Elithorn, A., Jones, D., Kerr, M. O., & Mott, J. (1960). A group version of a perceptual maze test. *British Journal of Psychology, 51*(1), 19-26.

Lee, D. N. (1965). *A psychological and mathematical study of task complexity in relation to human problem-solving using a perceptual maze test.* Unpublished doctoral dissertation, University of London, London, England.

Loevinger, J. (1957). Objective tests as instruments of psychological theory. *Psychological Reports, 3*, 635-694.

Penrose, L. S. (1944). An economical method of presenting matrix intelligence tests. *British Journal of Medical Psychology, 20*(2), 144-146.

Roger D. Carlson, Ph.D.
Research and Evaluation Assistant, Eugene Public Schools, Eugene, Oregon.

THE PERSONAL SKILLS MAP

Darwin B. Nelson and Gary R. Low. Corpus Christi, Texas: Personal Life Skills Center.

Introduction

The Personal Skills Map: A Positive Assessment and Personalized Learning Model (PSM) is a means of positive self-assessment of intrapersonal skills, interpersonal skills, career/life management skills, stress management, and problematic behaviors. The results of the PSM can help the client identify specific areas for personal change and growth.

Darwin B. Nelson, the senior author, is a counseling psychologist (Ph.D., 1968, East Texas State University) who collaborated with Gary R. Low, Ph.D., and Keith A. Taylor, M.S. (also both of East Texas State University). The authors were influenced by a number of the humanistic and holistic perspectives. The theoretical biases of the authors in the definition of mental health are ostensibly Rogers, Maslow, Jourard, Fensterheim, Jakubowski and Lange, Berne, Satir, Perls, Bandler and Grinder, Mahoney, Michenbaum, Ellis, Maltusby, Truax, Carkhuff, Lazarus, Benson, Friedman and Rosenman, and Pelletier. The authors note that their interpersonal skills training has been influenced by the work of James McHolland, Joe Hill, Bernard Guerney, Jakubowski and Lange, Watzlawick, Bandler and Grinder.

The PSM was developed from 1976 through 1978 and released to professionals in 1979. A number of research studies, mostly doctoral dissertations at Texas institutions, have used the PSM in applied situations since 1979. In their 1981 manual, the authors state that "In its sixth year of research and development, the PSM must still be viewed as an experimental instrument" (Nelson & Low, 1981).

The PSM adult version consists of 300 items that were drawn from an original pool of 1,300 items. Each item was determined to have content validity through the judgments of professionals as to what scale was most appropriate for its placement: intrapersonal skills (self-esteem, growth motivation, change orientation), interpersonal skills (assertion, aggression, interpersonal deference, interpersonal awareness, empathy), career/life management skills (drive strength, decision-making, time management, sales orientation, commitment ethic, stress management). The PSM was normed on a random sample of 1,400 normal adults.

Besides the main form, which is contained in a reusable booklet and used with separate answer sheets, there is also a 244-item self-scoring nonreusable form and a form that was developed for use with adolescents (PSM-A). The PSM has also been translated into the Finnish language. The present critique only pertains to the adult English-language version in the non-self-scorable format.

The PSM is contained within a 6-page test booklet, and answers are marked on a separate machine-scorable answer sheet. The 300 items are grouped in two parts; the first 63 items describe possible reactions to situations, and the remaining items are self-descriptions outside of situational contexts. The respondent is asked to rate each item in terms of being most descriptive, sometimes descriptive, and least descriptive of him- or herself. The scale is untimed and completion time ranges from 45 to 75 minutes.

The profile of the PSM, a computer-generated, full-color standard form called a "person map," lists all of the dimensions of the PSM: intrapersonal skills, interpersonal skills, career/life skills, personal communication style, and personal change orientation. Along each dimension an individual's standard score is graphically indicated. Standard scores below 40 are labeled as areas in need of change, those between 40 and 60 are labeled as skills that are developed, and those over 60 are labeled as skill strengths. On the reverse of the profile form is interpretive material for the user. The forms are designed to be given directly to the client.

Practical Applications/Uses

The PSM was developed out of a need for an assessment device to measure the degree to which one has developed positive and healthy life skills (intrapersonal, interpersonal, and career/life management). It is meant to be of use in human development education, individual and group counseling, and consultation and training that focuses on personal growth as a skill-building process. Moreover, it is meant to measure the presence of mental health skills rather than merely the absence of pathology.

The PSM is self-administered, and the manual contains statements that can be used to help examinees understand the directions. The authors warn that the test should *not* be used for unobtrusive assessment purposes. They also present research on the PSM indicating that responses can be faked to a significant degree.

Scoring is accomplished by sending the answer sheets to the Personal Life Skills Center, P.C. (formerly Institute for the Development of Human Resources) in Corpus Christi, Texas, or Castro Valley, California. Normally, computerized scoring services are prepaid with the answer sheets when ordered.

Technical Aspects

Concurrent validity was obtained by administering the scale to three groups and obtaining means and t ratios comparing them. Statistically significant differences were found between mental health professionals, normal adults, and persons voluntarily seeking counseling and psychotherapy services at outpatient treatment facilities.

Construct validity was obtained by scale-to-scale correlations with other scales such as the Personal Orientation Inventory, the Edwards Personal Preference Schedule, the 16PF, and the MMPI.

Test-retest reliability coefficients range from .64 to .94 on the various scales. Because the test is meant to detect change in personal skills that can be brought about by a number of sources, the PSM is not meant to reveal constant stable aspects of personality. Therefore, according to the authors, the PSM profiles should not be expected to remain stable over time.

Critique

One quite practical problem in using the PSM is that turnaround time for scoring is lengthy. (In this reviewer's experience, it can take two weeks to receive profiles—a problem that seems to defeat the purpose of computerized scoring). There is no remedy in hand scoring because keys are not released to professionals. The only alternative is a more expensive self-scoring form. The authors purport that this restrictiveness is due to research security: "The use of the PSM was highly restricted during the initial years of development (1976-79), and for the first two years of its use by professionals nationally (1979-81). This procedure was followed to assure the completion of large scale sampling and standardization studies, as well as extensive research by professionals external to the authors" (Nelson & Low, 1981, p. 7). Yet alternatives to having the PSM scored by the LSC are still unavailable. Further, publishers of other tests dealing with much more sensitive issues of mental health (e.g., the MMPI) that *do* purport to be unobtrusive measures of personality (and whose sensitivity *could* be compromised due to prior exposure to test takers) have seen fit to release scoring keys to professionals in trust that ethical standards will prevail. Likewise, such restrictive security does not explain why the publishers recently have issued a more expensive self-scoring version of the PSM. Presumably that, too, could compromise the test's security.

The heavy emphasis upon skills associated with business and what has recently been in fashion in popular psychology makes one wonder whether there were any serious attempts to develop the PSM based on the scientific literature in the area of personality research. Measurement of stress, time management skills, aggression, and assertion are expedient for the purposes of business and industry, however tangential to the scientific and theoretical study of the psychology of personality.

Two aspects of the technical development of the PSM seem oversimplified. First, scales were developed by means of face validity and judgments of professionals (content validity); why item performance was not factor analyzed and, by doing so, scales derived empirically remains a puzzle. As such, items and scales are arbitrary, and scales were chosen theoretically rather than empirically. Second, why the authors did not examine predictive validity using subjects who were thought to be developing the said skills also remains puzzling. Simply ascertaining statistically significant differences between arbitrarily chosen populations does not establish validity. In this reviewer's personal experience with the PSM, the test profiles lack discriminability between normal adults and thus do not seem to provide the wealth of individual information that scales like the MMPI provide. The best measure of validity that the PSM is able to provide is construct validity from correlations with scales on other personality tests.

In the PSM manual, Nelson and Low suggest that the PSM measures the "personal strengths and areas of needed change for personal growth and creative living" (Nelson & Low, 1981, p. 5), yet in their validity studies they fail to show how their scale is related to "personal growth." Further, there are no measures of creativity used to validate the scales selected. There are no correlations between the presence or absence of any particular skill and the presence or absence of creativity as measured by standard measures of creativity (e.g., Christiansen, Guilford, Merrifield, & Wilson, 1978; Torrance, 1984).

There are other extremely serious problems inherent in the PSM. The PSM purports to stress positive aspects of personality, yet it can be argued that the test is no more value-free than are tests such as the MMPI that stress negative aspects of personality. There is a mental health ethic inherent in the PSM. In fact, the authors have an 11-point list of items that characterize the "healthy personality" from their point of view. Not surprisingly, these fall into perfect correspondence with the "skill strengths" on their profile form. The authors' recognition and concern that the test can be "faked" implies that they can recognize an implicit "good" and "bad" in the outcomes of the scale. Faking implies a motive, for without one there would be no reason to "fake" the test. Therefore, the authors imply that there is a more desirable profile to be obtained on the PSM, that the PSM is relatively transparent to the respondent as to what that profile might be like and, therefore, some respondents may seek to avoid producing a negative profile.

The listing of the theoretical biases of the authors on the surface seems like a commendable way of "letting the buyer beware" and making the reader know that one is aware of one's own limitations as an observer, as if to abdicate one's own responsibility for biases by pointing them out. Yet the biases are still there. And it is important to note that, although the purpose of the PSM is allegedly positive, the underlying theme is no different than that of the MMPI—it draws attention to deficits, given an arbitrary standard of comparison.

The authors seem to implicitly represent a kind of eclecticism by the mentors who they list. If the authors are not implying that they are eclectic, then they are glossing over some very important theoretical differences between theorists listed (e.g., Rogers vs. Maslow vs. Michenbaum vs. Ellis vs. Lazarus vs. Perls vs. Benson vs. Freidman and Rosenman). Neither eclecticism nor homogeneity of thought are adequate rationale in listing those theorists to which the authors owe their debt. Rather, such a long and varied list implies that the authors have not really come to grips enough with their own theoretical orientations to ask some tough critical questions of the theories they ostensibly support.

Many, including Ruth Benedict (1934), Offer and Sabshim (1966), Michel Foucault (1965), and Thomas Szasz (1960) have been critical of a mental health ethic. The PSM tries to camouflage a mental health ethic for a developmental ethic. Many aspects of developmental psychology are value laden, but the very best of developmental psychology has been shown to be rather stable, endurable, entailing value-free events of change in the individual. And much of that is born of maturation rather than nurturance. The authors of the PSM are practitioners concerned more with *inducing* skill development—in other words, *training*, rather than scientific observation of ontogenetic change. Despite this, the PSM purports to be of use to consulting developmental psychologists.

The desire to work from a value-neutral framework, where one is not condemned for his or her failing, is a commendable one. Unfortunately Nelson and Low have missed their mark. Although cloaked in positive language, the very subjects that they chose to look at, as well as the implication that deficits require remediation implies a value framework. "Humanistic" frameworks seem to be very often condemning and are not value neutral.

As an aid in either positive adult development or in personal wellness, as it is advertised, the PSM leaves much to be desired. Both of these areas imply a kind of "normality in nature." In using the theoretically value-laden framework that it does, the PSM mistakes normal adult development for desirable adult development (from some arbitrary standard of preference), and personal wellness for desirable health—both ethic-laden rather than nature-laden states.

The major purpose for developing the PSM was to "construct a positive assessment instrument that would result in a self-description for the person which identified personal strengths and areas of needed change for personal growth and creative living" (Nelson & Low, 1981, p. 5). The nomenclature for the profile that the scale generates is called "mapping" out of an awareness of Korzybski's distinction between the "map" and the "territory," which warns that we not confuse the map for the territory.

Nelson and Low imply that their model is a comprehensive one but it is at best, simplistic. The authors were right to join Korzybski in cautioning that the map is not the territory. Maps can be either simple or complexly detailed, accurate or inaccurate. Models of human action can also be simplistic or complex, true or false. The Personal Skills Map does not adequately map the complex territory of human action.

References

Benedict, R. (1934). Anthropology and the abnormal. *Journal of General Psychology, 10,* 59-82.

Christiansen, P. R., Guilford, J. P., Merrifield, P. R., & Wilson, R. C. (1978). *Alternate uses.* Orange, CA: Sheridan Psychological Services.

Foucault, M. (1965). *Madness and civilization: A history of insanity in the age of reason.* New York: Pantheon.

Nelson, D. B., & Low, G. R. (1979). *The Personal Skills Map: A Positive Assessment and Personalized Learning Model.* Corpus Christi, TX: Institute for the Development of Human Resources.

Nelson, D. B., & Low, G. R. (1981). *Personal Skills Map: A Positive Assessment of Career/Life Effectiveness Skills: Manual.* Corpus Christi, TX: Institute for the Development of Human Resources.

Offer, D., & Sabshin, M. (1966). *Normality: Theoretical and clinical concepts of mental health.* New York: Basic.

Szasz, T. S. (1960). The myth of mental illness. *American Psychologist, 15,* 113-118.

Torrance, E. P. (1984). *Torrance Tests of Creative Thinking.* Bensenville, IL: Scholastic Testing Service.

Elizabeth Taleporos, Ph.D.
Associate Professor of Psychology, Long Island University, Brooklyn, New York.

POLITTE SENTENCE COMPLETION TEST
Alan J. Politte. Creve Coeur, Missouri: Psychologists and Educators, Inc.

Introduction

The Politte Sentence Completion Test (PSCT) is designed to elicit information about the personality characteristics of children. The instrument consists of a series of sentence stems which a child completes. The pattern of responses is intended to inform the examiner about the child's feelings and emotions.

The PSCT was developed over a 4 year period, during which time items were tried out on over 400 students. The first form of the instrument was published in 1971. It consisted of 35 sentence stems designed to tap the affective states of children in Grades 7-12. A second form of the instrument was published in 1974. This also consisted of 35 sentence stems, but the content of items on this form was chosen and determined to be more appropriate for measuring children in the elementary school grades, 1-6.

Practical Applications/Uses

The PSCT can be administered either individually or in groups. As noted earlier, it can be administered to children in Grades 1-12, and may also be given to those who are older than the typical twelfth grader but whose mental functioning is in the range of average first through twelfth grade students.

For the younger child, the examiner reads the sentence stem, asks the child to complete the sentence, and then records the response on the test form. For older children, the individual child can read the sentence stem and complete the sentence by writing in the blank space provided on the test form. The author states that anyone who can read at a level above second or third grade should be able to read the items and fill in their response by themselves.

Administration time is quite short. It is expected that an individual can read and complete the 35 items in about 15 minutes. In addition to providing space for recording responses, space is provided for recording basic demographic information about the child, including name, age, sex, grade, teacher's name, and date of testing. The test itself is given in typewritten form, and only minimal space seems to be available for recording responses. This may constrict the answers of an individual who is reading the items and writing in his or her own answers, rather than the person to whom the items are being read to.

The 35 items on each of the two forms appear to be appropriately chosen to elicit affective information. They include some obvious stems that ask directly about feelings and emotional times of the day, such as dreaming at night. Others are not so obvious and describe ordinary activities and events, such as schoolbus and lunchtime experiences. The first type clearly taps into the emotional aspects of the child's thinking; the second is more removed and thus may provide projective information that can reveal aspects of the child's affective state that he or she might not ordinarily share. Even though one cannot say much about personality structure and emotional status from responses to single sentence stems, clear patterns of responses to many such stems can reveal stable traits and themes that can describe typical problems or current stressors that affect a child's functioning.

The test manual provides all the information needed to use the instrument. It is written in a clear and straightforward manner, although only minimal information is given. The instrument is presented as a structured clinical tool, the responses to which may be interpreted as projective information that reveals patterns of personality functioning and themes of affective functioning. The clinician using the information must rely on his or her own experience with responses to instruments such as this to judge the degree to which the child's responses may be used as part of diagnosis or treatment. The items may prove useful as structured stimuli to initiate discussion with a child in order to provide a starting place for more in-depth probing of clinical interviews.

The test is designed to be used by a trained clinician, although with proper cautions, it can be administered by someone without training in clinical psychology. The administrator of the instrument must exercise subjective judgment in analyzing responses, both through his or her own experience and interpretation of psychological theories pertinent to projective assessment of personality. The author cautions users lacking clinical training to use the instrument only as a screening device, one which may prove useful for interviewing in a counselling and/or referral situation.

Technical Aspects

There are no standard psychometric data presented for either form of this instrument. The author states that no objective scoring system is available, and therefore no standard reliability and validity analyses have been attempted. Face validity is obvious for the instrument, and should, according to the author, suffice for a clinical instrument such as this. The instrument clearly is designed for use as a single tool in making judgments about a child's emotional life and does not present information that implies normative comparisons.

Many projective tests are used without standardization and without the support of an objective scoring system. Clinicians find these instruments useful as adjunctive aids in assessment and treatment, but of limited use when compared with those for whom reliability and validity information has been compiled. Certainly, elaborate scoring and diagnostic validity such as that obtained for other projective tests, such as the Thematic Apperception Test and the Rorschach, is not necessary. And certainly, the gathering of psychometric support is difficult, but a minimal effort using the Politte could substantially increase its acceptance and use by clinical psychologists. An initial estimate of test-retest reliability and interrater reliability should not be difficult to obtain in analyzing and interpreting information obtained from children about personality traits that presumably are stable over a relatively short period of time.

Critique

The Politte Sentence Completion Test presents a set of potentially useful sentence stems that can be used as standard stimuli to elicit projective information about personality structure and development in children. The broad age range that has been considered in its development is an attractive feature, since individuals can be tracked longitudinally and change noted following various periods of time and kinds of therapeutic interventions. More research is clearly needed to bring the instrument to the level at which it will be widely used and accepted as a reliable projective device that is a valid indicator of children's feelings and emotional states. Even though difficult, obtaining this additional information is clearly not impossible, as successful attempts have been made by others (e.g., Borgatta, 1961; Loevinger, Wessler, & Redmore, 1970; Rotter & Rafferty, 1950). As it stands now, the PSCT presently appears to offer nothing more than a format for clinicians to use in eliciting affective information about children, uninterpretable beyond the clinician's personal level of experience and integration of psychological theory. Additional research should be undertaken so that one may use this form in research and clinical settings.

References

Borgatta, E. F. (1961). Make a sentence test: An approach to objective scoring of sentence completions. *Genetic Psychology Monographs, 63,* 3-65.
Loevinger, J., Wessler, R., & Redmore, C. (1970). *Measuring ego development* (Vols. 1 & 2). San Francisco: Jossey-Bass.
Politte, A. J. (1971). *Politte Sentence Completion Test: Intermediate and secondary form.* Jacksonville, Illinois: Psychologists and Educators, Inc.
Politte, A. J. (1974). *Pollitte Sentence Completion Test: Elementary school form.* St. Louis, Mo.: Psychologists and Educators, Inc.
Rotter, J. B., & Rafferty, J. S. (1950). *Manual for the Rotter Incomplete Sentences Blank: College Form.* New York: The Psychological Corporation.

Glenn E. Snelbecker, Ph.D.
Professor, Psychological Studies, Temple University, Philadelphia, Pennsylvania.

Michael J. Roszkowski, Ph.D.
Research Psychologist, Research and Evaluation Department, The American College, Bryn Mawr, Pennsylvania.

POSITION ANALYSIS QUESTIONNAIRE
Ernest J. McCormick, P. R. Jeanneret, and Robert C. Mecham. West Lafayette, Indiana: Purdue University Bookstore.

Introduction

The Position Analysis Questionnaire (PAQ) is a standardized, quantifiable job analysis questionnaire that is "worker" rather than "work" oriented. This means that the unit of analysis is not the technology of the job but, rather, the underlying generalized behavior required to perform that job. The philosophy behind the instrument is that even though each job consists of a unique set of activities at the surface level, all jobs can be described with a finite set of "elements," and these elements can be quantified. Thus, jobs at different technological levels can be measured and compared on a common metric once the behaviors necessary for performance of the actual job task are identified, analyzed, and synthesized. Jobs analyzed with the PAQ are characterized by profile scores on these underlying dimensions.

The PAQ was designed to measure the underlying structure of virtually all jobs. It was intended to be a job analysis procedure that would be applicable in a wide range of jobs/positions in diverse work contexts. The PAQ focuses primarily on worker knowledge, skills, and abilities (broadly defined) needed to perform work.

The three developers of the PAQ are prominent industrial psychologists who have been affiliated at one time or another with Purdue University. Ernest T. McCormick received a bachelor's degree from Ohio Wesleyan University in 1933. After working as a chief occupational statistician for the Selective Service System and a Personnel Classification Officer in the Bureau of Naval Personnel during World War II, he attended Purdue University, earning an M.S. in 1947 and a Ph.D. in 1948, both in industrial/organizational psychology. Upon graduating, he remained at Purdue University as a faculty member of the Psychology Department, retiring in 1977 with the rank of Professor. At present, Dr. McCormick is Professor Emeritus in the Department of Psychological Sciences at Purdue. A Fellow of the American Psychological Association, Dr. McCormick is also certified by the American Board of Examiners in Professional Psychology (ABPP). During his long and productive career, Dr. McCormick has authored a number of textbooks dealing with industrial psychology, human factors engineering, and job analysis.

The two junior authors of the PAQ did their doctoral work under McCormick at

Purdue University and their dissertations involved the refinement of the PAQ. Robert Mecham earned his master's and doctoral degrees at Purdue University. He is currently Associate Professor of Business Administration at Utah State University and serves as director of operations for PAQ Services, Inc. He has been associated with both organizations since receiving his doctorate in 1970.

Paul R. Jeanneret received a bachelor's degree in psychology from the University of Virginia in 1962, a master's degree in general psychology from the University of Florida in 1963, and a Ph.D. in industrial/organizational psychology from Purdue University in 1969. Since graduating from Purdue, Dr. Jeanneret has worked as a management consultant, most recently in his own practice (Jeanneret & Associates) in Houston, Texas.

An extensive body of literature exists describing the PAQ's creation and refinement. Detailed historical information regarding the development of the PAQ is available in a number of technical reports issued by the Occupational Research Center of Purdue University (e.g., McCormick, Jeanneret, & Mecham, 1969), but these documents are not in general circulation. However, summaries of the overall research effort can be found in relatively recent books (McCormick, 1976, 1979) and journal articles (McCormick, DeNisi, & Shaw, 1979; McCormick, Jeanneret, & Mecham, 1972).

The PAQ was developed under a series of contracts between the Office of Naval Research and the Purdue Research Foundation, which holds the copyright on this instrument. The PAQ is an outgrowth of McCormick's earlier work with two scales, The Checklist of Work Activities and The Worker Activity Profile. The first version of the PAQ (Form A) was developed in the 1960s and released for practical applications in 1969. The current version of the PAQ is Form B, which has superceded Form A, but differs from it only moderately in terms of its basic nature, content, and format.

Formal computer techniques were made available for scoring and analysis purposes in 1973. When the computer techniques were operational, procedures were also arranged to accumulate a data bank of PAQ results. Thus, PAQ users can have individual or group records from a given situation compared with previous PAQ results for comparable jobs or positions. Analyses in the data bank are identified by job titles and job numbers from the *Dictionary of Occupational Titles* (U.S. Department of Labor, 1977).

The PAQ consists of 194 items called *job elements*. Responses for any given position are to be based on a face-to-face interview with a job incumbent or with someone who is intimately familiar with the job being analyzed (e.g., a supervisor who formerly worked in the job for a number of years). Administration, analysis, and interpretation of the PAQ results can provide quantified details and descriptions of jobs in terms of job elements and statistically derived job dimensions. Job dimension attributes are calculated from combinations of questionnaire item results. The 194 questionnaire items are contained in an easy-to-use 28-page booklet; responses for the job being analyzed are recorded on a separate optical-scan answer sheet.

The first 187 items serve as the main basis on which the job analyses are conducted. These 187 items relate to job activities, behaviors, requirements, or features of work situations. The last seven questionnaire items (i.e., items #188 through #194) concern financial compensation details, including the type of compensation method (e.g., salary, hourly wage, tips, etc.) and actual dollars for the respective compensation method(s). Thus, unless questions of comparable worth or compensation adjustments are raised, PAQ users may choose to focus primarily (or exclusively) on the first 187 items.

Most of the 187 items involve a 6-point scale, although some require only a 2-point rating ("does apply/does not apply"). The anchors for the 6-point scales vary across different clusters of items. Most of the ratings are made in terms of the respective items' "importance to this job"; other scales involve "extent of use," "amount of time," and "possibility of occurrence" (used with items dealing with physical hazards). For the 6-point scales, a "Does Not Apply" category also is included.

The *Job Analysis Manual* is an almost indispensable resource for anyone using the PAQ. It not only provides helpful suggestions about conducting job analysis interviews, but also offers instructions for selecting appropriate responses. The *Job Analysis Manual* gives users an overall description of the respective item sets, specifies and explains possible responses, and provides a framework of occupation "anchors" for each of the rating points. This latter information is essential in providing PAQ users with some broader perspective when making judgments about ratings for individual jobs. For example, item #98, "Hand-ear coordination," is classified under "3.6 Manipulative/Coordination Activities" among the 49 "Division 3" items involving "Work Output." The PAQ questionnaire booklet contains this description for item #98: "(T)he coordination of hand movements with sounds or instructions that are heard, for example, tuning radio receivers, tuning musical instruments by ear, piloting aircraft by control tower instructions, etc."

The *Job Analysis Manual* contains these response possibilities for item #98, "Hand-ear coordination," along with at least one anchor occupation for each response category as illustrated by the following: N = Does Not Apply, Head Teller; 1 = Very Minor, Electrician Helper; 2 = Low, Surveyor Helper; 3 = Average, Police Officer; 4 = High, Commercial Air Pilot; and 5 = Extreme, Piano Teacher. These anchor occupations for the responses provide valuable information for the job analyst, who ultimately must make the rating judgment, and indirectly for the interviewee, who typically needs assistance in gaining perspective about ratings for each of the questionnaire items. Using item #98 as an example, it is conceivable that *practically every respondent* will think that hand-ear coordination is involved in some way in a given job. The job analyst needs to provide some perspective about jobs more generally in selecting and recording responses for the particular job being analyzed.

The 187 items are organized in six major divisions:

1) Information Input (35 items): "Where and how does the worker get information that is used in performing the job?"

2) Mental Processes (14 items): "What reasoning, decision-making, planning, and information processing activities are involved in performing the job?"

3) Work Output (49 items): "What physical activities does the worker perform and what tools or devices are used?"

4) Relationships With Other Persons (36 items): "What relationships with other people are required in performing the job?"

5) Job Context (19 items): "In what physical and social contexts is the work performed?"

6) Other Job Characteristics (41 items): "What activities, conditions, or characteristics other than those described above are relevant to the job?"

The first 34 items in Division 6 clearly are needed for the job analyses. The last 7 items (items #188 through 194) deal with pay, income, and other financial compensation details and may or may not be needed for a particular PAQ project.

Various principal-components analyses by McCormick and his colleagues (see McCormick et al., 1979) have indicated that the 187 items on the PAQ can also be represented by 32 dimensions when each of the six divisions is analyzed separately, and 13 factors when the divisions are disregarded and the 187 items are analyzed all at once. However, only 12 of these 13 factors were interpretable:

1) Having decision, communicating, and general responsibilities;
2) Operating machines or equipment;
3) Performing clerical-related activities;
4) Performing technical-related activities;
5) Performing service-related activities;
6) Working regular day versus other work schedules;
7) Performing routine or repetitive activities;
8) Being aware of work environment;
9) Engaging in physical activities;
10) Supervising or coordinating other personnel;
11) Public or customer-related contacts; and
12) Working in an unpleasant, hazardous, or demanding environment.

A comprehensive set of materials and other resources are available for PAQ users. Administration materials include a 28-page questionnaire booklet and an answer sheet designed for optical scanning. These items are the "bare minimum" one needs to administer the PAQ; to conduct the PAQ in a manner that will lead to useful information, however, one needs to consult other PAQ resources.

Two resources provide administration information and technical details. The aforementioned *Job Analysis Manual* provides guidelines for the actual administration of the PAQ. It appears to have been written primarily for formally trained job analysts or for other users who have at least some minimal experience in conducting interviews and job analyses. It includes detailed instructions about conducting the interviews and completing the PAQ response forms.

The second resource is a 31-page *Technical Manual (System II)*. As the name implies, this manual contains information about the PAQ's development, reliability, and validity. The authors state that it includes "a discussion of the nature of the Position Analysis Questionnaire (PAQ), some background regarding its development, a summary of some of the research carried out with it, a discussion of certain of its potential applications, and a summary of the procedures that should be followed by an organization that is using it, or is considering its use" (McCormick et al., 1977, p. 1). Given the fact that it provides virtually no definitions and very little "cookbook" information, it appears to be written for readers with at least some minimal psychometric training and experience. In that respect, it contains the kinds of information typically found in the technical sections of test manuals.

A third resource, the *User's Manual (System II)*, provides detailed instructions for

330 Position Analysis Questionnaire

planning and conducting a PAQ project, including descriptions of various ways in which PAQ results can be analyzed, transformed, and examined. In the preface to this manual the authors state that this resource

> is intended primarily for organizations and individuals using the Position Analysis Questionnaire (PAQ) for some operational or research purpose. It is based in large part on the accumulated experience of many individuals and organizations with the PAQ, and explains some of the techniques found to be valuable when using PAQ data. In particular it provides information useful in preparing PAQ material for computer processing and in interpreting the data once processed. (McCormick, et al., 1977, p. 1)

Automated scoring of PAQ response forms and a rather wide range of computer-based analyses and interpretations are available from PAQ Services, Inc. When planning the types of analyses and interpretations needed for a given situation, users should refer to the *User's Manual* and to the PAQ Services "Processing Request Form and Price List." The Processing Request Form and Price List can serve somewhat as a guide to the sections of the *User's Manual* that one will need for a given PAQ project. PAQ Services periodically provides newsletters describing PAQ research and practical applications, and offers workshops (for a fee) that address matters concerning the administration and interpretation of the PAQ.

Readers may be interested in other forms of the PAQ which have been developed. There exists a German version, called PAQ Bd, the development and features of which are described in Frieling, Kannheiser, and Lindberg (1974) and Frieling (1977). In addition, items from the PAQ were used to develop a Coast Guard job inventory (Cornelius, Hakel, & Sackett, 1979). This instrument involved the creation of additional items, reduction in the number of response formats, and a lowering of the reading level. The latter modification was especially necessary because trained job analysts were not being used.

Practical Applications/Uses

Job analysis has come to be recognized as the cornerstone for most personnel functions within an organization (McCormick, 1976, 1979), and Ash and Levine (1980) have outlined the most common uses for the results of a job analysis. The authors of the PAQ seem to consider the instrument appropriate for many, but not all, of the applications expected from the job analysis process. There is a very extensive body of research literature that has either focused on the PAQ or has employed the PAQ to address a wide range of human resource development and management issues. The PAQ has been used, for research or practical purposes, on such matters as identification of appropriate tests for a given job, job evaluation and classification for wage and salary administration, comparability analyses for different jobs or for similar jobs in different work contexts, performance appraisal, detecting similarities and differences among jobs, forming job families, evaluating the extent to which a particular job "fits" with selected job families, examining questions concerning "validity generalization" across different job contexts, vocational counseling and career development, and so on. Because it detects the key attributes required of workers on a common scale, the PAQ is seen as particularly useful in choosing appropriate selection criteria and tests, determining wage allocations, making comparisons among jobs for employee transfer and job design purposes, and for forecasting personnel requirements (Harvey & Hayes, 1986; McCormick, 1976, 1979; McCormick et al., 1972; Mecham, 1983).

The PAQ has been used to analyze a multitude of jobs in numerous work contexts. By 1979, the PAQ data bank contained descriptions of over 25,000 positions (McCormick, DeNisi, & Shaw, 1979). The variety of jobs analyzed can be seen in the published analyses of some of these jobs, such as "homemaker" (Arvey & Begalla, 1975), "mentally retarded sheltered-workshop worker" (Townsen, Prien, & Johnson, 1974), "hospital volunteer" (Clark, 1985), and "setter in the plastics injection-moulding industry" (Sparrow, Patrick, Spurgeon, & Barwell, 1982). The PAQ has been used to classify into job families from as few positions as seven foreman jobs in a chemical processing plant (Cornelius, Carron, & Collins, 1979) to as many as 325 positions at a major insurance company (Colbert & Taylor, 1978; Taylor, 1978; Taylor & Colbert, 1978).

The usefulness of the PAQ has been compared to other job analysis methods, but with only a few exceptions (e.g., Cornelius et al., 1979; Madigan, 1985), most of these studies are based on the informed opinions of experienced job analysts rather than on more objective criteria. The most comprehensive surveys of the attitudes of job analysts have been conducted by Levine and his colleagues (Levine, Ash, & Bennett, 1980; Levine, Ash, Hall, & Sistrunk, 1983; Levine, Bennett, & Ash, 1979). These studies have shown that during the 1970s the PAQ was not popular in the public sector because personnel specialists were not familiar with this method, due to limited opportunities for training on how to use the technique and perhaps to the PAQ's non-job-specific language. Given the great attention the PAQ receives in the literature, the situation may have changed since these studies were completed.

The PAQ appears to be viewed by job analysts as being more effective for some purposes than others (Levine et al., 1983). From among seven job analysis methods, the PAQ was rated as the best method for job evaluation purposes, third best for job classification purposes, and fourth best for job description purposes. The PAQ was seen as the most practical of the seven methods in terms of (a) standardization, (b) being ready to use "off-the-shelf," (c) reliability, and (d) the time needed to complete the job analysis.

It was also found that most analysts (86%) prefer using a combination of job analysis methods rather than just one (Levine et al., 1983). The most frequently chosen companions for the PAQ were the "task inventory" and "critical incidents." An example in the literature of how the PAQ can be used in conjunction with the critical incidents technique is reported by Ronan, Talbert, and Mullet (1977). Here, the PAQ data were used primarily to pick the appropriate selection tests, while the critical-incident technique served as the basis for developing job performance standards.

In general, most (if not all) contemporary job analysis techniques, including the PAQ, can be described along two continuums: (1) whether they are work (task) oriented or worker oriented, and (2) whether they are position specific or standardized (Wright & Wexley, 1985). In this typology, the PAQ is generally regarded as worker-oriented and standardized. Wright and Wexley contend that each job analysis method is differentially effective for various purposes, and propose that the two-dimensional typology can be useful in matching the method to the purpose. In terms of this typology, the PAQ is most useful for selection, job evaluation, and career planning. It is less appropriate for the development of a performance appraisal system because it is neither sufficiently job specific nor work oriented.

The importance of job analysis has been brought to the forefront during the last 15 years in litigation revolving around charges of employment discrimination. The Equal Employment Opportunities Commission requires that an organization show "job-relatedness" in any personnel practices (e.g., selection, promotion, and termination) that have an adverse impact on minorities (EEOC, 1978). As proof of job-relatedness, the courts have consistently required evidence that an appropriate job analysis was conducted and that the results formed the basis for the organization's decisions (Feild & Holley, 1982; Kleiman & Faley, 1985; Thompson & Thompson, 1982). However, the question of what constitutes an acceptable job analysis is less clear given the rulings rendered by some judges. Nonetheless, a review of existing court decisions leads Thompson and Thompson (1982) to propose the following legally defensible standards for a job analysis: 1) it must be conducted on the exact job for which the selection device is to be used, 2) the tasks, duties, and activities constituting the job must be identified, and 3) the information must be collected from several sources by an expert job analyst.

The PAQ appears to satisfy these criteria, and there is already a proven "track-record" for the instrument in litigation involving equal pay (Jeanneret, 1980; Mecham, 1983). In recent court cases, the PAQ has been used both as a benchmark against which the fairness of another job evaluation system was judged, and as a basis for developing a job classification system considered equitable by the court (Jeanneret, 1980).

One *potential* legal shortcoming of the PAQ is that it does not focus on the "work." Its non-job-specific language may raise some questions in some judges' minds (Cornelius et al., 1979). It is not clear, given previous court decisions, whether both work-oriented and worker-oriented data need to be collected in order to show that an acceptable job analysis has been performed. Although there are precedents to show that the PAQ is looked upon favorably by the courts in job evaluation matters, its legal acceptability for all purposes still remains to be established. Prien (1977) advocates the combined use of both a task-(work-) oriented and a worker-oriented approach to a job analysis, and for some purposes, such as performance appraisal, it is probably prudent to use the PAQ in conjunction with a more work-oriented technique (e.g., critical incidents, task inventory).

Although the PAQ was designed to be used in analyzing virtually all jobs, there is evidence to suggest that the instrument may be better suited for the analysis of blue-collar, production-type jobs rather than of managerial, professional, and some technical positions because it fails to describe the latter comprehensively (Cornelius, DeNisi, & Blencoe, 1984; DeNisi, 1985; Harvey & Hayes, 1986; Taylor, 1978). Recognizing this problem, Mitchell and McCormick (1980) have developed a new instrument, the Professional and Management Position Questionnaire (PMPQ). This close relative of the PAQ consists of 197 items distributed across three sections (Job Functions, Personal Requirements, and Other Information). The 10 principal factors underlying this scale are different from those represented in the PAQ, indicating that the PAQ is not as universal as once believed.

Moreover, because the PAQ was designed to tap generic differences between jobs, there exist data indicating that the instrument may not be appropriate for situations where one needs to pick up subtle differences between jobs. For example, Cornelius et al. (1979) attempted to determine how many unique jobs underlie the seven foreman positions in a petrochemical factory. While two other job analysis methods suggested at least three different positions, the PAQ indicated that there was only one type of job across the seven positions. Research by Frieling (1977) with the German version of the PAQ has also shown that the PAQ may be better for differentiating among manual occupations than among clerical ones.

Job clustering results may have legal ramifications when one generalizes a selection procedure from one job to another. Thus, differences between job analysis methods in their relative "sensitivity" to similarities and differences among various jobs is an important consideration. However, Kleiman and Faley's (1985) analysis of recent court decisions leads them to conclude that judges are unconcerned about groupings within job titles (e.g., "desk" vs. "field" sergeant), so the PAQ's insensitivity to minor differences within a job title may not cause legal problems.

The authors indicate that their instrument can be completed by trained job analysts, personnel staff, or even by job incumbents and their supervisors. They recommend that the person completing the PAQ have at least six months' experience on the job, so that the respondent will be aware of the various facets of the job. Moreover, it is suggested that at least three respondents be contacted to provide information about any given position. This is sound advice, considering that the amount of information offered by a respondent influences the PAQ description made by an analyst (Arvey, Davis, McGowen, & Dipboye, 1982). By having at least three experienced respondents, the job analyst is more likely to obtain sound, comprehensive information about the position.

Although some studies have suggested that the PAQ can be completed appropriately by raters who are inexperienced with the instrument and naïve about the job (e.g., Smith & Hakel, 1979; Jones, Main, Butler, & Johnson, 1982), closer examination of the data (Harvey & Hayes, 1986; DeNisi, 1985; Cornelius et al., 1984) indicates that experience and expertise do have a positive effect on the quality of the job analysis. Robinson, Wahlstrom, and Mecham (1974) reported that PAQ ratings produced by job incumbents were less accurate than those generated by personnel department analysts, especially when blue-collar positions were being analyzed. The error tends to be systematic. Incumbents and supervisors rate most PAQ items higher than job analysts (Smith & Hakel, 1979). The inflation is especially marked for socially desirable items and is greatest among supervisors.

Smith and Hakel (1979) also found that when job incumbents and their supervisors complete the PAQ, the reliability of the information increases with the level of the position; thus, the ratings from incumbents and supervisors at higher job levels are more accurate than ratings from incumbents and supervisors at the lower levels. The reading level of the PAQ may be a factor in the latter finding. A readability analysis of the PAQ conducted by Ash and Edgell (1975) showed that a college degree is necessary to understand the directions as well as the items on this instrument.

Data reported by Taylor (1978) suggest that even when measures are taken to assure that reading level is not a problem for incumbents and supervisors completing the PAQ on their own, many incumbents and supervisors may be uncomfortable with this method of data collection. Of the 203 raters in Taylor's study, 88% felt that the instructions on how to use the PAQ are easy to understand, 71% believed that the format was easy to follow, and 71% considered the items easy to understand; however, only 44% were confident that they described the job thoroughly, and only 62% felt certain that they were accurate in describing the job.

Other potential sources of bias on the PAQ have been explored. Although it was reported that the sex of the analyst mattered, with female analysts assigning relatively lower scores to a job on most PAQ job dimensions (Arvey, Passino, & Lounsbury, 1977), this finding was not replicated (Arvey, Davis, McGowen, & Dipboye, 1982). While analysts tend to view incumbents who express less interest in their job more negatively than incumbents who express greater interest in their job, the PAQ descriptions made by the analysts were not affected markedly by the incumbent's level of interest in the job (Arvey et al., 1982).

As one reads the PAQ instructions and reviews the research carefully, it becomes apparent that the individual completing the instrument actually needs training and proficiency in using the PAQ, a broad understanding of jobs in general, and basic familiarity with interviewing techniques and issues. Otherwise, it is possible that item responses for a given job will be substantially higher (or, in some cases, lower) on each job element than is appropriate for the job being analyzed.

PAQ administration time can vary substantially, depending on a number of factors such as the job analysts' training and experience, the respondents' familiarity with the position and disposition to answer the questions succinctly, and the circumstances under which the PAQ is being administered. Taylor (1978), for example, studied PAQ administration times within a large insurance company. Supervisors and job incumbents, serving both as job analysts and informants for the positions, took an average (mean) of 91 minutes, with a standard deviation of 41 minutes, to complete the PAQ. However, compared to other job analysis techniques, the PAQ is relatively quick (Levine et al., 1983). Mecham (1983) cites an unpublished in-house study conducted at a bank indicating that, when the PAQ was administered for job evaluation purposes at that facility, the required information was collected by the manager in about 2½ hours using a group interview method and in approximately 5 hours using individual interviews. This amount of time was substantially shorter than under a traditional point-factor system, which required about 10 hours for the data collection phase.

Technical Aspects

Psychometric information about the PAQ is available from a variety of sources, stemming from the number of years and the rather diverse settings in which it has been used. The *Technical Manual (System II)* summarizes the reliability and validity data available at the time of publication (1977). Additional discussions of the PAQ's psychometric properties have been released in the *PAQ Newsletter,* which is identified as "Reporting research and practice with the Position Analysis Questionnaire," in PAQ Services Research Bulletins, and through informal papers and workshops offered by PAQ Services, Inc., staff members. Numerous other research reports—written not only by the PAQ developers but also by other researchers and practitioners—can be found in the industrial psychology literature.

The PAQ technical manual reviews information about the instrument's test-retest and interrater reliability. Apparently, due to the heterogeneous nature of the PAQ, internal consistency reliability was not considered. The test-retest reliability analysis reported in the manual was conducted at an insurance company and involved 69 analysts (incumbents and supervisors) rating 27 jobs two times, 90 days apart. The average test-retest reliability for the 427 pairs of ratings was .78. These data, unpublished at the time of the release of the technical manual, are described more fully in Taylor (1978) and Taylor and Colbert (1978).

Interrater reliability data from this same insurance company, based on 1,190 pairs of raters, resulted in an average correlation of .68, a somewhat lower figure than the test-retest reliability. Another interrater reliability study reported in the manual, using incumbents, supervisors, and analysts as raters, resulted in an interrater reliability of .79. The same average interrater reliability coefficient (.79) was reported with the German edition of the PAQ (Frieling et al., 1974).

A number of studies dealing with the interrater reliability of the PAQ have been conducted since 1977 and therefore are not reviewed in the technical manual. Cornelius, Carron, and Collins (1979) looked at agreements between a job analyst and foremen in a petrochemical plant. The median correlation was .59. Smith and Hakel (1979) calculated the following average interrater correlations on the PAQ in a state government setting involving 25 jobs: .59 for 42 pairs of job incumbents, .63 for 45 pairs of supervisors, and .63 for 33 pairs of job analysts. Madigan (1985) found the average interrater agreement between four experienced personnel professionals rating 20 positions in an education and information services organization to be .70. Trained municipal government job analysts studied by Harvey and Hayes (1986) rated 88 jobs with a median interrater reliability of .95.

The variation in the reported reliability of the PAQ can be attributed to a number of factors (Cornelius et al., 1984; Smith & Hakel, 1979). These include differences in the jobs sampled, the respondents' familiarity with the job as well as the PAQ, actual differences in a job with the same title, the level of the PAQ (i.e., job elements, division dimensions, overall dimensions) used for the computation of reliability, and different methods of calculating the reliability indicators.

One potentially disturbing finding to emerge from comparisons of agreements between different classes of raters using the PAQ is the high level of agreement sometimes found between raters who are "experts" about the job and those who are "naïve" about it (e.g., Smith & Hakel, 1979). Two explanations have been offered to account for this phenomenon (Cornelius et al., 1984): 1) the naïve raters in these studies (typically college students) may not be as ignorant about some jobs as investigators assumed, and 2) if many of the 187 items "do not apply" (N), then artifactually high estimates of reliability can result.

The reason for the overestimated reliability arises from the fact that, even to the casual observer, many of the items on the PAQ are obviously not applicable to a given job (e.g., operates submarines and rocket ships; Cornelius et al., 1984; Harvey & Hayes, 1986). Thus, two raters will find it easy to agree that such items should be marked "N" for "Does Not Apply," yet they may disagree entirely about the ratings on the other (non-N) items. If the number of items that do not apply is large, then agreement on the "N" items along with a corresponding disagreement on the remaining items can still result in a large interrater reliability coefficient. Cornelius et al. (1984) showed that when only the items that were not scored "N" were analyzed, then the level of agreement between "expert" and "naïve" raters dropped from a coefficient of .58 to .41.

The number of "N" items is thus a function of the particular job being analyzed. For the nine jobs examined by Cornelius et al. (1984), the percentage of "N" items was lowest for maintenance foreman (16%) and highest for college professor (48%). Within the 90 municipal jobs studied by Harvey and Hayes (1986), the average percentage of items rated "N" was 53%, but it ranged from a low of 25% (paramedic/ firefighter) to a high of 76% (accountant). Using Monte Carlo techniques, Harvey and Hayes (1986) showed that for a job with 53% obviously not applicable items, an interrater correlation coefficient of .75 could be achieved if raters simply responded randomly to the remaining items. The larger the number of "N" items, the better the performance of naïve raters and the higher the expected interrater reliability. A large number of "N" becomes a problem only if the job is not described comprehensively by the PAQ (e.g., managerial, professional positions). According to DeNisi (1985), using the instrument with jobs where more than 60 to 90 of the items are nonapplicable tends to mask differences between naïve and expert raters in their accuracy at describing the job.

In essence, the validity of a job analysis method can be established by showing that the instrument measures the named characteristics and that these characteristics are necessary for successful job performance (Prien, 1977). McCormick and his colleagues have emphasized the second validation strategy in their work. Data reported in the technical manual show that the PAQ dimension scores can predict aptitudes characteristic of various jobs and salaries for different occupations.

The aptitude data employed as the criteria in these validation studies have come primarily from the General Aptitude Test Battery (GATB), which is not readily available commercially. More specifically, the data reported in the technical manual deal with the PAQ's ability to predict two things: 1) mean GATB scores of incumbents in various occupations, and 2) the GATB validity coefficients for various occupations. The results indicate that the PAQ dimension scores can predict GATB scores quite well (shrunken multiple correlations in the low .70s on average), but are not as successful in predicting the GATB validity coefficients (mean shrunken multiple correlation of only .13). The least predictable were the psychomotor tests on the GATB (i.e., Finger Dexterity, Manual Dexterity). The regression of PAQ scores on commercially produced aptitude tests that were matched to comparable subtests of the GATB resulted in slightly lower levels of predictability (average multiple correlations in the upper .60s), perhaps because the tests were not perfect matches for their respective GATB counterparts.

A number of studies using compensation rates as criteria are reviewed in the technical manual. The PAQ scores correlate with salary (or point value of positions) in the high .80s to low .90s range. The convergent validity of the PAQ as a job evaluation method is discussed in the technical manual, showing high levels of correlation with other methods of determining compensation rates.

As with the PAQ's reliability, additional evidence for the instrument's validity can be found in the literature on personnel practices and industrial/organizational psychology. Madigan (1985) looked at the convergence of three methods of job evaluation (PAQ, point-factor system, and guide chart). The PAQ correlated .85 with the guide chart and .95 with the point-factor system. Smith and Hakel (1979) tried to predict salaries for 25 jobs in a state government using PAQ ratings provided by incumbents, supervisors, and analysts. The resulting multiple correlations were .67 (analysts), .58 (incumbents), and .51 (supervisors). These correlations were low compared to the figures reported in the technical manual, but comparable when corrected for restriction in range.

The PAQ has been found to be a good predictor of job satisfaction, particularly the intrinsic variety (Pritchard & Peters, 1974), and of job stress (Shaw & Riskind, 1983). The information-processing dimensions of the PAQ were shown to moderate the validities of the general intelligence, verbal ability, and numerical ability subtests of the GATB (Guttenberg, Avery, Osburn, & Jeanneret, 1983).

McCormick, DeNisi, and Shaw (1979) cross-validated the regression equations developed on the basis of the GATB to commercial tests measuring the same constructs. The correlation between the predicted and the actual mean test scores had a median value of .71. In a comparative study, Mecham (1985) predicted the mean scores on the GATB for various jobs using situationally specific, job component (PAQ-based), and Hunter's generalization approaches to validation; the median correlations for the three methods were .73, .70, and .45, respectively.

The technical manual also provides some data showing that the PAQ measures the named characteristics. Several factor analyses of the PAQ are discussed, and outside literature shows that the PAQ can be used to form meaningful job families (e.g., Jones et al., 1982). Some authors consider the convergence of ratings between different classes of raters (e.g., incumbents vs. analysts) as evidence of the PAQ validity. These studies, dealt with previously in the discussion of the PAQ's reliability, are available in the technical manual as well as in more recent publications.

Critique

The PAQ is one of the best known standardized job analysis methods. This instrument was carefully designed and, generally, the reliability and validity studies conducted bear this out. The PAQ's chief virtue is that it provides a common metric to compare different jobs or to compare the same job in different contexts. Moreover, the PAQ job analysis results routinely are identified in terms of the *Dictionary of Occupational Titles*, a widely used directory of job titles and characteristics. For potential PAQ users, its most serious limitations is that—contrary to what was intended—the PAQ is *not* equally appropriate for all jobs. Moreover, the PAQ appears to be better suited for some purposes (i.e., determination of appropriate selection tests and validity generalization of these tests) than for others (e.g., identifying specific criteria for performance appraisal); the developers of the PAQ acknowledged such limitations when the instrument was published. One can appropriately view the PAQ as a supplement, rather than a replacement, for other job-specific analytic procedures.

The psychometric research on the PAQ is quite extensive, but one must be careful in drawing firm conclusions about practical implications. For example, some of these studies have not involved trained job analysts, raising questions about the generalizability of their findings. Also, research findings *could* be limited to the specific jobs studied. There are an insufficient number of studies comparing the PAQ to other methods of job analysis. Some "conclusions" are based on the self-reported experiences and "opinions" of job analysts as the primary criteria. Another limitation for potential users is that much of the research on the PAQ's usefulness in selection is keyed to the GATB, a test that is not widely available. From the standpoint of a potential user, it would be valuable to have the PAQ applications stated in terms of more widely available aptitude tests. Based on the PAQ newsletters, PAQ workshops, and professional conference presentations abou the PAQ, it seems likely that there may be some on-going progress on these matters.

Readers who plan to use the PAQ should exercise caution in selecting and preparing job analysts who will administer it. The latter will need training and proficiency using the PAQ (including awareness of the limitations of the instrument), a broad understanding of jobs in general, and basic familiarity with interviewing techniques and issues. Fortunately, both the PAQ support services and external literature provide helpful information on these matters. It is *strongly* recommended that potential users read and follow the guidelines provided about the use of the PAQ. Once the instrument has been administered properly, the job characteristics and aptitude attributes are described with regard to the "local" positions being analyzed and, if desired, can be compared with PAQ Service's rather extensive national data bank.

References

Note: References with an * are recommended especially for potential PAQ users.

Arvey, R. D., & Begalla, M. E. (1975). Analyzing the homemaker job using the Position Analysis Questionnaire (PAQ). *Journal of Applied Psychology, 60,* 513-517.

Arvey, R. D., Davis, G. A., McGowen, S. L., & Dipboye, R. L. (1982). Potential sources of bias in job analytic processes. *Academy of Management Journal, 25,* 618-629.

Arvey, R. D., Passino, E. M., & Lounsbury, J. W. (1977). Job analysis results as influenced by sex of incumbent and sex of analyst. *Journal of Applied Psychology, 62,* 411-416.

Ash, R. A., & Edgell, S. L. (1975). A note on the readability of the Position Analysis Questionnaire. *Journal of Applied Psychology, 60,* 765-766.

*Ash, R. A., & Levine, E. L. (1980). A framework for evaluating job analysis methods. *Personnel, 57*(6), 53-59.

Clark, B. V. (1985). Analyzing the job of volunteer using the Position Analysis Questionnaire. *Dissertation Abstracts International, 45,* 2346B-2347B.

Colbert, G. A., & Taylor, L. R. (1978). Empirically derived job families as a foundation for the study of validity generalization. *Personnel Psychology, 31,* 355-364.

Cornelius, E. T., Carron, T. J., & Collins, M. N. (1979). Job analysis models and job classification. *Personnel Psychology, 32,* 693-708.

*Cornelius, E. T., III, DeNisi, A. S., & Blencoe, A. G. (1984). Expert and naïve raters using the PAQ: Does it matter? *Personnel Psychology, 37,* 453-464.

Cornelius, E. T., III, Hakel, M. D., & Sackett, P. R. (1979). A methodological approach to job classification for performance appraisal purposes. *Personnel Psychology, 32,* 283-297.

DeNisi, A. S. (1985, August). Comparative research in job analysis: Incumbents versus naïve raters. In E. T. Cornelius (Chair), *Comparative job analysis research*. Symposium conducted at the 93rd Annual Convention of the American Psychological Association, Los Angeles.

Equal Employment Opportunity Commission. (1978). Uniform guidelines on employee selection. *Federal Register, 35*(249), 12333-12336.

Feild, H. S., & Holley, W. H. (1982). The relationship of performance appraisal system characteristics to verdicts in selected employment discrimination cases. *Academy of Management Journal, 25,* 392-406.

Frieling, E. (1977). Occupational analysis: Some details of an illustrative German project. *International Review of Applied Psychology, 26,* 77-85.

Frieling, E., Kannheiser, W., & Lindberg, R. (1974). Some results with the German form of the Position Analysis Questionnaire (PAQ). *Journal of Applied Psychology, 59,* 741-747.

Guttenberg, R. L., Arvey, R. D., Osburn, H. G., & Jeanneret, P. R. (1983). Moderating effects of decision-making information-processing job dimensions on text validities. *Journal of Applied Psychology, 68,* 602-608.

Harvey, R. J., & Hayes, T. L. (1986). Monte Carlo baselines for interrater reliability correlations using the Position Analysis Questionnaire. *Personnel Psychology, 39,* 345-357.

Jeanneret, P. R. (1970). A study of the job dimension of "worker-oriented" variables and of their attribute profiles. *Dissertation Abstracts International, 30,* 5273B-5274B.

Jeanneret, P. R. (1980). Equitable job evaluation with the Position Analysis Questionnaire. *Compensation Review, 12*(1), 32-42.

Jones, A. P., Main, D. S., Butler, M. C., & Johnson, L. A. (1982). Narrative job descriptions as potential sources of job analysis ratings. *Personnel Psychology, 35,* 813-828.

*Kleiman, L. S., Faley, R. H. (1985). The implications of professional and legal guidelines for court decisions involving criterion-related validity: A review and analysis. *Personnel Psychology, 38,* 803-833.

Levine, E. L., Ash, R. A., & Bennett, N. (1980). Exploratory comparative study of four job analysis methods. *Journal of Applied Psychology, 65,* 524-535.

*Levine, E. L., Ash, R. A., Hall, H., & Sistrunk, F. (1983). Evaluation of job analysis methods by experienced job analysts. *Academy of Management Journal, 26,* 339-348.

Levine, E. L., Bennett, N., & Ash, R. A. (1979), Evaluation and use of four job analysis methods for personnel selection. *Public Personnel Management, 8,* 146-151.

Madigan, R. M. (1985), Comparable worth judgments: A measurement properties analysis. *Journal of Applied Psychology, 70,* 137-147.

McCormick, E. J. (1976). Job and task analysis. In M. D. Dunnette (Ed.) *Handbook of industrial and organizational psychology* (pp. 651-696). Chicago: Rand McNally.

*McCormick, E. J. (1979). *Job analysis: Methods and applications*. New York: Amacom.

McCormick, E. J., Jeanneret, P. R., & Mecham, R. C. (1969, January). *The development and background of the Position Analysis Questionnaire*. West Lafayette, IN: Occupational Research Center, Purdue University.

*McCormick, E. J., DeNisi, A. S., & Shaw, J. B. (1979). Use of the Position Analysis Questionnaire for establishing the job component validity of tests. *Journal of Applied Psychology, 64,* 51-56.

*McCormick, E. J., Jeanneret, P. R., & Mecham, R. C. (1972). A study of job characteristics and job dimensions as based on the Position Analysis Questionnaire (PAQ). *Journal of Applied Psychology, 56,* 317-368.

McCormick, E. J., Mecham, R. C., & Jeanneret, P. R. (1977). *Technical manual for the Position Analysis Questionnaire (PAQ; System II)*. West Lafayette, IN: Purdue University Book Store.

Mecham, R. C. (1970). The synthetic prediction of personnel test requirements and job evaluation points using the Position Analysis Questionnaire. *Dissertation Abstracts International, 31,* 2341B.

Mecham, R. C. (1983). Quantitative job evaluation using the Position Analysis Questionnaire. *Personnel Administrator, 28*(6), 82-88, 124.

Mecham, R. C. (1985, August). *Comparative effectiveness of situational, generalized and job component validation methods*. Paper presented at the 93rd annual convention of The American Psychological Association, Los Angeles, CA.

Mecham, R. C., McCormick, E. J., & Jeanneret, P.R. (1977). *User's manual for the Position Analysis Questionnaire (PAQ; System II)*. West Lafayette, IN: Purdue University Book Store.

Mitchell, J. L., & McCormick, E. J. (1980). *User's manual for the Professional and Managerial Position Questionnaire, System IV*. West Lafayette, IN: Purdue Research Foundation.

PAQ Services, Inc. (1977). *Position Analysis Questionnaire: Job analysis manual*. Logan, UT: Author.

Prien, E. P. (1977). The function of job analysis in content validation. *Personnel Psychology, 30*, 167-174.

Pritchard, R. D., & Peters, L. H. (1974). Job duties and job interests as predictors of intrinsic and extrinsic satisfaction. *Organizational Behavior & Human Performance, 12*, 315-330.

Robinson, D. D., Wahlstrom, O. W., & Mecham, R. C. (1974). Comparison of job evaluation methods: A "policy capturing" approach using the Position Analysis Questionnaire (PAQ). *Journal of Applied Psychology, 59*, 633-637.

Ronan, W. W., Talbert, T. L., & Mullet, G. M. (1977). Prediction of job performance dimensions: Police officers. *Public Personnel Management, 6*, 173-180.

Shaw, J. B., & Riskind, J. H. (1983). Predicting job stress using data from the Position Analysis Questionnaire. *Journal of Applied Psychology, 68*, 253-261.

Smith, J. E., & Hakel, M. D. (1979). Convergence among data sources, response bias, and reliability and validity of a structured job analysis questionnaire. *Personnel Psychology, 32*, 677-692.

Sparrow, J., Patrick, J., Spurgeon, P. C., & Barwell, F. (1982). The use of job component analysis and related aptitudes in personnel selection. *Journal of Occupational Psychology, 55*, 157-164.

*Taylor, L. R. (1978). Empirically derived job families as a foundation for the study of validity generalization: Study 1. The construction of job families based on the component and overall dimension of the PAQ. *Personnel Psychology, 31*, 325-339.

*Taylor, L. R., & Colbert, G. A. (1978). Empirically derived job families as a foundation for the study of validity generalization: Study II. The construction of job families based on company-specific PAQ job dimensions. *Personnel Psychology, 31*, 341-353.

*Thompson, D. E., & Thompson, T. A. (1982). Court standards for job analysis in test validation. *Personnel Psychology, 35*, 865-873.

Townsend, J. W., Prien, E. P., & Johnson, J. T. (1974). The use of the Position Analysis Questionnaire in selecting correlates of job performance among mentally retarded workers. *Journal of Vocational Behavior, 4*, 181-192.

U.S. Department of Labor. (1977). *Dictionary of occupational titles* (4th ed.). Washington, DC: U.S. Government Printing Office.

*Wright, P. M., & Wexley, K. N. (1985). How to choose the kind of job analysis you really need. *Personnel, 62*(5), 51-55.

Alice G. Friedman, Ph.D.
Postdoctoral Fellow, Pediatric Psychology, Department of Psychiatry and Behavioral Sciences, University of Oklahoma Health Sciences Center, Oklahoma City, Oklahoma.

C. Eugene Walker, Ph.D.
Professor, Director of Pediatric Psychology, Department of Psychiatry and Behavioral Sciences, University of Oklahoma Health Sciences Center, Oklahoma City, Oklahoma.

PRESCHOOL BEHAVIOR QUESTIONNAIRE
Lenore Behar and Samuel Stringfield. Durham, North Carolina: Lenore Behar.

Introduction

The Preschool Behavior Questionnaire (PBQ) was developed as a brief screening instrument to identify preschool-aged children who exhibit symptoms of behavioral/emotional problems. It was designed for use by teachers, mental health professionals, and child care workers. The questionnaire consists of 30 behavioral items that are rated on a 3-point scale according to whether the behavior "doesn't apply," "applies sometimes," or "certainly applies." Results yield a score for total behavioral disturbance and scores on three subscales: Hostile-Aggressive, Anxious-Fearful, and Hyperactive-Distractible. The Hostile-Aggressive (H-A) subscale assesses behaviors such as fighting, bullying others, kicking, and destroying property. The Anxious-Fearful (A-F) subscale assesses behaviors such as being fearful or unhappy and crying easily. The Hyperactive-Distractible (H-D) subscale includes items such as being inattentive and restless. According to the manual, scores in the upper 10% on the total scale or on any of the three subscales are suggestive of possible disturbance and warrant further examination.

The test materials consist of the questionnaire, test manual, and a score sheet for the rater. The questionnaire includes space for information about the child's age and sex as well as a space to record the length of time the rater has worked with the child. Directions for rating a child are clearly written and the questionnaire is easy to score. Raters must rely on their internal norms to make decisions about whether a particular behavior doesn't apply, applies sometimes, or most certainly applies to a given child. All items are assigned a score of 0, 1, or 2. The sum of the values assigned to each of the items constitutes the total score. Likewise, the sum of the values assigned to each item for each subscale represents the score for the subscales. The percentile ranks corresponding to scores on the total scale and each of the three subscales are on the score sheet.

This questionnaire was developed by Lenore Behar and Samuel Stringfield while they were working on a preschool project. Lenore Behar is currently chief of children's services in the Division of Mental Health Services at the North Carolina Department of Human Resources. She received a Ph.D. in clinical psychology from Duke University and was an assistant professor at the University of North Carolina in Chapel Hill at the time of test development. Samuel Stringfield worked as Dr. Behar's research assistant and has since received a Ph.D. from Temple University. According to the authors, the impetus for the development of the questionnaire was the need for a brief screening instrument for preschool children that would be capable of differentiating normal from disturbed behavior.

The current PBQ is a modified version of the Children's Behavior Questionnaire (Rutter, 1967). The earlier 26-item questionnaire was developed in England for use with elementary school-aged children. Ten additional items that represent problem behaviors frequently exhibited by preschool-aged but not older children were added to the item pool. These latter items were based on perusal of the available preschool questionnaires and on consultation with experienced preschool teachers (Behar, 1977). Following initial studies of the validity of the measure, the questionnaire was shortened to 30 items.

The original 36-item PBQ was standardized on a sample of 598 children ages 3-6. Of these, 496 were "normal" children selected from five preschools in Durham, North Carolina and two schools in Portland, Oregon. These children were selected because they attended a preschool not intended to serve a special segment of the population, such as the retarded, disturbed, or autistic. A second sample of 102 preschoolers was selected from 15 treatment programs throughout the country specifically intended for the care of emotionally disturbed children. No specific information is given about the socioeconomic status of either sample, except a comment by the authors that the sample "represented socioeconomic groups ranging from lower to upper-middle-class" families (Behar & Stringfield, 1974b). The sex and racial characteristics of the sample are described as "roughly comparable to the general population." Further specific information about subject selection for the deviant sample is absent except for a comment that retarded or autistic children were excluded. Included in the standardization sample statistics were data from 122 subjects (over 20% of total) for whom sex, age, and/or race were missing.

Practical Applications/Uses

The PBQ should be useful to teachers working in a preschool setting who need objective criteria to aid in the identification of children requiring further evaluation. The questionnaire was intended to be used by professionals to rate children ages 3-6 within the context of a peer group/class. Since development of the scale, the PBQ has been used for a number of purposes for which it was not originally intended, including use by parents, use with children younger and older than the standardization sample, and for assessing individual "target" children in a class (Behar, 1977). Because these uses represent a deviation from the standardization sample, Behar suggests that additional data are needed to evaluate the appropriateness of these applications.

Elevations on the overall score or on one of the three subscales of the PBQ indicate that a child exhibits behavior that may suggest behavioral problems. Such elevations should not be interpreted as a trait description of the child. The potential misuse of the questionnaire to label children is discussed in the manual and discouraged by the authors. The authors warn that interpretation should be extremely conservative. Results should be used only in collaboration with other data about the child and are only suggestive of the need for further evaluation.

The PBQ should be used only by examiners who are very familiar with the children they are rating. Behar and Stringfield (1974) reported that teachers and aides who had worked with the same children for nearly 20 weeks obtained moderate to high interrater reliabilities (mean coefficients were .84 for the overall scale; .81 for the H-A subtest; .71 for the A-F subtest; and .67 for the H-D subtest. However, interrater reliability between an aide and teacher who had worked with the children for only five weeks was considerably lower (coefficients .42 for the overall scale and .29 for the H-A, .55 for the A-F, and .30 for the H-D subscales.

A number of studies have used parents as respondents (Behar, 1977), but the results have been conflicting. Gray, Clancy, and King (1981) compared PBQ responses of mothers and preschool teachers for particular children and found the mother's response patterns differed substantially from those of the teachers. Gray, Clancy, and King concluded that the subscale scoring system developed from the original standardization sample is inappropriate for scoring parent responses. Conversely, Harwell (1972) reported significant similarities between teacher and parent ratings. However, this study used children "at the extremes of adjustment." Similarly, Campbell and Cluss (1982) reported moderate correlations between parent and teacher ratings in children who had been referred for behavior problems. It may be that correspondence between parent and teacher ratings on the PBQ is adequate only when the child exhibits behavioral extremes. Further work on standardization of the PBQ using parents as respondents is warranted before this questionnaire can be recommended for use in this manner.

Scoring of the PBQ is straightforward. Children who obtain elevations of 17 or above on the total scale, or 7, 4, and 4 on the three subscales (H-A, A-F, and H-D respectively) are considered to exhibit behavior that is out of the ordinary. No information is provided as to how these levels were determined except that they represent scores above the 90th percentile. An illustration of interpretation of the scale is provided in the manual.

Technical Aspects

The manual for the PBQ contains information about development, standardization, and initial validity studies of the instrument. A more detailed description of the validation process is presented in two journal articles (Behar, 1977; Behar & Stringfield, 1974).

The deviant group of children obtained significantly ($p \leq .0001$) higher scores on the PBQ than did the normal group in the initial standardization sample. The deviant group obtained a mean of 23.35 (s.d. = 7.3), while the group mean for the normal children was 9.12 (s.d. = 7.67). Chi square analysis applied to each test item indicated that 32 of the original 36 items differentiated between the normal and deviant population beyond the .01 level of significance. A multiple regression of .740 was obtained on the original scale, indicating that 53.9% of the total variance in the scale was accounted for by group differences. A principal-component root number/root plot factor analysis produced a three-factor solution. The orthogonal factors were varimax rotated. The three rotated factors accounted for 37.7% of the total variance of the PBQ. The first factor contained items related to behaviors such as fighting and bullying and was termed "Hostile-Aggressive." The second factor included items such as fearfulness and crying and was labeled "Anxious-Fearful." The third significant factor contained items related to poor attention span and was termed "Hyperactive-Distractible." Thus, these three factors constitute the three subscales of the test. The three factors are all moderately correlated, the highest correlation being H-A and H-D ($r = .50$, $p \leq .01$).

Four items that did not differentiate significantly between the two populations and two items that did not rank in the highest 25 on the stepwise multiple regression or have a factor loading higher than .55 on one of the three factors were eliminated from the item pool. The remaining 30 items constitute the current PBQ (Behar, 1977).

Significant differences were obtained for both race and sex upon examination of the responses on the original standardization sample using the remaining 30 items. Males scored significantly higher than females ($p \leq .001$) and blacks scored significantly higher than whites ($p \leq .01$). Significant differences for age were not obtained.

To assess the interrater and test-retest reliability of the measure, Behar (1977) conducted a second study using 80 children selected from a population of normal preschool children and nine children from a therapeutic preschool class. Each child was rated by both a teacher and a teacher's aide. Teacher/aide interrater reliabilities were .84 for the overall scale and .81 for the H-A subscale, .71 for the A-F subscale, and .67 for the H-D subscale. Test-retest reliability (measured by having the teachers and aides rate the same children after a 3- to 4-month period) was moderate to high (mean coefficient of .87 overall, and .93 for the H-A subscale, .60 for the A-F subscale, and .94 for the H-D subscale.

Campbell and Cluss (1982) provided support for the construct validity of the PBQ. Tests completed by teachers differentiated between a group of children referred for behavioral problems and a control group of children. Teachers rated the problem children as more hyperactive and aggressive than the controls. Observations of the children showed that problem children were less attentive during free play and more active, impulsive, and inattentive during structured tasks than were the controls. Follow-up (Campbell, Breaux, Ewing, & Szumowski, 1984) of these children one year later showed little change in the ratings on the PBQ. Children from the problem behavior group continued to have significantly higher scores on the total scale as well as on the Hostile-Aggressive and Hyperactive-Distractible subscales.

A number of studies have compared the PBQ with other measures and with behavioral observations. Hoge, Meginbir, Khan, and Weatherall (1985) reported a significant relationship between overall teacher PBQ score and overall PBQ scores completed by independent observers ($p \leq .05$), and between behavioral observation data and the overall teacher scores ($p \leq .05$). They also reported significant relationships between teacher ratings and corresponding observational data for the factors Hostile-Aggressive and Anxious-Fearful. Data did not support the convergent validity of the H-D factor. In one of the largest studies using the PBQ,

Fowler and Park (1979) failed to find a third factor (H-D found in other studies) in a factor analytic study of PBQ ratings by teachers on 701 normal children. Items representing the H-D factor in Behar and Stringfield (1974) loaded on the first factor in this study, using both the principal component and maximum likelihood methods of analysis.

In a study of the construct validity of the PBQ, Rubin and Clark (1983) examined the relationship among ratings on the three factors of the PBQ and observations of behavior, sociometric status, and social problem-solving among preschool-aged children. Each child was rated by a classroom supervisor on the PBQ, observed during free play, and administered a problem-solving task and a sociometric battery. Results showed that children who obtained elevated ratings on the three subscales of the PBQ exhibited less mature and more aggressive behaviors in the classroom, were less popular than their peers, and were more likely than peers to suggest negative strategies on the social problem-solving task. Overall, this study provides additional support that children rated highly on any of the factors evidence behavioral, sociometric, and sociocognitive characteristics that reflect the ratings.

In a study examining the concurrent validity of the PBQ, Stringfield and Woodside (1976) reported significant positive correlations among the PBQ, the California Preschool Competency Scale, and the Problem Checklist completed on 30 children.

Few studies have examined racial differences on the PBQ. Bruneau (1984) compared PBQ results of American Indians to those of whites and reported no significant differences. However, an insufficient amount of information was presented from which to draw conclusions about these results. In light of the racial differences reported by Behar (1977), further work in this area is warranted before the measure can be recommended for use with nonwhites.

Critique

Initial work on the PBQ suggests that it may be a valuable instrument for screening children who exhibit behavioral difficulties. It is brief, easy to administer and score, and provides a method against which to validate teachers' perceptions of the child (Fox, 1985). However, further work is needed in a number of areas before this instrument can be recommended without qualification. First, the standardization sample was small and an insufficient amount of information about the children's background was provided to judge whether the norms are appropriate for other samples. Behar (1977) indicates that additional work is underway on the standardization of the PBQ; however, these data are not currently available.

Another related problem is the criterion for classification of a child as in need of further evaluation. Gray, Clancy, and King (1981) report that the mean subscore and total scores in their sample of 128 normal preschool-aged children were significantly higher than those reported by Behar and Stringfield (1974). Use of the criteria presented in the manual for classifying a child as in need of further evaluation would have resulted in 30% of Gray et al.'s sample being so classified. Barnard and Eyers (1977) obtained similarly elevated scores on a sample of 179 children. There are no existing norms for the use of the PBQ with parents as respondents. There are some preliminary data to suggest that parents and teachers are not interchangeable (Gray, Clancy, & King, 1981). Further work on the standardization of the instrument using parents of disturbed and normal preschoolers is needed before the PBQ can be used appropriately this way.

Third, while significant race and sex differences were obtained in the initial analysis, separate norms are not presented. Rather, only one set of norms is presented and a 90th percentile cutoff is recommended for discriminating disturbed from normal children. Use of these norms on males and nonwhites may result in overrepresentation of these groups (and underrepresentation of others) as being in need of further testing.

Fourth, a portion of the initial standardization sample was comprised of children who had previously been diagnosed as disturbed. The teachers were not blind to the diagnoses. Consequently, ratings for the disturbed children on the PBQ may have reflected expectations rather than the actual behavior of the children. However, there are a few studies that have found correlations between elevations on the PBQ and behavioral observations that mirror the elevated factors. Further work on the construct and predictive validity of this scale is warranted.

Given these qualifications, most available research has shown the PBQ to have adequate psychometric properties. It appears to be a reliable, valid instrument that should be useful for screening preschool-aged children who exhibit problem behaviors. Further work on the standardization of the instrument would add significantly to the utility of the instrument.

References

This list includes text citations as well as suggested additional reading.

Anderson, D. R. (1981). Documentation of change in problem behaviors among anxious and hostile-aggressive children enrolled in a therapeutic preschool program. *Child Psychiatry and Human Development, 11*(4), 232-240.

Barnard, K., & Eyres, S. (1977). *Child health assessment: Part 2. Results of the first twelve months of life* (HEW Technical Report No. 77-114). Washington, DC: U.S. Government Printing Office.

Bates, J. E., & Bayles, K. (1984). Objective and subjective components in mothers' perceptions of their children from age 6 months to 3 years. *Merrill-Palmer Quarterly, 30*(2), 111-130.

Behar, L. B. (1977). The Preschool Behavior Questionnaire. *Journal of Abnormal Child Psychology, 5*(3), 265-275.

Behar, L., & Stringfield, S. (1974a). A behavior rating scale for the preschool child. *Developmental Psychology, 10*(5), 601-610.

Behar, L., & Stringfield, S. (1974b). *Manual for the Preschool Behavior Checklist*. Durham, NC: Lenore Behar.

Bruneau, O. J. (1984). Comparison of behavioral characteristics and self-concepts of American Indian and Caucasian preschoolers. *Psychological Reports, 54*, 571-574.

Burg, C., Hart, D., Quinn, P., & Rapoport, J. (1978). Newborn minor physical anomalies and prediction of infant behavior. *Journal of Autism and Childhood Schizophrenia, 8*(4), 427-439.

Campbell, S. B., & Breaux, A. M. (1983). Maternal ratings of activity and symptomatic behaviors in a nonclinical sample of young children. *Journal of Pediatric Psychology, 8*(1), 73-82.

Campbell, S. B., Breaux, A. M., Ewing, L. J., & Szumowski, E. K. (1984). A one-year follow-up study of parent-referred hyperactive preschool children. *Journal of the American Academy of Child Psychiatry, 23*(3), 243-249.

Campbell, S. B., & Cluss, P. (1982). Peer relationships of young children with behavior problems. In K. H. Rubin & H. S. Ross (Eds.), *Peer relationships and social skills in childhood* (pp. 323-352). New York: Springer-Verlag.

Fowler, P. C., & Park, R. M. (1979). Factor structure of the Preschool Behavior Questionnaire in a normal population. *Psychological Reports, 45,* 599-606.

Fox. R. A. (1985). The Preschool Behavior Questionnaire. In J. V. Mitchell, Jr. (Ed.), *The ninth mental measurements yearbook* (pp. 1189-1190). Lincoln, NE: Buros Institute of Mental Measurements.

Gray, C. A., Clancy, S., & King, L. (1981). Teacher versus parent reports of preschoolers' social competence. *Journal of Personality Assessment, 45*(5), 488-493.

Harwell, M. M. (1972). *How children are viewed.* Unpublished master's thesis, University of North Carolina, Chapel Hill.

Hoge, R. D., Meginbir, L., Khan, Y., & Weatherall, D. (1985). A multitrait-multimethod analysis of the preschool behavior questionnaire. *Journal of Abnormal Child Psychology, 13*(1), 119-127.

Klein, H. A. (1982). The relationship between children's temperament and adjustment to kindergarten and Head Start settings. *The Journal of Psychology, 112,* 259-268.

Lahey, B. B., Hammer, D., Crumrine, P. L., & Forehand, R. L. (1980). Birth order x sex interactions in child behavior problems. *Developmental Psychology, 16*(6), 608-615.

Rubin, K. H. (1982). Nonsocial play in preschoolers: Necessarily evil? *Child Development, 53,* 651-657.

Rubin, K. H., & Clark, M. L. (1983). Preschool teachers' ratings of behavioral problems: Observational, sociometric, and social-cognitive correlates. *Journal of Abnormal Child Psychology, 11*(2), 273-286.

Rutter, M. A. (1967). A children's behavior questionnaire for completion by teachers: Preliminary findings. *Journal of Child Psychology and Psychiatry, 8,* 1-11.

Stringfield, S., & Woodside, R. V. (1976, April). *Socioemotional screening instruments for the preschool child.* Paper presented at the Council for Exceptional Children, Chicago, IL.

Gene Schwarting, Ph.D.
Project Director, Preschool Handicapped Program, Omaha Public Schools, Omaha, Nebraska.

PRESCHOOL DEVELOPMENT INVENTORY

Harold Ireton. Minneapolis, Minnesota: Behavior Science Systems, Inc.

Introduction

The Preschool Development Inventory (PDI) is a screening instrument developed in 1984 for children aged 3 through 5½ years. It is presented in questionnaire form and is designed to be completed by the child's parent in order to indicate the child's current skills. The purpose of the inventory is to identify those children with developmental delays as well as problems that might have an impact on their ability to learn. The instrument consists of 60 items to measure general developmental levels as well as 24 items measuring problem behaviors, all in a "yes/no" format. There are also three open-ended questions regarding the child.

The author of the PDI, Dr. Harold Ireton, has been actively involved in research and assessment with young children for many years. The instrument was derived from research and experience with two other scales developed by Dr. Ireton: the Minnesota Child Development Inventory (1974) and the Minnesota Preschool Inventory (1979). The former is a 320-item questionnaire in a "yes/no" format, completed by the parent and intended to measure adaptive behavior of children ages 1 to 6 in eight areas. The latter is a 150-item questionnaire in a "yes/no" format that measures kindergarten readiness in 11 areas for children aged 4½ to 5½ years of age.

The manual for the PDI provides little information regarding the development and norming of the instrument. It is noted, however, that the developmental status items were derived from the general development scale of the Minnesota Child Development Inventory and were among the most age-discriminating on the MCDI.

Practical Applications/Uses

The PDI consists of a single scoresheet containing descriptive statements in incomplete sentence form. Responses are recorded by the parent by filling in circles marked "yes" or "no." Directions are short, asking the parent to describe the child's present, observed behavior. A heading provides space for name, sex, birthdate, date, age, parent's name and relationship to the child, and parent occupation and education. A portion of the reverse side of the form provides space for parental description of the child as well as concerns for development and a scoring form. The 5-page manual consists of background information, a description of the scale, scoring information, and a table of cutoff scores.

Item representation of various areas on the general development scale are as follows: language comprehension (19), expressive language (14), fine motor (9), self-help (9), personal-social (5), situation comprehension (2), and gross-motor (2). All "yes" responses are summed and contribute to an overall score, which is then compared to cutoff scores for children aged 3 to 5½ years.

The PDI is designed to perform as a screening instrument for young children in order to identify those with developmental delays or problems that could interfere with learning. As such, the inventory would be useful to educators, pediatricians, preschool teachers, Head Start counselors, physical and occupational therapists, speech therapists, and psychologists. Situationally, the PDI might be appropriate to utilize with children entering preschool or kindergarten, or simply to determine if the child's skills are within maturational expectations. The second section of the instrument, which lists unusual or problem behaviors, is designed to elicit information useful to discussion with the parent; however, both sections could be used this way, as could the three open-ended questions at the end of the questionnaire. Appropriate for all children aged 3-5½, it could be used with children having physical, language, cognitive, or sensory handicaps. However, the handicapping condition would significantly affect their scores, and there are no adaptations or adjusted norms available.

Administration consists of simply presenting the parent with the directions and answer sheet; thus, special training is not required of the examiner. There are no time limits, but it is estimated that completion would require less than 20 minutes. Scoring could be accomplished in 5 minutes, with minimal training required. Scoring of the general development scale consists of summing the "yes" responses and comparing this score to age-norm tables (boys, girls, or combined, at 3-month age intervals). A child is considered to be functioning below age-level expectations if the score is less than the average for children who are 25% younger. A code number of 1, 2, or 3 is assigned, with 1 indicating a score at or above the chronological age norm and 3 indicating a "possible problem."

The second section of questions represents problem behaviors, with 10 low-incidence behaviors to be scored. A code number of 1 is assigned for no positive responses, 2 for one or more positive responses, and 3 for one or more listed uncommon positive responses or for three or more overall "yes" responses.

A similar 1 to 3 code is scored to identify significantly negative or problem responses on the three open-ended questions. Again, score interpretation does not require extensive training.

Technical Aspects

Technical information regarding the PDI is not provided in the manual. The only data regarding the norm group is that it consisted of the mothers of 800 white children aged 6 months to 6½ years in Bloomington, Minnesota. Information on validity, reliability, date and procedures for norming, and development of cutoff scores are not presented. Dr. Ireton (personal communication, May 1, 1986) indicates that a study exploring the relationship between the PDI and the Developmental Indicators for the Assessment of Learning is nearing completion, however.

Critique

The author's caveat to utilize the PDI as a screening device is well taken, given the dearth of statistical information. The 25% delay indicated for delayed development is neither explained nor justified, and the usefulness of the cutoff scores without supportive data should be seriously questioned. The instrument might well be useful to obtain general information regarding a child's development, as a preliminary to formal evaluation or as a means to initiate discussion with a parent. More specific use of the PDI, such as to verify eligibility for placement or services, should be discouraged, while the establishment of local norms should be encouraged.

References

Eisert, E. C., Spector, S., & Shankaran, S. (1980). Mothers' report on their low-birth-weight infants' subsequent development in the Minnesota Child Development Inventory. *Journal of Pediatric Psychology, 5,* 353-364.

Gottfried, A. W., Guerin, D., Spencer, J. E., & Meyer, C. (1983). Concurrent validity of the Minnesota Child Development Inventory in a nonclinical sample. *Journal of Consulting and Clinical Psychology, 51,* 643-644.

Ireton, H. R. (1984). *Manual for the Preschool Development Inventory.* Minneapolis: Behavior Science Systems.

Ireton, H., Lun, K. S., & Kampen, M. (1981). Minnesota Preschool Inventory identification of children at risk for kindergarten failure. *Psychology in the Schools, 18,* 439-501.

Ireton, H. R., & Thwing, E. J. (1972). *Minnesota Child Development Inventory.* Minneapolis: Behavior Science Systems.

Ireton, H. R., & Thwing, E. J. (1979). *The Minnesota Preschool Inventory.* Minneapolis: Behavior Science Systems.

Ireton, H. R., & Thwing, E. J. (1980). *The Minnesota Infant Development Inventory.* Minneapolis: Behavior Science Systems.

Mardell, C., & Goldenberg, D. (1975). *Manual for Developmental Indicators for the Assessment of Learning.* Edison, NJ: Childcraft Education Corporation.

Metzer, L. J. (1983). Developmental attainment in preschool children: Analysis of concordance between parents and professionals. *Journal of Special Education, 17,* 203-213.

Richard Colwell, Ph.D.
Professor of Music and Education, University of Illinois at Urbana-Champaign, Urbana, Illinois.

PRIMARY MEASURES OF MUSIC AUDIATION
Edwin E. Gordon. Chicago, Illinois: G.I.A. Publications.

Introduction

Edwin Gordon's Primary Measures of Music Audiation comprise a music aptitude test for kindergarten and primary-grade children. The test consists of 80 pairs of musical stimuli, 40 tonal and 40 rhythm patterns, which are played from two cassette tapes. Electronic sounds generated by a synthesizer, which are somewhat similar to the sounds generated for the older Seashore Measures of Musical Talents, are used as stimuli. The task for the student is to determine whether the paired patterns are the same or different. Tonal patterns consist of musical phrases two to five tones in length with 13 two-tone patterns, 25 three-tone patterns, and 1 four- and 1 five-tone pattern. Patterns are voiced in the middle register and are based on tones from tonic, dominant, and subdominant chords. The tonal patterns are in major or minor tonality (no other modes are used). The two phrases are in the same key and tempo, and the metrical and rhythmic elements are identical. Wehner (1985) indicates that there is a discrepancy on three items with the keyed answer. The reviewer erred; the test is correctly keyed.

Rhythm patterns range from two to seven tones all sounded by the same pitch. Most patterns are four to six notes in length, which may make comparison of rhythm patterns more difficult than the tonal patterns. The rhythm patterns are almost devoid of silence—only one item contains a rest, and it is a thirty-second rest; thus students will likely not perceive this rest as having a specific duration in the rhythmic patterns test.

The patterns used in the test are drawn from those Gordon found to be the easiest in an earlier study in which his concern was the development of a taxonomy of tonal and rhythmic patterns. Whether the selection of easy or difficult patterns makes any difference in measuring aptitude is unknown; the length of the pattern is presumably important.

Edwin Gordon has devoted his professional career to investigating the role of music aptitude as it affects music instruction. Beginning with his doctoral dissertation in 1958, Gordon has focused his research efforts on identifying those elements and processes that impact upon a student's progress in learning to "hear" music. Gordon carefully developed a music aptitude test and a series of music achievement tests, investigated the limits of aptitude measurement (the Primary Measures of Music Audiation is a result of one of these extensions), and most recently has developed instructional sequences in instrumental and vocal music that are based upon his nearly two decades of research. In some respects, his work is rather specialized, and a student taught by the "Gordon system" is more likely to demonstrate achievement on one of his tests. To fully understand the results of Gordon's research, its strengths and weaknesses, one must know and understand Gordon as the consummate teacher. The flaws in his work are most often a result of his attempting to "teach" the reader or user of his research rather than carefully and objectively presenting and interpreting the data, a point that is developed later in this review. Even in the manual for his stabilized music achievement test, the Musical Aptitude Profile, Professer Gordon devotes many pages to suggestions about what should be done by the teacher for the student who scores below average on the test. If there is one student in a school whose score is less than it might be because his aptitude has not completely stabilized, Gordon wants the teacher to initiate an instructional campaign to change that student's score before it is too late.

Gordon's Musical Aptitude Profile was available for less than a year when teachers and researchers expressed a desire for a shortened version. One of Gordon's own doctoral students (Harrington) investigated the effect of giving less than the complete MAP. Teachers want to measure musical aptitude, but not badly enough to devote three 50-minute periods to giving the Musical Aptitude Profile. Omitting sections of the MAP to shorten the test was not satisfactory, and Gordon soon began to give attention to the possibility of constructing a new aptitude test, one that could be given to young children and administered in two 20-minute periods. Two reasons support his action. First, a market existed for an aptitude test for young children; young children are more readily available to researchers wishing to investigate musical phenomena. Second, the importance of music instruction and experiences for the very young child has not escaped educators. The power of these early experiences lends credibility to Gordon's argument that "aptitude" has not stabilized. Gordon devoted more than a year to the development of the Primary Measures of Music Audiation; this development was based on his extensive previous research with tonal and rhythmic patterns.

Gordon is famous in the music education profession for "coining" words. Audiation is perhaps his most famous word although keyality is another term attributed to Gordon. Audiation describes a musical phenomenon of critical importance to musicians and clarifies discussions that previously were muddled and involved.

The author is careful about describing the materials needed to take the test and how to record the answers on a profile card that comes as a part of the test package. The profile card is constructed in such a way that scores can be recorded twice a year for each age, kindergarten through third grade. Gordon recommends that the test be given at least four times during the primary grades and suggests that eight times (!) is even better for obtaining an accurate indicator of the student's aptitude. The manual is spiral bound and easy to use. The section of the manual needed to administer the test is color coded (green pages); the book lies flat and is durable, with a sturdy cover and quality paper. The information considered of lesser importance to the teacher is at the end of the book; unfortunately the validity section is placed here also, a section of extreme importance to one considering use of the test.

Practical Applications/Uses

The Primary Measures of Music Audiation are contained on two cassette tapes, one for the tonal test and one for the rhythm test. Each test requires 12 minutes of listening time. Student answer sheets have been designed with the young child in mind. Question numbers are not used; rather, the student finds his or her place on the test paper by identifying pictures of apples, shoes, cups, trees, hats, chairs, and so on. The student does not have to be able to read; he or she indicates a pair is "Same" by circling two smiling faces. "Different" is indicated by circling one frowning face and one smiling face. Two examples are given for each test. Gordon is very precise and thorough in his directions to the teacher and to the student. Ample test time is suggested in order that the questions of all students can be answered before the test begins. Gordon cautions against replaying any examples in the test, but does allow the teacher to stop the tape during the test administration to allow students extra time for marking their answer. This extra time may or may not affect the norms and other technical qualities of the test; no pertinent data have been gathered.

The PMMA is designed for kindergarten, first-, second-, and third-grade students, and all four levels of students were involved in the test development. One study used fourth-grade students, but these subjects were found to be too old to provide valid and reliable data. The test items are not overly difficult; kindergartners average 64% correct answers on the tonal test, a figure that rises to nearly 86% for the third-grade student. The rhythm test is slightly more difficult, with average difficulty indices ranging from .58 for kindergartners to .75 for third-grade students.

The PMMA can be administered and scored by the music teacher. The instructions are clear and professional with minute attention to detail. The author "insists" that the tonal pattern test must be given first although no empirical reasons are given for this ordering. Gordon's explanation is that students will better understand the testing task if they begin with the tonal patterns. Because computer scoring is not feasible for pictographic answer sheets, scoring of the test is done by hand. Templates allow the teacher to see if students have circled all of the answers or have pattern marked. The scoring templates are sturdy and reflect the general high quality of production that was involved in producing this product.

Although a composite score is computed, the primary interest of the author is that the examiner interpret test results using two scores, one for tonal patterns and one for rhythm patterns. Interpretation of test score data is straightforward in that raw scores are easily converted to norms. Gordon strongly suggests the development of local norms, although they are less likely to be used than published, national norms.

Technical Aspects

Four school systems were used to provide the data in the development of the Primary Measures of Music Audiation; the norms presented in the manual are from one school system in upstate New York (N = 873). One might more reasonably expect this type of sampling in the development of a criterion-referenced test than in the development of an aptitude test.

Gordon discusses content validity, concurrent validity, and congruent validity; however, he provides little data for any of these. For content validity, Gordon suggests that the test measures keyality and tempo within the tonal and rhythmic pattern discrimination. He accepts on face value that tone and rhythm are the two major components of aptitude; however, in his tonal and rhythm pattern research, the "ability of fourth grade students to hear pairs of patterns as being the same or different was found to have virtually no correlation with stabilized music aptitude as measured by the Musical Aptitude Profile" (1981, p. 73). This statement could be interpreted to mean that there is almost no relationship between developmental aptitude and Gordon's definition of true musical aptitude. The same data are used on page 90, however, to argue that scores from the PMMA are related to the MAP.

> The correlations between the *Musical Aptitude Profile* and the *Primary Measures of Music Audiation* are comparable to the longitudinal predictive validity coefficients reported for the *Musical Aptitude Profile*. Although not conclusive, thus far these data offer the strongest objective evidence of the validity of the *Primary Measures of Music Audiation*. (p. 90)

The data supporting the argument that Gordon is *not* measuring aptitude with the PMMA are more convincing than his concluding sentence in the manual stating that he is.

Concurrent validity is dismissed because of the difficulty of distinguishing between informal and formal music achievement on the one hand and innate music aptitude on the other (1979, p. 86). The author's point is that there can be no reliable criterion. If Gordon's statement were true, criterion-related validity would not be possible for any aptitude or intelligence test. The construction of all aptitude tests poses the same problem. Gordon focuses on the small correlation between PMMA scores and test scores on the Lorge-Thorndike Intelligence Tests, Stanford Achievement Test, and Metropolitan Readiness Test. Although of interest, this negative argument is not convincing as an indicator of validity. The case for congruent validity rests completely on the congruence between the test scores of 227 fourth-grade students on his two tests, PMMA and MAP.

The author is to be commended in providing both internal and test-retest reliability data. Internal reliability is especially high. Gordon's logic with the test-retest data is that a correlation of .60 between two administrations of the test a week apart seems good (high) to him, and a correlation of .51 between two parts of the test seems low—he argues that only 25% of the variance is common. The correlation between the two parts of the test of about .50 was confirmed by this reviewer's administration of the test, and a similar figure is found in at least two other studies. Additional care is needed in the drawing of conclusions from these data. The test-retest reliability computed by this reviewer using students in first and second grades was .61. The interval was one year. The combined grades contributed to a speciously high reliability; a test-retest reliability of .5 for a single grade is probable.

Of most interest to the technician is Table 5, Gordon's item analysis table for the two subtests. The items are shown to be very easy even for first-grade children. Twenty-four of the 40 items in the tonal test had a difficulty index of .80 and above; the average difficulty index for third grade is 85.6, an indication that most students obtain the correct answer. Computing his item discrimination by point biserial (the presumed method, as Gordon does not so state) provides impressive discrimination values. These unlikely, but possible, figures occur only when a test resembles a Guttman rating scale. Gordon's statement that "there is a considerable range of item difficulty levels for each test in all grades" (1979, p. 70) cannot be taken seriously; one difficult question (#19) hardly gives "considerable" range. Item 19 is the only item with a difficulty index of less than .5 for third-grade students. The point biserial formula used is not as much a measure of discrimination between those who know and those who do not know as it is a measure of the relationship between the individual item and the total score. These data, as suggested earlier, tend to explain the results Gordon obtained in his factor analysis as well as some of his other statistical data.

Critique

The manual for the Primary Measures of Music Audiation does not make a clear distinction between aptitude and achievement. The test's subtitle says it is an aptitude test when it is not, and some sections of the manual will mislead the casual reader. The essence of what Gordon says, however, is that aptitude is not sufficiently stable at this age, and an achievement test that is labeled "developmental music aptitude" should be given instead. In Gordon's defense, achievement is often too narrowly defined as that knowledge or skill, "systematically" taught, that can be measured. With children of this age (6-9) there may have been little systematic instruction; there has been, however, considerable music achievement. Gordon suggests that the terms *higher* and *lower* result from instruction, but making a comparison between *same* and *different* is more visceral. What he really means is that vocabulary must be taught and attached to concepts before higher and lower, louder and softer, and longer and shorter can successfully be used in testing students. Same and different, however, are terms that are learned very early in all cultures and can be satisfactorily used in measuring music achievement. His argument that tonal and rhythmic memory are not being measured is probably true, and the student probably does make a "gestaltist" decision about these two musical components. His statements, however, do not add up to a compelling argument for or against aptitude. Many musical decisions are made on the basis of a gestalt impression, and these impressions may be based upon systematic learning or impressions learned through systematic instruction.

Not only is the argument weak that same and different responses to tonal and rhythmic patterns constitute musical aptitude, Gordon makes no effort to justify the use of only these two components. He calmly suggests that if there are other factors (than tonal and rhythm patterns), they are presently unknown (1979, p. 79) and the reader is asked to accept the ability to make same and different distinctions as constituting the core of developmental music aptitude. Gordon finds it more successful to argue negatively rather than positively in defending his choice of tasks. His primary argument in this test, as it was in the Musical Aptitude Profile, is the low correlations with other school tests. For example, he indicates that scores on the PMMA correlate around .3 with Stanford's test in mathematics and reading. The basis of the argument being that if intelligence or other school achievement is not being measured, music aptitude is.

Gordon conducts a factor analysis that should be useful in indicating to the user the presence in the test of two main factors, pitch and rhythm. Unfortunately, the factor analysis is not conducted on the total test; rather, Gordon is intrigued with possible factors within the pitch and rhythm subtests. The result of the factor analysis is that the primary factor identified is whether the student answers "Same" or whether he or she answers "Different." Gordon's item analysis data indicate the probable futility of obtaining insights from this factor analysis, to which considerable manual space is devoted.

No review of Gordon's work is complete without documenting his primary concern for instruction, not for testing. Pages 50-64 of the manual are devoted to suggestions for teaching. Gordon is a good teacher, but he does make unsubstantiated statements in what is supposedly a scholarly test manual:

> "Unconscious listening to music is most important before the age of three" (p. 51)
> "Instrumental music should be played most of the time" (p. 52)
> "Parent or teacher singing to a child is of equal importance (to instrumental music)" (p. 52)
> "Rote singing probably contributes less than spontaneous singing to the development of a child's tonal aptitude" (p. 53)
> "There is a direct correspondence between the quality, quantity, and diversity of rhythm activities of a preschool child and rhythmic aptitude" (p. 54)
> "Large muscle movement should be encouraged" (p. 55)
> "There are two types of nonsingers; two types of out of tune singers" (p. 57)

He describes how to teach a rote song and much more. Some of the statements are logical, but none is supported by research.

Gordon seems reluctant to drop or change an item or item type once he has formulated his testing hypotheses, which fortunately are usually based on extensive and careful thought. An example of this penchant for stasis can be found in the PMMA, where all of the tonal items were retained throughout the test's development. A few rhythm items were changed because of that subtest's lower and less reliable score, but Gordon claims that even this revision had little effect on validity or reliability—an argument to his audience that he might just as well have stayed with the original rhythm items (1979, p. 19). It is important to note that Gordon operates within a single philosophy of music instruction and learning and that he makes every effort to be consistent.

The author repeatedly argues that the test is valid only during that period when the young child's music aptitude is in a state of flux. Once musical ability stabilizes, which for Professor Gordon is around the age of 9, the data from this test are no longer valid. The data are not valid even for primary-age children if their aptitude has already stabilized. A major use of the test results for Gordon is that scores from the test should serve a diagnostic function based on whether a student is in the high, middle, or low group on pitch and rhythm. This suggestion, however, has limited value, at least with third-grade students and perhaps with others as well. The test functions as a criterion-related achievement test with a ceiling that is rather easily attained. Missing a question lowers the percentile rank of third-grade students by 6%; thus a student who misses five questions on the rhythm test is at the 81st percentile, 6 questions at the 75th. Teachers with strong music programs will find the norm tables for third-grade students disconcerting and may believe that their students have not attained when, in fact, the ceiling effect is influencing their scores and their class rank.

This reviewer administered the test in two different communities and obtained scores even higher than the already "high" scores obtained by Gordon for his norms. Fewer than 15% of this reviewer's sample scored below 35 on the tonal test. The table of norms in the manual suggests that the test is inappropriate for third-grade students (too easy), but these are likely underestimated; the norms are most appropriate for first- and second-grade students. The test is not appropriate as an aptitude test for all of the recommended ages. The test does appear to measure the ability to distinguish same and different from an aural stimulus.

Gordon's final table correlating results of the PMMA with his MAP, especially when corrected for attenuation, is interpreted as a good indicator that *achievement* as measured by PMMA does have a respectable relationship to the student's aptitude as measured by Gordon's Musical Aptitude Profile.

References

Gordon, Edwin E. (1979). *Primary Measures of Music Audiation.* Chicago: G.I.A. Publications.
Gordon, Edwin E. (1981). *The manifestation of developmental music aptitude in the audiation of "same" and "different" as sound in music.* Chicago: G.I.A. Publications.
Wehner, Walter L. (1985). Primary Measures of Music Audiation. In J. V. Mitchell (Ed.), *The ninth mental measurements yearbook* (pp. 1206-1207). Lincoln, NE: The Buros Institute of Mental Measurements.

Dale Carpenter, Ed.D.
Associate Professor of Special Education, Western Carolina University, Cullowhee, North Carolina.

Ellen Hedrick Bacon, Ph.D.
Assistant Professor of Special Education, Western Carolina University, Cullowhee, North Carolina.

THE PYRAMID SCALES
John D. Cone. Austin, Texas: PRO-ED.

Introduction

The Pyramid Scales are criterion-referenced tests of adaptive behavior intended for moderately to severely handicapped individuals of all ages. The scales or subtests are organized into three areas, called *zones*: Sensory Zone, Primary Zone, and Secondary Zone. The Sensory Zone contains three scales, and the Primary and Secondary Zones consist of nine and eight scales respectively, for a total of 20 separate scales designed to measure the adaptive behavior of moderately to profoundly handicapped children in residential and public school settings. Eight specific behaviors are assessed in each scale; therefore, 160 specific behaviors can be measured with The Pyramid Scales.

The following scales comprise the Sensory Zone: Tactile Responsiveness, Auditory Responsiveness, and Visual Responsiveness. Tactile Responsiveness measures the subject's sensitivity and responsiveness to being touched or touching, such as having the feet stroked or touching soft or coarsely textured material. Auditory Responsiveness assesses behavioral reactions to sounds, such as turning the head toward the source of sound and responding to music or rhythms. Visual Responsiveness concerns behavioral response to visual stimuli, such as differences in light brightness and discriminating between dissimilar objects and symbols.

The scales that make up the Primary Zone are Gross Motor, Eating, Fine Motor, Toileting, Dressing, Social Interaction, Washing/Grooming, Receptive Language, and Expressive Language. The Gross Motor scale assesses the large muscle movement repertoire such as supporting self, walking, and participating in athletic activities. Eating is an evaluation of mastering basic mouth movements, using utensils, and selecting appropriate food. Fine Motor is concerned with small-muscle dexterity, such as grasping, drawing, and folding paper. Toileting ranges from remaining clean for a specified period of time to independently using the toilet, including adjusting one's clothing and flushing the toilet. Dressing involves cooperating when being dressed, partially dressing oneself, and caring for one's own clothing. Social Interaction includes such items as recognizing the presence of others, expressing feelings to others, respecting other's property, and interacting comfortably with members of the opposite sex. Washing/Grooming assesses basic grooming from cooperating when being bathed, to more advanced grooming, with a separate item for males and females (shaving for males and menstrual care for females). Receptive Language concerns response to language, such as comprehending one's own name to understanding stories. Expressive Language, the last of the Primary Zone scales, involves making basic sounds, imitating words, naming common objects, and asking simple questions.

The Secondary Zone is concerned with more advanced behaviors and includes Recreation and Leisure, Writing, Domestic Behavior, Reading, Vocational, Time, Numbers, and Money. Recreation and Leisure includes engaging in passive activities such as watching TV, playing with others, participating in organized activities (such as a team sport), and maintaining a hobby. Writing includes holding a pencil or crayon and writing correspondence. Domestic Behavior involves items such as picking up trash and toys, washing clothes, preparing meals, and keeping a yard neat. Reading assesses skills from attending to symbols to reading orally from printed text. Vocational is a work-oriented scale measuring working unsupervised for short periods, effective job performance, and locating and applying for jobs. Time involves understanding time concepts, knowing days of the week, using a calendar, and keeping appointments. Numbers is a math scale measuring basic arithmetic skills. The last scale in the Secondary Zone is Money, which involves knowing money values, counting change, using bank services, and budgeting.

The Pyramid Scales, originally known as The West Virginia Assessment and Tracking System, was developed in 1976 as a uniform method of evaluating elements of Title I programs in the West Virginia Department of Health. According to the author (Cone, 1984), the original version was field-tested on 338 subjects in a variety of residential programs, public schools, and community mental health centers. The initial version was revised in 1978 and was administered to over 1,000 handicapped persons ranging in age from infancy to over 70 years. The Pyramid Scales represent the third version of the instrument, and a Spanish language version has been developed. The present version is an attempt to go beyond instruments designed for more specific target groups limited by degree of handicap or type of setting. The instrument is designed to allow standard assessment across groups and settings.

The scales are both criterion- and curriculum-referenced and were designed to be used for general description, program planning, and evaluation. The author claims that they are especially useful in setting priority areas for individual education programs. Items have been selected from objective sets included in curricula for handicapped students, such as the Behavior Characteristics Progression, Brigance Inventories, Uniform Performance Assessment System, Learning Accomplishment Profile, Portage materials, Teaching Resources curriculum, Adaptive Behavior Scale, The West Virginia System, and others. The Pyramid Scales are most closely correlated with the curriculum of The West Virginia System, as each of the 20 areas in the system are represented in the scales. The West Virginia System curriculum consists of 414 subareas and over 5,000 objectives and method cards, which can be used in conjunction with the scales to allow a finer-tuned assessment and subsequent educational program.

The final 20 scales were chosen from a review of checklists reviewed by Walls, Werner, Bacon, and Zane (1977) and supplemented with areas representing lower level skills and important higher level skill areas such as recreation and leisure and vocational. The author chose not to include maladaptive behavior with the rationale that appropriate adaptive behavior (which was incompatible with maladaptive behavior) could be identified using the scales (Cone, 1984). Each of the 20 areas contains eight behaviors, which are arranged by difficulty level from very minimal performance levels to behavior indicative of relatively high levels of proficiency. Ordering of the items was based on empirical evidence collected during field-testing and revision. The scales generally tap behaviors ranging from birth to 7-8 chronological years, although higher items in some of the scales assess behaviors characteristic of persons of high-school age.

The Pyramid Scales consist of a manual and a combination answer and profile sheet. The one-page answer sheet has space for identifying information about the client and a place for responses to each of the 160 items. Also, space is provided for recording the percentage correct for each of the 20 areas. The one-page profile sheet, located on the back of the answer sheet, has space for the client's name, date, and plotting of percent of maximum possible score for each scale arranged by zone. Thus, administration of the scales requires the examiner to have access to the manual and the answer sheet. The scales with specific item information are printed in the manual along with directions for administration, scoring, and interpretation.

Practical Applications/Uses

The Pyramid Scales are designed to be used for general descriptive purposes, program planning, and evaluation. For descriptive purposes, the scales allow a user to obtain a profile of an individual's proficiency in the 20 areas assessed. For example, one could see from the profile whether a client was relatively more proficient in Primary Zone areas such as Toileting and Dressing than in Social Interaction and Receptive Language, or more proficient in Primary Zone areas than in Secondary Zone areas. Also, the scales provide a description of overall ability in adaptive behavior. Program planning for individuals and groups is possible by using the profile of scores to detect which areas need to be targeted for instruction or therapy. The scales can also be used to measure the progress of clients in a particular program or across settings. In this way the scales serve a summative evaluation purpose. According to Cone (1984), the scales have been used most frequently for program planning for handicapped persons.

Because of the criterion- and curriculum-referenced nature of The Pyramid Scales, interpretation and use differ from norm-referenced instruments. For example, scores for each scale represent a percentage of positively worded items that are true about the individual as compared to those that are false, ignoring those behaviors not observed or those for which the client is physiologically incapable. This means that if a client obtains a score of 75% for a particular scale and 85% for another scale, those results are meaningful only in the context of their relationship to each other, the behavior actually observed, the requirements of the setting, and the purpose for which the scales were administered. No arbitrary cutoff score is available to enable a test consumer to judge whether a client would be eligible for a certain program or needed programming in that area. Two clients could obtain a score of 100% for a particular scale, but one may not be as proficient in the area as another if some behavior items were not observed by the informant. Therefore, the manual cautions and instructs users about how to establish priority training areas depending on the criteria needed for functioning in certain environments, which must be determined.

Furthermore, pinpointing specific instructional objectives is not possible using The Pyramid Scales without further assessment with additional materials relevant to the curriculum of a particular program. The Pyramid Scales allow a user to specify current levels of performance necessary for general descriptive purposes and for establishing annual goals for clients. These appear to be the major purposes for which the scales are appropriate. Because the sensitivity of the scales to pre- and posttesting has not been established, the use of scales to measure progress is questionable, although they can be used to document the level of performance of handicapped clients in a given program.

The Pyramid Scales should be used to assess handicapped clients in educational settings, such as residential homes with a therapeutic mission and school settings. The scales were developed to assess moderately to profoundly handicapped children, but are appropriate for assessing the adaptive behavior of clients of all ages. The nature of the item content makes the scales most appropriate for handicapped children for whom adaptive behavior is of concern. The manual states that the wording of items may be adapted for hearing-impaired persons, visually impaired persons, and others with handicapping conditions. The author appropriately advises that any adaptations be undertaken with an understanding of the purpose for which the scores are to be used, as some uses would make adaptations meaningless (Cone, 1984).

The scales may be used by anyone involved in the habilitation of handicapped individuals, such as child-care workers, special educators, psychologists, and others. Administration can be completed by trained adults who are familiar with the purposes and procedures described in the manual. The scales can be administered in one of three modes: interview, informant, or direct observation. The manual states that the most frequent mode used is the interview mode. In this case a trained examiner interviews a person familiar and knowledgeable about the behavior of the client. This consists of asking the informant about the client's present behavior by reading the scale items or phrasing the items into normal conversational questions. The manual states that this should take from 30 to 50 minutes. The time required will depend on the skill of the interviewer, the client's behavior, and the familiarity of the informant with the client's behavior. Interviewers are advised to conduct the interview in an informal manner.

The informant mode involves having the informant read and complete the scales without the assistance of an interviewer, and the direct observation mode requires the person completing the scales to observe the client while assessing. There are no explicit directions for using the direct observation mode, and the manual discusses the obvious difficulty with this arrangement. Presently, this mode appears to be unsatisfactory because no data exist regarding the reliability and validity of all 20 scales using the direct observation mode.

The wide range of behaviors assessed by The Pyramid Scales requires that informants have a familiarity with the client resulting from both time spent observing his or her and opportunities to observe a wide range of behaviors. No data are present in the manual documenting the optimal characteristics of informants regarding quantity and quality of experience with the client. Also, similar information is missing regarding the characteristics of interviewers. Although items have been worded carefully and revised as a result of adequate field-testing, the relationship of informant to client and skills of interviewers and informants pose a concern regarding administration of the scales.

Scoring instructions are carefully presented in the manual. Scoring requires extensive familiarity with items and scoring format. Different procedures are used for scoring the scales of the Sensory Zone and for scoring the scales of the Primary and Secondary Zones. Each of the 24 items in the three areas of the Sensory Zone is written as a 4-point scale, but only one point is marked along the scale. For example, the item "Responds to sudden loud noise" requires the informant to determine if the client should be rated: 1) Has done so at least once, 2) Sometimes, 3) More often than not, or 4) Always. Also, two other response categories are provided: P (Physiologically incapable) and N (No opportunity to observe). Other items are marked using the same format. Primary and Secondary Zone scoring uses a different and more complicated format. Each of eight items for a scale includes four descriptors that must be scored. A sample item, "Drinks," includes the following descriptors: 1) Drinks at least some liquids, 2) Swallows liquids placed in mouth, 3) Uses cup or glass to drink from independently or if given help, 4) Uses cup or glass to drink from without assistance. Four ratings are possible for each descriptor—"True," "False," "Physiologically incapable," and "No opportunity to observe." Therefore, 32 items are addressed in each of the scales in the Primary and Secondary Zones, and eight items are addressed in the scales in the Secondary Zone.

Obtained scores for all scales are computed by determining the percentage of maximum possible score. Items marked "Physiologically incapable" or "No opportunity to observe" are subtracted from the maximum possible score. The maximum possible score for an area in the Secondary Zone would be 8x4 = 32 if no items were marked "P" or "N." As a score of 0-4 is possible for each item, a scorer would add the number of points received for each item, divide this sum by the maximum possible score (32 less 4 for each N or P) and multiply by 100 to get the area percentage score. The maximum possible score for an area in the Primary and Secondary Zones would be 32 if no items were marked "P" or "N." Because 32 different descriptors are responded to as "True" or "False," the number of "True" responses are added and divided by this maximum possible score (32) minus each N or P. The quotient is multiplied to obtain the area percentage score. Scores for each area can range from 0-100%. A computer program for scoring the scales and producing a profile is available for Apple II + computers from the author.

Interpretation is based on scores but requires linking interpretation to purpose for testing. Interpretation demands that the user keep in mind that the instrument is criterion- and curriculum-referenced. Scores obtained are area percentage correct of maximum possible scores determined by the number of items for which the client is physiologically incapable or for which the informant had no opportunity to observe. The only interpretation appropriate must be based on the relation of area scores to each other and to the goals of the program in which the client is placed or being considered (Sattler, 1982; Zucker, 1984-85). Descriptive purposes allow the user to determine levels of ability in each area assessed by examining percentage scores for each level. Programming purposes allow the user to target areas that yielded the lowest scores for the client, keeping in mind that higher level areas such as Money and Vocational are apt to have naturally occurring lower scores than lower level areas such as Eating and Dressing. Areas are generally arranged from lowest skill to highest skill, allowing users to target areas receiving the same scores in a developmental manner, training the lowest skill area before training the next lowest skill area.

Interpreting score results relies on several factors. As stated, the purpose for the assessment is primary. Interpretation must also relate to the goals of a particular program, as a low score in some areas may be inconsequential to the goals or concerns of a given program. Additionally, because scoring accuracy is dependent on the informant's knowledge of the client to a great extent and is influenced by the number of items not observed, the user must know how to interpret areas for which a significant number of items were marked "No opportunity to observe." Therefore, although scores might seem relatively easy to interpret, interpretation is dependent on a thorough understanding of adaptive behavior assessment and the particular scoring procedures used with The Pyramid Scales.

Technical Aspects

Evidence of reliability and validity for The Pyramid Scales is available in the manual. Reliability information addresses the agreement of informants using various modes, temporal stability, and internal consistency. Content, criterion-related, and construct validity information is reported. The user should keep in mind that the scales are criterion- and curriculum-referenced, and thus classical reliability and validity data should be interpreted in a different context than that of norm-referenced instruments.

Two small studies addressed the agreement of data obtained from informants and through direct observation. In the first, 59 developmentally disabled clients were observed along eight scales, and this information was correlated to information collected from teachers, aides, and house parents. Pearson product-moment correlations and mean percent agreement coefficients range from .68 to .90 and from .68 to .87, respectively, with means of .80 and .75. A second study investigated the agreement of direct observation as compared to teacher and parent informants and teacher informants compared to parent informants for five preschool handicapped children along 12 scales. The lowest mean correlation coefficient for the comparisons was .82, with the highest being .90, which demonstrated that direct observation for these scales compared favorably with informant produced data. Similarly, teacher informants compared favorably with parents for the scales evaluated. Data for all of the instrument's scales are not available.

Test-retest stabilty and internal consistency estimates were figured using 67 males and 55 females with mean ages of 16.7 and 17.7 years, respectively. Clients represented four different age groups, and testing intervals were approximately one year. Stability coefficients ranged from .58 for the Vocational area to .97 for the

Fine Motor area, with a mean of .88 for all scales and all age groups. The Kuder-Richardson 21 formula was used to compute internal consistency for the same group and the coefficient mean was .92 across all scales.

The author has drawn on the work of others to develop The Pyramid Scales as a means of measuring adaptive behavior. A review of the items and scales indicates that they include important domains in suffcient quantity and are stated with sufficient specificity to be useful to consumers concerned about the adaptive behavior of handicapped individuals. Specific consumers with predetermined purposes may find that the scales have varying degrees of content validity depending on their own needs and uses.

To demonstrate criterion-related validity, comparisons of The Pyramid Scales with the Slosson Intelligence Test, the Uniform Performance Assessment System (UPAS), and the Adaptive Behavior Scales are reported. The mean correlation coefficient showing comparison of The Pyramid Scales with the Slosson Intelligence Test was .42, using approximately 36 clients. Validity coefficients representing the correlation of scores for The Pyramid Scales with scores for the Uniform Performance Assessment System range from means of .76 to .87 for appropriate scales. Scores from The Pyramid Scales did not compare favorably (.10) with the scales of Inappropriate Behaviors on the UPAS; The Pyramid Scales include no area of maladaptive behavior. These comparisons were figured using a group of 16 or less preschool and elementary multiple-handicapped children. Scores for 50 moderately to severely handicapped clients were used to compare The Pyramid Scales and Part I of the Adaptive Behavior Scales. Mean validity coefficients range from .13 to .90, with great variability depending on the scales compared. These criterion-related validity coefficients generally show relatively high correlation with scales that purport to measure approximately the same behaviors.

Construct validity concerns whether the instrument adheres to a logically consistent theory by demonstrating scores that support the theory (Salvia & Ysseldyke, 1985). To demonstrate construct validity, the author has reported scores of various groups of individuals in different settings. The settings have different eligibility criteria and different programming emphases. If the instrument is sensitive to different adaptive behavior criteria and training, the clients in each setting should demonstrate different scores relative to the setting. Furthermore, if the scales are arranged hierarchically, most handicapped clients should show a developmental pattern of scores in which lower scores are obtained in the Secondary Zone than in the Primary and Sensory Zones. The author presents data that show that scores are generally developmental (Cone, 1984)—older clients obtain scores that are generally higher than younger clients, and most scores for both groups show that the scales are arranged hierarchically. Males and females have obtained similar scores. Clients in different programs have different score profiles. This includes a sample of psychiatric patients who were tested using the scales. These data support the construct validity of the instrument.

Reliability and validity have been established using procedures appropriate for norm-referenced instruments and useful for the purposes for which the instrument was designed. The user should be cautioned that most of the data used to establish reliability and validity were collected using earlier versions of the instrument. Additionally, performance criteria were determined using the curriculum of The West Virginia System and need to be determined for other curricula.

Critique

The Pyramid Scales appear to be carefully developed and should be useful as an aid to programming for handicapped clients by indicating relative strengths and weaknesses in adaptive behavior. Psychometric characteristics of the scales appear to be adequate, considering that the scales are criterion-referenced and to be used for programming. If the scales were to be used for eligibility or evaluation of program gains, data do not support their use. For example, no data are presented that show the reliability or validity of the scales in determining mastery or nonmastery of a certain area, a frequently mentioned purpose of criterion-referenced instruments (Livingston, 1977; Hambleton, Swaminathan, Algina, & Coulson, 1978). No information is reported that documents whether a client identified as a master in a given subdomain of The Pyramid Scales would be identified as a master using the same program criteria on a second administration. Although statistical procedures are available (Livingston, 1977; Hambleton et al., 1978), they have not been employed, perhaps because this information would only be pertinent to certain curricular programs and would not generalize to other programs. Mastery for one program in a particular area may not suffice as mastery in that area for another program. Likewise, the sensitivity of the instrument to individual growth in an area has not been adequately demonstrated and should probably be carried out in the context of a particular curricular program. Therefore, the utility of The Pyramid Scales for eligibility and/or evaluation must be assessed by each program user.

For descriptive purposes, the scales promise usefulness if the user is adequately familiar with the scales and if the informant has an adequate knowledge of the behavior of the client. Unfortunately, no benchmark exists to judge the adequacy of a user's knowledge both of the instrument and of adaptive behavior generally, and the informant's knowledge of the client's behavior specifically. More work needs to be done in these areas before standards are available regarding user qualifications. This is a common issue with adaptive behavior instruments (McLoughlin & Lewis, 1986; Salvia & Ysseldyke, 1985) and has been addressed in the manual so that consumers are aware of the problem.

The merit of The Pyramid Scales will be determined by further use, especially in programs that do not employ the West Virginia curriculum. Although Cone has attempted to devise an insrument that can be used across programs, more data are necessary in a wide range of programs, not tied to a particular curriculum and set of objectives, to determine the worth of the scales. The admirable quality of The Pyramid Scales is that the instrument has been carefully developed and field-tested and does not promise more than it is able to deliver. It has a flexibility essential to the assessment of adaptive behavior.

The Pyramid Scales offer special educators and others working with the severely handicapped a tool for recording and collecting salient information on an individual's development and education. The scale was carefully devised to measure, reliably and validly, the essential aspects of concern regarding severely handicapped clients. The scales should prove to be effective for summarizing and communicating information about a student and, as a starting point, for setting major educational goals.

References

Cone, J. D. (1984). *The Pyramid Scales: Criterion-Referenced Measures of Adaptive Behavior in Severely Handicapped Persons.* Austin, TX: PRO-ED.

Hambleton, R. K., Swaminathan, H., Algina, J., & Coulson, D. B. (1978). Criterion-referenced testing and measurement: A review of technical issues and developments. *Review of Educational Research, 48,* 1-47.

Livingston, S. A. (1977). Psychometric techniques for criterion-referenced testing and behavioral assessment. In J. D. Cone & R. P. Hawkins (Eds.), *Behavioral assessment: New directions in clinical psychology.* New York: Brunner/Mazel.

McLoughlin, J. A., & Lewis, R. B. (1986). *Assessing special students* (2nd ed.). Columbus, OH: Charles E. Merrill.

Salvia, J., & Ysseldyke, J. E. (1985). *Assessment in special and remedial education* (3rd ed.). Boston: Houghton Mifflin.

Sattler, J. M. (1982). *Assessment of children's intelligence and special abilities* (2nd ed.). Boston: Allyn & Bacon.

Walls, R. T., Werner, T. S., Bacon, A., & Zane, T. (1977). Behavior checklists. In J. D. Cone & R. P. Hawkins (Eds.), *Behavioral assessment: New directions in clinical psychology.* New York: Brunner/Mazel.

Zucker, S. (1984-85). Assessment of mental retardation. *Diagnostique, 10,* 115-127.

Theodore R. Cromack, Ed.D.
Director, Commodity Donation Demonstration Study, Virginia Polytechnic Institute and State University, Washington, D.C.

Jim C. Fortune, Ed.D.
Professor of Educational Research and Evaluation, Virginia Polytechnic Institute and State University, Blacksburg, Virginia.

A QUICK SCREENING SCALE OF MENTAL DEVELOPMENT

Katherine M. Banham. Murfreesboro, Tennessee: Psychometric Affiliates.

Introduction

A Quick Screening Scale of Mental Development consists of a series of statements of readily observable behavior that can be checked as true or false. The statements are grouped into five categories: 1) bodily coordination, 2) manual performance, 3) speech and language, 4) listening, attention, and number, and 5) play interests. Furthermore, the order in which the statements are arranged represents the developmental abilities of children between the ages of 6 months and 10 years.

The Quick Screening Scale was developed by Katherine M. Banham of Duke University and is distributed by Psychometric Affiliates. The manual (Banham, 1963) states that the scale was constructed "with a view to meeting the need of pediatricians, psychiatrists, and clinical psychologists for some practical device for quickly assessing, at least approximately, the level of mental development of young children brought to children's clinics for psychiatric or psychological examination" (p. 1). The test was normed on infants and children who had come in contact with the chief psychologist in the Division of Psychological Services of the North Carolina Department of Public Welfare and on grade school and kindergarten children at the Child Centered School in Durham, North Carolina. It would appear that the test has never been revised.

This test consists of four pages, with 16 items under each of the five aforementioned categories. The items are consistent in that there is one statement for each level beginning at 6 months of age and every 6 months thereafter up to age 6, then annually from age 7 to age 10. In addition to the test there is a six-page manual, which describes the test and provides the standardization information and technical data. The manual also includes directions describing how to administer and score each of the statements. Because the test is individually administered, the examiner is the only one who uses these materials. Considerable emphasis is given in the manual to the flexibility that the examiner has in administering the items; for example, the examiner may have the parents present or may ask the parents to leave the room for any or all portions of the test. The examiner may prefer to begin with the first section on bodily coordination, or he or she may prefer to start at some other point. Because it is a preliminary screening instrument and is an individually administered observation scale, there is no particular concern for standardization in administration.

The scale manual indicates that no special apparatus is required for administration and in fact some of the items are checked on the basis of parental report. Because this is merely a screening device, it may easily be administered on such an informal basis that neither the parent nor the child may be aware that a scale is being administered. The few items that are necessary to establish the appropriate developmental level for a child in each of the five areas are then averaged to represent the child's general mental level (GML), and this score is recorded on the booklet. The administrator is cautioned that the Quick Screening Scale is not a technique for precise mental measurement; however, an IQ (Intelligence Quotient) or DQ (Developmental Quotient) may be calculated by dividing the GML by the child's chronological age and thus estimate something that might be obtained in a more lengthy examination.

In reviewing the scale items, it would appear that in many instances observing the child in the room while collecting information from the parent would identify a number of the developmental levels. However, in other instances specific items would have to be administered. For example, the age 7 criteria for bodily coordination indicates that the child should "Crouch on toes, knees bent 45 degrees, arms out at sides, shoulder high, eyes closed [for] ten seconds." Similarly, there are drawing activities that the child is expected to perform and, at some levels in the speech and language section, the child must correctly pronounce certain words, name colors, and so on. The listening and attention category has a number of repeating-digits and repeating-digits-in-reverse-order items. In the play interest category, most of the items would have to be scored based on information given by the parents.

Practical Applications/Uses

The manual indicates that this scale was constructed to help meet the needs of pediatricians, psychiatrists, and clinical psychologists as a practical device for quickly assessing the mental development of young children. It is expected that preliminary screening by means of such a brief test would help evaluate the child's developmental level during the first interview and enable the physician to make a tentative recommendation pending a more complete examination. The five item groupings were intended to simplify the administration and to aid in diagnosis of developmental or other aberrations.

It is possible that as physicians and psychologists make use of such a quick screening device, it could help focus their general assessment, thereby aiding in the establishment of a remedial plan. A clinician in a mental health service might find this measure of some value in assessing a problem during a brief initial interview; however, the caveat provided in the manual must be very clearly kept in mind—that these quick screenings are certainly insufficient for classifying or establishing any long-term action plan.

A Quick Screening Scale of Mental Development 369

Because the score is readily apparent by identifying the statement representing the highest developmental age completed, the scoring "task" itself is extremely simple and occurs during administration. Guidelines for interpretation probably comprise the area of least clarity; it is assumed that the Quick Screening Scale would be administered by someone with considerable clinical judgment. The level of sophistication and training required of the examiner is not great except in terms of interpreting the data.

Technical Aspects

There is virtually no information available about this scale's validity and reliability, nor for how it has been used, even though it has been available for 23 years. (This reviewer contacted the author and was advised that she was not aware of any further uses of the scale beyond the two studies cited hereafter.) Validity consists of two pieces of evidence: the first, taken from the manual, indicates "most of these statements are adaptations from test items in scales of mental development that have already proved their usefulness and whose validity are well established" (Banham, 1963). Some scales mentioned include Gesell developmental schedules, the Oseretsky and the Lincoln-Oseretsky Motor Development Scales, the Stanford revision of the Binet-Simon Scale, the Goodenough Draw-A-Man test, and the Vineland Social Maturity Scale.

The second evidence of validity is presented in concurrent correlations with the Stanford-Binet, Form L-M ($r = 0.89$, $N = 58$) and the Cattell Infant Intelligence Scale ($r = 0.95$, $N = 13$), both of which were administered to children by the chief psychologist in the Division of Psychological Services of the North Carolina Department of Public Welfare. In both instances these children were below normal IQ in that the mean IQ for the Stanford-Binet group was 70 (with a standard deviation of 20) and for the Cattell the mean IQ was 75 (with a standard deviation of 27).

A test-retest (one-month interval) administration was conducted at the Child Centered School in Durham, North Carolina, and yielded a *rho* reliability coefficient of 0.93. The mean GML of the first test was 6 years, 10 months, and the retest was 7 years, 0 months. The chronological age of these children was 5 years, 10 months.

These coefficients are quite impressive; however, the validation took place in 1960 and 1962, and there appears to be no evidence of more recent usage or validation of these tests.

Critique

It would appear that this scale of mental development would be useful to validate one's professional judgment; however, an experienced child psychologist—or even a less trained individual working regularly with children—would have little difficulty obtaining results as adequate and accurate as these. If the instrument truly is helpful as a diagnostic scale, its primary usefulness might lay in that area. However, though it claims to be a diagnostic instrument, there is no evidence of validity or reliability for the individual categories. The most interesting aspect is that this scale continues to be carried in the publisher's catalog and is currently available, though there is no evidence of its continued usage.

References

Banham, M. (1963). *A Quick Screening Scale of Mental Development manual.* Munster, IN: Psychometric Affiliates.

Tim Roberts, Ed.D.
Associate Professor of Special Education, East Texas State University, Commerce, Texas.

REVISED BEHAVIOR PROBLEM CHECKLIST
Herbert C. Quay and Donald R. Peterson. Coral Gables, Florida: Herbert C. Quay, Ph.D.

Introduction

The Revised Behavior Problem Checklist (RBPC) is a scale purporting to measure the structure of deviant behavior associated with children and adolescents experiencing social-emotional problems. As the name implies, the RBPC is the revision of the Behavior Problem Checklist (BPC; Quay & Peterson, 1967). The original 55-item BPC was formulated from clinical observations and factor-analytic studies of child and adolescent behaviors. Items were developed to be descriptive of broad band dimensions of problematic behavior traits derived from clinically referred patients (Peterson, 1961) and juvenile delinquents (Quay, 1964). These items contributed to four primary independent factor dimensions: conduct disorders, anxiety-withdrawal, inadequacy-immaturity, and socialized delinquency. Over 100 studies have been published since 1967 demonstrating the utility of the BPC with a wide variety of handicapped and nonhandicapped populations, and the checklist has been translated into eight foreign languages (Quay & Peterson, 1983).

The revision, initiated in 1979, was undertaken primarily to strengthen the internal reliabilities for each of the four original dimensions, rather than to expand the number of dimensions. Furthermore, the authors sought to include behavioral traits of autistic and/or psychotic populations not addressed on the original checklist.

The utility of the RBPC, as indicated in the Interim Manual, includes screening for behavior problems, assessing the behavior of referred students, classifying juvenile offenders, evaluating the behavioral change associated with intervention programs, and collecting data for research purposes. Adult informants familiar with the behavior of the child or adolescent rate the intensity of 89 items on a trinary scale: 0 = behavior does not constitute a problem, 1 = behavior is perceived as a mild problem; or 2 = behavior constitutes a severe problem. Seventy-seven of the 89 items are distributed among four major and two minor social-emotional scales. The major scales consist of Conduct Disorders (CD), 22 items; Socialized Aggression (SA), 17 items; Attention Problems-Immaturity (AP), 16 items; and Anxiety Withdrawal (AW), 11 items. The minor scales are Psychotic Behavior (PB), 6 items and Motor Excess (ME), 5 items. Additionally, 12 items have been included for the research purpose of extending the age range of the checklist. These 12 items do not contribute to the RBPC scoring.

The RBPC consists of an Interim Manual accompanied by a 1984 Appendix, 20 checklists, and scoring templates. The checklist is divided into three components:

identifying information, checklist items, and a scoring summary. Identifying information consists of descriptive data regarding the subject's name or identification number, date of birth, sex, father's occupation, name of person completing the checklist, relationship of observer to the subject, and the date the checklist was completed.

The checklist is designed to be completed by any observer familiar with the subject. Items are listed and rated according to the observed severity of the behavior. Completion of the checklist rating can be accomplished in approximately 15 minutes.

Scoring templates (stencils) are provided for determining the raw scores for each of the four major and two minor scales. Raw scores for each of the six scales are entered onto the summary table at the bottom of the checklist. The authors suggest that raw scores can be converted into standard scores for interpretation; however, tables for converting raw scores into standard scores are not provided.

Practical Applications/Uses

The RBPC may be used in screening children and adolescents referred for behavior problems, as a component in the diagnosis of behavior disorders, and for differentiating among the behavioral traits or dimensions of students identified as behaviorally disordered. Preliminary comparisons between gifted, unselected public school students, school-identified handicapped, and clinical samples indicate that the RBPC differentiates between normal and atypical populations. A variety of research findings, reported in the Interim Manual and 1984 Appendix, indicate that the RBPC may be useful for differentiating some of the dimensional traits between samples of clinically served inpatients, behaviorally disordered students attending school at a mental health center, private school learning-disabled students, and male juvenile delinquents. Furthermore, data are presented on a representative sample from Auckland, New Zealand (Aman, Werry, Fitzpatrick, Lowe, & Waters, 1983).

Unlike other checklists designed for use in a specific setting (e.g., home, school, clinic, etc.), the RBPC can be completed by a variety of adults (e.g., parents, teachers, counselors, psychologists, physicians, etc.) familiar with the behavior of the targeted student. The open-ended format allows parents and professionals alike to rate all of the items. However, guidelines are not presented regarding the duration of the observation period prior to rating. All items are rated according to the degree of severity demonstrated by the subject. The zero rating is the only one that addresses the frequency of the behavior; the remaining two categories of mild (1) and severe (2) are based on the informant's perceived intensity of student misbehavior.

Scoring of the RBPC can be completed in 5 to 10 minutes with the use of the scoring templates. The RBPC uses an additive, weighted scoring system for the 77 scored items. Each scale has a minimum raw score of 0 and a maximum raw score of twice the number of items for that scale. These obtained scores must be interpreted by an examiner knowledgeable of the properties measured by the scale dimension, the relationship of each dimension to the remaining dimensions, and the magnitude of the obtained score relative to the reported age and sex mean scores for the normal and atypical populations presented in the Interim Manual and Appendix.

Technical Aspects

The technical aspects of the RBPC are presented in the Interim Manual, 1984 Appendix, and the professional literature, most notably Aman and Werry (1984), Aman et al. (1983), and Quay (1983). As the RBPC was developed to "strengthen the psychometric properties of the original" (Quay & Peterson, 1983, p. 1), an assumption of the authors is that the existing body of BPC literature can be applied, in part, to the RBPC. This assumption appears warranted as the item selection process and factor-analytic studies have produced similar constructs to those identified for the BPC (Cancelli, 1985).

Item selection consisted of including some items found on the BPC, extrapolating items from literature reviews, and developing new items addressing the specific needs of the original scales. This procedure yielded a 150-item checklist that was administered to four samples of handicapped students, then factor analyzed to select items consistently appearing and loading on one factor. Results of the factor analysis yielded four major and two minor dimensions. Finally, items with low alpha reliabilities were eliminated from the item pool.

Internal consistency for the six scales range from a low of .68 on the PB scale (elementary-aged school students) to a high of .95 on CD (developmentally disabled and elementary-aged groups). However, demographic information is limited for the developmentally disabled and nonexistent for the elementary-aged groups. Using an alpha coefficient of .80 as an acceptable criterion, the major scales meet this standard. The minor scales consistently fail to meet the criterion. These lowered coefficients on the minor scales may be due, in part, to a limited number of items (Quay, 1983).

Test-retest and interrater reliabilities are minimally acceptable. Achenbach and Edelbrock (1984) report that coefficients in the .70s and .80s are acceptable for teacher ratings of intervals not exceeding 6 months. Test-retest reliabilities for a group of elementary-aged students rated by their teachers at a 2-month interval produced acceptable coefficients of .83 and .79 for the SA and AP scales, respectively.

Interrater reliabilities generally produce lowered correlation coefficients, which may be due to differences in the informants or the demands of the environmental situations. Achenbach and Edelbrock (1984) report that agreement between informants observing subjects in similar environments tend to yield coefficients in the .60 to .80 range, while informants in differing environments tend to produce coefficients ranging from .20 to .50. The average inter-teacher correlation coefficients for a developmentally disabled sample indicate that all scales met the criterion for differing environments. Inter-parent correlation, similar environments, resulted in only the AW scale (.55) failing to meet the criterion.

Validity is the most impressive aspect of the RBPC (Lahey & Piacentini, 1985). The wealth of BPC-related research and the RBPC item selection process has resulted in an internally consistent instrument measuring at least four dimensions of behavior. Criterion-related validity was established through the BPC. Consequently, it is not surprising that the RBPC and BPC are highly correlated on the four major scales. The reported correlation coefficients of the major scales, with a possible exception of the AP scale, account for a considerable amount of variance, thereby supporting the RBPC. However, examination of the PB minor scale indicates a considerable amount of unexplained variance. Criterion-related validity data are not available for the ME scale.

Construct validity was determined through the use of contrasting groups and diagnostic validity procedures. The RBPC scales have been shown to discriminate normal from clinical groups (Quay & Peterson, 1983, 1984). Significant differences were found to exist between a limited clinical sample (66 males, 33 females) and an unselected normal sample (293 males, 273 females). However, the composition of these samples were not reported, and no attempt was made to screen out identified special education students from the unselected group (Quay & Peterson, 1983). The RBPC scales were also correlated with peer nominations of classroom behavior, direct playground observations, and academic achievement (Quay & Peterson, 1983). Peer-nominated aggression produced moderate coefficients with the SA, AP, and PB scales (range .36 to .44) and a strong coefficient with the CD scale (.72). Likability produced moderate negative coefficients with CD (−.39) and AP (−.41). The AW scale (.39) correlated with peer-nominated withdrawal. Direct observation of playground behavior indicated that initiating aggression correlated with CD (.60) and negatively with AW (−.34). Negative correlations existed between cooperating and CD (−.45) and AP (−.49). The PB scale correlated with being alone and being with peers .34 and −.38, respectively. SA failed to correlate significantly with any of the direct observation categories and ME failed to correlate with gross motor activity (.00). However, ME *did* correlate with rough and tumble play (.35) and being unoccupied (−.36).

The failure of the ME scale to correlate with gross-motor activity calls into question the validity of this scale. Support for the retention of the ME scale has been provided by Lahey, Schaughency, Strauss, and Frame (1984). However, Lahey, Schaughency, Frame, and Strauss (1985) question the homogeneity of the AP scale items for differentiating between subjects identified as attention-deficit disordered with and without hyperactivity.

The RBPC has been examined to determine what, if any, relationship existed between the six scales and group measures of ability and achievement. Significant negative coefficients were found to exist between language ability (range −.26 to −.44), total ability (range −.21 to −.47), and the major scales. The PB scale (−.14) was also found to correlate significantly with total ability. Nonlanguage abilities produced significant negative correlations for the CD (−.15), SA (−.15), and AP (−.30) scales. The AW scale (−.07) failed to produce a significant relationship with nonlanguage abilities. With the effects of intelligence partialed out, only the AP scale produced consistent significant negative correlations with reading (−.19), arithmetic (−.20), and total achievement (−.28). Quay and Peterson (1983) conclude that AP is differentially related to academic achievement, a finding supporting the AP scale as a measure of attentional problems and immaturity.

Diagnostic validity has been established by comparing DSM-III (American Psychiatric Association, 1980) categories to the behavioral ratings for the six RBPC scales. DSM-III diagnostic categories for an inpatient sample were collapsed to form three broad-based classifications of psychotic, externalizing, and internalizing behaviors; RBPC ratings were conducted independently from DSM-III diagnosis, and then analysis of variance procedures were applied. The RBPC scales were found to differentiate, either singly or in combination with other scales, subjects in the broad-based classifications (Quay, 1983; Quay & Peterson, 1983).

The lack of a normative sample is the most distracting feature of the RBPC. Quay and Peterson (1983) state that the collection of representative national norms "would be an undertaking beyond our capacities" (p. 8). They advocate the development of local norms and provide reference points (Quay & Peterson, 1983) to serve as a guide for the numerical interpretation of the scores on each scale. These reference points provide means and standard deviations for the six RBPC scales and establish a metric for comparative purposes. One reference group is an unselected sample of public school students from three states in Grades K-8 (N = 869) and a sample of parochial high school students from one state in Grades 9-12 (N = 99). This sample was reported to be from predominately working- and middle-class families, an ethnic composition estimated to be 90% or greater Anglo, and with no inner-city representation. The means and standard deviations for a second sample of unselected elementary students in Grades K-6 (N = 566) were reported for establishing contrasting group validity. However, even less demographic information is available for this sample (Lahey & Piacentini, 1985). A representative sample is provided from Auckland, New Zealand (Aman et al., 1983). While several of the means are similar to the reference samples, substantial differences also exist (Lahey & Piacenti, 1985).

Reference point means and standard deviations are also provided for a wide range of exceptional student samples rated by professional personnel and a child psychiatric inpatient and outpatient sample rated by their parents. The exceptional student samples rated by professional personnel include behaviorally disordered students attending a Canadian mental health center, fourth-grade gifted students, institutionalized male juvenile delinquents, learning-disabled students attending a private school, and university laboratory students. Only for the delinquent sample is minimal demographic information provided. Descriptions for the remaining exceptional samples provide less information regarding composition. These reference points are used to compare the obtained gender scores to standard deviation units above the mean of the reference normative sample and to the mean scores of three clinical samples.

Critique

The RBPC is the extension on an established, well-documented standard (BPC) used in the identification of students at high risk for behavior disorders. Its test-retest reliability coefficients are marginally acceptable for the major scales, and interrater reliabilities fall within an acceptable range. Internal consistency measures are well established for the major scales. Lahey and Piacentini (1985) indicate that when compared to other teacher rating scales of problematic behavior, the reliability of the RBPC is satisfactory.

The RBPC purports to measure independent dimensions of problematic behavior in students exhibiting social/emotional characteristics associated with behavior disorders. The empirical support of the RBPC seems impressive (Lahey & Piacentini, 1985). Using contrasting and diagnostic validity, the construct validity of the RBPC is convincing. Construct validity evidence suggests the major scales measure independent dimensions of problematic behavior. The SA and AP major scales seem to lose some of their differentiating power with presumably more mildly disturbed students served in special education classes. Cancelli (1985) points out, however, that evidence has not been provided supporting the minor scales. Diagnostic validity has been established by DSM-III diagnostic classifications. Some evidence is presented supporting the RBPC as an aid for DSM-III diagnosis.

Cancelli (1985) and Lahey and Piacentini (1985) address the serious limitations imposed on score interpretation due to the lack of a normative sample. The authors readily recognize these limitations, encourage professionals using the RBPC to establish local norms, and provide reference points for clinical, school identified, and unselected normal samples (Quay & Peterson, 1983). However, these reference points for the normal groups are formulated on either unselected, ethnically undifferentiated, or predominately Anglo samples. The one exception is the male juvenile delinquent sample: reference points are provided for a group consisting of 46% white and 54% black. Utilizing any of these reference points for interpretive purposes would seem to create a tenuous position for those professionals charged with diagnosis and placement of students referred for possible intervention services.

The development of local norms without reference to a normative sample seems questionable due, in part, to cultural and ethnic differences within communities, transient populations, and the lack of behavioral stability across situational variables. While local norms provide a viable component for supplementing national norms, local norms should not supplant national norms, as they frequently have little relevance outside of specific geographical areas (i.e., urban ghetto, suburban, rural, etc.). Local norms seem best utilized for within group analyses, either to compare students of dominant or minority cultures to previous test findings for measuring intervention gain or to examine a specific group for establishing a validation of observed behavior. Without consideration of national norms coupled to local norms, professionals responsible for diagnosing behavior disorders may be contributing to the misrepresentation of students, dominant or minority, in need of services.

The RBPC is to be completed by a knowledgeable observer (Quay & Peterson, 1983). No specific criteria are given either for the duration of the observational period prior to rating or regarding who should rate the subject for what decisions (Cancelli, 1985). RBPC items are not environmentally keyed. Therefore, casual observations by adults tangential to the referral, assessment, or intervention processes may not provide reliable and valid observations of student behavior. Also, guidelines are not provided to assist the observer in determining if the frequency of behavior is subsumed when rating the severity of behavior.

In summary, the RBPC has good internal consistency, cautiously acceptable reliability, and acceptable construct validity. The RBPC appears better at differentiating between normal and seriously disturbed students than among students typically found in special education classes. However, the major limitations of the RBPC are the lack of a well-defined normative sample, specifications for completing the checklist, and the specific contributions made by the minor scales. These limitations, while effecting the interpretation of the RBPC, fail to negate the four independent dimensions of behavior commonly associated with emotional disturbance. Further, the RBPC remains one of the more valid instruments for identifying students experiencing social-emotional disorders.

References

Achenbach, T. M., & Edelbrock, C. S. (1984). Psychopathology of childhood. *American Review of Psychology, 35,* 227-256.

Aman, M. G., & Werry, J. S. (1984). The Revised Behavior Problem Checklist in clinic attenders and non-attenders: Age and sex effects. *Journal of Clinical Child Psychology, 13,* 237-242.

Aman, M. G., Werry, J. S., Fitzpatrick, J., Lowe, M., & Waters, J. (1983). Factor structures and norms for the Revised Behavior Checklist in New Zealand children. *Australian and New Zealand Journal of Psychiatry, 17,* 345-360.

American Psychiatric Association. (1980). *Diagnostic and statistical manual of mental disorders* (3rd ed.). Washington, DC: Author.

Cancelli, A. A. (1985). Revised Behavior Problem Checklist. In J. V. Mitchell, Jr., (Ed.), *The ninth mental measurement yearbook* (pp. 1274-1276). Lincoln, NE: Buros Institute of Mental Measurements.

Lahey, B. B., & Piacentini, J. C. (1985). An evaluation of the Quay-Peterson Revised Behavior Problem Checklist. *Journal of School Psychology, 23,* 285-289.

Lahey, B. B., Schaughency, E. A., Frame, C. L., & Strauss, C. C. (1985). Teacher ratings of attention problems in children experimentally classified as exhibiting attention deficit disorders with and without hyperactivity. *Journal of the American Academy of Child Psychiatry, 24,* 613-616.

Lahey, B. B., Schaughency, E. A., Strauss, C. C., & Frame, C. L. (1984). Are attention deficit disorders with and without hyperactivity similar or dissimilar disorders? *Journal of the American Academy of Child Psychiatry, 23,* 302-309.

Peterson, D. R. (1961). Behavior problems in middle childhood. *Journal of Consulting Psychology, 25,* 205-209.

Quay, H. C. (1964). Dimensions of personality in delinquent boys as inferred from the factor analysis of behavior ratings. *Child Development, 35,* 477-484.

Quay, H. C. (1977). Measuring dimensions of deviant behavior: The Behavior Problem Checklist. *Journal of Abnormal Child Psychology, 5,* 277-287.

Quay, H. C. (1983). A dimensional approach to behavior disorder: The Revised Behavior Problem Checklist. *School Psychology Review, 12,* 244-249.

Quay, H. C., & Peterson, D. R. (1979). *Manual for the Behavior Problem Checklist.* (Available from Herbert C. Quay, Ph.D., P.O. Box 248074, Coral Gables, FL 33124)

Quay, H. C., & Peterson, D. R. (1983). *Interim manual for the Revised Behavior Problem Checklist.* (Available from Herbert C. Quay, Ph.D., P.O. Box 248074, Coral Gables, FL 33124)

Quay, H. C., & Peterson, D. R. (1984). *Appendix I for the interim manual for the Revised Behavior Problem Checklist.* (Available from Herbert C. Quay, Ph.D., P.O. Box 248074, Coral Gables, FL 33124)

Donald Mowrer, Ph.D.
Professor of Speech and Hearing Science, Arizona State University, Tempe, Arizona.

RILEY ARTICULATION AND LANGUAGE TEST: REVISED
Glyndon D. Riley. Los Angeles, California: Western Psychological Services.

Introduction

The purpose of the Riley Articulation and Language Test (RALT) is to facilitate screening articulation and language skills of children ages 4 through 7. Two scores are obtained, allowing the examiner to evaluate articulation and language skills according to norms provided. A diagnostic examination is recommended for those who fail any part of this test.

The author, Dr. Glyndon D. Riley, has published several articles about testing children but has focused more on diagnosis of stuttering behaviors than on articulation and language development (Riley, 1972; Riley & Riley, 1979, 1980). Aside from an instrument designed to measure stuttering behavior, Riley also developed a Motor Problems Inventory published in 1971.

The first report concerning the RALT was presented as a paper at an American Speech and Hearing Association convention (Riley, 1965), followed by the published test (Riley, 1966) and a revision five years later (Riley, 1971). An evaluation of the revised edition was written by O'Toole (1979), which includes a language proficiency measure and an intelligibility estimate not included with the first instrument. Also, the first-grade sample population has been expanded, but standardization data are still interpolated from adjacent age subgroups. The revised edition includes norms for a Head Start population (age 4) not referenced in the original test.

Norms were derived for males and females in two socioeconomic groups, low and mid levels, but these levels are not defined. The normative population included 332 children from kindergarten, 74 from first grade, and 67 from second grade. Norms are not provided for Head Start children. Norms include median scores and a cutoff score for the lowest 10% in each group studied. The range of cell size is from 10 to 100 children. No norms are provided for boys or girls in first grade who make up the middle socioeconomic group.

The test consists of a 5-page manual and a 4-page test booklet. No pictures or other stimulus materials are needed. The examiner evokes speech responses by asking the child questions or requiring imitative vocal responses. Children are tested individually by an examiner, who should have sufficient knowledge of phonetics to be able to distinguish among sound substitutions, distortions, and omissions in the initial and final positions of words. While practically no skilled knowledge of language development or analysis is required to administer the language test, special training would be required to interpret the results.

Three subtests are included: 1) a language proficiency and intelligibility test, 2) an articulation profile, and 3) a language profile. The first subtest consists of a subjective evaluation (normal, somewhat abnormal, and severely abnormal) of the child's ability to use language and follow verbal instructions. The child is asked to tell a story or to answer simple questions to determine if he or she can be understood. The child is given instructions to see how well he or she can follow verbal commands. A simple score is obtained, but norms are not provided because the intent is to make only a gross judgment about language reception and production.

The second subtest, Articulation Function, requires the child to repeat each of the following words: *shoe, fish, this, smooth, rabbit, car, sun,* and *bus*. Four phonemes are tested (ʃ, ð, r, s) in the initial and final positions. These phonemes were selected to represent articulation proficiency, because most children who misarticulate these sounds were found by the author to be in need of speech therapy. If the child misarticulates the sound in one position but not the other, less points are deducted. If the child can be stimulated to produce the misarticulated sound correctly, less points are deducted. Finally, if a sound is distorted rather than substituted or omitted (except for /ð/), less points are deducted. Consequently, an attempt is made to take consistency of error, stimulatability, and type of error into account in weighting scores of each misarticulation. An articulation loss score is derived by subtracting the total loss scores from 100 to produce the functional articulation score.

Language Function, the third subtest, consists of six sentences, each more complex than the previous one. The child is allowed two additional tries to repeat each sentence if the first attempt is incorrect. No points are deducted if the first response is correct; however, points are deducted for incorrect subsequent tries. A functional loss score is derived by subtracting this score from 100.

Practical Applications/Uses

The chief value of the RALT is that it allows the professional to determine the adequacy of a child's articulation and language skills in a short time. It could be used as a means of sorting those whose articulation and language skills are within a normal range from those whose skill level is below the norm. Results could determine whether a communication problem is present and, if so, establish some degree of severity. Results could also help determine which children should receive additional speech testing. After all, this is the basic function of a screening device. The examiner must be somewhat skilled in making judgments about language ability and analysis of sound errors. Consequently, this reviewer would feel uncomfortable with anyone except a speech/language pathologist administering this test. The directions are easy to follow, but the skills needed to evaluate verbal responses are somewhat complex. Nowhere in the test is it suggested that anyone except a speech/language pathologist administer and score the test. Obviously, the RALT is designed to be used with children who are entering a school environment.

The test was designed to be given to lower and middle socioeconomic groups. No mention is made of the test's use with special populations such as the blind, hearing handicapped, bilingual, mentally handicapped, and so on. Also, no mention is made of allowances for dialects, deprived environments, or other handicapping conditions. Using the scoring system provided by the author, individuals with handicapping conditions may be penalized unjustly. Evidently the author's intent was to design a test to be used with the majority of the population that most speech/language pathologists encounter in the public schools.

The setting for test administration could be in a classroom under quiet conditions, but ideally children should be tested in separate rooms where noise is not a factor. The manual is clearly written and the answer form is easy to follow, giving the examiner ample space to record test results. No other materials are needed; the examiner only needs a supply of record forms to administer the test (after reading the manual, of course).

Scoring is simple, as is comparing the resultant scores with articulation and language function norms. Cutoff scores allow the examiner to determine quickly whether a child passes or fails the test. The author suggests that results of the test can provide indications of central nervous system damage, mental retardation, or physical anomalies. Frankly, this reviewer feels screening tests like this one tell us only one thing—whether the individual has a speech problem. Any judgment beyond this simple conclusion seems to me to be unwarranted.

Technical Aspects

Unfortunately, no data are presented regarding the exact ages or geographic and ethnic background of the population on which this test was standardized. Therefore, the normative data are limited in their usage. The author refers to two studies that were conducted to establish reliability of the RALT, one of 76 preschool children (presumably enrolled in Head Start programs), the other of 41 second-grade children. A correlation of .81 was obtained on test-retest reliability in the first study; the second study, which investigated interexaminer reliability, demonstrated adequate clinical reliability. In a third study cited by the author, the Templin-Darley Test identified 10 out of 29 mentally handicapped children as being in need of retesting while the RALT identified 13, resulting in a correlation of .75. Finally, the RALT was compared with teacher judgments about children in need of language therapy. The correlation in this case was .65. Evidently none of these studies were published and no statements are made regarding who conducted the studies or what controls were used. Reliability and validity information concerning this test appears to be weak at best.

Critique

The basic rationale Riley used to score articulation responses appears to be valid. She took into account many important factors used in rating severity of articulation disorders (type of error, consistency, developmental factors, etc.) to derive score loadings. This is a difficult task, considering only four sounds are tested. The rationale used to evaluate language responses is not so complete, given what we know about language today. More than any other factor, the language evaluation section dates this test by nearly two decades.

As screening tests go, the RALT appears to be a useful test for the speech/language pathologist who wishes to determine quickly which children are in need of further testing. It was not intended to be used as a diagnostic tool. The test's weakest point lies in the normative data provided, which gives the examiner little valuable information. O'Toole (1979) concluded that the RALT's biggest drawback was that it provided the speech/language pathologist with little information to aid in writing Individual Education Plans, whereas other screening tests (e.g., the McDonald Deep Test of Articulation, the Goldman-Fristoe Test of Articulation) provide more useful information. Nevertheless, as a screening test the RALT appears to provide the professional with a quick means of sorting two populations: those who most likely will have an articulation or language problem, and those whose speech skills are probably adequate as long as one is working with non-minority groups.

References

O'Toole, T. (1979). The Riley Articulation and Language Test (RALT). In F. L. Darley (Ed.), *Evaluation of appraisal techniques in speech and language pathology.* Reading, MA: Addison-Wesley.

Riley, G. D. (1965, October). *Construction and standardization of a quick screening test.* Paper presented at the meeting of the American Speech and Hearing Association, Chicago.

Riley, G. D. (1966). *The Riley Articulation and Language Test.* Los Angeles: Western Psychological Services.

Riley, G. D. (1971). *The Riley Articulation and Language Test: Revised.* Los Angeles: Western Psychological Services.

Riley, G. D. (1971). *Motor Problems Inventory.* Los Angeles: Western Psychological Services.

Riley, G. D. (1972). A stuttering severity instrument for children and adults. *Journal of Speech and Hearing Disorders, 37,* 314-322.

Riley, G. D., & Riley, J. (1979). A component model for diagnosing and treating children who stutter. *Journal of Fluency Disorders, 4,* 279-293.

Riley, G. D., & Riley, J. (1980). Motoric and linguistic variables among children who stutter: A factor analysis. *Journal of Speech and Hearing Disorders, 45,* 504-514.

Russell H. Lord, Ed.D.
Associate Professor of Educational Psychology, Eastern Montana College, Billings, Montana.

RILEY MOTOR PROBLEMS INVENTORY
Glyndon D. Riley. Los Angeles, California: Western Psychological Services.

Introduction

The stated goal of the Riley Motor Problems Inventory (RMPI) is to provide "a quantified system of observation of neurological signs from which . . . nonmedical personnel can (1) decide on the need for referral and (2) measure the motor component as a factor in any related syndrome" (Riley, 1980, p. 1). In the author's view, a " 'motor factor' has been noted by clinicians in children with speech, reading, and learning disorders and seems to have become a recurring theme" (p. 1). The RMPI is meant to serve as a screening device in early selection decisions identifying children who might need more thorough and sophisticated examination by more highly trained personnel. Though designed to serve both clinical and research purposes, the RMPI's primary emphasis certainly seems to be in the service of clinical decision-making.

The RMPI was developed by Glyndon D. Riley and was published by Western Psychological Services in 1972 as the Motor Problems Inventory. Although the test manual shows both an original 1972 copyright and a 1976 revision (with a third printing in February, 1980), a master's thesis by J. Riley (1971) used a Motor Problems Inventory in studying children who stuttered, and a 1980 article by Riley and Riley used and cited a 1971 Motor Problems Inventory by G. Riley and published by Western Psychological Services. The test manual makes reference to a 1967 experimental form, but lack of a citation makes examination of that form unlikely. Some confusion thus exists about the exact history of the RMPI.

Items included on the RMPI were selected from among the numerous procedures typically used "by speech and language pathologists and the routine neurological examination" (p. 1). All of these tasks were selected according to the criteria of being "simple enough for general use," involving "readily observable" abnormal responses, and having been "a part of some traditional examining procedure" (p. 1). There are three speech and language tasks, three fine motor tasks, and four gross motor tasks.

The 1980 manual does not discuss any updating of the normative base, any of the changes implemented in the revision, any reasons for the revision, nor any alternative forms of the test. Evidently, however, some revision occurred, for the manual refers to scores from the Small Muscle Coordination, Laterality, and General sections, but present normative data exist only for Oral, Fine Motor, and Gross Motor subtests.

Ten motor tasks, each accompanied by a checklist representing deviation from "normal performance," comprise the RMPI. Because the RMPI is intended to screen for additional examination, the tasks are relatively easy and a normal child should encounter little difficulty accomplishing them. The tasks and their accompanying checklists are printed together on the back of the Record Form, which is used to administer, score, and interpret the RMPI. The front of the Record From provides the examiner with the summary of scores procedures along with the normative data used to interpret the results of the RMPI. The author states that the normative data (which do not extend beyond eight-year-old respondents) can be used for older children and even adults (p. 4). He states on the same page that, although children under age four should not have their performances scored, "an experienced clinician can detect the difference between normal and abnormal performance" (again without the benefit of normative data). The one-page Record Form is quite clear and easy to use, making the scoring and interpretation straightforward and uncomplicated.

The three Oral Motor Tasks include two oral tasks (one requiring the rapid repetition of a single syllable and a second that requires repeating a trio of syllables) and one that involves rapid, alternating, lateral movements of the respondent's protruded tongue. The Fine Motor Tasks require the child to complete three different activities. The first involves having the child look through a hole in a piece of paper and then play catch with paper that has been wadded up, and the second and third both assess finger dexterity and coordination. The Gross Motor Tasks subtest consists of four activities: bilateral hand/arm movement, a hopping task, a balancing activity, and whole body movement in walking/running/skipping. For each of these, the examiner must observe carefully in order to complete each task's checklist correctly.

Practical Applications/Uses

As stated in the manual, the RMPI is intended to identify children who exhibit "the so-called 'soft' neurological signs" (p. 4) by providing the previously cited "quantified system of observation of neurological signs from which speech pathologists, psychologists, learning specialists, and other nonmedical personnel can (1) decide on the need for referral and (2) measure the motor component as a factor in any related syndrome." The RMPI is intended to differentiate children whose overall speech difficulties are independent of motor dysfunction from children having a "significant motor component participating in the overall syndrome" (p. 4). In fact, the manual states that "the major purpose it has served is to help determine the extent to which a given speech or language disorder . . . includes a motor component" (p. 5). The author also states that high scores on the RMPI are useful in differentiating between neurogenic and psychogenic disorders (p. 4).

The intended settings for the RMPI are those in which clinicians are working with "children with speech, reading, and learning disorders" (p. 1). Indeed, the manual states (p. 5) that the RMPI has been used "routinely by several school districts," "in several Head Start projects," "by many college clinics, hospitals, and public school speech clinicians," and "as a screening instrument for children being considered for special education classes"—but no specific references are cited for the reader/user to check. These examples would seem to establish reasonable parameters for applications of the RMPI, in terms of settings as well as subjects for whom it might prove useful.

Administration of the RMPI requires no unusual equipment—only an appropriate testing area large enough for performance of the large motor tasks, table and chairs, several sheets of unlined paper, crayon or pencil (depending upon the child's age), a watch readable in seconds, and the RMPI Record Form. The entire exam generally is completed in 10 minutes or less, and scoring is straightforward and quickly completed.

Examiners using the RMPI are expected to be "trained personnel in the several disciplines concerned" (p. 1), which is further delineated only by references to "speech pathologists," "psychologists," "learning specialists," and "other nonmedical personnel." Given that "the results should be analyzed qualitatively as well as quantitatively" (p. 5), it seems unreasonable to expect that persons lacking rather extensive training in the neurological aspects of speech could interpret the RMPI accurately.

Scoring is virtually included in the administration procedures, for the examiner is directed to circle appropriate items on the checklist accompanying each task as the item is performed by the subject. Transcription of the circled numbers to the appropriate places on the Record Form is straightforward and free from any likelihood of errors. Machine or computer scoring is not discussed, and seem quite unnecessary, given the simplicity of the Record Form.

Interpretation should, it seems, be consistent with the intent to provide a quantified assessment system, but the later requirement of qualitative analysis complicates the process. The normative data provide Median, 10%, and 2% categories for each of the three subtests (Oral, Fine Motor, and Gross Motor). These categories are used to distinguish the normal child (Median) from the child having "relevant" motor component involvement in his or her speech difficulty. Children whose performance places them at the 10% (10 out of 100) cutoff are to be referred for further testing, while those at the 2% (2 out of 100) "are almost certain" to have motor problems affecting their speech problems. Interpretation following these established cutoffs seems to be clear enough so that any personnel justifiably using the RMPI should have no difficulty interpreting the results. The "qualitative" analysis mentioned in the manual, however, could cause problems for examiners attempting diagnosis and inference beyond their expertise.

Technical Aspects

Having been available since 1967 in one form or another, the RMPI should have much more substantial reliability, validity, and normative data than it does. In one of the revisions, it seems that at least some additional technical data would have been gathered, analyzed, and reported, but apparently they were not.

Test-retest reliability, which yields a measure of the degree to which any test measures consistently from one time to another with the same respondents, is reported as .77 on a clinic population of 24 children. Interscorer reliability, or the extent to which different scorers produce similar judgments based on the same respondent behaviors, is reported as .91. Both of these statistical values have a maximum value of 1.0, so they seem quite high. However, the interscorer figure was based on only 15 clinicians rating the RMPI responses of only five children; in such small samples, extreme values can occur more easily than in larger samples (Kerlinger, 1986). Additionally, the test-retest figure of .77, based upon the "same clinic population of 24 children" (p. 6) who were used in one of the validity studies reported, is considerably lower than the figures generally recommended as as minimal (.90 and .95 respectively) for making decisions affecting individuals (Anastasi, 1982; Kaplan & Saccuzzo, 1982). These are the only reliability data provided in the manual, and seem too few for the long time the RMPI has been available.

Validity, or the extent to which a test can reasonably be expected to accomplish the task its user claims it accomplishes, is predicated upon though not guaranteed by reliability. Three validity studies are reported in the manual, but none of them are referenced for the potential user to evaluate prior to use. The factor analysis study discussed in the manual compared MPI (apparently the earlier version of the RMPI) data with other measures of neurological impairment. Not knowing when these data were collected is a major concern in view of the rapid increase in knowledge and techniques relevant to neuropsychology during the last ten years. Additionally, because a large number of diverse procedures are subsumed under the generic name "factor analysis" (the manual tells nothing about the procedures used), such information really tells nothing certain about RMPI validity. The second reported validity study found the "Small Muscle Coordination, Laterality, and General sections" (p. 6) of the RMPI to be correlated with the Bender-Gestalt (a long-standing test of perceptual motor integrity). This reviewer did not find these subtests listed or explained in the manual, and hence is quite uncertain about the value of this validity study. The third study reported a statistically significant correlation between RMPI results and the "organic signs" (p. 6) of the Human Figure Drawing Test for 24 children, aged five to 11. However, no mention is made as to whether the scorers were "blind" as they scored the two tests or whether these 24 children were the same sample used to establish RMPI reliability—both of which raise serious questions as to the confidence one should place in these data.

The research populations are unknown, even to the number of subjects included in the major study (factor analysis). With 149 measures, however, the number of subjects should have been very large just to meet the criteria for using factor analytic procedures. The characteristics of the subjects used for validity data and norms must be made available to potential test users so that they can judge the appropriateness of the test instrument for use with their intended subjects.

Operating in support of the RMPI is the fact that its items were selected from traditional examination procedures (Beaumont, 1983; Golden, 1981). This gives the test a sound, rational basis for validity, but, in this case, that basis is not supported by the additional empirical data that are absolutely crucial.

The reliability and validity data provided in the manual raise at least as many questions as they answer and are not as substantial as they should be, given both the length of time the RMPI has been available and the decisions an examiner might make with it. With its current technical data base, the examiner must proceed cautiously in terms of decisions based on RMPI results.

Critique

When used with children already experiencing speech/language difficulties in order to determine "which . . . need further evaluation of their neurological integrity" (p. 5), the RMPI possesses "some of the attributes of a good screening device" (Chissom, 1978, p. 1430). It has an acceptable rational basis, as its items come from already established examination procedures and its directions, administration and scoring procedures, Record Form, and guidelines for interpretation are clearly stated and easy to follow.

Several of its author's claims, however, are overstated and lack supportive documentation, which is a concern. It is especially troubling that norms are not provided for certain age groups claimed to be appropriately assessed by the RMPI. It is also troubling when claims such as the following are made without documentation: "High scores on the RMPI are usually associated with the so-called 'soft' neurological signs and thus are useful in differentiating between neurogenic and psychogenic disorders" (Riley, 1980, p. 4). Such assertions, when made without sufficient supportive references, should cause serious concern on the part of any careful examiner. Many uses in different settings are claimed, but again, there are no substantiating references to allow the careful examiner to evaluate such uses for him- or herself. Along with these problems, there is a definite deficiency in the reliability and validity data provided. Not only is there the previously mentioned lack of published reports, but what is presented in the manual is insufficient.

In summary, this reviewer would recommend caution in using the RMPI for diagnoses, educational placements, or similar purposes. Although it does possess the clarity, simplicity of administration/scoring/interpretation, and inexpensive costs desirable in a screening instrument, the RMPI lacks sufficient technical strength to justify significant decisions on its data alone.

References

This list includes text citations and suggested additional reading.

Anastasi, A. (1982). *Psychological testing* (5th ed.). New York: Macmillan Publishing Co.
Beaumont, J. G. (1983). *Introduction to neuropsychology.* New York: The Guilford Press.
Chissom, B. S. (1978). Motor Problems Inventory. In O. K. Buros (Ed.), *The eighth mental measurements yearbook* (pp. 1412-1413). Highland Park, NJ: The Gryphon Press.
Filskov, S. B., & Boll, T. J. (Eds.). (1981). *Handbook of clinical neuropsychology.* New York: John Wiley & Sons.
Gaddes, W. H. (1980). *Learning disabilities and brain function: A neuropsychological approach.* New York: Springer-Verlag.
Golden, C. J. (1981). *Diagnosis and rehabilitation in clinical neuropsychology* (2nd ed.). Springfield, IL: Charles C. Thomas.
Kaplan, R. M., & Saccuzzo, D. P. (1982). *Psychological testing: Principles, applications, and issues.* Monterey, CA: Brooks/Cole.
Kerlinger, F. N. (1986). *Foundations of behavioral research* (3rd ed.). New York: Holt, Rinehart, & Winston.
Lezak, M. D. (1976). *Neuropsychological assessment.* New York: Oxford University Press.

Riley, J. (1971). *Language profiles of thirty-nine children who stutter grouped by performance on a Motor Problems Inventory*. Unpublished master's thesis, California State University-Fullerton.

Riley, G. D. (1980). *Riley Motor Problems Inventory manual* (revised 1976). Los Angeles: Western Psychological Services.

Riley, G. D., & Riley, J. (1980). Motoric and linguistic variables among children who stutter: A factor analysis. *Journal of Speech and Hearing Disorders, 30,* 504-513.

Allan L. LaVoie, Ph.D.
Professor of Psychology, Davis & Elkins College, Elkins, West Virginia.

ROSENZWEIG PICTURE-FRUSTRATION STUDY
Saul Rosenzweig. Odessa, Florida: Psychological Assessment Resources, Inc.

Introduction

The Rosenzweig Picture-Frustration Study (P-FS; Rosenzweig, 1978d) or, by its full name, the Rosenzweig Picture-Association Method for Assessing Reactions to Frustration (Rosenzweig, 1981d), has the character of a limited-domain projective test. Guttman (1973) describes it as a structured projective test that yields scores on several dimensions of frustration tolerance and aggression. It may be used with individuals or with groups, and the style of testing is response completion. More simply, it is referred to as a semiprojective test in recognition of the fact that only frustration responses are measured in very specific circumstances.

The P-FS attempts to measure a person's reactions to visually presented situations that most people would consider frustrating (e.g., missing a train or being splashed by mud). In addition to the visual stimulus, there is a verbal comment by one of the figures portrayed, then the examinee responds verbally for the other person in the scene. The verbal reactions are scored in a variety of ways, including the direction of aggression: extraggressive, intraggressive, or imaggressive (i.e., minimizing the frustrating aspect of the situation); and the type of aggression: obstacle-dominance (in which the frustrating obstacle is the focus of the reaction), etho-defense (in which the aim is to defend or maintain the self), and need-persistence (in which a solution to the frustration is sought). The three directions of aggression, when crossed by the three types of aggression, produce nine "factors" (Rosenzweig, 1978d) that can be scored. As an example of a factor, consider a response that is intraggressive and etho-defensive; the manual calls this factor Intropunitive (p. 5). In addition to these nine factors, there are two variant factors involving denial. Other scores include the Group Conformity Rating, which provides a measure of normal or typical responding to frustration, and various trend and pattern scores.

A major difficulty with all of the scores has to do with what Rosenzweig (1978d, p. 34) calls levels of response. As with any other projective device, the examiner assumes that the person taking the test identifies with the frustrated individual and responds from some deep level of personal organization. No measure of depth of response exists for the P-FS. The examinees may be giving shallow, socially desirable answers, or answers based on what they have observed in other people. In the former instance, which seems plausible given the results of Govia and Velicer (1985), a large part of the P-FS could be replaced with a series of direct questions. Rosenzweig (1978d, p. 17) provides for an Inquiry following the test, partly to estimate the level of responding and partly to disambiguate questionable responses, but the Inquiry is rarely performed in the published studies and would at best be a rough guide to degree of projection or level of consciousness.

Saul Rosenzweig, born in 1907, is Emeritus Professor at Washington University in St. Louis. He received his degrees from Harvard University and has spent his career at the Harvard Psychological Clinic, Worcester State Hospital (where his name was associated with the Tautometer), Western State Psychiatric Institute, and finally at Washington University. His biography indicates 180 published works in areas ranging from the history of medical psychology to experimental psychodynamics. His earlier research, influenced by psychoanalysis, attempted to confirm in the laboratory Freud's ideas about repression. This led to his work on aggression as a topic relevant to psychoanalysis and capable of being realistically studied in the laboratory.

The P-FS was created in the 1930s as part of a battery of tests of aggression that included a behavioral test, two multiple-choice tests of real and ideal reactions to frustration, and the precursor to the present test. The other parts of the battery did not stand up to empirical investigation (Rosenzweig, 1978b). These other early tests tended to produce more stereotyped responses with little variation among individuals, though as Bjerstedt (1965) notes, keeping them in the battery might have helped with the problem of differentiating levels of response by providing an index of conscious responding.

The current adult form was copyrighted in 1964 and consists of items unchanged from the 1945 test description. The 24 items are now in their fifth decade and show some signs of age, particularly in the clothing styles and automobiles that are depicted in the cartoons. Each item consists of a crudely drawn cartoon showing a frustrating situation. The box over the speaker on the left carries the verbal cue to which the examinee responds by writing in the empty box over the frustrated figure on the right. Scoring the written responses is conducted via comparison with a large sample of responses to each cartoon contained in the supplemental manuals for adults, adolescents, and children (Rosenzweig, 1978a, 1981a, 1981b).

Along with the test form, one receives a scoring blank on which individual item scores are entered. From the item scores one can compile the conformity score, trend scores, factor scores, and so on. Few articles in the recent literature use anything but category or factor scores, but for idiodynamic purposes the detailed scoring blank would be useful.

The Children's Form has been designed for use with examinees in the age range from 4 to 13 years. The Adolescent Form is used in the age range from 12 to 19 years, and may also, "with the necessary precautions, be employed as parallel" to the Adult Form (Rosenzweig, 1981a, p. 4).

The P-FS has been adapted, translated, and/or standardized for use in French, German, Hindi, Italian, Japanese, Portuguese, Spanish, and Swedish. Pirated versions are available in Chinese, Finnish, Polish, and Russian, but Rosenzweig reports that they "are unsuited to cross-cultural research on a comparable basis" (1981d, p. 122).

Practical Applications/Uses

A large variety of applications for this instrument have shown up in the literature. The P-FS may be used to measure changes in frustration states, typical reactions to frustration, changes in frustration tolerance due to therapy, developmental trends in reactions to and tolerance of frustration, and cultural influences on expressions of frustration. Clinically it may be used in conjunction with other assessment tools to investigate the idiodynamics of an individual, but the reliabilities of the scores are too low to permit accurate individual interpretations without corroborating evidence (see Bjerstedt, 1965). With skillful inquiry and cooperative examinees, the P-FS can yield information about degree of self-conscious frustration levels, about defense mechanisms and, of course, about relative strengths of id, ego, and superego.

Recently published applications also cover a large number of topics. Using the P-FS, Weinstein and deMan (1982) measured the effects of a vegetarian diet versus a diet including meat on frustration levels. Several investigators have used the P-FS to study effects of abuse on children (Kinard, 1982a, 1982b; Straker & Jacobson, 1981) and to study the personalities of the abusing parents (Tsiantis, Kokkevi, & Agathanos-Marouli, 1981; Wright, 1976). White (1975) and Govia and Velicer (1985) used the P-FS as a criterion against which to judge the performance of other measures of aggressive reactions. Benton, Kumari, and Brain (1982) used the P-FS to confirm the hypothesis that aggressiveness and hypoglycemia are interrelated, while in similar work Perini, Rauchfleisch, and Bühler (1985) found that the P-FS could help to identify types of hypertension. Other recent work examined the effects of video games on aggressive ideation (Graybill, Kirsch, & Esselman, 1985), the effects of long-term intensive coaching on aggressiveness in sports-gifted children (Raviv, 1980), and the recidivism rates of youthful offenders (Spellacy & Brown, 1984).

An original purpose of the test was to provide the means to validate the theory of frustration Rosenzweig has been developing for 50 years (see, e.g., Rosenzweig, 1981c). That purpose may still be served by the P-FS. Other experimental purposes may also be well served; for example, the test could be used as a manipulation check, to create individual difference variables, to provide the dependent variable, or to serve as an independent criterion measure.

The most common published procedure for administering the P-FS Adult Form has been in groups without Inquiry. The administrator reads the directions as the examinees follow in their booklets. Each person works independently until, when finished, the booklet is turned in. The examiner notes the total time to completion, as very slow or very fast times may indicate considerable conflict and defensiveness. Response times for each item would seem to be more useful information for this purpose, especially when the P-FS is used idiodynamically (see Challman, 1953; Bjerstedt, 1965), but that information is not collected. Total time in this reviewer's experience varies from 5 minutes to about 20 minutes. If the administrator must read the captions and record the answers, as with young children, more time will be necessary.

The scoring tends to be very straightforward, because no deep or subtle interpretations are necessary. Once the supplemental manuals have been studied and the various scoring categories and factors committed to memory, scoring consists of comparing an answer with the samples given. For experienced scorers, a scoring blank can be completed in 10-15 minutes. Occasionally one will find an unscorable answer, particularly if no Inquiry had been conducted. One answer may also be scored on two factors.

Only the Inquiry requires a skilled examiner; otherwise, the test can be administered by a clerical worker. The Inquiry begins when the examinee is asked to read aloud each answer so that hidden meanings can be detected, perhaps through the use of irony or sarcasm. The examiner may ask what the person had in mind when that answer was written, or whether such a thing had ever happened personally, in an effort to find what level of projection was operating. The manuals contain no guides or sample answers to assist interpretation of levels, and at best the whole procedure is a dubious, post facto method for gleaning a little extra information. Incidentally, while the cartoons are crudely drawn to facilitate identification with the frustrated figure, some examinees may make it clear during Inquiry that they are answering as they think the cartoon figure would, and not as they would. One example, of a response by a 10-year-old girl on Children's Form item #4: "He is a nasty boy, and he said, 'You're lying, you could if you wanted to.'" No provision is made to score her response differently than if she had spoken for herself.

Alternative scoring systems have been used. To illustrate briefly, Kinard (1982a) scored the cartoons with adult-child interactions separately from the child-child cartoons and found different scores with a sample of abused children. Bjerstedt (1965), who has noted several discrepancies in the test forms, such as unequal representation of sex roles, has suggested other procedures, including the use of intensity ratings, scoring separately ego versus superego blocking items, and scoring male frustrator items separately from female frustrator items. Very little systematic research has been published that deals with different administrative and scoring procedures.

Norms are available for either the category scores, such as Extraggression, or for factor scores, such as the earlier example of Intropunitive. The supplemental manuals report them as means and standard deviations for various age groups. Only the young adult samples are adequate, as the samples are too small for most other age groups. For the range from 50 to 80 years, the mean is based on only 79 subjects. There are only 36 children ages 4 and 5, and only 23 ages 6 and 7. As these clearly provide no useful normative information, local norms would have to be established or the literature wold have to be exhaustively surveyed to find enough comparison data (e.g., with abused children).

The Group Conformity Rating (GCR), expressed as a percentage of stereotyped responding, provides a rough measure of socialization. The total pattern of the GCR (i.e., the normal test pattern) is in the first place Extrapunitive, in which blame or hostility is turned onto the other person, and in the second place Impunitive, in which blame for the frustration is evaded (Rosenzweig, 1978d). It seems odd that the norm against which to judge socialization should consist of such behaviors. But as the norms for the GCR are also small, too much importance should not be attached to it.

Given the difficult problem of levels of projection and the serious shortcoming of too-small norm samples, scores ought to be considered very carefully in the light of all other information available.

Technical Aspects

Some controversy surrounds the reliability of the P-FS. When assessed with the standard technique of split-halves, the various scores tend to be unacceptably inconsistent. Rosenzweig (1978c) has even reported negative correlations between the halves of Obstacle-Dominance on the Children's Form. On the Adult Form with female subjects, Rosenzweig, Ludwig, and Adelman (1975) report that the halves of the Intraggression scale correlate -.47 and the halves of the Need-Persistence scale correlate -.04. In the latter study, the average split-half reliability was .32 for males and females combined. The comparable figure for the Children's Form was .43 (Rosenzweig, 1978c).

Rosenzweig correctly maintains that the standards for projective techniques are different than for objective tests (e.g., Rosenzweig, Ludwig, & Adelman, 1975). After all, the point of ambiguous items is to call out from a person a variety of impulses. There are other solutions to this problem, however, such as that of Wagner, Alexander, Roos, and Prospero (1985) to maximize split-half coefficients, or perhaps to score in the split-halves only those items with high frequencies for a particular category. With psychometrically guided item selection the internal consistencies could certainly be increased with probably no reduction in validity. There is other evidence that item-level work ought to be carried out with the P-FS. For example, items 7, 9, 13, 14, 15, 18, 20, and 24 show no Intropeditive (Intraggression by Obstacle-Dominance) samples in the Adult Form Supplement (Rosenzweig, 1978a). Clarke, Rosenzweig, and Fleming (1947) report that four items, even after two revisions of the scoring samples and with highly trained scorers, produced interscorer disagreement at least 20% of the time (items 8, 12, 16, and 17). The GCR, the closest thing to an objective test, also suffers from low consistency, with averages around .30 to .40.

On the other hand, both interrater agreement and test-retest stability tend to be better than average. With some exceptions (e.g., Govia & Velicer, 1985), interrater agreement ranges from 75% to 85%. Test-retest stability seems to average about .5 for children and adults (see Rosenzweig, 1978c; Rosenzweig, Ludwig, & Adelman, 1975). Both sets of values are very acceptable.

Validity has been even more difficult to evaluate conclusively. Rosenzweig and Adelman (1977) argue persuasively that construct validity must be the ultimate yardstick for the P-FS. They summarize evidence showing regular developmental patterns, score responsiveness to frustrating conditions, and so on (see also Pareek, 1964; Rosenzweig, 1981d; Rosenzweig & Rosenzweig, 1976). That evidence does not of itself convince. There are a number of negative reports in the literature (i.e., failures of prediction) such as Lester (1970), Spellacy and Brown (1984), and Straker and Jacobson (1981), to name a few. Even some of the supportive studies contain disquieting notes. Govia and Velicer (1985) found a significant negative correlation between social desirability scores and Extraggression, and a significant positive correlation between social desirability and Imaggression. Perhaps in this study respondents were answering at a conscious level. Wright (1976) noted that parents who batter their children score higher on Imaggression, higher on the GCR, and lower on Extraggression, again suggesting a pattern of conscious impression management. Perini, Rauchfleisch, and Buhler (1985) demonstrated relationships between pattern of hypertension and some of the P-FS scores, but 13 of 16 relevant comparisons were nonsignificant. Coché and Meehan (1979) found that the various scoring categories did not align themselves into independent factors. Finally, Winefield (1981) reports that under increasing stress her subjects showed a reduction in Extraggression compared to control subjects, a finding that might more easily be rationalized if it had turned out the other direction.

To summarize the validity studies, the case is the same as noted by Bjerstedt (1965) more than two decades ago: there are promising results and unexpected inconsistencies. Obviously, more research must be performed to decide the question more definitively, but the research should be concerned with the difficulties noted earlier regarding level of projection, size of norm samples, and inconsistent items.

Critique

With more than 500 published studies in the P-FS bibliography, one could reasonably have expected a clearer answer to the question of how good a test it was. To summarize the foregoing material, the Rosenzweig Picture-Frustration Study has adequate reliability though low item consistency, promising but not certain construct validity, and regrettable problems. Some of these problems, clearly identified by Bjerstedt (1965), could have been and should have been remedied long ago. The norms are not useful as they exist in the manuals, the items have problems from logical and empirical viewpoints, and no solution has been found to the problem of identifying at what level of consciousness the examinee has been responding. At least two of these problems have been addressed in foreign adaptations (see Perini, Rauchfleisch, & Buhler, 1985).

Should one use the P-FS? According to its author (S. Rosenzweig, personal communication, June 22, 1986), millions of copies of the test have been sold during the past 30 years, so at least some professionals believe the answer is yes, though Lubin, Larsen, and Matarazzo (1984) don't list it among the 30 most commonly used psychological tests in this country. If you have a need for a test that will allow you to explore an individual's reactions to frustrating situations and are not bothered by the problems mentioned, the P-FS can lead to interesting results. And if you are interested in a tool that can add information to what you know from other assessment procedures, again the P-FS deserves serious attention. It cannot obtain definitive information about an individual and one should not try to use it for that purpose. For experimental applications it merits attention, and if one is interested in working to update and improve the P-FS, it should prove very rewarding. This reviewer believes it could easily become a very effective and widely used test.

References

Benton, D., Kumari, N., & Brian, P. F. (1982). Mild hypoglycemia and questionnaire measures of aggression. *Biological Psychology, 14,* 129-135.

Bjerstedt, A. (1965). Rosenzweig Picture-Frustration Study. In O. K. Buros (Ed.), *The sixth mental measurements yearbook* (pp. 511-515). Highland Park, NJ: The Gryphon Press.

Challman, R. C. (1953). Rosenzweig Picture-Frustration Study. In O. K. Buros (Ed.), *The fourth mental measurements yearbook* (pp. 240-242). Highland Park, NJ: The Gryphon Press.

Clarke, H. J., Rosenzweig, S., & Fleming, E. E. (1947). The reliability of the scoring of the Rosenzweig Picture-Frustration Study. *Journal of Clinical Psychology, 3,* 364-370.

Coché, E., & Meehan, J. (1979). Factor and cluster analyses with the Rosenzweig Picture-Frustration Study. *Journal of Personality Assessment, 43,* 39-44.

Govia, J. M., & Velicer, W. F. (1985). Comparison of multidimensional measures of aggression. *Psychological Reports, 57,* 207-215.

Graybill, D., Kirsch, J. R., & Esselman, E. D. (1985). Effects of playing violent versus nonviolent video games on the aggressive ideation of aggressive and nonaggressive children. *Child Study Journal, 15,* 199-205.

Guttman, L. (1973). A partial-order scalogram classification of projective techniques. In M. Hammer, K. Salzinger, & S. Sutton, (Eds.), *Psychopathology* (pp. 481-490). New York: Wiley.

Kinard, E. M. (1982a). Aggression in abused children: Differential response to the Rosenzweig Picture-Frustration Study. *Journal of Personality Assessment, 46,* 139-141.

Kinard, E. M. (1982b). Experiencing child abuse: Effects on emotional adjustment. *American Journal of Orthopsychiatry, 52,* 82-91.

Lester, D. (1970). Attempts to predict suicidal risk using psychological tests. *Psychological Bulletin, 74,* 1-17.

Lubin, B., Larsen, R. M., & Matarazzo, J. D. (1984). Patterns of psychological test usage in the United States: 1935-1982. *American Psychologist, 39,* 451-454.

Pareek, U. N. (1964). *Developmental patterns in reactions to frustration.* New York: Asia Publishing House.

Perini, C., Rauchfleisch, U., & Bühler, F. R. (1985). Personality characteristics and renin in essential hypertension. *Psychotherapy and Psychosomatics, 43,* 44-48.

Raviv, S. (1980). The influence of genetics, age and training on the reaction to frustration in sport gifted children. *International Journal of Sport Psychology, 11,* 202-214.

Rosenzweig, S. (1945). The Picture-Association method and its application in a study of reactions to frustrations. *Journal of Personality, 14,* 3-23.

Rosenzweig, S. (1976). Aggressive behavior and the Rosenzweig Picture-Frustration (P-F) Study. *Journal of Clinical Psychology, 32,* 885-891.

Rosenzweig, S. (1978a). *Adult Form supplement.* St. Louis: Rana House.

Rosenzweig, S. (1978b). *Aggressive behavior and the Rosenzweig Picture-Frustration Study.* New York: Praeger.

Rosenzweig, S. (1978c). An investigation of the reliability of the Rosenzweig Picture-Frustration (P-F) Study Children's Form. *Journal of Personality Assessment, 42,* 483-488.

Rosenzweig, S. (1978d). *The Rosenzweig Picture-Frustration (P-F) Study: Basic manual.* St. Louis: Rana House.

Rosenzweig, S. (1981a). *Adolescent Form supplement.* St. Louis: Rana House.

Rosenzweig, S. (1981b). *Children's Form supplement.* St. Louis: Rana House.

Rosenzweig, S. (1981c). Toward a comprehensive definition and classification of aggression. In P. F. Brain & D. Benton (Eds.), *Multidisciplinary approaches to aggression research* (pp. 17-22). Amsterdam: Elsevier/North-Holland Biomedical Press.

Rosenzweig, S. (1981d). The current status of the Rosenzweig Picture-Frustration Study as a measure of aggression in personality. In P. F. Brain & D. Benton (Eds.), *Multidisciplinary approaches to aggression research* (pp. 113-125). Amsterdam: Elsevier/North-Holland Biomedical Press.

Rosenzweig, S., & Adelman, S. (1977). Construct validity of the Rosenzweig Picture-Frustration Study. *Journal of Personality Assessment, 41,* 578-588.

Rosenzweig, S., Ludwig, D. J., & Adelman, S. (1975). Retest reliability of the Rosenzweig Picture-Frustration Study and similar semiprojective techniques. *Journal of Personality Assessment, 39,* 3-12.

Rosenzweig, S., & Rosenzweig, L. (1976). Guide to research on the Rosenzweig Picture-Frustration (P-F) Study, 1934-1974. *Journal of Personality Assessment, 40,* 599-606.

Spellacy, F. J., & Brown, W. G. (1982). Prediction of recidivism in young offenders after brief institutionalization. *Journal of Clinical Psychology, 40,* 1070-1074.

Straker, G., & Jacobson, R. S. (1981). Aggression, emotional adjustment, and empathy in the abused child. *Developmental Psychology, 17,* 762-765.

Tsiantis, J., Kokkevi, A., & Agathanos-Marouli, E. (1981). Parents of abused children in Greece: Psychiatric and psychological characteristics. *Child Abuse and Neglect, 5,* 281-285.

Wagner, E. E., Alexander, R. A., Roos, G., & Prospero, M. K. (1985). Maximizing split-half reliability estimates for projective techniques. *Journal of Personality Assessment, 49,* 579-581.

Weinstein, L., & deMan, A. F. (1982). Vegetarianism vs. meatarianism and emotional upset. *Bulletin of the Psychonomic Society, 19,* 99-100.

White, W. C., Jr. (1975). Validity of the overcontrolled-hostility (O-H) scale: A brief report. *Journal of Personality Assessment, 39,* 587-589.

Winefield, H. R. (1981). Anger expression in the Picture-Frustration Study under stressful conditions. *Journal of Personality Assessment, 45,* 370-374.

Wright, L. (1976). The "sick but slick" syndrome as a personality component of parents of battered children. *Journal of Clinical Psychology, 32,* 41-45.

Doris L. Redfield, Ph.D.
Associate Professor of Psychology, Western Kentucky University, Bowling Green, Kentucky.

ROSS TEST OF HIGHER COGNITIVE PROCESSES
John D. Ross and Catherine M. Ross. Novato, California: Academic Therapy Publications.

Introduction

The Ross Test of Higher Cognitive Processes was designed to measure the abilities referred to by Bloom (1967) in *Taxonomy of Educational Objectives, Handbook I: Cognitive Domain* as *analysis, synthesis,* and *evaluation.* These three abilities comprise the top three tiers in Bloom's six-tier hierarchy of cognitive abilities: *analysis* is the ability to break down a whole object or idea into its component parts; *synthesis,* considered to require higher level cognitive abilities than analysis, is the ability to combine component parts or ideas to create a whole or solution; and *evaluation,* the highest level of thinking described by Bloom, is the ability to make quantitative and qualitative judgments.

The Ross Test of Higher Cognitive Processes, hereafter referred to as the Ross Test, was developed by John and Catherine Ross. John Ross has a master of arts degree in psychology from the University of Washington and is currently a consultant residing in Utah. Catherine Ross has a master of education degree with an emphasis in elementary education from the University of Washington and is currently a school administrator in the state of Washington.

Following a review of existing tests, Ross and Ross concluded that "no comprehensive instruments for assessing the higher-level thinking skills of students in the intermediate grades were available" (Ross & Ross, 1976b, p.4). Hence, between September 1974 and June 1976, they developed the Ross Test.

There is one form of the Ross Test, and it was specifically developed and normed for use with both gifted and normal students in Grades 4 through 6. The test was first published in 1976 and has not been revised. However, the test manual (Ross & Ross, 1976b) has been revised to include the once-separate *Statistical Supplement.*

The Ross Test is a pencil-and-paper test consisting of 105 multiple-choice items divided into eight subtests or "sections." The test may be administered individually or to groups. Sections I (Analogies, 14 items), III (Missing Premises, 8 items), and VII (Analysis of Relevant and Irrelevant Information, 14 items) reportedly assess analysis abilities corresponding to subsections 4.20, 4.10, and 4.20, respectively, of Bloom's taxonomy. Sections IV (Abstract Relations, 14 items), V (Sequential Synthesis, 10 items), and VIII (Analysis of Attributes, 15 items) reportedly assess synthesis abilities corresponding to the taxonomic subsections 5.30, 5.10, and 5.30, respectively. Sections II (Deductive Reasoning, 18 items), and VI (Questioning Strategies, 12 items) reportedly measure evaluation abilities corresponding to subsections 6.10 and 6.20.

Practical Applications/Uses

The Ross Test, in conjuction with other measures, might be resonably used to screen students for placement in special programs (e.g., programs for the gifted, programs focusing on thinking skills). Typically, screening for placement in special school programs includes tests of achievement and ability or IQ. The Ross Test cannot substitute for either of these measures; however, it may provide useful information regarding students' ability to analyze, synthesize, and evaluate information.

Another use of the Ross Test is to assess students' relative strengths and weaknesses in the abilities to analyze, synthesize, and evaluate information so that appropriate remediation or enrichment might be provided. Scores indicating that a student's "higher cognitive processes" are not functioning at expected levels imply that instruction in those processes may be warranted. Likewise, scores indicating that a student is a high-level processor imply that instruction requiring and encouraging such processing may be the methodology of choice.

The Ross Test might also be used to evaluate educational programs. For instance, the test might be used to judge the effectiveness of curricula or instructional methodology designed to teach those higher-order thinking skills purportedly measured by the test (i.e., aspects of analysis, synthesis, and evaluation as defined by Bloom).

For the most part, instructions provided for the test administrator and to the students are sufficiently simple and clear. While it appears that no extraordinary training is required to administer or score the test, "it is recommended that administration be done only by certificated teachers, counselors, school psychologists, or other qualified testing personnel" (Ross & Ross, 1976b, p. 4). Students may mark their answers directly on the 32-page test booklet or on a separate answer sheet, which is hand-scored using an overlay of keyed responses. The test is administered in two sittings. Sections I through V are administered in one sitting, allowing 63 minutes of working time; sections VI through VIII are administered in a second sitting, allowing 58 minutes of working time. Time limits are based on an 85% completion rate for gifted students and a 55% completion rate for nongifted students in the test norming sample. Instructions to the student and working of examples require a reasonable amount of additional time. The amount of time to be allowed between sittings is not specified.

The Ross Test is objectively scored; the scoring procedure is simple and straightforward. Raw scores for each subtest and the total test are obtained by counting the number of correct responses. Raw scores may be converted to percentile rank equivalents for nongifted as well as gifted populations in Grades 4 through 6, whether testing occurs in the fall or spring of the year.

Average scoring time is 10-15 minutes. Scoring answers recorded directly on test booklets is more time-consuming than scoring the separate answer sheets using the available scoring overlay.

Percentile scores are relatively easy to interpret, provided that it is clearly understood that students obtaining the same raw scores share ranks or intervals along the score scale. Therefore, it is possible for students obtaining perfect raw scores to obtain percentile scores of less than 99 if other students also obtained perfect scores. Likewise, if more students obtain higher raw scores at the time of posttesting compared to pretesting, it is possible for a student to obtain a higher raw score but a lower percentile score at the time of posttesting.

Commendably, the Ross Test does not claim to provide a measure of intelligence or achievement; hence, neither IQ nor grade equivalent scores are provided (nor would they be appropriate).

Technical Aspects

The Ross Test was normed on 527 gifted and 610 nongifted students enrolled in fourth-, fifth-, and sixth-grade classes in nine public school districts throughout Washington state. All students in the gifted sample had obtained IQ scores of 125 or above on a standardized IQ test, in most instances the Lorge-Thorndike Intelligence Test (Thorndike, Hagen, & Lorge, 1966) or had been identified via case studies. Approximately 4% of the nongifted sample had been identified as gifted and were maintained as part of the nongifted or "normal" sample.

Some of the students in each of the norming samples were tested in the fall (September and October); the remainder were tested in the spring (May and June). Therefore, gifted and nongifted students in Grades 4, 5, or 6 may be compared to a norm whether they are tested during the fall or spring.

Reliability studies (Ross & Ross, 1976b) are restricted to split-half and test-retest reliability. Odd-even split-half reliability of the total test, after correction using the Spearman Brown prophecy formula, is reported as .92 ($p < .001$). The test manual does not specify whether the resulting coefficient is based on the gifted and/or nongifted groups. However, personal communication with J.D. Ross (July 9, 1986) verified that reliability was assessed using the total sample ($N = 1,137$).

A test-retest reliability coefficient of .94 ($p < .001$) is reported in the test manual. This coefficient is based on retesting an available 91 out of 100 selected students after three days. The procedures for selecting students for retesting are not specified and could not be clarified via personal communication.

Ross and Ross (1976b) offer four "correlations" as evidence of "construct validity." These correlations are meant to reflect the relationship between total scores obtained on the Ross Test and "students' chronological ages, age differentiation, group (gifted vs. non-gifted) differentiation, and correlation with an intelligence test" (p. 20).

Chronological age. The correlation between Ross Test scores and chronological age was .674 ($N = 339$). How chronological age was defined and how the 339 students were selected is not reported in the manual, but personal communication (J.D. Ross, July 9, 1986) indicated that age was measured in months; sample selection procedures were not able to be clarified.

Age differentiation. "The age differentiation method of construct validity also showed the test to be related to chronological age" (Ross & Ross, 1976b, p. 20). Evidence of this relationship consists of a table reporting mean scores and standard deviations for each grade level in the standardization sample divided into groups by IQ (gifted vs. nongifted), grade (fourth vs. fifth vs. sixth), time of testing (fall vs. spring), and test section (sections I-VIII and total test).

It is implied but not stated that all 1,137 students in the gifted and nongifted norm groups participated in the age-differentiation study. However, personal communication with J.D. Ross did not clarify sample size. Further, it is not clear how the data provided show the test to be related to chronological age. The data presented in the manual tables suggest that age and grade were synonymously treated. It seems that the intent of the data analysis was to show that different age groups, apparently defined as grade in school, obtain significantly different scores on the Ross Test. However, results of statistical tests of significant differences between groups are not reported.

Group differentiation. Presumably, differential performance of gifted and nongifted students was assessed to demonstrate that groups expected to differ in performance would actually differ. Such comparisons are sometimes used to demonstrate the convergent validity of instruments when appropriate, alternative measures are not available (Sabers & Whitney, 1976). It is reported that "in every one of the 54 possible instances of comparison, the performance of the gifted students on the Ross Test was superior to that of the non-gifted with all differences being statistically significant at the .05 level of confidence or better" (Ross & Ross, 1976b, p. 21). The 54 comparisons refer to differences obtained by gifteds versus nongifteds on the eight sections of the Ross Test and the total Ross Test score (nine scores per student) at each grade level (three grade levels) for both fall and spring testings (two testings). Therefore, nine scores × three grade levels × two testings = 54 comparisons. While difference scores between gifted and nongifted students are reported for all 54 comparisons, how the difference scores were statistically evaluated and the results of such evaluation is not reported. It is implied that all 1,137 students were included in this aspect of the validity study; however, personal communication did not clarify sample size.

Intelligence test scores. Finally, "a study was made comparing students' performance on the Ross Test with the Lorge-Thorndike Intelligence Test to (1) investigate the relationship of higher-level thinking skills to intelligence and (2) ascertain if the Ross Test was a test of general intelligence" (Ross & Ross, 1976b, p. 22). For nongifted students, the correlation coefficient representing the relationship between scores on the Ross Test and the Lorge-Thorndike Intelligence Test was .397; for gifted students, $r = .156$. It is reported that "a statistically significant relationship may exist between IQ and use of higher-level thinking skills in the regular student population of the intermediate grades" (Ross & Ross, 1976b, p. 22). Whether $r = .397$ is statistically significant is not reported and is not determinable because the number of students on whom it was based is not reported. It is doubtful that all 1,137 students in the norming sample had been tested using the Lorge-Thorndike Intelligence Test (see Ross & Ross, 1976b, p. 19). However, the statistical significance of $r = .397$ need not be an issue. A correlation of such magnitude may be of little practical significance, accounting for only 16% of the variance shared between the two sets of test scores. The authors have hereby shown reasonable evidence of discriminant validity. That is, the Ross Test does not appear to measure what it should not measure (viz., IQ).

Item-total point biserial correlations are offered as indices of discrimination (D). Discrimination indices reflect the degree to which individual items differentiate high scorers on the total test from low scorers. Relatively high item-total correlations indicate relatively good discrimination; relatively low (< .20) item-total correlations add little to the test's discriminating power (Nunnally, 1978).

Difficulty indices (i.e., percent of examinees passing an item) are also provided. As the difficulty index (p) increases, item ease (the opposite of difficulty) increases; likewise, as the difficulty index decreases, item ease decreases.

The discrimination and difficulty indices are not reported separately for gifted versus nongifted students or for grades. The number of subjects used to calculate the indices is not reported. However, personal communication revealed that the item analyses were conducted prior to the norming studies. The sample used for the item analyses consisted of approximately 600 students from a school district in Washington state "highly loaded" with gifted students. These students did not participate in the norming studies. Approximately 200 items were administered. The "best" items ($N = 105$) were selected for inclusion in the published version of the Ross Test (Ross & Ross, 1976a). The 105-item published version of the Ross Test was used for the norming, reliability, and validity studies.

Discrimination indices of the 105 selected items, based on analysis of the original 200 items administered to a total of 600 gifted and nongifted subjects, ranged from .20 (items 28, 78, and 84) to .52 (item 7). The median point biserial item-total correlation was .30. Difficulty indices ranged from .13 (item 87) to .89 (item 21), which may suggest a ceiling effect. That is, nearly all gifted students ($N =$ unknown) may have answered low difficulty items correctly. The median difficulty index was .63. Clearly there is a need to cross-validate the item characteristics of the Ross Test, especially because item analyses were not based upon the 1,137 subjects in the norming groups.

Critique

There are two general concerns regarding use of the Ross Test. One concern is substantive in nature and revolves around the definition of higher cognitive processes; the other is technical in nature and revolves around the samples upon whom norms, reliability, and validity are based.

The publisher advertises the Ross Test as assessing "abstract and critical thinking skills among gifted and nongifted students" (Academic Therapy Publications, 1985-86, p. 6). However, it is important that the test user realizes the limitations of the Ross Test for assessing such skills. First, the test is based on Bloom's (1967) taxonomy, which represents but one conceptualization of higher-order thinking. Prominent theoreticians/researchers (e.g., Ennis, 1985; Gagne, 1977) provide different, equally plausible conceptualizations.

Second, only six of the eight subsections encompassed by the analysis, synthesis, and evaluation levels of Bloom's taxonomy are represented by the Ross Test.

Specifically, sections 4.30 (analysis of organizational principles) and 5.20 (production of a plan or proposed set of operations) are not represented by the Ross Test. Also, the number of test items representing the included subsections of Bloom's taxonomy is inconsistent. Taxonomy subsections 4.10 (analysis of elements), 4.20 (analysis of relationships), 5.10 (production of unique communication), 5.30 (derivation of a set of abstract relations), 6.10 (judgments in terms of internal evidence), and 6.20 (judgments in terms of external criteria) are represented by 8, 28, 10, 29, 12, and 18 items, respectively. In other words, the various aspects of higher order thinking as defined by Bloom are either not represented or may be over- or under-represented by the Ross Test.

Ross and Ross (1976b) explain the unequal number of items per test section as follows:

> The Ross Test has been carefully designed to concentrate its main emphasis on a student's ability to deal with abstractions on a verbal basis. The ability to conceptualize a verbal abstraction and see relationships within and around it is a major component of all of the higher cognitive processes. Analysis of quantitative and symbolical data—assessed in Sections VII and VIII—while also certainly requiring higher cognitive skills, does not involve this kind of verbal facility and, therefore, is represented by relatively fewer items in the total instrument. (p. 6)

Together, test sections VII (14 items) and I (14 items) purportedly represent subsection 4.20 of Bloom's taxonomy; test sections VIII (15 items) and IV (14 items) purportedly represent subsection 5.30 of the taxonomy. Sections VII and VIII, therefore, do not contain significantly more items than their verbally oriented counterparts (viz., sections I and IV). Neither do sections VII and VIII contain relatively fewer items than other sections (e.g., section III = 8 items; section V = 10 items; section VI = 12 items). In fact, only section II (18 items) contains more than 15 items.

The aforementioned explanation offered by Ross and Ross for differential numbers of items across test sections is puzzling. Granted, an examination of test items reveals a decided emphasis on verbal reasoning; however, it seems that Sections VII and VIII contribute to a comparative overrepresentation of items designed to measure taxonomy subsections 4.20 (analysis of relationships) and 5.30 (derivation of a set of abstract relations).

Examination of the test items suggests that, overall, the various test sections have reasonable face validity for assessing abilities at their corresponding levels of Bloom's taxonomy. Additional examination of the items suggests that the Ross Test may be biased in favor of students having at least average reading skills, adequate experience and knowledge bases, and relative strengths in verbal reasoning. Consequently, the test may be biased against students having limited reading skills, inadequate knowledge or experience levels, and relative strengths in spatial, symbolic, or numerical reasoning.

It is clear that the 537 gifted and 610 nongifted students included in the norming studies were selected from nine school districts throughout the state of Washington. However, how the students were selected and the demographic makeup of the sample are not reported. Therefore, the external validity of the norming data is questionable. Because the reliability and validity studies were apparently conducted with students or subsamples of students participating in the norming groups, reliability and validity data may also be of questionable external validity.

The appropriateness of the provided norms requires evaluation by individual test users. When the two norming samples (gifted vs. nongifted) were subcategorized by grade (fourth vs. fifth vs. sixth) and time of testing (fall vs. spring), subgroup sizes ranged from $N = 76$ to $N = 136$. Considering that selection procedures were not specified and that the demographic makeup of the norming groups is unknown, the relatively small subsample sizes may limit the external validity of the norms.

While norms are provided for gifted and nongifted groups, reliability coefficients are not. Failure to report separate reliability coefficients is unfortunate because the test may yield lower discrimination indices and higher difficulty indices for gifted students than for nongifted students, thereby differentially influencing reliability for the separate groups.

The use of an odd-even split-half technique may have yielded a biased estimate of reliability ($r = .92$). Even numbers of items occur within all but Section VII of the test, and all items within a section were designed to measure the same construct. A more conservative measure of total test internal consistency would likely have been yielded by KR-20 or coefficient alpha.

Reliability coefficients are not reported for each of the eight sections of the test. The failure to report such coefficients is curious because means and standard deviations are reported for each test section by subgroups of students. Also, reliabilty of the various test sections should influence the test user's interpretation of students' relative strengths and weaknesses.

Standard errors of measurement are not reported and cannot be readily calculated because the reliability coefficient reported for the Ross Test is based on the entire test, while the reported standard deviations are based upon test sections. Standard deviations for the total score are reported by grade and time of testing, but to determine the overall standard deviation related to the overall reliability coefficient, the number of students per subgroup (grade × time of testing) is required but not explicitly reported. If all 1,137 students included in the norming studies were included in the internal consistency reliability study, then the number of students per subgroup is determinable. However, it is not stated that all 1,137 students actually participated in the reliability study. The ommission of standard errors of measurement from the technical data is unfortunate because those data are required to determine the reliability of individual student's scores as well as the reliability of the differences between scores obtained by a student. The reliability of difference scores is important to the appropriate assessment of relative strengths and weaknesses.

The test-retest reliability coefficient ($r = .94$) is not easily interpretable because it is based on 91 available students out of 100 selected students and retesting occurred after only three days. How the 100 students were selected is not clear; hence, their representativeness may be suspect. A three-day time lapse may be inappropriate because the level of thinking is a relatively stable construct and forgetting items on a test such as the Ross Test after only three days is improbable.

The model for investigating what Ross and Ross call construct validity is not clear. A theoretically sound case is presented for correlating chronological age with Ross Test scores. However, the resultant coefficient ($r = .674$) is difficult to interpret because it was based on 339 students. How the students were selected is not reported. Overrepresentation of gifted students would restrict the range of test scores, thereby providing an overly conservative estimate of the relationship. It would be useful to determine the relationship separately for gifted and nongifted students.

The purpose of the age differentiation study is not clear. Presumably, the intent was to show that students of different ages would score differently on the Ross Test. If so, the purpose is redundant with the correlation of Ross Test scores with chronological age. The data provided as evidence for "age differentiation" consists of means and standard deviations by grade, not age. No correlation coefficient and/or results of between or among group comparisons (e.g., ANOVA) are reported.

A major concern regarding the group (gifted vs. nongifted) differentiation study is the nature of the 54 comparisons. Average differences between gifted and nongifted student performance are reported by test section, grade, and time of testing, "with all differences being statistically significant at the .05 level of confidence or better" (Ross & Ross, 1976b, p. 21). How the difference scores were "compared" is not clear. If multiple t-tests were used, it is certain that some of the differences are due to chance alone (see Hays, 1973; Myers, 1972). If a priori contrasts or ANOVA procedures were used, presentation of a summary table is critical to the appropriate interpretation of the comparative data.

The relationship between IQ and Ross Test scores were separately calculated for gifted ($r = .156$) and nongifted ($r = .397$) students. The statistically nonsignificant correlation coefficient yielded for the gifted group should be interpreted in light of their restricted range of intelligence test scores and, perhaps, Ross Test scores.

Test validity is logically and statistically dependent upon test reliability, which is dependent on item properties such as discrimination and difficulty. Because the Ross Test is separately normed for gifted and nongifted students, it is important that the item properties be known for the separate groups. Unfortunately, the discrimination and difficulty indices are reported for the groups combined, and the combined group used to determine item properties was separate from the groups used for the norming, reliability, and validity studies (J.D. Ross, personal communication, July 9, 1986). When difficulty indices range as high as .89, as they do for the Ross Test, it is possible that nearly all gifted students made correct responses, thereby limiting the test's ability to make discriminations among gifted students.

Time limits were based on 85% completion rates for gifted students and 55% completion rates for nongifted students. Given that speed of processing is a characteristic of gifted students (Maker, 1982; Webb, Meckstroth, & Tolman, 1982), the Ross Test may in effect be a speeded test for nongifted students.

The test manual indicates that the Analysis of Attributes subtest consists of 10 items (p. 5). There are actually 15 items.

It is suggested in the manual that students participating in an experiment or evaluation study be instructed to circle the letters "EXP" (designating experimental group) or "CON" (designating control group) on the front of their test booklets (p. 7). This practice may serve to bias test performance.

On page 17 of the test manual, the reader is referred to a *Statistical Supplement*. However, there is no longer such a supplement; the technical data are included in the manual.

If students are required to respond on separate answer sheets and not mark in the test booklets, it could be important that they be provided with "scratch" paper. Even with such provision, students allowed to mark directly on the test booklet may be at an advantage due to the visual transport required by some items.

Scoring time could be decreased by numbering the items consecutively within test sections rather than continuously throughout the entire test.

The Ross Test provides a step in the needed directions of developing objective measures of thinking abilities not measured by traditional achievement and/or intelligence tests and providing norms for nontraditional populations (i.e., gifted students). The integrity of the test could be markedly improved by ensuring the representativeness of or adequately describing the characteristics of the norming samples, ensuring that the test is not biased against minority or disadvantaged students, providing a conservative overall measure of internal consistency, providing reliability coefficients and standard errors of measurement for each test section and each norming sample, validating the test content via a content validation study, systematically continuing construct validation studies, and conducting cross-validation studies. Information regarding the test's convergent and discriminant properties with regard to each norming sample is needed.

References

This list includes text citations and suggested additional reading.

Academic Therapy Publications. (1985-86). *Catalog*. Novato, CA: Author.

Bloom, B.S. (Ed.). (1967). *Taxonomy of educational objectives, handbook I: Cognitive domain*. New York: David McKay Co.

Callahan, C.M., & Corvo, M.L. (1980). Validating the Ross Test for identification and evaluation of critical thinking skills in programs for the gifted. *Journal for the Education of the Gifted*, 4(1), 17-26.

Ennis, R.H. (1985). A logical basis for measuring critical thinking skills. *Educational Leadership*, 45(2), 44-48.

Gagne, R.M. (1977). *The conditions of learning* (3rd ed.). New York: Holt, Rinehart & Winston.

Hays, W.L. (1973). *Statistics for the social sciences* (2nd ed.). New York: Holt, Rinehart & Winston.

Krichev, A. (1978). Test review: Ross Test of Higher Cognitive Processes. *Psychology in the Schools*, 15(1), 145-146.

Lee, L.A., & Karnes, F.A. (1983). Correlations between the Cognitive Abilities Test, Form 3, and the Ross Test of Higher Cognitive Processes for gifted students. *Perceptual and Motor Skills*, 56(2), 421-422.

Maker, C.J. (1982). *Teaching models in education of the gifted*. Rockville, MD: Aspen Systems.

Myers, J.L. (1972). *Fundamentals of experimental design*. Boston: Allyn & Bacon.

Nunnally, J.C. (1978). *Psychometric theory* (2nd ed.). New York: McGraw-Hill.

Ross, J.D., & Ross, C.M. (1976a). *Ross Test of Higher Cognitive Processes*. Novato, CA: Academic Therapy Publications.

Ross, J.D., & Ross, C.M. (1976b). *Ross Test of Higher Cognitive Processes manual*. Novato, CA: Academic Therapy Publications.

Sabers, D.L., & Whitney, D.R. (1976). *Suggestions for validating rating scales and attitude inventories* (Technical Bulletin No. 19). Iowa City: University of Iowa, Evaluation and Examination Service.

Thorndike, R.L., Hagen, E.P., & Lorge, I.D. (1966). *Lorge-Thorndike Intelligence Tests, Multilevel Edition*. Boston: Houghton Mifflin.

Webb, J.T., Meckstroth, E.A., & Tolman, S.S. (1982). *Guiding the gifted child*. Columbus, OH: Ohio Psychology.

Travis A. Carter, Ed.D.
Associate Professor of Counselor Education, University of North Florida, Jacksonville, Florida.

SCHOOL AND COLLEGE ABILITY TESTS II & III
Educational Testing Service. Monterey, California: CTB/ McGraw-Hill.

Introduction

The School and College Ability Tests II and III (SCAT II & III) are group-administered tests designed to measure basic verbal and quantitative abilities as well as the general academic ability of students in Grades 4 through 14 (SCAT II) and 4 through 12 (SCAT III). The tests measure those general abilities associated with academic success in public and private schools.

The SCAT has a history of more than 30 years of development by the staff of Educational Testing Services (ETS). Between 1955 and 1979, a number of revisions were published: SCAT II in 1966 and 1973, and SCAT III in 1979. SCAT II and SCAT III were standardized and normed concurrently with the Sequential Tests of Educational Progress (STEP) II and III. In each revision, samples were selected to reflect the variables that define school populations by geographic regions, social class, ethnic group, and community size. SCAT III represents an added effort to reduce bias by further refining the norming sample, selection of more culture-free test items, and reporting male and female scores as one rather than separately. Such revisions are intended to assess academic ability more accurately and to respond to the continuing changes in the field of education.

SCAT II tests are available at four levels of difficulty with two parallel forms for each level. Forms 4A and 4B are for elementary Grades 3 (spring) through 6 (fall). Forms 3A and 3B are for middle school Grades 6 (spring) through 9 (fall). Forms 2A and 2B are for high school Grades 9 (spring) through 12 (fall). Forms 1A and 1B are for college freshmen (fall) through sophomore level (spring). All of the forms are available in the SCAT III except Forms 1A and 1B. There are no special forms of the test available in languages other than English or for the visually impaired.

SCAT II and III are designed to be administered in 40 minutes. The verbal and quantitative tests each require 20-minute timed periods. This permits completion of the whole test in an academic class period.

The SCAT Series II supplies an informative handbook that describes preparation for testing, clear administration and scoring directions, and score interpretation principles. Test booklets for each level, hand- and machine-scored answer sheets, and "Student Preview" handouts are available.

The SCAT II handbook provides detailed specific directions on preparation for and administration of the tests. Detailed attention is given to selecting the testing room, seating arrangements, the importance of scheduling, advance announcements, materials needed, and management of the test material inventory. All these standardized directions are very important in achieving test scores that may be meaningfully compared to the scores of the standardized norming sample.

The Student Preview is designed to prepare students for the testing experience by informing them, in age- and situation-appropriate language, of the purpose of the test. They are told they will receive a booklet, separate answer sheet, and that no one is expected to know all the answers. They are advised to work carefully, manage their time, record their answers accurately, guess if they do not know the answer, and not worry about being wrong. Three examples of verbal and three examples of quantitative test items are included for practice; correct answers are provided so each student can score the practice preview. This preview experience is designed to reduce anxiety and promote self-confidence during the testing period.

SCAT II elementary-level booklets contain both the Verbal and Quantitative subtests. The directions repeat the information and advice included in the preview handout and advise students not to open the booklet until instructed. Page 2 includes two examples of verbal test items with the correct answer appropriately marked. This demonstrates the format of the test items and the correct way to record answers on the answer sheet.

Every verbal test item follows the same format. The item begins with two words connected by a colon and printed in bold black letters. The directions state that these words go together in some way, and the student's task is to select from the four options (A-D) the two words connected by a colon that have a similar relationship. By using this format the test developers produced verbal items that require very little reading with only five word pairs (or 10 words) required for each question. Pages 3 and 4 contain 50 of these analogy questions, which comprise Part I of SCAT II. The test items are arranged in three columns, and directions are printed at the top and bottom of each page when necessary.

Page 5 gives directions and three examples of Part II of SCAT II, the Quantitative subtest. The examples are presented with marked answers and explanations of why the answers are correct. Two parts make up each test item. Each part is listed in either Column A or Column B. The student must decide which column item is greatest, or if they are equal. This permits three possible answers: Column A, Column B, or the two columns are equal. Fifty test items are printed on pages 6 and 7. The test items include such examples as addition problems, mph on a speedometer, minutes before or minutes after an hour, and distance around various geometric shapes. Directions to stop and wait until time is called are printed at the end of page 7.

SCAT II Form 3A and 3B booklets for middle school students are printed in the same format as the elementary booklets. There are also the same number of pages in each part, with the same number of items. The only noticeable difference is in the difficulty of the analogies and quantitative comparisons. As one would expect, the items in both parts are more challenging. Though they are progressively more demanding, they appear to be age and situation appropriate.

The SCAT II Form 2A and 2B booklets for high school students also have the same format and become appropriately more demanding. The only difference is in Part II, in which an eighth page is added to accommodate the longer, more complex quantitative problems.

SCAT II Forms 1A and 1B booklets for college examinees follow the format of Forms 3 and 4 of the elementary and middle school levels. The only difference evidenced is in the difficulty of the verbal and quantitative items. The standardization of the booklet format and instructions over a 10-year period would probably have the positive effect of permitting an experienced student to perform in such a way as to more accurately reflect academic ability as measured by the SCAT II Series.

Answer sheets used in SCAT II administration include IBM 850 and 1230, for which punchout stencils are available for handscoring, and an ETS issue of an NCS Trans-Optic sheet. These answer sheets require students to use grids to enter information and blacken "bubbles" at the elementary level, and at other levels to blacken spaces between parallel lines to code in their answers to test questions.

The raw score for each part of the SCAT II test is the number of right answers. Three raw scores are generated on each answer sheet: Verbal, Quantitative, and Total. These may be different from form to form; however, developed ability can be compared between forms by translating raw scores from each form to a converted score. The handbook reports that converted scores have the same meaning and thus permit comparison of developed ability over a 10-year period (assuming a student was administered at least the first and last forms). Converted scores are also reported as percentile ranks. This permits estimating verbal, quantitative, and overall academic ability development in relation to a norming group. The SCAT II handbook provides data necessary for comparison with the national norm group for every grade, 4 through 14. There are also national school-mean norms that permit comparison with the means of a local school.

Probably the most important test score generated by the SCAT II will be that which is indicated on a percentile band. Anastasi (1968, p. 96) considers representing student performance on these bands outstanding, because it permits communication of the lack of significance of score differences when the bands overlap. This reviewer has found interpretation of the meaning of differences between scores easily communicated to parents, students, and faculty when using these graphic representations. In effect, the percentile band recognizes that all tests approximate reality. The bands fairly represent the probability of error without destroying the practical use of the results.

Practical Applications/Uses

The SCAT II and III are designed to measure students' academic ability in the verbal and quantitative areas as well as general ability. The same objective, to predict academic performance, is defined as the objective of every edition. As an educator and practicing psychologist, this reviewer has had occasion to participate in selection and placement of students in programs of learning designed to promote optimum development. Individualizing instructional programs, designing school curricula to target defined levels of ability, and evaluating student achievement all require reliable measures of academic ability. The SCAT II and III provide such measures in grades 4 through 14 for average English-speaking students.

The SCAT II and III can be administered individually or in groups under the direction of an educator or psychologist. The directions for administration are easy to understand, communicate, and follow. Either the Verbal or Quantitative subtest may be given, scored, and interpreted separately. This permits assessment of either area of ability conveniently and quickly when necessary. A subtest can be administered and scored for an individual in approximately 30 minutes. The whole test can be administered and scored for an individual in about an hour. Such economy of time is very valuable in a guidance office, mental health clinic, psychologist's office, and college counseling center.

Group administration can require more time, but the actual testing can be accomplished within an academic period (50 minutes) when the preparation and administration directions are followed. This can be an invaluable consideration when designing a program of assessment for a school; it is quite convenient to plan and administer testing programs when the testing does not interrupt more than one class period. It also permits testing in classroom or auditorium to accommodate small and large groups.

This reviewer has hand-scored individual answer sheets and plotted the scores on report forms in 10 to 15 minutes. Group scoring is best accomplished by a scoring service. In such cases, arrangements can be made to have results returned within about three weeks after they are shipped. The reports can be provided on gummed labels for filing and on individual forms for group interpretation. In recent years, colleges, local schools, and school systems have begun using small optical-mark scanners that are used with microcomputers to score their own tests. This equipment is inexpensive and permits ready access to scores and school analyses.

Interpretation of SCAT scores is based on objective evidence that is as reliable as any group-administered standardized test of academic ability. However, judgment decisions made on the basis of the test information will be only as good as the professional and personal decision-making abilities of the persons involved in the process. To accommodate the demands of such decision processes, ETS has provided a variety of scores that lend themselves to the nature of the presenting problem. When raw scores are translated into converted scores they "represent the same level of developed ability regardless of the form or level . . ." (Educational Testing Service, 1973, p. 9). This permits comparison of developed ability of individuals over periods of time ranging up to as many as 10 years. Percentile ranks permit the comparison of individual students to performance of age and grade peers in the national sample. Stanine scores permit grouping of students by academic ability in cases in which educational progress is promoted by such programming of instruction.

School administrators, guidance counselors, classroom teachers, psychologists, and other professionals with a knowledge of testing will find these scores easy to understand and use. In those cases where local norms are provided, school peer comparisons provide additional useful information in planning and administrative decisions. When fine discriminations must be made, the nature of error in measurement is graphically demonstrated in the percentile band scores. In such cases, there is a standard error of measurement placed on a percentile rank scale above and below the individual rank. Arranged beside each other, the Verbal and Quantitative rankings can be compared. If the bands overlap the scores are considered basically the same. Such comparison permits more accurate understanding of the limits imposed by error in interpreting and using standardized test scores.

Technical Aspects

The 1973 SCAT II handbook (and other editions) includes a technical report. Standardization procedures and statistical analyses to assure reliability and validity of the SCAT Series scores are described. Efforts are made to identify meaningful and capricious score differences, equate the parallel forms at every level, and provide scores that can be compared from test to test whatever the form, level, or series.

Norming sample tables report the percentages and sizes of various subgroups, regional representations, and school levels. These are combined to form the national norming sample. Many reliability scores are presented, and the procedures and methods of statistical analysis are described and explained.

As is often the case in such technical analyses, some experts have criticized ETS over the years for some of their procedures and technical reports. The criticism most often raised concerns the weakness (i.e., incompleteness) of the validity data supporting the SCAT Series. The validity questions raised concern achievement of the stated purpose of the SCAT Series. The handbook (1973, p. 67) states that the test's "predictive validity is of primary importance," then describes a procedure that is more appropriately considered concurrent validity—not predictive validity—as observed by S. David Farr as early as 1968. Passow and Schiff (1985, p. 1318) agree with Farr and add, "Reviewers of SCAT in both the *Seventh* MMY and *Eighth* MMY have suggested that its usefulness is 'severely limited by a lack of information pertaining to validity.'" These criticisms are directed toward the technical report. These same reviewers suggest that even the high validity reported for predicting STEP and SAT scores are suspect because the tests were all normed together on the same sample at the same time.

While this reviewer respects these criticisms and agrees that more reliability and validity support data should be included in the technical report, a computer search of such studies over the past three decades removes doubt about the SCAT Series meeting its stated objective of predicting academic performance in schools and colleges.

Critique

In their review, Passow and Schiff (1985) recognize the long history and observe that the SCAT Series "has been a staple in school testing programs. It is a well conceived and designed test. SCAT Series III continues the series as a useful instrument. . ." (p. 1318).

This reviewer has used the SCAT in schools and colleges and has been satisfied with the reliability and validity of the results. The tests are easily administered and scored, and interpretation is much more meaningfully achieved when using the percentile bands. Another valuable aid has been the directions in the handbook for establishing local norms. Included is a very practical worksheet in Table A-2 that demonstrates how to organize the data for convenient computation.

As a measure of academic ability the SCAT Series has made a significant contribution to education and other human service programs over the past 25 years, and the revisions have kept in step with the very rapid changes that have characterized the period. Though the test items have not always satisfied the need for face validity demanded by some consumers, the tests have provided the opportunity to accomplish their defined purpose very well with economy of effort, time, and other resources.

In this reviewer's opinion the publisher should continue to make this various series available, and in future editions include in their technical report the validity research data requested by many worthy critics. Such additions would increase the professional dignity of a test series that is already held in very high esteem.

References

Anastasi, A. (1968). *Psychological testing.* (3rd ed.) New York: Macmillan.

Educational Testing Service. (1973). *SCAT Series II handbook.* Princeton, NJ: Educational Testing Service.

Farr, S. D. (1972). Cooperative School and College Ability Tests. In O.K. Buros (Ed.), *The seventh mental measurements yearbook* (pp. 660-662). Highland Park, NJ: The Gryphon Press.

Passow, A. H. (1985). School and College Ability Tests. In J. V. Mitchell, Jr. (Ed.), *The ninth mental measurements yearbook* (p. 1317). Lincoln, NE: Buros Institute of Mental Measurements.

Timothy M. Osberg, Ph.D.
Associate Professor of Psychology, Niagara University, Niagara University, New York.

THE SELF-CONSCIOUSNESS SCALE
Allan Fenigstein, Michael Scheier, and Arnold Buss.
Washington, D.C.: American Psychological Association.

Introduction

The Self-Consciousness Scale (SCS; Fenigstein, Scheier, & Buss, 1975) is a 23-item paper-and-pencil measure of dispositional self-attention processes. Building upon the work of Duval and Wicklund (1972), which extensively examined the role of the *state* of self-awareness in regulating social behavior, Fenigstein et al. intended to develop a scale assessing the *disposition* to be self-attentive, which they labeled *self-consciousness*. Although the authors' original goal in developing the measure was to examine the potential relationship of individual differences in self-attention processes to psychotherapy preferences, the scale has since been adopted for use by many other independent researchers and explored for its relationship to diverse areas of psychological functioning. In fact, a recent search of the *Social Sciences Citation Index* indicated that more than 230 studies using the scale have been conducted in the ten years following the test's publication.

At the time the test was developed, Allan Fenigstein and Michael Scheier were doctoral candidates at the University of Texas-Austin working with faculty member Arnold Buss. Fenigstein is now at Kenyon College in Ohio, and Scheier is currently at Carnegie-Mellon University in Pittsburgh. After developing a pool of 38 items to tap the domain of self-consciousness, the scale was administered to an initial sample of 212 undergraduate men and women. A factor analysis indicated that three factors accounted for the bulk of the variance in test responses. The final 23-item version of the measure thus includes three subscales that tap two separate aspects, called *private* and *public* self-consciousness, as well as a third dimension, *social anxiety*. All items included in the scale are responded to using a 5-point Likert scale ranging from 0 ("extremely uncharacteristic") to 4 ("extremely characteristic"). Three items are reverse scored because greater agreement indicates lower levels of the characteristic assessed.

The private self-consciousness subscale measures the tendency to direct attention to one's own thoughts, feelings, and motives (e.g., "I'm always trying to figure myself out"; "I'm generally attentive to my inner feelings"). The public self-consciousness subscale assesses awareness of oneself as a social object (e.g., "I'm concerned about the way I present myself"; "I'm usually aware of my appearance").

The assistance of Beryl Smith in conducting the literature search on which this review is based is gratefully acknowledged. Appreciation is also extended to Amy Davis for her help in preparing the manuscript.

The social anxiety subscale measures concern over one's performance in social situations (e.g., "It takes me time to overcome my shyness in new situations"; "I get embarrassed very easily").

The scoring of the SCS is straightforward and simple. Subscale scores are obtained by adding the numerical responses to the items included on each subscale. Total score is calculated by adding the three subscale scores.

The widespread interest in the SCS has led to the development of a Japanese version (Sugawara, 1984), and at least two attempts to revise the SCS based on updated assessments of the scale's factor structure (Burnkrant and Page, 1984; Spana, Rich, & Robertson, 1985). The Burnkrant and Page (1984) study, in particular, suggested the existence of two separate aspects of private self-consciousness, which they labeled *self-relectiveness* and *internal state awareness*. In addition, they suggested that five of the scale's original items be dropped to compensate for some weaknesses identified in their attempt to duplicate the scale's original factor structure.

One of the scale's original authors has even raised a potential shortcoming in the use of the SCS. Scheier and Carver (1985), acknowledging the successful use of the test in numerous studies using college student samples, noted that they and other researchers had experienced some difficulty in using the SCS with noncollege samples. They identified two problems with samples drawn from the general population: respondents' difficulties comprehending the content of some of the items and their apparent problems in responding to items using the "extremely uncharacteristic" to "extremely characteristic" rating scale. To address these shortcomings, Scheier and Carver developed a revised version of the SCS for use in research with noncollege samples. Several items were rewritten and one was dropped from the original measure. In addition, the format for eliciting responses was changed to a 4-point Likert scale with endpoints labeled "not at all like me" (0) and "a lot like me" (3). Results indicate the revised measure possesses psychometric properties similar to those of the original SCS, suggesting that it is a viable substitute when research participants from the general population are to be used.

Practical Applications/Uses

The extensive body of research exploring the mediating role of self-attention processes in behavior through use of the SCS attests to the wide variety of potential uses of the scale. Early research employing the SCS determined that individuals high in private self-consciousness are more aware of (Scheier & Carver, 1977) and react more intensely to (Scheier, 1976) their transient affective states. People high in public self-consciousness were shown to be more sensitive to peer group rejection (Fenigstein, 1979). In addition, both early and more recent investigations have shown that private and public self-consciousness moderate the congruence between self and peer assessments of the individual (Cheek, 1982; Underwood & Moore, 1981; Wymer & Penner, 1985) as well as the fit between self-assessments and actual behavior (Osberg & Shrauger, in press; Scheier, 1980; Scheier, Buss, & Buss 1978; Shrauger & Osberg, 1982; Turner, 1978; Turner & Peterson, 1977; Wymer & Penner, 1985).

In addition to the studies exploring the role of self-consciousness in mediating basic social psychological processes, a number of other studies using the SCS have addressed more applied issues of interest to clinical and counseling psychologists and researchers interested in consumer behavior. Two studies of potential interest to the latter group explored the relationship of self-consciousness to makeup use (Miller & Cox, 1982) and to focus on clothing interests (Solomon & Schopler, 1982). Hull and his associates (Hull & Young, 1983; Hull, Levenson, Young, & Sher, 1983) have used the SCS with a more clinical focus in developing a self-awareness model of alcohol consumption. Herbertt and Innes (1982) assessed the relationship between scores on the SCS and coronary-prone behavior, while Andersson, Orrell, and Puente (1984) employed it to examine self-attention processes in acute and chronic schizophrenics. Franzoi and his colleagues have used the SCS to determine that individuals high in private self-consciousness are more self-disclosing, which seems to mitigate against loneliness (Franzoi & Davis, 1985) and enhance marital satisfaction (Franzoi, Davis, & Young, 1985). Thus, the SCS has proven to be a useful tool in exploring a variety of both basic and applied issues in a clinical and social psychological research.

Although the ease of administering and scoring the SCS suggests that little psychometric sophistication is required on the part of the potential user, a word of caution may be in order. Osberg (1985) found that an administrative order effect on SCS scores occurs when the scale is administered as a part of a battery of tests. This study determined that individuals who respond to the SCS last in a battery tended to score higher on the private subscale and slightly lower on the public subscale than those administered the scale first. For this reason, potential users should consider administering the scale by itself or in a uniform fashion to all participants to control for this possibility.

Technical Aspects

In the original article introducing the SCS, Fenigstein et al. (1975) provided data suggesting the scale possessed adequate reliability. Two-week test-retest correlations for the subscale and total scores ranged from .73 to .84 in a sample of 84 subjects. Scheier and Carver (1985) provide similar data attesting to the test-retest reliability of the revised SCS. Four-week reliability estimates for the revised SCS ranged from .74 to .77 in a sample of 135 subjects. Scheier and Carver (1985) also present internal consistency estimates for both the SCS and revised SCS. Cronbach alphas for the original SCS ranged from .69 to .79 as compared to .75 to .84 for the revised SCS, suggesting that the revised version of the scale for use with general populations compares favorably to the original.

Normative data for the SCS are reported in Fenigstein et al. (1975) and in Carver and Glass (1976). Fenigstein et al. report subscale and total score means and standard deviations separately for college men and women. Normative data for the revised SCS based on a college sample are reported by Scheier and Carver (1985). As yet, no complete norms for noncollege samples are available for the revised SCS, although the authors presented subgroup norms for samples of male coronary-bypass patients and menopausal women.

Validity data relevant to the SCS are voluminous. Two reports examined the scale's convergent and discriminant validity (Campbell & Fiske, 1959). Carver and Glass (1976) found that social anxiety scale scores correlated negatively with IQ, activity level, and sociability. No association with test anxiety scores was found, suggesting that this subscale is specific in its assessment of social anxiety. Private self-consciousness scores showed no association with IQ, need achievement, test anxiety, activity level, impulsivity, emotionality, or sociability. Public self-consciousness evidenced a similar pattern, except for weak positive associations with the latter two characteristics.

Turner, Scheier, Carver, and Ickes (1978) in part replicated the findings of Carver and Glass (1976), suggesting that the SCS provides subscale and total scores that are distinct from conceptually unrelated constructs. In addition, private self-consciousness scores were positively associated with scores on measures of thoughtfulness and mental imagery. None of the subscale scores correlated significantly with a measure of socially desirable responding, and only minimal associations were found between subscale scores and Snyder's (1974) Self-Monitoring Scale, which suggests that the SCS taps a conceptually distinct construct. Finally, a recent report by Osberg and Basta (1984) found that private self-consciousness scores showed only a weak association to scores on Cacioppo and Petty's (1982) Need for Cognition Scale (see Heesacker, 1985), suggesting the conceptual distinctiveness of these two constructs. On the whole, the convergent and discriminant validity of the SCS seem well supported.

Numerous other studies supporting the validity of the SCS have been reported in the literature. Some of these studies are briefly referred to in the Practical Applications/Uses section of this review. More extensive coverage of research studies employing the SCS are provided by Buss (1980), Carver and Scheier (1981), and Scheier and Carver (1983). A brief review of some of the studies that have appeared subsequent to these reviews follows.

Several recent studies have examined the relationship of individual differences in self-consciousness to behavior in performance-related situations. Baumeister (1984) found high total self-consciousness scorers experience more disruption in performance on tasks of an automatic or overlearned nature. Baumeister, Hamilton, and Tice (1985) determined that when subjects hold private expectancies of success, performance is improved, while audience expectations of success tend to lower performance. Furthermore, these effects were found to be more pronounced in subjects low in total self-consciousness. Carver, Antoni, and Scheier (1985) examined the relationship between self-consciousness and the seeking of ability-diagnostic information. Individuals high in private self-consciousness were found to be more likely to seek out normative information after success and avoid normative information after failure relative to others.

A number of other studies explored the relationship of self-consciousness to such phenomena as reward allocation, the processing of self-relevant information, and egocentric focus on the self in day-to-day interactions. Kernis and Reis (1984) found that public and private self-consciousness related to standards adhered to in reward allocation. People high in public and low in private self-consciousness conformed more to an external (equity) standard of justice, while those low in public and high in private conformed more to an internal (equality) standard of justice.

Agatstein and Buchanan (1984) had subjects, separated by whether they were elevated in public or private self-consciousness, process trait labels using a public, private, or non-self-referent processing strategy. Subjects recalled more words processed with a strategy congruent with their predominant self-consciousness subscale score. Finally, Fenigstein (1984) found that subjects high in private self-consciousness were more likely to overperceive themselves as targets of actions in daily interactions.

Critique

The SCS is perhaps one of the most heuristic personality assessment devices published in the last 20 years. The scale itself and the theory on which it is based have been a fecund source of research hypotheses for investigators in diverse areas such as personality, clinical, and social psychology. The widespread validity data available support not only the technical sophistication of this scale, but also the importance of the theoretical construct that it taps in regulating social behavior. It is especially encouraging that a revised version of the scale, possessing psychometric properties comparable to those of the original, is available for use with a broader range of populations.

References

Agatstein, F. C., & Buchanan, D. B. (1984). Public and private self-consciousness and the recall of self-relevant information. *Personality and Social Psychology Bulletin, 10,* 314-325.

Andersson, C., Orrell, T. D., & Puente, A. E. (1984). Self-consciousness in acute and chronic schizophrenics. *Psychological Reports, 55,* 569-570.

Baumeister, R. F. (1984). Choking under pressure: Self-consciousness and paradoxical effects of incentives on skillful performance. *Journal of Personality and Social Psychology, 46,* 610-620.

Baumeister, R. F., Hamilton, J. C., & Tice, D. M. (1985). Public versus private expectancy of success: Confidence booster or performance pressure. *Journal of Personality and Social Psychology, 48,* 1447-1457.

Burnkrant, R. E., & Page, T. J. (1984). A modification of the Fenigstein, Scheier, and Buss Self-Consciousness Scales. *Journal of Personality Assessment, 48,* 629-637.

Buss, A. H. (1980). *Self-consciousness and social anxiety.* San Francisco: Freeman.

Cacioppo, J. T., & Petty, R. E. (1982). The need for cognition. *Journal of Personality and Social Psychology, 42,* 116-131.

Campbell, D. T., & Fiske, D. W. (1959). Convergent and discriminant validation by the multitrait-multimethod matrix. *Psychological Bulletin, 56,* 81-105.

Carver, C. S., Antoni, M., & Scheier, M. F. (1985). Self-consciousness and self-assessment. *Journal of Personality and Social Psychology, 48,* 117-124.

Carver, C. S., & Glass, D. C. (1976). The Self-Consciousness Scale: A discriminant validity study. *Journal of Personality Assessment, 40,* 169-172.

Carver, C. S., & Scheier, M. F. (1981). *Attention and self-regulation: A control theory approach to human behavior.* New York: Springer-Verlag.

Cheek, J. M. (1982). Aggression, moderator variables, and the validity of personality tests: A peer-rating study. *Journal of Personality and Social Psychology, 43,* 1254-1269.

Duval, S., & Wicklund, R. A. (1972). *A theory of objective self-awareness.* New York: Academic Press.

Fenigstein, A. (1979). Self-consciousness, self-attention, and social interaction. *Journal of Personality and Social Psychology, 37,* 75-86.

Fenigstein, A. (1984). Self-consciousness and the overperception of self as a target. *Journal of Personality and Social Psychology, 47,* 860-870.

Fenigstein, A., Scheier, M. F., & Buss, A. H. (1975). Public and private self-consciousness: Assessment and theory. *Journal of Consulting and Clinical Psychology, 43,* 522-527.

Franzoi, S. L., & Davis, M. H. (1985). Adolescent self-disclosure and loneliness: Private self-consciousness and parental influences. *Journal of Personality and Social Psychology, 48,* 768-780.

Franzoi, S. L., Davis, M. H., & Young, R. D. (1985). The effects of private self-consciousness and perspective taking on satisfaction in close relationships. *Journal of Personality and Social Psychology, 48,* 1584-1594.

Heesacker, M. (1985). The Need for Cognition Scale. In D. J. Keyser & R. C. Sweetland (Eds.), *Test critiques* (Vol. III, pp. 466-474). Kansas City, MO: Test Corporation of America.

Herbertt, R. M., & Innes, J. M. (1982). Type-A coronary-prone behavior pattern, self-consciousness, and self-monitoring—A questionnaire study. *Perceptual and Motor Skills, 55,* 471-478.

Hull, J. G., & Young, R. D. (1983). Self-consciousness, self-esteem, and success-failure as determinants of alcohol consumption in male social drinkers. *Journal of Personality and Social Psychology, 44,* 1097-1109.

Hull, J. G., Levenson, R. W., Young, R. D., & Sher, K. J. (1983). Self-awareness-reducing effects of alcohol consumption. *Journal of Personality and Social Psychology, 44,* 461-473.

Kernis, M. H., & Reis, H. T. (1984). Self-consciousness, self-awareness, and justice in reward allocation. *Journal of Personality, 52,* 58-70.

Miller, L. C., & Cox, C. L. (1982). For appearances sake: Public self-consciousness and makeup use. *Personality and Social Psychology Bulletin, 8,* 748-751.

Osberg, T. M. (1985). Order effects in the administration of personality measures: The case of the Self-Consciousness Scale. *Journal of Personality Assessment, 49,* 536-540.

Osberg, T. M., & Basta, J. C. (1984, August). *Some correlates of the need for cognition.* Paper presented at the annual meeting of the American Psychological Association, Toronto.

Osberg, T. M., & Shrauger, J. S. (in press). Self-prediction: Exploring the parameters of accuracy. *Journal of Personality and Social Psychology.*

Scheier, M. F. (1976). Self-awareness, self-consciousness, and angry aggression. *Journal of Personality, 44,* 627-644.

Scheier, M. F. (1980). Effects of public and private self-consciousness on the public expression of personal beliefs. *Journal of Personality and Social Psychology, 39,* 514-521.

Scheier, M. F., Buss, A. H., & Buss, D. M. (1978). Self-consciousness, self-report of aggressiveness, and aggression. *Journal of Research in Personality, 12,* 133-140.

Scheier, M. F., & Carver, C. S. (1977). Self-focused attention and the experience of emotion: Attraction, repulsion, elation, and depression. *Journal of Personality and Social Psychology, 35,* 625-636.

Scheier, M. F., & Carver, C. S. (1983). Two sides of the self: One for you and one for me. In J. Suls & A. Greenwald (Eds.), *Psychological perspectives on the self* (Vol. 2, pp. 123-157). Hillsdale, NJ: Lawrence Erlbaum.

Scheier, M. F., & Carver, C. S. (1985). The Self-Consciousness Scale: A revised version for use with general populations. *Journal of Applied Social Psychology, 15,* 687-699.

Shrauger, J. S., & Osberg, T. M. (1982). Self-awareness: The ability to predict one's future behavior. In G. Underwood (Ed.), *Aspects of consciousness* (Vol. 3, pp. 267-313). London: Academic Press.

Snyder, M. (1974). Self-monitoring of expressive behavior. *Journal of Personality and Social Psychology, 30,* 526-537.

Solomon, M. R., & Schopler, J. (1982). Self-consciousness and clothing. *Personality and Social Psychology Bulletin, 8,* 508-514.

Spana, R., Rich, A., & Robertson, D. (1985, March). *Factorial validity of the self-consciousness scale.* Paper presented at the annual meeting of the Eastern Psychological Association, Boston.

Sugawara, K. (1984). An attempting to construct the Self-Consciousness Scale for Japanese. *Japanese Journal of Psychology, 55,* 184-188.

Turner, R. G. (1978). Consistency, self-consciousness, and the predictive validity of typical and maximal personality measures. *Journal of Research in Personality, 12,* 117-132.

Turner, R. G., & Peterson, M. (1977). Public and private self-consciousness and emotional expressivity. *Journal of Consulting and Clinical Psychology, 45,* 490-491.

Turner, R. G., Scheier, M. F., Carver, C. S., & Ickes, W. (1978). Correlates of self-consciousness. *Journal of Personality Assessment, 42,* 285-289.

Underwood, B., & Moore, B. S. (1981). Sources of behavioral consistency. *Journal of Personality and Social Psychology, 40,* 780-785.

Wymer, W. E., & Penner, L. A. (1985). Moderator variables and different types of predictability: Do you have a match? *Journal of Personality and Social Psychology, 49,* 1002-1015.

Jack L. Bodden, Ph.D.
Psychologist, Olin E. Teague Veterans' Center, Temple, Texas.

THE SELF-DIRECTED SEARCH
John L. Holland. Odessa, Florida: Psychological Assessment Resources, Inc.

Introduction

The Self-Directed Search (SDS) is a self-administered, self-scored, and self-interpreted vocational counseling measure. It consists of four main parts involving the use of a number of scales and ratings. As a whole, the SDS attempts to simulate the vocational counseling experience.

The SDS was created by John L. Holland, Ph.D., representing an outgrowth of his theory of vocational choice (Holland, 1959; 1966). Holland began with the premise that people view the world in terms of occupational stereotypes, and these stereotypes reveal something about the individual and his or her career choices. Over a period of more than 35 years Holland has revised not only his theory of vocational choice but also the SDS. His theory and the SDS have been utilized and refined by an extensive body of empirical research.

Holland's purpose in developing the SDS was to create a "scientifically sound and practical simulation of the vocational counseling experience" (Holland, 1985b, p. v). He hoped to accomplish this goal by developing a self-administered, self-scored, and self-interpreted vocational assessment booklet and a compatible file of occupational possibilities. Part of his motivation to develop the SDS was his desire to develop an inventory that would avoid the problems involved in separate answer sheets, mailing, scoring, and so on.

The origin of the SDS can be traced to the Vocational Preference Inventory (VPI), which Holland developed in 1953, prior to the first presentation of his theory of vocational choice (1959). The VPI was used to define six theoretical personality types (Realistic, Investigative, Social, Conventional, Enterprising, and Artistic). The next step in the process was defining occupational environments according to VPI profiles (1966). In 1969, Holland published his "Hexagonal Ordering" concept, which showed that the correlation between the six theoretical typologies could best be represented by a hexagon so that distances between the six points on the hexagon were inversely proportional to the correlations among the six types). These preliminary steps led to the publication of the first version of the SDS in 1971. Some format changes, a simplified scoring procedure, the inclusion of the seventh revision of the VPI, and the addition of 50 job titles to the Occupations Finder comprised the revision published in 1977. The 1985 edition, which is the subject of this review, is the latest refinement of the SDS. This edition includes updated items, rewritten directions for scoring the test (designed to improve scoring accuracy), and a doubling of the number of occupations in the Occupations Finder (from 500 to more than 1,100). There is also a new form (Form E), which was developed for

420 The Self-Directed Search

adolescents and adults with limited reading skills. Form E has simplified scoring procedures and is shorter than the standard SDS. In addition, a special version of the SDS has been developed for use with the blind.

Research investigations with the SDS have been done in a number of foreign countries. These studies have reportedly demonstrated the validity of the theory as well as the utility of the instrument (Holland, 1985b). However, there are no foreign language versions available to the general test user.

The SDS consists of two main components: 1) the Assessment Booklet and 2) the Occupations Finder. There is also a supplementary booklet entitled *You and Your Career* (Holland, 1985c), which provides additional background on the instrument, the theory, and suggestions for enriching the experience provided by the SDS.

The heart of the SDS is the Assessment Booklet (which incorporates the VPI). The booklet includes four sections: 1) Activities (six scales of 11 items each), 2) Competencies (six scales of 11 items each), 3) Occupations (six scales of 14 items each), and 4) Self-Estimates (two sets of six ratings, each rating corresponding to a type). There is a fifth part to the Assessment Booklet, entitled "Occupational Daydreams," which does not actually contribute to the formal scoring of the SDS; however, the occupations listed in the "Daydreams" section are coded and can be compared with the SDS personality code.

The Occupations Finder includes 1,156 occupational titles (comprising 99% of the workers in the United States). The occupations are arranged according to personality types and subtypes. Each occupational subtype is arranged according to the level of general educational development (GED) that an occupation requires according to the *Dictionary of Occupational Titles* (Department of Labor, 1977).

Each of the four main parts of the Assessment Booklet contain six clusters of items, which correspond to and determine the score for each of Holland's personality types. The personality types (based on Holland's early work on vocational titles, occupational stereotypes, and personality) follow:

1) *Realistic:* a practical, mechanically inclined individual who may be somewhat lacking in social skills;

2) *Investigative:* a scientifically oriented, intellectual person who may lack leadership ability;

3) *Artistic:* an imaginative, creative person who may lack clerical, practical skills;

4) *Social:* a people-oriented individual whose strength is his or her social skills;

5) *Enterprising:* an individual with sales and leadership skills; and

6) *Conventional:* a person who likes orderly pursuits but may lack artistic ability.

The Activities section includes items to which the user responds with "L" (like) or "D" (dislike). Items include interests such as "Fix electrical things" and "Sell something." The Competencies section asks the user to indicate whether or not he or she can perform a given activity well. Items include examples like "I can type 40 words per minute." The Occupations section consists of occupational titles (and is actually the VPI). Users indicate whether they like or are interested in a particular occupation. Self-Estimates include two scales, on which the user rates his or her perceived ability on dimensions such as Manual Skill or Scientific Ability.

The participation of the examiner or counselor in the testing process with the SDS is intended to be nominal. Depending on the age, education, and sophistication of the group or individual using the SDS, the person who administers the instrument may do no more than mail out the instrument or simply serve as a monitor for groups, answering questions and assisting with scoring. Holland encourages monitoring counselors to be trained vocational counselors or psychologists, knowledgeable about psychological assessment and vocational counseling. For the most part the examiner assists in administration or scoring problems and provides vocational guidance to the few who may require additional assistance. It should be noted that Holland never proposed that the SDS would replace vocational counselors or other vocational assessment instruments; rather, he hoped to develop an instrument that, under ideal conditions, would require little or no attention and time from the highly trained professional. The SDS provides an experience that may in itself be sufficient vocational counseling for some individuals; however, it may also stimulate others to ask for more information or even professional counseling.

Although no clear-cut upper and lower age limits have been established, Holland (1985b) states that the SDS can be used for persons 15 years of age and older. The test may be taken individually (and in private) or in groups having one monitor for every 25-30 persons. The reading difficulty level is estimated to be at the seventh- to eighth-grade level using a standard readability formula.

When the user completes the SDS, he or she is guided through the scoring process, which is actually a rather simple process of adding scale subtotals or rating values. The answer sheet is the booklet itself. The scoring process results in a summary or profile code, which is comprised of the three highest values for the six types (e.g., Investigative, Social, and Artistic, or I-S-A). After determining the profile code, the user looks up the occupations listed under the corresponding code in the Occupations Finder (which for an I-S-A would include occupations such as physician, nurse, and educational psychologist). For most people, the process is relatively simple and takes less than 50 minutes.

Practical Applications/Uses

The SDS is designed to multiply the number of people a vocational counselor can serve and to provide a vocational counseling experience for people who may not need or have access to a professional counselor. The SDS eliminates the need—or at least the time—required to administer, mail, score, interpret, and give unnecessary feedback/counseling.

The SDS is intended to give a user an indication of his or her personality type (or style) and a list of occupations that are congruent or compatible with that personality style. The test does not, as Holland points out, tell an individual what jobs he can or should do. Some awareness of Holland's theory can be helpful to the potential user and this information is given in simple terms in *You and Your Career* (Holland, 1985c). The counselor could also provide explanations to those who want an understanding of the rationale of the test.

Holland (1985b) proposes that the SDS can be used with a very wide range of persons. He states that it could serve perhaps as many as 50% of the students and adults who have only a minimal need for vocational assistance. It can and has been used in schools (high school and college), adult centers, correctional institutions, employment offices, women's centers, business, and industry. All of these uses have been evaluated by research and found appropriate.

The SDS is suited to the needs of vocational counselors, counseling and clinical psychologists, and other mental health professionals who have some training in psychometrics, personality theory, and vocational theory. As the examiner serves primarily in a back-up role, the amount of professional training he or she needs depends largely on how the test is to be used.

The SDS has been used in many settings, countries, and by a wide variety of users. The only limitations to its use would be with subjects less than 15 years of age or persons who have no interest in vocational self-exploration. This reviewer suspects that the SDS will always find its greatest use in college counseling centers and high school guidance offices. A considerable amount of research indicates that the SDS is a highly adaptable and pragmatic instrument.

The SDS is suitable for administration individually, in groups, or through the mail. The setting can be anyplace that is relatively quiet. Holland (1985b) states that private settings appear to be conducive to greater individual involvement with the SDS.

Unlike the majority of psychological tests, which are designed to provide data about the user and must be handled from administration to interpretation by a highly skilled professional examiner, the SDS is entirely self-administered, self-scored, and self-interpreted. The instructions to the examinee are quite clear and easy to follow. Form E is especially simple. It is this reviewer's opinion that very few individuals would have difficulty understanding how they are supposed to respond to the SDS.

It is in the area of scoring where most questions and concern have arisen. The booklet gives succinct scoring instructions, the required operations are quite simple (nothing more complicated than adding small numbers), and the scoring procedures, when followed correctly, lead the examinee to a determination of his or her 3-point summary of personality code. However, Holland (1985b) and other reviewers (e.g., Gelso, Collins, Williams, & Sedlacek, 1973) have expressed concern about scoring errors. The manual cites one study of college students in which 60% of the men and 63% of the women made no scoring errors; however, about 83% of both men and women correctly identified their 3-point summary code (even if they made an error along the way). Whether scoring errors are significant enough to raise serious questions as to how truly self-scoring and self-administering the SDS actually is cannot be answered unequivocally. This reviewer believes the scoring instructions are very clear, but monitoring and double-checking by a counselor or monitor is still advisable.

All scoring is accomplished by counting scale totals; no templates are needed. A machine version has been developed for large-scale research studies, but this version is less desirable because self-scoring is an integral part of the SDS's effort to simulate the vocational counseling experience.

In order to interpret the SDS, the examinee is instructed to look up the occupations listed in the Occupations Finder under his or her summary code. Finally, the examinee is given some suggestions for further reading and exploration. The entire process should require no more than 45-50 minutes. The only limitation is that users who are curious about the "hows and whys" of the summary code and the occupational grouping that corresponds to their code may be left with some unanswered questions. Some of these questions could be answered if the student has access to *You and Your Career*. Other questions, such as what the examinee should do if he or she obtains a rare or an undifferentiated summary code (i.e., little or no difference between the top three scores that comprise the code), may require additional input from the psychologist or counselor.

Technical Aspects

According to Holland (1985b), the current version of the SDS is more reliable than the 1977 revision. Measures of internal consistency (Alpha) generally range from about .70 to .93. Test-retest reliability (1-4 weeks) for the 1977 edition (using a sample of high school students) ranged from .56 to .95. The manual does not report test-retest data on the 1985 edition but states that it should be good because of the high intercorrelations between the 1977 and 1985 editions.

In general, the 1985 version of the SDS has shown adequate evidence of its reliability with a diverse group of subjects, and it will probably prove to be as stable as the 1977 edition once test-retest correlations are reported.

Holland (1985b) refers to more than 400 studies of construct validity on the 1971 edition alone. A comparison of concurrent validities of the 1977 and 1985 editions, which involved comparing the examinee's summary code with his or her stated vocational choice, yielded agreement scores ranging from 44% to 70% for the 1977 edition and from 48% to 62% for the 1985 edition. Holland suggests that the concurrent validity of the two editions is probably comparable.

Predictive validity studies based upon the 1971 edition showed moderate support. These validity studies compared SDS summary codes with expressed vocational choice one and three years after taking the SDS. Kappa values ranged from .24 ($p < .001$) to .33 ($p < .001$). Percent correct prediction values ranged from 26.6% to 72.4% in the studies cited by Holland (1985b).

An in-press study cited by Holland (1985b), in reviewing concurrent and predictive validity studies, indicates that most interest inventories have "hit rates" (i.e., predicting stated vocational choice from test profile scores) in the range of 40% to 55% in a six-category scheme. If so, the SDS is comparable to other interest measures in this regard.

In addition to reliability and validity data, Holland (1985b) cites what he calls "effects and outcome data." Studies reported in this section of the manual show that the SDS has the expected positive effect on its user's self and vocational understanding, and also creates more career choice options. Moreover, several studies have found the SDS to "equal the influence of professional counselors" (p. 51).

The SDS appears to possess reliability and validity that are on a level with other vocational interest measures. In addition, a number of studies have also demonstrated its apparent utility.

Critique

This reviewer has been familiar with the theory and research conducted by John Holland for a number of years and has been impressed with the utility of the SDS and the theory on which it rests. As when it was first introduced, the revised SDS fills a genuine need in the vocational counseling field.

424 The Self-Directed Search

John Holland is to be commended for the thorough and thoughtful way in which the SDS manual is constructed. Not only does it cover the theory and rationale upon which the instrument was built, it goes on to discuss administration, scoring, and practical applications. The manual anticipates commonly asked questions regarding the SDS and includes a particularly good section on interpretation and uses of test results. In short, this manual could well serve as a model for other developers of vocational interest inventories.

The SDS is strongly recommended for its practical as well as research value. Holland's theory of career development is probably one of the more viable theories and the SDS is a logical outgrowth of his theory.

References

This list includes text citations and suggested additional reading.

Department of Labor. (1977). *Dictionary of occupational titles* (4th ed.). Washington, DC: U.S. Government Printing Office.

Gelso, C. J., Collins, A. M., Williams, R. O., & Sedlacek, W. E. (1973). The accuracy of self-administration and scoring of Holland's Self-Directed Search. *Journal of Vocational Behavior, 3*, 375-383.

Gottfredson, G. D., Holland, J., & Ogawa, D. K. (1982). *Dictionary of Holland occupational codes.* Palo Alto, CA: Consulting Psychologists Press.

Holland, J. L. (1959). A theory of vocational choice. *Journal of Counseling Psychology, 6*, 35-45.

Holland, J. L. (1966). *The psychology of vocational choice.* Waltham, MA: Blaisdell.

Holland J. L. (1973). *Making vocational choices: A theory of careers.* Englewood Cliffs, NJ: Prentice-Hall.

Holland, J. L. (1985a). *Making vocational choices: A theory of vocational personalities and work environments.* Englewood Cliffs, NJ: Prentice-Hall.

Holland, J. L. (1985b). *The Self-Directed Search, professional manual.* Odessa, FL: Psychological Assessment Resources, Inc.

Holland, J. L. (1985c). *You and your career.* Odessa, FL: Psychological Assessment Resources, Inc.

Holland, J. L., & Gottfredson, G. D. (1976). Using a typology of persons and environments to explain careers: Some extensions and clarifications. *The Counseling Psychologist, 6*, 20-29.

Osipow, S. H. (1973). *Theories of career development.* New York: Appleton-Century-Crofts.

Raymond G. Johnson, Ph.D.
Professor and Co-Chair, Department of Psychology, Macalester College, St. Paul, Minnesota.

SHIPLEY INSTITUTE OF LIVING SCALE
Walter C. Shipley. Los Angeles, California: Western Psychological Services.

Introduction

The Shipley Institute of Living Scale (SILS), more commonly known as the "Shipley-Hartford," has been extensively used by clinical psychologists for nearly half a century. The test consists of two parts, a group of 40 multiple-choice vocabulary items and a set of 20 open-ended series that require the person to abstract a rule with which to determine the next element in the list. A Vocabulary and an Abstraction score may be obtained; intellectual impairment is purportedly indicated when the Abstraction score is considerably lower than expected from the Vocabulary score. The paper-and-pencil test takes less than 20 minutes and may be self-administered and scored by a clerk. A new version is available for microcomputers; the computer administers the test, scores it, and produces a multipage report.

The test was devised by Walter C. Shipley and was originally known as the Shipley-Hartford Retreat Scale. After the institution modified its name, Shipley changed the test title to the Shipley Institute of Living Scale. Articles in the literature are evenly divided between the two titles. The test was published by Shipley and his family for several decades. In recent years the publisher has been Western Psychological Services.

Shipley (1953) states that his test was "inspired" by the work of Harriet Babcock, who had devised an individually administered scale to assess mental deterioration. Babcock (1930) assumed that vocabulary is relatively more resistant to deterioration than speed and performance tests, and used the vocabulary list from the Stanford-Binet as a measure of intellectual level. She compared a person's tested vocabulary level with 24 sets of items. These ranged from memory for designs to learning paired associates, from memory of a paragraph to picture recognition, and from Knox Cubes to timed responses to general information questions. On the basis of the vocabulary score, an expected score is projected for each of the other subtests. Deterioration or impairment may be inferred when actual scores fail to reach the expected level. Babcock's tests are clinical instruments administered

---

The reviewer wishes to thank Robert A. Zachary, former director of clinical assessment at Western Psychological Services, for graciously allowing me to examine a prepublication draft of the revised manual for the Shipley Scale. It is due to be published in the fall of 1986. The final version of that manual may be somewhat different from what is cited in this review.

426 Shipley Institute of Living Scale

individually, allowing the psychologist to observe and make qualitative judgments about the person's performance in addition to the quantitative comparison.

Shipley's goal was to follow Babcock's model "with a view to measuring the same sort of thing on a group-test basis" (1953, p. 751). He wanted a self-administered test that could be given quickly and objectively (1940). He realized that it would be difficult to devise group tests of recent memory; therefore, he chose to use abstract thinking as the ability manifesting rapid deterioration, taking as his guide the sorting tests devised by Kasanin and Hanfmann. Shipley (1953, p. 752) describes his abstraction items as requiring the subject "to induce some principle common to a given series of components and then to demonstrate his understanding of this principle by continuing the series."

Each Abstraction item is a series of letters or numbers followed by blanks indicating the number of characters in the answer. Three items similar to those in the test follow:

1. A C E G I _
2. bib bib   part trap   269 _ _ _
3. 234 162 45 81 315 43_

Instructions are to complete each series and to place the appropriate answer in the blanks. (Answers to the above items are K, 962, and 2.) The individual must infer a rule that governs placement of the elements in the list and then use that rule to determine the next item. The Abstraction score is the number of items correct multiplied by two; thus, scores on this subtest can range from 0 to 40.

The Vocabulary section consists of 40 items. The individual's task is to select the synonym of a word from a set of four alternatives. Vocabulary items have this form:

1. SHIP   animal   tree   knife   boat
2. INANE   slender   timely   silly   damp

The Vocabulary score is the number correct plus one for every four omitted to provide a guessing correction, and scores can range from about 10 to 40.

A total score is the sum of the Vocabulary and the doubled Abstraction score. The original 1940 manual provides tables to derive Vocabulary Age, Abstraction Age, Mental Age, and Conceptual Quotient. A new manual being developed by the publisher (Zachary, 1986) reports these scores but discourages their use. The new manual provides age-corrected T-scores for Vocabulary and Abstraction based on a new normative sample of psychiatric patients. It also provides a new impairment index, the Abstraction Quotient (AQ). The new manual gives an extensive review of relevant literature and many suggestions for appropriate use of the instrument.

Practical Applications/Uses

Each part of the scale has a 10-minute time limit, but because an individual rarely needs that much time the test is often considered a power test. A number of psychiatric institutions have used the Shipley as part of an admissions test battery that often includes the MMPI and a sentence completion device. The psychologist may have the results from these instruments before ever seeing the patient.

The Shipley-Hartford Vocabulary score is usually interpreted as a rough estimate of the individual's intellectual level. The general population mean appears to be in the upper 20s, while bright normals score in the low 30s. The Vocabulary test has a low ceiling and does not distribute persons well at the upper end, and the range is restricted at the lower end as well. A person not answering any item or guessing blindly at all items will obtain a score of 10. Obviously the examinee needs to be able to read some English to earn points. Low scores may be due to language problems, inability to concentrate or follow directions, low intelligence, or other factors. In the original manual, Shipley cautions against the use of the deterioration index (the Conceptual Quotient) with persons of subnormal intelligence; he feels the index should not be used when the Vocabulary score is less than 23. Garfield (1947) maintains that the Shipley-Hartford, and especially the Abstraction scale, is too difficult for persons of below average intelligence. He tested 350 men in a disciplinary barracks who had Wechsler-Bellevue IQs ranging from 50 to 106 and found that mental age scores based on the Shipley-Hartford were lower than those based on the Wechsler.

The Abstraction scale has a low ceiling. In this reviewer's experience using the test as a demonstration instrument in undergraduate classes, Abstraction always yields a negatively skewed distribution. The vagaries of the Shipley distribution probably matter little when used in conjunction with other information to develop clinical hypotheses, but when used in place of the WAIS to estimate IQ or to assess "brain damage" of an individual, the Shipley by itself is inadequate.

Motivation may be a problem in test performance. When high school students were grouped by responses to the question, "How important is it that you do well?", there were no group differences in performance. Poorly motivated chronic schizophrenics, on the other hand, had lower scores than well-motivated patients (Schalock & Wahler, 1968).

An Abstraction score considerably lower than a Vocabulary score may reflect reduced intellectual efficiency, though such an interpretation must take into account other information developed about the individual, such as age, social history, and motivation, as well as anxiety level, psychotic mentation, or possible brain damage.

The Shipley is frequently used in research studies, sometimes as a selection or matching variable, less often as a dependent variable. In recent years it has been particularly popular in the alcoholism literature.

Technical Aspects

In constructing his test, Shipley (1953) used students rather than psychiatric or neurological patients. His initial sample comprised 462 youth from three educational levels: high school freshmen, high school juniors and seniors, and college upperclassmen. This sample was given preliminary forms containing 24 abstraction items and one of three vocabulary lists containing about 40 items each. An item analysis of the abstraction items was performed to select the 20 items that best differentiated students from the three educational levels. Each item in the abstraction test was then matched with two vocabulary items that matched the abstraction item in percent passing at each educational level. The result was a 40-item vocabulary test and a 20-item abstraction test of approximately equal difficulty for this sample that differentiated on the basis of educational level and age.

The Conceptual Quotient is not quite the same as the ratio of Abstraction Age to Vocabulary Age times 100. Shipley continued to follow Babcock's (1930) procedure and constructed a CQ table by first finding the median abstraction age that accompanied each vocabulary age in the normative group. This predicted abstraction age is divided by the obtained abstraction age, then multiplied by 100 to obtain the CQ.

In the new Shipley manual, Zachary (1986) summarizes criticism of age-equivalent and ratio scores. While the concept of mental age allowed Alfred Binet to develop his revolutionary instrument, the notion has outlived its usefulness. Age-equivalent scores are not appropriate for adults, the regression procedures used are arbitrary, variability around the age curve is ignored, no normative information is provided, and the concept of mental age contains misleading connotations. The new manual, however, continues to report Shipley's original Vocabulary Age and Abstraction Age.

Zachary also notes the deficiency in ratio IQs; namely that they may have different variances at various age levels, and that deviation IQs are used in the Wechsler tests and more recently in the Stanford-Binet. The new manual continues to report the CQ, while at the same time strongly criticizing it and recommending that it not be used—an undesirable compromise between selling and science that the publisher feels compelled to make. Zachary has devised a new impairment index, the Abstraction Quotient, which will be described later in this review.

Scherer (1949) found no differences between individual and group administration of the Shipley. Zachary (1986) reports that no differences were obtained between a computer-administered Shipley and the paper-and-pencil version.

An alternate form of the Abstraction scale has been devised by Horlick and Monroe (1954). While the items contain letters and numbers that are different from the original, the rules to be induced are identical to Shipley's version. It is of little use; practice effects remain.

In the literature, Shipley results have been reported in a variety of ways: raw scores for Vocabulary, Abstraction, and total; mental age equivalents of each; IQ transformations; and Conceptual Quotients.

To develop mental-age norms Shipley (1940, 1946) used a sample of 1,046 students who had previously been given standardized group intelligence tests. This group included 572 grammar school pupils in Grades 4 through 8, 257 high school students in Grades 9 through 12, and 217 college students. The college students were given the Otis test, while school records provided mental-age scores from various tests for the other students. On the basis of these results, tables of Vocabulary Age, Abstraction Age, and Conceptual Quotient were developed.

Table 1 lists several studies that have reported mean raw scores. Examination of the table suggests that persons who score above 30 on both subtests may be considered to be of above-average intelligence. Persons in the lower 20s and below on each subtest have difficulty with these kinds of tests and related tasks. The data in Table 1 are not a representative sample of the normal population but include more educated groups. Across these samples median Vocabulary raw score is 31.5 and median Abstraction raw score is 28.3. To the extent that we can generalize from these samples, we may expect normally functioning adults to score on average

Table 1

Shipley-Hartford Mean Raw Scores for Several Nonpsychiatric Samples

Sample	Voc (SD)	Abs (SD)
812 British "normals"[1]	22.8 (8.5)	20.7 (9.0)
485 jr.-sr. high school students[2]	26.4 (5.4)	28.3 (7.3)
65 psychiatric aides[3]	28.1 (5.3)	22.5 (8.9)
43 student nurses[4]	30.5 (2.8)	33.5 (4.3)
56 student nurses[5]	32.5 (2.9)	35.1 (3.8)
200 hospital staff[6]	33.8 (4.2)	28.3 (6.5)
40 medical students[7]	34.7 (3.5)	36.4 (3.3)
60 teachers[8]	34.9 (3.4)	28.3 (4.1)
MEDIAN	31.5	28.3

Sources: [1]Slater (1943); "Approximately random sample of the normal adult population" of Britain, "old men and imbeciles not included"; [2]Palmer (1964); [3]Sines (1958); [4]Shaw (1966); [5]Ruiz and Krauss (1967); [6]Kraus, Chalker, and Macindor (1967), includes nurses, clerks, technicians, and domestic staff in Australia; [7]Jones (1974), medical school students volunteering to participate in alcohol ingestion study; and [8]Garfield and Blek (1952), median of three groups of unmarried female teachers ages 20-30, 40-50, 60-70.

about 3 points higher on the Vocabulary than on the Abstraction portion. Such a figure is consistent with the difference psychiatric patients show on discharge, as will be noted.

Spearman rank-order correlations between means and standard deviations for the samples in Table 1 are .62 for Vocabulary and .99 for Abstraction. Thus as the means get higher, the standard deviations get lower because of the low test ceiling and the resulting piling up at the top of the curve. High as well as low scores on the Shipley are more subject to distortion than scores in the midrange.

The new norms presented in the revised manual (Zachary, 1986) are based on a sample studied by Paulson and Lin (1970) comprising 290 mixed psychiatric patients drawn from three sources: 160 clinic patients from the Neuro-Psychiatric Institute of the UCLA Medical Center (a low SES group with some neurological cases); 60 patients from private psychiatric practices in Los Angeles (an upper-middle-class group); and 70 patients from private files of psychologists at NPI-UCLA (also upper middle class). Each group contained both out- and inpatients, but the proportions were not reported. The only criterion for selection was that each person had taken both the Shipley and the WAIS. The sample contains approximately equal numbers of men and women. The youngest examinees in the sample are 16 years old and a small proportion are over 54 years. The mean age is 34.9, but, reflecting the positive skew, the median is about 30 and Q is roughly equal to 10. This sample obtained a Vocabulary mean of 29.2 (SD = 6.0) and an Abstraction mean of 22.0 (SD = 10.1).

The new manual has tables of age-corrected T-scores for Vocabulary and

Abstraction based on this sample. It has age-based tables for estimating WAIS and WAIS-R IQs. The Abstraction Quotient (AQ), a new impairment index, based on the difference between Vocabulary and Abstraction scores, is also reported. To obtain the AQ, a predicted Abstraction score is compared to the actual Abstraction score. The predicted score is derived from a regression equation that uses Vocabulary score, age, and educational level and is reported as a standard score with a mean of 100 and an SD of 15. The AQ is an improvement over the CQ, because the latter was strongly influenced by age (e.g., Garfield & Fey, 1948).

Because the new norms are based on a sample of psychiatric patients, the Abstraction T-scores and the AQ will tend to overestimate an individual's functioning. Zachary and Huba (1985) have developed a table, reprinted in the manual, listing the statistical uniqueness of the various T-score combinations, correcting for the correlation between the two subtests. A more useful table for clinicians would be a normative table for predicted Abstraction scores. (I could not find the SE(est) for Abstraction score predictions in the manual [Zachary, 1986]).

Shipley assessed the reliability of his scales with a sample of 322 Army recruits. The odd-even correlations were .87 (Vocabulary), .89 (Abstraction), and .92 (total score). Manson and Grayson (1947) obtained similar figures; they calculated Spearman-Brown reliabilities for 1,262 prisoners as .82 for Vocabulary and .92 for Abstraction. Thus, internal consistency appears satisfactory.

Retest reliabilities are more difficult to interpret; a practice effect should be evident over short intervals. Most studies of retest reliability have used small samples and intellectually homogeneous groups (nurses or college students) whose mean scores are over 30 on each Shipley subtest. The resulting restriction of range should attenuate reliability coefficients. Retests of three samples of nurses (Ns of 43, 56, and 19) over a 3-month period yielded coefficients for Vocabulary of .54, .77, and .60, and for Abstraction of .47, .63, and .61 (Shaw, 1966; Ruiz & Krauss, 1967; Goodman, Streiner, & Woodward, 1974). Reliabilities of the total score were .62, .74, and .63. Another study using 40 undergraduates found total score reliability of .80 over a 45-day period (Martin, Blair, Stokes, & Lester, 1977).

The practice effect found in these studies (Shaw, 1966; Ruiz & Krauss, 1967; Goodman et al., 1974) tended to be less than one point for Vocabulary but about two to four points for Abstraction. The latter differences could be greater in more heterogeneous samples; with Abstraction means over 37 for student nurses on 3-month retest, the test ceiling left little room for the practice effect.

A study of 181 state hospital patients who retook the Shipley on readmission following an average interval of 14 months found a retest reliability coefficient of .73 (Stone, 1965b). The estimated IQs rose from 103.8 to 105.7. Moreover, Schalock and Wahler (1968) administered the Shipley weekly to chronic schizophrenics and to high school students. Over repeated testings the students' scores improved while the patients' scores did not.

Thus, while internal consistency reliability measures are satisfactory, coefficients of stability reach only moderate levels. Interpretation of these data is complicated because of the homogeneity of some of the samples used, the low test ceiling, practice effects, and possible motivation problems among patient groups.

Several studies have reported the intercorrelations of the Vocabulary and the Abstraction tests in samples ranging from high school students to "normal" British adults, to psychiatric and nonpsychiatric patients. The results ranged from .31 to .71 with a median correlation of .53 (Eisenthal & Harford, 1971; Kish, 1970; Mason & Ganzler, 1964; Palmer, 1964; Paulson & Lin, 1970; Pishkin, Lovallo, Lenk, & Bourne, 1977; Salzman, Goldstein, Atkins, & Babigian, 1966; Slater, 1943).

A number of studies have shown that results on the Shipley-Hartford are strongly related to age. Among adolescents there is a positive correlation between age and Vocabulary and Abstraction scores, reflecting Shipley's strategy of selecting items that differentiated students of various grades or ages. In his study of junior and senior high school students, Palmer (1964) found correlations with age of .58 for Vocabulary and .47 for Abstraction.

The results reported by Tarter and Jones (1971) indicate the different trends among adults. VA patients under 45 years have Vocabulary scores of 27.4, and patients between 46 and 60 have a score of 29.3. On Abstraction, the younger patients score 19.4 and the older patients score 17.6. Hoffmann and Nelson (1971) grouped alcoholics into three age groups, 18-44, 45-54, and 55-67, and found decreasing Conceptual Quotients of 84, 74, and 67. Another study at the same state hospital (Jansen & Hoffmann, 1973) showed that CQ also increases with IQ and with educational level. Their ANOVA results were highly significant and no interaction was found. Corotto (1966) tested several hundred psych-tech trainees. His ANOVA showed no interactions, but main effects of age of Vocabulary, Abstraction, and CQ.

Salzman et al. (1966) report a correlation of -.45 between age and Abstraction. They found that when they controlled for age the Shipley-Hartford differences between various neurotic and psychotic admissions to a university psychiatric unit washed out. Mason and Ganzler (1964) obtained a correlation of -.29 between Abstraction and age, with a positive correlation of .18 between Vocabulary and age. Eisenthal and Harford (1971) obtained age correlations with Vocabulary and Abstraction of .07 and -.33 in 100 hospitalized VA patients.

To examine age differences on the Shipley in a nonpsychiatric group, Garfield and Blek (1952) studied a group of unmarried women who were or had been teachers. They had three groups, each with 20 persons, aged 20-30, 40-50, and 60-70. Vocabulary means were higher in the older groups (31.3, 34.9, and 37.6), while Abstraction remained constant or showed some decrease (31.6, 28.3, 29.2).

Any interpretation of the Shipley-Hartford must consider the factor of age. Among adults we may expect that older samples will have slightly higher Vocabulary scores and considerably lower Abstraction scores and CQs. The T-score values presented in the new manual (Zachary, 1986) are age corrected, as is the Abstraction Quotient.

Stone and Chambers (1965) found no gender effect among over 2,500 state hospital patients; Paulson and Lin (1970) found none in the 290 mixed psychiatric patients used for the new norms. But at least two studies have reported gender differences. Pauker (1975) began with 54 males and 62 females. Both inpatients and outpatients were represented. He matched them by age and WAIS Full Scale IQ and found that females had higher Shipley total scores than males: 47.4 to 42.2. Palmer (1964) tested almost 500 junior and senior high school students and found the girls to be slightly but consistently higher than the boys, especially on Abstraction. Corotto (1966) found no gender differences in his sample of psych-tech trainees, and by and large there is an assumption implicit in the literature that gender differences are not significant.

Contrary to the expectation of some, educational level seems more related to Abstraction than to Vocabulary. Kish and Ball (1969) randomly selected subjects from VAH files, omitting chronic brain syndrome patients. They divided the sample into persons with no more than a grade school education and those who have gone to high school. The groups did not differ in age. Vocabulary scores for the two groups were identical (24.5 and 25.2), but the groups differed on Abstraction (11.4 and 16.6) and CQ (72.7 and 81.0).

A recent study at the Institute for Living in Hartford obtained means considerably higher than those found at state and VA hospitals. The authors (Phillips, Phillips, & Shearn, 1980) had two groups of patients, 23 schizophrenics and 36 nonschizophrenics. The Vocabulary means for these groups were 28.5 and 32.1, and the Abstraction means were 27.0 and 27.2. The higher mean scores as compared with state hospital and VA groups probably reflect the higher educational level, lower age, and better functioning of this more select group.

Eisenthal and Harford (1971) obtained Vocabulary and Abstraction correlations with social class of .44 and .41 on a sample of VAH patients. Among high school students Palmer (1964) found correlations of .29 and .20.

Clearly, scores on the Shipley reflect demographic variables, particularly age and SES. Such a condition is not unique to the Shipley-Hartford. Demographic variables (age, gender, race, education, occupation) of the WAIS normative group explain over half the variance of WAIS Full Scale IQs (Wilson et al., 1978). Shipley-Hartford scores must always be interpreted with respect to age and social history.

A number of studies have calculated the correlation between Wechsler-Bellevue or WAIS Full Scale IQs and Shipley-Hartford total scores (Garfield & Fey, 1948; Lewinski, 1946; Monroe, 1966; Sines, 1958; Sines & Simmons, 1959; Stone & Ramer, 1965; Suinn, 1960; Wahler & Watson, 1962; Weins & Banaka, 1960; Wright, 1946). These studies used psychiatric inpatients and outpatients as well as aides. These correlations range from .65 to .90 with a median of .76. Thus, the Shipley total score typically explains over one-half the Wechsler Full Scale IQ variance, even though the range has been restricted both by omitting those low scoring individuals who cannot read the Shipley, and by the low ceiling of the test.

Prado and Taub (1966) tested 59 VA patients and almost as many employees or applicants. They recommend the Shipley as a screening instrument, noting that of the persons who had at least an average Shipley, all had at least an average WAIS.

A number of investigators have developed regression equations and tables, some with age corrections, to estimate WAIS Full Scale IQs from Shipley total scores. As Zachary (1986) points out, these equations are most accurate for midrange scores. Most will tend to underestimate IQs above 115.

Dennis (1973) did a cross-validation of a number of these prediction equations on a sample of 37 psychiatric patients. He found correlations between Shipley-predicted and actual WAIS FSIQs to range from 0.716 to 0.792, and the SE(est) ranged from 7.68 to 8.79. The best of these estimates is age corrected, but even it provides 95% confidence intervals (1.96 × 7.68) that range about two standard deviations of IQ [(X-15.05) < X < (X+15.05)]. With so much error, pinpoint estimates are inappropriate.

The most recent attempts to develop WAIS FSIQ and now WAIS-R FSIQ estimates have been by the publisher, apparently to be used with a computer scoring and interpretive program and as part of a new manual (Zachary, Crumpton, & Spiegel, 1985; Zachary, Paulson, & Gorsuch, 1985; Zachary, 1986). They have brought the SE(est) down to 5.75 for the WAIS-R on a cross-validation sample providing 95% confidence intervals of ± 11.3 or about 1.5 standard deviations of IQ. The authors recognize the problem when they state that while the Shipley is "useful for general intellectual screening, it should not be used to make more fine-grained discriminations in the higher and lower IQ scores" (p. 537). They still provide a table with increments as low as one IQ point. Instead of reporting that the estimated WAIS-R IQ of a 40-year-old man with a Shipley Total Score of 60 is 102, why not have the table show the 95% confidence limits of 91 and 113? The table would then be less subject to misuse. If Zachary et al. and the publisher are concerned about the deficiencies at the top and bottom of the Shipley, their energies would be better spent revising the instrument to obtain better spread at the extremes.

The conversion tables provided in the Zachary articles go down to a Shipley Total Score of zero. With the multiple-choice format and guessing correction on the Vocabulary test, a "zero" score is 10. What do scores less than 10 mean?

Responsible clinicians will use the WAIS when a more refined individual assessment is needed. Converting the Shipley score to an estimated WAIS IQ should not be encouraged in clinical practice, although such conversion may have usefulness in research. The new manual and scoring programs will probably stimulate more WAIS estimates.

Palmer (1964) found the Shipley Vocabulary and Abstraction subtests to correlate .77 and .64 with the STEP-SCAT academic achievement tests in 151 high school students. Eisenthal and Harford (1971) correlated the Shipley Vocabulary and Abstraction scores with the Raven Progressive Matrices in 100 VA hospital patients and obtained coefficients of .57 and .67. The Shipley has been found to correlate approximately .4 with the Quantitative score of the Porteus Mazes (Bennett, 1956; Sutker, Moan, & Swanson, 1972); Bennett found nonsignificant correlations with Porteus Qualitative scores. Martin, Blair, Sadowski, and Wheeler (1981) obtained a .39 correlation between total score on the Shipley and the Intellectual Efficiency scale of the California Psychological Inventory.

Table 2 lists mean Vocabulary and Abstraction raw scores for several psychiatric samples. It is a heterogeneous bunch, ranging from state hospital patients of the 1940s and soldiers referred for evaluation to contemporary private hospital patients. Both inpatients and outpatients of varying ages are represented. The studies are ranked by Vocabulary means. From the table one may infer poor functioning among city hospital alcoholics, deterioration and motivational problems in long-time state hospital patients, lack of deterioration in servicemen referred largely for behavior problems, and higher functioning among the younger, better-educated patients at a private psychiatric facility. The median across the samples in Table 2 is 28.0 for Vocabulary and 18.7 for Abstraction, a difference of about 9 points.

Three studies compared Shipley-Hartford scores taken at admission and later at discharge of psychiatric patients (Kobler, 1947; Lewinsohn & Nichols, 1964; Gold-

Table 2

Shipley Scale Mean Raw Scores for Several Psychiatric Samples

Sample	Voc (SD)	Abs (SD)
376 alcoholic inpatients[1]	24.2 (nr)	15.5 (nr)
50 state hospital patients[2]	24.8 (6.2)	12.5 (9.3)
977 naval psychiatric patients[3]	24.8 (6.9)	18.2 (nr)
251 VAH psychiatric patients[4]	25.8 (7.1)	16.6 (10.0)
100 VAH psychiatric patients[5]	27.7 (nr)	15.6 (nr)
99 VA MH clinic patients[6]	27.7 (6.0)	20.3 (10.8)
886 state hospital admissions[7]	28.0 a	18.0 a
100 psychological referrals[8]	28.0 a	29.5 a
86 psychiatric outpatients[9]	28.4 (7.2)	21.4 (10.2)
23 schizophrenic patients[10]	28.5 (8.5)	27.0 (9.6)
150 VAH psychiatric patients[11]	28.8 (6.6)	19.4 (9.7)
290 *mixed psychiatric patients[12]*	*29.2 (6.0)*	*22.0 (10.1)*
44 psychiatric outpatients[13]	29.4 (5.4)	18.1 (10.6)
36 non-schizophrenic patients[14]	32.1 (5.2)	27.2 (8.8)
MEDIAN	28.0	18.7

a: Scores reported as Vocabulary Age and Abstraction Age.
Sources: [1]Dalton and Dubnicki (1981), city hospital patients; [2]Magaret and Simpson (1948), patients aged 40-50 years; [3]Wright (1946), neuropsychiatric unit of naval hospital; [4]Sines (1958); [5]Zachary, Crumpton, and Spiegel (1985); [6]Sines (1958); [7]Stone (1965a), all new admissions to state hospital; [8]Lewinski (1946), men referred for psychological evaluation; [9]Zachary, Paulson, and Gorsuch (1985); [10]Phillips, Phillips, and Shearn (1980), private hospital, young, educated; [11]Eisenthal and Harford (1971); [13]*Paulson & Lin (1970), the new normative sample;* [13]Zachary, Paulson, and Gorsuch (1985); and [14]Phillips, Phillips, and Shearn (1980), private hospital, young, educated.

stein & Salzman, 1967). The results are shown in Table 3. From admission to discharge median Vocabulary scores went from 27.5 to 28.8, while median Abstraction scores went from 20.6 to 26.3. Psychiatric patients in the acute phase of their disorder on admission show a diminution of intellectual efficiency as represented in lowered Abstraction scores. At discharge these Abstraction scores rise to normal levels. The Vocabulary scores at discharge have increased only a point or two, while the Abstraction scores have increased 3 to 6 points.

In a study of factors related to improvement of mental hospital patients, Lewinsohn (1967) used a variety of measures and outcome criteria. He found that Shipley Vocabulary scores were not related to the outcome measures, but that improvement in Abstraction was related to financial security and father's occupational level. Jansen and Nickles (1973) compared Shipley scores of patients with two or more admissions with patients who had been admitted but once; they found no differences in IQ or CQ.

Table 3

Shipley-Hartford Mean Raw Scores on Admission and Discharge for Several Psychiatric Samples

	Admission		Discharge	
Sample	Voc(SD)	Abs(SD)	Voc(SD)	Abs(SD)
100 Army psychiatric patients[1]	26.5 (6.4)	20.1 (9.8)	27.7 (6.3)	25.4 (9.9)
45 psychiatric patients[2]	28.1 (nr)	21.0 (nr)	28.3 (nr)	27.1 (nr)
45 nonschizophrenic patients[3]	29.1 (6.1)	24.2 (9.4)	30.2 (6.2)	27.6 (8.8)
44 schizophrenic patients[4]	26.9 (8.3)	18.1 (9.3)	29.4 (8.0)	21.6 (10.5)
MEDIAN	27.5 (6.4)	20.6 (9.4)	28.8 (6.3)	26.3 (9.9)

Sources: [1]Kobler (1947); [2]Lewinsohn and Nichols (1964); [3]Goldstein and Salzman (1967); [4]Goldstein and Salzman (1967).

Braff and Beck (1974) compared depressed patients with schizophrenic patients in a run of consecutive admissions. On Vocabulary and Abstraction the depressed patients scored 28.0 and 18.7, while the schizophrenics had 23.0 and 10.8. Normal controls from a local church with similar SES had means of 31.5 and 32.3. The depressed patients were considerably older than the schizophrenics and the controls, making more salient the impairment of the schizophrenics as represented by their low Abstraction score. Abrams and Nathanson (1966) studied intellectual deterioration by retesting schizophrenics who had been hospitalized for over 6 years since the initial testing. Both Vocabulary and Abstraction showed statistically significant decreases, Vocabulary by 2-3 points and Abstraction by 4-5 points. It seems too short a time for aging to have a major effect, but motivational change may well have occurred together with or as part of the schizophrenic process.

Murray, Page, Stotland, and Dietze (1970) found a correlation of -.52 between Shipley vocabulary scores and the Phillips scale of process-reactive schizophrenia. Lewinsohn (1963) used a regression procedure to control for age and vocabulary level and found that schizophrenics, especially chronics, tended to score lower than psychiatric and normal controls. Pishkin, Lovallo, Lenk, and Bourne (1977) studied cognitive dysfunction in schizophrenics. The Shipley scores had a correlation of about -.5 with errors on the Whitaker Index of Schizophrenic Thinking, and correlations over -.7 with errors on a rule learning task. Knight, Epstein, and Zielony (1980) also compared the Shipley with the Whitaker Index. They found correlations of -.32 with Vocabulary and -.43 with Abstractions.

Psychiatric patients have lowered Abstraction scores on admission that are on average improved at discharge. The results lend support to the construct validity of the test as a measure of intellectual impairment. Schizophrenics show lower scores than other patients on both Vocabulary and Abstraction.

Shipley and Burlingame (1941) ranked Conceptual Quotients for various diagnostic groups and found that psychoneurotics had a mean CQ of 93, which was similar to normals (CQ = 100). The CQs of functional psychotics ranged from 75 to 85, while CNS syphilitics had the lowest score (CQ = 58).

Other empirical studies of brain-damaged patients do not lend much support for the Shipley as a subtle measure of impairment. Robinson (1946) found the CQs of lobotomized schizophrenics to be no different from control schizophrenics. Winfield (1953) estimated IQs from General Classification Tests taken by men entering service with IQs estimated from the Shipley taken after they suffered brain trauma and found no differences. Nine Klinefelter's syndrome (a congenital endocrine condition) cases were found in the military and had a mean Conceptual Quotient of 103.5 (Barker & Black, 1976). No test showed deficit or dysfunction in these individuals who as servicemen were a highly selected sample from the Klinefelter's population. Canter (1951) challenged the validity of the CQ when he found no measured deterioration in multiple sclerosis patients. Ross and McNaughton (1944) examined 90 head-injured patients and reported that the Shipley "in our series showed no relation to severity of the injury or to the electroencephalographic or pneumoencephalographic evidence of cerebral damage except in cases of extreme injury" (p. 259).

The expectation that psychological test scores should have a linear relationship with EEG or morphological measures is not justified, especially when extreme cases have been omitted. It is impossible to say whether the aforementioned negative results represent test misses or the recuperative function of the brain. Negative results may indicate that the Shipley is insensitive to impairment resulting from brain malfunction or injury. Negative results may also reflect that no significant intellectual impairment has occurred. To validate a test of intellectual impairment, independent evidence of deterioration (psychometric, behavioral, social history) is needed.

Several studies have looked at the ability to abstract in selected groups of subjects with hypothetically impaired abstracting ability. Malerstein and Beldon (1968) matched 10 Korsakoff's syndrome (polyneuritica psychosis) patients with 10 alcoholic controls on age, gender, education, and WAIS Vocabulary. The controls had Shipley Vocabulary and Abstraction means of 31.3 and 23.0, while the Korsakoff's patients had means of 31.8 and 10.7. Black (1973) found that patients with diffuse brain damage had lower Conceptual Quotients than patients with penetrating missile wounds, 79.2 to 92.7. WAIS Full Scale IQs showed a similar difference. Black (1976) found that subjects with frontal lesions had better scores on a number of WAIS measures than subjects with posterior lesions. Shipley-Hartford CQs were in the same direction (94.6 and 88.09), but were not significantly different. Lyle and Gottesman (1977) followed up the offspring of Huntington's disease patients and attempted to ascertain premorbid psychometric indicators of the Huntington's gene. They found that Shipley-Hartford total score had a point-biserial correlation of .41 with the criterion (still normal, late onset, early onset). Over these groups Vocabulary declined slightly, but there was a marked difference in Abstraction between the still-normal group and those who showed the Huntington's symptoms.

Aita, Armitage, Reitan, and Rabinovitz (1947) compared 70 veterans with brain damage with 61 controls who were on the same wards. While 46% of the brain-injured patients had pathological CQs, so did 26% of the controls. The groups had similar Vocabulary scores, but differed on Abstraction (22.2 and 17.7). The authors found little relationship between the Shipley and the Hunt-Minnesota Test and concluded that the Shipley was of "doubtful validity" for diagnosing brain damage. Armitage (1946) pointed out that the Conceptual Quotient is not valid for diagnosing brain damage; both false negatives and false positive are produced.

Among the general run of psychiatric patients there appears to be no relationship between Shipley scores and number of Bender figures recalled (Aaronson, Nelson, & Holt, 1953). However, while comparing "brain-damaged" patients with schizophrenics, Watson (1968) found correlations with the Shipley of .58 with the Bender, .60 with the Graham-Kendall, and .46 with BVRT correct. Parker (1957) tested 30 brain damaged soldiers and compared their results with control patients. The mean age of each group was in the mid-20s. He used a variety of tests: Bender-Gestalt, Goldstein-Scheerer sorting, Wechsler Memory Scale, and Block Design. Only Block Design differentiated the groups—on the Shipley the controls had a lower CQ than the brain-damaged subjects! Garfield and Fey (1948) found no relationship between Shipley Conceptual Quotient and a Wechsler-Bellevue Hold-No Hold Index; the age corrected correlation was .13.

Inferring brain damage on the basis of psychological test results involves using some scores as indicators of the client's premorbid level of functioning and then comparing other scores to that level. There are a large number of possible comparison standards and many potential measures of functioning. The Shipley provides only one of each. Yates (1954, 1956) questions the assumption that vocabulary level may be used as the measure of previous intellectual functioning. He argues that spurious organic scores may be obtained when using such a procedure. He also questions the "rather curious (assumption) that organic deterioration is similar to the deterioration accompanying age" (1954, p. 368).

From the studies done with neurological patients and those performed with psychiatric patients, one must conclude that low Abstraction scores and low Conceptual Quotients are not pathognomic of brain damage. In clinical situations the Shipley is useful as a screening instrument, but one cannot diagnose brain damage on the basis of this test alone. This reviewer is not the first to point out that vague terms such as "brain damage" or "organicity" need much more specific definition in order to clarify the relationships between brain lesions and psychological functioning.

Critique

The Shipley-Hartford is a useful device to make a rough assessment of intellectual functioning. It taps some of the same abilities as the Wechsler tests. Hunt (1949, p. 456) found the Shipley to be

> . . . as satisfactory as, if not more so than, the other available measures. Brevity and ease of administration are definitely in its favor. The answers on the Abstraction Test also offer relatively rich material for clinical interpretation despite the pencil-and-paper nature of the test. Some weakness develops at the lower ranges of intelligence, suggesting the need for further extension at this level. (p. 456)

Ives (1949) concludes her review,

> ... for screening purposes or to supplement information from other tests, the Shipley scale provides valuable information regarding impairment in abstract thinking when restricted to the select group for which it is suited—above average in intelligence, reasonably well educated with no language handicaps, test-sophisticated, not too disturbed to be cooperative, and preferably young. (p. 45)

Armitage (1946) concludes that "as a screening device is the only possible way in which [the Shipley-Hartford] can profitably be employed. . . . To determine the presence or absence of intellectual impairment, regardless of its cause, the test is of value" (p. 16). Filskov and Leli (1981) feel that short tests such as the Shipley can be used only as "adjunctive" measures "since validity data regarding their sensitivity to brain deficits have not been evaluated" (p. 558).

Yates (1972) concludes his review of the test by saying

> The test, used with due caution because of possible confounding factors listed above [failure to control in the standardization data, for confounding variables such as age, sex, educational level, and the effects of slowness or responding], remains a useful screening device or indicator of change where more intensive or direct experimental investigation is not possible (p. 322).

The new Shipley manual is a major improvement; all users of this test should obtain a copy. It provides a comprehensive review of the Shipley literature and is replete with cautions about the appropriate use of the instrument.

Users of the Shipley need to be aware of the characteristics of the new normative sample when making inferences on the basis of T-scores. These norms are based on a group of psychiatric patients who may be slightly above average in SES, but who manifest some performance deficit in Abstraction. The decision to use psychiatric patients as the normative group may not have been wise. Clinicians are accustomed to interpreting roughly equal Vocabulary and Abstraction scores as showing no evidence of deterioration. The new norms tend to minimize impairment. Consider a 35-year-old man with a high-school education: suppose his scores were the same as the medians in Table 3 as he entered and left the hospital. His admission raw scores for Vocabulary and Abstraction of 28 and 21 correspond to T-scores of 45 and 48. His discharge scores of 29 and 26 have T-scores of 47 and 53. The Abstraction Quotient on admission would be 99 and on discharge it would be 106. A more accurate picture of his functioning would have been an admission AQ in the low 90s and approximately 100 on discharge. Clinicians will need to look to their own experience to see whether their interpretations of Shipley results are greatly modified on the basis of these new norms.

The computerized version of the Shipley will now print out a 6-page report that, despite the caveats of the manual, are certain, I fear, to be misused.

In the new manual, Zachary lists several directions for future research on the Shipley. They include study of the AQ, establishing its norms, conducting validity studies with criterion groups and correlations with other measures, and relating the Shipley to brain scans. Goals for the Shipley should be more modest. It cannot replace the Halstead-Reitan, the Michigan, or the idiosyncratic test batteries used by clinicians, and validity data for these batteries are difficult to come by.

Clinical and research users should be cautioned against overinterpreting results from the Shipley and consider the following:

1. The results are affected by age. Older samples have slightly higher Vocabulary scores but considerably lower Abstraction scores; test development was done with samples of students. Yates (1954, p. 367) calls the standardization of the Shipley "completely inadequate" because only young, intelligent normals were used.

2. The new norms are age and education corrected, but are based on psychiatric patients rather than normals; thus, an Abstraction T-score of 50 may imply some impairment. The T-scores and the AQ should be used with caution.

3. The test is inappropriate for low IQ persons or individuals with language handicaps.

4. The Shipley also has a low ceiling and will not spread high IQ subjects.

5. Shipley results may be lowered by poor motivation of the examinee. The test is self-administered, and motivational level cannot be evaluated by the clinician.

6. Retest reliabilities are only moderate. This may be because of the shortness of the test, low ceiling and high base, uncontrolled motivational variables, or the homogeneity of the samples used.

7. Although correlations with WAIS FSIQ are about .7 to .8, estimates based on the Shipley should be used with caution. Under the best of circumstances, the 95% confidence intervals of the IQ estimates are 1.5 standard deviations of IQ.

8. Relatively low scores on the Abstraction section may reflect diminished intellectual efficiency. Schizophrenics, for example, tend to score lower on Abstraction than other psychiatric patient groups, and chronic schizophrenics lower yet.

9. A relatively low Abstraction score or low Conceptual Quotient or low Abstraction Quotient is *not* pathognomic of intellectual impairment resulting from brain damage.

The Shipley-Hartford is useful as a screening instrument, but it cannot replace more intensive individual devices to assess individual intellectual functioning. We can do no better than conclude with Shipley's own caution:

> [The application of the scale] is pretty well restricted to use with individuals of at least average intelligence who are reasonably well educated and are without language handicaps. (1953, p. 755)

The scale should not be used as a final, definitive measure of intellectual impairment. Instead, it should be used as a preliminary screening device to call to the attention of clinicians those individuals who may be functioning at a lowered level in an important area of their thinking and therefore need to be studied more carefully. Where impairment is indicated in the test score, only further clinical evaluation will determine whether the impairment is genuine and, if so, to what it is attributable.

References

Aaronson, B. S., Nelson, S. S., & Holt, S. (1953). On a relation between Bender-Gestalt recall and Shipley-Hartford scores. *Journal of Clinical Psychology, 9,* 88.

Abrams, S., & Nathanson, I. A. (1966). Intellectual deficit in schizophrenia: Stable or progressive. *Diseases of the Nervous System, 27,* 115-117.

Aita, J., Armitage, S. G., Reitan, R. M., & Rabinovitz, A. (1947). The use of certain psychological tests in the evaluation of brain injury. *Journal of General Psychology, 37,* 25-44.

Armitage, S. G. (1946). An analysis of certain psychological tests used for the evaluation of brain injury. *Psychological Monographs, 60* (Whole No. 277).

Babcock, H. (1930). An experiment in the measurement of mental deterioration. *Archives of Psychology, 18* (Whole No. 117).

Barker, T. E., & Black, F. W. (1976). Klinefelter syndrome in a military population. *Archives of General Psychiatry, 33,* 607-610.

Bennett, H. J. (1956). The Shipley-Hartford Scale and the Porteus Maze test as measures of functioning intelligence. *Journal of Clinical Psychology, 12,* 190-191.

Black, F. W. (1973). Cognitive and memory performance in subjects with brain damage secondary to penetrating missile wounds and closed head injury. *Journal of Clinical Psychology, 29,* 441-442.

Black, F. W. (1976). Cognitive deficits in patients with unilateral war-related frontal lobe lesions. *Journal of Clinical Psychology, 32,* 366-372.

Braff, D. L., & Beck, A. T. (1974). Thinking disorder in depression. *Archives of General Psychiatry, 31,* 456-459.

Canter, A. H. (1951). Direct and indirect measures of psychological deficit in multiple sclerosis. *Journal of General Psychology, 44,* 3-50.

Corotto, L. V. (1966). Effects of age and sex on the Shipley-Institute of Living Scale. *Journal of Consulting Psychology, 30,* 179.

Dalton, J. L., & Dubnicki, C. (1981). Sex, race, age, and educational variables in Shipley-Hartford scores of alcoholic inpatients. *Journal of Clinical Psychology, 37,* 885-888.

Dennis, D. M. (1973). Predicting Full Scale WAIS IQs with the Shipley-Hartford. *Journal of Clinical Psychology, 29,* 366-368.

Eisenthal, S. & Harford, T. (1971). Correlation between the Raven Progressive Matrices Scale and the Shipley Institute of Living Scale. *Journal of Clinical Psychology, 27,* 213-215.

Filskov, S. B., & Leli, D. A. (1981). Assessment of the individual in neuropsychological practice. In S. B. Filskov & T. J. Boll (Eds.), *Handbook of clinical neuropsychology* (pp. 545-576). New York: Wiley.

Garfield, S. L. (1947). The Shipley-Hartford Retreat Scale as a quick measure of mental status. *Journal of Consulting Psychology, 11,* 148-150.

Garfield, S. L., & Blek, L. (1952). Age, vocabulary level, and mental impairment. *Journal of Consulting Psychology, 16,* 395-398.

Garfield, S. L., & Fey, W. F. (1948). A comparison of the Wechsler-Bellevue and Shipley-Hartford scales as measures of mental impairment. *Journal of Consulting Psychology, 12,* 259-264.

Goldstein, R. H., & Salzman, L. F. (1967). Cognitive functioning in acute and remitted psychiatric patients. *Psychological Reports, 21,* 24-26.

Goodman, J. T., Streiner, D. L., & Woodward, C. A. (1974). Test-retest reliability of the Shipley-Institute of Living Scale: Practice effects or random variation. *Psychological Reports, 35,* 351-354.

Hoffmann, H., & Nelson, P. C. (1971). Personality characteristics of alcoholics in relation to age and intelligence. *Psychological Reports, 29,* 143-146.

Horlick, R. S., & Monroe, H. J. (1954). A study of the reliability of an alternate form of the Shipley-Hartford Abstraction scale. *Journal of Clinical Psychology, 10,* 381-383.

Hunt, W. A. (1949). Shipley-Institute of Living Scale for Measuring Intellectual Impairment. In O.K. Buros (Ed.), *The third mental measurements yearbook* (p. 456). Highland Park, NJ: The Gryphon Press.

Ives, M. (1949). Shipley-Institute of Living Scale for Measuring Intellectual Impairment. In O.K. Buros (Ed.), *The third mental measurements yearbook* (pp. 456-457). Highland Park, NJ: The Gryphon Press.

Jansen, D. G., & Hoffmann, H. (1973). The influence of age, intelligence, and educational level on Shipley-Hartford Conceptual Quotients of state hospital alcoholics. *Journal of Clinical Psychology, 29,* 468-470.

Jansen, D. G., & Nickles, L. A. (1973). Variables that differentiate between single- and multiple-admission psychiatric patients at a state hospital over a 5-year period. *Journal of Clinical Psychology, 29,* 83-85.

Jones, B. M. (1974). Cognitive performance of introverts and extraverts following acute alcohol ingestion. *British Journal of Psychology, 65,* 35-42.

Kish, G. B. (1970). Alcoholics' GATB and Shipley profiles and their interrelationships. *Journal of Clinical Psychology, 26,* 482-484.

Kish, G. B., & Ball, M. E. (1969). Low education level as one factor producing a verbal-abstract disparity on the Shipley-Institute of Living Scale. *Journal of Clinical Psychology, 25,* 183-184.

Knight, R. A., Epstein, B., & Zielony, R. D. (1980). The validity of the Whitaker Index of Schizophrenic Thinking. *Journal of Clinical Psychology, 36,* 632-639.

Kobler, F. J. (1947). The measurement of improvement among neuropsychiatric patients in an Army convalescent facility. *Journal of Clinical Psychology, 3,* 121-128.

Kraus, J., Chalker, S., & Macindoe, I. (1967). Vocabulary and chronological age as predictors of "abstraction" on the Shipley-Hartford Retreat Scale. *Australian Journal of Psychology, 19,* 133-135.

Lewinski, R. J. (1946). The Shipley-Hartford Scale as an independent measure of mental ability. *Educational and Psychological Measurement, 6,* 253-259.

Lewinsohn, P. M. (1963). Use of the Shipley-Hartford Conceptual Quotient as a measure of intellectual impairment. *Journal of Consulting Psychology, 27,* 444-447.

Lewinsohn, P. M. (1967). Factors related to improvement in mental hospital patients. *Journal of Consulting Psychology, 31,* 588-594.

Lewinsohn, P. M., & Nichols, R. C. (1964). The evaluation of changes in psychiatric patients during and after hospitalization. *Journal of Clinical Psychology, 20,* 272-279.

Lyle, O. E., & Gottesman, I. I. (1977). Premorbid psychometric indicators of the gene for Huntington's disease. *Journal of Consulting and Clinical Psychology, 45,* 1011-1022.

Magaret, A., & Simpson, M. M. (1948). A comparison of two measures of deterioration in psychotic patients. *Journal of Consulting Psychology, 12,* 265-269.

Malerstein, A. J., & Beldon, E. (1968). WAIS, SILS, and PPVT in Korsakoff's syndrome. *Archives of General Psychiatry, 19,* 743-750.

Manson, M. P., & Grayson, H. M. (1947). The Shipley-Hartford Retreat Scale as a measure of intellectual impairment for military prisoners. *Journal of Applied Psychology, 31,* 67-81.

Martin, J. D., Blair, G. E., Sadowski, C., & Wheeler, K. J. (1981). Intercorrelations among the Slosson Intelligence Test, the Shipley-Institute of Living Scale, and the Intellectual Efficiency Scale of the California Psychological Inventory. *Educational and Psychological Measurement, 41,* 595-598.

Martin, J. D., Blair, G. E., Stokes, E. H., & Lester, E. H. (1977). A validity and reliability study of the Slosson Intelligence Test and the Shipley Institute of Living Scale. *Educational and Psychological Measurement, 37,* 1107-1110.

Mason, C. F., & Ganzler, H. (1964). Adult norms for the Shipley Institute of Living Scale and Hooper Visual Organization Test based on age and education. *Journal of Gerontology, 19,* 419-424.

Monroe, K. L. (1966). Note on the estimation of the WAIS Full Scale IQ. *Journal of Clinical Psychology, 22,* 79-81.

Murray, M. D., Page, J., Stotland, E., & Dietze, D. (1970). Success on varied tasks as an influence on sense of competence. *Journal of Clinical Psychology, 26,* 296-298.

Palmer, J. O. (1964). A restandardization of adolescent norms for the Shipley-Hartford. *Journal of Clinical Psychology, 20,* 492-495.

Pauker, J. D. (1975). A gender difference and a caution in predicting WAIS IQ from Shipley-Hartford scores. *Journal of Clinical Psychology, 31,* 94-96.

Paulson, M., & Lin, T-T. (1970). Predicting WAIS IQ from Shipley-Hartford scores. *Journal of Clinical Psychology, 26,* 453-461.

Phillips, W. M., Phillips, A. M., & Shearn, C. R. (1980). Objective assessment of schizophrenic thinking. *Journal of Clinical Psychology, 36,* 79-89.

Pishkin, V., Lovallo, W. R., Lenk, R. G., & Bourne, L. E., Jr. (1977). Schizophrenic cognitive dysfunction: A deficit in rule transfer. *Journal of Clinical Psychology, 33,* 335-342.

Prado, W. M., & Taub, D. V. (1966). Accurate prediction of individual intellectual functioning by the Shipley-Hartford. *Journal of Clinical Psychology, 22,* 294-296.

Robinson, M. F. (1946). What price lobotomy? *Journal of Abnormal and Social Psychology, 41,* 421-436.

Ross, W. D., & McNaughton, F. L. (1944). Head injury: A study of patients with chronic post-traumatic complaints. *Archives of Neurology and Psychiatry, 52,* 255-269.

Ruiz, R. A., & Krauss, H. H. (1967). Test-retest reliability and practice effect with the Shipley-Institute of Living Scale. *Psychological Reports, 20,* 1085-1086.

Salzman, L. F., Goldstein, R. H., Atkins, R., & Babigian, H. (1966). Conceptual thinking in psychiatric patients. *Archives of General Psychiatry, 14,* 55-59.

Schalock, R. L., & Wahler, H. J. (1968). Changes in Shipley-Hartford scores with five repeated test administrations: Statistical conventions vs. behavioral evidence. *Psychological Reports, 22,* 243-246.

Scherer, I. W. (1949). The psychological scores of mental patients in an individual and group testing situation. *Journal of Clinical Psychology, 5,* 405-408.

Shaw, D. J. (1966). The reliability of the Shipley-Institute of Living Scale. *Journal of Clinical Psychology, 22,* 441.

Shipley, W. C. (1940). A self-administering scale for measuring intellectual impairment and deterioration. *Journal of Psychology, 9,* 371-377.

Shipley, W. C. (1946). *Shipley-Institute of Living Scale; Manual of directions and scoring key.* Hartford: Institute of Living.

Shipley, W. C. (1953). Shipley-Institute of Living Scale for measuring intellectual impairment. In A. Weider (Ed.), *Contributions toward medical psychology: Theory and psychodiagnostic methods* (Vol. 2, pp. 751-756). New York: Ronald.

Shipley, W. C., & Burlingame, C. C. (1941). A convenient self-administering scale for measuring intellectual impairment in psychotics. *American Journal of Psychiatry, 97,* 1313-1325.

Sines, L. K. (1958). Intelligence test correlates of Shipley-Hartford performance. *Journal of Clinical Psychology, 14,* 399-404.

Sines, L. K., & Simmons, H. (1959). The Shipley-Hartford Scale and the Doppelt Short Form as estimators of WAIS IQ in a state hospital population. *Journal of Clinical Psychology, 15,* 452-453.

Slater, P. (1943). Interpreting discrepencies. *British Journal of Medical Psychology, 19,* 415-419.

Stone, L. A. (1965a). Recent (1962-1964) psychiatric patient validation norms for the Shipley-Institute of Living Scale. *Psychological Reports, 16,* 417-418.

Stone, L. A. (1965b). Test-retest stability of the Shipley-Institute of Living Scale. *Journal of Clinical Psychology, 21,* 432.

Stone, L. A., & Chambers, A., Jr. (1965). The distribution of measured adult intelligence in a state psychiatric hospital population. *Psychology, 2,* 27-29.

Stone, L. A., & Ramer, J. C. (1965). Estimating WAIS IQ from Shipley Scale scores: Another cross-validation. *Journal of Clinical Psychology, 21,* 297.

Suinn, R. M. (1960). The Shipley-Hartford Retreat Scale as a screening test of intelligence. *Journal of Clinical Psychology, 16,* 419.

Sutker, P. B., Moan, C. E., & Swanson, W. C. (1972). Porteus Maze test qualitative performance in pure sociopaths, prison normals, and antisocial psychotics. *Journal of Clinical Psychology, 28,* 349-352.

Tarter, R. E., & Jones, B. M. (1971). Absence of intellectual deterioration in chronic alcoholics. *Journal of Clinical Psychology, 27,* 453-454.

Wahler, H. J., & Watson, L. S. (1962). A comparison of the Shipley-Hartford as a power test with the WAIS verbal scale. *Journal of Consulting Psychology, 26,* 105.

Watson, C. G. (1968). The separation of NP hospital organics from schizophrenics with three visual motor screening tests. *Journal of Clinical Psychology, 24,* 412-414.

Wiens, A. N., & Banaka, W. H. (1960). Estimating WAIS IQ from Shipley-Hartford scores: A cross-validation. *Journal of Clinical Psychology, 16,* 452.

Wilson, R. S., Rosenbaum, G., Brown, G., Rourke, D., Whitman, R., & Grisell, J. (1978). An index of premorbid intelligence. *Journal of Consulting and Clinical Psychology, 46,* 1554-1555.

Winfield, D. L. (1953). The Shipley-Hartford vocabulary test and pre-trauma intelligence. *Journal of Clinical Psychology, 9,* 77-78.

Wright, M. E. (1946). Use of the Shipley-Hartford test in evaluating intellectual functioning of neuropsychiatric patients. *Journal of Applied Psychology, 30,* 45-50.

Yates, A. (1954). The validity of some psychological tests of brain damage. *Psychological Bulletin, 51,* 359-379.

Yates, A. (1956). The use of vocabulary in the measurement of intellectual deterioration—A review. *Journal of Mental Science, 102,* 409-440.

Yates, A. (1972). Shipley-Institute of Living Scale for Measuring Intellectual Impairment. In O.K. Buros (Ed.), *The seventh mental measurements yearbook* (p. 322). Highland Park, NJ: The Gryphon Press.

Zachary, R. A. (1986). *Shipley-Institute of Living Scale manual* (revised). Pre-publication draft.

Zachary, R. A., Crumpton, E., & Spiegel, D. E. (1985). Estimating WAIS-R IQ from Shipley Institute of Living Scale. *Journal of Clinical Psychology, 41,* 532-540.

Zachary, R. A., & Huba, G. J. (1985). Simplified formula and table for the unusualness of combinations of subtest scores on the Shipley Institute of Living Scale. *Journal of Clinical Psychology, 41,* 832-833.

Zachary, R. A., Paulson, M. J., & Gorsuch, R. L. (1985). Estimating WAIS IQ from the Shipley Institute of Living Scale using continuously adjusted age norms. *Journal of Clinical Psychology, 41,* 820-831.

Robert C. Reinehr, Ph.D.
Assistant Professor of Psychology, Southwestern University, Georgetown, Texas.

SOMATIC INKBLOT SERIES
Wilfred A. Cassell. Anchorage, Alaska: Aurora Publishing Company.

Introduction

The Somatic Inkblot Series (SIS) is a series of inkblots printed in black, gray, and red on white cards that are slightly smaller than those used in the Rorschach. Blots that suggest anatomical structure have been selected. The series has been in development since 1965 and was originally intended as an attempt to develop a quantifiable technique for the investigation of body awareness.

The SIS has undergone considerable development and revision (including several name changes) since its inception. Originally called the Projective Index of Body Awareness, the name was changed to Cassell's Somatic Inkblots in 1969. At that time over 30 different scores were described in the manual. The current version consists of a set of twenty cards; nine of the cards are black and white, three are red and white, and eight are black, red, and white. The purpose of the test is to provide enough similarity to anatomical structure to evoke anatomical responses, but not so much as to limit responses to the naming of body parts.

Practical Applications/Uses

Administration is similar to standard Rorschach administration, although inquiry is more detailed and attends particularly to those instances in which the subject did not respond to the anatomical cues provided by the blot. It is also suggested that responses be used as stimuli for spontaneous associations and that an unstructured interview then be conducted in which "associations to the associations can be explored" (Cassell, 1980).

The blots are accompanied by a book, *Body Symbolism and the Somatic Inkblot Series,* (Cassell, 1980), which also serves as a test manual. The book is actually a fairly wide-ranging discussion of body symbolism and the relationship of SIS responses to many clinical concerns. Manual-like material is scattered throughout the book, although it is concentrated in the early portion.

Scoring criteria are presented for four separate clinical scales: Pathologic Anatomy Score (PAS), Anxiety-Threat Rating (ATR), Depression (D), and Movement Responses (MR). Normative data are provided for the frequency of occurrence of various content categories for each card, based on the responses of 168 volunteers. Both males and females, adults and adolescents, were included, but no information is given as to the number of each in the sample. No normative data are given for any of the previously mentioned four scales, nor for most of the other scales that are mentioned in the book. The scattering of scale descriptions throughout the book makes it very difficult to construct a list of the scores that the author envisions obtaining from the test. There is no section that summarizes the scoring categories, and the location of the scoring criteria is not indexed. In addition to those previously noted, at least four other scales are described in varying amounts of detail. The author does not discuss in detail the use of any score. He favors the ideographic or individual case approach and feels that this is the most appropriate approach at this preliminary stage of test development.

The discussion in the book is basically psychoanalytic, as are the various interpretations of responses. Much of the book is given over to the discussion of illustrative case histories, over 70 of which are presented in various degrees of detail. Scores are seen primarily as supplementary to the interpretation of content, the SIS serving to stimulate the production of dynamically important fantasy material. Used in this manner, the SIS is designed to elicit material that may be used either as a beginning point for psychotherapy or to generate descriptive statements about the respondent. The SIS is thus seen by the author both as an assessment technique and as a special kind of interview situation.

Technical Aspects

As an assessment tool in the traditional psychometric sense, the SIS is particularly lacking, but, of course, this is true of many other projective techniques. Essentially no standardization or validation information is available. *The Ninth Mental Measurements Yearbook* (Mitchell, 1985) lists only two publications relating to the SIS, both by the test author (Cassell, 1971, 1972). Neither of these studies provides psychometric information regarding the test or the scoring categories, both articles relying instead upon the case history method. There is a considerable body of research by the test author relating to the general concept of body awareness and utilizing all or part of the SIS as stimulus materials, but little scoring or standardization material beyond that contained in the book/test manual is presented in these studies.

Critique

The near total lack of availability of psychometric information limits the use of the SIS to research situations. In spite of its rather long history, the test does not meet any of the criteria outlined in *Standards for Educational and Psychological Testing* (AERA, APA, & NCME, 1985). The original intention to provide quantifiable information regarding body awareness seems to have been abandoned, or at least postponed, in favor of an interpretive case history approach. Until normative data become available, the technique must be considered to be essentially a special interview technique rather than a test.

References

American Educational Research Association, American Psychological Association, & National Council on Measurement in Education. (1985). *Standards for Educational and Psychological Testing*. Washington, DC: American Psychological Association.

Cassell, W. A. (1971). Body consciousness in exhibitionism. *British Journal of Projective Psychology and Personality Study,* 16(1), 21-31.

Cassell, W. A. (1972). Individual differences in somatic perception: A projective method of investigation. *Advances in Psychosomatic Medicine, 8:* 86-104.

Cassell, W. A. (1980). *Body symbolism and the somatic inkblot series.* Anchorage: Aurora Publishing Co.

Mitchell, J. V., Jr. (Ed.). (1985). *The ninth mental measurements yearbook.* Lincoln, NE: Buros Institute of Mental Measurements.

Leonard S. Milling, Ph.D.
Assistant Professor of Psychology, Department of Psychiatry, The Medical College of Ohio, Toledo, Ohio.

STANFORD HYPNOTIC CLINICAL SCALE FOR CHILDREN
Arlene H. Morgan and Josephine R. Hilgard. Des Plaines, Illinois: American Society of Clinical Hypnosis.

Introduction

The Stanford Hypnotic Clinical Scale for Children (SHCS:C) is a brief standardized measure of children's responsiveness to hypnotic suggestions. Hypnotic responsiveness or hypnotic susceptibility is defined as the probability that a subject will respond to hypnotic suggestions. The SHCS:C is an individual behavioral measure of hypnotic responsiveness designed for children 4 to 16 years of age. The test includes standardized administration procedures, a quantitative scoring system, and age-graded norms.

The SHCS:C was developed by Arlene H. Morgan, Ph.D., and Josephine R. Hilgard, M.D., Ph.D., at the Laboratory of Hypnosis Research of Stanford University. Drs. Hilgard and Morgan are well-known as pioneers in the area of hypnosis. Both have written extensively on various topics in hypnosis, including hypnotic susceptibility.

The SHCS:C was designed to be a brief measure of responsiveness appropriate for clinical practice with emotionally-disturbed and physically-ill children. Consequently, test items were developed according to three criteria. First, a limited number of items were included so that administering the entire scale would require no more than 20 minutes. Second, items sufficiently varied in difficulty were selected so that the scale would have discriminative power. Finally, items were developed to be interesting to children and to have direct relevance to clinical intervention.

The standard version of the SHCS:C of children aged 6 to 16 years utilizes a traditional relaxation/eye closure trance induction. It consists of the following seven items: hand lowering, arm rigidity, visual TV, auditory TV, dream, age regression, and post-hypnotic suggestion. A modified version of the scale for younger children aged 4 to 8 years employs an imagination/eyes open induction and deletes the post-hypnotic suggestion item. SHCS:C items sample the three domains commonly thought to comprise the hypnotic responsiveness construct: cognitive, motor, and challenge areas. However, at least two-thirds of scale items sample the cognitive content area, thereby underrepresenting challenge and motor domains. As for representativeness of item difficulty, no systematic data have been presented regarding the pass/fail ratios of individual items. However, Hilgard and LeBaron (1984) have observed on the basis of their clinical practice that the SHCS:C possesses an insufficient number of difficult items, thus rendering the scale relatively insensitive to individual differences among more highly responsive children. Overall, the SHCS:C may have signficant limitations in the representativeness of item content and item difficulty.

Procedures for administering the two versions of the scale are described in *The American Journal of Clinical Hypnosis* (Morgan and Hilgard, 1978/1979). These procedures include verbatim induction methods and hypnotic suggestions. Each item is scored according to a pass/fail dichotomy, yielding a total score range of 0 to 7 for the standard version and 0 to 6 for the modified version. Behavioral referents describing passing responses for each item are provided in the test directions as well as in a scoring booklet.

Normative information organized by age categories and type of induction (i.e., standard vs. modified) are provided for the SCHS:C (Morgan & Hilgard, 1978/1979). The standardization sample for these norms consisted of 182 children aged 2 to 14 years, drawn from the local secondary and elementary schools. Several deficiencies are noted in these norms. First, demographic information describing the representativeness of the standardization sample is not presented. Second, although the SCHS:C is intended for use with children up to 16 years of age, norms are not presented for age categories beyond 14 years. Third, in the 3- to 4-year age range, one group of children was used as the normative sample for both relaxation and imagination inductions. This procedure may have benefited subjects' performance during the latter imagination induction, thereby distorting the norms. Fourth, the lack of standard deviations or comparable statistics make interpretation of individual results difficult. Finally, inclusion of the seventh item during the imagination induction compromises these norms for use with the modified (i.e., imagination/eyes open), six-item version of the scale.

Practical Applications/Uses

The SHCS:C is a valuable clinical and research tool for assessing children's hypnotic responsiveness. It is one of very few published measures of hypnotic responsiveness constructed specifically for use with children (for another, see Cooper & London, 1978/1979). As a brief scale, the SHCS:C is particularly well-suited for use with children, especially emotionally disturbed or medically ill children who may lack the necessary attention and energy to complete longer instruments. Because a broad range of psychological and medical problems are amenable to hypnotherapy, the SHCS:C may be valuable in clinical settings to determine the potential utility of hypnosis relative to other interventions. However, hypnotherapists often elect to rely on their subjective judgments about responsiveness rather than to utilize a standard instrument. As a research tool, the SHCS:C may be of considerable use for studying individual differences in hypnotic responsiveness among children.

Technical Aspects

To demonstrate psychometric adequacy, a behavioral measure of hypnotic responsiveness must possess interexaminer reliability, test-retest reliability, and internal consistency. Unfortunately, such studies of the SHCS:C have not been undertaken. Consequently, the reliability of the scale is unknown.

As for scale validity, Chronbach and Meehl (1955) have argued that a series of experiments varying persons, situations, and construct referents must be conducted to establish the construct validity of a scale. Thus, research utilizing the SHCS:C offers a commentary on the validity of the scale. To date, only two such studies have appeared in the empirical literature. Both experiments utilized the SHCS:C to predict responsiveness to hypnotherapeutic intervention. Hilgard and LeBaron (1982) employed hypnosis with children to successfully reduce distress associated with painful bone marrow aspirations. Hypnotic responsiveness as measured by the SHCS:C was significantly related to reductions in self-reported and observed pain and anxiety. In a somewhat similar study, Zeltzer, LeBaron, and Zeltzer (1984) used hypnosis to successfully reduce children's nausea and vomiting secondary to chemotherapy. However, measured hypnotic responsiveness was unrelated to treatment outcome. Together, these preliminary studies provide mixed support for the validity of the SHCS:C.

Critique

The SHCS:C demonstrates considerable promise as a measure of children's hypnotic responsiveness. The scale evidences a number of strengths. First, the SHCS:C can be administered in a brief period of time, making it ideal for use with children, particularly emotionally disturbed or medically ill youngsters who may be unable to sustain the attention and energy required by more lengthy instruments. Second, the SHCS:C can be used with a wide age range of children. Indeed, the modified version employing the imagination/eyes open induction is particularly appropriate for use with very young children. Finally, the scale is easily administered and scored according to detailed instructions.

On the other hand, the SHCS:C suffers from a number of psychometric deficiencies. First, the content of items tends to overrepresent cognitive referents and underrepresent motor and challenge referents. A second problem is the underrepresentation of difficult items, rendering the SHCS:C relatively insensitive to differences among more highly responsive children. Third, currently available normative information for the scale is inadequate. Fourth, empirical evidence of test-retest reliability, interrater reliability, and internal consistency is completely lacking. Finally, the SHCS:C possesses no better than preliminary evidence of construct validity.

Overall, the SHCS:C is a brief standardized measure of children's hypnotic responsiveness that evidences a number of significant weaknesses. However, the scale may serve useful research and clinical purposes if the practitioner is mindful of the scale's limitations. Future studies of scale reliability and validity will be needed to demonstrate the psychometric adequacy of the SHCS:C. Finally, redeveloping scale normative information, as well as adding a few new items to increase the representativeness of item content and difficulty, would help to make the SHCS:C a more valuable measure of children's hypnotic responsiveness.

References

This list includes text citations and suggested additional reading.

Chronbach, L. J., & Meehl, P. E. (1955). Construct validity in psychological tests. *Psychological Bulletin, 52,* 281-302.
Cooper, L. M., & London, P. M. (1978/1979). The Children's Hypnotic Susceptibility Scale. *The American Journal of Clinical Hypnosis, 21,* 170-184.
Gardner, C. G., & Olness, K. (1981). *Hypnosis and hypnotherapy with children.* Orlando, FL: Grune and Straton.
Hilgard, J. R., & LeBaron, S. (1982). Relief of anxiety and pain in children and adolescents with cancer: Quantitative measures and clinical observations. *International Journal of Clinical and Experimental Hypnosis, 30,* 417-422.
Hilgard, J. R., & LeBaron, S. (1984). *Hypnotherapy of pain in children with cancer.* Los Altos, CA: William Kaufman, Inc.
Milling, L. S., & Walker, C. E. (1986). The Children's Hypnotic Susceptibility Scales. In D. J. Keyser and R. C. Sweetland (Eds.), *Test critiques* (Vol. IV, pp. 162-171). Kansas City, MO: Test Corporation of America.
Morgan, A. H., & Hilgard, J. R. (1978/1979). The Stanford Hypnotic Clinical Scale for Children. *The American Journal of Clinical Hypnosis, 21,* 148-169.
Zeltzer, L., LeBaron. S., & Zeltzer, P. M. (1984). The effectiveness of behavioral intervention for reduction of nausea and vomiting in children and adolescents receiving chemotherapy. *Journal of Clinical Oncology, 2,* 683-690.

Carl G. Willis, Ed.D.
Counseling Psychologist, University of Missouri, Columbia, Missouri.

STANTON SURVEY
Carl S. Klump. Chicago, Illinois: Stanton Corporation.

Introduction

The Stanton Survey is a paper-and-pencil self-report inventory designed to assess the probable honesty, criminality, or integrity of a job applicant. It is an instrument used by organizations as a part of a personnel selection process; however, it is restricted to the pre-employment setting. The Stanton Survey is used in employment situations where the propensity to steal is encouraged by the opportunity to do so. No claims are made for measurement of variables such as ambition, aptitude, likeability, promotability, or violence proneness.

There seem to be three basic assumptions underlying the Stanton Survey. First, people engaged in past criminal behaviors are apt to continue to behave in this same manner. Second, criminally active people form attitudes and behaviors differing from adults not engaged in such deviant activities. Third, individuals involved in deviancy and counterproductivity are able to defend their behaviors through rationalization; they possess a greater tolerance for others who behave distrustfully and deviantly.

On the basis of a score on the Stanton Survey, an applicant is placed in one of three risk categories. A Low Risk applicant is one whose previous behavior was minimally or not at all dishonest, even when the opportunity to engage in such behavior was present. The High Risk individual possesses an attitude that condones dishonesty, that does not recognize the moral wrongness of theft; theft is excusable to this person. Marginal Risk applicants fall in between and, if employed, should receive direct supervision. They do not create theft situations, but they may be more inclined to take advantage of opportunities for theft.

Carl Stanton Klump, developer of the Stanton Survey, is a professional polygrapher and criminologist. In the 1950s, Klump worked with John Reid in developing polygraph examinations, attempting to determine the honesty or dishonesty of individuals. Carl Klump and James Walls founded the Chicago Professional Polygraph Center over 20 years ago and soon afterward formed the Stanton Corporation.

The first copyright on the Stanton Survey was in 1964. Based on copyright dates, at least 15 revisions have been constructed through 1985. Some of these revisions appear as format changes as opposed to actual content modifications. While the test has over two decades of use, its early development was based on a general concept of honesty/dishonesty. Over the years, criminality and integrity have also been used as reference points to describe what the Stanton Survey measures. In reviewing the materials provided, there seems to be a very distinct shift in current writing or research from a strong early association of the Stanton Survey with polygraph examination to almost a non-association. The current research (Hay, 1981; Hom & Harris, 1986; Kpo, 1984) seems to be primarily aimed at attempts to provide a factor structure as a theoretical basis of honesty testing, albeit somewhat later than the early development. In this situation, the practical use of the Stanton Survey preceded development of a theoretical model. Several foreign language forms are available and others are under development.

When the cost of a polygraph examination and the considerable questions, both legal and ethical, concerning its utility were considered, Klump and Walls sought different modalities to assess honesty. According to Klump, paper-and-pencil honesty tests developed as ". . . business world spinoffs from academic criminologists' efforts to study and understand human behavior" (1983a, p. 63). To Klump, the idea behind a written honesty test is ". . . disarmingly straightforward. Ask people the right questions about their past behavior and current attitudes, and honest individuals will answer critical questions differently . . ." (Klump, 1983b, p. 63.) than those who are apt to pilfer or dip in the till.

Walls (1986) indicates that more than 1.5 million job applicants have been evaluated by the Stanton Survey in the past 20 years. He notes that over two million honesty tests of all varieties are given each year, up from one million in 1981.

The Stanton Survey is similar to other honesty or theft-proneness instruments on the market. In total, it is a 20-page booklet consisting of five sections. The first section is an authorization that an applicant must sign, which allows an employer a reasonable check of the answers for truth and completeness. The second section contains a personal/educational/employment history similar to some employment applications. However, more emphasis seems to be placed on negative or disciplinary actions than a typical job application. The third section consists of questions targeted towards an applicant's addictive behaviors and views (i.e., alcohol, drugs, gambling). The fourth section is really an open page which requests a handwritten response detailing the examinee's goals, why he or she should be hired, good and bad points, and how his or her performance will improve for the employer.

The fifth section, and perhaps the most important, is an attitude questionnaire of 74 items, 73 of which are objectively scored and contain from 2 to 11 possible responses. These items explore attitudes toward honesty and actual past behavior in this area. There is also one open-ended question that, rather than asking for a yes/no response, requires the respondent to express his or her opinion on the subject of honesty. Actual item examples may be found in Linsen (1983) and Ganguli (1985). All objective items are marked on a top sheet of an NCR-type form with the responses and processing directions on the second sheet.

Fifteen of the 73 objective questions also request a subjective reply or explanation. Various research indicate a range of 70-74 items are scored.

An interesting facet is the numbering of the attitude items. The actual printed sequence in the Stanton Survey booklet is from 1-84, with the omission of items numbered 15, 31, 44, 60, 67-71, and 75. The fact that these 10 items are omitted would suggest that an earlier edition of the Stanton Survey might have contained 84 items. This numbering system could possibly confuse some applicants. No information is available on the numbering mystery.

According to Klump (1983b), "Each question has been carefully tested and selected for its capability to distinguish honest and dishonest respondents" (p. 64), yet no item statistics are available to support this contention. Perhaps this sheds some light on the numbering omissions, as items may have been dropped due to poor discrimination.

Practical Applications/Uses

The examiner's role in this administration is not major. However, biographical questions might need some explanation because there are differences in legally allowable questions between Canada and the United States and between several states within the United States. Emphasis must be given to having all questions answered completely.

On the back page of the booklet, the directions for the examiner (INTERVIEWER) stress that "ALL 'Explain' lines" have been answered: "THESE WRITE-IN ANSWERS ARE MOST IMPORTANT." One must insist on complete answers. By implication, perhaps the subjective responses are more important than the objective SS score. Yet the research reports basically deal with the SS score.

By the nature of the publications (Klump, 1983a, 1983b, 1984a, 1984b; Linsen, 1983; Walls, 1986) and research populations (Hay, 1981; Kpo, 1984), there is a strong suggestion that the major target populations for use of the Stanton Survey are in the retailing, service, and production areas of business firms and organizations where merchandise, supplies, and money could be stolen. As many of the positions are at lower salary levels, many of the job applicants would be young, perhaps first-time job seekers. Some of the questions on the Stanton Survey might not be within range of the life experiences or literary expertise of all job seekers, and some of the forced choice items may not be answerable (honestly!).

Another issue may be the reading level of test takers. Many job seekers may not have good reading skills. Estimated completion time is 40-45 minutes; however, 1 hour should be allowed.

Gorsuch (1986) has recently reported the growing phenomena of increasing numbers of psychometric instruments that are scored only by service organizations or computer programs that provide no access to scoring keys. The Stanton Survey is such an instrument. When keys are not available, Gorsuch considers it essential that the scoring service provide internal consistency reliabilities on each group of tests scored and that samples of items that correlate well with the total test be given in the manual if content validity is claimed. These two suggestions were not supported by any materials available to this reviewer.

The 73 items are scored by the Stanton Corporation to obtain three scale scores: numerical base (NB), admissions score (AS), and the Stanton Survey score (SS). The NB score is the attitude toward theft based on 52 dichotomous items. The NB items assess an applicant's approval of dishonest behaviors, rationalizations of theft, beliefs about the prevalence of theft in society, and contemplation of theft (Harris, 1985). The higher the NB score, the more one is viewed as approving of dishonest behavior. The AS score is the sum of the 18 multiple-choice admission items weighted by a factor of 5, 10, or 15, based on the magnitude of the admissions to previous thefts [i.e., a composite of three classes of admissions (petty, marginal, severe) weighted differentially]. These items openly solicit self-reports of theft and association with criminal elements. The weightings were derived intuitively by expert judgment (Kpo, 1984). The SS score is the sum of NB plus AS. Applicants are assigned into one of the three risk categories (low, marginal, or high) based on their SS score.

The personal/educational/employment, the addictive behaviors/views, the handwritten goals, and the subjective portion of the attitude section are not objectively scored. Klump (1983b) states that "The test also includes an evaluation of the phraseology used in responding to the open-ended questions" (p. 64). These answers are categorized by their similarity to responses given by honest and dishonest people.

Technical Aspects

In terms of reliability, internal consistency measures of .91 (n = 1,806; Klump & Perman, 1976) and of .92 (n = 1,000; Harris, 1986) are reported. Grimsley (1986b) reports a .92 coefficient using test-retest reliability for 51 college students with at least 6 months work experience. The students were assessed twice, 6 weeks apart. Both reliability coefficients, NB = .92 and AS = .90, were acceptable.

Although Hay (1981), Kpo (1984), Harris (1985), Hom and Harris (1986), and Harris and Kpo (1985) have concluded through factor analytic procedures that several dimensions (General Theft, Opportunistic Theft, Pervasiveness, Leniency, Employee Discounting, Employee Theft, and Association) exist in the Stanton Survey, there is no apparent incorporation of these dimensions in scoring, reporting, or interpretation of the results. Only the overall SS is reported in the validation studies. However, Hay (1981) does report that 65 of the items carried a .30 or higher loading on at least one of the seven factors using a Varimax Rotated Matrix.

Reed (1982) used a combination of interview and polygraph data as an independent criteria of honesty. The Stanton Survey was first administered to 259 individuals who were then ranked as low, marginal, or high risk. The same individuals were then interviewed and administered a polygraph examination covering the same material as in the Stanton Survey. Actual admissions of dishonesty were compiled, and the applicants were again rated. Based on the Stanton Survey, approximately 90% of the low risk applicants would have been hired, and over 90% of the high risk applicants would have been rejected. Grimsley (1986a) studied 587 applicants for jobs in retail stores with a subsample of 85 reporting that they had been fired from a previous job. Candidates from the subsample were assigned to the low, marginal, and high risk categories. While male applicants reported similar rates of being fired independent of the risk category, female applicants were mostly in the high risk category.

The predictor variable, or attitude toward theft/honesty, and the criterion variable, admissions to previous theft, are both contained in the Stanton Survey. Two validation studies summarizing data from many organizations are reported. Kpo (1984) reported on 34 validity studies from 10 different position titles with a total sample size of 3,482. The mean observed validity coefficient was .70. Only three of the 34 validity coefficients were below .61, with 31 others between .61–.90. The three low coefficients were reported by small sample sizes. Harris and Kpo (1985) examined the generalizability of the Stanton Survey across 8,807 job applicants and 10 occupations in the retail industry. The overall validity coefficient was .70, with coefficients for the 10 occupations ranging between .65–.79. The authors state that "The high validity index found in the present study attests to the transportability of the honesty trait across situations" (p. 7).

Since 1983, Bagus (1986) reports that 7,030 applicants across the United States from a wide variety of industries were studied. Individual affirmative action studies on between 100 to 500 applicants for many firms were pooled into one large study. Fairness of the Stanton Survey across ethnic, sex, and age lines fell within federal guidelines. However, younger applicants were found to be more likely to fail the test than older applicants. Failure rates were highest for applicants in their teens and early twenties.

Only one reference (Walls, 1986) provides any data with reference to addictive behavior. In this case, 68% of job applicants categorized as high risk admitted to a history of marijuana use, 9% to cocaine, and 14% to uppers. No other reports or data are provided to substantiate any portion of the Stanton Survey except the Attitude section.

Critique

Honesty is a poorly defined construct with no concensual definition in the literature. Recent efforts have begun to provide some basis of dimensionality for the Stanton Survey, but the theoretical underpinnings are not yet incorporated into practical use. Most research has focused only on predictive abilities.

Based on the material provided by the Stanton Corporation, which was extensive, and on published literature from bibliographic sources, an interesting dichotomy is apparent. No research articles could be found in the professional psychological publications after 22 years of marketing the Stanton Survey. Only three references in the published literature appear to be written by psychologists, two reviews in *The Ninth Mental Measurements Yearbook* (Ganguli, 1985; Wheeler, 1985) and a letter to the editor by Smith (1983). Smith, in response to Klump (1983b), made a good suggestion. "In security matters, we psychologists defer to the expertise of the security professional. I would hope that the security professional would look to psychologists for assistance with assessment" (p. 10). Yet in the last 4 years at least six articles were published (Klump, 1983a, 1983b, 1984a, 1984b; Linsen, 1983; Walls, 1986) in trade journals, perhaps as marketing efforts.

The Stanton Survey is woefully in need of a test manual to compile and integrate the large amount of data into a usable standard format. The number of recent corporate and unpublished manuscripts seems to reflect a decision by the Stanton Corporation, with the assistance of psychometricians and psychological researchers, to produce a better product; however, significant attention should also be paid to sections other than the Attitude portion, where there is a current paucity of information pertaining to its use. No explanation is available as to the use of the very extensive personal data, self-description, and "Explain" items. No item statistics were available, and no norms are presented. There is a lack of follow-up validations from on-the-job investigations as well as long-term follow-up studies. No studies are reported relating the instrument to other psychological constructs or tests.

Clearly, the content and questions of the Stanton Survey point up the need for studies on faking or social desirability. Social desirability could result in a spurious correlation coefficient if it correlated with both the independent and dependent variables, or it could provide a suppression effect if it contaminated only one of the variables.

Lastly, this reviewer wonders about the legal and ethical questions that could apply to the user and the applicant in that the Stanton Corporation maintains files of very personal "theft" admissions for over 1.5 million job applicants.

References

This list includes text citations and suggested additional reading.

Bagus, K. (1986). *Results of the combined affirmative action data study*. Charlotte, NC: Stanton Corporation.

Ganguli, H. C. (1985). The Stanton Survey and the Stanton Survey Phase II. In J. V. Mitchell, Jr. (Ed.), *The ninth mental measurements yearbook* (pp. 1470-1472). Lincoln, NE: The Buros Institute of Mental Measurements.

Gorsuch, R. L. (1986). Psychometric evaluation of scales when their scoring keys are unavailable. *Professional Psychology: Research and Practice, 17*, 399-402.

Grimsley, D. L. (1986a). *Frequency of admitted termination of employment on a pre-employment honesty test*. Unpublished manuscript, University of North Carolina, Charlotte.

Grimsley, D. L. (1986b). *Test-retest reliability of the Stanton Survey*. Unpublished manuscript, University of North Carolina, Charlotte.

Harris, W. G. (1985). *An investigation of the Stanton Survey using a validity generalization model*. Chicago, IL: Stanton Corporation.

Harris, W. G. (1986). *Stanton Survey: A preliminary test manual*. Unpublished manuscript. Charlotte, NC: Stanton Corporation.

Harris, W. G., & Kpo, W. R. (1985). *Generalizability of a measure of honesty*. Unpublished manuscript. Charlotte, NC: Stanton Corporation.

Hay, D. W. (1981). *An exploration of the dimensionality of a personnel selection instrument designed to measure honesty*. Unpublished master's thesis, Illinois Institute of Technology, Chicago.

Hom, A. E., & Harris, W. G. (1986). *A component model of honesty testing*. Charlotte, NC: Stanton Corporation.

Klump, C. S. (1983a). How you can reduce employee theft. *Drug Topics, 127*, 42-45.

Klump, C. S. (1983b). Honest employees: Find them and keep them. *Security Management, 8*, 63-64.

Klump, C. S. (1984a). Awareness and action are critical in stopping costly employee theft. *Independent Restaurants, 46*, 76-78.

Klump, C. S. (1984b). Honesty testing. *Security World, 21*, 71-74.

Klump, C. S., & Perman, S. (1976). *A survey of criminal and non-criminal behavior traits*. Chicago: Stanton Corporation.

Kpo, W. (1984). *Application of validity generalization to honesty testing*. Unpublished master's thesis, Illinois Institute of Technology, Chicago.

Linsen, M. A. (1983). An ounce of prevention can offer profit protection. *Progressive Grocer, 62*, 85-88.

Reed, H. B. C. (1982). *Stanton Survey: Description and validation manual*. Chicago: Stanton Corporation.

Smith, W. A. (1983). Letter to Editor. *Security Management, 8*, 10.

Walls, J. D. (1986, May). Survey shows drug users to be dishonest employees. *Discount Store News*, p. 220.

Wheeler, K. G. (1985). The Stanton Survey and the Stanton Survey Phase II. In J. V. Mitchell, Jr. (Ed.), *The ninth mental measurements yearbook* (pp. 1472-1473). Lincoln, NE: The Buros Institute of Mental Measurements.

Alexinia Y. Baldwin, Ph.D.
Associate Professor of Curriculum and Education of the Gifted, Graduate School of Education, State University of New York at Albany, Albany, New York.

STRUCTURE OF INTELLECT LEARNING ABILITIES TEST-FORM P (PRIMARY)

Mary Meeker and Robert Meeker. Los Angeles, California: Western Psychological Services.

Introduction

The Structure of Intellect Learning Abilities Test-Form P (Primary) is a variant of the standard Structure of Intellect Learning Abilities Test (SOI-LA). It has been scaled down so that it is appropriate for use with children in kindergarten through the third grade. It can also be used with children as young as four years of age. According to the 1985 SOI-LA manual, Form P, which was formerly named the Process and Diagnostic Test, is now known as the Primary Form P. This title will be used hereafter to refer to this test.

The Primary Form P contains 11 subtests that assess the student's reading skills and cognitive style, providing a profile of strengths and weaknesses for kindergarten through third-grade students. It is divided into two areas, processing abilities and diagnostic abilities, under which the 11 subtests are grouped. The subtests listed under processing abilities are Cognition of Figural Units (CFU); Cognition of Figural Classes (CFC); Cognition of Semantic Units (CMU); Memory of Symbolic Units-Audio (MSU-A); Convergent Production of Figural Units (NFU); and Memory of Figural Units (MFU). Those subtests listed under diagnostic abilities are Cognition of Semantic Relations (CMR); Cognition of Semantic Systems (CMS); Evaluation of Figural Units (EFU); Convergent Production of Symbolic Transformations (NST); and Cognition of Symbolic Systems (CSS). Five of the subtests measure figural abilities; symbolic and semantic abilities are measured by three subtests each.

The Primary Form P is based on the philosophy that all students have intelligence, but these intelligences can vary in kind and amount. According to the authors, this diagnostic test can be used to recommend instructional strategies necessary for appropriately developing the abilities that are shown to be weak and enhancing those considered to be strong.

Authors Mary and Robert Meeker have based their work on research that comes from the theory of intelligence proposed by J. Paul Guilford (1959, 1967). They have adapted the Guilford model to education and, according to Meeker (1969), there are two educational problems to which the test can be applied: 1) a philosophical perspective, which comes from the realization that there is an acceleration of subject matter itself (this growth means that there is a need to "unlock" the mental capacities of students so that they will be able to employ these abilities in acquiring this

Structure of Intellect Learning Abilities Test-Form P (Primary)   459

rapidly changing knowledge), and 2) a pedagogical perspective, which comes from a need on the part of the teacher to focus his or her instruction on the needs of the student.

Mary Meeker extended Guilford's research by developing tests and related curriculum and instructional strategies based on the Structure of Intellect model. She was joined by Robert Meeker in the development of these tests and intervention strategies.

The Guilford theory is represented in a morphological model. This model depicts intelligence as having three dimensions: 1) mental operations, 2) content or information, and 3) products. Each of these dimensions has subcategories that, according to Guilford, give a total picture of the many intelligences, singularly or in combination, that a person can possess. According to his model, which is represented by a cube with three intersecting dimensions, there are 120 separate entities that can be identified as intellectual processing abilities.

The Meekers have designed the "parent" SOI-LA test and all the subtests, including the Primary Form P, to give a detailed profile of learning abilities by assessing a maximum of 26 of the 120 possible intellectual abilities. They have concentrated on abilities that are needed for success in school-related curriculum. The Primary Form P includes those abilities that are considered to be on a maturational level for the examinees.

The trigram that codes each ability uses three letter symbols, with the first letter representing operations, the second representing contents, and the third representing products (e.g., Cognition of Figural Units is represented as CFU). In the case of convergent and semantic, the first letter is not used in order to avoid confusion; instead, the letter N for convergent and M for semantic are used.

Primary Form P takes 1 to 1½ hours to administer. The directions for each subtest include information on what the specific test proposes to assess (e.g., subtest CFU is a test of visual closure). The student is tested on the ability to recognize familiar figures that are partially obscured.

According to guidelines in the manual, this test can be given individually to examinees in kindergarten through third grade who cannot read or write. Reading ability is not a factor in the test because children are read the directions and the items they are to work with in order to give their answers.

Primary Form P is a 15-page booklet in which examinees record their answers. The cover provides a table of percentiles that match the scores of each of the eleven SOI categories to the grade level. This percentile rank is also matched to an evaluation hiearchy, which has seven levels: disabling, 6 %ile; limiting, 16 %ile; low average, 34 %ile; average, 50 %ile; high average, 66 %ile; superior, 84 %ile; and gifted, 94 %ile. This table is organized horizontally for the 11 categories, with vertical columns for seven score intervals for the lowest and highest possible score listed under each. When the appropriate score interval for a student is circled, a connecting line can be drawn to form a profile that graphically shows the highs and lows and also indicates the percentile for each of the 11 categories and the corresponding ability evaluation level. On the back of the booklet there is a chart that includes spaces for the dates on which training in each of the areas included on the test is completed. This chart suggests that the test is useful for diagnosis and prescription.

460 Structure of Intellect Learning Abilities Test-Form P (Primary)

Whereas Primary Form P is a separate test, directions are included in the comprehensive manual used for all of the variant forms of the SOI-LA test. Scoring stencils for each of the subtests of this form are included in a notebook. These are convenient, clear-plastic overlays for each subcategory. Each stencil includes the scoring techniques for each test. The profiles on each test give a good picture of the student's abilities and can be completed by the examiner; however, a more sophisticated analysis, with a computer printout of each category, subareas of each trigram, and activities necessary for developing or strengthening a particular area, can be secured from the publisher.

Directions for the examiner regarding needed materials are included in the test manual. Soft lead pencils and, in some instances, crayons are used by examinees. Price of the test was not included in the material sent for review; however, this information can be secured from Western Psychological Services, publishers of the test.

Practical Applications/Uses

Primary Form P can be used as a diagnostic tool because its subtests, when reorganized into learning factors, related groupings (such as reading and writing abilities), and creativity, give specific learning needs of the individual. Use of this test on very young children provides an opportunity for early diagnosis and correction of faults. While it can be an effective tool for psychologists, the Primary Form P can also be used efficiently by the classroom teacher who is not a certified psychologist.

Technical Aspects

This test was normed on students in Kindergarten through Grade 3. The norming population included 270, 424, 432, and 396 students respectively. Information from the 1982 technical data manual (p. 1) indicates that this norming, which was done in 1982, included six school districts representing six states: Florida, Indiana, Oklahoma, Pennsylvania, Texas, and Washington.

The test-retest (3-week interval) correlation at each grade level showed a reasonable correlation, with the subtests CFU, CMS, and NST showing the highest correlation. The figural, symbolic, and semantic content ability scores showed a very high test-retest reliability. The total test-retest reliability, which included subtests and content ability scores, ranged from .81 to .94 across the four grade levels. This is a high correlation and would lead one to certify immediately that the tests are reliable; however, this reviewer would like to have reviewed a total test-retest correlation that did not include the three content ability scores—figural, symbolic, and semantic.

The total test-retest reliability indicates that the Primary Form P can be reliable for children as young as those in kindergarten; however, the low subtest CSS correlations indicate that this particular subtest should not be used alone.

The Primary Form P does not have separate content validity information listed in materials under review. As this form is taken from the Basic SOI test, one must rely upon the validity data of the SOI-LA test forms A & B.

Structure of Intellect Learning Abilities Test-Form P (Primary)

According to the 1985 manual, the content validity of the SOI-LA test is verified by the close relationship of the test to the research by J. Paul Guilford (p. 91). The manual contains a table that lists the number of tests and the University of Southern California (USC) Psychological Laboratory Report number, which outlines the research by Guilford used to verify the SOI factors represented in these tests (p. 92).

As another source of content validity, the authors cite a 20-year research period in which a link was established between certain of Guilford's factors and school learning. In this reviewer's opinion, the rationale and verification of content validity, which I feel is adequate, applies to the Primary Form P test also.

Criterion validity, which is specifically related to Primary Form P, is not listed, but criterion validity for the subtests of Forms A & B—some of which are included in Primary Form P—is given in terms of diagnostic utility, concurrent validity, predictive ability, and construct validity for the SOI-LA tests:

Diagnostic utility. Several studies quoted by the authors showed the use of the tests on blacks, Hispanics, and American Indians. There is also evidence that the tests could be used to indicate the level of ability of these students in particular clusters of factors deemed important for school success.

Concurrent validity. Concurrent validity is based on the fact that nine of the SOI-LA subtests are related to reading achievement and 12 are seen as precursors or predictors of arithmetic achievement. Several studies quoted in the manual showed the correlation between the SOI subtests and the Peabody Individual Achievement Test (PIAT) and several other tests.

Predictive validity. There is no research noted indicating the predictive validity of the Primary Form P.

Construct validity. As is true with content validity, construct validity for this form is dependent on the parent test. According to the SOI-LA manual, construct validity is based on studies that have verified the construct validity of groups of subtests (e.g., DFU, DMU, DSR, Thompson & Anderson, 1983; MSU-A, MSS-V, MSS-A, MSI, CFS, and CFT, Maxwell, 1981), and a factor analysis of the 26 subtests in forms A and B (Gorsuch, 1983). This analysis also included the operations, content, and product portion of the Structure of Intellect model. The manual points to construct validity of the Guilford model, which is the conceptual base for the test, as supportive evidence for the construct validity of all forms of the SOI-LA.

Critique

The Primary Form P of the SOI-LA test battery is a diagnostic prescriptive device, which when used with other instruments can be an effective tool for use in education. Its use as an identification tool for the gifted has been reviewed in articles by Clarizio and Mehrens (1985), and O'Tuel, Ward, and Rawl (1983). These reviewers expressed concern about information given by the test authors regarding the use, interpretation, and validity of the tests. They have expressed a need for more supportive data regarding the validity and reliability of the tests. On the other hand, Roid (1985) discussed the strengths of the SOI approach, although specific mention of Primary Form P was not made.

In the case of the Primary Form P, this reviewer found that much of the data needed for informed decision-making was not available. The 1985 manual was centered around the total test battery. It is evident that the rationale or support for the validity of Primary Form P is inextricably tied to the validity of the entire test battery; however, it would be helpful to decision-makers if each of the separate batteries had substantiating evidence for their use for the particular population and area to be tested.

Primary Form P is also used to rate the performance level of each of the intellectual trigrams. Page 66 of the manual provides a scale that gives the examiner a range of abilities to count if the district requires a certain percentile in the range of 3-10% of its students to be identified as gifted. No explanation of this breakdown is included in the test materials, so the use of this process might be risky for a school district. Using this breakdown with other test information is recommended and is defensible in the event that districts are forced to verify each aspect of their testing procedure.

Whereas this test is easy to administer, the usefulness of the test to diagnosticians or school districts is dependent upon how well they understand the meaning and the relationship to learning of each of the trigrams as well as each separate factor included in the tests. For Primary Form P, this would be 11 trigrams and 14 different factors.

The examiner must be careful in administering the test because the directions for the NFU subtest ask children to look at the top of the page for the test, when actually it is in the middle of the page. The directions for MFU can also be confusing. Therefore, the directions should be carefully reviewed in order to be sure students understand. There is also a need for information regarding the levels of score to be expected before continuing the last section of the test.

Given these concerns, Primary Form P should serve as a starting point for intervention. Its use as a sole indication of abilities might be questioned in terms of psychometric evidence, but the rationale for using tests that examine more than what has been learned in school is evidenced in recent studies and the theoretical proposal of Sternberg (1984), Gardner (1983), and others.

References

This list includes text citations and suggested additional reading.

Besel, G. (1980). *Structure of intellect pilot program*. Unpublished manuscript. (Available from SOI Institute, 343 Richmond St., El Segundo, CA 90245)

Clarizio, H., & Mehrens, W. (1985). Psychometric limitations of Guilford's structure of intellect model for identification and programming of the gifted. *Gifted Child Quarterly, 29*(3), 113-120.

Coffman, W. E. (1985). Structure of Intellect Learning Abilities Test. In J. V. Mitchell, Jr. (Ed.), *The ninth mental measurements yearbook* (pp. 1486-1488). Lincoln, NE: Buros Institute of Mental Measurements.

Cunningham, C., Thompson, B., Alston, H., & Wakefield, J. (1978). Use of SOI abilities for prediction. *Gifted Child Quarterly, 22*(4), 506-512.

Gardner, H. (1983). *Frames of mind: The theory of multiple intelligences*. New York: Basic Books.

Gorsuch, R. (1983). *Factor analysis* (2nd ed.). Hillsdale, NJ: Lawrence Erlbaum.

Guilford, J. (1959). Three faces of intellect. *American Psychologist, 14*, 469-479.

Guilford, J. (1967). *The nature of human intelligence*. New York: McGraw-Hill.

Kent, A. (1981). *Differences between high-skilled first-grade readers and control group non-readers on three tests*. Unpublished manuscript. (Available from SOI Institute, 343 Richmond St., El Segundo, CA 90245)

Leton, D. A. (1985). Structure of Intellect Learning Abilities Test. In J. V. Mitchell, Jr. (Ed.), *The ninth mental measurements yearbook* (pp. 1488-1489). Lincoln, NE: Buros Institute of Mental Measurements.

Meeker, M. (1969). *The structure of intellect: Its interpretation and uses*. Columbus, OH: Charles E. Merrill.

Meeker, M., Meeker, R., & Roid, G. (1985). *Structure of Intellect Learning Abilities Test (SOI-LA) manual*. Los Angeles: Western Psychological Services.

O'Tuel, F., Ward, M., & Rawl, R. (1983). The SOI as an identification tool for the gifted: Windfall or washout? *Gifted Child Quarterly, 27*(3), 26-134.

Roid, G. (1985). Limitations of the test reviewing process: A response to Clarizio and Mehrens. *Gifted Child Quarterly, 29*(3), 121-123.

Sternberg, R. (1984). What should intelligence tests test? Implications for a triarchic theory of intelligence for intelligence testing. *Educational Researcher, 13*(3), 5-15.

Anne H. Widerstrom, Ph.D.
Associate Professor of Early Childhood Special Education, University of Colorado at Denver, Denver, Colorado.

TEST OF EARLY LANGUAGE DEVELOPMENT
Wayne P. Hresko, D. Kim Reid, and Donald D. Hammill. Austin, Texas: PRO-ED.

Introduction

The Test of Early Language Development (TELD) is a standardized measure of the form and content of young children's expressive and receptive language. The test was designed for use with children ages three to seven in order 1) to identify those who are performing at a level significantly below that of their peers, 2) to plan for and evaluate a child's participation in an instructional program, or 3) to conduct research related to preschool children's acquisition of language.

The TELD is derived from a developmental psycholinguistic theory of child language that is representative of current thinking in the field. As such, it is valuable for teachers and clinicians as well as for those engaged in research. The authors of the TELD have credentials in the fields of children's language and test development. Wayne P. Hresko, currently chair of the Division of Special Education at North Texas State University, earned a Ph.D. in special education from Temple University. D. Kim Reid, associate professor of special education at the University of Texas, has specialized in the study of young children with problems in language development since completing her doctoral work at Temple University. Donald D. Hammill has several statistically sound tests to his credit, including the Test of Language Development (TOLD), the Test of Written Spelling (TWS), and the Basic School Skills Inventory (BSSI). Dr. Hammill, president of PRO-ED, publishers of the TELD, is a former member of the special education faculty at Temple University. All three authors hold a psycholinguistic perspective on language development, which forms the basis for the TELD. Published by the same authors is the Test of Early Reading Ability (TERA; Reid, Hresko, & Hammill, 1981), which is intended as a companion test to the TELD.

In the introduction to this test, the authors state that the TELD was designed to fill the gap that existed in an important assessment domain: young children's spoken language. They note that until the development of the TELD there was a lack of well-constructed standardized measures of young children's language based on current theoretical perspectives.

The TELD was designed to provide a means of identifying children in need of more intensive clinical evaluation. The authors state that both clinical observation and standardized testing should be included in a comprehensive and accurate assessment of a child's language abilities. As a standardized test, the TELD was not intended to replace, but rather to complement, systematic, naturalistic observation.

In developing the TELD, the authors chose a model of language acquisition based on the work of Bloom and Lahey (1978), which identifies three dimensions of language—form (syntax, morphology, phonology), content (semantics), and use (pragmatics). The dimensions measured by the TELD are form and content, because use is assessed more accurately through clinical observation. In addition, the TELD measures both expressive and receptive modes of communication.

A 370-item experimental edition of the TELD was developed and administered to 200 children living in upstate New Jersey. The resulting item data were analyzed; as a result of that analysis a second version of the test, reduced to 70 items, was administered to a group of 100 children in north central Texas. Following a second item analysis the number of test items was reduced to 38. This became the final version of the TELD. The appropriateness of the item selection was tested by conducting a third analysis on randomly selected test protocols, 100 at each age level (three years through seven years). This analysis yielded coefficients of discrimination that were significantly beyond the 1% confidence level.

The standardization sample consisted of 1,184 children who were fairly representative of the nation as a whole, both geographically and socioeconomically, with consideration given to sex, race, and parental occupations; that is, the sample represented a slightly more urban and more southern population than national data would indicate, with more parents in white-collar occupations than in blue-collar ones.

The TELD was copyrighted in 1981 and has not been revised. The following year a Spanish version was published, Prueba del Desarrolo Inicial del Lenguaje (PDIL; Hresko, Reid, & Hammill, 1982), which was standardized on a sample of Spanish-speaking children living in Mexico, Puerto Rico, and the United States.

Practical Applications/Uses

The TELD manual describes test administration, scoring and interpretation, and specific instructions for administering each test item. The manual also provides information concerning development of the test, its validity, and its reliability. With a pad of scoring forms and a set of picture cards used in administering some of the items, the test comes packaged in a slim 6" x 10" box, which makes it easy to handle and store. This simple and effective packaging is a distinct asset; the TERA and the PDIL come packaged in similar fashion.

The picture cards are simple line drawings in black and white. Some of the illustrations are of minority children, but most represent white, middle-class people and customs. This may be of some concern when administering the test to children from low socioeconomic or minority backgrounds.

The test consists of 38 items individually administered, with no time limit. It is suggested that all items be administered orally during a single session, yielding a single overall raw score. Each test item is labeled as testing either *expressive* or *receptive* language and either *form* or *content*. As noted, the test is appropriate for use with children ages 3-0 to 7-11. The authors state that the TELD may be used with special-needs children not represented in the norming groups (e.g., deaf or retarded children, or those below three or older than eight years of age) if certain precautions are followed (such as establishing specific norms for these groups).

Extensive experience in test administration is not required for this measure; administering the TELD is easy and the manual is clear and explicit. Under each item a specific procedure is described, including the exact words to be said by the examiner. For example, the examiner might show the child one of the picture cards and say, "Show me the -----." The child must point to the correct picture. Scoring criteria are specifically stated for each item: "The child must point correctly to two of the three pictures to receive credit for this item."

The examinee receives one point for each correct item; partial credit is not given. This makes scoring simply a matter of recording the child's pass/fail performance on the scoring sheet, establishing basal and ceiling levels, and computing a raw score. The basal level is that point where the child passes five items in a row, and the ceiling is established when the child misses five items in a row. Each age group begins the test at a different item number: the first nine items are administered only to three-year-olds, four-year-olds begin the test at item 10, whereas seven-year-olds begin at #25. This means that there are only 14 items available for administering to seven-year-olds. The authors note in their discussion of item difficulty that the TELD test items appear to be most acceptable for children at the middle ages (four-, five-, and six-year-olds).

The raw score can be converted to a Language Quotient (LQ), a percentile score, or an age equivalent by referring to tables in the back of the manual. These scores are listed for each child on an individual scoring sheet, along with information concerning the child's name, sex, age, school, teacher, referring agent, and the examiner's name and title. The child's age in years and months is computed at the time of testing, and a place for this information is also provided on the scoring sheet. On the back of the single 5"x8" sheet is an item profile, which allows the child's performance to be plotted according to mode (expressive vs. receptive) and feature (content vs. form). This profile is useful for identifying strengths and weaknesses in language performance. Also on the reverse side of the scoring sheet is a short "Interpretations and Recommendations" section and a place for the examiner to list any special environmental conditions (noise, temperature) that might have interfered with the testing process.

Interpretation of TELD scores centers on the Language Quotient, designed with a mean of 100 and a standard deviation of 15. The LQ is interpreted in a fashion similar to the intelligence quotient yielded by the Wechsler tests; for example, the average range is represented by a score falling between one standard deviation below and above the mean (85-115). Therefore, below average scores are those from 70 to 84 (two standard deviations below the mean) and scores from 55 to 69 (three standard deviations below the mean) are considered poor.

The manual states that a low LQ on the TELD should be treated as a hypothesis to be investigated, and the authors stress that other information concerning the child's language functioning should be gathered, including further testing and clinical observation, before the child is labeled language-delayed or -disordered. This is consistent with the primary purpose of the TELD, which is to screen young children who may be in need of special educational programming in language development.

The information yielded by the item profile and the Language Quotient can be supplemented by the percentile score and the language age, thus providing an efficient and accurate indication of the child's receptive and expressive language abilities.

Average testing time per child on the TELD is 15 to 20 minutes. Scoring takes another 10 minutes, making this a very efficient screening test.

Technical Aspects

According to the manual, reliability for the TELD was established by examining error variance associated with content sampling and time sampling. To assess the amount of test error due to content, the internal consistency reliability of the items was investigated using Cronbach's (1951) coefficient alpha. Coefficient alphas were computed on 500 children, 100 from each of the five age groups, and both these reliability coefficients and the associated standard errors of measurement are reported in the manual for each age group.

The five coefficient alphas range from .88 to .92, well above the .80 level established by Anastasi (1976) and others as the magnitude necessary for a reliable test. The standard error of measurement in each case rounds to two raw score points; the small size of the SEM also supports the test's reliability.

To assess the amount of test error due to time, the stability reliability of the items was investigated using a test-retest model. A group of 177 children from the five age groups was administered the TELD twice, with a two-week interval between administrations. The two scores were correlated, yielding reliability coefficients for each age group ranging from .72 to .87.

Three types of validity are reported for the TELD: content, criterion-related, and construct. Content validity is reported by the authors to consist of item validity tested through item analysis. In this analysis, described in an earlier section of this review, the internal consistency of the test was ascertained by correlating each item with the total test score. The authors report that these validity coefficients (coefficients of discrimination) are significant at each age level of the test beyond the 1% level of confidence.

To establish the criterion-related validity of the TELD, scores were correlated with several well-known measures of expressive and receptive language in young children: the Preschool Language Scale (Zimmerman, Steiner, & Pond, 1979), the Test of Language Development (Newcomer & Hammill, 1977), the Metropolitan Readiness Test (Hildreth, Griffiths, McGauvran, 1969) and the Metropolitan Achievement Test (MAT; Durost, Bixler, Wrightstone, Prescott, & Barlow, 1970). The resulting coefficients ranged from .46 with the Zimmerman scale (three-year-olds) to .80 with the Test of Language Development (six-year-olds). The highest correlations (.66, .80, .67, .75, and .58) were found with five- and six-year-olds. No criterion-related validity is reported in the manual for four-year-olds or seven-year-olds. Although all the coefficients were reported as significant beyond the 1% level, it appears that the TELD's greatest strength may be in use with five- and six-year-olds.

In order to establish the construct validity, TELD scores were correlated with those of several intelligence (Slosson, 1963), reading (TERA, MAT, Test of Reading Comprehension [Brown, Hammill, & Wiederholt, 1978]) and readiness (MRT) tests. As with criterion-related validity, construct validity correlations are more numerous for five- and six-year-olds than for the other three age groups. Only one correlation each is reported for three-, four-, and seven-year-olds. Nevertheless, all correlation coefficients reported are high, ranging from .34 to .82 with a median of .54.

Further evidence of the TELD's good construct validity is offered in a study that attempted to determine whether the test could differentiate between children with normally developing language skills and children who were diagnosed as "communication disordered." A group of 17 of the latter were administered the TELD. The mean LQ for this group was 76, which represents a discrepancy approaching two standard deviations below the mean and which supports the TELD's ability to discriminate between normally functioning and language-delayed children. Unfortunately, ages for this group of communication-disordered children were not reported, so it is impossible to say whether this aspect of construct validity is applicable to all five age groups.

A final means for examining the test's construct validity is to ascertain whether it measures language skills in a developmental sense (i.e., whether test scores correlate with chronological age). This is indeed the case, as evidence is provided through the use of Pearson product-moment correlations that as children increase in age, so do their mean scores on the TELD.

The TELD manual provides strong evidence of reliability and validity for children ages three through seven. It is especially useful for five- and six-year-olds, according to the data, but this does not mean that it is not a reliable and valid instrument for all the age groups for which it is intended.

Critique

The TELD and the PDIL are relatively new instruments about which little has thus far been written. They are soundly constructed tests that appear to have strong appeal for teachers and clinicians as initial screening tests. For this purpose they are gaining wide acceptance, most particularly in educational settings.

While apparently most suitable for use with four-, five- and six-year-olds, these tests are also appropriate for three- and seven-year-olds. Their intended purpose, to fill the need for a well-constructed test of spoken language for use with preschool children, seems well met. In general, the tests seem most appropriate for use with children from middle-class backgrounds, but reliability and validity data demonstrate that they provide accurate information for children from other backgrounds as well.

An added advantage of the TELD is the fact that it can be combined in a screening program with its companion test, the Test of Early Reading Ability (reviewed elsewhere in this volume), for an accurate assessment of a child's written and spoken language abilities.

References

Anastasi, A. (1976). *Psychological testing*. New York: Macmillan Publishing Co.
Bloom, L., & Lahey, M. (1978). *Language development and disorders*. New York: John Wiley & Sons.

Brown, V., Hammill, D., & Wiederhold, J. L. (1978). *The Test of Reading Comprehension.* Austin, TX: PRO-ED.

Cronbach, L. (1951). Coefficient alpha and the internal structure of tests. *Psychometrika, 16,* 297-334.

Durost, W., Bixler, H., Wrightstone, J., Prescott, G., & Barlow, I. (1970). *The Metropolitan Achievement Tests.* New York: Harcourt, Brace, Jovanovich.

Hildreth, G., Griffiths, M., & McGauvran, M. (1969). *The Metropolitan Readiness Tests.* New York: Harcourt, Brace, Jovanovich.

Hresko, W., Reid, D. K., & Hammill, D. (1982). *Prueba del Desarrollo Inicial del Lenguaje.* Austin, TX: PRO-ED.

Newcomer, P., & Hammill, D. (1977). *The Test of Language Development.* Austin, TX: PRO-ED.

Reid, D. K., Hresko, W., & Hammill, D. (1981). *The Test of Early Reading Ability.* Austin, TX: PRO-ED.

Slosson, R. (1963). *Slosson Intelligence Test for Children and Adults.* East Aurora, NY: Slosson Educational Publications.

Zimmerman, I., Steiner, V., & Pond, R. (1979). *Preschool Language Scale.* Columbus, OH: Chas. E. Merrill.

Anne H. Widerstrom, Ph.D.
Associate Professor of Early Childhood Special Education, University of Colorado at Denver, Denver, Colorado.

TEST OF EARLY READING ABILITY

D. Kim Reid, Wayne P. Hresko, and Donald D. Hammill. Austin, Texas: PRO-ED.

Introduction

The Test of Early Reading Ability (TERA) is a standardized measure of young children's proficiency in the interpretation of written language. The test was designed for use with children ages three to seven in order 1) to identify those children who are significantly behind their peers in the development of reading, 2) to document children's progress in learning to read, 3) to serve as a measure in research projects, and 4) to suggest instructional practices.

The TERA is based on the theoretical work of K. Goodman and Y. Goodman (1979), who have described the nature of early reading as related to the child's symbolic development in the Piagetian sense and to the child's early awareness of the importance of print and an interest in making sense out of it. The authors of the TERA note that children are spontaneously motivated at an early age to find meaning in print, to learn the alphabet and its uses, and to discover the conventions associated with written language (e.g., page turning, left-right orientation). These characteristics of early reading form the basis for the TERA, making the test representative of current thinking in the field of written language and making it useful for teachers, clinicians, and researchers.

The authors of the TERA have credentials in the fields of children's language and test development. Dr. Reid has specialized in the study of young children with problems in oral and written language using Piagetian and psycholinguistic theoretical approaches. Dr. Hresko was the primary author of the Test of Early Language Development (TELD), companion to the TERA. Dr. Hammill has several statistically sound tests to his credit, including the Test of Language Development (TOLD), the Test of Written Spelling (TOWS), and the Basic School Skills Inventory (BSSI). All three authors hold a psycholinguistic perspective on oral and written language development, which is the basis for the TERA.

The TERA, like its counterpart the TELD, was designed to provide a device which can be used to identify children in need of more intensive clinical evaluation. The authors state that both clinical observation and standardized testing should be included in a comprehensive and accurate assessment of a child's reading abilities. As a standardized test, the TERA was not intended to replace but rather to complement systematic, naturalistic observation.

A 270-item edition was developed and administered to 100 children living in upstate New Jersey. The resulting item data were analyzed; as a result of that analysis a second version of the test, reduced to 76 items, was administered to a group of 150 children residing in the Dallas/Fort Worth area. Following a second item analysis, the number of test items was reduced to 50, the final version of the TERA.

The appropriateness of the item selection was tested by conducting a third item analysis on 500 randomly selected test protocols, 100 at each age level, three years through seven years. This analysis yielded coefficients of discrimination that were significant beyond the 1% confidence level. However, the coefficient of discrimination for the 3-year-old group was below the .30 criterion for acceptability, and the authors do not recommend using the TERA with children below age 3-10. Item difficulty analysis revealed that the TERA is most acceptable for 5- and 6-year-olds, too difficult for 3- and 4-year-olds, and too easy for 7-year-olds.

The standardization sample consisted of 1,184 children who were fairly representative of the nation as a whole, both geographically and socioeconomically, with consideration given to sex, race, and parental occupation; that is, the sample represented a slightly more urban and more southern population than national data would indicate, and more white-collar occupations as opposed to blue-collar for the parents of the sample children than national statistics show.

Practical Applications/Uses

The TERA manual describes test administration, scoring and interpretation, and specific instructions for administering each test item. The manual also provides information concerning development of the test, its validity, and its reliability. With a pad of scoring forms and a set of picture cards used in administering some of the items, the test comes packaged in a slim 6" x 10" box, which makes it easy to handle and store. This simple and effective packaging is identical to that of the two companion tests of the TERA, the TELD and its Spanish-language version, Prueba del Desarrolo Initial del Lenguaje (PDIL).

The test consists of 50 items individually administered. It is suggested that the TERA is most useful with children who are between the ages 4-0 and 7-11, who are English speakers, and who can understand the directions and respond to the items. While these criteria may seem self-evident, the authors are concerned that the test not be used with children whose native language and/or sociocultural background may penalize their test performance. It is stated that the TERA may be used with special needs children not represented in the norming groups, such as deaf or retarded children, or those below 4 or older than 8 years of age if certain precautions are followed. These may include the establishment of specific norms for these groups.

Test administration is simple, and the manual is easy to follow. Extensive experience in test administration is not required, although the authors naturally suggest that adequate familiarity with the test manual be acquired by anyone wishing to administer the TERA. Under each item a specific procedure is described, including the exact words of the examiner. For example, item #2 on the test asks the examiner to show the child a picture card depicting a book and say to the child, "Show me the top of the book. Point to it." Scoring criteria are specifically stated. In the previous example, the child must "clearly indicate by pointing to the top of the book" in order to receive credit for the item.

472 Test of Early Reading Ability

The child receives one point for each correct item; partial credit is not given. Similar to the TELD, the TERA is scored on a simple pass/fail basis. The child's raw score is computed from the basal and ceiling levels established by passing five items in a row and failing five in a row. The test performance is recorded on a simple, one-page scoring sheet. Each age group begins with a different item; 4-year-olds begin at item #5, 7-year-olds at item #30. This eliminates the necessity of administering a large number of unnecessary items to older children.

Like the TELD, the raw score is converted to a quotient (the Reading Quotient or RQ), a percentile score, or an age equivalent by referring to tables in the manual. These scores are listed on the individual scoring sheet for each child, along with demographic information. On the reverse side of the scoring sheet is an item profile, which allows the child's performance to be plotted according to strengths and weaknesses in the three areas of meaning, alphabet knowledge, and print conventions. Also included is a short "Interpretations and Recommendations" section and a place for the examiner to list any special environmental conditions that might have adversely affected the child's performance.

Interpretation of TERA scores centers on the Reading Quotient, designed with a mean of 100 and a standard deviation of 15. The RQ is interpreted in a fashion similar to the Intelligence Quotient yielded by the Wechsler tests (i.e., the average range is represented by a score falling between one standard deviation below and above the mean [85-115]). Below average scores thus are those from 70 to 84 (two standard deviations below the mean) and scores from 55 to 69 (three standard deviations below the mean) are rated poor.

The manual states that a low Reading Quotient on the TERA should be treated as a hypothesis to be investigated, and the authors stress that other information concerning the child's language functioning should be gathered, including further testing and clinical observation, before it is determined that the child has a reading problem. This is consistent with the primary purpose of the TERA, which is to screen young children who may be in need of special instruction in reading.

The information yielded by the item profile and the Reading Quotient can be supplemented by the percentile score and the language age, thus providing an efficient and accurate indication of the child's written language abilities.

Average testing time per child on the TERA is 15 to 20 minutes. Scoring takes another 10 minutes, making this an efficient screening test.

Technical Aspects

According to the manual, reliability for the TERA was established by examining error variance associated with content sampling and time sampling. To assess the amount of test error due to content, the internal consistency reliability of the items was investigated using Cronbach's (1951) coefficient alpha. Coefficient alphas were computed on 500 children, 100 from each of the five age groups, and reliability coefficients and the associated standard errors of measurement were reported in the manual for each age group. The five coefficient alphas range from .87 to .96, well above the .80 level established by Anastasi (1976) and others as the magnitude necessary for a reliable test. The standard error of measurement in each case rounds to two raw score points; the small size of the SE_m also supports the test's reliability.

To assess the amount of test error due to time, the stability reliability of the items was investigated using a test-retest model. A group of 177 children from the five age groups was administered the TERA twice, with a two-week interval between administrations. The two scores were correlated, yielding reliability coefficients for each age group ranging from .82 to .94. Highest correlations were for ages 4, 5, and 6 years.

Three types of validity are reported for the TERA: content, criterion-related, and construct. Content validity is reported by the authors to consist of item validity tested through item analysis. In this analysis, described in an earlier section of this review, the internal consistency of the test was ascertained by correlating each item with the total test score. The authors report that these validity coefficients (coefficients of discrimination) are significant at each age level of the test beyond the one percent level of confidence.

To study the TERA's criterion-related validity, scores were correlated with those of the Reading subtest from the Metropolitan Achievement Tests (using 6-year-old children as subjects) and with the Composite Score from the Test of Reading Comprehension (using 7-year-old children as subjects). The resulting coefficients were .66 and .52, respectively. These coefficients were significant beyond the 1% level of confidence and were sufficiently large to demonstrate the TERA's criterion-related validity. It should be noted that no data are reported for the other age groups.

To establish the construct validity of the TERA, its scores were correlated with several well-known measures of reading, language, and school readiness for young children: the TELD (Hresko, Reid, & Hammill, 1981), the Preschool Language Scale (Zimmerman, Steiner, & Evatt, 1979), the Test of Language Development (Newcomer & Hammill, 1977), the Metropolitan Readiness Test (Hildreth, Griffiths, & McGauvran, 1969) and the Metropolitan Achievement Test (Durost, Bixler, Wrightstone, Prescott, & Barlow, 1970). The resulting coefficients ranged from .37 to .82 with a median of .57, and were all significant at less than the 5% level.

Further evidence of the TERA's construct validity is a small study that attempted to determine whether the test could differentiate between children who read well and children who were diagnosed as "learning disability/reading disorders." A group of 19 of the latter 6- or 7-year-old white males was administered the TERA. The mean Reading Quotient for this group was 82, which represents a discrepancy of more than one standard deviation below the mean and which supports the TERA's ability to discriminate between normally functioning and language-delayed children.

A final means for examining the test's construct validity was to ascertain whether it measures reading in a developmental sense (i.e., whether test scores correlate with chronological age). This is indeed the case, as evidence was provided through the use of Pearson product-moment correlations that as children increase in age, so do their mean scores on the TERA.

In summary, the TERA manual provides good evidence of reliability and validity for children ages 4 through 7, and is especially useful for 5- and 6-year-olds, according to the data.

Critique

Although the TERA by itself provides a useful screening test for early readers, it is probably most effective when used in conjunction with its counterpart, the Test of Early Language development.

The TELD and the TERA are relatively new instruments about which little to date has been written. They are soundly constructed tests that appear to have strong appeal for teachers and clinicians as a means of initial screening. For this purpose they are gaining wide acceptance, most particularly in educational settings.

While they seem most suitable for use with 4-, 5- and 6-year-olds, they are also appropriate for 7-year-olds, and the TELD may be administered to 3-year-olds. Their intended purpose, to fill the need for well-constructed tests of spoken and written language for use with preschool children, seems well met. In general, the two tests seem most appropriate for use with children from middle class backgrounds, but reliability and validity data demonstrate that they provide accurate information for children from other backgrounds as well.

References

Anastasi, A. (1976). *Psychological testing.* New York: Macmillan.

Cronbach, L. J. (1951). Coefficient alpha and the internal structure of tests. *Psychometrika, 16,* 297-334.

Durost, W., Bixler, H., Wrightstone, J., Prescott, G., & Barlow, I. (1970). *The Metropolitan Achievement Tests.* New York: Harcourt, Brace Jovanovich.

Hildreth, G. W., Griffiths, M., & McGauvran, M. E. (1969). *The Metropolitan Readiness Tests.* New York: Harcourt, Brace Jovanovich.

Goodman, K., & Goodman, Y. (1979). Learning to read is natural. In L. B. Resnick & P. A. Weaver (Eds.), *Theory and practice of early reading* (Vol. 1). Hillsdale, NJ: Lawrence Erlbaum Associates.

Newcomer, P., & Hammill, D. (1977). *The Test of Language Development.* Austin, TX: PRO-ED.

Zimmerman, I., Steiner, V., & Evatt, R. (1979). *Preschool Language Scale.* Columbus, OH: Charles E. Merrill.

Robert L. Heilbronner, Ph.D.
Postdoctoral Fellow, Clinical Neuropsychology, University of Oklahoma Health Sciences Center, Oklahoma City, Oklahoma.

E. Wayne Holden, Ph.D.
Postdoctoral Fellow, Pediatric Psychology, University of Oklahoma Health Sciences Center, Oklahoma City, Oklahoma.

TEST OF FACIAL RECOGNITION-FORM SL
A. L. Benton, M. W. Van Allen, K. Hamsher, and H. S. Levin. New York: Oxford University Press.

Introduction

The Test of Facial Recognition-Form SL (TFR) is a 54-item test that requires the matching of unfamiliar faces under different conditions of stimulus presentation. It was developed by Arthur Benton and his colleagues at the University of Iowa to provide a standardized, objective procedure for assessing the capacity to identify and discriminate unfamiliar faces. The overall goal of the authors' research on this test was to determine whether or not impaired facial recognition was an autonomous deficit or one manifestation of a pervasive visuoperceptive disability.

The TFR was initially developed by Arthur Benton and Maurice Van Allen in 1968. A short form was later produced by Benton, Harvey Levin, and Kerry Hamsher in 1975. A comprehensive manual for use with the test was first published in 1978 by Benton, Van Allen, Hamsher, and Levin. All four authors were involved in scholarly work in the area of neuropsychology at the University of Iowa during the period of test development. Dr. Benton has made significant contributions to the field of clinical neuropsychology since 1934, publishing over 100 articles, chapters, and books. He is also responsible for the development of a number of carefully constructed and documented clinical tests in neuropsychology (Benton, Hamsher, Varney, & Spreen, 1983). Dr. Van Allen was a neurologist who worked closely with Benton on a number of studies designed to bridge the gap between neurology and psychology. Drs. Levin and Hamsher trained under Benton. Dr. Levin is currently at the University of Texas Medical Branch at Galveston and is well known for his work with closed head injury. Dr. Hamsher is in the Department of Neurology at the University of Wisconsin and continues to publish extensively in the field of clinical neuropsychology.

The TFR was first employed in a study of brain-damaged patients in which the relationship between facial recognition and such factors as locus and type of lesion, visual field defect, and aphasia were investigated (Benton & Van Allen, 1968). Other tests of facial recognition had been developed to study prosopagnosia (the failure to recognize the faces of familiar persons), but previous tests made demands upon an individual's immediate memory and involved the simultaneous matching of faces (Warrington & James, 1967; De Renzi, Faglioni, & Spinnler, 1968).

476 Test of Facial Recognition-Form SL

The same cognitive and perceptual processes that are involved in the recognition of familiar faces were assumed to be measured by tests using unfamiliar faces as stimuli. Despite early findings that both types of agnosias were associated with disease of the right cerebral hemisphere (Hecaen & Angelergues, 1962; De Renzi & Spinnler, 1966), it became clear that the two deficits were not identical and that their relationship needed more specification. The adequate performance of prosopagnosic patients on tests requiring the discrimination of unfamiliar faces provided additional evidence that the two types of disabilities were dissimiliar (Benton & Van Allen, 1972). Recent research has also demonstrated that the anatomical foci of the damage resulting in the two agnosias are different (Benton, 1980).

The first part of the TFR (six responses) requires matching identical front view photographs of faces. The subject is presented with a single front-view photograph and is instructed to identify it on a display of six front-view photographs underneath the stimulus photograph. In the second part of the test (24 responses), the subject is required to match a front-view photograph with three-quarter view photographs of the same person on a multiple-choice display. In the third part (24 responses), the subject matches front-view photographs of the same person that have been taken under different lighting conditions.

The test is assembled in a spiral-bound booklet. Each stimulus and its corresponding response choices are presented on two facing pages, with the single stimulus photograph above the six response pictures. The subject is encouraged to hold and manipulate the test booklet to his best advantage. The test is arranged so that the 13 stimulus and response pictures that comprise the Short Form are presented first. These are labeled items 1 through 27 (pages 1-13). Combined with these items, the latter nine stimulus response pictures (pages 14-22) comprise the 54 items in the Long Form. A record sheet is used for recording and scoring responses.

To begin testing, the examiner says, "You see this woman? Show me where she is on this picture", (pointing to the multiple choice display below). After the subject points or verbally responds, the examiner records correct responses by checking the appropriate items on the answer sheet and records errors by circling the numbers on the right side of the record form. For items 7 through 27 and the remaining items on the Long Form (items 28-54), the examiner says "You see this woman? She is shown three times on this picture. Show me where she is. Find three pictures of her." The examiner records the subject's responses in the same manner as before. The Long Form contains 54 responses with each response assigned a score of 1. A minimum score of 25 is expected by chance; therefore, the effective range of Long Form scores is considered to be 25 to 54. For the Short Form, the effective range of scores is 11 to 27.

The record form includes spaces for each correct response and a column to document the nature of an incorrect response. It also includes Short Form to Long Form conversion scores and corrections to adjust for age and education. Once the score is obtained, the examiner can classify the subject's performance according to the following range of scores: Normal (41-54), Borderline (39-40), Moderately Impaired (37-38), and Severely Impaired (below 37). Mean administration time is approximately 7 minutes for the Short Form and approximately 15 minutes for the Long Form.

Normative standards for the TFR are based on the performance of 286 control patients aged 16-74 years (Benton, Hamsher, Varney, & Spreen, 1983). One sample of subjects (N = 96) was seen on the neurological, neurosurgical, and medical services of the University of Iowa Hospitals. No patient in this group had a history of brain disease, psychiatric disorder requiring hospitalization, or a history suggesting mental deficiency dating back to childhood. A second sample (N = 90) was comprised of normal subjects aged 60-74 years who had volunteered to participate in a study of aging.

The test manual (Benton, Van Allen, Hamsher, & Levin, 1978) reported that the performance of subjects aged 16-56 years did not appear closely related to intelligence (the correlation between the Shipley-Hartford Vocabulary Test and the TFR for 25 control subjects was .20). Subsequent evidence based on a larger and older sample of subjects indicated that educational level was related to performance. Data obtained from subjects aged 55-74 years demonstrated a mean 1.9-point difference between the performance of those with 12 or more years of education and those with 6 to 11 years of education.

The difference favoring the higher educated group was statistically significant. In the 16- to 54-year-olds, however, the difference between education levels was not significant. Because of this, an education correction of two points was added to the Long Form raw scores of the 55 and over control subjects with less than 12 years of education. With educational levels controlled, the mean performance of subjects in the 65- to 74-year-old range was 1.2 points below the mean performance level of subjects in the 55- to 64-year-old range. In addition, subjects 55 to 64 years old performed, on the average, 1.6 points below the subjects in the 16- to 54-year-old group. Consequently, an age correction of one point was added to the Long Form scores of subjects between the ages of 55-64 years, and two points were added to the raw scores of subjects 65 to 74 years old. A subsequent study by Roberts and Hamsher (1984) reported that TFR performance is relatively independent of racial bias.

Two hundred sixty-six Iowa public school children were administered the TFR and abbreviated Wechsler Intelligence Scale for Children (WISC). Their ages ranged from 6-14 years, their grade placement ranged from Kindergarten to Grade 7, and their prorated WISC Full Scale IQs ranged from 85 to 116. Results demonstrated an increase in performance level as a function of age. A consistent rise in scores from age 6 to age 14 was found, and the mean score of the 14-year-olds was nearly identical to that of young adults. To explain the slight increments in performance level of children between the ages of 7 and 9, the authors cited evidence from other research suggesting that children under the ages of 9 or 10 process facial information in a "piecemeal" fashion, while older children process this information in a "configurational" manner (Carey & Diamond, 1977).

Practical Applications/Uses

The TFR was designed to measure an individual's capacity to identify unfamiliar faces. Impaired facial recognition is not routinely seen in the majority of neuropsychological evaluations. It is rarely, if ever, the primary presenting problem of a patient undergoing neuropsychological testing. Moreover, it does not appear to be as "psychosocially salient" as prosopagnosia, the inability to recognize the faces of familiar persons. However, impaired facial recognition does manifest itself within the context of other visual-spatial deficits, which are common symptoms of a number of organic and psychiatric conditions. Consequently, the most useful application of the TFR would be within a battery of tests designed to qualitatively assess defects in the processing of visual-spatial stimuli. For example, if a patient demonstrated significantly impaired ability on the Performance subtests of the WAIS-R or on Halstead-Reitan tests that are purported to measure the integrity of the nondominant cerebral hemisphere, the TFR could be of use in identifying the nature of the functional impairments and, quite possibly, have utility in localizing the lesion. Because of its sensitivity to comprehension defects in patients with posterior left-hemisphere lesions, the TFR might also be of use in determining whether these patients process faces in a sequential verbal-linguistic manner or by utilizing a simultaneous visual-spatial approach. These data would have important implications for rehabilitation planning. Unlike cognitive and neuropsychological tests requiring a verbal or written response, a patient without the capacity for such responses can take the TFR. As such, it may prove particularly useful with patients who have expressive speech deficits, or for those persons with motor difficulties or writing problems.

Technical Aspects

Recent progress in the remediation of cognitive deficits resulting from cerebral impairment has prompted significant changes in the relative emphases placed upon the psychometric characteristics of neuropsychological tests. The technical adequacy of neuropsychological tests no longer rests solely on their ability to identify brain-damaged patients within psychiatric populations or to detect, lateralize, and localize cerebral impairment. The validity and reliability of such tests as measures of specific cognitive functions have assumed increasing importance in test construction and in the application of test results to rehabilitation and treatment planning.

The authors have concluded that the TFR is a valid measure of right-hemisphere damage, particularly in the posterior portions, and left-hemisphere damage when language comprehension deficits are present. In their original validation study, Benton and Van Allen (1968) found significant differences between the mean scores of subjects with cerebral impairment and controls, regardless of the hemispheric location of the lesion. Over 66% of subjects with right-hemisphere damage, however, scored within the defective range, while only 13% of subjects with left-hemisphere damage obtained similarly defective performances. No significant associations were found between test performance and visual-field defects, aphasia, intrahemispheric locus of lesion, and type of lesion. More recent research by the authors has extended their original conclusions regarding the sensitivity of the test to left-hemisphere impairment (Benton, 1980; Hamsher, Levin, & Benton, 1979). Similar to previous results, defective performances were associated with lesions of the right hemisphere, particularly the posterior portions, in nonaphasic brain-damaged subjects. Furthermore, high rates of defective performance (38%) were obtained by left-hemisphere-damaged subjects who displayed oral language comprehension deficits. Intrahemispheric locus of lesion was not significantly associated with performance in the latter group of subjects.

Additional support for validity as a measure of cerebral impairment, irrespective of hemispheric location of damage, has been reported. Levin, Grossman, and Kelly (1977) found a significant association with extent of closed head injury. Defective performances were reported for 50% of patients who were comatose for greater than 24 hours following injury, while only 12% of patients who were not comatose, or comatose for less than 24 hours, obtained scores within the defective range. These results are supported by the essentially normal performance of a patient who had sustained a mild closed head injury and was tested prior to participating in a memory retraining program (Crosson & Buenning, 1984).

In addition to sensitivity to severity of closed head injury, it has been reported that the TFR is a valid measure of more generalized cerebral impairment. In two investigations of a series of patients who had undergone cerebral hemispherectomy for intractable seizures as children (Strauss & Verity, 1983; Verity et al., 1982), all patients scored within the defective range of performance regardless of the hemisphere that was removed. Bentin, Silverberg, and Gordon (1981) reported that the mean score for a group of patients with Parkinson's disease (M = 40) was lower than the mean score for controls (M = 44). Moreover, the mean score for a group of demented patients (M = 34) in the same study was lower than the parkinsonians and was within the defective range. High rates of defective performances by demented subjects were also reported by Eslinger and Benton (1983), who found that 58% of demented subjects scored within the defective range on the TFR.

In contrast to the previously cited investigations, three studies have failed to support the validity of the TFR as a measure of cerebral impairment. Mean scores for right-hemisphere-damaged and left-hemisphere-damaged subjects were within the normal range in one investigation (Bentin & Gordon, 1979), but the right-hemisphere damaged patients were inferior to the left-hemisphere damaged group. In addition, scores for two patients with infarctions in the left hemisphere and accompanying moderate to severe language comprehension deficits were within the normal range (Silverberg & Gordon, 1979), and the score of a patient with a right-hemisphere tumor was at the 90th percentile of normal performance (Bowers & Heilman, 1984). The former result, however, is limited by the absence of statistical tests, and the generalizability of the latter results is questionable due to the small number of subjects investigated.

Aging and psychiatric disorders are important moderator variables to consider in the evaluation of the neurodiagnostic validity of the TFR. Rates of impaired performance have been reported to increase to 10 to 14% in normal subjects beyond the age of 70 years (Benton, Eslinger, & Damasio, 1981). These results, however, contrast strongly with a previously cited investigation, which reported that 58% of demented subjects within the age range of 60 to 81 years obtained defective scores (Eslinger & Benton, 1983). The typical decline in performance associated with aging that is obtained with nonverbal neuropsychological measures is apparent, but it also appears that the test is sensitive to diagnosable cerebral impairment in aged individuals.

Psychiatric illness has a differential impact on the performance of the TFR, depending upon the condition investigated. The mean score of a group of pseudoneurological patients was essentially equivalent to the mean score reported for the normative population (Levin & Benton, 1977). Similarly, schizophrenics were not found to differ significantly from controls in another investigation (Silverberg-Shalev, Gordon, Bentin, & Aranson, 1981). Depression and anorexia nervosa, however, have been associated with increased rates of defective performance. Prior to electrocunvulsive therapy (ECT), 17% of depressed subjects scored within the defective range (Kronfol, Hamsher, Digre, & Wiziri, 1978) and 10% of anorexics obtained scores within the defective range during hospitalization for treatment (Hamsher, Halmi, & Benton, 1981).

Minimal attention has been devoted to investigating the TFR as a measure of cognitive function. This is surprising, given the controversy over the relationship between the discrimination of unfamiliar faces and prosopagnosia. A case study by Benton and Van Allen (1972) indicated that prosopagnosia and TFR performances are dissociable. A postencephalitic patient who was blatantly prosopagnostic scored within the normal range on the TFR.

This does not, however, clearly explicate the cognitive components that are being tapped by the TFR. Explorations of relationships with different cognitive measures are necessary to appropriately validate the test. The test manual (Benton, Van Allen, Hamsher, & Levin, 1978) asserts that scores are independent of general intelligence, based on a nonsignificant correlation with the Shipley-Hartford Vocabulary Test (p. 5). In addition, Benton and Gordon (1971) reported a moderately significant positive correlation between test scores and the ability to discriminate different brightness patterns, independent of intellectual level and the ability to discriminate complex forms. They also reported nonsignificant correlations with verbal tasks and significant positive correlations with visuoconstructive tasks. Broadly construed, these results support the validity of the TFR as a measure of visuoperceptive function(s). The population investigated in the latter study, however, consisted of young adult retardates (IQ = 42 to 70), which limits significantly the generalizability of the results to a normal adult population.

It is important to note that no attempt has been made to formally evaluate the reliability of the TFR. Part-whole correlations between the Long Form and Short Form have been reported to be above .88 (Levin, Hamsher, & Benton, 1975), providing ancilliary evidence for internal consistency and evidence for the validity of Short Form to Long Form score conversions. The absence of further information on reliability is a glaring omission in the development of the Short and Long Forms of this test and hampers significantly its continuing use.

Critique

The majority of the literature on the TFR has addressed its validity as a measure of cerebral impairment. Although results clearly indicate sensitivity to brain damage, the magnitude of hit rates are relatively low, contraindicating the use of the test as a single-screening measure of cerebral impairment. (It should be emphasized, however, that the TFR was not designed to be a screening for the detection of brain damage, but instead as a measure of a specific visuocognitive task performance with implications for the locus of brain damage as well as for the behavioral status of the patient.) The TFR does appear to be differentially sensitive to lateralized brain damage and TFR scores may have some diagnostic value in the lateralization of lesions. Therefore, TFR scores may have neurodiagnostic utility within a battery approach to neuropsychological assessment, but no published investigation has specifically examined this issue. As is the case with a number of assessment instruments in clinical neuropsychology, minimal attention has been devoted to the reliability of the TFR and its validity as a measure of cognitive function(s). More information is needed on these latter topics to enhance the interpretation of test results and to increase the utility of the TFR in the areas of rehabilitation planning and cognitive remediation.

Another area in need of further investigation is the relationship of TFR performance to prosopagnosia in particular and to other forms of visual agnosia in general. Although test scores clearly have neuropsychological significance, their relevance to the area of visual-perceptual processing and the classification of visual agnosias remains unclear. Furthermore, the impact of impaired discrimination of unfamiliar faces on an individual's psychosocial/interpersonal functioning has yet to be determined. Test interpretation would be enhanced significantly by more comprehensive information on the role of TFR performance within the total context of comprehensive approaches to neuropsychological assessment.

References

Bentin, S., & Gordon, H. W. (1979). Assessment of cognitive asymmetry in brain damaged and normal subjects: Validation of a test battery. *Journal of Neurology, Neurosurgery, and Psychiatry, 42,* 715-723.

Bentin, S., Silverberg, R., & Gordon, H. W. (1980). Asymmetrical cognitive deterioration in demented and parkinsonian patients. *Cortex, 17,* 533-544.

Benton, A. L. (1980). The neuropsychology of facial recognition. *American Psychologist, 35,* 176-186.

Benton, A. L., Eslinger, P. J., & Damasio, A. R. (1981). Normative observations on neuropsychological test performances in old age. *Journal of Clinical Neuropsychology, 3,* 33-42.

Benton, A. L., & Gordon, M. C. (1971). Correlates of facial recognition. *Transactions of the American Neurological Association, 96,* 146-150.

Benton, A. L., Hamsher, K. deS., Varney, N. R., & Spreen, O. (1983). *Contributions to neuropsychological assessment: A clinical manual.* New York: Oxford University Press.

Benton, A. L., & Van Allen, M. W. (1968). Impairment in facial recognition in patients with cerebral disease. *Cortex, 4,* 344-358.

Benton, A. L., & Van Allen, M. W. (1972). Prosopagnosia and facial discrimination. *Journal of the Neurological Sciences, 15,* 167-172.

Benton, A. L., Van Allen, M. W., Hamsher, K., & Levin, H. S. (1978). *Test of Facial Recognition-Form SL Test Manual.* Department of Neurology, University of Iowa Hospitals and Clinics.

Bowers, D., & Heilman, K. M. (1984). Dissociation between the processing of affective and nonaffective faces: A case study. *Journal of Clinical Neuropsychology, 6,* 367-379.

Carey, S., & Diamond, R. (1977). From piecemeal to configurational representation of faces. *Science, 196,* 312-314.

Crosson, B., & Buenning, W. (1984). An individual memory retraining program after closed head injury: A single-case study. *Journal of Clinical Neuropsychology, 6,* 287-301.

DeRenzi, E. P., Faglioni, P., & Spinnler, H. (1968). The performance of patients with unilateral brain damage on facial recognition tasks. *Cortex, 4,* 17-34.

DeRenzi, E. P., & Spinnler, H. (1966). Facial recognition in brain-damaged patients. *Neurology, 16,* 145-152.

Eslinger, P. L., & Benton, A. L. (1983). Visuoperceptual performances in aging and dementia: Clinical and theoretical implications. *Journal of Clinical Neuropsychology, 5,* 213-220.

Hamsher, K. deS., Halmi, K. A., & Benton, A. L. (1981). Prediction of outcome in anorexia nervosa from neuropsychological status. *Psychiatry Research, 4,* 79-88.

Hamsher, K., Levin, H. S., & Benton, A. L. (1979). Facial recognition in patients with focal brain lesions. *Archives of Neurology, 36,* 837-839.

Hecaen, H., & Angelergues, R. (1962). Agnosia for faces. *Archives of Neurology, 7,* 92-100.

Kronfol, Z., Hamsher, K., Digre, K., & Waziri, R. (1978). Depression and hemispheric functions: Changes associated with unilateral ECT. *British Journal of Psychiatry, 132,* 560-567.

Levin, H. S., & Benton, A. L. (1977). Facial recognition in "pseudoneurological" patients. *Journal of Nervous and Mental Disease, 164,* 135-138.

Levin, H. S., Grossman, R. G., & Kelly, J. (1977). Impairment in facial recognition after closed head injuries of varying severity. *Cortex, 13,* 119-130.

Levin, H. S., Hamsher, K., & Benton, A. L. (1975). A short form of the Test of Facial Recognition for clinical use. *Journal of Psychology, 91,* 223-228.

Roberts, R. J., & Hamsher, K. (1984). Effects of minority status in facial recognition and naming performance. *Journal of Clinical Psychology, 40,* 539-545.

Silverberg, R., & Gordon, H. W. (1979). Differential aphasia in two bilingual individuals. *Neurology, 29,* 51-55.

Silverberg-Shalev, R., Gordon, H. W., Bentin, S., & Aranson, A. (1981). Selective language deterioration in chronic schizophrenia. *Journal of Neurology, Neurosurgery, and Psychiatry, 44,* 547-551.

Strauss, E., & Verity, L. (1983). Effects of hemispherectomy in infantile hemiplegics. *Brain and Language, 20,* 1-11.

Verity, C. M., Strauss, E. H., Moyes, P. D., Wada, J. A., Donn, H. G., & Lapointe, J. S. (1982). Long-term follow-up after cerebral hemispherectomy: Neurophysiologic, radiologic, and psychological findings. *Neurology, 32,* 629-639.

Warrington, E. K., & James, M. (1967). An experimental investigation of facial recognition in patients with unilateral cerebral lesions. *Cortex, 3,* 317-326.

Michael D. Franzen, Ph.D.
Director of Neuropsychology, West Virginia University Medical Center, Assistant Professor of Behavioral Medicine and Psychiatry, West Virginia University School of Medicine, Morgantown, West Virginia.

TEST OF PERCEPTUAL ORGANIZATION
William T. Martin. Creve Coeur, Missouri: Psychologists and Educators, Inc.

Introduction

The Test of Perceptual Organization, originally entitled the Test of Abstract Reasoning, was designed as a measure of abstract reasoning. Preliminary data from a pilot study using normal children and adults led to a revised scoring system. The conceptualization of the test as a measure of attention span, psychomotor functioning, and abstract reasoning followed the initial validation study. The test was written by William T. Martin, who developed it from a test known as the Map for Communications Experiments, which was used by the personnel department of St. Paul Hospital in Dallas, Texas (Martin, 1967). The origin of the test is unknown. It was renamed the Test of Perceptual Organization in order to suggest the variety of situations in which it can be used.

Practical Applications/Uses

The Test of Perceptual Organization is a paper-and-pencil assessment instrument that has a ten-minute time limit in administration. It consists of a 22-page manual, a test booklet, a scoring key, and profile sheets. The test booklet is a series of 10 instructions, each increasing in difficulty. The instructions refer to locations on a grid map, which is printed on a subsequent page. The subject is to read the instructions and then place an "X" corresponding to a location described.

The manual suggests that the test can be scored using both objective and subjective scoring procedures. The objective scoring procedures are facilitated by the scoring key, which is a template. The template fits over the grid map with the correct locations for each response. Correct responses are given a score of three points. If the "X" is not placed per the instructions, one point is deducted. Quick completions can earn up to five extra points. The total score can vary from +35 to –19 points.

Subjective scoring involves examination of the protocol for the presence of free associations, spontaneous writings, bizarre drawings, poor motor coordination, or "other effects." Unfortunately, the manual does not describe any of these subjec-

---

The reviewer would like to acknowledge the significant and substantial contributions of Stanley Smith to the writing of this chapter.

tive scoring categories. The only interpretation of these signs is a suggestion to follow with additional assessment.

The manual recommends the test in the initial evaluation of clinical and counseling clients and further suggests that it could be useful as a clinical research instrument. The areas of suggested sensitivity are in abstract reasoning, psychomotor functioning, and the ability to follow instructions.

Technical Aspects

Reliability has not been extensively evaluated for this instrument. Because of the nature of the Test of Perceptual Organization, the manual states that it is likely to have practice effects, resulting in low test-retest reliability. Although this may turn out to be the case, it is an empirical question and therefore should be investigated. In the one study conducted, 13 student nurses were administered the instrument twice in a 7-day period. The correlation between the scores was .17, and there was a significant difference between the scores obtained on the two occasions. The small sample used in this investigation precludes the possibility of generalizing from the results, but it does suggest that the author may be correct in his assessment of test-retest reliability. It is possible that the results of the test may be more stable in an impaired population. However, this needs to be evaluated. In addition, though the order of the items is said to reflect increasing difficulty, the correctness of the order should be evaluated using an index of item difficulty.

There are data that can be used in an evaluation of the validity of the test as a measure of abstract reasoning. The Test of Perceptual Organization correlates .46 with the Abstract Reasoning Test of the Differential Aptitude Test in a sample of 48 normal college students (Martin, 1967). In the same sample, the Test of Perceptual Organization correlated .31 with the Proverbs Test (Martin, 1967). Both correlations are low, indicating that shared variance with other measures of abstract reasoning is approximately 9-18%. Moreover, the Test of Perceptual Organization correlated .61 with the Bender Visual Motor Gestalt Test in a sample of 20 subjects, which included various diagnoses (Martin, 1974). Validation of the suggested uses of the test is needed.

The manual presents interpretative strategies for the obtained profiles, but these are in need of empirical validation. Furthermore, the other constructs purported to be measured by the test need to be investigated, including concentration and the ability to follow instructions. Although the face validity of the test is apparent, the determination of construct validity requires additional empirical data.

References

Martin, W. T. (1967). Analysis of the abstracting function in reasoning using an experimental test. *Psychological Reports, 21,* 593-598.
Martin, W. T. (1974). *Test of Perceptual Organization: Manual.* Jacksonville, IL: Psychologists and Educators, Inc.

Connie K. Varnhagen, Ph.D.
Research Associate, Centre for the Study of Mental Retardation, The University of Alberta, Edmonton, Canada.

TEST OF WRITTEN SPELLING
Stephen C. Larsen and Donald D. Hammill. Austin, Texas: PRO-ED.

Introduction

The Test of Written Spelling (TWS-2; Larsen & Hammill, 1986) is a norm-referenced test designed to assess the spelling of students in Grades 1 through 12. The TWS-2 employs the dictated-word method of spelling assessment and is comprised of two subtests. The first subtest assesses spelling for "predictable" words (those which conform to common English orthographic rules), while the second subtest assesses spelling for "unpredictable" words (those which do not conform to orthographic rules). Test results are reported in terms of standard scores and percentiles. The TWS-2 is a revision of an earlier test, the Test of Written Spelling (TWS; Larsen & Hammill, 1976).

The development of the TWS-2 is based on both the rule-governed nature of English orthography and the many irregularities encountered in English spelling. Larsen and Hammill (1986) cite a comprehensive study by Hanna, Hanna, Hodges, and Rudorf (1966) as a basis for the particular structure of the TWS-2. Hanna et al. programmed a computer to predict the spelling of 17,000 frequently used words on the basis of some 2,000 orthographic spelling rules. The computer predicted the correct spelling for only 49.8% of the words. However, of the remaining words, 37% were spelled with only one error in rule application. In the TWS-2 manual, Larsen and Hammill cite the Hanna et. al findings in order to emphasize that, with certain exceptions, English spelling is essentially rule governed in terms of phoneme-grapheme correspondence regularities. Nonetheless, there are many common words that do not conform to orthographic rules. The "predictable" words subtest of the TWS-2 consists of words that can be spelled by correct application of orthographic rules and the "unpredictable" words subtest consists of words that violate orthographic spelling rules.

In addition to attending to construct validity by including predictable and unpredictable words subtests, the TWS-2 was developed with attention to criterion-based validity in terms of written spelling proficiency. Other commercially produced spelling tests often employ either a multiple-choice format of assessment, in which the student must recognize the correct spelling among a series of distractor items, or a proofreading format, in which the student must recognize incorrectly spelled words (Shores & Yee, 1973). Arguing that a major goal of spelling instruction is to teach children how to write words correctly, Larsen and Hammill employ a dictated words format in which the student must actually spell the test words. Thus, the testing format of the TWS-2 is more directly related to the

486 Test of Written Spelling

criterion of being able to write correctly than many other commonly used spelling tests.

The TWS-2 is a revision of an earlier dictated-word test, the TWS (Larsen & Hammill, 1976). Like the TWS-2, the TWS consisted of predictable and unpredictable words subtests. The criterion used for selecting predictable words was that the orthographic rule governing the spelling had applied at least 50% of the time in the Hanna et al. (1966) study. For example, the study revealed that a one-syllable word with a long /a/ sound in the middle would be spelled with an *a* in the middle and a silent *e* at the end of the word (as in *made*) 87% of the time. Conversely, the word would be spelled with *ai* (as in *maid*) much less of the time. The criterion used for selecting unpredictable words was that the word could not be spelled correctly with any of the 2,000 rules used in the Hanna et al. study.

The words used in the TWS were selected from ten popular basal readers to ensure that the tested words were actually representative of words taught in school. The TWS contained 35 predictable words and 25 unpredictable words and was designed for use with students in Grades 1 through 8.

The TWS was revised for two reasons: to expand the test for use with upper-level students (i.e., Grades 9-12) and to strengthen the weak reliability of the test at the lower age ranges. For the TWS-2, various words were selected from current basal readers and the EDL reading core vocabulary list (Taylor et al., 1979) for use with the lower grade levels, and from the EDL lists for the upper grade levels (for which basal readers are not written). A total of 145 predictable and unpredictable words were originally selected. These were reduced through item analysis to a final version of the TWS-2 that contained 100 words (50 predictable and 50 unpredictable).

The experimental words in the TWS-2 were administered to students in first through twelfth grade using the dictated-word test format. Two measures of item analysis were used: through item discrimination procedures, words that did not have a point biserial correlation with the total test score of greater than .3 were eliminated; through item difficulty procedures, words that could not be spelled correctly by 15% of the sample, or were spelled correctly by more than 85% of the sample, were eliminated.

The final 100-word version of the TWS-2 was standardized on 3,805 students in first through twelfth grade in 15 states. Characteristics of the normative population were roughly comparable to national characteristics with respect to sex, race, ethnicity, geographic area, and urban versus rural residence. The resulting normative tables are reported in the manual in terms of standardized scores (also referred to as quotients) with a mean of 100 and a standard deviation of 15, and in terms of percentiles based on scores obtained from the normative population.

Practical Applications/Uses

The TWS-2 was developed to serve as "a well-standardized, valid, and reliable spelling test with a sound theoretical base" (Larsen & Hammill, 1986, p. 3). The stated uses of the TWS-2 include identifying spelling ability, diagnosing and isolating spelling strengths and difficulties in order to provide appropriate spelling instruction, and measuring progress in spelling.

The TWS-2 was developed for use in a school setting and is easily administered.

The TWS-2 should also prove to be a viable research tool as the earlier version, the TWS, has been used in several research settings. For example, Carpenter (1983) used the TWS in a factor-analytic study of spelling error patterns distinguishing average and reading disabled elementary students. Gerber (1984) used the TWS as an aid to diagnose spelling difficulties experienced by a severely learning disabled fifth-grade student and was able to develop a remediation program that significantly improved the student's spelling performance.

Other innovative uses of the TWS have been made in research settings. Hasselbring and Crossland (1982) developed a computerized version of the TWS. The test words are presented via tape recorder controlled by a microcomputer, thereby eliminating the need for a teacher or other examiner to administer the test. The student enters the words into the computer, which scores and interprets the test results. Varnhagen and Gerber (1984) also developed a computerized version of the TWS and have compared both versions of the test in order to emphasize differences in performance and test-taking processes between paper-and-pencil tests and their computerized counterparts.

The manual describes procedures for either individual or group administration of the TWS-2. Due to the particular procedures for determining basal and ceiling performance levels, however, group administration is a complex task. The instructions for individual administration are quite clear and can be mastered with little practice.

The procedure for presenting each word follows a standard dictated-word test format: 1) The examiner says the word in isolation (e.g., "bed"), then 2) says a sentence in which the word is used ("She slept in a bed."), and 3) repeats the word in isolation ("bed"). A pronunciation guide and context sentence are provided in the manual for each word. The student spells the word on a response form developed for use with the TWS-2.

Entry levels are provided for different grade levels. The examiner begins testing at the appropriate entry level and continues until the last word in the list is spelled or until ceiling performance has been reached. (The ceiling level is defined as that point at which the student misspells five consecutive words.) If the student fails to spell the first five words correctly, the examiner returns to the words below the entry level words and presents words in reverse order to determine the student's basal performance. In testing for basal performance, the examiner continues testing downward until the first word is presented or the student spells five consecutive words correctly. The predictable subtest words are presented first, followed by the unpredictable subtest words. The manual reports that testing can usually be accomplished in 15-25 minutes. Young students may be tested in two or more sessions.

The instructions for test administration may initially appear somewhat complex; however, the manual provides several detailed examples that help clarify the testing procedures. The instructions for group administration are, on the other hand, quite confusing and the examiner is instructed to "attempt to administer enough items to ensure that the students achieve basals and ceilings" (Larsen & Hammill, 1986, p. 6). The manual states that students for whom group administration did not reveal basal or ceiling performance must then be tested individually (p. 6). Criteria are suggested for determining which words to present in a group setting in order

488 Test of Written Spelling

to maximize the possibility of obtaining clear basal and ceiling performance for each student.

Scoring of the TWS-2 is objective and easily accomplished. Each correctly spelled word is credited one point. Incorrectly spelled words receive no credit. Unreadable words must be respelled by the student in order to be scored. All unpresented words below the basal level are scored as correct and all unpresented words above the ceiling level are scored as incorrect. The manual explains the scoring procedure by citing the same examples used to clarify the administration procedure.

Interpretation of TWS-2 scores is the weakest chapter of the TWS-2 manual. Although the test is relatively quick and easy to score and interpret, there are several difficulties with the manual and the Summary/Response Form that may confuse a novice test interpreter.

Three scores are obtained with the TWS-2: raw scores, standard scores, and percentiles. Raw scores represent the number of words spelled correctly on the predictable and unpredictable words subtests and the total number of correctly spelled words. These scores are entered on the Summary/Response Form provided for administering and interpreting the TWS-2. The student's exact age must then be obtained in order to determine standard scores and percentiles, the two norm-referenced scores that are reported with the TWS-2.

Standard scores are simple transformations of the raw scores to a distribution having a mean of 100 and a standard deviation of 15. The standard scores for performance on each subtest and for total performance are found by comparing age and number of correctly spelled words in tables provided in the manual. Percentiles represent the percentage of students in the same age range scoring at an equal or lower level. Percentiles for the two subtests and for total performance are determined by comparing age and standard score values in an additional table provided in the manual.

This progression of converting from raw to standard scores, and from standard scores to percentiles, follows a common procedure, and the tables are clearly and easily laid out in the manual. However, the Summary/Response Form reverses the order of standard scores and percentiles from the order of progression used in the tables. This may confuse the novice examiner and lead to incorrect reporting and interpretation of test results. In addition, the terms "standard scores" and "quotients" are used interchangably, both in the manual and on the Summary/Response Form. The terminology should be consistent, because test interpreters familiar with the original TWS may confuse a standard score reported in the TWS-2 with a spelling quotient, a questionable measure that was reported with the 1976 TWS version.

Both the standard score and percentile rank measures represent an improvement over the grade equivalent, spelling age, and spelling quotient measures reported with the TWS; the earlier measures tended to be misinterpreted and misused. In addition, the standard scores allow for a comparison of the TWS-2 with other spelling tests by simply converting the other tests to an equivalent distribution. Instructions for transforming other scores are provided in the manual and space is provided on the Summary/Response Form for plotting the profiles of TWS-2 and other test scores.

The TWS-2 manual provides brief examples of how to interpret standard score profiles obtained for predictable words, unpredictable words, and total performance. Larsen and Hammill (1986) describe several common patterns of performance, relate each to potential spelling difficulties the student may be experiencing, and provide vague instructional suggestions for remediation. The spelling patterns presented are: below average achievement throughout the test, very low achievement throughout the test, average achievement on the predictable words subtest and low achievement on the unpredictable words subtest, and low achievement on the predictable words subtest and average achievement on the unpredictable words subtest. Determination of what constitutes average, low, and very low achievement is not detailed, and remedial suggestions are inadequate for a test designed to serve as a diagnostic instrument.

Technical Aspects

Test validity of the TWS-2 was established through measures of content, criterion-related, and construct validity. Content validity of the test was examined using a sample of first- through twelfth-grade students drawn from the standardization population. Median item discrimination for predictable and unpredictable words combined ranged from .48 (for the first-grade words) to .70 (for the twelfth-grade words). Median item difficulty for the total test ranged from 0% (for the first-grade words) to 83% (for the twelfth-grade words). In general, item discrimination coefficients were comparable for the predictable and unpredictable words, whereas item difficulty measures were slightly higher for predictable words than they were for unpredictable words.

The item discrimination values are quite good, indicating that the TWS-2 words can be used to discriminate between good and poor spellers. As expected, the discrimination values increase with age—presumably, the differences between good and poor spellers increase as a function of experience and instruction in spelling.

The other measure of content validity, item difficulty, is less adequate. The mean percentages of item difficulty are generally in the unacceptable range for first through third grade and approach the unacceptable range for twelfth grade. With the exception of the third-grade predictable words, the words designed for use with the lower grade levels are much too difficult and on the average are spelled correctly by less than 15% of the students. The original TWS suffered from a similar degree of unacceptable item difficulty in the lower levels. This problem was one of the factors that prompted the revision of the TWS. (In defense of the TWS-2, spelling is very difficult to assess at the lower grade levels, in part because of the wide variability in initial spelling instruction and the inexperience of these young students.) At the upper age range, the TWS-2 suffers the opposite problem: the words, particularly the predictable words, are too simple and are spelled correctly by an average of over 80% of the students. Thus, content validity at the lower and upper age ranges is suspect due to the extreme values of item difficulty.

Measures of concurrent validity were used to evaluate the criterion-related validity of the TWS-2. Correlations between spelling of words included in both the TWS and the revised TWS-2 (27 predictable subtest words and 22 unpredictable

Test of Written Spelling

subtest words were carried over from the TWS to the TWS-2) as well as the remaining words of the TWS-2 are .91 for the predictable words subtest, .93 for the unpredictable words subtest, and .93 for the total test. On the basis of these high correlations, Larsen and Hammill (1986) argue for the equivalence of the two test forms and, therefore, that the concurrent validity of the TWS-2 is comparable to the concurrent validity reported for the original 1976 version.

In order to measure concurrent validity of the TWS, a sample of fourth-grade students was administered the TWS and four other standardized spelling tests. Correlations between TWS performance and performance on three of the other tests were quite high. Taking into account the imperfect reliability of each test, the correlations ranged from .82 to .97 for the spelling subtests of the Durrell Analysis of Reading Difficulty, the Wide Range Achievement Test, and the California Achievement Test.

The TWS had lower correlations with the fourth test, the SRA Achievement Series Spelling test, ranging from .72 to .81. These lower correlations are possibly the result of the format of the SRA test used in determining concurrent validity, which uses a multiple-choice proofreading rather than a dictated-word format. Various studies, however, provide conflicting evidence with regard to the importance of testing formats in the assessment of spelling ability. For example, Northby (1936) and Nisbett (1939) found little difference between different forms of spelling tests, whereas Brody (1944) and Allan and Ager (1965) found notable differences in performance on tests measuring spelling production (e.g., dictated-word tests) versus spelling recognition (e.g., multiple-choice tests). On the other hand, production tasks such as the TWS-2 have been found to have a higher correlation with the criterion of correct spelling in written work than recognition tests such as the SRA (Croft, 1982).

In an independent evaluation of concurrent validity, Carpenter and Carpenter (1978) obtained very low correlations of the TWS with the California Achievement Test (CAT) for fourth-grade students. The correlation between predictable scores and CAT spelling was .31, and the correlation between unpredictable words and the CAT was .28. Although the authors admit that the TWS has poor concurrent validity due to the low correlations with the CAT spelling subtest scores, they point out that this evaluation may not be entirely valid because the two tests were administered 8 months apart and during different school years.

The final measure of test validity reported for the TWS-2 is construct validity. Larsen and Hammill (1986) argue that the TWS-2 scores should be related to age, ability, and to each other. TWS-2 scores do increase with age and are highly significantly correlated with age; the correlations between age and predictable subtest scores, unpredictable subtest scores, and total test scores are .62, .63, and .64, respectively. The TWS-2 is also reported to discriminate between ability groups. A study of learning disabled students averaging at least one standard deviation below the mean for the standardization population on each of the subtests and on the total test is reported in the manual. In addition, Carpenter (1983) used the TWS to obtain good discrimination in terms of error patterns between average and reading disabled elementary school children. Finally, Larsen and Hammill emphasize that the relatively high item discrimination values reported with content validity would be difficult to obtain in tests with poor construct validity.

Test reliability of the TWS-2 was examined through measures of internal consistency, standard errors of measurement, and test-retest reliability. Internal consistency coefficient alphas from the normative data ranged from .86 to .97 for the separate predictable and unpredictable subtests, and from .92 to .98 for total test performance. Associated standard error of measurement estimates, necessarily accounting for a maximum of 8% of the variance in the scores, ranged from one to three words for the separate predictable and unpredictable words scores and from two to four words for the total score. Finally, 1-week test-retest reliability on a sample of students in first through eighth grade ranged from .86 to .98 for the separate subtests and from .91 to .99 for the total score.

The magnitude of these correlations of reliability are all sufficient and demonstrate good reliability for the TWS-2. The reliability of the TWS-2 is greatly improved from that of the TWS, particularly at the first and second grade levels. Thus, the revised TWS-2 may be considered quite accurate in terms of assessing spelling ability, even at the lower grade levels.

Critique

The TWS-2 is a theoretically based spelling test. The predictable words subtest is predicated on the Hanna et al. (1966) finding that the spelling of many English words conforms to regular orthographic rules, while the unpredictable words subtest recognizes that many words are irregular and cannot be spelled by the application of orthographic rules. This theoretical base is a sound one. There is much evidence suggesting that orthographic rules are used, even by young children, to spell words (cf. Baron, Treiman, Wilf, & Kellman, 1980; Marsh, Friedman, Welch, & Desberg, 1980); indeed, Read (1971, 1975) found that prior to exposure to formal spelling instruction, young children invent their own rules to govern spelling. However, it is not clear that differential knowledge of rules is related to differential spelling ability (cf. Boder, 1973; Baron et al., 1980; Barron, 1980). Thus, although the TWS-2 may be an adequate measure for the assessment of spelling achievement, it may not be an appropriate diagnostic instrument.

One reason for this difficulty may lie in the narrowness of the theoretical framework of the TWS-2. Spelling a word correctly involves more than the application of orthographic rules or rote memorization of irregular words. Spelling involves many additional processes and skills, including an awareness of phoneme-grapheme correspondence (cf. Ehri, 1980; Frith, 1980; Gerber & Hall, 1982; Treiman, 1985), phonemic analysis (cf. Baron et al. 1980; Ehri, 1980; Gerber & Hall, 1982), and problem-solving and metacognitive skills (cf. Gerber & Hall, 1982; Hall, 1984; Lydiatt, 1984; Nulman & Gerber, 1984)—to name only a few. It is likely that these factors and many others interact in the spelling of a word. Therefore, in order to diagnose spelling difficulties adequately, many interrelated factors must be taken into consideration. Further research is necessary to isolate and understand how these different factors contribute to spelling ability and disability. The TWS-2 does, however, appear adequate for pinpointing deficiencies in application of certain orthographic rules and in memory for irregularly spelled common words.

In terms of test construction, the TWS-2 also represents a vast improvement over the original TWS. Although the administration of the TWS-2 is somewhat more involved, the information may be more valuable in terms of spelling assessment. Certainly the reporting of performance on the TWS-2 in terms of standard scores and percentiles is more appropriate and useful than the reporting of TWS performance in terms of grade equivalents, spelling ages, and spelling quotients. Certain aspects of test validity, in particular the content validity of the test at lower and upper grade levels, are somewhat suspect; however, the reliability of the test is commendable.

In summary, the TWS-2 is a remarkably well-constructed spelling test and represents a vast improvement over the original. Although the test has demonstrable value for assessing spelling ability, it has somewhat limited diagnostic utility. Further research is necessary to develop a spelling test that can adequately pinpoint a student's spelling disability.

References

Allan, D., & Ager, J. (1965). A factor analytic study of the ability to spell. *Educational and Psychological Measurement, 25,* 153-161.
American Psychological Association. (1974). *Standards for educational and psychological tests.* Washington, DC: Author.
Baron, J., Treiman, R., Wilf, J. F., & Kellman, P. (1980). Spelling and reading by rules. In U. Frith (Ed.), *Cognitive processes in spelling* (pp. 159-194). New York: Academic Press.
Barron, R. W. (1980). Visual and phonological strategies in reading and spelling. In U. Frith (Ed.), *Cognitive processes in spelling* (pp. 195-213). New York: Academic Press.
Boder, E. (1973). Developmental dyslexia: A diagnostic approach based on three atypical reading-spelling patterns. *Developmental Medicine and Child Neurology, 15,* 663-687.
Brody, D. S. (1944). A comparative study of different forms of spelling tests. *The Journal of Educational Psychology, 35,* 129-144.
Carpenter, D. (1983). Spelling error profiles of able and disabled readers. *Journal of Learning Disabilities, 16,* 102-104.
Carpenter, D., & Carpenter, S. (1978). The concurrent validity of the Larsen-Hammill Test of Written Spelling in relation to the California Achievement Tests. *Educational and Psychological Measurement, 38,* 1201-1205.
Croft, A. C. (1982). Do spelling tests measure the ability to spell? *Educational and Psychological Measurement, 42,* 715-723.
Cronbach, L. J. (1970). *Essentials of psychological testing* (3rd ed.). New York: Harper & Row.
Ehri, L. C. (1980). The development of orthographic images. In U. Frith (Ed.), *Cognitive processes in spelling* (pp. 311-338). New York: Academic Press.
Frith, U. (1980). Unexpected spelling problems. In U. Frith (Ed.), *Cognitive processes in spelling* (pp. 495-515). New York: Academic Press.
Gerber, M. M. (1984). Techniques to teach generalizable spelling skills. *Academic Therapy, 20*(1), 49-58.
Gerber, M. M., & Hall, R. J. (1982). Development of spelling in learning disabled and normally achieving children. *Monograph for the Society of Learning Disabilities and Remedial Education.*
Hall, R. J. (1984). Orthographic problem-solving. *Academic Therapy, 20*(1), 67-75.
Hanna, P. R., Hanna, J. S., Hodges, R. G., & Rudorf, E. H. (1966). *Phoneme-grapheme correspondences to spelling improvement.* Washington, DC: Office of Education, United States Department of Health, Education, and Welfare.
Hasselbring, T. S., & Crossland, C. L. (1982). Application of microcomputer technology to spelling assessment of learning disabled students. *Learning Disability Quarterly, 5,* 80-82.

Larsen, S. C., & Hammill, D. D. (1976). *Test of Written Spelling*. Austin, TX: PRO-ED.
Larsen, S. C., & Hammill, D. D. (1986). *TWS-2: Test of Written Spelling*. Austin, TX: PRO-ED.
Lydiatt, S. (1984). Error detection and correction in spelling. *Academic Therapy, 20*(1), 33-40.
Marsh, G., Friedman, M., Welch, V., & Desberg, P. (1980). The development of strategies in spelling. In U. Frith (Ed.), *Cognitive processes in spelling* (pp. 339-353). New York: Academic Press.
Nisbett, S. D. (1939). Non-dictated spelling tests. *British Journal of Educational Psychology, 9*, 29-44.
Northby, A. S. (1936). A comparison of five types of spelling tests for diagnostic purposes. *Journal of Educational Research, 29*, 339-346.
Nulman, J. A. H., & Gerber, M. M. (1984). Improving spelling performance by imitating a child's errors. *Journal of Learning Disorders, 17*, 328-333.
Read, C. (1971). Preschool children's knowledge of English phonology. *Harvard Educational Review, 41*, 1-34.
Read, C. (1975). *Children's categorization of speech sounds in English*. Urbana, IL: National Council of Teachers of English.
Shores, J. H., & Yee, A. H. (1973). Spelling achievement tests: What is available and needed? *The Journal of Special Education, 7*, 301-309.
Stanley, J. C. (1971). Reliability. In R. L. Thorndike (Ed.), *Educational measurement* (2nd ed., pp. 356-442). Washington, DC: American Council on Education.
Taylor, S., Frankenpohl, H., White, C., Nieroroda, B., Browning, C., & Birsner, E. (1979). *EDL core vocabularies in reading, mathematics, science, and social studies*. New York: EDL, a division at Arista.
Treiman, R. (1985). Phonemic awareness and spelling: Children's judgments do not always agree with adults'. *Journal of Experimental Child Psychology, 39*, 182-201.
Varnhagen, S., & Gerber, M. M. (1984). Use of microcomputers for spelling assessment: Reasons to be cautious. *Learning Disability Quarterly, 7*, 266-270.

Robert H. Bauernfeind, Ph.D.
Professor of Education, Northern Illinois University, DeKalb, Illinois.

TESTS OF ADULT BASIC EDUCATION
CTB/McGraw-Hill. Monterey, California: CTB/McGraw-Hill.

Introduction

The Tests of Adult Basic Education (TABE) comprise an objective (multiple-choice and true/false) measure of skills in reading, mathematics, and language/editing. These skills are needed by adults for two reasons: 1) to pass the GED high school graduation equivalency test and 2) to "function to our society" (*TABE Technical Report*, 1978, p. 1).

The 1976 edition of the TABE was developed through direct adaptation of test materials appearing in the 1970 edition of the California Achievement Tests (CAT). There were occasional changes in the test items to give them an "adult flavor," but the changes were so minimal that the publisher elected to apply the CAT national norms to the TABE raw scores.

The test materials are entirely visual and entirely oriented to appropriate use of the English language. According to the publisher, a large-print edition is available from the American Printing House for the Blind.

The TABE program consists of six test booklets, two each (Form 3 and Form 4) at three levels of difficulty: Level E (Easy), Level M (Medium), and Level D (Difficult).* There are enough major differences between Level E and the other two levels to warrant separate reviews for all three. Administration includes a Practice Exercise and a Locator Test, the latter for determining which level is appropriate to administer. The publisher states that TABE results can be used to place students in the *Lessons for Self-Instruction in Basic Skills* (LSI; multilevel programmed work texts in reading, mathematics, and English).

Level E (Easy). Color-coded green, Level E is remarkably different from the other two levels. First, it covers reading and mathematics only—no language/editing. Secondly, all answers are recorded in the test booklet—no separate answer sheet is provided. Thirdly, all of the questions seem to be drawn from real life; there are no aberrations designed to please a textbook author somewhere.

Level E Reading consists of 85 items: Word recognition (20), Vocabulary-in-context (20), Alphabetization (5), a Table of Contents (3), an Index (2), and Comprehension of Short Stories (35). Testing time, with breaks, runs about 1 hour, 15 minutes. A person attaining a 50% correct raw score will be given a national Grade Equivalent of 2.5. National Grade Equivalents run from 1.0 to 5.5—somewhat short of the 8.2 that is approximately equivalent to a GED passing score of 45.

Level E Mathematics consists of 117 items: Addition (20), Subtraction (16), Multiplication (20), Division (16), Concepts (30), and Story Problems (15). Testing time, with breaks, requires about 1 hour, 15 minutes. A person attaining a 50% correct

---

*This critique cites items and data from the Form 3 tests at each level.

raw score will be given a national Grade Equivalent of 2.3. National Grade Equivalents run from 1.0 to 5.5, again somewhat short of the 8.2 that approximates a GED passing score of 45.

Level M (Medium). This level, color-coded blue, does include a test of language/editing, and also includes a separate answer sheet. National Grade Equivalents run from 3.0 to 10.0, so a person scoring very high on these tests would seem to have good chances of exceeding the GED passing score of 45.

Level M Reading consists of 82 items: Vocabulary-in-context (40), a Table of Contents (3), an Index (3), Comprehension of Short Stories (28), and a bewildering set of problems involving 12 men in a two-way classification scheme (8). Testing time, with breaks, will run about 1 hour, 15 minutes. A person attaining a 50% correct raw score will be given a national Grade Equivalent of 4.7.

Level M Mathematics consists of 108 items: Addition (12), Subtraction (12), Multiplication (12), Division (12), Fractions (20), Concepts (25), and Story Problems (15). Testing time runs approximately 1 hour, 35 minutes. A person attaining a 50% correct raw score will be given a national Grade Equivalent of 4.6.

Level M Language consists of a 32-item Spelling test and a Mechanics test comprising 109 items: Capitalization (38), Punctuation (42), and Standard English (29). The Standard English test is presented in a true/false format; all of the other tests are multiple choice. Testing time for the Spelling Test is about 15 minutes, and a 50% correct raw score will be given a national Grade Equivalent of 4.3. Testing time for the Mechanics tests, with breaks, runs about 55 minutes, and a 50% correct raw score will be given a national Grade Equivalent of 5.2.

Level D (Difficult). Color-coded brown, Level D is closely akin to Level M with a comprehensive Language test and a separate answer sheet. National Grade Equivalents run from 5.0 to 12.9, so a person scoring high on this test would have excellent chances of exceeding a GED passing score of 45.

Level D Reading consists of 85 items: Vocabulary-in-context (40), a Table of Contents (3), an Index (3), Comprehension of Short Stories (30), and a bewildering set of problems involving which-capital-letter-belongs-between-which-two-capital-letters (9). Testing time, with breaks, requires about 1 hour, 10 minutes. A person attaining a 50% correct raw score will be given a national Grade Equivalent of 6.9.

Level D Mathematics contains 98 items: Addition (12), Subtraction (12), Multiplication (12), Division (12), Concepts (35), and Story Problems (15). Testing time, with breaks, will run about 1 hour, 15 minutes. A person attaining a 50% correct raw score will be given a national Grade Equivalent of 7.4.

Level D Language consists of a 32-item Spelling test and a Mechanics test containing 100 items: Capitalization (40), Punctuation (32), and Standard English (28). The Standard English test is presented in a true/false format; the others are multiple choice. Testing time for the Spelling test is about 10 minutes, and a 50% correct raw score converts to a national Grade Equivalent of 7.0. Testing time for the Mechanics tests, with breaks, runs about 50 minutes, and a 50% correct raw score converts to a national Grade Equivalent of 6.3.

At all three levels the examiner's responsibilities are quite simple: he or she is to make certain that each student understands the practice problems and the use of separate answer sheets. The authors recommend that at least one proctor be present for every 15 students. The examiner and proctors are to help students who become confused with the test materials, but they are *not* to help students with the test questions.

Practical Applications/Uses

The TABE authors intend that the test will be used with poorly educated adults who wish to improve themselves in the kinds of basic skills just described. They write that

> TABE can be used to provide pre-instructional information about a student's level of achievement in the basic skills of reading, mathematics, and language; to identify areas of weakness in these skills; to measure growth in the skills after instruction; to involve the student in appraisal of his or her learning difficulties; and to assist the teacher in preparing an instructional program to meet the student's individual needs. (*TABE Examiner's Manuals*, 1976, p. 1)

The national Grade Equivalent scores were, of course, derived from studies of elementary and high school students. However, the authors clearly have had a good deal of experience with ABE (Adult Basic Education) students.

TABE is a group test. Given enough competent proctors, the testing sessions should run fairly smoothly. Level E will require about 2½ hours administration time; Level M, about 4 hours; and Level D, about 3½ hours. Considering that poorly educated people will be taking the tests, this reviewer would recommend that Level E be given over two days, and that Levels M and D be given over the course of three days.

The authors provide an answer key (one correct answer per item) for each test booklet. These keys are readily adaptable for hand scoring. Hand scoring also may be accomplished by using Scoreze® answer sheets, which also give subskill diagnostic information.

Technical Aspects

Reliability estimates for the TABE scores appear to be quite satisfactory. Although Kuder-Richardson estimates will vary greatly depending on the make-up of the local Adult Basic Education (ABE) group, they typically should run in the .80's or possibly the low .90's.

The authors show data for between-levels equating studies for elementary school children. For Levels E and M in Grade 4, the alternate-levels reliabilities averaged around .80; for Levels M and D in Grade 6, the alternate-levels reliabilities averaged around .85.

The TABE authors also show same-form and alternate-form test-retest reliabilities for ABE students, averaging around .75 to .80 (*TABE Technical Report*, 1978, p. 16). If ranking studies and/or growth studies are judged to be important, these reliability estimates are certainly satisfactory.

But "validity" is a different matter. The TABE battery is promoted as a device to predict scores on the high school equivalency GED battery—and to predict a student's ability to "function in our society." It appears to this reviewer that the TABE does neither very well.

When we use tests to predict similar tests, we should be able to obtain validity coefficients of .80 or higher. In the one GED study reported by the authors, the TABE Mean Scale Score correlated only .56 with the GED Mean Standard Score (N = 359). While a TABE Grade Equivalent score of 8.2 suggests a 50:50 chance of attaining a GED Standard Score of 45, one must attain a TABE Grade Equivalent of 11.6 or higher to have a near 100% probability of attaining a GED Standard Score of 45 (*TABE Technical Report*, 1978, p. 18). The two testing programs thus seem rather remote from each other.

As for "content validity," many of the TABE items seem terribly remote from "real life"; this point will be developed in the following sections of this review.

Critique

The TABE materials are attractively printed; the equating work has been done with professional skill; the reliabilities appear to be adequate; and the authors have provided an Expanded Standard Score Scale as an alternative to Grade Equivalent interpretations.

So, what are the negatives? To answer this question, we need to remember that TABE will be given to poorly educated Americans who want to "make it" in America. They wish to be upwardly mobile; they care; and they probably believe that the items presented in the TABE represent the kinds of skills they must master in order to "make it" in America.

On a 10-point scale, this reviewer would rate Level E a "10." All of the items seem to be important. Even those sections of the Reading test that have the story on one page and some of the questions on the reverse remind us that, in real life, we often must extend our comprehensions from one page to another—in books, magazines, and newspapers. So, although Level E gets a "10," it also gets us to a Grade Equivalent of only 5.5—short of effective functioning.

This reviewer gives Level M a "5." For one thing, a raw score of zero will get you a Grade Equivalent of 3.0. Obviously, this was an editorial goof, but some test administrators are going to accept that 3.0 as a legitimate measurement.

In addition, the "content validity" appears shaky. The Reading test seems all right up to the two-way classifications of members of relay teams (the last eight items). My colleagues in reading assure me that they cannot relate these materials to success in reading a story or an editorial.

The capitalization, punctuation, and expression problems seem to be real; the errors actually slow us down in our reading. Many of the spelling problems, however, seem to be nitpicking.

The Mathematics test also drifts away from real life. Examinees are led to believe that $2/5 \times 5/8$ is a vital skill, and worse, that you won't succeed in life unless you can figure out that $4/5 \div 3/10$ is somehow $2^2/_3$.

And, if you master all of these Level M skills, you will be given a Grade Equivalent score of 10.0—still short of a near-guarantee that you can now pass the high school equivalency GED test.

Level D also gets a "5." This time a raw score of zero will get you a Grade Equivalent of 5.0—but of course this *is* a more difficult test.

The Reading test seems to be all right up to the section involving capital letters in

498   Tests of Adult Basic Education

a sequential arrangement. The task is confusing; one item (#42) involves a double negative, and, after you master the tasks, you will *not* have advanced as a reader of books, newspapers, or magazines.

The comments about the Level M Mathematics test apply to Level D as well. Those who can figure that $6 \div 4/5$ yields $7\frac{1}{2}$ *somethings* are no better prepared for adult life than those who cannot.

All of the items in Level E appear to be oriented to reality. This reviewer would endorse Level E for use in ABE programs. The problem is that Level E gets you to a Grade Equivalent of only 5.5, short of satisfactory performance on the GED and probably short of adequate performance in everyday life.

This reviewer cannot, however, endorse Levels M and D in their present form. I think we should not suggest to poorly educated young and middle-aged Americans that attainment of some of the above cited skills will open doors of opportunity. They won't, and users of the Level M and Level D tests should carefully show their clients which skills *are* important and which skills are not.

References

This list contains text citations as well as suggested additional reading.

Buros, O. K. (Ed.). (1972) *The seventh mental measurements yearbook.* Highland Park, NJ: The Gryphon Press.
Tests of Adult Basic Education, examiner's manuals. (1976). Monterey, CA: CTB/McGraw-Hill.
Tests of Adult Basic Education, technical report. (1978). Monterey, CA: CTB/McGraw-Hill.

Note: In 1986 CTB/McGraw-Hill announced publication of a new edition of TABE. This edition provides two forms—Forms 5 and 6—at each of four levels: E (Easy); M (Medium); D (Difficult); and A (Advanced). Each level, including Level E, covers reading, language, and mathematics. The publisher has asked, however, that Forms 5 and 6 not be reviewed until a technical report has been published.

Jeanette N. Cleveland, Ph.D.
Assistant Professor of Psychology, Colorado State University, Fort Collins, Colorado.

TESTS OF MENTAL FUNCTION IN THE ELDERLY
Ives Laboratory, Inc. Philadelphia, Pennsylvania: Wyeth Laboratories.

Introduction

The Tests of Mental Function in the Elderly propose to assess the mental functions of the elderly through a series of short subtests on 10 areas of mental function: general orientation, sentence learning, counting backwards, mental control, digit retention, 5-minute memory, digit copying, associated learning, simple arithmetic, and general knowledge. The test is designed to take approximately 10 minutes to complete.

Originally published by Ives Laboratory and now by Wyeth Laboratories, the Tests of Mental Function in the Elderly are intended to provide the physician with a way of increasing the "reliability of his own evaluation of the mental impairment" (Ives Laboratory, Inc., 1978) of the elderly, rather than provide a detailed psychometric examination. Although the information accompanying the test does not indicate the year of test development, the sample scoring sheet is dated 1978, and the test booklet was issued in 1979. The test booklet indicates that the intended population is the elderly; however, there is no definition or specification of the term, *elderly*.

The 10 subtests are printed on 10 5"x8½" pages. The subtests are enclosed in a folder that has four brief paragraphs explaining a) the objective of the set of tests (targeted/worded for the physician), b) the areas that the test covers, c) a caution regarding the use of these tests, and d) a brief, nontechnical interpretation of the test outcome.

Each of the subtests has its own set of instructions. The examiner, presumably a physician or a physician's assistant, is an integral part of the test. In nine of the subtests, the examiner provides oral instructions to the individual. In one subtest only, the test-taker responds in writing. The written instructions for each subtest are intended to inform the examiner of the procedure for test administration. For 90% of the test, individuals respond aloud.

Subtest 1, General Orientation, is intended to assess the individual's general orientation for time and place. The examiner reads instructions to the test-taker and then asks three very simple questions, such as "What time of day is it?" The three questions are scored as either correct or incorrect. On the back of the subtest, there is a brief comment section describing what the subtest is intended to assess. There is also a brief section intended to assist the physician in interpreting the responses. Acceptable scores for General Orientation are stratified by three age groups (60-69,

70-79, and 80 +). If the individual is unable to achieve the stated number of correct answers expected in an age category, then he or she has failed the subtest and receives an "impaired" assessment.

Subtest 2 is called Sentence Learning. The examiner instructs the individual to listen to a sentence and then to repeat it. The test-taker is allowed five opportunities to repeat the sentence correctly. The subtest is scored in terms of the number of repetitions required to repeat the sentence accurately. Again, a comment section on the back of the test describes what capacity it is intended to assess. Again, the interpretation of the score is stratified according to the three age categories. Generally, more repetitions are acceptable as the individual's age increases chronologically. If the individual requires more repetitions than indicated for the age category, he or she fails the test. Similar to the first subtest, the final score here is either "impaired" or "not impaired."

Subtest 3 attempts to assess concentration by having the individual count backward. The time it takes to complete the test and the number of errors made are recorded. A time limit is set, and if the individual does not complete the count within the specified time, he or she receives an "impaired" assessment. Further, the test-taker receives a failing score when he or she commits more errors than expected in his or her age category.

Subtest 4, Mental Control, also is designed to assess concentration. The individual's concentration is assessed in two parts. First, the individual is asked to count in a specified interval (e.g., 2,4,6,8, and so on) until he or she reaches a certain number. Next, the subtest requires the individual to subtract a specific number from another number (e.g., subtract 6 from 80) and to continue subtracting that value from the result until he or she reaches zero. The test-taker is assessed on the time taken to complete each item and the number of errors made on each item. An individual fails an item if he or she exceeds the time limit for the item or if the number of errors is greater than expected by individuals in the specific age category.

Subtest 5, Digit Retention, is intended to assess both concentration and short-term memory. It consists of two parts. First, the individual is instructed to repeat a series of numbers. The size of the set of numbers increases by one with each successful repetition. This procedure is followed for a maximum of six sets of numbers. The procedure is discontinued when the individual fails to repeat the digits correctly. The second part of the subtest requires the individual to repeat a set of numbers backward. If repeated correctly, the individual is presented with a larger set of numbers to repeat backwards. The procedure is followed using up to five sets of numbers. At the point where the individual incorrectly repeats the digits, the second part of the test is discontinued. Thus, this subtest is similar to digit span tests that are used in many intelligence tests. The minimum passing scores are stratified by the three age categories on the back of the subtest. The score is computed by adding the length of the series of numbers correctly repeated forward and backward. Test-takers do not pass the subtest when their score is less than expected for the age category or when the difference between the number of digits correctly repeated forward or backward is greater than three.

Subtest 6, 5-Minute Memory, requires the individual to repeat from memory essential details of a brief story presented by the examiner/physician. The subtest

Tests of Mental Function in the Elderly 501

proposes to assess retention and memory. Approximately 5 minutes after the story is presented, the examiner asks the individual what the story was about. The individual receives one point for each sentence "more or less" correctly remembered in content. Scoring is therefore more subjective in this subtest. Similar to all previous subtests, scoring is stratified on the back of the subtest according to the three age categories. However, unlike the scores presented in each category, the scores in 5-Minute Memory indicate the maximum points that reflect impairment rather than the number of points needed to pass or receive a "not impaired" score.

Subtest 7, the Digit Copying test, is intended to be a psychomotor speed test. It is the only subtest that requires a written response from the individual. The respondent is given a set of numbers and is asked to copy each number as quickly as possible under the one printed on the page. After a specified interval, the individual is stopped and the number of digits copied is counted. If the individual copied less than the minimum number, he or she receives an "impaired" score. The minimum number needed to pass is the same for all age groups of the elderly.

Subtest 8, Associated Learning, is designed to assess an individual's ability to learn new word associations. The examiner reads three pairs of words. The individual is then given a cue word (one word in a pair) and asked what word was associated with it. If the test-taker answers correctly, the examiner proceeds to the next cue word. If the response is incorrect, the correct response is provided and the next cue word is given. This procedure is followed until the cue words for the three pairs are presented three times each. The cue words are presented in an order specified on the record sheet. The word pairs differ in terms of logical or natural association. Therefore, for two pairs, a correct response is scored two points, while a correct response to the third pair is scored one point. Minimum passing scores are stratified by the three age categories presented on the back of the subtest.

Subtest 9, Simple Arithmetic, is a two-question scale assessing simple arithmetic skills. All elderly individuals are expected to answer both questions correctly. According to the response interpretation on the back of the subtest, one incorrect answer *suggests* impairment while two incorrect responses are "clearly indicative of impairment of mental functions." It is not clear how to score this test if the test-taker misses only one question.

Subtest 10, is a four-question General Knowledge test. One point is given for each correct response. Impairment is indicated when less than three correct answers are given. Minimum acceptable scores are not stratified by age category.

On the back of each subtest, there is a caution that an impairment of mental functions cannot be assessed on the basis of one subtest outcome alone. Therefore, record sheets are provided for the examiner. The individual's responses/scores on each of the 10 subtests are recorded on the record sheet. For each of the subtests, the examiner assesses whether the individual's responses reflected "impaired" or "not impaired" behavior. If the individual received five or more "not impaired" assessments, he or she is assessed as "not impaired"; on the other hand, six or more "impaired" scores reflect an assessment of impairment.

Practical Applications/Uses

With the increasing number of elderly persons in our society, the general objective of this type of test is a worthwhile and necessary one. However, it is unclear what the test developer means by impairment of mental ability. The test may be intended to assess a deficit in an individual's mental capacity or it may be intended to assess mental ability as it contributes to life-functioning impairment. There is certainly a need for tests assessing the latter. However, the developers of the Tests of Mental Function in the Elderly do not adequately articulate what it is they are trying to measure.

The test booklet states that the appropriate subjects for the test are the elderly; however, as mentioned previously, no chronological age definition of *elderly* is provided, although the age stratification of responses suggests 60 years and older. Further, it is unclear if another appropriate population includes late-middle-aged persons (i.e., 55 to 65 years) who have had strokes, chronic physical illnesses, and so on, conditions that may impair mental and life functioning. That is, it is not clear whether the test is assessing impairment resulting from an illness (chronic or acute) or impairment resulting from an aging process. Because the developer does not state whether the test is intended to assess impairment of mental ability potential or capacity or life functioning impairment, there is some confusion about the appropriate subject population.

The Tests of Mental Function in the Elderly are administered individually. As the test description does not indicate a medical specialty, this reviewer assumes that users may include general practitioners and internists, as well as neurologists. It is doubtful that the former have had appropriate training for such a test. Further, unless physicians have had training in or a practice involving the treatment of geriatric patients, there is an ethical concern that the test requires skills and knowledge that go beyond the competencies of many general practice physicians.

Another administration concern involves the standardization of an examiner. Because the test is purported to take only 10 minutes, and due to its straightforward format, it may be administered by physician's assistants, nurses, nurses aides, and so on. Although other types of examiners may not influence the accuracy of the test outcomes, this flexibility inadvertently defeats the objective of the test, which is to assist *physicians* in making more reliable mental function assessments.

A third concern is that such tests administered in physician's office (or in a clinic) may be extremely anxiety-producing for most elderly individuals. It is likely that such a test environment will yield more "impaired" evaluations than if the test were administered in a more familiar environment with more practical, familiar items (especially if the goal is to assess the life-functioning impairment of the individual).

Finally, it is stated that the test takes approximately 10 minutes to administer. It is unlikely that this time frame is realistic, given that one of the subtests involves a memory task with a 5-minute interval.

Scoring instructions for 9 of the 10 subtests are clearly stated. For subtest 5, it is not clear whether an individual fails the subtest if one of the two items is answered incorrectly. As the final outcome of the test is a dichotomous evaluation of "impaired" or "not impaired," one ambiguously derived subtest score may move an individual from the "not impaired" to the "impaired" category. Therefore, the examiner must exercise caution when interpreting scores on each subtest. For the majority of subtests, the minimum acceptable scores are provided by age category. However, for others, the scores reflect impairment and are unacceptable scores.

This may increase the possibility of examiner errors in recording responses. Further, there is no rationale given for the minimum acceptable scores in general or for the scores in the three age categories.

This reviewer has two concerns about the final test outcome. First, all subtests are weighted equally in importance to mental functioning. For example, an individual may receive impaired scores on Counting Backwards, Mental Control, Digit Retention, Digit Copying, Associated Learning, and Simple Arithmetic. The individual's final assessment would be that he or she was impaired. However, an individual who fails only the orientation and general knowledge subtests would pass the test. Given the nature of these last two subtests, failing them would be a clearer indication of impairment than failing the six listed above.

A second concern about the interpretation of the final test outcome is that it is not clear what the assessment actually reflects. Does it mean that the individual has diminished mental capacity (cannot perform optimally on a test), or does it mean that the individual can no longer live without supervision? The concern raised here is one that relates to criterion-related and construct validity of the test. These concerns are discussed in the next section.

Technical Aspects

The 10 subtests and record sheets are enclosed in a folder that provides a brief description of the test. There is no description of the procedures used in the subtest development. No technical report or test manual is available to offer data on the reliability, validity, and usefulness of this instrument. It is not substantiated, then, that the test does assist the physician in increasing the reliability of his or her own assessments. In fact, two characteristics of the test suggest to this reviewer that the test may have unacceptable reliability. First, the subtests are very short, typically one to four items. For exmaple, Sentence Learning involves one sentence, Simple Arithmetic has two items, and Mental Control also consists only of two items. With so few items to assess a construct, subjects' responses may vary greatly from a scale that consists of more items that tap the area. A score on one or two items may be more a function of the idiosyncratic characteristics of the item(s) than the construct that it was intended to measure. The second reliability concern involves the method of scoring the test. If the test were reliable, the dichotomous scoring method would still restrict the variability in test scores and lose valuable subject information, therefore limiting the reliability index.

Although seven subtest scores are stratified by age, there is no statistical justification or norms provided to support the accuracy of such stratification. That is, no criterion-related information is provided on the test. Therefore, it is difficult to determine whether the test accurately distinguishes between impaired and nonimpaired individuals either in general or by age category. There is no statement on approximately what proportion of the elderly population is expected to fail the test. Further, this reviewer is particularly concerned with what the test developers intend to measure with this instrument. Because they do not articulate the test domain, it is difficult to determine what construct the test is intended to assess and how successfully it measures it. Before the test is promoted, the construct or test domain requires fuller explication followed by construct validation data.

As this test is intended for use with the elderly population, the content of the test items may require special consideration. In the gerontology literature, there is concern that the elderly may view the content of test items as trivial or irrelevant to their life functioning and, as a consequence, perform less well on such tests (Demming & Pressey, 1967). Therefore, test items should be constructed carefully to reflect both relevant activities and the skills needed to perform such activities in the older population.

Critique

Until demonstration of test reliability and validity are provided, the Tests of Mental Function in the Elderly require tentative use and extreme caution in interpretation. Test examiners or users should not rely solely on this test to make judgments about an individual's mental or life functioning. The complete absence of test reliability and validity data is a substantial oversight and should be corrected immediately. Therefore, this reviewer would not recommend the use of the test until such data are collected and reliability and validity demonstrated.

References

Anastasi, A. (1982). *Psychological testing* (5th ed.). New York: Macmillan Publishing Company.
Baltes, P. B., & Schaie, K. W. (1974, October). Myth of the twilight years. *Psychology Today,* pp. 35-40.
Birren, J. E. (1974). Translation of gerontology—from lab to life: Physiology and speed of response. *American Psychologist, 29,* 808-815.
Charness, N. (Ed.) (1985). *Aging and human performance.* New York: John Wiley & Sons.
Demming, J. A., & Pressey, S. L. (1967). Tests "indigenous" of the adult and older years. *Journal of Consulting Psychology, 2,* 144-148.
Ives Laboratory, Inc. (1978). *Tests of Mental Function in the Elderly.* New York: Author.
Schaie, K. W. (1974). Translations in gerontology—from lab to life: Intelligence functioning. *American Psychologist, 29,* 802-807.

Ellis D. Evans, Ed.D.
Professor of Educational Psychology, College of Education, University of Washington, Seattle, Washington.

THINKING CREATIVELY IN ACTION AND MOVEMENT

E. Paul Torrance. Bensenville, Illinois: Scholastic Testing Service, Inc.

Introduction

Thinking Creatively in Action and Movement (TCAM) is a brief, untimed observational measure of young children's improvisational psychomotor behavior intended to assess creative thinking. Designed for use with children ages 3 to 8, this individually administered measure consists of four major activities, covering moving through space, pretending, inventing alternative uses for a common object, and improvising with a common object. These activities are claimed to reveal aspects of creative thinking without necessitating expressive language. Results are said to enable the early identification of individual strengths and facilitate the nurturance of long-term creative development. By implication, TCAM is proposed for possible use in screening for giftedness at the preschool level on grounds that the kinesthetic modality is viewed as the most natural and most frequently practiced for children of this age.

Development of the TCAM began in 1975 under the direction of E. Paul Torrance, a long-standing student of creativity whose research on ideas about the nature and development of creativity span several decades (e.g., Torrance, 1962, 1979). TCAM represents the latest of Torrance's attempts to originate measures of creativity for use in research and education (Torrance, 1974; Torrance, Khatena, & Cunnington, 1973). In contrast to these earlier measures, TCAM is designed exclusively and especially for work with preschool children. Torrance (1981) believes that adults have too often overlooked or underestimated the creative capabilities of these younger children. He further believes that inappropriate measurement practices are partly to blame for misleading adult perceptions of young children's creativity. For Torrance, the central measurement problem is that most creativity assessments are ill suited to the preschool child's development level, in that too much emphasis is placed upon formal testing to which young children are unaccustomed (including a requirement for elaborate language skills, or even literacy). Torrance also criticizes past measures of early creative ability for their low reliability, administrative encumbrances, and low relationships to creativity measures during middle childhood and beyond.

TCAM is an attempt to minimize these problems in three specific ways. First, the principal modality for measurement is kinesthetic expression, which is viewed as inherently natural and spontaneous for children in all cultures. TCAM consistently places emphasis on a child's ability to act out solutions to problems. Verbal responses are not required, although they are acceptable in lieu of or in conjunction with kinesthetic expressions at the child's preference. Second, TCAM provides for "warm-up" procedures in a game-like context to establish motivation for testing. These procedures are followed by testing activities that are sufficiently meaningful and novel to challenge children's improvisational abilities without inducing reticence or fatigue. Finally, the nemesis of impractical measurement is largely defeated by utilizing tasks that are easy to administer and score. Examiner training requirements are low, as are equipment and time costs.

TCAM was published in final, singular form in 1981. There has been no revision. Test norms are based on the performances of 1,896 children from ages 3 to 8 residing in 11 different states and Guam. Four sets of activities or exercises are guided by scripted instructions in English. A separate data recording and scoring protocol is used for each child.

Activities with each individual child are first initiated and demonstrated by the examiner in a private room. Materials needed are a table and chair to enable response recording, the administration booklet and scoring sheet, a wastebasket, and a supply of paper cups. The first activity, "How Many Ways," requires the child to think up and enact a variety of ways for moving from one side of the room to another (e.g., hopping, rolling, walking backwards). Boundaries for starting and stopping are marked by strips of colored tape or any distinctive objects preferred by the examiner. Activity 1 is introduced by an explanation and demonstration of the task. Thereafter, the examiner's task is to encourage, observe, and record all of the child's responses. Technically speaking, no time limit is imposed on Activity 1, but normally it will consume about 5 minutes. Each way of movement shown by the child is listed on the protocol sheet, and scoring for Activity 1 takes place after testing.

Activity 2, called "Can You Move Like?", involves six different "pretending" scenarios. Action begins with movement to portray four different animals and objects (e.g., a rabbit being chased, a tree moving in the wind). This combination of movement tasks is followed by two situations in which the child pretends a role relationship with inanimate objects (e.g., driving a car). For each situation, the examiner reads a question to prompt the child's pretending. The child's movement is then rated immediately on a 5-point scale (1 = no movement; 5 = excellent). Activity 2 is the only TCAM activity scored during the enactment process.

Activity 3, "What Other Ways?", requires an ample supply of paper cups and a wastebasket. The task, again initiated and modeled by the examiner, involves devising and enacting as many different ways as possible for putting the cup in the wastebasket. During the enactment process, the examiner must record each way on the scoring protocol. This improvisational theme continues for Activity 4, whereby the child again uses one or more paper cups to illustrate different uses for this presumably commonplace object. Each cup use is recorded by the examiner as the child's activity unfolds.

For reasons unspecified in the TCAM manual, the examiner is instructed to record the time lapsed for each of the four activities. However, time data do not figure into scoring. According to the manual, each test administration normally requires about 15 minutes. The individual test protocol form provides separate pages for each activity record, plus a face sheet for child-identifying data and score summaries.

Practical Applications/Uses

The stated purpose of TCAM is to identify special creative abilities of young children as a first step toward the nurturance of these abilities. The TCAM author believes that a fuller understanding of conditions to facilitate creative development can be reached through its use. Specifically, creative ability is conceptualized in terms of three test response criteria: originality or uniqueness of responses, fluency or sheer number of relevant responses, and imagination or pretending in relation to specific role definitions. Under Torrance's direction, the development of this measure has involved a relatively simple process: administer TCAM to children ages 3 to 8 for the purpose of describing age trends and variability in creative expression. Any given child for whom a question about this type of creative performance is relevant can be quickly tested, then compared to a norm group. More broadly, TCAM provides a convenient tool for researchers concerned with questions about possible antecedents and correlates of creativity, as well as the impact of environmental conditions on the growth of creativity.

Strictly speaking, TCAM is designed for and normed primarily on young, normal, white and black English-speaking children; thus, for meaningful score interpretation, its use is confined to this segment of the childhood population. According to Torrance (1981), however, TCAM can be used with exceptional children. In support of this claim are TCAM studies, largely unpublished, that include disadvantaged black children (Haley, 1979), deaf children (Lubin, 1979), emotionally disturbed children (Paget, 1979), and intellectually handicapped children (Cropley, 1986). Such studies exemplify an apparently popular experimental use of TCAM in creativity research.

To reiterate, TCAM must be administered individually to a child in a private setting sufficiently large to accommodate gross-motor movement. The test manual itself specifies no special training requirements for an examiner, but certain basic skills seem imperative, including technique to establish rapport, ensure clarity in communication, model tasks appropriately, maintain motivation for testing, and sustain satisfactory pacing. Guidelines for test administration are relatively direct and simple. Aside from response scoring and interpretation, the most obvious challenges to an examiner's effectiveness are the preliminary warm-up activities and means for deciding when and how best to terminate testing. The manual specifies that testing time will normally take from 10 to 30 minutes. Some children will need more time, perhaps up to 45 minutes, depending on their rate and style of response.

The testing time issue is critical for users of TCAM. Excepting Activity 2, which specifies a limit of six items, TCAM has no ceiling. For Activities 1, 3, and 4, the scoring protocol provides space for recording up to 30 responses each. Technically speaking, however, completion of the protocol form does not necessarily signify that testing should be terminated. The extent to which a child may reach or surpass this 30-response accommodation as well as how quickly a child may respond may depend to an unknown degree upon examiner technique and judgment. This issue is critical because each response for Activities 1, 3, and 4 is scored for both fluency (total number of acceptable responses) and originality (statistical uniqueness). These are not mutually exclusive scoring criteria because as fluency increases, the probability of originality may also increase. By extending or moving to terminate testing time, an examiner may partly control response output, thereby influencing a child's score in nonstandard fashion. This potential weakness in testing procedure must be heeded carefully by TCAM users. In short, no standard criterion for terminating the test is provided. Instead, the examiner is advised to exercise discretion and "to avoid dragging out the testing time to 45 or 60 minutes" (Torrance, 1981, p. 12). Otherwise, TCAM seems not to pose major problems for administration.

Potential problems also emanate from the wide latitude and considerable ambiguity in guidelines for TCAM response scoring and interpretation. Careful examiner preparation is advised in relation to two characteristics in the scoring guide. First, directions for the concurrent scoring of Activity 2 should be mastered prior to any test administration. Second, lists of illustrative responses and their point values (0-3, depending upon uniqueness) are provided in Activities 1, 3, and 4, and should be studied in advance. Scoring standards for these activities are derived from test performances of 500 children, ages 3 to 7, a group that may have been independent of the main normative sample.

For any test administration, hand recording and scoring of a child's responses is necessary. Activities 1, 3, and 4 require that responses first be recorded as they occur. This is done by counting (or preferably listing and then counting) the child's responses. Once the test is completed, response scoring is determined by applying the fluency and originality criteria. *Fluency* refers to the sheer number and combinations of ways in which a child performs the particular activity. *Originality* is determined by the statistical frequency or infrequency of various responses that occurred in the aforementioned group of 500 children. Any response not shown by this sample must be judged by the examiner as "adequate, relevant, and appropriate" (Torrance, p. 15) to qualify for scoring. If so judged, a response not on the model list automatically qualifies as unique and is awarded maximum credit (3 points). An examiner also has freedom to award bonus credit (4 points) for any rare, artistically choreographed routine that a child may perform.

In contrast to Activities 1, 3, and 4, Activity 2 is scored in process and involves only one category: imagination. A score range of 1-5 points applies to each of six "pretend" movement situations. This requires an individual rating by the examiner for each situation. Ratings are summed to provide the imagination score, which is then recorded on the face sheet of the test protocol for each child.

Similarly, fluency and originality scores are recorded separately for Activities 1, 3, and 4. All three fluency and originality scores are summed to provide total scores. Together with the imagination score, these raw scores provide a basis for conversion to standard scores with a mean of 100 and a standard deviation of 20. Separate conversion tables are provided for 3-, 4-, 5-, and 6-year-olds. Conversion scores are not available for 7- and 8-year-olds; only raw score means and standard deviations are reported. Because these latter two groups involved unspecified numbers of "developmentally delayed" and "intellectually gifted" children, a

TCAM user is cautioned about the meaning of these normative data. Regardless, use of both raw scores and conversion scores can define an individual creativity profile for fluency, originality, and imagination. Although stemming from scores based upon a rather extensive list of model responses and their point values, this profile will necessarily reflect some degree of clinical judgment by the examiner.

Technical Aspects

Clinical judgments notwithstanding, the TCAM manual states that "interscorer reliability is easily maintained through careful use of the scoring guide at a level in excess of .90" (Torrance, 1981, p. 6). Several interscorer reliability studies are cited to support this claim, including a sample of 30 second-grade children (Bolen, 1976) and 68 records from children whose performances were scored by Torrence and/or one or more research assistants. These reliability coefficients clustered in the high .90s for both fluency and originality but, excepting Bolen, are not differentiated by age or grade level.

Evidence for other important forms of reliability is limited. Torrance (1981) reports one "preliminary study" of test-retest reliability involving a group of 20 children, ages 3 to 5. Based upon a 2-week interval for testing, an overall stability coefficient of .84 was obtained. Predictably, subtest reliability was substantially lower: Activity 1 = .71, Activity 2 = .79, Activity 3 = .67, and Activity 4 = .58. The meaningfulness of a test-retest reliability coefficient is questionable because TCAM is designed to measure inventiveness. If a child has performed to full capacity during the first administration, a second administration is likely to pull many of the same responses, thus measuring memory or reproductive skill, not creativity in the original sense. Moreover, motivation for a repetition of the same test may suffer, as indicated by Cropley's (1986) work with handicapped children. A much stronger procedure for establishing meaningful reliability would involve using an alternative form of TCAM.

Lacking an alternative form, there is no coefficient equivalence to strengthen the case for TCAM reliability. The TCAM manual also lacks information about *interrater* reliability, a statistic most germane to Activity 2 because of the in-process ratings involved. An independent report of interrater reliability is favorable to TCAM (Cropley, 1986). This reliability was computed on preschool handicapped children whose TCAM responses were observed and recorded simultaneously by two judges trained for 10 weeks to achieve high reliability. Resultant interrater reliability coefficients were .93 for imagination, .98 for originality, and .99 for fluency. Lacking an equivalent form and data relevant to different age levels, part of the TCAM reliability story remains untold. But satisfactory interscorer reliability seems attainable with informed guidance from the scoring guide. Preliminary evidence suggests that high interrater reliability can be achieved for TCAM as well.

Validity evidence for TCAM is somewhat more problematic. Torrance (1981) candidly admits that a direct and meaningful validity study was not conducted prior to TCAM publication. Construct validation is perhaps most at issue. For one thing, TCAM is not clearly anchored in a coherent and comprehensive theory of creativity. For another, TCAM scores are not clearly linked to any independent criterion for creative ability. Torrance speaks to the criterion problem in two differ-

510 *Thinking Creatively in Action and Movement*

ent ways. First, he rejects the use of teachers' ratings of creativity as an external on grounds of low reliability. Second, he observes that other existing measures of young children's creativity (themselves showing dubious validity) involve different response modalities, thus rendering useless their comparative value for TCAM. A user is left to infer validity from Torrance's test rationale, personal experience, and "scattered bits of evidence" included in the test manual.

This scattered evidence comes mostly from unpublished studies, including doctoral dissertations by Torrance's students, sundry ancedotes, and personal communications. Collectively, such evidence is indirectly relevant to concurrent validity. Young children's TCAM scores show a positive and significant correlation with independent measures of children's humor, achievement of socioemotional objectives in a developmental curriculum, and self-concept (Torrance, 1981). A preliminary claim for discriminant validity is based upon a weak correlation of TCAM scores with measures of intelligence, cooperation, preschool attendance, and socioeconomic status (Torrance, 1981). Race and sex differences in TCAM performance are nil. More revealing is the finding that increases in TCAM scores are associated with learning experiences consistent with theoretical predictions about conditions for creative growth, including problem-solving sociodrama and creative movement exercises (Torrance, 1981).

As measured by rate of published empirical studies since 1981, Torrance's call for rigorous and creative TCAM validity studies has been met with slow progress. Recent studies come mostly from the ranks of doctoral dissertations and offer little validity support for TCAM. For example, Sears (1982) found that teachers and their professional aides generally agreed on their ratings of children's creative talents, but these ratings differed measurably from the children's TCAM scores. Rogers (1984) found no meaningful relationship between preschool children's TCAM scores, cognitive style as measured by the Preschool Embedded Figures Test, or their use of structured or unstructured play materials. Rush (1984) found no reliable differences in TCAM scores between 3- and 5-year-old children who participated in a Montessori or an open educational model preschool curriculum. Similarly, Christie (1983) reports that preschool children's fluency scores—but not their originality or imagination scores—increased as a function of both academic and play-skills tutorial program experience. It seems fair to conclude that these studies have not reinforced the validity of TCAM. Neither do they provide any independent interscorer reliability data.

Critique

This state of affairs about the technical adequacy of measures is not unusual for the assessment of young children's creativity. In fact, TCAM exemplifies most of the fundamental problems associated with creativity measurement in general. Most creativity researchers seem to agree on the importance of fluency, originality, and inventiveness as hallmarks of creativity. But persistent debate continues about creativity as ability, style in approaching and managing problems, interests and attitudes, personality attributes, and so on (Hocevar, 1981). One might expect the spectre of construct validity to haunt TCAM at least for the near term. Evidence about the relationship of young children's kinesthetic expressiveness and their later creative achievement is needed, evidence that requires time-consuming longitudinal research. In addition, rigorous methods of substantiating TCAM reliability via interrater checks and a coefficient of equivalence using an alternate test form are recommended. Meanwhile, scant data suggest that kinesthetic expressiveness can be influenced by training. Thus, to the extent that divergent kinesthetic skills are valued by parents and educators, TCAM has utility for evaluating attempts to enhance these skills.

Even so, users need to attend carefully to the problems in administration, scoring, and interpretation mentioned earlier. The importance of a warm-up procedure prior to TCAM administration, cues for which are not always made explicit in the manual, is a case in point. Some children, especially those who tend toward shyness or fearfulness, will require special attention. Use of TCAM with a socially inhibited child could be very misleading because the role of personal-social variables in TCAM performance is largely unknown. A further limitation involves the TCAM norm group. TCAM confidence is perhaps most satisfactory for 4- and 5-year-olds whose norm sample size numbers 920 and 537, respectively. Considerably smaller norm samples represent the remaining age levels: age 3 = 91, age 6 = 155, age 7 = 117, and age 8 = 76. TCAM performance comparisons for any given child with the age 3 or age 8 samples seem tentative indeed.

Finally, a TCAM user is cautioned to approach Activity 2 ("Can You Move Like?") with a critical eye. Although this activity purports to measure imagination, the "pretending" tasks seem actually to require convergent, not divergent, production. Even though elaborations (e.g., sound effects and facial expressions) figure into the rating of this activity, a child's score is a function of how accurately the movement of an animal or object can be modeled. At issue is whether imaginative but focused role-playing constitutes a genuine creative ability.

In its present form, TCAM is best considered in a formative stage of development. Although unique in its approach to creativity measurement, TCAM shows uncertain validity and usefulness. Reliability evidence is satisfactory, although somewhat incomplete, as are normative data for the total age range for which TCAM was designed. Training is advisable for users of TCAM, especially for scoring and interpretation. On balance, however, the measure seems not to pose major problems in terms of administrative usability. TCAM cannot yet be recommended for use in educational decisions about individual children, but may have some value in exploratory research about creativity and psychomotor development.

References

Bolen, L. M. (1976). *Effects of race, sex, and kindergarten attendance on the creative thinking of second graders.* Unpublished manuscript, Eastern Carolina University, Greenville, NC.

Christie, J. F. (1983). The effects of play tutoring on young children's cognitive performance. *Journal of Educational Research, 76*(6), 326-330.

Cropley, C. (1986). *Divergent thinking in young handicapped children.* Unpublished doctoral dissertation, University of Washington, Seattle.

Haley, G. L. (1984). Creative response styles: The effects of socioeconomic status and problem-solving training. *Journal of Creative Behavior, 18*(1), 25-40.

Hocevar, D. (1981). Measurement of creativity: Review and critique. *Journal of Personality Assessment, 45*(5), 450-464.

Lubin, E. N. (1979). *Motor creativity of preschool deaf children*. Unpublished doctoral dissertation, Texas Women's University, Denton, TX.

Paget, K. (1979). Creativity and its correlates in emotionally disturbed preschool children. *Psychological Reports, 44*, 595-598.

Rogers, M. S. (1984). *Creativity and play materials: The origins and development of creativity in preschool children*. Unpublished doctoral dissertation, Texas A&M University, College Station, TX.

Rush, N. M. (1984). *A comparison of the effects of two child-centered models of educational intervention on three selected creative abilities of preschool children*. Unpublished doctoral dissertation, Catholic University of America, Washington, DC.

Sears, M. H. (1982). *Intellectual and creative talents in young children as perceived by teachers, teacher aides, and parents*. Unpublished doctoral dissertation, Temple University, Philadelphia.

Torrance, E. P. (1962). *Guiding creative talent*. Englewood Cliffs, NJ: Prentice-Hall.

Torrance, E. P. (1974). *The Torrance Tests of Creative Thinking*. Levington, MA: Personnel Press.

Torrance, E. P. (1979). Unique needs of the creative child and adult. In A. H. Passow (Ed.), *The gifted and the talented: Their education and development* (pp. 352-371). Chicago: University of Chicago Press.

Torrance, E. P. (1981). *Thinking Creatively in Action and Movement*. Bensenville, IL: Scholastic Testing Service.

Torrance, E. P., Khatena, J., & Cunnington, B. F. (1973). *Thinking Creatively with Sounds and Words: Research Edition*. Bensenville, IL: Scholastic Testing Service.

Roger D. Carlson, Ph.D.
Research and Evaluation Assistant, Eugene Public Schools, Eugene, Oregon.

THREE MINUTE REASONING TEST
A. D. Baddeley. Austin, Texas: Psychonomic Society, Inc.

Introduction

The Three Minute Reasoning Test (TMRT) was developed by A. D. Baddeley in order to fill the need for a measure of "higher mental processes" that was relatively easy to administer in a short period of time. The need for such a test is particularly apparent in research areas that investigate the effects of environmental stresses or drugs on human performance.

The TMRT consists of 64 sentences and letter pairs. The subject is to determine as quickly as possible whether the sentence expresses the true relationship between the letter pair. Examples of such items are

1. A follows B—BA True or False?
2. B precedes A—AB True or False?
3. A is followed by B—AB True or False?
4. B is not followed by A—BA True or False?
5. B is preceded by A—BA True or False?
6. A does not precede B—BA True or False?

The test is comprised of all 64 possible combinations of the following six binary conditions: 1) positive or negative, 2) active or passive, 3) true or false, 4) precedes or follows, 5) A or B mentioned first, and 6) letter pair AB or BA. The score on the test is the total number of items correct.

A description of the test and its construction, the instructions to be given to subjects, and a research summary outlining validity and reliability has been published by the author (Baddeley, 1968), so the user need only consult the short journal article in order to construct and administer the test.

Professor Baddeley, who is now at Experimental Psychology Laboratory, University of Sussex, developed the test while at the prestigious Applied Psychology Research Unit in Cambridge, England.

Practical Applications/Uses

The TMRT was developed out of the need to offer a short, easily administered reasoning test of acceptable validity, reliability, and sensitivity to supplement already existing measures of motor skill and simple addition, which are used in studies of human performance of environment stress or drugs.

Technical Aspects

Many cognitive theorists have used differences in speed in types of performance as a way to derive inferences about human cognition (e.g., Clark & Chase, 1972; Carlson & Kost, 1977; Carlson & Schacke, 1980; Carlson, Setley, & Lerman, 1982). The assumption that basic mechanisms of mental processing (or thought) take time underlies the development of the TMRT. For example, Clark and Chase (1972) found that, other things being equal, negative sentences take longer to respond to than positive sentences, passives longer than actives, and false longer than true.

Baddeley cites not only the face validity of the TMRT, but also a correlation of +.59 with performance on the British Army Verbal Intelligence Test ($p < .001$) in a study of 29 enlisted men. Baddeley cites a study in which 18 subjects were tested twice on successive days, which yielded a mean correlation of +.80 between performance on the two days. Practice effects are reasonably small after the initial trial. Five successive administrations yielded a mean difference of only nine points.

The author reports that the sensitivity of the test is good, as demonstrated with the test administered under less than optimal conditions (divers repeated taking the test while intoxicated in nitrogen narcosis studies, automobile drivers took an auditory version, and another sample was administered in the presence of white noise).

Critique

Sternberg (1986) has recently pressed for a notion of intelligence based theoretically on what we know about human cognitive processing (as compared to those that are empirically derived or inferred from performance on an eclectic set of "power" items). The moderately high correlations between the TMRT and other generally accepted tests of intelligence gives the TMRT a degree of construct validity. It might be argued that Baddeley was indeed ahead of his time in 1968 when he developed this test, which truly bridges the experimental psychology laboratory and the applied domain. Such a test is a timely and welcome addition to those developed using solely atheoretical, empirically derived approaches.

It is commendable that the TMRT attempts to ground itself in the work of cognitive science by measuring a quality of performance that cognitive psychologists have come to regard as an aspect of intelligence. The test is timely in the sense that it is a coherent attempt at measuring the processes of cognition, based on a homogeneous set of items derived from rather stable and known findings about how human cognition works, rather than from intuition and "common sense." Because the TMRT uses a homogeneous set of items, one knows *precisely* what one is measuring.

Several questions about the TMRT need to be asked. Is performance on the TMRT simply another "power" test because the person is required to perform against a time standard? Is rapidity of execution a large component of what is ordinarily referred to as "intelligence"? Perhaps the correlations of the TMRT to traditional tests of intelligence are as instructive about the "power" aspects of traditional tests as they are about the TMRT. The sentences processed in the TMRT are tasks that most adult people *can do,* quickly or not. Whether they can do them quickly is another question.

The TMRT is based upon a coherent theoretical structure that may in fact be either right or wrong. It makes no pretense of measuring anything beyond the ability to make grammatical transformations quickly. Whether or not this is related to any kind of "central processing" ability, i.e., "intelligence," is another question, which, aside from establishing "construct validity," is by and large, beyond the scope of the test developer. The fact that the TMRT does show construct validity, is evidence that it does measure what is ordinarily regarded by psychometrists as "intelligence" *as measured by established intelligence tests*.

Baddeley found that differences between individuals correlate with traditional measures of intelligence. He assumed that the basic processes (or "mechanisms") of intelligence account for those individual differences in performance. Therefore overall speed of processing a number of sentences of this sort is thought to reflect individual differences in the speed at which the mechanisms process information. Is the speed of solving problems the same thing we mean when we speak of intelligence? Intelligence tests were first designed to measure success in schools. Does speed assure such success? Is essentially work efficiency what it takes to be successful in school? Or are processes which process *quality* involved?

Is it legitimate to attempt to understand "culture-free" aspects of mental functioning by means of a medium of the culture—namely language? "Mental functioning" in itself may be a cultural construction taken from the analogue of a mechanistic processing model. Gardner (1986) also has been encouraging psychologists and educators to look to the specific *types* of performance which we call "intelligent" alluding to the point that there might be many qualitatively different kinds of "intelligence." Gardner seems to assume intelligences to be things or substances—a process of reification which treats "intelligent" as an adjective modifying people rather than as an adverb modifying performance.

Ulrich Neisser has provided an important corrective to the study of intelligence by suggesting that we go beyond the laboratory for more "ecologically valid" approaches in our understanding of what comprises "intelligence" by examining acts of intelligence in their natural contexts. Ecologically sensitive cognitive psychologists such as Neisser (1976) have moved beyond demonstrating performances of restrictive tasks in restrictive environments by arranging new tasks in new environments that result in novel performances—true instances of novelty. While an important step away from the practices of traditional cognitive researchers of which Baddeley is a representative, Neisser nonetheless believes that the discovery of intelligence overrides criticisms by philosophers of language (such as Wittgenstein, 1953; Foucault, 1970; and Ryle, 1949) by assuming that there is, like Gardner, some *thing* to discover to which the word "intelligence" applies. What constitutes a "discovery," Neisser fails to recognize, is that what is recognized as "discovery" is determined by the discursive acts of people in social interaction rather than in some "pure" form unveiled by acts by scientific inquiry.

Success in school is probably more dependent upon *knowledge* and familiarity and adeptness at various qualitatively different subject matters than mere speed of execution. Only such special school tasks as those that take place on the athletic field or gymnasium, the old fashioned spelling bee, mathematical power tests, the quiz bowl, or, of course, standardized tests of aptitude or achievement are speed determined. But most of traditional North American scholastic curriculum has little to do with speed of execution. Thus such intrusions into the curriculum in a sense bastardize the nature of schooling. Using time-dependent measures to assess qualities that were not taught by the clock is not a fair appraisal of human ability. Where training is against the clock and development can occur (as it often does in athletic skill building), such appraisal is valid. The rapid processing of sentences is not one of those areas covered in traditional curriculum. A person who we say is intelligent is a person who *can do,* not "can do quickly."

Until we begin to assess intelligence by specifying meaning in contexts and performance we will continue only to develop "power" tests of intelligence with problems similar to projective tests of personality. In projective tests meaning-free stimuli elicit meaningful personality attributes—in "power" tests, meaningful stimuli elicit meaning-free "data" void of content. Intelligent living generates meaningful content as understood in a social context—not "data."

References

Baddeley, A. D. (1968). A Three Minute Reasoning Test Based on Grammatical Transformation. *Psychonomic Science, 10,* 341-342.

Carlson, R. D., & Kost, R. S. (1977, April). *The effect of differential syntactic structure of Baddeley Reasoning Test items on reaction time.* Paper presented at the meeting of the Eastern Psychological Association, Boston.

Carlson, R. D., Setley, M. A., & Lerman, J. A. (1982). Ocular position in sentence-picture comparisons. *Perceptual and Motor Skills, 54,* 291-297.

Carlson, R. D., & Schacke, J. H. (1980). Visual vs. auditory encoding of linguistic material in comparison of sentences and pictures. *Perceptual and Motor Skills, 51,* 1051-1058.

Clark, H. H., & Chase, W. G. (1972). On the process of comparing sentences against pictures. *Cognitive Psychology, 3,* 472-517.

Foucault, M. (1970). *The order of things.* New York: Pantheon.

Gardner, H. (1986). *The education of multiple intelligences.* Paper presented at the meeting of the American Educational Research Association, San Francisco.

Neisser, U. (1976). *Cognition and reality: Principles and implications of cognitive psychology.* San Francisco: Freeman.

Ryle, G. (1949). *The concept of mind.* London: University Library.

Sternberg, R. (1986). *The education of multiple intelligences.* Paper presented at the meeting of the American Educational Research Association, San Francisco.

Wittgenstein, L. (1953). *Philosophical investigations.* Oxford: Blackwell.

Jim C. Fortune, Ed.D.
Professor of Educational Research and Evaluation, Virginia Polytechnic Institute and State University, Blacksburg, Virginia.

Theodore R. Cromack, Ed.D.
Director, Commodity Donation Demonstration Study, Virginia Polytechnic Institute and State University, Washington, D.C.

THE 3-R's TEST

Nancy S. Cole, E. Roger Trent, Dena C. Wadell, Robert L. Thorndike, and Elizabeth P. Hagen. Chicago, Illinois: Riverside Publishing Company, Inc.

Introduction

The 3-R's Test is a battery of group-administered achievement tests distributed under a 1982 copyright to Riverside Publishing Company of Chicago, Illinois. Introductory materials appearing in each of the teacher's manuals for the tests report that the achievement test series grew out of school district requests for brief, reliable measurement in the basic subject areas of reading, mathematics, and language arts. In response to these district needs, achievement tests of reading and mathematics for Grades K-12 and of language arts for Grades 3-12 were developed. All of the items contained in these tests were based on objectives that are commonly sought at each grade level.

The 3-R's Test is available in three editions: the Class-Period Edition, the Achievement Edition, and the Achievement/Abilities Edition. The achievement tests in the Achievement Edition and in the Achievement/Abilities Edition are the same tests and are available in two equivalent forms.

The Class-Period Edition was authored by Nancy S. Cole, Professor of Education at the University of Pittsburgh; Dr. E. Roger Trent, test development coordinator in the Ohio Department of Education; and Dena C. Wadell, editorial consultant for Wadell Associates. The tests for each grade level were developed under three guiding principles: "1. The test would measure the most fundamental objectives in the school curriculum. 2. The test would address the three central content areas of reading, language arts, and mathematics. 3. The test would be as short as possible and still produce reliable scores for use by teachers and school administrators" (Cole, 1982b, p. 7). The tests for Grades K-12 require approximately 50 minutes for administration and include 16 items to measure reading objectives and 15 items to measure mathematics objectives. The tests for Grades 3-12 require approximately 40 minutes for administration and each includes 17 items to measure reading objectives, 14 items to measure language objectives, and 12 items to measure mathematics objectives.

The Achievement Edition has the same authors as the Class-Period Edition. The tests in the Achievement Edition were designed to cover a broader range of content and to be administered as survey tests within two sessions. The contents and administration times are shown by grade levels in Table 1.

Table 1

Achievement Edition: Objectives Covered, Number of Items, and Administration Time by Subject Area and Grade Level

Grade Level	Reading Objectives	Items	Time	Language Objectives	Items	Time	Mathematics Objectives	Items	Time
K	19	30	50				27	29	40
1	21	30	50				27	29	40
2	10	35	55				31	30	50
3	17	50	45	32	40	35	32	35	35
4	22	50	45	34	40	35	33	35	35
5	22	50	45	33	40	35	34	35	35
6	22	50	45	34	40	35	33	35	35
7	20	50	45	33	40	35	33	35	35
8	25	50	45	34	40	35	33	35	35
9/10	23	50	45	35	40	35	34	35	35
11/12	24	50	45	34	40	35	33	35	35

The Achievement/Abilities Edition was authored by Cole, Trent, Wadell, and Robert L. Thorndike and Elizabeth P. Hagen, both professors of psychology and education at Columbia University. The achievement tests are identical to the tests in the Achievement Edition (Reading, Language, Mathematics); however, this edition is accompanied by a test to measure verbal ability and a test to measure quantitative ability. The Verbal Abilities test is composed of a 25-item word identification subtest and a 25-item analogy subtest, which have a combined administration time of 30 minutes. The Quantitative Abilities test comprises a 25-item comparison of quantity subtest and a 25-item series completion subtest, which have a combined administration time of 30 minutes.

Practical Applications/Uses

The emphasis of the testing strategy for The 3-R's Test is an efficient coverage of the fundamental objectives that are common to students in Grades K-12. All three editions generate reliable composite raw scores in reading, mathematics, and language arts (except for the three primary grades). These raw scores can be converted into percentile ranks, which permit individual test performance comparisons to national norm groups who took the same form and level of the test. The raw scores can also be converted into stanine and normal curve equivalent scores. Both of these scores permit student-to-student comparisons and individual subject-to-subject comparisons. The normal curve equivalent scores are more precise than the stanines and are more appropriate for use with parametric statistics.

The raw scores can also be converted to two across-grade scores, the grade development score and the expanded standard score. Both of these permit estimation of student growth. The grade development scores are analogous to grade equivalent scores and are more useful in reporting to parents and teachers. "At grade level" for the grade development score is defined by the test authors "as performing on content designed for a particular grade in the same way that the average student performed nationally on the same content" (Cole, 1982b, p. 12). The expanded standard score is defined as representative of the "scores that a student would achieve if all levels of The 3-R's Test could have been administered to the same child" (Cole, 1982b, p. 12). The authors present a table of suggested score uses in the technical manuals.

It appears to these reviewers that the Class-Period Edition tests are useful only as general achievement thermometers. These tests cover a limited number of the primary objectives at a given grade level, cover these objectives with but a single item, and generate only a meaningful composite score. Their use for diagnostic purposes or for the evaluation and analysis of instruction are certainly suspect. Although little testing time is required, they appear to produce limited utility.

The achievement tests for the remaining two editions present a wider range of potential utility. These tests do cover a much wider range of objectives at each grade level and contain enough items within each subtest to produce reliable subtest scores. The objectives covered by each test appear representative of a meaningful amount of the curriculum for the respective grade level and content area. Again, time investment is held at a minimum. Although the objectives are, for the most part, measured by single items, the objectives appear to portray a more intact curricular continuum, making limited diagnostic uses possible.

A near-ideal use for these tests appears to be as a criterion instrument in the evaluation of the regular school program. The Achievement/Abilities Edition, with the additional convenience of independent testing of abilities, the efforts that have been made to minimize undesirable test bias, and the availability of the expanded standard scoring method, appears especially appropriate for use in the evaluation of regular school programs.

Riverside Publishing Company test scoring services have been designed to facilitate the use of the instruments by teachers and administrators. In the reporting of scores, the scoring service makes available five score conversions, scores by subtest, and expected outcome estimates. In addition to the reporting of scores, the publishers also provide an item analysis summary, a classroom report by objectives measured for each student, and a summarized school administrator report. The technical manuals are written in simple, easily understood language with explanations that are geared to the novice test user.

Technical Aspects

The development procedures for the 3-R's involved professional item writers who wrote more than 6,000 items across the three content areas for the 11 test levels. The items were then administered to a national sample of 27,112 students representatively proportional in racial/ethnic background and sex to the national population (Cole, 1982a). The tryout sample appears to average better than 200 students taking each item. Item analysis was performed on the tryout sample results, and item selection was made by content requirements constrained by the statistical performance in the item analysis.

The tests were then standardized and normed on a spring sample of 85,000 students and a fall sample of 32,500 students (Cole, Trent, & Wadell, 1982). Again, these samples were chosen proportional to national marginals on racial/ethnic background and sex. Panel reviews and analyses were utilized to minimize undesirable biases. The tests include provisions for out-of-level testing, provided that the span of testing does not exceed two levels above or below the referent grade level.

Both split-half and K-R 20 reliability coefficients were calculated for each set of meaningful raw scores. In Table 2 the K-R 20 estimates are reported by grade level and content area. The split-level estimates appear slightly higher or equal to the K-R 20 estimates, which are adequate.

Table 2

K-R 20 Reliability Estimates by Grade Level and Content Area

Test Level	Grade Level	Class-Period Composite	Achievement Reading	Language	Mathematics	Ability Verbal	Quantitative
6	K	.79	.77		.81		
7	1	.84	.85		.82		
8	2	.86	.91		.80		
9	3	.90	.73	.91	.86	.89	.84
10	4	.90	.92	.91	.93	.90	.86
11	5	.88	.92	.88	.81	.91	.86
12	6	.88	.93	.89	.82	.91	.86
13	7	.90	.93	.88	.81	.91	.88
14	8	.87	.90	.87	.84	.90	.89
15	9	.88	.90	.86	.86	.91	.90
16	10	.88	.90	.87	.87	.91	.90
17	11	.87	.89	.85	.86	.92	.90
18	12	.87	.90	.84	.86	.92	.90

The primary validity consideration in an achievement test is that of content validity, which is evidenced through the test construction procedures. The 3-R's Test was developed in accordance to the rigor of up-to-date and appropriate test development procedures. The validity of the use of the test depends on whether the content tested is what is desired to be tested or if the body of content in the test is representative of the content that is in use. Each of the teacher's manuals (Cole, Trent, & Wadell, 1982; Cole, Trent, Wadell, Thorndike, & Hagen, 1982) explicitly describes the objectives tested in each level of content. Appropriate use of the test can be made through a review of the objectives tested as they relate to the objectives intended in the application.

In the technical manuals, the brief report of comparisons of The 3-R's Test scores with those of other achievement tests show reasonable and expected levels of correspondence. Several specific validity studies which add to the mounting evidence of the validity foundation of these tests are briefly described in *The 3-R's Test Technical Manual for the Achievement/Achievement and Abilities Edition* (Cole, 1982a).

Critique

The 3-R's Test is an excellent example of what can be accomplished by properly applied testing expertise. The Achievement Edition tests provide reliable estimates of general achievement in the three basic content areas with minimum expenditure of testing time. The tests are configured to provide useful research and general evaluative instruments for application to the regular school program.

The achievement tests were limited intentionally in content scope and in item replications across content objectives. The users of these tests must keep in mind these limitations in their applications of them; precise diagnostic uses are just not possible. Instead, the tests serve well as general criteria and indicators.

Overall, the tests in the two achievement editions are excellent for the limited purposes for which they were designed. The publishers have presented the tests with clear and easily understandable administration and interpretation materials, an ample and creative set of options for scoring, and an effective technical support system. However, these reviewers question the general utility of the Class-Period Edition tests, as the tests in the other two editions provide much greater utility for a minor addition of time.

References

Cole, N. S. (1982a). *The 3-R's Test technical manual for the Achievement/Achievement and Abilities Edition*. Chicago: Riverside Publishing Co.

Cole, N. S. (1982b). *The 3-R's Test technical manual for the Class-Period Edition*. Chicago: Riverside Publishing Co.

Cole, N. S., Trent, E. R., & Wadell, D. (1982). *The 3-R's Test Class-Period Edition teacher's manual*. Chicago: Riverside Publishing Co.

Cole, N. S., Trent, E. R., Wadell, D., Thorndike, R. L., & Hagen, E. P. (1982). *The 3-R's Test Achievement/Achievement and Abilities Edition teacher's manual for levels 13-18*. Chicago: Riverside Publishing Co.

Kenneth T. Wilburn, Ph.D. *Chairperson, Division of Educational Services and Research, College of Education and Human Services, University of North Florida, Jacksonville, Florida.*

TIME PERCEPTION INVENTORY
Albert A. Canfield. La Crescenta, California: Humanics Media.

Introduction

The Time Perception Inventory (TPI) is an objective instrument designed to assess the ways in which individuals view ther use of time and the general frame of reference they use in thinking about their world. There are two sets of materials provided: 1) the actual inventory, which is used for administration and scoring, and 2) an accompanying manual, which describes the purpose, rationale, and interpretation of the inventory.

The TPI was developed by Albert A. Canfield (1980) for use by consultants analyzing time management problems. No review of related research or theoretical background is included in the test manual. However, the test does follow the general theories associated with time awareness and its relationship to personal time management skills as reported by Kostick (1961) and Mackenzie (1971). Related materials, such as the Time Use Analysis, the Time Problems Inventory, and the Supervisory Practices Inventory, are available from Humanics Media.

The Time Perception Inventory is divided into two parts. The first part contains 10 items relative to the ways in which individuals feel about themselves in certain situations. For example, the examinees might be asked how often they feel there are not enough hours in the day to get their jobs done. Respondents rate themselves on a four-point scale (*rarely, occasionally, frequently,* or *a great deal*).

The second part of the inventory consists of eight items. Respondents are asked to assess what time reference they utilize in their day-to-day thinking—the past, the present, or the future.

The test can be group-administered or self-administered. No special training is needed to give or take the test, and no separate answer sheets are needed. The examinee checks the appropriate box in the test booklet, which results in the answer being recorded onto the scoring page. The scoring page includes directions for scoring and interpretation of the results. The average client can finish the test in five minutes.

The manual explains why specific items were selected and the meaning of each part of the inventory. A discussion is provided as to the possible interpretation of a high or low score for each section. Normative data is provided so an individual might relate his or her score to the scores of others that have previously completed the inventory. In addition, the manual provides a general discussion of the concept of time frames and their relationship to emotional predispositions. The manual also addresses the application of time awareness concepts to business people.

Practical Applications/Uses

The Time Perception Inventory could serve as a structured tool for consultants working with clients on time management and personal-efficiency-related problems. It could also serve as an introductory activity to the general topic of time management in a variety of business and educational settings. In addition, the test could be used as a discussion tool to help a client verify his or her self-perception as a baseline for future developmental activities.

Technical Aspects

No validity or reliability studies of the TPI are reported in the inventory or the manual. No information is presented on the norming group. The items on the test appear to have face validity, but there is no empirical evidence presented on the construct or criterion-referenced validity of this scale. There are no coefficients of any type or standard errors of measurement included for the two scales.

Critique

The Time Perception Inventory can only be used on an informal basis. The scale does not adhere to the standards set for educational and psychological tests; therefore, it is of limited value as a counseling or research tool. Users need to recognize that the test only has face validity—no evidence of the construct or criterion-referenced validity is presented. No background is presented of the literature that supports the constructs measured in this instrument. No description of the norming group is included. If the Time Perception Inventory is continued to be marketed, the author needs to provide supporting evidence and meet accepted professional standards.

References

American Psychological Association (1985). *Standards for educational and psychological testing.* Washington, DC: Author
Canfield, A. A. (1980). *Time Perception Inventory.* Ann Arbor, MI: Humanics Media.
Kostick, M. M. (1961). *Profile for Kostick's Perception and Preference Inventory.* Brookline, MA: Author.
MacKenzie, R. A. (1972). *The time trap.* New York: AMACOM.

John C. Daresh, Ph.D.
Assistant Professor of Educational Administration, Department of Educational Policy and Leadership, The Ohio State University, Columbus, Ohio.

TIME PROBLEMS INVENTORY
Alfred A. Canfield. La Crescenta, California: Humanics Media.

Introduction

According to management consultant Peter Drucker, one of the most critical tasks facing the individual who wishes to function as an effective executive is the ability to control time effectively (Drucker, 1967). This observation may be coupled with the fact that nearly every recent survey of professional educators has shown that, among the factors that comprise the most frustrating characteristics of their daily work life, time management is an enduring concern. School administrators in particular frequently note that the inability to manage and control their schedules often prohibits them from accomplishing their objectives. It is because of this consistently perplexing problem that the field of management has seen a great deal of attention paid to the ways in which leaders of organizations might learn how to budget the precious resource of time more effectively (Mackenzie, 1972). It was to add to this material designed to analyze the use of time that the Time Problems Inventory was created by Albert Canfield.

The stated purpose of this inventory is simply to help people identify the reasons why they waste time while performing their jobs in an organization. The test consists of 48 items that have been selected as the most descriptive and representative issues related to time problems encountered typically by administrative and managerial personnel. With this broad focus, there is no attempt made to suggest that the instrument need be considered appropriate for educators alone; rather, private sector managers and public administrators outside of education might well consult the findings derived from this test as a way to analyze and better understand their personal use of time.

The Time Problems Inventory measures the extent to which an individual's behavior might be classified as "time-wasting" according to four dimensions. These dimensions include measures of a person's likelihood of demonstrating difficulties of personal management and control in the areas of priority-setting, planning, delegating to subordinates, and engaging in self-discipline. The assumption, of course, is that the fact that a manager experiences problems in any or all of these four areas will be a way to determine how he or she wastes time.

The inventory also assumes that, by presenting items that focus on larger categories of potential time-wasting activities instead of specific potential time-saving techniques, the individual respondent will have a greater opportunity to identify, utilize, and evaluate techniques that are directly related to his or her major problem areas rather than generic time-management problems.

This inventory may provide a foundation for considering the application of many specific time-saving techniques. These techniques are normally presented as part of in-service training sessions and workshops provided to assist administrators with developing more effective time-management skills. The designers of the test note, however, that it may be used by individuals who wish to apply its results in developing a personal profile for use in self-improvement settings. In such cases, individuals must contact the company that distributes the instrument to purchase a copy of scale descriptions offering individual interpretations of the instrument results.

Practical Applications/Uses

Whether the Time Problems Inventory is utilized in a workshop setting or by an individual respondent, procedures for administration are the same. The manual states that the test requires approximately 25 minutes to complete, score, and analyze so that profiles of time-wasting dimensions can be determined.

This inventory is a self-report device in which the respondent must indicate, on a 5-point scale, the extent to which each of the 48 statements describes something that he or she typically experiences "Not at all" (at one end of the scale) to "Quite a lot" (at the other end of the scale). After all items have been rated according to this process, the respondent follows the directions for self-scoring. Scores are derived based on numerical equivalents for the five items on the rating scale, and the respondent is then able to determine separate subscores for each of the four dimensions of the test: priorities, planning, delegation, and self-discipline. These subscores are then used to develop a personal "Time Problems Profile," wherein personal scores are compared with those of a national norm-reference group. According to the inventory's designers, the higher an individual's score appears as a point in his or her profile, the more likely it is that a particular dimension represented by that point will indicate an area for improvement of time management skills.

The actual question/answer forms utilized in the administration of this instrument are a simplified self-report and scoring device. The 48 items related to time utilization are printed in the space of two inner pages of the question booklet, along with a series of boxes reflecting the five-point response scale. This material is printed on treated paper that transfers pencil marks made on the first page to a second layer that, when peeled from the response pages, reveals a scoring grid. To score his or her answers, the respondent merely looks down the columns of boxes that show check marks copied from the first sheet. The columns are arranged according to the four dimensions of time management. A tally of scores in each of the four columns provides total values for each dimension.

On the reverse of the scoring sheet, a table shows the national norm-reference group scores and equivalent percentile rankings for each dimension. The respondent plots his or her scores on the table and can then see a profile of time management skills that may need improvement. In addition to these items, the question/answer forms also include brief narrative descriptions of important characteristics of each of the four time-management dimensions.

The accompanying manual provides a brief review of the administration and scoring procedures, with instructions to be issued to respondents that they not examine the scoring grid in advance and that they should remember that the test results will be of value to them only if they answer all questions as objectively and honestly as possible.

There is little doubt that the issue of effective time management is viewed increasingly as a topic of great concern to administrators in all types of organizations. Thus, the Time Problems Inventory is a useful tool for those who would like to identify more clearly the general areas of management practice that are likely to waste more time than would others. It may be argued that the four dimensions of effective management that are measured here (priorities, planning, delegation, and self-discipline) are far from exhaustive terms that indicate what administrators need to do in order to be successful. Nevertheless, the four dimensions are sufficiently descriptive of good management practices that they can be seen as guides to further improvement of individuals in leadership roles. For example, an indication that a manager needs to refine his or her ability to encourage workers in the organization to carry out practices without constant supervision (delegation) may serve as a valuable observation that will help not only the individual administrator to budget time more effectively, but may also be a benefit to the organization. Executives who know how to work well with subordinates tend to be able to elicit more in the way of productivity from their employees.

The Time Problems Inventory appears to be an instrument that is simple to use and takes very little time to complete. In return, the user is able to gain important insights into his or her behavior in an organization. Although the emphasis is on the test's applicability to administrative and managerial performance, there are only slight limitations to its use by anyone. For example, all people are faced with the need to prioritize, plan, and engage in self-discipline, regardless of whether they are in positions of leadership or not. The only items that would appear to be difficult to assess by nonmanagers are those that deal with delegation. Those not in administrative roles would find it nearly impossible to respond directly to items that deal with the ways in which one works with organizational subordinates. This limitation is noted in the accompanying manual; however, it is not a major limitation on the usefulness of the overall inventory. In cases where nonmanagers respond, they may be directed to ignore their scores in the category related to delegation. The scoring and analysis of the other three dimensions can still provide respondents with insights into their behavior.

Technical Aspects

The inventory's manual provides little information concerning the technical aspects of the instrument. All that are indicated are descriptive statistics gathered as a result of a pilot test. As indicated in the manual, the following tables reveal the means and standard deviations for each of the four subscales, and also preliminary data related to subscale intercorrelations:

Table 1

Scale Descriptive Statistics
N = 79

	Mean	Standard Deviation
Priorities	26.5	11.9
Planning	23.0	10.6
Delegation	19.1	9.2
Discipline	27.2	11.5

Table 2

Scale Data Correlations
(Pearson rs)
N = 79

	Planning	Delegation	Discipline
Priorities	.75	.51	.71
Planning		.52	.70
Delegation			.50

The lack of technical information poses several disturbing questions. First, there is no indication if the pilot test sample used to generate the descriptive statistics (Table 1) and scale correlations (Table 2) was representative of managers across the nation or if it was a regional, random sample that did not necessarily include administrative or managerial personnel. Second, there is no description offered of the national norm reference groups that served as the basis of data provided in the Time Management Profile feature of the scoring sheet. It would be much more helpful, for example, if respondents could know how they compare to those in approximately identical roles. A third general limitation of the technical specifications provided is that there is no information about the overall validity and reliability of the instrument. How does a user know if the items assigned to the Delegation subscale have been sufficiently tested to determine if they truly measure that characteristic of time management? Finally, no information is given to explain why the four dimensions were selected as the basis for time management skill development.

Critique

Despite the limitations of the technical features (or at least the descriptions available of those features), this appears to be a very useful instrument. This inventory addresses an issue of significant and enduring concern to those in administrative and managerial roles in schools and many other organizations. In addition, with the exception of the concept of "delegation," the Time Problems Inventory might easily be adapted for use with anyone. Insights into the ways in which people go about planning, setting priorities, and maintaining self-discipline are helpful to all employees.

An interesting feature of the inventory is that it clearly may be used by individuals who respond to the items alone, without the benefit of follow-up discussion. It is apparent, however, that an even more satisfying way to approach the results is within a larger discussion of time management. Therefore, a potential application of this instrument exists in the area of management consultant/development work. As the designers note, it is likely that the Time Problems Inventory will be used frequently in large group training sessions and workshops. That is, indeed, an appropriate use of this instrument.

References

Canfield, A. A. (1980). *Time Problems Inventory manual.* Ann Arbor, MI: Humanics Media.
Drucker, P. F. (1967). *The effective executive.* New York: Harper & Row.
Mackenzie, R. A. (1972). *The time trap.* New York: McGraw-Hill.

Ardelina Albano Baldonado, R.N., Ph.D.
Associate Professor of Nursing, Loyola University of Chicago, and Assistant Dean and Director, Undergraduate Nursing Program, Marcella Niehoff School of Nursing, Chicago, Illinois.

TRAIT EVALUATION INDEX
Alan R. Nelson. Larchmont, New York: Martin M. Bruce, Ph.D., Publishers.

Introduction

The Trait Evaluation Index (TEI) is a multitrait, forced-choice, self-report instrument. It consists of 125 triads of hyphenated adjectives and positive-sounding words descriptive of "normal" personality variables. The TEI has 22 basic trait scales grouped into six clusters (based on their scale intercorrelations). In addition to the 22 basic trait scales are seven supplemental scales for overall adjustment, consistency, masculine/feminine orientation, job satisfaction, employment stability, and productivity/creativity.

The TEI assumes that personality is a multidimensional entity that is best described by the individual. The author, Alan R. Nelson, contends that issues of validity such as acquiescence, deviance, and social desirability were taken into consideration during instrument development. These were achieved by presenting the examinee only positive and valenced adjectives/words. Additionally, "invasion of privacy" was minimized by not using personal and negative words or statements to elicit the examinee's intrapersonal and interpersonal behavioral perceptions or self-image.

Personality assessment began in 3000 B.C. with the ancient Chinese practice of palmistry. This was followed by phrenology and physiognomy. From these early beginnings came the development of empirically based theories formulated for the understanding and prediction of human behavior. Present study and understanding of human behavior is approached from different theoretical viewpoints and interpretations of the *core* and *peripheral* aspects of man's nature. The core of the personality may be conceived as the tendencies and directions of human functioning; the peripheral aspects are learned, are present in *some* rather than *all* people, and are specific rather than general in their effect upon behavior (Maddi, 1968, P. 228).

Personality is also defined in terms of characteristics directly observable in behavior, based on the ways in which persons interact with each other or the roles individuals adopt and ascribe to themselves. According to Allport (1937), personality is a dynamic organization of the psychological systems that determine an individual's unique adjustment to his environment. On the other hand, contemporary research in personality dimensions is based on conceptual portraits of man's psychological nature through the researcher/theorist's personal interpretation. Assessment models used include biological, experimental, social, psychometric, and computer models. The TEI is but one of the many tools (based on theoretical framework; e.g., Murray's need-press system) used to provide a valid measure of trait systems and personality theories. It is useful in understanding the content and structure of an individual's personality derived from self-perception or self-image.

The TEI is a one-piece, fold-over instrument consisting of a three-column list of 125 adjective triads. The front page bears the name of the instrument, the directions for administration and an example of accurate marking of the separate answer sheet, the author's name, the publisher, the publisher's address, and the copyright date. The instrument has a one-page answer sheet that fits well over the 24 IBM scoring stencils. Scoring is clearly described in the manual and is easily done by hand. There are two profile sheets; one provides graphic normative scales for business/industry population, and the other offers percentiles for comparison of the individual's scores with male and female college students. On the reverse of each profile sheet are descriptions of each trait in addition to those traits with which each is negatively correlated. The six trait categories are determined by their intercorrelations.

The examinee's task is to select which one of the groups of traits in the triads is the *most* descriptive and the *least* descriptive of the self as currently perceived by the examinee. The words/adjectives are commonly used, so their meaning should present no difficulty to college and postcollege populations. The test instrument is self-administering and can be done individually or in groups. According to the manual, the instrument is *Level B* (i.e. users must have a general knowledge of psychological testing, etc.); hence, formal training in psychology, personality, test construction, statistics, and psychometrics are required of the user.

Practical Applications/Uses

The TEI has potential for use in career counseling, job placement, and evaluation when used with other validation studies. Like other personality tests, it is a tool useful for understanding the individual's self-perceptions and current functioning within a given context and time. A school psychologist, a college counselor, or a placement/recruitment officer may want to use the instrument to help identify the individual's predilection towards a cluster of behaviors. For example, when a high school senior takes the test and scores high in consistency, the school counselor then proceeds to assess the other scores that may be predictive of college success for a particular discipline. Thus, examinees who score high in adaptability, responsibility, productivity/creativity, ambition, motivational drive, propriety, and verbal and intellectual orientation may be counseled into professions that demand eloquence, wit, moral/ethical behavior, high responsibility, and accountability (e.g., sales/marketing, social work, law). Likewise, the manual indicates that extreme scores in the Over-all Adjustment scale suggest the possibility of neurotic or malingering behavior. Hence, the psychologist may find the instrument useful for counseling and referral purposes.

Administration of the TEI is simple; it is essentially self-administering. It is untimed, but requires an average of 40 minutes to complete in industrial and college situations.

Scoring the answer sheet is easily done. The manual gives succinct directions on scoring the variables of traits. The answer sheet, which is one page, is placed over the stencil for a particular scale. There are 24 IBM stencils for the 24 scales/personality dimensions: Adaptability, Ambition, Benevolence, Caution, Compliance, Courtesy, Dynamism, Elation, Fairmindedness, Feminine Orientation, Independence, Intellectual Orientation, Masculine Orientation, Motivational Drive, Perception, Personal Adequacy, Propriety, Responsibility, Self Confidence, Self Control, Self Organization, Sincerity, Social Orientation, and Verbal Orientation. The score is the sum of the marks for the most and least descriptive of self for the particular scale.

The Consistency score and the Over-all Adjustment scores are computed without using a stencil. The Consistency score is computed by adding the total number of duplicated responses to each of the eight triads. Each triad has an exact duplicate. For each of the eight triads the examinee has two responses per item, one *most* and one *least*. Each repeated response in an item with a corresponding item alternative merits one score. Thus, a response of *most* and *least* in an item duplicated in the corresponding alternative item is given a score of two. Maximum score is 16. The Over-all Adjustment score is computed by summing the raw scores from four scales: Elation, Personal Adequacy, Self Confidence and Self Control.

Interpretation of obtained scores from ipsative instruments are accompanied with caution. The TEI manual provides guidelines and acknowledges the fact that findings (scores) are relative rather than absolute. The TEI measures validity of responses by the score obtained in the Consistency scale. A score of eight or less suggests invalid scores. Of note are the suggested meanings of low or high scores in the Over-all Adjustment scale: a low score suggests limited self-confidence, pervading pessimism, poor control of emergency measures, and inadequate self-image; conversely, a high score suggests emotional control, self-assurance, ego strength, optimism, and a sense of well-being. Extreme scores are suggestive of malingering or a neurotic personality (Nelson, 1968, p. 25.).

For a psychological portrait of the examinee, the TEI has two profile sheets. One profile sheet provides graphic normative scales for business/industry populations. The other offers percentiles for comparison of the examinee's scores with male or female college students. On the reverse of each profile sheet are descriptions of each trait in addition to those traits with which each is negatively correlated. The traits are grouped into five based on their intercorrelations. Sincerity (a miscellaneous scale) was designated Group Six.

Overall, inferential interpretation of scale scores and profile should be cross-validated in situations where findings are applied, and most especially in relation to selection and evaluation in academic, business, industry, or similar settings.

Technical Aspects

Personality theories and psychometric theory guided the development of the TEI. Thus, construct, content, and concurrent validity (and cross-validation of the supplementary scales) were carefully addressed by Nelson. To assess validity, test-retests were done, initially among 87 college students attending various schools in the New York metropolitan area. The first test administration consisted of the 22 basic scales of the TEI, while the retest was on the scale descriptions without reference to any of the trait scales. The reliability coefficients obtained ranged from 0.52 to 0.79, with one exception (Adaptability = 0.31). Using 49 college students, concurrent validity was established by correlating the TEI scores with six scales of the Gordon Survey of Interpersonal Values. In addition to the above procedures, item-scales correlations were also established. All items were significant at the .05 level or higher (Nelson, 1968, p. 12). Social desirability for the adjectives in each triad was controlled by using forced-choice methodology (Braun & Seamon, 1969; Nelson, 1968, p. 5).

Scale intercorrelations were also computed separately, using a sample of 135 coeds and 71 male college students and from a nationwide sample of 1,081 engineers. Results from both sample groups were highly correlated (i.e., mean average [college] was .26 and [engineers] .28). Lastly, the TEI was also significantly correlated with total scores and/or selected scales of the following instruments: Association Adjustment Inventory, Guilford-Zimmerman Temperament Survey, Minnesota Multiphasic Personality Inventory, and Edwards Personal Preference Schedule.

Reliability of the TEI was established using business/industrial and academic populations. The Spearman-Brown prophecy formula was used to estimate the split-half (for college students) and odd-even reliabilities (business/industrial group). For both groups, the reliability coefficients were "well within the range typical for such inventories, and in many instances, somewhat higher" (Nelson, 1968, p. 23).

Critique

The TEI was rationally developed with substantive approach to test construction. The instrument is easily self-administered; that is, the examiner's presence is not necessary. The use of positive-sounding adjectives and avoiding "personal" intrusion would make the instrument appealing for extensive use in research and counseling situations. However, its wide usage among the norm-related populations was not supported by a body of literature. It is possible that the literature computer search did not tap the appropriate resources or data bases.

This reviewer has both self-administered the instrument provided by the publisher and administered it to a couple of first-year college students and first-year-in-the-job sales/marketing samples, concurring with one general comment made by the examinees: "The test is monotonous, redundant, and annoying." This comment was based not only on the eight pairs of adjective triads (eight mirror images), but also on the multiple use of words in the 125-item triads. For example, the words *agreeable* and *willing* were used five times each, the words *accurate* and *careful* four times each.

First-year college students are aware that the use of duplicate words checks for consistency of responding; thus, the instrument reveals the intent for which the test is given. Hence, the examinee may respond to the items just to "please" the examiner or may truly reveal self-image. Additionally, the directions for taking the test instruct the examinee to select the words that describe "you as you are now." Taken literally, the examinee will respond to the items according to "here and now" rather than a more stable, consistent over time and well-developed image of self. Responses based on a transient self-image impacted by stress or crisis, such as the loss of a loved one or a job termination, may be useful in certain instances (e.g., counseling or referral).

Scoring by using the IBM templates is a simple task. Once mastered, it takes an average of 15 minutes to score the 24 scales and the supplementary scales. However, this method would be time consuming for large samples. With the advent of personal computers and university-wide computer main frames, it is instructive for the developer of this instrument to change the scoring methodology, making it adaptable to computer technology.

Although the literature search did not provide evidence of an extensive use of the TEI, this reviewer recommends its use in research for the personality dimensions it measures, both for not being too cumbersome to administer, and for its apparent validity and reliability. The TEI is useful for correlating personality profiles with college success and job satisfaction/stability. To a lesser extent, the instrument may be useful for prediction purposes for it lends itself to the social and behavioral sciences (although the norm groups were unidentified-discipline college groups and business/industry).

References

Allport, G. W. (1937). *Personality: A psychological interpretation*. New York: Holt and Rinehart.
Braun, J. R., & Seamon, J. (1969). Control for social desirability in the Trait Evaluation Index. *Journal of Projective Techniques and Personality Assessment, 33*(3), 279-280.
Maddi, S. (1968). *Personality theories: A comparative analysis*. Homewood, IL: Dorsey Press.
Nelson, A. R. (1968). *Examiner's manual: Trait Evaluation Index*. Larchmont, NY: Martin M. Bruce Publishers, Ph.D.

Michael D. Franzen, Ph.D.
Director of Neuropsychology, Assistant Professor of Behavioral Medicine and Psychiatry, West Virginia University School of Medicine, Morgantown, West Virginia.

TRITES NEUROPSYCHOLOGICAL TEST BATTERY
Ronald Trites. Lafayette, Indiana: Lafayette Instrument Company, Inc.

Introduction

The Trites Neuropsychological Test Battery is not a novel battery of tests. Instead, it is a collection of tests which were developed in a number of different neuropsychological assessment contexts. Many of these tests will be familiar to clinical neuropsychologists, as they include the Halstead Category test, the Tactual Performance test, the Finger Tapping test, the Speech Sounds Perception test, the Seashore Rhythm Test, the Trail Making test, and other tests such as the Wide Range Achievement Test (WRAT), the Wechsler Memory Scale, the Wechsler Adult Intelligence Scale (WAIS), and the House-Tree-Person Technique.

Ronald Trites, author of the battery manual (Trites, 1977), explains that much of the Trites battery was developed by Halstead and Reitan. Hallgrim Klove and Charles Matthews modified the original set of tests, which Trites then adapted for his own uses. The manual does not detail what changes were made; however, an examination of the battery indicates that the changes were largely inclusions of additional procedures. Because Trites worked in Canada, the instructions in the manual are given in both English and French.

The Trites battery has three forms, each of which is related to the age of the intended subject. The adult form is intended for subjects 15 years of age and older, the midrange form is intended for subjects between the ages of 9 and 15 years, and the children's form is intended for subjects between the ages of 5 and 9 years. The manual states that any of the three forms can take from 6 to 12 hours to complete. For each of the three forms, there is a suggested short form, which the author states should take no longer than 4-5 hours even with difficult subjects.

Practical Applications/Uses

The battery for adult subjects is comprised of the WAIS, the WRAT, the Wechsler Memory Scale, the ABC Vision Test, the House-Tree-Person Technique, the Minnesota Multiphasic Personality Inventory, the Halstead Category Test, the Tactual Performance Test, the Finger Tapping test, the Speech Sounds Perception Test, the Seashore Rhythm Test, Trails A and B, the Klove sensory exam, the Wisconsin Aphasia Screen (a modification of the Wepman Aphasia Screen), the Foot Tapping test, the Grooved Pegboard, the Motor Steadiness Battery, the Dynamometer, visual field examination, a Roughness Discrimination Exam, tactile form recognition, a lateral dominance examination, a test of left-right discrimination, the Knox Cube Test, and a dichotic listening test.

The midrange battery includes the age-appropriate forms of the Halstead-Reitan tests plus the dichotic listening test, Knox Cube Test, and Motor Steadiness Tests of the adult form; the Myklebust Pupil Rating Scale, the Conner's Parent and Teacher Questionnaires, the Missouri Children's Picture Series, the Vineland Social Maturity Scale, the Children's and the High School Personality Questionnaires, the Peabody Picture Vocabulary Test, Raven's Progressive Matrices, and the Boston Children's Medical Center Anthropometric Chart.

The children's form includes the tests from the midrange battery plus the Developmental Drawings Procedure, the Frostig Developmental Test of Visual Perception, and the Illinois Test of Psycholinguistic Abilities. The battery is quite expensive; if all the tests are purchased, the cost can amount to more than $3,000.00.

Technical Aspects

The manual does not provide norms for the adult battery; however, norms are provided for the other two forms. These are based on subjects who were referred to the neuropsychology laboratory at the Royal Ottawa Hospital. Subjects were excluded if they were mentally retarded or if they carried a neurological diagnosis. Consequently, the children in the normative group had diagnoses of learning disabilities, hyperactivity, speech disabilities, or psychological problems. There were 75 5-year-olds, 118 6-year-olds, 147 7-year-olds, 145 8-year-olds, 103 9-year-olds, 109 10-year-olds, 73 11-year-olds, 68 12-year-olds, 56 13-year-olds, and 61 14-year-olds. In addition, norms for the same age groups for some of the same tests are quoted from Spreen & Gaddes (1969) and Knights (1966).

Although these norms are useful in describing the type of subject referred to the Royal Ottawa Hospital, they do not provide any information as to how to interpret the results of the testing. For that purpose, norms derived from a "normal" normative group (a group without identified problems) are needed. This is particularly true because there are known neurological and neuropsychological deficits associated with several of the diagnoses, including learning disabilities, hyperactivity, and psychiatric disorders.

The intended use of the battery appears to be a full-scale neuropsychological evaluation. In order to obtain information regarding the reliability and validity of the tests included in this battery, however, one would have to turn to the literature on the individual tests. There is apparently no literature available on the relation of these tests to one another or on the validity of diagnoses drawn through the combined use of these tests. The manual does not reference any of the literature related to these tests. In the adult form, the calculation of the Average Impairment Index is recommended, but no information is provided as to how this information can be integrated with the results of the other tests not included in the impairment index.

There are rules presented for prorating scores when not all of the tests are given; however, these rules have not been validated. Another problem is that the norms are given separately for English-speaking and French-speaking subjects. For the motor tests, this is not a problem. However, it is a major problem for tests such as the Speech Sounds Perception test, which is identical for the two languages. Cultural experience plays a large role in the subject's ability to perceive and produce certain speech sounds, but this does not seem to have been taken into account in the development of the Trites battery.

Critique

Overall, the manual does not provide enough information for the Trites Neuropsychological Test Battery to be useful in settings other than that in which it was developed. Basic reliability and validity research needs to be conducted before this battery can be recommended for widespread clinical use.

References

Knights, R. M. (1966). Normative data on tests for evaluating brain damage in children from 5 to 14 years of age (Research Bulletin No. 20). Ottawa: University of Western Ontario.

Spreen, O., & Gaddes, W. H. (1969). Developmental norms for 15 neuropsychological tests age 6 to 15. *Cortex, 5,* 171-191.

Trites, R. L. (1977). *Neuropsychological Test manual.* Lafayette, IN: Lafayette Instrument Co.

Raymond E. Webster, Ph.D.
Assistant Professor and Director, School Psychology Training Program, East Carolina University, Greenville, North Carolina.

Theodore W. Whitley, Ph.D.
Associate Director, Division of Research, Department of Emergency Medicine, East Carolina University, School of Medicine, Greenville, North Carolina.

THE VISUAL-AURAL DIGIT SPAN TEST
Elizabeth M. Koppitz. Orlando, Florida: Grune & Stratton, Inc.

Introduction

The Visual-Aural Digit Span Test (VADS) was designed to assess childrens' short-term memory (STM) recall capacity for digit strings presented visually and aurally. The unique aspect of the VADS is its attempt to evaluate STM capacity as it relates to the nature of the response that the child must give. These responses are given either orally or written by the child on a sheet of paper.

The test was derived from the author's 15 years of experience as a school psychologist working with learning-disabled children. On the basis of these experiences, Koppitz (1977) identified a "close relationship between children's reading, spelling, and arithmetic achievement and their functioning in intersensory integration and recall" (p. xi). Although not explicitly stated by Koppitz, the theoretical rationale and empirical foundation underlying this observation are based heavily on the work of Birch and Belmont (1964), who examined the intersensory integration and transfer of information in both skilled and disabled readers. The results from these studies have been seriously questioned during the past 20 years. But, more recent research (Webster, 1979, 1980) has suggested that learning-disabled children do exhibit different STM capacity and learning efficiency as a function of the way the material is presented (visual and auditory) in combination with the manner in which they are required to produce the material learned (verbal and written).

The VADS was developed as a brief standardized alternative to more elaborate, individually administered intelligence tests that include STM as one component of several subtests measuring global cognitive ability and potential. The entire test package consists of a hardcover test manual containing a good deal of supporting research that reflects the role of STM in reading and learning, a set of 26 stimulus cards containing digit strings ranging in length from two to seven digits printed in black ink on a white background, and test scoring sheets. The examiner must provide blank sheets of unlined white 8½" x 11" paper and a pencil with an eraser for the written output subtests. A stopwatch or wristwatch with a sweep second hand is needed to limit the exposure of visually presented digit strings to 10 seconds.

In terms of the development of this instrument, Koppitz mentions briefly that the experimental edition of the VADS was used extensively by herself and colleagues. There is no indication of the number or type of revisions the instrument underwent or how the present format was selected.

The VADS is described in the test manual as a diagnostic instrument for children between the ages of 5½ and 12 years. The only academic requirements for the child are the ability to recognize single digits and to reproduce them orally and in written form. The examiner's role is typical in that it involves establishing rapport, communicating directions, ensuring that the child understands the instructions, presenting the stimulus cards, and recording verbal responses and accompanying behaviors during the test.

The VADS consists of four subtests, administered in the following sequence: Aural-Oral (A-O), Visual-Oral (V-O), Aural-Written (A-W), and Visual-Written (V-W). The maximum length of the digit strings is seven items. Koppitz (1977) argues that any student who can remember a seven-digit string possesses "a well-functioning short-term memory" (p. 10). Research by Miller (1956), Simon (1974), and Spitz (1972) on the STM capacity of adolescents and adults is presented as further support for this ceiling on the length of the strings. Such reasoning seems appropriate and acceptable.

Digits are presented at the rate of one per second in the aural subtests. In the visual subtests, the child is shown each card for 10 seconds. Oral responses are recorded by the examiner on the printed answer sheet. Written responses are recorded by the child on a blank sheet of paper. Children are asked to write the numerals 1 through 9 on the top of the paper before responding in the written output mode and to sign their names on the test protocol at the conclusion of the test to get a handwriting sample. There is no explanation of how the handwriting sample is to be used or evaluated.

Testing begins with the three-digit string in the A-O, V-O, and V-W subtests for children aged 5½ to 6 years or who are mentally retarded. If the child fails the first string, a second three-digit string is presented. If that is failed, the child is then given the two-item string. Two failures at this level conclude testing. If the child is successful on either of these strings, he is then given the four-item string.

The three-item string is used as the starting point in the A-W subtest for children between the ages of 5½ to 7 years. With this subtest, only children aged 8 to 12 years are started with the four-digit string. In the three remaining subtests, the four-item string is used for 7- to 9-year-olds and the five-item string for children older than 10 years. The reason for different starting points on the A-W subtest is not given. For all subtests, the child is given two opportunities to recall different digit strings of the same length. Success on either string advances the child to the next longer string. Testing is discontinued when the child fails to recall correctly both strings of a given length.

The score for each subtest equals the longest digit sequence recalled without error. Three different sets of scores are computed: one score for each of the four subtests, six scores for various combinations of the subtest scores, and a total test score. The six subtest combination scores describe STM functioning according to how the material was presented (aural or visual), the response made by the child (verbal or written), and intersensory and intrasensory integration of the two input modes and output modes.

Combination scores are computed by summing the raw scores from the four subtests as follows:

Aural Input = A-O and A-W;
Visual Input = V-O and V-W;
Oral Expression = A-O and V-O;
Written Expression = A-W and V-W;
Intrasensory Integration = A-O and V-W; and
Intersensory Integration = V-O and A-W.

The VADS total test score is derived from the sum of the raw scores from all four subtests. There is no comparison of ordered and unordered recall capacity. Only ordered recall is measured.

Koppitz (1977) makes a number of statements regarding what each of these subtests and combination scores measure (pp. 55-57); however, there is a paucity of data supporting these assertions. The manual cites a correlation study of 26 fourth-graders (Carr, 1974 in Koppitz, 1977) in which subtests and combination scores were correlated with each other and with total test score. Because total test score has a 25% dependency on each subtest score, it is not surprising that all of the measures were significantly correlated with total test score.

The scoring sheet is one page. The front side is to summarize test results and includes space to record information about the number of reversals made during recall, as well as behavior and attitude. The reverse side summarizes instructions for the examiner, lists the digit strings for each subtest, and is used to record student responses. Subtest and combination raw scores are converted to corresponding percentile scores for age and grade level. The total test score is transformed into an age-level equivalent score. One part of the scoring sheet is reserved to list the frequency and type of reversals made by the child during recall.

Practical Applications/Uses

During the past 15 years, an increasing number of studies have identified the critical role of STM in reading and general learning. The precise role and operation of STM in cognitively based disabilities remains a moot point. Webster (1986) has summarized at least four different perspectives regarding STM processing by disabled learners. Some studies have shown that disabled learners have less STM capacity than average learners (Perfetti & Lesgold, 1977), while others have shown that the between-group differences reflect temporal ordering difficulties by the disabled students and not overall capacity limitations (Bakker, 1972). Still other studies suggest that modality-specific deficits in either the visual or auditory modality account for the learning problems of students (Kirk & Kirk, 1971). Finally, another group of researchers have tried to explain learning problems in terms of poor intersensory transfer of information (Birch & Belmont, 1964). Of all these viewpoints, the one receiving the least consistent empirical support has been the intersensory transfer hypothesis.

A second issue in the role of STM in learning disabilities involves the procedures used to estimate STM capacity. The use of digit recall has been, and continues to be, an accepted procedure among many test developers, yet research has shown that digit recall tends to be higher than recall of consonants, particularly nonrhyming consonants (Webster, 1981). Subsequently, using digit strings to measure STM capacity is likely to produce a spuriously high and inaccurate estimate of a person's true STM recall capacity.

Finally, the significance of number and letter reversals in learning disabilities remains controversial. Some (Orton, 1925, 1937) have argued that such strephosymbolic errors indicated interhemispheric transfer problems. More recently, such reversals have been interpreted as representing inadequate learning by the child who lacks knowledge about the distinctive features that characterize and distinguish similar letters and numerals.

The VADS is presented as a measure of STM recall capacity. Three types of information about a child are obtained from the test: the child's attitudes and behaviors during the test, the quality of the test protocol, and the VADS scores for each subtest. A six-page, well-presented chapter in the test manual addresses some of the major behaviors and characteristics that the examiner might observe during testing. However, most of these appear to reflect clinical observations by the test author rather than empirically derived data that establish a relationship between learning styles and strategies. In fact, the chapter is a good refresher for experienced psychometrists who wish to refamiliarize themselves with the qualitative aspects involved in testing.

The VADS would be useful in both educational and psychological settings in which the emphasis is on diagnostic evaluation. No special training for the examiner is necessary beyond familiarity with the specific instructions and mechanics of VADS administration. The only qualifications for the examiner would be some formalized specific training and experience with test administration in general.

The instrument is designed for individual administration in a setting relatively free from distractions. Instructions are presented clearly on pages 12 to 14 in the test manual. The VADS can be used with children who have visual or hearing sensory impairments provided that the subtests administered avoid testing in the impaired modality. Total testing time varies from 10 to 15 minutes, depending on the child being evaluated.

Scoring is a straightforward procedure involving transfer of subtest raw scores to the scoring summary sheet. Normative tables are located in the back of the test manual and are available at varying age increments beginning at 5 years, 6 months and concluding at 12 years, 11 months. The norm tables between ages 5 years, 6 months and 6 years, 11 months are presented in 6-month intervals. At 7 years, 0 months the tables are stratified according to 1-year intervals. Only five percentile ranks are presented in these tables—10, 25, 50, 75, and 90.

Appendix C in the VADS test manual offers similar normative tables by grade level. The tables begin with kindergarten and conclude at sixth grade. The format of the tables is identical to that described for the age-level normative tables. The total test score is converted to an age level equivalent, the norms for which are presented in Appendix B of the manual. Hand scoring should take no longer than 10 minutes.

Technical Aspects

Reliability data for the VADS are presented in a two-paragraph section on pages 57 and 58 of the test manual. Koppitz used the test-retest method with two groups of youngsters who had been identified as learning disabled and/or behaviorally disordered. The groups were distinguished by age rather than disability. Group 1, with 35 members, was comprised of children ages 6 to 10 years. The second group included 27 children between the ages of 11 and 12 years. With a retest interval of 1 day to 15 weeks and a mean interval of 6.5 weeks, product-moment correlations ranged from .74 to .92 for the younger group and .72 to .90 for the older group. Koppitz accepts these figures as indicative of satisfactory reliability of the instrument. A review of the literature failed to identify any studies examining the reliability of the VADS.

The lack of specificity in the initial reliability study and the widely varying time interval make interpretation of these data difficult. Although the two groups were comprised of exceptional children, the final distinction between groups was on the basis of age. However, no rationale is offered for the age split selected. The correlation coefficients are certainly acceptable. The use of the test-retest method is appropriate and an improvement over typical split-half procedures, which are nothing more than measures of internal consistency rather than reliability. However, the methodological problems inherent in the reliability study obscure the utility of the data.

The test manual does not include a section dealing specifically with the validity of the VADS; the test user is forced to search other sections of the manual to address this issue. Chapters 8 through 12 present a variety of studies examining the relationship between VADS performance and performance on intelligence tests and on the Bender-Gestalt. Studies examining the relationships between VADS performance and school achievement are reported as well, and there is also a chapter devoted to the diagnostic patterns of VADS scores. Collectively, the user may infer information about the validity of the VADS. These chapters may also be viewed as providing some evidence about the discriminative validity of the test.

A between-groups design was used to examine the degree to which VADS performance distinguished learners dichotomized along a variety of variables. A chi-square analysis was performed on each individual subtest from the VADS. Significant differences between groups are interpreted as supporting the instrument's discriminative utility. The apparent reasoning underlying this approach seems to be that it is important for a diagnostic instrument to differentiate categories of learners. This rationale is not stated explicitly in the manual. Rather, Koppitz states that the key question is "how close is the relationship between VADS Test scores and school achievement?" (Koppitz, 1977, p. 72). If that is the question the author intended to answer, then the statistical analyses and methodological procedures used as described in the manual are inappropriate. The chi square does not specify relationships; it merely identifies between-group differences. Subsequently, the author has failed to address the initial question that she posed.

The more appropriate question for a diagnostic instrument might be "To what degree does the instrument distinguish between and among various groups of achievers?" The chi-square analysis does not answer this question either. It would be more appropriate to use multivariate procedures like a discriminant analysis, multiple regression analysis, and/or a multivariate analysis of variance to respond to such concerns.

Several studies were found in the literature review that purported to examine

542 Visual-Aural Digit Span Test

the concurrent validity of the VADS with the WRAT (Koppitz, 1977), the Comprehensive Test of Basic Skills (Koppitz, 1977), and the Test of General Ability (Koppitz, 1975). The same methodology described in the test manual was used in all these studies. In like manner, the author concluded that significant between-group differences supported the diagnostic usefulness of the VADS.

The test manual includes a section of the relationship between VADS test scores and WISC intelligence test data. Correlations with the major IQ score scales are low to moderate for each VADS subtest, which suggests that the VADS is measuring some construct or skill that differs in a substantial way from mere intelligence. Correlations with the WISC Digit Span subtest range from .57 to .69, which is rather surprising. The VADS A-O subtest correlates only .61 with WISC Digit Span. A-O is identical to this WISC subtest in terms of the input-output combination and the use of the same type of stimulus items.

In summary, the basic prerequisites for any psychological test are the adequacy of its reliability and validity. Koppitz has failed to exercise the necessary precision and rigor to establish the VADS as meeting minimally acceptable levels. The test manual offers a plethora of information about what appear to be empirical studies of the VADS. Unfortunately, these studies fall short of providing adequate evidence of reliability and validity.

Finally, there are no data presented to support the variety of subtests and combinations that comprise the VADS. The usefulness of these scores could be clarified, and the possible number of scores generated could be compacted through the use of factor analysis. Such a procedure could yield a more useful and practical interpretation of the scores.

Critique

The approach underlying the VADS is novel. It attempts to evaluate the learning styles and characteristics of children in a process-oriented manner. Such a testing strategy minimizes reliance on simple quantitative analysis of test data. Both attention to the interactive nature of the learning process and recognition that the way a child is asked to respond can influence learning and retention are extremely important. In these respects, the VADS is a significant step beyond traditional measurement procedures.

The instrument clearly provides a quick estimate of short-term memory recall capacity for digits. The consumer can readily compare the child's ability for visual and auditory presentations. Thus, if the child shows modality-specific learning preferences, the VADS may be quite useful in identifying them.

The ultimate question becomes what can the test consumer do with these data, aside from stating whether the child is a visual learner or an auditory learner. The validity of the VADS is questionable. This does not mean that future research will not establish its validity. However, appropriate validity estimates have not been provided. Because it distinguishes children with cognitive disabilities from those functioning at expected levels, such a diagnostic test should have discriminative validity. Using chi-square analysis to illustrate between-group differences is not sufficient to convince the consumer that the test possesses discriminative validity.

Another important issue is the degree to which VADS performance relates to, or even can predict, actual school achievement in the major subject areas of reading and mathematics. There are no data available on the VADS's predictive validity or on its concurrent validity with actual school performance or achievement as measured by standardized achievement testing. If these types of criteria are not appropriate, then some real-life criteria must be identified against which the VADS can be evaluated. In short, the test user needs to know the degree to which VADS performance is related to other kinds of real criteria in an empirical manner. Statements by the test author that essentially are founded in "expertise through the process of practical experience" are simply not acceptable. Perhaps one of the major problems with the VADS is the large number of statements made throughout the manual about what the test measures without providing sufficient, or in some cases any, supporting documentation. The following example serves to illustrate this point.

On page 76 in the test manual, Koppitz cites a study conducted by Hurd (1971) using 36 children in one investigation and 24 in a second. The children were divided into two groups, good and poor learners. A total of 18 *t*-tests resulted in some significant between-group differences in the two investigations. Koppitz interprets these data as "strong support for the hypothesis that most of the VADS measures are related to school achievement in the primary grades." She then goes on to note that her research with fifth-graders revealed "very different findings." In this study, Koppitz (cited on pages 76-77 in the manual) conducts 66 individual chi-square analyses on a group of 26 fifth-grade students. On page 78, she concludes that "the VADS test measures the mechanics of learning, such as perceptual-motor integration, sequencing, and recall; these mechanics are essential for school achievement." It is difficult for the reader to understand how such conclusions can be drawn on the basis of these kinds of procedures and analyses. Until further well-conducted research can be conducted that begins to address some of these issues, the usefulness of the VADS appears to be limited.

References

Bakker, D. (1972). *Temporal order in disturbed reading: Developmental and neuropsychological aspects in normal and reading-retarded children*. Rotterdam: Rotterdam University Press.

Birch, H., & Belmont, L. (1964). Auditory-visual integration in normal and retarded readers. *American Journal of Orthopsychiatry, 34*, 852-861.

Carr, M. (1974). *Relationships between the Bender Visual-Motor Gestalt Test, the Visual-Aural Digit Span Test, and the Arithmetic Subtests of the Wechsler Intelligence Scale for Children the Wide Range Achievement Test*. Professional paper, Texas Christian University.

Kirk, S., & Kirk, W. (1971). *Psycholinguistic learning disabilites: Diagnosis and remediation*. Urbana: University of Illinois Press.

Koppitz, E. (1975). Bender Gestalt Test, Visual-Aural Digit Span Test and reading achievement. *Journal of Learning Disabilities, 8*, 154-157.

Koppitz, E. (1977). *The Visual-Aural Digit Span Test*. New York: Grune & Stratton.

Miller, G. (1956). The magical number seven, plus or minus two: Some limits on our capacity for processing information. *Psychological Review, 63*, 81-97.

Orton, S. (1925). "Word-blindness" in school children. *Archives of Neurology and Psychiatry, 14*, 581-615.

Orton, S. (1937). *Reading, writing and speech problems in children*. London: Chapman and Holt.

Perfetti, C., & Lesgold, A. (1977). Discourse comprehension and sources of individual differences. In P. Carpenter & M. Just (Eds.), *Cognitive process in comprehension*. Hillsdale, NJ: Lawrence Erlbaum Associates.

Simon, H. (1974). How big is a chunk? *Science, 183*, 483-488.

Spitz, H. (1972). A note on immediate memory for digits: Invariance over the years. *Psychological Bulletin, 78*, 183-185.

Webster, R. (1979). Visual and aural short-term memory capacity deficits in mathematics disabled students. *Journal of Educational Research, 72*(5), 277-283.

Webster, R. (1980). Short-term memory in mathematics-proficient and mathematics-disabled students as a function of input modality/output modality pairings. *Journal of Special Education, 14*(1), 67-78.

Webster, R. (1981). *The Learning Efficiency Test manual*. Novato, CA: Academic Therapy Publications.

Webster, R. (1986). Memory and learning: A case study. *Academic Therapy, 21*(5), 526-530.

Robert J. Drummond, Ph.D.
Program Director, Counselor Education, University of North Florida, Jacksonville, Florida.

VOCATIONAL PREFERENCE INVENTORY

John L. Holland. Odessa, Florida: Psychological Assessment Resources, Inc.

Introduction

The Vocational Preference Inventory (VPI)—1985 Revision is an objective, pencil-and-paper personality interest inventory composed of 160 occupational titles. The inventory is based on Holland's (1985a) career development theory and has 11 scales, including his Realistic, Investigative, Artistic, Social, Enterprising, and Conventional dimensions, which are utilized in many inventories assessing vocational interests.

John L. Holland is one of the leading career development theorists and researchers. His theory is explained in the revised edition of *Making Vocational Choices: A Theory of Personality Types and Work Environments*. His Self-Directed Search (1985c) is one of the most widely used tools in vocational and career counseling.

The Vocational Preference Inventory was first published in 1953 and has been revised and refined through eight editions. The VPI scales have been constructed in a series of rational-empirical steps rather than by a direct empirical method employing defined criterion groups (Holland, 1985b, p. 15). Attention was given to item discrimination studies and internal consistency analysis. Six major scales were refined and in some cases renamed. Certain scales, such as the Aggressiveness scale, were eliminated, while others, such as the Masculinity, Infrequency, and Acquiescence scales, were added. In the 1977 edition all sex-biased occupational titles were eliminated; for example, fire*man* became fire*fighter*. The number of items has been revised from the original 300 to the current 160. In the 1985 revision the order of the first six scales was changed to coincide with the order on the Self-Directed Search. Four items on the test were also revised to increase the response rate by females and the scale homogeneity.

The VPI consists of 160 occupational titles, which are printed in double columns on the front and back of the test sheet. Examinees are told that it is an inventory of their feelings and attitudes toward many types of work. They record their answers on a separate sheet by filling in the appropriate circle. There are two circles, one containing a *y* (yes) and the other an *n* (no). Novelist, Accountant, Band Director, Automobile Mechanic, Internist, and File Clerk are types of occupations similar to those listed on the VPI.

The VPI can be either individually, group-, or self-administered. No special training is necessary for the examiner, for the profile sheet allows the examiner to plot the raw scores into T-scores without using the tables in the manual. The VPI has been used with high school and adult groups. Holland states that the person to be tested should be over 14 years of age and have at least normal intelligence (Holland, 1985b, p. 1).

Practical Applications/Uses

The Vocational Preference Inventory can be used by the psychologist, counselor, or educator as an interest and career assessment inventory for high school and college students or adults. The first six scales correspond to the major personality dimensions of Holland's theory of vocational choice and the scales on his Self-Directed Search. It is a quick method to assess personality type, providing useful information at low cost with brief testing and scoring time. Holland states that "without exception, the VPI should be used and interpreted only in combination with other psychosocial information such as age, sex, educational level, field of training, and current occupational status" (1985b, p. 1). Holland indicates (1985b, p. 1) that the VPI has four main uses: 1) a brief personality inventory for high school and college students as well as employed adults, 2) a helpful addition to a battery of personality inventories, 3) an interest inventory, and 4) an assessment technique for the investigation of career theory and behavior.

The VPI has 11 scales: Realistic, Investigative, Artistic, Social, Enterprising, Conventional (the six main dimensions in Holland's theory), Self-Control, Masculinity/Femininity, Status, Infrequency, and Acquiescence. The test is used by counselors and psychologists in career counseling functions as well as in research context. There are no special forms available for handicapped groups such as the blind, but the inventory could be administered orally. Most individuals can complete the test in 15 to 30 minutes.

There is a single scoring stencil for ten of the scales. The Acquiescence Scale is scored by counting the number of "yes" responses given to items 1 through 30. It only takes about a minute to score each test.

There are good back-up materials to facilitate the interpretation of VPI results. The scales are described adequately in the manual and other of Holland's publications such as *Making Vocational Choices* (1985a). If the examiner has not only a background in testing and test interpretation but also in career development theory, the more adequate and proper the interpretation of the protocol should be.

Technical Aspects

Holland presents evidence of the construct validity of his six major scales and also reports studies that correlate the VPI with tests such as the California Personality Inventory, the Sixteen Personality Factor Questionnaire, the Edwards Personal Preference Schedule, the Guilford-Zimmerman Temperament Survey, and the Allport-Vernon-Lindzey Study of Values. He states that factor-analytic studies have also supported the relative independence of the scales, concluding that the VPI scales have the ability to discriminate among a wide variety of criterion groups. There is evidence of both the predictive and criterion-referenced validity of the test.

Reliability data are not as extensively presented. Holland compared the equivalence of the sixth and seventh revisions. The six major scales for samples of men and women have coefficients ranging between .89 and .97. He also presents reliability coefficients between two short research forms; correlations between these forms for the six major scales ranged from .61 to .84 for women (121) and .64 to .81 for men (152). The standard error of measurement for the six major 14-item scales ranged from .80 to 1.16, with 2.00 for Infrequency and 3.32 for Acquiescence.

Critique

In general, the changes to the eighth or 1985 revision of the Vocational Preference Inventory itself were minor and involved revising four occupational titles. The manual does update literature concerning the test and provides a comparison and discussion of the VPI and SDS. No reliability data are presented on the eighth edition, and no new norms.

Rounds (1985) concluded that the manual for the seventh edition of the VPI did not provide enough evidence for the validity and reliability of the scale and he did not recommend the seventh edition for any of the practical applications suggested by Holland in the manual. The issues that Rounds felt needed resolution were the rationale for selecting the 11 personality dimensions, the unidimensionality of the scales, the reliability for individual assessment, and the accuracy and utility of using the instrument in applied settings (1985, p. 1684).

On the other hand, Vacc and Pickering (1985) concluded that the seventh revision of the VPI was an improved edition and recommended it as a helpful instrument for career exploration. They felt that the manual needed to be updated by including recent studies, eliminating the sex-biased language, and presenting validity information of the seventh revision. They also found inconsistencies among the test form, profile sheet, and manual.

The eighth edition has addressed several of the issues identified by previous reviewers but has neglected some others. The manual has been updated and sex-biased language has been omitted; however, no validity, reliability, or normative data are presented for the new edition. There is a section on profile interpretation and some illustrative interpretations given, but no intercorrelations between the scales are presented for the new edition nor standard errors of measurement for each of the scales. In this reviewer's search of the literature concerning the VPI, a computer search identified 145 available studies. The literature tends to support the constructs included in Holland's theory. For example, Care and Naylor (1984) examined high school student preferences in 30 Australian schools and found data consistent with Holland's model. They reported a strong association between interest in school subjects and vocational interests as well as an empirical basis for classifying school subjects in terms of interest themes. Miller, Karriker, and Pilgreen (1984) used Holland's consistency theory to predict behavior and attitude toward problem-solving and found confirming evidence.

This reviewer has used the VPI in both group and individual counseling situations. In general, the theory and constructs tend to make sense to the clients, but many times their profiles don't. Nevertheless, the VPI can be a good springboard for discussion and facilitates career counseling. It should be remembered, as Holland pointed out, that one needs to interpret the VPI keeping other factors in mind. Although Holland purports that the VPI is a personality measure, users must be

548 Vocational Preference Inventory

cautious. Other, more established measures might be better for personality assessment. Moreover, this reviewer finds that subjects often fail to check many of the items on the scale, so a limited sample is obtained of the domains being measured.

Under certain circumstances, recognizing its limitations, the VPI can be a useful tool for career counseling, interest measurement, and for research purposes.

References

Care, E., & Naylor, F. (1984). The factor structure of expressed preferences for school subjects. *Australian Journal of Education, 28,* 145-153.

Holland, J. L. (1985a). *Making vocational choices: A theory of personality types and work environments.* Englewood Cliffs, NJ: Prentice-Hall.

Holland, J. L. (1985b). *Manual for the Vocational Preference Inventory* (1985 Ed.). Odessa, FL: Psychological Assessment Resources.

Holland, J. L. (1985c). *Professional manual for the Self-Directed Search.* Odessa, FL: Psychological Assessment Resources.

Holland, J. L. (1985d). *The Occupations Finder.* Odessa, FL: Psychological Assessment Resources.

Miller, M., Karriker, C. S., & Pilgreen, J. C. (1984). Personality consistency and perceived problem-solving behavior and attitudes: An extension of Holland's typology. *Journal of Employment Counseling, 21,* 162-167.

Rounds, J. B. (1985). Vocational Preference Inventory. In J. V. Mitchell, Jr. (Ed.), *The ninth mental measurements yearbook,* (pp. 1683-1684). Lincoln, NE: The Buros Institute of Mental Measurements.

Vacc, N. A., & Pickering, J. (1985). Vocational Preference Inventory. In J. V. Mitchell, Jr. (Ed.), *The ninth mental measurements yearbook* (pp. 1684-1685). Lincoln, NE: The Buros Institute of Mental Measurements.

Nu Viet Vu, Ph.D.
Associate Professor, Medical Education, Southern Illinois University School of Medicine, Springfield, Illinois.

WACHS ANALYSIS OF COGNITIVE STRUCTURES
Harry Wachs and Lawrence J. Vaughn. Los Angeles, California: Western Psychological Services.

Introduction

The Wachs Analysis of Cognitive Structures (WACS) test consists of a series of sensory-based and body movement tasks designed to assess different aspects and levels of cognitive development in preschool children. These tasks require the children's intelligent use of their vision, hearing, and motor coordination in order to identify, reproduce, and construct concepts such as object colors, shapes, and designs, and to perform various large motor movements.

The WACS was designed by Harry Wachs, an optometrist, and Lawrence Vaughan, a specialist in testing and measurement. Most of the items presently in the WACS were derived from an earlier inventory of tasks developed by Wachs over a period of 13 years, and which had been used as a guide for designing curriculum for normal and impaired children. Up to 1971, no effort had been made to collect and develop the normative data for the inventory, nor to standardize and validate it. Such efforts were only completed in 1976.

The WACS is based on Jean Piaget's theory of knowledge acquisition and his cognitive developmental stages. Specifically, the instrument focuses on the preoperational thinking stage characterized by the child's development of symbolic thinking, and progression from a primarily sensorimotor type of thinking towards a more "operational" or theoretical one. According to the authors, during this preoperational stage (which extends from about age 2 to about age 7), thinking is not mental in the sense that we understand higher intellectual activity. Rather, it takes place in a more physical or developmental form, in reaction and instinct; "hence, it is best understood to actually be 'body and sense' thinking" (Wachs & Vaughn, 1977). This type of thinking is manifest in the child's intelligent use of his or her sensorimotor functions and is considered essential for later development of theoretical thinking. For instance, in many intellectual activities such as reading comprehension, the sensorimotor functions (e.g., visual functioning) are almost prerequisite for the child's cognitive development and acquisition of knowledge. Given the important role of the sensorimotor functions in cognitive development, the WACS was designed to assess the various levels of these functions. The present test specifically includes those tasks that are considered measurements of different levels of a child's body and sense functions, which do not stabilize until primary school age.

As a guide for developing and standardizing the original inventory, the authors have set forth seven content domain test specifications and seven criteria for selecting test items. These selection criteria dictated that the items selected should be valid, administrable by personnel without special professional training, susceptible to easy and objective scoring, and should not require lengthy administration. The process for selecting the test items consisted first of eliminating those items in the original inventory that did not meet the test domain specifications and selection criteria. This step resulted in retaining 15 of the 21 original items for further consideration and refinement. Once these items were identified, the next step in the item selection process was to review a set of test items that met the test content specifications but was not included in the original version. This process resulted in the selection of six additional tasks that are included in the inventory. The rationale behind the selection and design of each of those selected tasks is provided by the authors in the test manual.

The refined inventory was first field-tested with a group of 54 children to verify the adequacy of its administration time, determine whether differences in children's performance were a function of their age, and obtain a preliminary item analysis of the test items.

Normative data were obtained from a sample of 743 children. This sample consisted of approximately 100 children or more in each of the five-months interval age groups ranging from 3 years, 0 months, to 5 years, 11 months. (Only the group of 5 years, 6 months, to 5 years, 11 months, had a sample size of 221 children because of their availability.) Each group consisted of a near-equal sample of male and female children. Several other characteristics of the normative sample were noted: 1) the children were from three East Coast, one Midwest, and one Southern school; 2) 60% of the children were urban residents and 40% were suburban; 3) 86% were Caucasian and approximately 14% were ethnic minorities, mainly black; and 4) 85 to 90% of the children were enrolled in either public or private schools. The socioeconomic status of the children's families was not systematically examined and was estimated by the authors to be equally distributed across all levels.

For diagnostic purposes, the authors have proposed a supplemental set of evaluation tasks that would allow the examiners to do a more in-depth analysis of the child's sensorimotor functions and skills. Tasks were suggested for each of the following seven functions: Discriminative Ocular movement, Discriminative Digital movement, Discriminative Tongue movement, Rhythm, Auditory Thinking, Receptive Language Processing, and Logical Reasoning. For each function, the authors describe how to assess them, their relative importance to the child's cognitive development, and the respective performance observed for each age group. Given the complexity of the assessed functions and skills and the unavailability of standard norms and scoring criteria, the authors caution examiners to have a good understanding of the developmental aspects of those functions and skills before they use the supplementary tasks for diagnostic purposes.

The WACS is designed to assess a child's stage of development in various selected body-and-sense thinking tasks. The purpose of the test is to evaluate not only the external manifestation of the child's action, but to derive from it the developmental level of the cognitive scheme underlying that action. The test is mainly nonverbal, can be administered in 30 to 45 minutes, and is designed for children 3 to 6 years of age. The WACS is individually administered and consists mainly of one-on-one interactions between the examiner and the child. The test package comes with a manual, all the necessary equipment required for each test item, and individual record booklets and profile sheets for recording, scoring, and interpreting observed performance.

In general, the test is organized so that the tasks that use the same test equipment have the same mode of response, and those that measure related behaviors are grouped together. The tasks are also ordered progressively, from the easiest to the most difficult. The test is composed of four subtests, each of which consists of several tasks. The four subtests are: Identification of Objects, Object Design, Graphic Design, and General Movement.

Identification of Objects (6 tasks/28 possible points): This subtest requires the child to do visual, auditory, and hand identification of object shapes and/or colors. These tasks are organized for data reporting purposes into three item clusters: Color Identification (2 tasks), Shape Identification (2 tasks), and Hand Thinking (2 tasks). The visual color identification task is used as a warm-up exercise and is not included in the actual scoring.

NOTE: To alleviate any possible confusion that could be created by the authors' classification of tasks by subtest, then tasks by item cluster, it should be noted that although the authors described and scored the test by subtest, they reported the test validity and reliability data by subtest and item cluster. An item cluster is a grouping of tasks within the subtest itself.

Object Design (6 tasks/38 possible points): The first task requires the child to stack square blocks on their broad side, narrow side, and in the shape of a bridge. The second task has the child duplicate six different block designs that become successively more complex in form and number. The third task requires the child to duplicate six successively complex visual patterns, which the examiner provides by placing colored pegs in a pegboard. The last three tasks require the child to match and place solid and split geometric shapes or forms into their respective slots in an empty formboard. For the split forms task, the forms are cut into two or three pieces, like a jigsaw puzzle, and the child must match them on the formboard. These six tasks are organized into five item clusters: Block Stacking (1 task), Block Design (1 task), Pegboard (1 task), Solid Formboard (1 task), and Split Formboard (2 tasks).

Graphic Design (5 tasks/48 possible points): In the first two tasks, the child is required to draw various shapes or graphic operations from verbal instructions, then from visually presented pictures. In the third task, the child is asked to perform a series of graphic operations such as drawing between lines, tracing lines, connecting dots, tracing along templates, and drawing a person. In the last two tasks, the child is asked to reproduce eight geometric patterns by using four sticks. One type of reproduction is directly made on the presented patterns, and the other requires the child to duplicate the patterns separately from the pattern model. These five tasks are organized into five item clusters: Form Reproduction (1 task), Form Copy (1 task), Graphic Control (1 task), Sticks-on (1 task), and Sticks-off (1 task).

General Movement (7 tasks/28 possible points): In the first two tasks, the child is required to move parts of his or her body individually or simultaneously in response to the examiner's touch. The last five tasks require the child to integrate body movement in imitation of the examiner: balancing on one foot, hopping forward and backward, skipping, catching a ball, walking on a line, and walking crisscross on each side of a line. These seven tasks are organized into two item clusters: Body Lifts (2 tasks) and Balance (5 tasks).

Performance is observed and directly recorded and scored by the examiner in the record booklet. The performance is then summarized on the profile sheet. This sheet reports the child's performance on the four subtests in terms of percentile ranks, and "Clinical Age Expecteds" within his or her chronological age group. If the WACS is administered repeatedly to a child at different chronological ages, his or her performance can also be assessed and charted in terms of individual progress and development on the Profile Sheet.

Practical Applications/Uses

It takes approximately one hour to administer and score the WACS for each examinee. One of the attractive aspects of the test is that its exercises include objects that are familiar to children and are similar to the kinds of activities used in most preschool programs. The added advantage in using the WACS is that its exercises or activities are standardized, so that the teacher's assessment and evaluation of a child's performance can be made readily and objectively.

By definition the WACS is used to assess a child's level of readiness in sensorimotor functioning, which is considered necessary for the effective development of cognitive functioning. From that perspective, and given the types of sensorimotor functioning included in the WACS, the test is most informative and useful when used with children between the ages of 3 years, 0 months, and 4 years, 5 months, as most older children (as shown by the normative data) have already acquired those sensorimotor functions.

Although the WACS was designed to be administered to English-speaking children between ages 3 and 6, the instrument was also tried out with small samples of children in non-Western cultures and to small groups of deaf, mentally impaired, and non-English-speaking immigrant children. The method of administration varied for these latter groups. While some groups were not administered the tasks that required use of language labels, others received the entire test; one group had the test administered in its native language and others had their test mimed or signed. Although the use of mime in place of verbal instructions appears to be a viable alternative in nontypical situations, it needs to be further standardized and verified—making any bias in the observed performance less possible. Overall comparisons of the subjects' mean performance obtained on the translated WACS (e.g., Labrador Indians) with the mean performance obtained on a comparable English-speaking group (in this case the test-retest sample) indicate that the two means are about the same. This suggests that translating the WACS may be a more viable alternative for its administration than miming it: the observed performance can be more readily compared and assessed in terms of cultural differences alone than in terms of both cultural and language differences.

The conditions for appropriate administration of the test are outlined in the test manual. These consist of the importance of giving the test activities in the specified order, setting the testing room to allow maximum comfort and to avoid all distracting factors, and building a good, nonthreatening rapport with the child. The authors' specific directions on what to do when a child fails to respond to the first item of a task or obviously does not understand the verbal instructions are very helpful to the test administrator in readjusting the test administration. Overall, the directions for administering the test are detailed and clear, but there are a few exceptions. The authors' suggestions on using the "basic line approach" in administering the test are not quite clear because they do not indicate which activities they consider to be the "simplest" and can be omitted from the test when it is administered to the older children. The other part that is not clear involves the description of the materials used for the color and shape identification tasks. If the test administrator tries to read the directions for administering the test without the test materials (e.g., blocks) available, it is difficult to determine whether the colored blocks are of the same shape or whether the blocks of various shapes are also of the same color. This is an important aspect to specify because it could create confounding factors in the test administration. If, in the shape identification task, each shape has different colors, the child could match the block by color rather than by shape. Finally, it is not clear in the formboard matching task whether the performance of a child who matches by trial-and-error should be scored as a failure or as an acceptable performance.

The WACS scores consist of four subtest scores, each of which is the sum of the scores of all the tasks within that subtest. For most subtests (I, II, and IV), the child's performance can be recorded and readily hand-scored during test administration. For Subtest III, which consists of reproducing graphic designs, the authors have provided helpful examples and criteria of what is considered an acceptable or unacceptable performance or reproduction. The reasons that underlie those scoring criteria should be further explained in order to facilitate the scoring of reproductions that are not represented on the provided examples.

For test score interpretation, the raw scores on each of the four WACS subtests are converted into their corresponding standard scores (with a mean of 50 and standard deviation of 10) and percentile ranks. Children's total performance on the test is expressed in terms of a subtest average standard score and its corresponding percentile rank. Using the provided norm tables, children's standard score and percentile rank on each of the subtests and on the total test can be interpreted and compared to performance of children in the same age category. A child's functioning level can also be interpreted in terms of "Clinical Age Expected" or the developmental age corresponding to the child's level of functioning. So, for example, the Clinical Age Expected on a subtest for a 4 years-0 month child could be 4 years and 8 months; this can be interpreted that his development is 8 months more than expected. It is not clear from the test manual whether the data the authors use to develop the range of Clinical Age Expecteds are based on the normative sample or whether they are derived from common observations and experiences working with children.

Although the authors have suggested that in-depth study of the individual item cluster scores can allow the examiner to diagnose the child's strengths and weaknesses and to plan the curriculum accordingly, no concrete or direct suggestions are provided; the test examiner is referred instead to the text *Thinking Goes to School*

Wachs Analysis of Cognitive Structures

by Furth and Wachs (1974). As the most important use of the WACS is to plan appropriate curriculum, it is unfortunate that the authors do not specify those curriculum activities that would assist the child in developing functions on which he or she has scored low.

Technical Aspects

Findings obtained from the WACS reliability and validity studies are presented in the test manual. Reported reliability data include internal consistency, test-retest reliability, interrater scoring reliability, and standard error of raw score means.

Based on the norming sample, the internal consistency reliabilities for both the total test and each of the item clusters are relatively satisfactory. Although the authors' use of Cronbach's alpha coefficient and the communality values (derived from the principal component analysis) is appropriate to determine the internal consistency of the total test and the item clusters respectively, the advantages of using the item communality values (i.e., proportion of common factor variance) over the Cronbach's alpha index to calculate the reliability of the item clusters are neither evident nor explained. Furthermore, interpretation of the reliabilities of the item clusters is difficult because it is not clear from the table and from the provided description whether the common factor that is used to obtain the communality values is the total test or the subtest scores. If the common factor used for the item cluster reliability is the subtest, then the authors should calculate the internal consistency for individual subtests rather than for the item cluster; the subtest internal consistency indexes are more meaningful because the score results and other reliability data are reported by subtests instead of by item clusters.

The test-retest reliabilities, which were obtained by administering and re-administering the WACS within 10 to 14 days to 64 children, ranged from .76 to .96 for the four subtests and the total test. The relatively high interrater reliability ($r=.942$) is based on a very small sample of raters ($n=2$) and subjects ($n=10$) and needs to be further verified with a larger sample. Finally, although the authors used the standard error of raw score means as an index of test reliability, these results could also be considered and interpreted as evidence of construct validity because the standard errors were found to decrease with the higher age groups.

The obtained validity data for the WACS include data on its content, concurrent, predictive, and construct validities. Because the provided description of the various sensorimotor functions assessed in the WACS and how they may affect children's development and cognitive functioning is general and global in nature, the validity data and obtained evidence reflect that same nature. For example, to assess the test content validity, the authors' review of the literature on sensorimotor functions only indicated that in general these functions are found to be related to "deficits in development," or children's "concept development," "concept formation," and "general development" (Wachs & Vaughn, 1971). It has never been clear how these functions specifically could influence the cognitive activities and which activities could be more affected than others.

Similar generality in the findings is also found in the predictive validity studies. For example, the children's sensorimotor functions were found to have moderate to minimal correlations with the teachers' ratings of their overall performance on language arts, mathematics, and general orientation. Finally, evidence from the factor analysis in the construct validity study suggested that the WACS mainly assesses a general sensorimotor functioning. This functioning is basically represented by one general factor on which 13 of the 15 item clusters loaded.

Overall, the evidence reported by the authors on the content, concurrent, predictive, and construct validities are relatively adequate and appropriate. Furthermore, better understanding and interpretation of the results obtained for the predictive validity study can be achieved if the authors would elaborate on the used rating method, the specific number of ratings obtained per child, and the index of the observed interrater reliability. Similarly, the authors should have described in more detail the tests (e.g., McCarthy Scale of Children's Abilities and Wechsler Preschool and Primary Scale of Intelligence) that they selected to use to establish the WACS concurrent validity. Absence of these descriptions makes the interpretations of the correlations obtained between these tests and the WACS hard to interpret.

Critique

The WACS is not widely used, and it is therefore difficult to assess its value. Published studies reporting the use of the instrument are not available. However, the instrument is valued for its ability to identify "children who will be under stress as a result of being placed in kindergarten or first grade before they are psychologically and/or physiologically ready" (C. Sweeney, personal communications, 1985).

Overall the WACS appears to be a good test that can be used to assess children's readiness for preschool, because the sensorimotor functions that are assessed are commonly used and emphasized in most Western preschool and kindergarten programs. The test is more useful and informative when used with children 3 to 4 years old rather than with older children, because most older children have already acquired those functions. In general, the administration, scoring, and interpretation of the test results are simple and do not require special training. With a few exceptions, the authors' directions for the test administration and scoring are clear, and the provided validity and reliability data are adequate.

References

Furth, H. G., & Wachs, H. (1974). *Thinking goes to school*. New York: Oxford University Press.
Wachs, H., & Vaughan, L. J. (1977). *Wachs Analysis of Cognitive Structures—Manual*. Los Angeles: Western Psychological Services.

G. Cynthia Fekken, Ph.D.
Assistant Professor of Psychology, Queen's University, Kingston, Canada.

WELSH FIGURE PREFERENCE TEST

George Welsh. *Palo Alto, California: Consulting Psychologists Press, Inc.*

Introduction

The Welsh Figure Preference Test (WFPT) is a nonverbal, objectively scored measure of personality designed for respondents who are not amenable to testing with conventional personality inventories. The 400 black-and-white stimulus figures comprising the WFPT have been combined into scales that assess dimensions relevant to clinical work and research as well as scales relevant to creativity and originality. Although the WFPT was originally designed to measure psychiatric disorders, it has also become well known for its scale of aesthetic judgment, namely, the Barron-Welsh Art Scale (BWAS).

In his preface to the 1980 manual, George Welsh describes three key influences on his development of the WFPT. The first was his awareness of the need for a language-independent personality instrument, which Welsh realized during his clinical involvement with foreign POWs immediately after the Second World War. Second, the increasing popularity of the MMPI at that time underlined the merits of objective test scoring. Finally, the empirical strategy of scale construction provided the theoretical underpinnings for using nonverbal stimuli as the basis for a personality test. That is, the empirical approach to test construction de-emphasizes specific test item content, focusing instead on the ability of items to discriminate among given diagnostic categories. Thus, scales are built from items that elicit significantly different response patterns from individuals identified with one or another distinct psychiatric disorder. Undiagnosed patients are subsequently categorized on the basis of the similarity of their scale scores to those of the known groups.

In the context of his doctoral dissertation project in the late 1940s, Welsh selected 200 freehand and ruled figures to serve as the items for a test of psychopathology. The items were drawn in india ink on 3"x5" white cards. The respondent's task was to sort the cards into "like" and "dislike" piles. Subsequently, the pool of items on the WFPT has been expanded to 400. These items differ on such dimensions as complexity, symmetry, angularity, and shading, ranging from triangles or squares to figures containing many lines of varying thickness and shades. The format of the current version of the WFPT is a reusable booklet accompanied by a separate answer sheet with numbered spaces for "like" or "dislike" responses. General directions for responding to the WFPT are printed in the booklet, although it would be quite appropriate for the examiner to explain the instructions and the task involved. Similarly, directions for using the answer sheet are given at the top of the answer page. The answer sheet has a rather crowded appearance, in part because of the limited area reserved for recording over 30 WFPT scale scores. No independent profile sheet is available.

Practical Applications/Uses

The constructs measured by the WFPT scales are related to various psychopathological dimensions (e.g., anxiety, repression, overall adjustment, intellectual efficiency, etc.) as well as to nonpsychopathological dimensions (e.g., femininity, creativity, childlike preferences, etc.). The scales designed to measure these constructs were derived according to either an empirical or a rational approach. Empirical scales were constructed from items showing differential endorsement rates for contrasted groups, such as men and women, or neuropsychiatric patients and nonhospitalized adults. Rational scales combine items using a priori criteria (i.e., the formal, structural properties of the items or the judgment of experts that certain items reflect a particular domain).

The meaning of the WFPT empirical and rational scale scores was further elucidated from intercorrelations with other psychological instruments, most notably the MMPI, the California Psychological Inventory, and Terman's (1956) Concepts Mastery Test. The construct validity of the BWAS and of the Revised Art Scale (RAS) was examined in various independent studies of creativity and originality. In addition to substantive scales, the WFPT contains "validating" scales that bear on the respondent's test-taking attitude. The Dislike scale is the total number of items placed in the dislike category, and a high score in this category may be related to careless responding, maladjustment, or nonconformity. A measure of individual response consistency is afforded by the Repeat scale, which is comprised of 20 repeated items. Finally, four measures of conformance, which assess the similarity of the responses to the preference consensus of normative groups, are available.

Due to the popularity of the Barron-Welsh Art Scale and its alternate, the Revised Art Scale, the particular items comprising these two scales are made available in a separate test booklet. The WFPT manual provides keys for scoring the BWAS and the RAS, both from the context of the entire 400-item WFPT and from the context of the 86-item booklet. Three attendant problems make use of the reusable booklet somewhat convoluted. First, the test item booklet is labeled "Barron-Welsh Art Scale," although it contains Revised Art Scale items as well. This is not necessarily clear to the novice test user. Second, the answer sheet described earlier bears the dual title "Welsh Figure Preference Test or Barron-Welsh Art Scale." The first 86 response places on the answer sheet may be employed with the shortened item set and the remaining 314 places left blank. This makeshift strategy can be confusing and could lead to careless responding errors. A distinct 86-item answer sheet would seem highly preferable. Third, the WFPT manual describes the Art Scales, but no single chapter is clearly and explicitly devoted to them. The reader must skip from section to section of the manual to gather relevant information. Further, the coverage of empirical literature on the Arts Scales is cursory because an extensive review is published elsewhere (i.e., Welsh, 1975). Collating all the Art Scale material into a single chapter or a complementary manual would make the information on this popular subtest more readily accessible.

The administration of the WFPT is straightforward and the role of the examiner is usually minimal. Clear directions for responding make the test essentially self-administering. The difficulty level of the WFPT is quite low because no verbal response is required and the task is inherently simple. Thus, the WFPT is applicable to a wide variety of respondents. Besides adults, the WFPT may be used with children, mentally retarded individuals, non-English-speaking or illiterate persons, and deaf or mute persons. The examiner may read or translate the instructions and may record responses or adapt the test back to a card-sorting format if necessary. Few populations are totally unamenable to testing with the WFPT, the obvious exceptions being the visually or perceptually handicapped.

The WFPT has potential applicability in clinical settings, in educational and vocational counseling centers, and in research programs. The psychopathological constructs measured by the WFPT have the greatest relevance to psychiatric assessment. The nonverbal WFPT may provide an alternative format for testing individuals who are unable to respond to verbal tests because of language or intellectual barriers or because depression or infirmity prevent maintainance of the required attention. The WFPT may be uniquely suited for use in schools or treatment centers for the developmentally handicapped or hearing impaired, or in clinics drawing minority language or illiterate clients. The major educational uses of the WFPT are related to the creativity indices, especially the BWAS and RAS. These Art Scales may identify gifted or nongifted students in need of specialized training or they may be used to evaluate the outcome of a special education program. The vocational counseling role is derived from the ability of the Art Scales to classify creative versus noncreative persons within an occupation. To the extent that success in certain occupations depends on creativity, the BWAS and RAS may provide one piece of data in an assessment package about the suitability of an individual for an occupation.

Welsh (1980) divided the research studies utilizing the WFPT into those that emphasize the constructs underlying the scales and those that focus on the stimulus items. The first research approach involves intercorrelating WFPT scales with other measures in order to elucidate the scales' meaning. For example, the creativity indices have been related to intelligence, personality characteristics such as personal complexity, social attitudes, and to numerous indices of artistic merit or judgment. The second research approach involves factor analyzing the WFPT items for divergent samples to explicate their underlying structure. Largely due to their nonverbal nature, the WFPT items have also been employed in research on general response strategies (Sechrest & Jackson, 1962) and on role playing (Kroger & Turnbull, 1970). Similarly, the stimulus figures on the WFPT have been adapted for studies of perception, cognition, and memory. Other research applications might include investigating the verbal/nonverbal distinction in personality testing and cross-cultural personality comparisons.

Professionals who might employ the entire WFPT include clinical psychologists, psychiatrists, and researchers studying psychopathology, anthropology, sociology, or cross-cultural psychology. For educators, program evaluators, and vocational counselors interested in assessing creativity, the Art Scales on the WFPT may be useful. Administration of the WFPT does not require professional training. Any responsible person can be taught to administer the test in either an individual or group format. No special facilities are required for presenting the WFPT other than a reasonably quiet locale.

The manual outlines the WFPT administration procedure clearly, even indicating where the examiner may wish to make minor modifications. Questions likely to be asked of the administrator are noted, as are strategies for responding to them. Ordinarily, WFPT administration should not take more than 40 to 50 minutes. The professional user should be able to master scoring within two hours. Presentation of the scoring in the manual is not always straightforward. For example, some scoring information is described in the section entitled "Scale Descriptions," some in "Lists of Scored Item Responses by Scale," and still other scoring data are contained in special tables. (A little redundancy in the manual would be useful in this regard.)

Actual calculation of scale scores involves counting those item responses that correspond to the scale key. Handscoring may be conducted at the clerical level and could require up to one hour to complete, particularly if all 30 scales are scored. To facilitate scoring, the author recommends constructing templates from unused answer sheets or writing a computer program. No scoring services are currently offered by either the test developer or publisher.

Interpretation of the WFPT results is based on objective data (i.e., standard scores). Reprinted in the manual appendix are tables of T-scores and percentiles derived from general norms. These tables provide data for the 10 WFPT scales meant to encompass the main sources of test variance. The test interpreter may also calculate standard scores for other scales from the normative information reported for numerous and diverse subject groups. With the exception of the creativity indices, no formal construct definitions are associated with the scales. Rather, interpretation is guided by a description of the scale derivation and its intercorrelations and by representative case histories. To illustrate, consider the FM scale, which was constructed to differentiate between female and male respondents. Empirical results supporting the scale's discriminating power are provided. The nature of the construct tapped by the FM items is elucidated by intercorrelations with demographic information (e.g., age and education), with other WFPT scales (e.g., creativity indices), and with published measures of masculinity-femininity and intelligence tests. In addition, a series of illustrative cases are presented to exemplify which personality characteristics may be inferred from the basic 10-scale profile, which includes the FM scale. Six cases involve psychiatric patients and four concern the profiles of professionals who have obtained differential standing on the creativity indices.

Interpretation of WFPT results requires formal training in psychological testing. Psychologists, psychiatrists, psychometrists, and educators are best qualified to offer interpretations of WFPT results for the following reasons. First, the interpreter must be well versed in the use and calculation of standard scores. (Provision of relevant statistical formulae for converting raw to standard scores and some examples would have been a handy and practical addition to the manual.) Second, the interpreter must be able to select the appropriate normative group against which to make individual comparisons. For example, 46 and 52 sets of normative data are provided for the Barron-Welsh Art Scale and the Revised Art Scale, respectively. No explicit guidelines exist for selecting the appropriate comparison group or for dealing with potential interpretive confounds, such as age and sex differences. Finally, interpreting the WFPT scales depends to a large extent on familiarity with other psychological instruments. The manual makes numerous references to Rorschach scoring categories, MMPI and CPI scales, various intelligence tests, and so on. Broad knowledge of the research literature on the WFPT scales, which in the case of the Art Scales is extensive, would be an important aspect for understanding the underlying constructs.

Technical Aspects

Reliability studies of the WFPT have emphasized test-retest stability rather than internal consistency per se. Scale homogeneity is viewed as a matter of secondary importance within the empirical test construction strategy, which focuses primarily on a scale's ability to predict relevant criteria. Welsh (1980) reports stability data for a sample of 32 adolescents who were retested after a one-year interval. Test-retest coefficients for eight of the 10 basic profile scales plus the Revised Art Scale range from .29 to .79. The lower values may be due to restriction of range in the scale scores or due to genuine change, notes Welsh (1980, p. 45). Previous research (cf. Welsh, 1959) found higher test-retest correlations for the same scales, albeit over a shorter time period. The manual also provides anecdotal information on the stability of the 10 basic scales in the form of specific test and retest scores for four individuals retested after intervals of up to 22 years. Although the manual data are promising, it would be misleading to conclude that the test-retest stability of the 30 or more WFPT scales has been demonstrated.

The Art Scales form a clear exception to the foregoing rule: empirical data strongly indicate that the Art Scales show adequate stability. The 6-month test-retest stability of the BWAS was estimated at .91 and .75 for patients in psychotherapy and for college students, respectively (Welsh, 1975). RAS reliability coefficients over .90 were obtained in a study in which scores were derived from a 40-item card sort version and from a shortened 144-item booklet version of the WFPT. The two versions were administered in counterbalanced order to groups of students, one week apart. Similarly, test-retest correlations, based on RAS scores derived from a paired comparison format completed several weeks apart, were .75 for two independent student samples (Welsh, 1975).

Despite Welsh's (1980) argument to the contrary, the internal consistency of the WFPT scales demands evaluation if individual differences in scale scores are to be meaningfully interpreted. Limited data regarding scale homogeneity are available. The odd/even split-half reliability of the BWAS was found to be .96 for 80 nonartists (Barron & Welsh, 1952). A .96 index of internal consistency was also associated with respondents' tendency to "like" or "dislike" the WFPT items, supporting the internal consistency of the Dislike scale. Alternatively, this index may indicate the pervasiveness of a general stylistic determinant of responding. Finally, properties of the stimulus items, such as complexity or endorsement probability, show strong consistency across the 20 repeated items on the WFPT. Welsh (1980, p. 47) claims that this information bears on the internal consistency of the RP scale. However, internal consistency is commonly defined in terms of item response cohesiveness, whereas these data indicate that ratings of item characteristics are stable. Overall, the internal consistency of the WFPT is inadequately researched. Scales, including empirically derived scales, must manifest adequate homogeneity if differences in individual scores are to be explicated in terms of an underlying construct.

An issue of particular interest in the context of the nonverbal WFPT concerns its underlying structure. Will WFPT scales cluster in a fashion similar to verbal measures of psychopathology? How will creativity indices be related to scales reflecting psychiatric dysfunctioning? No scale intercorrelation matrix is provided in the manual (Welsh, 1980). Rather, the reader is presented with an overview of a series of factor analyses designed to uncover the underlying structure of the WFPT. The first analysis was based on 15 rationally constructed scales, derived from the responses of 61 psychiatric patients to the original 200-item card sort version. Other analyses were based on scale scores calculated from the 400-item version. The intercorrelations among 29 scales were analyzed separately for 528 male adolescents and for 628 female adolescents. Forty-six scale scores were examined for 54 Chamber of Commerce managers, as were 32 scale scores for 114 hospitalized psychiatric patients.

Factor analytic techniques are entirely appropriate for evaluating test dimensionality; unfortunately, so many problems plague the report of these analyses that little information of use can be derived. First, WFPT scales show substantial item overlap, which violates one of the basic assumptions of factor analysis. At the very least, this difficulty must be acknowledged when offering factor interpretations. Second, the ratio of subjects to variables is totally inadequate in the Chamber of Commerce managers analysis, and questionable in the case of the original 15-scale analysis. Third, a description of the factor analytic methods employed is entirely lacking. No mention is made regarding what was placed in the diagonal of the correlation matrix, the criterion for factor extraction, the percentage of variance accounted for by the solution, or whether factors were rotated to maximize interpretability. Finally, the lists of factor loadings reprinted in the manual have been abbreviated, apparently to include only those loadings for salient scales. The strategy guiding this abbreviation procedure is never detailed. In the absence of complete factor loading data, Welsh's (1980) discussion of the comparability of solutions across samples is extremely difficult to evaluate.

Evaluation of WFPT validity requires a discussion of potential response style confounds. One obvious stylistic confound for the WFPT scales might be a general tendency to "like" or "dislike" all items. Such a response style would distort scores on scales that are not balanced with regard to the number of keyed "like" and "dislike" responses. In fact, the majority of scales on the WFPT have substantially different numbers of items keyed "like" and "dislike." For example, responding "dislike" to all items on the BWAS will yield a score near the mean score for artists. Similarly, Van de Castle (1962) reports a .78 correlation between an unbalanced version of the Perceptual Maturity Scale and the number of dislike responses. Welsh (1980) argues that most respondents do not show evidence of extreme stylistic responding, as indexed by the DL (or Dislike) validity scale. At least one scale, the Revised Art Scale, which has been balanced in terms of "like" and "dislike" items, shows a correlation over .90 with the original BWAS. There are no obvious sex differences in the tendency to dislike items, nor are scores on the DL Scale related to intelligence. On the other hand, extreme groups on the DL scale may make more careless errors or may have an atypical pattern of responding as evidenced by a somewhat elevated MMPI profile.

By far the most extensively validated scales are those measuring creativity and originality, especially the BWAS and the RAS. Fekken (1985) concluded that the Art Scales are indeed able to discriminate between criterion groups, such as artists and nonartists, or persons designated as creative and noncreative within an occupation. Nonetheless, individual predictive accuracy appears to be relatively low. The Art Scales have demonstrated adequate empirical divergence from irrelevant measures (e.g., intelligence tests), but show little convergence for other standardized creativity measures. Attempts have been made to explicate the construct underlying the Art Scales by proposing various theoretical paradigms. Barron (1952, 1953) related high scores to preference for complexity, interpreting both as indicative of a single personality style. However, Ridley (1977) and Moyles, Tuddenham, and Block (1965) have questioned whether the relevant stimulus property is complexity or another dimension, such as asymmetry or communicability. Welsh (1975) developed a personality typology that incorporated originality, intelligence, and personality style. Although promising, this model has not yet been subjected to extensive empirical study.

The scales comprising the basic WFPT profile have also been studied empirically. For example, the ability of the FM scale to discriminate between males and females has been demonstrated in various studies. Similarly, scores on the movement scale, made up of items judged relevant to the Rorschach "movement" concept, have been correlated with Rorschach movement scores in two independent studies (Welsh, 1980). Rational scales, such as the Figure-ground, Black shading, and Cross-hatched lines scales, were constructed from items sharing formal characteristics and obviously require no cross-replication. More important, though, is the task of cross-validating the scales' interpretations. Because the items have no inherent psychological meaning or necessary relationship to the construct they tap, Welsh (1980) derived scale labels and descriptions from patterns of intercorrelations with other, validated scales.

Generally, scale interpretations were based on six to 10 reasonably large samples differing in age, sex, intellectual ability, and psychiatric standing. Welsh (1980) then integrated the data from the various samples and criterion questionnaires to elucidate the construct underlying the scale. Such a strategy for validating the scales might be convincing, except that few actual correlations are reported in the manual. Rather, extreme groups on a particular WFPT scale have their scores on a series of MMPF or CPI scales compared. For example, 17 students scoring between 42 and 49 on the MV scale had significantly higher IQ test scores than 16 subjects scoring between 18 and 25 on the MV scales. These extreme groups were drawn from a sample of approximately 400 high school students (Watson, 1963, as cited in Welsh, 1980). This approach is problematic if one wishes to interpret middle scores on the WFPT scale. Further, the specific findings vis-à-vis the sample and the particular criterion tests are never replicated. A study with regular high school students indicates that high MV scores are associated with certain CPI scores, and another study with gifted adolescents gives evidence that high MV scores are related to MMPI depression and hypochondriasis.

The extent to which these disparate findings replicate is not addressed. An additional concern is the lack of study of the validity of various score configurations across all 10 basic profile scales. The modest data available on the profile scales, in combination with the absence of any systematic evaluation of the remaining 20 WFPT scales, yield the conclusion that evidence for the validity of the WFPT is not persuasive.

Critique

Developing a nonverbal measure of personality is both interesting and useful. Potentially, the WFPT could constitute an easily administered, objectively scored, standardized measure of psychiatric disorders to be employed with individuals not amenable to more conventional personality inventories. The normative data provided for the WFPT are generally more than adequate. Unfortunately, other than for the Art Scales, there are few data available bearing on the reliability and validity of the WFPT scales. The most plausible reason for this is the extensive empirical research required to elucidate the nature of the concept reflected in scales comprised of items without inherent meaning. WFPT scale composition must be cross-replicated and extended to other relevant, contrasted groups. The scales must be correlated with previously validated scales and cross-validated, and they must fit into an appropriate nomological network. These are simply the general criteria for establishing the construct validity of a test, but the process is complicated for WFPT scales by the absence of clearly explicated constructs to guide the process. The entire validation procedure might be expected to entail considerable trial and error, because fortuitous findings (i.e., those that fail to cross-replicate) become misleading avenues for further research.

Test development strategies that have evolved since the original conceptualization of the WFP have placed strong emphasis on the construct tapped by a scale. Generally, the more modern strategies have incorporated both empirical criteria and theoretical construct definitions. When applied to verbal stimuli, construct-oriented approaches tend to yield more valid tests than strictly empirical approaches (Broughton, 1984; Jackson, 1975). Furthermore, adapting the strategy to nonverbal stimuli shows highly encouraging results. In one study, nonverbal items were designed to be meaningfully related to the construct. For example, a stick figure climbing a mountain reflected a thrill-seeking dimension. Subjects rated the descriptive accuracy of the items for a target. Theoretically related items showed internal consistency and predictive validity for criteria defined a priori (Paunonen & Jackson, 1979). These findings would argue that the blind empiricism that characterized the WFPT development is by no means a necessary concomitant of constructing nonverbal personality inventories.

References

Barron, F. (1952). Personality style and perceptual choice. *Journal of Personality, 20*, 385-401.
Barron, F. (1953). Complexity-simplicity as a personality dimension. *Journal of Abnormal and Social Psychology, 48*, 162-172.
Barron, F., & Welsh, G. S. (1952). Artistic perception as a factor in personality style: Its measurement by a figure-preference test. *Journal of Psychology, 33*, 199-203.

Broughton, R. (1984). A prototype strategy for the construction of personality scales. *Journal of Personality and Social Psychology, 47,* 1334-1346.

Fekken, G. C. (1986). Barron-Welsh Art Scale. In D. J. Keyser & R. C. Sweetland (Eds.), *Test Critiques: Volume IV* (pp. 59-67). Kansas City: Test Corporation of America.

Jackson, D. N. (1975). The relative validity of scales prepared by naive item writers and those based on empirical methods of personality scale construction. *Educational and Psychological Measurement, 35,* 361-370.

Kroger, R. O., & Turnbull, W. (1970). Effects of role demands and test-cue properties on personality test performance: Replication and extension. *Journal of Consulting and Clinical Psychology, 35,* 381-387.

Moyles, E. W., Tuddenham, R. D., & Block, J. (1965). Simplicity/Complexity or Symmetry/Asymmetry? A re-analysis of the Barron-Welsh Art Scales. *Perceptual and Motor Skills, 20,* 685-690.

Paunonen, S. V., & Jackson, D. N. (1979). Nonverbal trait inference. *Journal of Personality and Social Psychology, 37,* 1645-1659.

Ridley, D. R. (1979). Barron-Welsh scores and creativity: A second look. *Perceptual and Motor Skills, 49,* 756-758.

Sechrest, L., & Jackson, D. N. (1962). The generality of deviant response tendencies. *Journal of Consulting Psychology, 26,* 395-401.

Terman, L. M. (1956). *Manual, The Concept Mastery Test.* New York: The Psychological Corporation.

Van de Castle, R. L. (1962). Perceptual immaturity and acquiescence among various developmental levels. *Journal of Consulting Psychology, 26,* 167-171.

Welsh, G. S. (1959). *Preliminary manual: The Welsh Figure Preference Test* (research ed.). Palo Alto, CA: Consulting Psychologists Press.

Welsh, G. S. (1975). *Creativity and intelligence: A personality approach.* Chapel Hill, NC: Institute for Research in Social Science.

Welsh, G. S. (1980). *Manual: Welsh Figure Preference Test.* Palo Alto, CA: Consulting Psychologists Press.

Linda Mezydlo Subich, Ph.D.
Assistant Professor of Psychology, The University of Akron, Akron, Ohio.

WORK INTEREST INDEX
M.E. Baehr, R. Renck, R.K. Burns, and R.W. Pranis. Park Ridge, Illinois: London House Press.

Introduction

The Work Interest Index (WII) was developed to assess in a nonverbal fashion the relative strength of an individual's work interests in 12 areas. It also provides scores for examinees' variability of interests and the aspiration level of their work interests. This brief and pictorial interest test is easily administered and scored and is recommended by its authors for a variety of personnel, counseling, and guidance uses.

Melany E. Baehr, Ph.D., Richard Renck, Ph.D., and Robert K. Burns, Ph.D., of the Industrial Relations Center of the University of Chicago, built on the work of William Cottle (1950) in their construction of the WII in order to fill the need for a nonverbal occupational interest test. Cottle had identified what he believed were five bipolar interest factors that explained the underlying dimensions of the Kuder and Strong interest tests.

Baehr and her colleages used this premise in an analysis of 4,000 jobs for the U.S. Employment Service (1956). They classified each job by the two most relevant of Cottle's 10 possible job interest factors. They then noted that, of the 45 possible combinations of factor pairs, many were either antithetical or rare. Consequently, they chose 14 pairs of interests for inclusion in the initial form of the WII.

In developing scales for the original WII's 14 occupational interest combinations, 10 items were chosen for each proposed combination. The items were pictorial representations of some fundamental aspect of a job that involved the relevant interests. The black-and-white line drawings were judged by a 10-member panel for their pictorial adequacy and clarity.

These 14 scales and 140 items comprised the original WII, but were later reduced to 12 scales of 8 items (for a total of 96 items) through factor analytic techniques. These 96 items comprise the currently published version of the WII that was recently reprinted in 1980. A manual and normative data were published by Baehr, Renck, Burns, and Pranis in 1965. The 1965 norm group included 674 industrial personnel such as salesmen, foremen, executives, and government auditor supervisors. Since 1965, however, there have been no further revisions and little if any work on the WII by its authors or anyone else.

The WII is a seven-page booklet that may be used with or without a separate answer sheet. The first page provides space for demographic information and includes the directions for completing the inventory; the other six contain a total of 96 pictures arranged in four rows and columns on each page. The pictures are all black-and-white line drawings of a man engaged in some sort of work activity. The principal figure is usually highlighted with shading and may be working with things, people, or both. Each picture is numbered and includes two boxes in the lower right-hand corner marked "L" (like) and "D" (dislike) for respondents to indicate their interest in the activity pictured.

Scoring sheets are required for those administrations during which subjects mark their responses in the test booklet. These sheets are one page and subjects' responses must be transferred onto them. They provide a means of organizing responses for calculation of raw scores for the 12 factors and two other special scores. Although test directions indicate that separate answer sheets may be used, no mention of them is made in the manual. Standard score profiles are also discussed in the manual but profile sheets evidently do not exist and must be user-constructed.

The WII is primarily self-administered, with the examiner's role limited to distribution and collection of materials and the reading of directions. It is intended for anyone in the seventh grade or older who has the minimal language skills necessary to comprehend the simple instructions.

Practical Applications/Uses

The WII purports to assess an individual's occupational interests across a broad spectrum of work areas. The 12 factor scores tap the following interests: professional and technical areas that are primarily therapeutic (f1), social and verbal tasks (f2), authority and prestige (f3), artistic and interpretive pursuits in the performance arts (f4), artistic and stylized pursuits requiring creation of a product (f5), artistic and creative pursuits that manipulate ideas (f6), technical and scientific areas (f7), clerical and routine tasks (f8), business contact situations with formalized interactions (f9), personal service and persuasive endeavors (f10), mechanical and production tasks requiring dexterity (f11), and control of massive equipment (f12). Also measured are individuals' flexibility of interest and aspiration level. Flexibility is operationally defined as variability of interests, while aspiration level is the average status score of the occupations in which one expresses interest. This latter definition was adapted by the authors of the WII from the work of Warner (1960).

Baehr et al. (1965) suggest that the WII may be used in industry by personnel officers for selection and placement. They also recommend the test to mental health and employment counselors for use with their clients' career and life planning. Finally, the WII is also suggested to be helpful in school guidance programs with students from the seventh grade upward. These varied applications appear to span most standard situations requiring information about an individual's occupational interests.

While the recommended applications of the WII would seem to indicate that it would be useful and appropriate for anyone with minimal language facility who is over the age of 12, there may be certain individuals for whom it is less appropriate. In particular, the WII may be less appropriate for persons who are unfamiliar with work settings and tasks, those who may be of minority racial and/or cultural backgrounds, and women. The latter two groups may be problematic primarily because of the white male stimulus person depicted in the test booklets and the lack of normative data on the relevance of the WII for women and minorities.

Administration of the WII is easily accomplished. Individuals or groups may take this untimed test in any available setting that allows for a quiet place to work, including the person's own home. In a business or agency setting the test may be proctored by anyone familiar with the materials and test format. The suggested format for administration is merely one of passing out booklets, requesting that subjects complete the demographic information section, reading aloud the directions and answering questions, instructing subjects to answer items as quickly as possible, and collecting materials when subjects are finished. The test should take about 15 minutes and the major skill required of the proctor may be the ability to deflect questions about what the pictures represent; the manual directions state that no interpretations of the pictures may be given and subjects should answer on the basis of what they see.

Scoring instructions are clearly presented in the manual, and again no special expertise is required for this task. Some minimal training with the scoring sheets and directions should provide enough background for a secretary or assistant to accomplish scoring of the WII. With such training it should take no more than 10 minutes to transfer a subject's responses accurately and score the protocol.

The scoring procedure requires that the 4x4 matrix of responses on each page be transferred to the scoring sheet with only the "L" responses recorded. The columns of each page's matrix are designated I, II, III, and IV on the score sheet, and for each item there is a space for the indication of an "L" response and an accompanying aspiration score that may range from 10 to 50. When all "L" responses have been transferred to the score sheet, the number of such responses in each column for each page are summed, as are the aspiration scores for these "L" responses. To obtain the 12 factor scores, the scorer then adds the "L" sums from column I of pages 2 and 3 to obtain factor 1, column II of pages 2 and 3 to obtain factor 2, column III of pages 2 and 3 to obtain factor 3, column IV of pages 2 and 3 to obtain factor 4, column I of pages 4 and 5 to obtain factor 5, etc. The sum of these raw scores provides the flexibility score, and the sum of all aspiration values for "L" responses is divided by the flexibility score to provide the mean aspiration level score for the testee. Standard scores and percentiles for all raw scores are provided in an appendix to the WII manual.

While the test booklets indicate that computer-scored answer sheets may be used, all scoring information in the manual refers to the hand-scoring method. No mention is made of whether a computerized scoring program is available commercially. However, it would seem to be a simple procedure to write such a program given the straightforward nature of the scoring system.

The major problems likely to be encountered in scoring the WII are inaccurate transfers of responses and errors in the calculations of sums. The former problem is minimized by the design of the answer sheet, which mimics the test booklet's spacing and format, while the latter may be minimized through the scorer's use of a cross-check system for all sums. Less critical, but somewhat annoying, are the absence of spaces on the score sheet for recording either the standard scores or percentiles that correspond to the raw scores and the lack of a profile sheet on which to graph the subject's standard score pattern.

Interpretation of WII results is based primarily on the subject's obtained standard scores and the associated percentiles. Interpretive procedures are therefore fairly objective and clear cut. Subjects are given information about the relative strength of their interests in the 12 factors, their aspiration level, the variability of their interests, and the ways in which these scores compare to the population sample on which the WII was normed. The manual also suggests that interest profiles should be examined, but little guidance is provided for how this may be done. In general, the WII authors recommend that interpretations take into account whether the profile is flat or well-differentiated, whether scores are elevated or depressed, what relationships exist between the subject's aspiration level and abilities, what latitude is available for matching the subject to interesting occupational areas, and what similarities there are between the subject's profile and the nine occupational group profiles provided in the manual. Basic interpretations of WII results therefore require minimal training, although experience with numerous profiles would allow for greater sophistication in recognizing common or distinctive profiles.

Technical Aspects

Neither a search of the literature nor the WII manual provide much in the way of evidence for the test's reliability and validity. It would appear that the original work done in constructing the WII and its manual is all that is available. Unfortunately, the reliability evidence for the WII is thus limited to the report of internal-consistency reliability noted in the manual. Kuder-Richardson 20 values for the 12 factor scores and the flexibility score range from .65 (for the personal service and persuasive area) to .93 (for the flexibility score), with most values in the mid .70s to .80s. While these are acceptable KR-20 values, there is certainly a need for further studies of the WII's internal-consistency reliability as well as its test-retest reliability.

Validity analyses of the WII include the factor analysis of the original 140 items (this was the analysis used to determine the final 96 items) and the analyses of variance used to examine the discriminating ability of the WII when used with nine different occupational groups. The original factor analysis resulted in the construction of 12 factors, nine of which were each made up of eight items that loaded at least .30 on their respective factor and did not load significantly on any other factor. Three factors, however, had fewer than the eight items desired per scale. Factors 2, 5, and 10 had only six, four, and four items respectively that met the required criteria. To remedy this situation, items not assigned to other factors were chosen by the authors of the WII for inclusion in factors 2, 5, and 10. These choices were made with an eye to the consistency of item content with the factor's definition. Judgments were checked by examining a correlation matrix of all 140 items, the correlations between items and the beta-weight factor scores, and the correlations between items and the unit-weight factor scores. These checks were deemed satisfactory by the WII authors to support the resultant factor structures of 2, 5, and 10, but cannot entirely compensate for the contrived construction of these three factors.

The examination of occupational groups' score patterns on the WII scales was accomplished with one-way analyses of variance for each of the 12 factor scores, with the independent variable being membership in one of the nine occupational groups. Results indicated significant differences between occupation groups for nine of the 12 factors at the .001 level and for one factor at the .05 level. Post-hoc t-tests on factor scores of the 36 possible combinations of occupational pairs for each of these 10 factors indicated that the number of significant differences in pairs ranged from 5 (for factor 5) to 23 (for factor 11). Profiles of the groups' score patterns are also provided, but without any analysis of whether the total patterns differ statistically. Once again, while these analyses of variance provide some evidence for the power of the WII to differentiate between occupational groups, it is certainly neither comprehensive nor incontestable. No examination is made, for example, of whether the factor differences between the various occupational groups are consistent with either job descriptions or any theoretical rationale.

In general, then, both the reliability and validity evidence for the WII are weak. The major deficits are the lack of test-retest data, the methodologically dated and somewhat piecemeal construction of the WII factors, the incomplete examination of how meaningfully the test differentiates between occupational groups, the lack of predictive validity studies, and the limited sample on which the test was normed.

The norming sample data were obtained prior to 1964 from 674 persons (demographics are unknown) who were already in a number of specific occupational areas. These persons and their areas were top-level management executives in sales and production ($n = 49$), middle-management executives ($n = 40$), junior executives in training for production positions ($n = 50$), junior executives in training for finance positions ($n = 104$), foremen from metal, chemical, petroleum, and food industries ($n = 68$), hourly employees from the chemical industry ($n = 128$), salesmen from food companies and industry ($n = 103$), professional engineers and chemical engineers ($n = 67$), and government auditor supervisors ($n = 65$). No rationale is provided for why these persons were chosen and one suspects that they happened to be available, rather than theoretically relevant. Other problems with this sample are the somewhat heterogeneous nature of the nine groups, the unequal sample sizes, and the lack of demographics on them.

A critique of the statistical procedures used in the validity and reliability studies provides further support for some of the problems previously noted. To a certain extent the statistics used are limited by their age in that at the time the WII was constructed, the best available factor analysis program could accomodate only 125 of the 140 items, so 15 items were simply omitted. Also, in the analyses of variance and subsequent t-tests no effort was made to control for spurious results due to the multiple comparisons, a problem that today is alleviated with use of multivariate techniques. Unequal ns are another difficulty in that no information is provided in the manual as to whether any correction was made for these group size differences. Finally, certain factors appear to have restricted ranges that could affect the other statistical analyses (e.g., for factor 9, a raw score of 0 still places the person in the 18th percentile).

Critique

While the Work Interest Index was constructed to fill an important need in the realm of assessment, it unfortunately falls far short of its goal of providing a primarily pictorial method of interest assessment. It seems to be an example of a test that has attractive materials but lacks psychometric substance.

The major criticisms of the WII have been stated before (Shertzer, 1985; Tenopyr, 1985). It suffers from inadequate reliability and validity data as well as flaws in its construction. Many of the most important pieces of psychometric support for a test that aims to assist in selection, placement, and career guidance (e.g., predictive validity, test-retest reliability) are nonexistent. In addition, what validity and reliability data do exist are sketchy and quite outdated.

The WII's norm group, too, fails to meet good rules of test construction. It appears to have been chosen with little theoretical rationale, its composition is poorly described, and it has not been expanded or updated in 25 years. At the very least, a potential user of the WII would need to consider gathering local norms to make any use of this test.

The WII materials are also in need of updating (Shertzer, 1985). The pictures are visibly dated, encompass jobs that in some cases are obsolete, are indicative of a white male bias in a test that is not directed only toward white males, and are sometimes too vague to be truly representative of the intended occupation. The manual, too, needs to be revised, as it contains sexist language, confusing and sometimes incomplete explanations of statistical procedures, and a perhaps unethical absence of vital validation evidence.

In summary, while the concept behind the WII is a good one (there is certainly a need for such a pictorial interest inventory), the realization of that concept is a major disappointment. It is a test that should be used with extreme caution (if at all) by personnel, guidance, and counseling professionals. Until new validation studies and norms are obtained, the Work Interest Index is not a test on which to base important decisions about persons' lives.

References

Baehr, M. E., Renck, R., Burns, R. K., & Pranis, R. W. (1965). *Work Interest Index: Test administration manual*. Chicago: University of Chicago, Industrial Relations Center.

Baehr, M. E., Renck, R., & Burns, R. K. (1980). *The Work Interest Index*. Chicago: University of Chicago, Industrial Relations Center. (Original publication in 1959)

Cottle, W. C. (1950). A factorial study of the Multiphasic, Strong, Kuder, and Bell inventories using a population of adult males. *Psychometrika, 15*, 25-47.

Shertzer, B. (1985). Work Interest Index. In J. V. Mitchell, Jr. (Ed.), *The ninth mental measurements yearbook* (pp. 1777-1778). Lincoln, NE: Buros Institute of Mental Measurements.

Tenopyr, M. L. (1985). Work Interest Index. In J. V. Mitchell, Jr. (Ed.), *The ninth mental measurements yearbook* (pp. 1778-1779). Lincoln, NE: Buros Institute of Mental Measurements.

United States Employment Service. (1956). *Estimates of worker trait requirements for 4000 jobs as defined in the Dictionary of Occupational Titles*. Washington, DC: U.S. Government Printing Office.

Warner, W. L. (1960). *Social class in America*. New York: Harper & Bros.

INDEX OF TEST TITLES

AAMD Adaptive Behavior Scale, School Edition, I:3
Academic Instruction Measurement System, IV:3
ACT Assessment, The, I:11
Actualizing Assessment Battery I: The Intrapersonal Inventories, II:3
Actualizing Assessment Battery II: The Interpersonal Inventories, III:3
Adaptability Test, I:29
Adaptive Behavior Inventory for Children, III:13
Adjective Check List, I:34
Adjustment Inventory, The: Adult Form, I:41
Adolescent Emotional Factors Inventory, II:12
Adolescent Multiphasic Personality Inventory, V:3
Adolescent Separation Anxiety Test, III:30
Adult Basic Learning Examination, II:16
Adult Neuropsychological Questionnaire, V:6
Adult Personal Adjustment and Role Skills, II:23
Advanced Progressive Matrices, I:47
Affects Balance Scale, II:32
AH5 Group Test of High Grade Intelligence, IV:7
AH6 Group Tests of High Level Intelligence, I:51
Alcadd Test, V:9
Analysis of Coping Style, II:35
Analysis of Readiness Skills, IV:11
Arizona Articulation Proficiency Scale: Revised, IV:15
Arlin Test of Formal Reasoning, II:40
Armed Services Vocational Aptitude Battery, I:61
Assessment of Basic Competencies, II:45
Association Adjustment Inventory, I:70
Attitude to School Questionnaire, V:21
Attributional Style Questionnaire, IV:20
Auditory Discrimination Test, IV:33
Auditory Memory Span Test/Auditory Sequential Memory Test, IV:39
Autism Screening Instrument for Educational Planning, I:75
Balthazar Scales of Adaptive Behavior I: Scales of Functional Independence, IV:42
Balthazar Scales of Adaptive Behavior II: Scales of Social Adaptation, II:56
Barber Scales of Self-Regard for Preschool Children, IV:48
Barron-Welsh Art Scale, IV:58
Basic Achievement Skills Individual Screener, II:63
Basic Educational Skills Test, V:26
Basic Occupational Literacy Test, I:83
Basic School Skills Inventory—Diagnostic, IV:68
Basic School Skills Inventory—Screen, IV:76
Basic Screening and Referral Form for Children With Suspected Learning and Behavioral Disabilities, A, II:68
Basic Skills Assessment Program, 1978 Edition, IV:79
Battelle Developmental Inventory, II:72
Beck Depression Inventory, II:83
Behavior Evaluation Scale, IV:87
Behavior Rating Instrument for Autistic and Other Atypical Children, III:43
Behavior Rating Profile, IV:92
Behavioral Academic Self-Esteem, III:35
Behavioral Deviancy Profile, IV:103
Behaviour Assessment Battery, 2nd Edition, IV:107

572 Index of Test Titles

Bem Sex-Role Inventory, III:51
Bender Visual Motor Gestalt Test, I:90
Benton Revised Visual Retention Test, III:58
Bexley-Maudsley Automated Psychological Screening, II:88
Bipolar Psychological Inventory, II:95
Birth to Three Developmental Scale, III:68
Blacky Pictures, The, I:99
Blind Learning Aptitude Test, V:32
Boehm Test of Basic Concepts, I:106
Booklet Category Test, The, I:113
Boston Diagnostic Aphasia Examination, I:117
Botel Reading Inventory, V:37
Bracken Basic Concept Scale, I:125
Brief Index of Adaptive Behavior, III:75
Brigance Inventories, The, III:79
Bristol Social Adjustment Guides, II:104
British Ability Scales, I:130
Bruininks-Oseretsky Test of Motor Proficiency, III:99
Burks' Behavior Rating Scale, II:108
Bzoch-League Receptive-Expressive Emergent Language Scale, The, V:43
California Achievement Tests, Forms C & D, III:111
California Child Q-Set, III:125
California Phonics Survey, II:113
California Psychological Inventory, I:146
California Q-Sort, III:133
California Verbal Learning Test, I:158
Callier-Azusa Scale: G Edition, IV:119
Canadian Cognitive Abilities Test, V:48
Canadian Tests of Basic Skills, IV:127
Career Assessment Inventory, II:128
Career Decision Scale, II:138
Career Development Inventory, IV:132
Career Maturity Inventory, I:164
Carlson Psychological Survey, IV:144
Cattell Infant Intelligence Scale, IV:149
Center for Epidemiologic Studies Depression Scale, II:144
Central Institute for the Deaf Preschool Performance Scale, IV:157
Child Abuse Potential Inventory, V:55
Child Anxiety Scale, III:139
Child Behavior Checklist, I:168
Child Behavior Rating Scale, III:145
Children's Adaptive Behavior Scale-Revised, II:161
Children's Apperception Test, I:185
Children's Depression Inventory, V:65
Children's Human Figure Drawings, Psychological Evaluation of, I:189
Children's Hypnotic Susceptibility Scale, IV:162
Children's Personality Questionnaire, I:195
Children's Version/Family Environment Scale, III:152
Clarke Reading Self-Assessment Survey, IV:172
Classroom Environment Index, III:158
Claybury Selection Battery, II:169
Clifton Assessment Procedures for the Elderly, II:175
Clinical Analysis Questionnaire, I:202
Clinical Evaluation of Language Functions, IV:176
Clymer-Barrett Readiness Test, IV:183
Coloured Progressive Matrices, I:206
Columbia Mental Maturity Scale, II:182

Index of Test Titles 573

Communication Screen, The: A Pre-school Speech-Language Screening Tool, II:191
Communicative Abilities in Daily Living, IV:189
Communicative Evaluation Chart from Infancy to Five Years, IV:195
Comprehensive Ability Battery, I:214
Comprehensive Assessment Program: Achievement Series, III:164
Comprehensive Developmental Evaluation Chart, III:171
Comprehensive Drinker Profile, III:175
Comprehensive Test of Adaptive Behavior, V:73
Comprehensive Tests of Basic Skills, Forms U and V, III:186
Computer Operator Aptitude Battery, II:198
Computer Programmer Aptitude Battery, II:204
Comrey Personality Scales, IV:199
Cooper-McGuire Diagnostic Word Analysis Test, III:198
Coopersmith Self-Esteem Inventories, I:226
COPSystem Interest Inventory, V:76
Creativity Assessment Packet, II:211
Creativity Attitude Survey, III:206
Criterion Test of Basic Skills, IV:213
Culture Fair Intelligence Test, I:233
Culture-Free Self-Esteem Inventories for Children and Adults, II:216
Culture Shock Inventory, III:209
Curtis Completion Form, V:83
Daberon Screening for School Readiness, V:86
Decision-Making Organizer, V:90
Denver Developmental Screening Test, I:239
Depression Adjective Check Lists, III:215
Detroit Tests of Learning Aptitude-Primary, V:94
Detroit Tests of Learning Aptitude-2, II:223
Developmental Activities Screening Inventory-II, V:100
Developmental Indicators for the Assessment of Learning-Revised, IV:220
Developmental Test of Visual-Motor Integration, IV:229
Devereux Adolescent Behavior Rating Scale, III:221
Devereux Child Behavior Rating Scale, The, II:231
Devereux Elementary School Behavior Rating Scale, V:104
Diagnostic Achievement Battery, II:235
Diagnostic Reading Scales: Revised 1981 Edition, IV:238
Diagnostic Skills Battery, IV:245
Differential Aptitude Tests, III:226
Dyslexia Determination Test, V:109
Dyslexia Screening Survey, The, II:241
Early School Personality Questionnaire, III:246
Early Screening Inventory, II:244
Eby Elementary Identification Instrument, IV:251
Edinburgh Picture Test, IV:256
Education Apperception Test, IV:259
Educational Development Series, IV:264
Edwards Personal Preference Schedule, I:252
Ego-Ideal and Conscience Development Test, V:113
Ego State Inventory, II:255
Eight State Questionnaire, III:251
Elizur Test of Psycho-Organicity: Children & Adults, III:255
Embedded Figures Test, I:259
Emotions Profile Index, IV:274
Employee Aptitude Survey Tests, I:266
Evaluating Communicative Competence: A Functional Pragmatic Procedure, V:118
Expressive One-Word Picture Vocabulary Test: Upper Extension, IV:278

574 Index of Test Titles

Extended Merrill-Palmer Scale, I:274
Eysenck Personality Inventory, II:258
Eysenck Personality Questionnaire, I:279
Family Environment Scale, II:263
Family Relations Test: Children's Version, IV:281
Family Relationship Inventory, IV:294
Famous Sayings Test, V:128
Five P's: Parent Professional Preschool Performance Profile, The, III:261
Flanagan Aptitude Classification Tests, II:275
Flanagan Industrial Tests, II:282
Flint Infant Security Scale, III:271
Florida Kindergarten Screening Battery, The, II:288
Flowers Auditory Test of Selective Attention, III:276
Flowers-Costello Tests of Central Auditory Abilities, V:137
Forer Structured Sentence Completion Test, IV:300
Forty-Eight Item Counseling Evaluation Test: Revised, III:282
Foster Mazes, IV:307
Four Picture Test, III:288
Frenchay Dysarthria Assessment, III:293
Frostig Developmental Test of Visual Perception, II:293
Fuld Object-Memory Evaluation, I:288
Fullerton Language Test for Adolescents, V:141
Full-Range Picture Vocabulary Test, II:299
Fundamental Interpersonal Relations Orientation-Behavior (B) and Feelings (F), I:284
Gates-MacGinitie Reading Tests, The, Second Edition, IV:310
Gates-McKillop-Horowitz Reading Diagnostic Tests, II:303
General Aptitude Test Battery, V:150
General Clerical Test, III:296
Geriatric Depression Scale, V:168
Gesell Preschool Test, II:310
Gesell School Readiness Test, II:314
Gifted and Talented Screening Form, III:302
Gilmore Oral Reading Test, IV:320
Goldman-Fristoe Test of Articulation, V:172
Goldman-Fristoe-Woodcock Auditory Skills Test Battery, IV:327
Goldman-Fristoe-Woodcock Test of Auditory Discrimination, III:304
Goldstein-Scheerer Tests of Abstract and Concrete Thinking, I:295
Goodenough-Harris Drawing Test, II:319
Goodman Lock Box, III:310
Gordon Personal Profile Inventory, II:326
Gray Oral Reading Tests-Revised, V:179
Group Embedded Figures Test, V:189
Group Inventory for Finding Creative Talent, II:332
Hall Occupational Orientation Inventory, I:300
Halstead-Reitan Neurological Battery and Allied Procedures, The, I:305
Hand Test, The, I:315
Harding W87 Test, IV:334
Harrington-O'Shea Career Decision-Making System, The, I:322
Healy Pictorial Completion Test, IV:341
High School Personality Questionnaire, III:319
Hiskey-Nebraska Test of Learning Aptitude, III:331
Holtzman Inkblot Technique, I:328
Home Observation for Measurement of the Environment, II:337
Hooper Visual Organization Test, III:340
Hopelessness Scale, V:198
House-Tree-Person Technique, I:338

Index of Test Titles

Houston Test for Language Development, The, V:203
Howell Prekindergarten Screening Test, V:209
Human Information Processing Survey, III:344
Illinois Test of Psycholinguistic Abilities-Revised, I:354
Impact Message Inventory, III:349
Impact of Event Scale, III:358
Incomplete Sentences Task, II:347
Individual Phonics Criterion Test, V:212
Individualized Criterion Referenced Test—Reading, III:367
Inferred Self-Concept Scale, IV:351
Informal Reading Inventory, II:350
Instrument Timbre Preference Test, V:216
Interpersonal Language Skills Assessment: Final Edition, V:221
Inventory of Individually Perceived Group Cohesiveness, IV:354
Iowa Tests of Educational Development, I:364
IPAT Anxiety Scale, II:357
IPAT Depression Scale, I:377
I.P.I. Aptitude-Intelligence Test Series, II:363
Jackson Personality Inventory, II:369
Jesness Behavior Checklist, V:226
Jesness Inventory, The, I:380
Joseph Pre-School and Primary Self-Concept Screening Test, V:230
Kahn Intelligence Test, III:375
Kahn Test of Symbol Arrangement, II:376
Kaufman Assessment Battery for Children, I:393
Kaufman Developmental Scale, IV:357
Kaufman Infant and Preschool Scale, II:383
Kaufman Test of Educational Achievement, IV:368
Kendrick Cognitive Tests for the Elderly, II:388
Kent Infant Development Scale, III:380
Kohs Block Design, II:392
Kuder General Interest Survey, Form E, II:395
Kuder Occupational Interest Survey, Form DD, I:406
Learning Disability Rating Procedure, V:237
Learning Efficiency Test, V:244
Learning Styles Inventory, II:402
Leiter Adult Intelligence Scale, II:411
Leiter International Performance Scale, I:411
Life Event Scale—Adolescents, III:383
Life Event Scale—Children, III:388
Life Interpersonal History Enquiry, III:392
Life Skills, Forms 1 & 2, II:416
Lindamood Auditory Conceptualization Test, IV:376
Loevinger's Washington University Sentence Completion Test, III:395
Lollipop Test, The: A Diagnostic Screening Test of School Readiness, II:426
Lorge-Thorndike Intelligence Test/Cognitive Abilities Test, The, I:421
Louisville Behavior Checklist, II:430
Luria-Nebraska Neuropsychological Battery, III:402
Luria-Nebraska Neuropsychological Battery, Form II, IV:382
Make A Picture Story, II:436
Marital Satisfaction Inventory, III:415
Martinez Assessment of the Basic Skills, II:441
Maslach Burnout Inventory, III:419
Mathematics Anxiety Rating Scale, I:436
Maudsley Personality Inventory, IV:387
Maxfield-Buchholz Social Maturity Scale for Blind Preschool Children, IV:390
McCarthy Scales of Children's Abilities, IV:394

576 Index of Test Titles

McCarthy Screening Test, II:446
Memory-For-Designs Test, II:451
Merrill-Palmer Scale, II:457
Metropolitan Achievement Test: 5th Edition, III:427
Metropolitan Language Instructional Tests, III:434
Metropolitan Readiness Tests, II:463
Michigan Alcoholism Screening Test, III:439
Michigan Picture Test—Revised, III:447
Michigan Screening Profile of Parenting, IV:400
Mill Hill Vocabulary Scale: 1982 Edition, IV:408
Miller Analogies Test, IV:414
Miller Assessment for Preschoolers, I:443
Millon Adolescent Personality Inventory, IV:425
Millon Behavioral Health Inventory, III:454
Millon Clinical Multiaxial Inventory, I:455
Minnesota Child Development Inventory, II:472
Minnesota Importance Questionnaire, II:481
Minnesota Infant Development Inventory, V:252
Minnesota Multiphasic Personality Inventory, I:466
Minnesota Percepto-Diagnostic Test, III:461
Minnesota Satisfaction Questionnaire, V:255
Minnesota Satisfactoriness Scales, IV:434
Miskimins Self-Goal-Other Discrepancy Scale, V:266
Missouri Children's Picture Series, I:473
Modern Language Aptitude Test, V:271
Modified Vigotsky Concept Formation Test, II:491
Mooney Problem Check List, II:495
Mother-Child Relationship Evaluation, IV:440
Motor Steadiness Battery, I:478
Mullen Scales of Early Learning, IV:444
Multidimensional Aptitude Battery, II:501
Multilingual Aphasia Examination, V:278
Multiple Affect Adjective Check List-Revised, IV:449
Myers-Briggs Type Indicator, I:482
My Vocational Situation, II:509
Need for Cognition Scale, III:466
Nelson-Denny Reading Test, Forms E and F, III:475
Nelson Reading Skills Test, The, IV:453
Neurological Dysfunctions of Children, II:517
Neuropsychological Status Examination, I:491
Neuroticism Scale Questionnaire, V:283
New Sucher-Allred Reading Placement Inventory, The, IV:458
Non-Language Multi-Mental Test, II:530
Non-Verbal Reasoning, IV:463
Normative Adaptive Behavior Checklist, V:287
Object Relations Technique, IV:469
O'Brien Vocabulary Placement Test, The, V:290
Occupational Environment Scales, Form E-2, II:535
Offer Self-Image Questionnaire for Adolescents, V:297
Ohio Vocational Interest Survey: Second Edition, IV:478
Omnibus Personality Inventory, I:494
Ordinal Scales of Psychological Development, II:543
Organic Integrity Test, IV:484
Organizational Climate Index, The, II:551
Otis-Lennon School Ability Test, I:499
Parent Attachment Structured Interview, II:559
Parenting Stress Index, I:504

Index of Test Titles 577

Partner Relationship Inventory, V:303
Patterned Elicitation Syntax Test, II:562
Peabody Developmental Motor Scales and Activity Cards, V:310
Peabody Individual Achievement Test, III:480
Peabody Picture Vocabulary Test—Revised, III:488
Perceptual Maze Test, V:314
Performance Efficiency Test, III:496
Personal Skills Map, The, V:318
Personality Inventory for Children, II:570
Personality Research Form, III:499
Personnel Selection Inventory, III:510
Phonemic Synthesis, III:521
Picture Spondee Threshold Test, IV:493
Piers-Harris Children's Self-Concept Scale, I:511
Politte Sentence Completion Test, V:323
Polyfactorial Study of Personality, IV:496
Porteus Mazes, II:579
Position Analysis Questionnaire, V:326
Preschool Behavior Questionnaire, V:341
Preschool Development Inventory, V:348
Preschool Language Assessment Instrument, III:526
Primary Measures of Music Audiation, V:351
Process For The Assessment of Effective Student Functioning, A, II:584
Profile of Adaptation to Life, II:594
Profile of Mood States, I:522
Projective Assessment of Aging Method, III:539
Proverbs Test, II:603
Psychiatric Diagnostic Interview, IV:501
Psychological Screening Inventory, IV:509
Psychosocial Pain Inventory, III:542
Psychotic Inpatient Profile, II:607
Pyramid Scales, The, V:358
Quick Neurological Screening Test, II:621
Quick Screening Scale of Mental Development, A, V:367
Quick Test, I:530
Quick Word Test, IV:516
Reading-Free Vocational Interest Inventory-Revised, II:627
Reid Report/Reid Survey, II:631
Reitan Evaluation of Hemispheric Abilities and Brain
 Improvement Training, II:637
Reitan-Indiana Neuropsychological Test Battery for Children, I:536
Revised Behavior Problem Checklist, V:371
Reynell-Zinkin Scales: Developmental Scales for Young Handicapped Children
 Part 1—Mental Development, III:546
Riley Articulation and Language Test, V:378
Riley Motor Problems Inventory, V:382
Ring and Peg Tests of Behavior Development, IV:519
Roberts Apperception Test for Children, I:543
Rogers Personal Adjustment Inventory-UK Revision, II:642
Rokeach Value Survey, I:549
Rorschach Inkblot Test, IV:523
Rosenzweig Picture-Frustration Study, V:388
Ross Test of Higher Cognitive Processes, V:396
Roswell-Chall Auditory Blending Test, IV:553
Roswell-Chall Diagnostic Reading Test of Word Analysis Skills:
 Revised and Extended, II:646
Rothwell-Miller Interest Blank, IV:560

578   Index of Test Titles

Rotter Incomplete Sentences Blank, II:653
Scales of Independent Behavior, III:551
Schedule of Recent Experience, II:661
School and College Ability Tests II & III, V:406
School Apperception Method, III:564
School Behavior Checklist, IV:565
School Environment Preference Survey, I:555
School Interest Inventory, II:674
School Motivation Analysis Test, III:567
School Readiness Screening Test, II:681
School Readiness Survey, IV:570
School Social Skills Rating Scale, IV:578
Schubert General Ability Battery, III:579
Schutz Measures, The, I:559
SCL-90-R, III:583
Scott Mental Alertness Test, IV:585
S-D Proneness Checklist, I:568
SEARCH: A Scanning Instrument for the Identification of Potential
    Learning Disability, II:689
Self-Conciousness Scale, The, V:412
Self-Directed Search, The, II:697
Self-Directed Search, (1985 Revision), The, V:419
Self-Esteem Questionnaire, II:707
Self-Rating Depression Scale, III:595
Senior Apperception Technique, III:604
Sequenced Inventory of Communication Development-Revised, II:714
Sequential Assessment of Mathematics Inventories: Standardized Inventory, IV:590
Sequential Tests of Educational Progress, I:578
Shipley Institute of Living Scale, V:425
Shorr Imagery Test, I:593
Sixteen Personality Factor Questionnaire, IV:595
Sklar Aphasia Scale: Revised 1983, IV:606
Slingerland Screening Tests for Identifying Children with Specific Language Disability,
    IV:611
Slosson Drawing Coordination Test, IV:620
Slosson Oral Reading Test, IV:623
Smith-Johnson Nonverbal Performance Scale, II:723
Social Behaviour Assessment Schedule, III:608
Somatic Inkblot Series, V:444
Southern California Motor Accuracy Test, Revised, III:615
Spadafore Diagnostic Reading Test, IV:627
SRA Nonverbal Form, IV:635
SRA Pictorial Reasoning Test, III:621
SRA Verbal Form, IV:642
Standard Progressive Matrices, I:595
Stanford-Binet Intelligence Scale: Form L-M, I:603
Stanford Diagnostic Mathematics Test, I:608
Stanford Early School Achievement Test: 2nd Edition, I:614
Stanford Hypnotic Clinical Scale for Children, V:447
Stanford Hypnotic Susceptibility Scale, II:729
Stanford Profile Scales of Hypnotic Susceptibility, Revised Edition, I:623
Stanton Survey, V:451
State-Trait Anxiety Inventory, I:626
State-Trait Anxiety Inventory for Children, I:633
Steps Up Developmental Screening Program, III:628
Strong-Campbell Interest Inventory, II:737
Stroop Color and Word Test, II:751

Index of Test Titles 579

Structure of Intellect Learning Abilities Test-Form P (Primary), V:458
Study of Values, I:641
Suicide Probability Scale, IV:649
Survey of Interpersonal Values, II:759
Survey of Organizations, II:765
Survey of Personal Values, II:773
Survey of School Attitudes, III:633
Symbolic Play Test: Experimental Edition, IV:656
System of Multicultural Pluralistic Assessment, I:648
Tactual Performance Test, III:640
Taylor-Johnson Temperament Analysis, I:652
Temperament and Values Inventory, I:660
Tennessee Self Concept Scale, I:663
Test Anxiety Inventory, I:673
Test Anxiety Profile, I:682
Test of Auditory Comprehension, III:647
Test of Cognitive Skills, II:780
Test of Early Language Development, V:464
Test of Early Reading Ability, V:470
Test of English as a Foreign Language, III:655
Test of Facial Recognition-Form SL, V:475
Test of Language Development, IV:659
Test of Listening Accuracy in Children, III:669
Test of Nonverbal Intelligence, II:787
Test of Perceptual Organization, V:483
Test of Written Language, I:688
Test of Written Spelling, V:485
Tests of Adult Basic Education, V:494
Tests of Mental Function in the Elderly, V:499
Thematic Apperception Test, II:799
Thinking Creatively in Action and Movement, V:505
Thinking Creatively with Sounds and Words, IV:666
Three Minute Reasoning Test, V:513
3-R's Test, The, V:517
Thurstone Temperament Schedule, II:815
Time Perception Inventory, V:522
Time Problems Inventory, V:524
Trait Evaluation Index, V:529
Trites Neuropsychological Test Battery, V:534
United States Employment Service Interest Inventory, III:673
Utah Test of Language Development-Revised, I:707
Verbal Language Development Scale, I:712
Vineland Adaptive Behavior Scales, I:715
Visual-Aural Digit Span Test, V:537
Vocational Preference Inventory, V:545
Wachs Analysis of Cognitive Structures, V:549
Watson-Glaser Critical Thinking Appraisal, III:682
Ways of Coping Scale, III:686
Wechsler Adult Intelligence Scale, I:720
Wechsler Adult Intelligence Scale-Revised, I:728
Wechsler Intelligence Scale for Children-Revised, I:740
Wechsler Memory Scale, I:750
Wechsler Preschool and Primary Scale of Intelligence, III:698
Welsh Figure Preference Test, V:556
Wesman Personnel Classification Test, III:711
Western Aphasia Battery, The, II:819
Western Personality Inventory, II:826

Index of Test Titles

Western Personnel Tests, III:714
Whitaker Index of Schizophrenic Thinking, III:717
Wide Range Achievement Test-Revised, I:758
Wide Range Intelligence-Personality Test, I:762
Wide Range Interest-Opinion Test, IV:673
Wisconsin Card Sorting Test, IV:677
Wonderlic Personnel Test, The, I:762
Woodcock-Johnson Psycho-Educational Battery, IV:683
Woodcock Language Proficiency Battery, English Form, III:726
Woodcock Reading Mastery Tests, IV:704
Word Association Test, III:736
Word Test, The, II:831
Work Interest Index, V:565
Work Values Inventory, II:835

INDEX OF TEST PUBLISHERS

Academic Therapy Publications, 20 Commercial Boulevard, Novato, California 94947; (415) 883-3314—[II:621; IV:172, 213, 278, 627; V:237, 244, 396]
American College Testing Program, (The), 2201 North Dodge Street, P.O. Box 168, Iowa City, Iowa 52243; (319)337-1000—[I:11]
American Foundation for the Blind, 15 West 16th, New York, New York 10011; (212)620-2000—[IV:390]
American Guidance Service, Publisher's Building, Circle Pines, Minnesota 55014; (800) 328-2560, in Minnesota (612)786-4343—[I:322, 393, 712, 715; III:99, 304, 480, 488; IV:327, 368, 704; V:172]
American Orthopsychiatric Association, Inc., (The), 1775 Broadway, New York, New York 10019; (212)586-5690—[I:90]
American Psychiatric Association, *American Journal of Psychiatry,* 1400 K Street, N.W., Washington, D.C. 20005; (202)682-6000—[III:439]
American Psychological Association, *Journal of Consulting and Clinical Psychology,* 1200 Seventeenth Street, N.W., Washington, D.C. 20036; (202)955-7600—[V:198, 412]
American Society of Clinical Hypnosis, *The American Journal of Clinical Hypnosis,* 2250 E. Devon, Ste. 336, Des Plaines, Illinois 60018; (312)297-3317—[V:447]
American Testronics, P.O. Box 2270, Iowa City, Iowa 52244; (319)351-9086—[III:164]
ASIEP Education Company, 3216 N.E. 27th, Portland, Oregon 97212; (503) 281-4115—[I:75; II:441; V:86]
Associated Services for the Blind (ASB), 919 Walnut Street, Philadelphia, Pennsylvania 19107; (215)627-0600—[II:12]
Aurora Publishing Company, 1709 Bragaw Street, Ste. B, Anchorage, Alaska 99504; (907)279-5251—[V:444]
Australian Council for Educational Research Limited, (The), Radford House, Frederick Street, Hawthorn, Victoria 3122, Australia; (03) 819 1400—[IV:560]
Behar, Lenore, 1821 Woodburn Road, Durham, North Carolina 27705; (919)733-4660—[V:341]
Behavior Science Systems, Inc., Box 1108, Minneapolis, Minnesota 55440; no business phone—[II:472; V:252, 348]
Book-Lab, 500 74th Street, North Bergen, New Jersey 07047; (201)861-6763 or (201)868-1305—[V:209]
Brink, T.L., 1044 Sylvan, San Carlos, California 94070; (415)593-7323—[V:168]
Bruce, (Martin M.), Ph.D., Publishers, 50 Larchwood Road, Larchmont, New York 10538; (914)834-1555—[I:70; IV:496; V:529]
Cacioppo, (John T.), Department of Psychology, University of Iowa, Iowa City, Iowa 52242; no business phone—[III:466]
Callier Center for Communication Disorders, The University of Texas at Austin, 1966 Inwood Road, Dallas, Texas 75235; (214)783-3000—[IV:119]
Center for Child Development and Education, College of Education, University of Arkansas at Little Rock, 33rd and University, Little Rock, Arkansas 72204; (501)569-3422—[II:337]
Center for Cognitive Therapy, 133 South 36th Street, Room 602, Philadelphia, Pennsylvania 19104; (215)898-4100—[II:83]
Center for Epidemiologic Studies, Department of Health and Human Services, 5600 Fishers Lane, Rockville, Maryland 20857; (301)443-4513—[II:144]

582 Index of Test Publishers

Chapman, Brook & Kent, 1215 De La Vina, Suite F, Santa Barbara, California 93101; (805) 962-0055—[IV:183]

Childcraft Education Corporation, 20 Kilmer Road, Edison, New Jersey 08818; (800)631-5652—[IV:220]

Clinical Psychology Publishing Company, Inc., 4 Conant Square, Brandon, Vermont 05733; (802)247-6871—[III:461]

Clinical Psychometric Research, 1228 Wine Spring Lane, Towson, Maryland 21204; (301) 321-6165—[II:32; III:583]

College Hill Press, Inc., 4284 41 St., San Diego, California 92105; (619)563-8899—[III:293]

Communication Research Associates, Inc., P.O. Box 11012, Salt Lake City, Utah 84147; (801)292-3880—[I:707; III:669]

Communication Skill Builders, Inc., 3130 N. Dodge Blvd., P.O. Box 42050, Tucson, Arizona 85733; (602)323-7500—[II:191, 562; V:118]

Consulting Psychologists Press, Inc., 577 College Avenue, P.O. Box 60070, Palo Alto, California 94306; (415)857-1444—[I:34, 41, 146, 226, 259, 284, 380, 482, 623, 626, 663, 673; II:23, 56, 113, 263, 293, 509, 594, 697, 729; III:35, 51, 125, 133, 349, 392, 419; IV:42, 58, 132, 162, 570; V:141, 189, 226, 303, 556]

C.P.S., Inc., Box 83, Larchmont, New York 10538; no business phone—[I:185; III:604]

Creative Learning Press, Inc., P.O. Box 320, Mansfield Center, Connecticut 06250; (203) 423-8120—[II:402]

Croft, Inc., Suite 200, 7215 York Road, Baltimore, Maryland 21212; (800)638-5082, in Maryland (301)254-5082—[III:198]

CTB/McGraw-Hill, Publishers Test Service, Del Monte Research Park, 2500 Garden Road, Monterey, California 93940; (800)538-9547, in California (800)682-9222, or (408)649-8400—[I:3, 164, 578; II:517, 584, 780; III:186; IV:79, 238; V:406, 494]

Curriculum Associates, Inc., 5 Esquire Road, North Billerica, Massachusetts 01862-2589; (800)225-0248, in Massachusetts (617)667-8000—[III:79]

Delis, (Dean), Ph.D., 3753 Canyon Way, Martinez, California 94553—[I:158]

Devereux Foundation Press, (The), 19 South Waterloo Road, Box 400, Devon, Pennsylvania 19333; (215)964-3000—[II:231; III:221; V:104]

Diagnostic Specialists, Inc., 1170 North 660 West, Orem, Utah 84057; (801)224-8492—[II:95]

DLM Teaching Resources, P.O. Box 4000, One DLM Park, Allen, Texas 75002; (800)527-4747, in Texas (800)442-4711—[II:72; III:68, 521, 551, 726; IV:376, 493, 683; V:310]

D.O.K. Publishers, Inc., 71 Radcliffe Road, Buffalo, New York 14214; (716) 837-3391—[II:211]

Economy Company, (The), P.O. Box 25308, 1901 North Walnut Street, Oklahoma City, Oklahoma 73125; (405)528-8444—[IV:458]

Educational Activities, Inc., P.O. Box 392, Freeport, New York 11520; (800)645-3739, in Alaska, Hawaii, and New York (516)223-4666—[V:290]

Educational and Industrial Testing Service (EdITS), P.O. Box 7234, San Diego, California 92107; (619)222-1666—[I:279, 522, 555; II:3, 104, 258; III:3, 215; IV:199, 387, 449; V:76]

Educational Assessment Service, Inc., Route One, Box 139-A, Watertown, Wisconsin 53094; (414)261-1118—[II:332]

Educational Development Corporation, P.O. Box 45663, Tulsa, Oklahoma 74145; (800) 331-4418, in Oklahoma (800)722-9113—[III:367]

Educational Testing Service (ETS), Rosedale Road, Princeton, New Jersey 08541; (609) 921-9000—[III:655]

Educators Publishing Service, Inc., 75 Moulton Street, Cambridge, Massachusetts 02238-9101; (800)225-5750, in Massachusetts (800)792-5166—[IV:195, 611]

Elbern Publications, P.O. Box 09497, Columbus, Ohio 43209; (614)235-2643—[II:627]

Index of Test Publishers **583**

El Paso Rehabilitation Center, 2630 Richmond, El Paso, Texas 79930; (915)566-2956—[III:171, 628]

Elsevier Science Publishing Company, Inc., 52 Vanderbilt Avenue, New York, New York 10017; (212)867-9040—[III:358]

Essay Press, P.O. Box 2323, La Jolla, California 92307;(619)565-6603—[II:646; IV:553]

Evaluation Research Associates, P.O. Box 6503, Teall Station, Syracuse, New York 13217; (315)422-0064—[II:551; III:158]

Foreworks, Box 9747, North Hollywood, California 91609; (213)982-0467—[III:647]

Foundation for Knowledge in Development, (The), KID Technology, 11715 East 51st Avenue, Denver, Colorado 80239; (303)373-1916—[I:443]

G.I.A. Publications, 7404 South Mason Avenue, Chicago, Illinois 60638; (312)496-3800—[V:216, 351]

Grune & Stratton, Inc., Orlando, Florida, 32887-0018; (800)321-5068, (305)345-4500—[I:189; II:819; III:447, 526; IV:523; V:537]

Guidance Centre, Faculty of Education, University of Toronto, 252 Bloor Street West, Toronto, Ontario, Canada M5S 2Y3; (416)978-3206/3210—[III:271]

Halgren Tests, 873 Persimmon Avenue, Sunnyvale, California 94807; (408)738-1342—[I:549]

Harding Tests, Box 5271, Rockhampton Mail Centre, Q. 4701, Australia; no business phone—[IV:334]

Harvard University Press, 79 Garden Street, Cambridge, Massachusetts 02138; (617)495-2600—[II:799]

Hiskey, (Marshall S.), 5640 Baldwin, Lincoln, Nebraska 68507; (402)466-6145—[III:331]

Hodder & Stoughton Educational, A Division of Hodder & Stoughton Ltd., P.O. Box 702, Mill Road, Dunton Green, Sevenoaks, Kent TN13 2YD, England; (0732)50111—[IV:256]

Humanics Limited, 1182 W. Peachtree Street NE, Suite 201, Atlanta, Georgia 30309; (602)323-7500—[II:161, 426]

Humanics Media, 5457 Pine Cone Road, La Crescenta, California 91214; (818)957-0983—[V:522, 524]

Industrial Psychology Incorporated (IPI), 515 Madison Avenue, New York, New York 10022; (212)355-5330—[II:363]

Institute for Personality and Ability Testing, Inc. (IPAT), P.O. Box 188, 1602 Coronado Drive, Champaign, Illinois 61820; (217)352-4739—[I:195, 202, 214, 233, 377; II:357; III:139, 246, 251, 319, 567; IV:595; V:283]

Institute for Psycho-Imagination Therapy, c/o Joseph Shorr, Ph.D., 111 North La Cienega Boulevard #108, Beverly Hills, California 90211; (213)652-2922—[I:593]

Institute for Psychosomatic & Psychiatric Research & Training/Daniel Offer, Michael Reese Hospital and Medical Center, Lake Shore Drive at 31st Street, Chicago, Illinois 60616; (312)791-3826—[V:297]

Institute of Psychological Research, Inc., 34, Fleury Street West, Montreal, Quebec, Canada H3L 1S9; (514)382-3000—[II:530]

Instructional Materials & Equipment Distributors (IMED), 1520 Cotner Avenue, Los Angeles, California 90025; (213)879-0377—[V:109]

International Universities Press, Inc., 315 Fifth Avenue, New York, New York 10016; (212)684-7900—[III:736]

Jamestown Publishers, P.O. Box 6743, 544 Douglass Avenue, Providence, Rhode Island 02940; (800)USA-READ or (401)351-1915—[V:212]

Jastak Associates, Inc., 1526 Gilpin, Wilmington, Delaware 19806; (302)652-4990—[I:758, 762; IV:673]

Jossey-Bass, Inc., Publishers, 433 California Street, San Francisco, California 94104; (415)433-1740—[III:395]

584 Index of Test Publishers

Kent Developmental Metrics, 126 W. College Avenue, P.O. Box 3178, Kent, Ohio 44240-3178; (216)678-3589—[III:380]

Kovacs, Maria, Ph.D., University of Pittsburgh, School of Medicine, Western Psychiatric Institute and Clinic, 3811 O'Hara Street, Pittsburgh, Pennsylvania 15213-2593; no business phone—[V:65]

Krieger, (Robert E.), Publishing Company, Inc., P.O. Box 9542, Melbourne, Florida 32901; (305)724-9542—[III:30]

Ladoca Publishing Foundation, Laradon Hall Training and Residential Center, East 51st Avenue & Lincoln Street, Denver, Colorado 80216; (303)296-2400—[I:239]

Lafayette Instrument Company, Inc., P.O. Box 5729, Lafayette, Indiana 47903; (317)423-1505—[V:534]

Lake, (David S.), Publishers, 19 Davis Drive, Belmont, California 94002; (415)592-7810—[II:241]

Lewis, (H.K.), & Co. Ltd., 136 Gower Street, London, England WC1E 6BS; (01)387-4282—[I:47, 206, 595; IV:408]

LinguiSystems, Inc., Suite 806, 1630 Fifth Avenue, Moline, Illinois 61265; (800)ALL-TIME, in Illinois (309)762-5112—[II:831; V:221]

London House Press, 1550 N. Northwest Highway, Park Ridge, Illinois 60068; (800)323-5923, in Illinois (312)298-7311—[III:510; IV:463; V:565]

Marathon Consulting and Press, P.O. Box 09189, 575 Enfield Road, Columbus, Ohio 43209-0189; (614)237-5267—[II:138, 535]

Martinus Nijhoff, Postbuss 566, 2501 CN, Lange Voorhout, 9-11, The Hague, Netherlands; (070)469 460—[III:288]

Medical Research Council, Department of Psychological Medicine, Royal Free Hospital, Pond Street, London, England NW3 2QG; (01)794-0500—[V:314]

Merrill, (Charles E.), Publishing Company, 1300 Alum Creek Drive, Box 508, Columbus, Ohio 43216; (614)258-8441—[I:125; II:35; IV:3, 176, 590]

Modern Curriculum Press, Inc., 13900 Prospect Road, Cleveland, Ohio 44136; (216)238-2222—[IV:229; V:37]

Monitor, P.O. Box 2337, Hollywood, California 90028; no business phone—[V:21, 113]

NCS Professional Assessment Services, P.O. Box 1416, Minneapolis, Minnesota 55440; (800)328-6759, in Minnesota (612)933-2800—[I:455, 466, 660; II:128; III:454; IV:425]

Nelson Canada, 1120 Birchmount Road, Scarborough, Ontario M1K 5G4, Canada; (416) 752-9100—[II:350; IV:127; V:48]

Neuropsychology Laboratory, University of Wisconsin, University Hospitals, Madison, Wisconsin 53711; no business phone—[I:478]

NFER-Nelson Publishing Company Ltd., Darville House, 2 Oxford Road East, Windsor, Berkshire SL4 1DF, England; (07535)58961—[I:51, 130; II:88, 169, 388, 642; III:546, 608; IV:7, 281, 469, 656]

Organizational Tests (Canada) Ltd., Box 324, Fredericton, New Brunswick, Canada E3B 4Y9; (506)459-8366—[III:209]

Oxford University Press, 200 Madison Avenue, New York, New York 10016; (212)679-7300—[V:475]

Pacific Psychological, 710 George Washington Way, Suite G, Richland, Washington 99352; (800)523-4915—[V:3]

Peacock, (F.E.), Publishers, Inc., Test Division, 115 N. Prospect Road, Itasca, Illinois 60143; (312)773-1590—[IV:516]

Pediatric Psychology Press, 2915 Idlewood Drive, Charlottesville, Virginia 22901; (804) 973-5680—[I:504]

Index of Test Publishers 585

Perceptual Learning Systems, P.O. Box 864, Dearborn, Michigan 48121; (313)277-6480—[III:276; V:137]

Personal Life Skills Center, 1201 Second Street, Corpus Christi, Texas 78404; (512)883-6442—[V:318]

Plenum Press, *Cognitive Therapy and Research*, 233 Spring Street, New York, New York 10013; (212)620-8000—[IV:20]

PRO-ED, 5341 Industrial Oaks Boulevard, Austin, Texas 78735; (512)892-3142—[I:688; II:223, 235, 787; IV:68, 76, 87, 92, 189, 659; V:43, 94, 100, 179, 358, 464, 485]

Programs for Education, Inc., Dept. W-16, 82 Park Avenue, Flemington, New Jersey 08822; (212)689-3911—[II:310, 314, 681]

Psychodiagnostic Test Company, Box 859, East Lansing, Michigan 48823; no business phone—[IV:484]

Psychodynamic Instruments, c/o Gerald Blum, Dept. of Psychology, University of California, Santa Barbara, California 93106; no business phone—[I:99]

Psychological Assessment and Services, Inc., P.O. Box 1031, Iowa City, Iowa 52240; no business phone—[I:473]

Psychological Assessment Resources, Inc., P.O. Box 98, Odessa, Florida 33556; (813)977-3395—[I:113, 491; II:288; III:175, 542; IV:677; V:6, 278, 388, 419, 545]

Psychological Corporation, (The), A Subsidiary of Harcourt Brace Jovanovich, Inc., 555 Academic Court, San Antonio, Texas 78204; (512)299-1061—[I:47, 106, 117, 206, 252, 295, 328, 494, 499, 595, 608, 614, 648, 720, 728, 740, 750; II:16, 63, 175, 182, 319, 326, 436, 446, 463, 495, 579, 653; III:13, 58, 226, 296, 427, 434, 633, 682, 698, 711; IV:149, 320, 394, 414, 478; V:271, 287]

Psychological Publications, Inc., 5300 Hollywood Boulevard, Los Angeles, California 90027; (213)465-4163—[I:654; IV:294]

Psychological Services, Inc., 3450 Wilshire Boulevard, Suite 1200, Los Angeles, California 90010; (213)738-1132—[I:266]

Psychological Test Specialists, Box 9229, Missoula, Montana 59805; no business phone—[I:530; II:299, 376, 451, 603; III:375; V:128]

Psychologists and Educators, Inc., 211 West State Street, Jacksonville, Illinois 62650; (217) 243-2135—[I:568; III:206; V:323, 483]

Psychometric Affiliates, 1620 East Main Street, Murfreesboro, Tennessee 37130; no business phone—[IV:519; V:367]

Psychonomic Society, Inc., *Psychonomic Science*, 2904 Guadalupe, Austin, Texas 78705; (512)476-9687—[V:513]

Psytec, Inc., P.O. Box 300, Webster, North Carolina 28788; (704)227-7361—[V:55]

Purdue University Bookstore, P.O. Box 3028, Station 11, 360 State Street, West Lafayette, Indiana 47906; (317)743-9618—[V:326]

Quay, Herbert C., Ph.D., P.O. Box 248185, University of Miami, Coral Gables, Florida 33124; (305)284-5208—[V:371]

Reid Psychological Systems, 233 North Michigan Avenue, Chicago, Illinois 60601; (312) 938-9200—[I:631]

Reitan Neuropsychology Laboratory, 1338 East Edison Street, Tucson, Arizona 85719; (602)795-3717—[I:305, 536; II:637; III:640]

Research Psychologists Press, Inc., 1110 Military Street, P.O. Box 984, Port Huron, Michigan 48061-0984; (800)265-1285, in Michigan (313)982-4556—[II:369, 501; III:499; IV:144, 509]

Riverside Publishing Company, (The), 8420 Bryn Mawr Avenue, Chicago, Illinois 60631; (800)323-9540, in Alaska, Hawaii, or Illinois call collect (312)693-0040—[I:421, 603, 641; II:416, 674, 835; III:475; IV:11, 310, 453; V:517]

586 Index of Test Publishers

Rocky Mountain Behavioral Science Institute, Inc. (RMBSI), P.O. Box 1066, Fort Collins, Colorado 80522; no business phone—[I:436, 682; V:266]

Roll, (Samuel), Ph.D., 5712 Osuna N.E., Albuquerque, New Mexico 87109; no business phone—[II:559]

Scholastic Testing Service, Inc. (STS), 480 Meyer Road, P.O. Box 1056, Bensenville, Illinois 60106; (312)766-7150—[I:300; II:45; III:75, 344; IV:245, 264, 666; V:90, 505]

Schubert, (Herman J.P. & Daniel S.P.), 500 Klein Road, Buffalo, New York; no business phone—[III:579]

Science Research Associates, Inc. (SRA), 155 North Wacker Drive, Chicago, Illinois 60606; (312)904-7000—[I:29, 364, 406; II:198, 204, 275, 282, 395, 759, 773, 815; III:620; IV:635, 642]

Slosson Educational Publications, Inc., P.O. Box 280, East Aurora, New York 14052; (800) 828-4800, in New York (716)652-0930—[II:40; III:152; IV:251, 578, 620, 623]

Special Child Publications (SCP), P.O. Box 33548, Seattle, Washington 98133; (206)771-5711—[II:216]

Springer Publishing Company, 200 Park Avenue South, New York, New York 10003; (212) 475-2494—[III:539, 564, 686]

Stanford University Press, Stanford, California 94305; (415)497-9434—[II:737]

Stanton Corporation, 5701 Executive Center Drive, Suite 300, Charlotte, North Carolina 28229; (800)528-5745, in North Carolina (704)535-0060—[V:451]

Stoelting Company, 1350 S. Kostner Avenue, Chicago, Illinois 60623; (312) 522-4500—[I:274, 288, 411; II:255, 347, 383, 392, 411, 457, 491, 751; III:43, 302, 310, 496; IV:103, 157, 307, 341, 354, 357, 585; V:203, 230]

Stress Research Company, P.O. Box 307, St. Clairsville, Ohio 43950; (614)695-4805—[III:383, 388]

Teachers College Press, Teachers College, Columbia University, 1234 Amsterdam Avenue, New York, New York 10027; (212)678-3929—[II:244, 303]

Test Analysis and Development Corporation, 2400 Park Lane Drive, Boulder, Colorado 80301; (303)666-8651—[II:707; IV:400]

T.O.T.A.L. Child, Inc., 244 Deerfield Road, Cranston, Rhode Island 02920; (401)942-9955—[IV:444]

Union College, Character Research Project, 207 State Street, Schenectady, New York 12305; (518)370-6012—[IV:48]

United Educational Services, Inc., P.O. Box 357, East Aurora, New York 14052; (800)458-7900—[V:26]

United States Department of Defense, Testing Directorate, Headquarters, Military Entrance Processing Command, Attn: MEPCT, 2500 Green Bay Road, North Chicago, IL 60064; (800)323-0513, in Illinois call collect—(312)688-6908—[I:61]

United States Department of Labor, Division of Testing, Employment and Training Administration, Washington, D.C. 20213; (202)376-6270—[I:83; III:673; V:150]

University Associates, Inc., Learning Resources Corporation, 8517 Production Avenue, P.O. Box 26240, San Diego, California 92121; (619)578-5900—[I:559; II:765]

University of Illinois Press, 54 E. Gregory Drive, Box 5081, Station A, Champaign, Illinois 61820; institutions (800)233-4175, individuals (800)638-3030, or (217)333-0950—[I:354; II:543; V:32]

University of Minnesota Press, 2037 University Avenue S.E., Minneapolis, Minnesota 55414; (612)373-3266. Tests are distributed by NCS Professional Assessment Services, P.O. Box 1416 Minneapolis, Minnesota 55440; (800)328-6759, in Minnesota (612)933-2800—[I:466]

University of Vermont, College of Medicine, Department of Psychiatry, Section of Child, Adolescent, and Family Psychiatry, 1 South Prospect Street, Burlington, Vermont 05401; (802)656-4563—[I:168]

Index of Test Publishers 587

University of Washington Press, P.O. Box 85569, 4045 Brooklyn Avenue N.E., Seattle, Washington 98105; (206)543-4050, business department (206) 543-8870—[II:661, 714]

Valett, (Robert E.), Department of Advanced Studies, California State University at Fresno, Fresno, California 93740; no business phone—[II:68]

Variety Pre-Schooler's Workshop, 47 Humphrey Drive, Syosset, New York 11791; (516) 921-7171—[III:261]

Vocational Psychology Research, University of Minnesota, Elliott Hall, 75 East River Road, Minneapolis, Minnesota 55455; (612)376-7377—[II:481; IV:434; V:255]

Walker Educational Book Corporation, 720 Fifth Avenue, New York, New York 10019; (212) 265-3632—[II:689]

Western Psychological Services, A Division of Manson Western Corporation, 12031 Wilshire Boulevard, Los Angeles, California 90025; (213)478-2061—[I:315, 338, 511, 543, 663; II:108, 430, 570, 607, 723, 826; III:145, 255, 282, 340, 402, 415, 615, 714, 717; IV:15, 33, 39, 259, 274, 300, 351, 382, 440, 501, 565, 606, 649; V:9, 73, 83, 378, 382, 425, 458, 549]

Wonderlic, (E.F.), & Associates, Inc., P.O. Box 7, Northfield, Illinois 60093; (312)446-8900—[I:769]

Wyeth Laboratories, P.O. Box 8616, Philadelphia, Pennsylvania 19101; (215)688-4400—[V:499]

Zung, (William W.K.), M.D., Veterans Administration Medical Center, 508 Fulton Street, Durham, North Carolina 27705; (919)286-0411—[III:595]

INDEX OF TEST AUTHORS/REVIEWERS

Aaron, P. G., II:288
Abeles, N., I:117
Abidin, R. R., test I:504
Abrams, N. E., III:296
Abramson, L. Y., test IV:20
Achenbach, T. M., test I:168
Acker, C., test II:88
Acker, W., test II:88
Ackerman, T. A., III:164
Adair, F. L., I:226, 762
Adams, C. H., V:113
Adams, G. L., tests V:73, 287
Adams, G. R., V:297
Affleck, G., II:661, III:583
Allen, L., II:495
Allen, N. P., II:594
Allport, G., test I:641
Allred, R. A., test IV:458
Almond, P. J., test I:75
Alvarez, W., test III:358
Alvermann, D. E., IV:453
Ammons, C. H., tests I:530, II:299
Ammons, R. B., tests I:530, II:299
Anchin, J. C., test III:349
Anderhalter, O. F., tests IV:245, 264
Anderson, L. P., III:383, 542
Anderson, R. M., test IV:195
Anselmi, D., V:203
Anthony, J., test IV:281
Anton, B. S., V:109
Arick, J. R., test I:75
Arlin, P. K., test II:40
Arnold, P. D., test III:621
Arwood, E., IV:264
Ashton, P., II:681
Auld, F., II:169, 357
Ayabe, H. I., I:614
Ayres, A. J., test III:615
Bacon, E. H., IV:68, V:237, 358
Baddeley, A. D., test V:513
Baehr, M. E., test V:565
Baldonado, A. A., V:529
Baldwin, A. Y., V:458
Ball, B., test IV:103
Ball, R. S., tests I:274, II:457
Balla, D. A., test I:715
Balow, I. H., tests III:427, 434
Balthazar, E. E., tests II:56, IV:42
Bangs, T. E., test III:68
Banham, K. M., tests IV:519, V:367
Barber, L. W., test IV:48
Bardwell, R., II:363, IV:649

Barker, D. G., I:185
Barona, A., I:328
Barrett, M., test II:831
Barrett, T. C., test IV:183
Barron, F., test IV:58
Bartos, R. B., test IV:48, 183
Bascom, H. L., test IV:294
Bascue, L. O., III:415
Bass, A. R., I:83
Bass, B. M., test V:128
Battle, J., test II:216
Bauernfeind, R. H., IV:76, V:76, 494; test IV:264
Bauman, M. K., test II:12
Beatty, L. S., test I:608
Beck, A. T., tests II:83, V:198
Becker, R. L., test II:627
Bell, H. M., test I:41
Bellak, L., tests I:185, III:604
Bellak, S. S., tests I:185, III:604
Bem, S. L., test III:51
Bender, L., test I:90
Bene, E., test IV:281
Bennett, G. K., test III:226
Bennett, J. M., test III:475
Bennett, L. M., III:68, 628, IV:368
Benson, J., III:139
Benson, P. G., II:481, III:209
Benton, A., test III:58
Benton, A. L., tests V:278, 475
Berg, E. A., test IV:677
Berg, P. C., II:350
Berlin, L. J., test III:526
Berry, K. E., test IV:229
Bieger, G. R., II:463, III:51
Black, D., test IV:578
Black, K. N., III:380
Blagden, C. M., test V:221
Blank, M., test III:526
Bloch, J. S., test III:261
Block, J., tests III:125, 133
Block, J. H., test III:125
Blum, G. S., test I:99
Blum, L. H., test II:182
Bodden, J. L., I:315, V:419
Boehm, A. E., test I:106
Bolton, B., I:214, II:835, III:673, IV:434, V:255
Bonner, B., I:239
Boodoo, G. M., II:441
Borgatta, E. F., test IV:516
Borrebach, D. E., II:282

588

Botel, M., test V:37
Bower, E. M., test II:584
Boyd, H. F., test II:35; III:75
Bracken, B. A., test I:125
Bradley, M., II:299
Bradley, R. H., test II:337
Bradlyn, A. S., V:252
Brantley, J. C., I:3, II:104
Braun, J. R., I:377, 593
Brigance, A., tests III:79
Briggs, K. C., test I:482
Brink, T. L., test V:168
Broen, W. E., test II:570
Broughton, S. F., IV:92
Brown, G. M., test II:113
Brown, J. I., test III:475
Brown, L., test IV:578
Brown, L. L., tests II:787, IV:92
Brown, S. W., II:182
Brown, W., test IV:213
Bruce, M. M., test I:70
Bruininks, R. H., tests III:99, 551
Bryant, B. R., test V:94
Buchholz, S., test IV:390
Buck, J. N., test I:338
Buktenica, N. A., test IV:229
Bunch, M. B., III:111
Burgemeister, B., test II:182
Burks, H. F., test II:108
Burns, R. K., test V:565
Buss, A., test V:412
Bzoch, K. R., test V:43
Cacioppo, J. T., test III:466
Caine, T. M., test II:169
Caldwell, B. M., test II:337
Caldwell, J. R., II:263
Callahan, C. M., IV:251
Campbell, B. M., IV:469
Campbell, D. P., test II:737
Campbell, N. J., II:697
Canfield, A. A., tests V:522, 524
Cantwell, Z. M., III:319, 567, V:189
Capron, E. W., III:13
Carlson, K. A., test IV:144
Carlson, R. D., II:310, 314, III:171, IV:334, V:318, 513
Carney, C. G., test II:138
Carpenter, D., IV:68, 213, V:358
Carr, D., tests III:171, 628
Carroll, J. B., test V:271
Carroll, J. L., V:104
Carter, T. A., V:406
Cassell, R. N., tests III:145, V:113
Cassell, W. A., test V:444
Cattell, A. K. S., test I:233
Cattell, M. D., test III:319
Cattell, P., tests IV:149
Cattell, R. B., tests I:195, 202, 214, 233,

II:357, III:246, 251, 319, 567, IV:595, V:283
Chall, J. S., tests II:646, IV:553
Chaplin, W. F., I:626, II:3, III:3
Chase, C. I., I:189
Chesebro, P. A., II:63
Chew, A. L., test II:426
Childs, R., I:130
Chin-Chance, S. A., I:614
Chirico, B. M., test III:349
Cicchetti, D. V., test I:715
Clarke, J. H., test IV:172
Cleveland, J. N., V:499
Cliff, E., test II:303
Cliff, S., tests III:171, 628
Clymer, T., test IV:183
Coan, R. W., test III:246
Coddington, R. D., tests III:383, 388
Cohen, M. J., IV:620, 623
Cohen, S. H., IV:620, 623
Cole, C. W., test I:682
Colligan, R. C., II:472
Collins, C. S., test I:614
Colwell, R., V:216, 351
Comrey, A. L., test IV:199
Cone, J. D., test V:358
Connors, G. J., III:439
Cooper, J. L., test III:198
Coopersmith, S., tests I:226, III:35
Cornbleet, J. A., test IV:87
Corsini, R. J., tests IV:463, 516
Cosden, M. A., I:511, II:653, III:145, IV:229
Costello, A., test IV:656
Costello, M. R., test V:137
Cottle, W. C., test II:674
Cottrell, A. B., test II:113
Crabtree, M. C., test V:203
Craig, J. R., III:510
Craig, R. C., I:364
Crites, J. O., tests I:164, IV:478
Cromack, T. R., III:427, 434, IV:79, V:367, 517
Cull, J. G., test IV:649
Cunnington, B. F., test IV:666
Curran, J. P., test III:251
Curtis, D., test II:235
Curtis, J. W., test V:83
Daiger, D. C., test II:509
Danzer, V. A., test V:86
Daresh, J. C., V:524
Dattore, P. J., III:736
Davis, D. D., III:30, 454
Dean, R. S., I:113, II:621, III:340, IV:259, V:6
DeFilippis, N. A., test I:113
Delis, D., test I:158
Deluty, R. H., I:41, 70
Deni, J. R., II:235
Derogatis, L. R., tests II:32, III:583
Devins, G. M., II:144

Index of Test Authors/Reviewers

DeVito, A. J., I:673
Dodson, S., test III:68
Dole, A. A., II:347
Dole, J. A., I:106
Dole, N. S., test V:517
Dolliver, R. H., I:284
Domino, G., I:146
Downs, J., test IV:578
Droege, R. C., I:322
Droppleman, L., test I:522
Drummond, R. J., I:195, 252, II:258, III:246, 633, IV:351, V:226, 545
Duckworth, J. C., I:466
Dugan, R. D., II:765
Dunn, L(eota) M., test III:488
Dunn, L(loyd) M., tests III:480, 488
Duthie, B., test V:3
Dyer, C. O., II:369, IV:704
Dyer, F. J., III:310, IV:425
Eby, J. W., test IV:251
Edelbrock, C., test I:168
Edell, W. S., I:568
Edwards, A. L., test I:252
Edwards, J. E., II:198, 204
Edwards, J. R., test III:75
Elbert, J. C., III:698
Elenz-Martin, P., test V:90
Elithorn, A., test V:314
Elizur, A., test III:255
Elliott, C. D., test I:130
Ellsworth, R. B., tests II:23, 594
Enderby, P. M., test III:293
Esquivel, G. B., I:206, II:689
Essex-Sorlie, D., I:688
Estabrook, G. E., I:125
Evans, E. D., IV:570, V:505
Evans, J., test IV:213
Eysenck, H. J., tests I:279, II:258, IV:387
Eysenck, S. B. G., tests I:279, II:258
Fagley, N. S., I:682
Fakouri, M. E., II:40
Farr, R., tests III:427, 434
Federman, E. J., test III:349
Fekken, G. C., I:34, II:211, III:717, IV:58, V:556
Feldt, L. S., test I:364
Fenigstein, A., test V:412
Fewell, R. R., test V:100
Fischler, I., II:530, III:344
Fitts, W. H., test I:663
Fitzpatrick, R., I:266
Flanagan, J. C., tests II:275, 282
Fletcher, J., test II:288
Flint, B. M., test III:271
Florell, J. L., IV:195
Flowers, A., tests III:276, V:137
Folio, M. R., test V:310
Folkman, S., test III:686

Ford, J. S., test I:266
Forer, B. R., test IV:300
Fortune, J. C., III:427, 434, IV:79, V:367, 517
Foster, R., test I:3
Foster, W. S., test IV:307
Frankenburg, W. K., test I:239
Franzen, M. D., II:388, 637, III:402, IV:382, V:278, 483, 534
Frary, R. B., I:164
Fredrickson, L. C., II:319
French, J., III:447
Friedman, A. F., I:279
Friedman, A. G., V:341
Friedrich, W. N., I:543
Fristoe, M., tests III:304, IV:327, V:172
Frost, B. P., II:45
Frostig, M., test II:293
Fruchter, D. A., III:711
Fry, E., test V:212
Fudala, J. B., test IV:15
Fuld, P. A., test I:288
Fuller, G. B., test III:461
Gallini, J., IV:341
Gallivan, J., IV:127
Galluzzo, G. R., IV:578
Ganiere, D., V:266
Gardner, E. F., tests I:608, 614, II:16
Gardner, M. F., test IV:278
Gates, A. I., test II:303
Geers, A. E., test IV:157
Geisinger, K. F., I:11, IV:414, V:150
Gellman, E. S., III:186
Gerber, M. F., test V:86
Gerber, S., II:603
Getto, C. J., test III:542
Gilberts, R., test III:35
Gill, M., test III:736
Gill, W. S., test IV:649
Gilleard, C. J., test II:175
Gillis, J. S., test III:139
Gilmore, E. C., test IV:320
Gilmore, J. V., test IV:320
Glaser, E. M., test III:682
Goh, D. S., II:293
Golden, C. J., tests II:751, III:402, IV:382
Goldenberg, D. S., test IV:220
Golding, S. H., test V:26
Goldman, R., tests III:304, IV:327, V:172
Goldstein, K., test I:295
Goodenough, F. L., test II:319
Goodglass, H., test I:117
Goodman, J. F., test III:310
Gordon, E. E., tests V:216, 351
Gordon, L. V., tests I:555, I:326, 495, 759, 773
Gorenstein, E. E., III:175
Gorham, D. R., test II:603
Gorrell, J., II:543, IV:519

Index of Test Authors/Reviewers 591

Gorusch, R. L., test I:626
Gough, H. G., tests I:34, 146
Graham, F. K., test II:451
Grant, D. A., test IV:677
Gray, C. A., V:230
Gray, J., tests III:171, 628
Gray, J. W., III:340
Green, C. J., tests III:454, IV:425
Greig, M. E., test IV:264
Griffin, J. R., test V:109
Grimsley, G., test I:266
Gudmundsen, G., test IV:493
Guglielmo, R., III:35
Guidubaldi, J., test I:72
Gunn, R. L., test III:714
Gurtman, M. B., III:595
Hagen, E. P., tests I:421, V:48, 517
Hager, P. C., IV:683
Hagin, R. A., test II:689
Haimes, P. E., test III:221
Hakstian, A. R., test I:214
Hall, L. G., test I:300
Halstead, W., tests I:305, III:640
Hambleton, R. K., III:475
Hammeke, T. A., tests III:402, IV:382
Hammill, D. D., tests I:688, II:223, IV:68, 76, 92, 659, V:94, 464, 470, 485
Hamsher, K. de S., tests V:278, 475
Hanna, G. S., tests III:475, IV:453
Hansburg, H. G., test III:30
Hanson, R. A., IV:3, 11
Harding, C. P., test IV:334
Harmon, C., test III:521
Harnisch, D. L., I:608
Harrington, R. G., II:72, 244, 787, III:99, 551
Harrington, T. F., test I:322
Harris, D. B., tests I:511, II:319
Hartsough, C. S., test II:584
Harvey, P. D., III:125
Hathaway, S., test I:466
Headen, S. W., I:522
Healy, W., test IV:341
Heaton, R. K., test III:542
Hedrick, D. L., test II:714
Heesacker, M., II:674, III:466
Heiby, E. M., I:750
Heilbronner, R. L., V:475
Heilbrun, A., Jr., test I:34
Heim, A. W., tests I:51, IV:7
Helfer, R. E., test IV:400
Henson, F. O., III:68, 628, IV:368
Herman, D. O., V:32
Herrin, M. S., test III:75
Hertzog, C., II:815
Herzberger, S., II:661, III:358, 583, 686, IV:20
Hicks, L. E., III:133

Hieronymus, A. N., test IV:127
Hilgard, E. R., tests I:623, II:729
Hilgard, J. R., test V:447
Hill, B. K., test III:551
Himelstein, P., I:202, II:559
Hirsch, S., test III:608
Hirsh, H. R., I:29
Hiskey, M. S., test III:331
Histe, P. A., test I:494
Hoepfner, R., test V:21
Hoffmeister, J. K., tests II:707, IV:400
Hogan, J., III:615
Hogan, T. P., tests III:427, 434, 633
Holden, E. W., III:698, IV:400, V:475
Holden, R. H., I:603, 715, II:627, III:564, IV:444, V:3, 83
Holden, R. R., II:826, III:461, IV:144, V:198
Holland, A. L., test IV:189
Holland, J. L., tests II:509, 697, V:419, 545
Holloway, A. J., test II:198
Holmes, T. H., test II:661
Holtzman, W. H., test I:328
Hooper, H. E., test III:340
Hoover, H.D., test IV:127
Horne, M. D., II:113, IV:553
Horowitz, M. J., test III:358
Hoskins, C. N., test V:303
Houtz, J. C., IV:666
Howard, K. I., test V:297
Hresko, W. P., tests V:464, 470
Huard, S. D., IV:172
Huberty, T. J., II:161
Huck, S. W., I:51
Hudak, M. A., II:402
Hufano, L. D., III:221
Huisingh, R., test II:831
Hunt, J. McV., test II:543
Hunt, T., I:406, II:275, III:714
Hutson, B. A., IV:357
Hutt, M. L., test III:437
Hutton, J. B., IV:87, 565
Hutton, J. G., Jr., II:326
Ireton, H., tests II:472, V:252, 348
Jackson, D. N., tests II:369, 501, III:499
Jackson, S. E., test III:419
Jacobson, M. G., V:21
Jeanneret, P. R., test V:326
Jamison, C. B., I:274, II:241, IV:33
Jastak, J. F., tests I:758, 762, IV:673
Jastak, S., tests I:758, IV:673
Jaynes, W. E., IV:635
Jeffrey, P. M., test II:642
Jenson, W. R., I:75
Jesness, C. F., tests I:380, V:226
Jex, J. L., test III:669
Johansson, C. B., tests I:660, II:128
Johns, E., test III:319

Index of Test Authors/Reviewers

Johns, J. L., V:290
Johnsen, S. K., test II:787
Johnson, D. L., tests III:302, IV:354
Johnson, G. O., test II:35
Johnson, M. B., test IV:683
Johnson, R. E., test II:723
Johnson, R. G., II:607, V:425
Johnson, S. D., Jr., IV:132
Jones, A. P., II:551
Jones, D., test V:314
Jones, J. D., tests I:707, III:669
Jones, M., test IV:107
Jordaan, J. P., test IV:132
Jordan, F. L., test IV:570
Jorgensen, C., test II:831
Joseph, J., test V:230
Justice, E. M., III:158
Kahn, T. C., tests II:376, III:375
Kalish, B. I., test III:43
Kamons, J., test IV:310
Kaplan, E., test I:117, 158
Karlsen, B., test II:16
Katoff, L., test III:380
Katz, J., test III:521
Kaufman, A. S., tests I:393, IV:368
Kaufman, H., tests II:383, IV:357
Kaufman, J., II:12
Kaufman, K., I:633
Kaufman, K. L., V:55
Kaufman, N. L., tests I:393, IV:368
Kearney, P. A., II:584
Keith, T. Z., II:446, IV:394
Kelble, E. S., IV:11, V:86
Kellerman, H., test IV:274
Kendall, B. S., test II:451
Kendrick, D. C., test II:388
Kennedy, V. E., V:244
Kertesz, A., test II:819
Khatena, J., test IV:666
Kicklighter, R. H., test II:161
Kiernan, C., test IV:107
Kiesler, D. J., test III:349
Killian, G. A., I:338, II:751, IV:469
King, J. E., tests I:363, IV:635
King, M., test IV:127
Kirk, S. A., test I:354
Kirk, W. D., test I:354
Kirnan, J. P., V:150
Kleiman, L. S., III:496
Klein, S. P., test V:21
Klinedinst, J. E., test II:570
Klove, H., test I:478
Klump, C. S., test V:451
Knapp, L., test V:76
Knapp, R. R., test V:76
Kobos, J. C., III:288
Koch, W. R., I:233

Kohs, S. C., test II:392
Konopasky, R. J., II:95
Koppitz, E. M., tests I:189, V:537
Koschier, M., test II:138
Kovacevich, D. A., III:79
Kovacs, M., test V:65
Kowalski, R. L., test IV:310
Kramer, J., test I:158
Krauskopf, C. J., I:720
Krug, D. A., test I:75
Krug, S. E., tests I:377, III:567
Kuder, G. F., tests I:406, II:395
Kuhns, J. W., test II:517
Kyle, E. M., test III:349
Lachar, D., test II:570
Lambert, N., tests I:3, II:584
Lane, H. S., test IV:157
Langley, M. B., test V:100
Lanyon, B. P., test II:347
Lanyon, R. I., tests II:347, IV:509
Larsen, S. C., tests I:688, V:485
Larson, A. D., III:331
Laughlin, J. E., test I:377
LaVoie, A. L., I:99, 259, II:255, III:251, 302, IV:256, V:388
Lawshe, C. H., test I:29
Layton, L. L., V:94
Layton, T. L., IV:176, 659
Lazarus, R. S., test III:686
League, R., test V:43
Lee, C. C., I:300
Lehman, R. A. W., test III:542
Leigh, J. E., tests IV:68, 76, 87
Leiter, R. G., tests I:411, II:411
Leland, H., test I:3
Lennon, R. T., test I:499
Lerner, H., IV:523
Lerner, J. V., II:108
Lerner, P. M., IV:523
Lester, D., test V:198
Leton, D. A., I:536
Levin, H. S., test V:475
Levitt, E. E., I:466
Lewis, J. F., tests I:648, III:13
Lewis, L, III:640
Likert, R., test II:765
Lindamood, C. H., test IV:376
Lindamood, P. C., test IV:376
Lindeman, R. H., test IV:132
Linder, T., I:443, IV:220
Lindquist, E. F., tests I:364, IV:127
Lindzey, G., test I:641
Llabre, M. M., I:436, 595
Lockwood, J., test II:559
Loeb, H. W., II:457
Loevinger, J., test III:395
Lonborg, S. D., V:9

Index of Test Authors/Reviewers 593

London, P., test IV:162
Long, T. R., test III:496
Loper, A. B., II:68
Lord, R. H., II:517, IV:484, V:382
Lorge, I., tests I:421, II:182, 530
Lorr, M., tests I:522, II:607
Loser, C. P., IV:327
Lovell, M. R., I:473, II:570
Low, G. R., test V:318
Low, T. W., IV:440
Lowe, M., test IV:656
Lubin, B., tests III:215, IV:449
Lundell, K., test IV:213
Lurie, L., V:168
Lushene, R. E., test I:626
Lyons, T., test V:86
MacGinitie, R. K., test IV:310
MacGinitie, W. H., test IV:310
Madden, R., tests I:608, 614, II:16
Majers, K., test II:416
Malgady, R. G., II:56, 216
Mallinson, G., test IV:264
Mallinson, J., test IV:264
Manson, M. P., tests II:826, III:714, V:9
Mardell-Czudnowski, C. D., test IV:220
Margolis, J., IV:611
Markwardt, F. C., Jr., test III:480
Marlatt, G. A., test III:175
Martin, W. T., tests I:568, V:483
Martinez, D., test II:441
Maslach, C., test III:419
Mason, P. J., V:303
Massey, J., test IV:570
Matey, C., I:411, II:723
Matheny, P. A., test IV:195
Matuszek, P., I:51
Maxfield, K. E., test IV:390
McArthur, D. S., test I:543
McCabe, S. P., I:455, II:128
McCall, W. A., test II:530
McCallum, R. S., test III:75
McCampbell, E., test I:113
McCarley, D. G., test II:255
McCarney, S. B., test IV:87
McCarthy, D., tests II:446, IV:394
McCarthy, J. J., test I:354
McCarthy, P. R., II:707, III:349
McConnell, N. L., test V:221
McConnell, T. R., test I:494
McCormick, E. J., test V:326
McDaniel, E. L., test IV:351
McGauvran, M. E., test II:463
McGuire, M. L., test III:198
McInnis, C. E., V:48, 271
McKay, T., test IV:310
McKee, M. G., I:559, II:729, III:206
McKillop, A. S., test II:303

McKinley, J. C, test I:466
McKinney, B., I:504
McMahon, F. B., Jr., test III:282
McMurry, R. N., tests III:621, IV:635
McNair, D. M., test I:522
Meagher, R. B., Jr., tests III:454, IV:425
Mealor, D. J., III:546
Mecham, M. J., tests I:707, 712, III:669
Mecham, R. C., test V:326
Meeker, M., test V:458
Meeker, R., test V:458
Melendez, F., test V:6
Meisels, S. J., test II:244
Mercer, J. R., tests I:648, III:13
Merenda, P. F., IV:199
Merrifield, P., test I:274
Merrill, M. A., test I:603
Merz, W. R., Sr., I:393, II:436, III:255
Metalsky, G. I., test IV:20
Michaelson, R. B., test IV:294
Miles, M., test IV:195
Miller, H. R., IV:501
Miller, K. M., test IV:560
Miller, L. C., tests II:430, IV:565
Miller, L. J., test I:443
Miller, M. D., III:271
Miller, W. R., test III:175
Miller, W. S., test IV:414
Miller-Tiedeman, A., test V:90
Milling, L. S., I:239, IV:162, V:447
Millon, T., tests I:455, III:454, IV:425
Milner, J., test V:55
Mira, M., III:331, IV:281
Miskimins, R. W., test V:266
Monroe, N. E., IV:189
Mooney, K. C., I:168, 380
Mooney, R. L., test II:495
Moos, B. S., test II:263
Moos, R. H., test II:263
Morency, A., test IV:39
Morgan, A. H., test V:447
Morrison, L. P., test I:652
Morse, D. T., II:416
Mowrer, D., V:378
Mowrer, D. E., IV:15
Mueller, D. J., I:549, II:759, 773
Mulgrave, N. W., II:175, IV:408
Mullen, E. M., test IV:444
Murphy, K. R., I:61, 769
Murray, D. J., test I:130
Murray, H. A., test II:799
Mutti, M., test II:621
Myers, I. B., test I:482
Myers, R. A., test IV:132
Nelson, A. R., test V:529
Nelson, D. B., test V:318
Newberg, J., test II:72

Newcomer, P. L., tests II:235, IV:659
Newland, T. E., test V:32
Nicassio, P. M., II:35
Nihira, K., test I:3
Northrop, L. C., III:282
Nurss, J. R., test II:463
Nymann, C., tests III:171, 628
Ober, B., test I:158
O'Brien, J., test V:290
Oetting, E. R., test I:682
Offer, D., test V:297
Offermann, L. R., III:419
Ofsanko, F. J., V:128
Oltman, P. K., test V:189
Organist, J. E., IV:673
Orme, C. E., II:144
Osberg, T. M., III:608, V:412
O'Shea, A. J., test I:322
Osipow, S. H., tests II:138, 435
Ostrov, E., test V:297
Othmer, E., test IV:501
Otis, A. S., test I:499
Pace, L. A., IV:354
Palormo, J. M., test II:204
Papenfuss, J. F., test IV:264
Parker, R., IV:274
Parkison, S. C., V:109
Pattie, A. H., test II:175
Pauker, J. D., test I:473
Pearlman, R. C., III:521, V:137
Pearson, L. S., test I:130
Penick, E. C., test IV:501
Pennock-Román, M., III:226
Perachio, J. J., test II:562
Perkins, M. J., test III:349
Perry, K. M., III:367
Peterson, C., test IV:20
Peterson, D. R., test V:371
Peterson, R. A., I:504, 522
Petty, R. E., test III:466
Petzel, T. P., II:411, III:215
Phillips, S. E., I:578, III:655
Phillipson, H., test IV:469
Piers, E. V., test I:511
Pino, C. J., test III:152
Platt, S., test III:608
Plutchik, R., test IV:274
Polite, K., II:231
Porter, R. B., test I:195
Porteus, S. D., test II:579
Powell, B. J., test IV:501
Power, P. G., test II:509
Pranis, R. W., test V:565
Prather, E. M., test II:714
Prescott, G. A., tests III:427, 434
Preston, J. M., I:354
Price, G. E., I:555

Procidano, M. E., II:337, III:152
Puente, A. E., IV:677
Purisch, A. D., tests III:402, IV:382
Quatrano, L. A., V:90
Quay, H. C., test V:371
Rabetz, M., test III:539
Rabinowitz, W., I:641
Rapaport, D., test III:736
Rasinski, T. V., V:37
Rattan, A. I., IV:259, V:6
Rattan, G., I:113, II:621, V:6
Raven, J. C., tests I:47, 206, 595, IV:408
Reddin, W. J., test III:209
Redding, S., tests III:171, 628
Redfield, D. L., V:396
Reid, D. K., tests V:464, 470
Reinehr, R. C., I:758, V:444
Reinking, D., II:303
Reisman, F. K., test IV:590
Reitan, R. M., tests I:305, 535, II:637, III:640
Renck, R., test V:565
Renzulli, J. S., test II:402
Reuter, J. M., II:383, III:43, V:43; test III:380
Reynell, J., test III:546
Richmond, B. O., test II:161
Riley, G. D., tests V:378, 382
Rimm, S. B., test II:332
Roberts, G. E., test I:543
Roberts, T., V:371
Roberts, V. A., III:526
Robinette, M. S., III:669
Robinson, J. H., III:79
Rodrigues, M. C., test IV:11
Roe, A. V., test II:95
Roe, B. D., test II:350
Rokeach, M., test I:549
Roll, E. J., test II:559
Roll, S., test II:559
Rorschach, H., test IV:523
Rose, S. A., test III:526
Rosenbach, J. H., I:648
Rosenbaum, R., I:158, 288
Rosenzweig, S., test V:388
Ross, C. M., test V:396
Ross, J. D., test V:396
Roswell, F. G., tests II:646, IV:553
Roszkowski, M. J., V:326
Rothermel, R. D., II:570
Roth, R. M., test IV:440
Rothwell, J. W., test IV:560
Rotter, J. B., test II:653
Ruch, F. L., test I:266
Russell, S. C., III:726
Ruttenberg, B. A., test III:43
Ryan, J. J., IV:585
Ryan, R. M., II:799
Santos de Barona, M., IV:103

Sapon, S. M., test V:271
Satz, P., test II:288
Sax, G., I:421
Scannell, D. P., test IV:127
Schaefer, C. E., test III:206
Schafer, R., test III:736
Scheerer, M., test I:295
Scheier, I. H., tests II:357, V:283
Scheier, M., test V:412
Schell, L. M., test IV:453
Schinka, J. A., test I:491
Schneider, C., test IV:400
Schoenfeldt, B. B., II:646, III:198, IV:320
Schrank, F. A., I:660
Schreiner, R., test IV:453
Schubert, H. J. P., test III:579
Schutz, W., tests I:284, 559, III:392
Schwarting, G., IV:390, 656, V:209, 348
Seashore, H. G., test III:226
Seat, P. D., test II:570
Segel, R. C., test V:26
Seidenberg, M., I:478
Seligman, M. E. P., test IV:20
Selzer, M. L., test III:439
Semel, E., test IV:176
Semmel, A., test IV:20
Serwatka, T. S., IV:157, 493
Shellhaas, M., test I:3
Sherbenou, R. J., test II:787
Shipley, W. C., test V:425
Shneidman, E. S., test II:436
Shorr, J. E., test I:593
Shostrom, E. L., tests II:3, III:3
Siegel, L. J., V:65
Silver, A. A., test II:689
Silverstein, A. B., I:295
Simmonds, V., test I:51
Simon, C. S., test V:118
Simons, N., test III:152
Sines, J. O., test I:473
Sines, L. K., test I:473
Sklar, M., test IV:606
Slaney, R. B., II:138
Slawinowski, M. J., test III:152
Slingerland, B. H., test IV:611
Sloan, T. S., III:392, 539
Slosson, R. L., tests IV:620, 623
Smail, D., test II:169
Small, J. R., I:652
Smith, A. J., test II:723
Smith, J., test V:314
Smith, J. K., test III:164
Smith, K. J., II:714
Smith, L. H., test II:402
Smitheimer, L. S., II:191, 562, V:118
Smitherman, H. O'N., II:376
Snelbecker, G. E., V:326

Snider, J. L., IV:238, 278
Snider, K. P., IV:238, 278
Snyder, D. K., test III:415
Solomon, I. L., test III:564
Somwaru, J. P., test II:45
Sones, R. A., test IV:259
Sowell, E. J., IV:590
Spache, G. D., test IV:238
Spadafore, G. J., tests IV:627, V:237
Spadafore, S. J., test V:237
Sparrow, S. S., test I:715
Spalding, N. V., test II:621
Speilberger, C. D., tests I:626, 633, 673
Spivack, G., tests II:231, III:221
Spokane, A. R., test II:535
Spotts, J., tests II:231, III:221
Spruill, J., I:728
Sprunger, J. A., IV:42
Stahl, S. A., IV:310
Stahlecker, J. E., V:100
Stark, R. H., test IV:496
Starr, B. D., tests III:539, 563
Starr, C. D., III:304
Steen, P. test III:367
Stehouwer, R. S., II:83, 223
Sterling, H. M., test II:621
Stern, G. G., tests II:551, III:158
Sternberg, L., IV:119
Stick, S. L., V:141
Stillman, R. (Ed.), test IV:119
Stock, J., test II:72
Stoker, H. W., IV:245
Stone, M., I:491, 623, II:392, IV:387, V:314
Stone, R. E., Jr., IV:606
Stoodt, B. D., IV:458, 627
Stott, D. H., test II:104
Stott, L. H., test I:274
Strain, L. B., V:179
Streiner, D. L., II:88, III:375, IV:509
Strickland, G. P., test V:21
Striffler, N., test II:191
Strong, E. K., test II:737
Strotman, D., test III:367
Stuempfig, D. W., V:26
Subich, L. M., V:565
Sucher, F., test IV:458
Suinn, R. M., test I:436
Sullivan, A. P., III:35
Sundberg, N. D., II:579, 642
Super, D. E., tests II:835, IV:132
Svinicki, J., test II:72
Swartz, J. D., I:530, III:604, V:73, 287
Sweney, A. B., tests III:567, IV:560, 642
Swerdlik, M. E., II:293
Swift, M., test V:104
Switzky, H. N., IV:107
Taggart, B., test III:344

Index of Test Authors/Reviewers

Taggart, W., test III:344
Takooshian, H., III:621, IV:463
Taleporos, E., V:283, 323
Tarbox, A. R., III:439
Tarrier, R. B., test I:300
Taylor, J. S., I:707, 712
Taylor, M. F., III:293
Taylor, R. L., IV:119
Taylor, R. M., test I:652
Teas-Hester, E., III:261, V:221
Templer, D. I., II:32, IV:449
Tennen, H., II:661, III:358, 583, 686, IV:20
Terman, L. M., tests I:603, II:530
Theimer, K., IV:294
Thompson, A. S., test IV:132
Thompson, D. N., IV:307, 516
Thompson, J. M., test IV:259
Thorndike, R. L., tests I:421, V:48, 517
Thornton, G. C., III, II:16
Thorum, A. R., test V:141
Thurstone, L. L., tests II:815, IV:642
Thurstone, T. G., tests II:815, IV:642
Thwing, E., tests II:472, V:252
Tien, H. C., test IV:484
Tiffin, J., test I:29
Tinsley, H. E. A., II:509, III:499
Tobin, A. R., test II:714
Torrance, E. P., tests III:344, IV:666, V:505
Trapp, E. P., II:430
Trent, E. R., test V:517
Trexler, L., test V:198
Trites, R., test V:534
Troy, M. E., II:780
Tzeng, O. C. S., II:737
Umberger, F. G., II:819, III:488, V:172
Uzgiris, I. C., test II:543
Vail, N., test IV:264
Valett, R. E., tests II:68, 241
Van Allen, M. W., test V:475
van Lennep, D. J., test III:288
Varnhagen, C. K., V:485
Vaughn, L. J., test V:549
Venn, J. J., V:310
Vernon, P. A., I:47, 740, II:501
Vernon, P. E., test I:641
Vestre, N. D., test II:607
Vincent, K. R., III:388, 395, 480
Volger, W. H., test IV:11
von Baeyer, C., test IV:20
Vu, N. V., V:549
Wachs, H., test V:549
Wadell, D. C., tests II:416, V:517
Wagener, J. M., II:451
Wagner, E. E., test I:315
Wakefield, J. F., II:332
Walker, C. E., I:239, 633, IV:162, 400, V:55, 303, 341

Walker, W. J., test III:158
Walsh, J. A., I:663
Walsh, W. B., I:494
Walton, H. N., test V:109
Wang, P. L., test II:491
Ward, D. G., II:23, IV:496
Warren, J., III:579
Warren, N. D., test I:266
Waryas, P., test IV:493
Watson, G., test III:682
Watts, K. P., test I:51
Weatherman, R. F., test III:551
Weaver, S. J., IV:281
Webster, H. D., test I:494
Webster, R. E., IV:300, V:537; test V:244
Wechsler, D., tests I:720, 728, 740, 750, III:698
Weinberg, R., test IV:103
Weiner, M. B., test III:539
Weissman, A., test V:198
Weitzenhoffer, A. M., tests I:623, II:729
Wellman, M. M., III:58
Wells, G. B., II:831
Welsh, G., tests IV:58, V:556
Wenar, C., test III:43
Wepman, J. M., tests IV:33, 39
Wesman, A. G., tests III:226, 711
Weyman, A., test III:608
Whatley, J. L., IV:149
Wheeler, J. P., test III:75
Whitaker, L. C., test III:717
Whitley, T. W., IV:300, V:537
Whitworth, R. H., I:90, 305
Wholeben, B. E., IV:595
Wick, J. W., test III:164
Widerstrom, A. H., V:464, 470
Wiederholt, J. L., test V:179
Wiig, E., test IV:176
Wijesinghe, O. B. A., test II:169
Wilburn, K. T., V:522
Williams, F. E., test II:211
Williams, J. A., II:395
Williams, J. D., II:395
Williams, R. E., III:388, 395, 480
Williams, R. H., I:499
Willig, S., test II:191
Willis, C. G., I:482, II:631, V:451
Wilner, N., test III:358
Wilson, J. F., test IV:11
Windmiller, M., test I:3
Winer, J. L., test II:138
Winter, D., test II:169
Wirt, R. D., test II:570
Wiske, M. S., test II:244
Witkin, H., test I:259
Witkin, H. A., test V:189
Wittes, S., test IV:172

Wnek, L., test II:72
Woehlke, P. L., II:426, 491, III:682
Wolf, E. G., test III:43
Wolf, F. M., II:594
Wolpert, E. M., IV:48, 183
Wonderlic, E. F., test I:769
Woodcock, R. W., tests III:304, 551, 726, IV:327, 683, 704
Wright, E., test V:48
Yanico, B., II:535; test II:138
Yates, J. T., III:276
Yonge, G. D., test I:494
Young, E. C., test II:562
Zachman, L., test II:831
Zimmerman, B. R., III:647
Zimmerman, D. W., IV:7
Zinkin, P., test III:546
Zinna, D. R., IV:376, V:212
Zlotogorski, Z., IV:39, V:168
Zuckerman, M., test IV:449
Zung, W. W. K., test III:595

SUBJECT INDEX

PSYCHOLOGY

Child and Child Development

Barber Scales of Self-Regard for Preschool Children, IV:48
Behavior Rating Instrument for Autistic and Other Atypical Children, III:43
Birth to Three Developmental Scale, III:68
Bzoch-League Receptive-Expressive Emergent Language Scale, The, V:43
Callier-Azusa Scale: G Edition, IV:119
Cattell Infant Development Scale, IV:149
Communicative Evaluation Chart from Infancy to Five Years, IV:195
Comprehensive Developmental Evaluation Chart, III:171
Denver Developmental Screening Test, I:239
Extended Merrill-Palmer Scale, I:274
Flint Infant Security Scale, III:271
Kahn Infant and Preschool Scale, II:383
Kent Infant Development Scale, III:380
Maxfield-Buchholz Social Maturity Scale for Blind Preschool Children, IV:390
McCarthy Scales of Children's Abilities, IV:394
Merrill-Palmer Scale, II:457
Miller Assessment for Preschoolers, I:443
Minnesota Child Development Inventory, II:472
Minnesota Infant Development Inventory, V:252
Ordinal Scales of Psychological Development, II:543
Preschool Development Inventory, V:348
Quick Screening Scale of Mental Development, A, V:367
Reynell-Zinkin Scales: Developmental Scales for Young Visually Handicapped Children
 Part 1—Mental Development, III:546
Ring and Peg Tests of Behavior Development, IV:519
Smith-Johnson Nonverbal Performance Scale, II:723
Steps Up Developmental Screening Program, III:628
Symbolic Play Test: Experimental Edition, IV:656
Vineland Adaptive Behavior Scales, I:715

Intelligence and Related

Advanced Progressive Matrices, I:47
Clifton Assessment Procedures for the Elderly, II:175
Coloured Progressive Matrices, I:206
Columbia Mental Maturity Scale, II:182
Culture Fair Intelligence Test, I:233
Foster Mazes, IV:307
Full-Range Picture Vocabulary Test, II:299
Goodenough-Harris Drawing Test, II:319
Healy Pictorial Completion Test, IV:341
Kahn Intelligence Test, III:375
Kendrick Cognitive Tests for the Elderly, II:388
Leiter Adult Intelligence Scale, II:411
Leiter International Performance Scale, I:411
Mill Hill Vocabulary Scale: 1982 Edition, IV:408
Multidimensional Aptitude Battery, II:501
Non-Language Multi-Mental Test, II:530
Porteus Mazes, II:579
Quick Test, I:530

Subject Index 599

Shipley Institute of Living Scale, V:425
Slosson Drawing Coordination Test, IV:620
Slosson Oral Reading Test, IV:623
Standard Progressive Matrices, I:595
Stanford-Binet Intelligence Scale: Form L-M, I:603
Test of Nonverbal Intelligence, II:787
Wechsler Adult Intelligence Scale, I:720
Wechsler Adult Intelligence Scale-Revised, I:728
Wechsler Intelligence Scale for Children-Revised, I:740
Wechsler Preschool and Primary Scale of Intelligence, III:698

Marriage and Family: Family

Adaptive Behavior Inventory for Children, The, III:13
Children's Version/Family Environment Scale, III:152
Family Environment Scale, I:263
Family Relations Test: Children's Version, IV:281
Family Relationship Inventory, IV:294
Life Event Scale-Children, III:388
Life Interpersonal History Enquiry, III:392
Michigan Screening Profile of Parenting, IV:400
Mother-Child Relationship Evaluation, IV:440
Parent Attachment Structured Interview, II:559
Parenting Stress Index, I:504
Partner Relationship Inventory: Research Edition, V:303
Wisconsin Card Sorting Test, IV:677

Marriage and Family: Premarital and Marital Relations

Marital Satisfaction Inventory, III:415

Neuropsychology and Related

Adult Neuropsychological Questionnaire, V:6
Behaviour Assessment Battery, 2nd Edition, IV:107
Bender Visual Motor Gestalt Test, I:90
Benton Revised Visual Retention Test, III:58
Bexley-Maudsley Automated Psychological Screening, II:88
Booklet Category Test, The, I:113
Boston Diagnostic Aphasia Examination, I:117
California Verbal Learning Test, I:158
Developmental Test of Visual-Motor Integration, IV:229
Elizur Test of Psycho-Organicity: Children & Adults, III:255
Fuld Object-Memory Evaluation, I:288
Goldstein-Scheerer Tests of Abstract and Concrete Thinking, I:295
Halstead-Reitan Neuropsychological Battery and Allied Procedures, The, I:305
Hooper Visual Organization Test, III:340
Houston Test for Language Development, The, V:203
Kahn Test of Symbol Arrangement, II:376
Luria-Nebraska Neuropsychological Battery, III:402
Luria-Nebraska Neuropsychological Battery, Form II, IV:382
Memory-For-Designs Test, II:451
Minnesota Percepto-Diagnostic Test, III:461
Modified Vigotsky Concept Formation Test, II:491
Motor Steadiness Battery, I:478
Multilingual Aphasia Examination, V:278
Neurological Dysfunctions of Children, II:517
Neuropsychological Status Examination, I:491
Organic Integrity Test, IV:484
Perceptual Maze Test, V:314

600 Subject Index

Quick Neurological Screening Test, II:621
Reitan Evaluation of Hemispheric Abilities and Brain Improvement, II:637
Reitan-Indiana Neuropsychological Test Battery for Children, I:536
Riley Motor Problems Inventory, V:382
Southern California Motor Accuracy Test, Revised, III:615
Tactual Performance Test, III:640
Test of Facial Recognition-Form SL, V:475
Test of Perceptual Organization, V:483
Tests of Mental Function in the Elderly, V:499
Trites Neuropsychological Test Battery, V:534
Wechsler Memory Scale, I:750
Western Aphasia Battery, The, II:819

Personality: Adolescent and Adult

Actualizing Assessment Battery I: The Intrapersonal Inventories, II:3
Actualizing Assessment Battery II: The Interpersonal Inventories, III:3
Adjective Check List, I:34
Adjustment Inventory, The: Adult Form, I:41
Adolescent Emotional Factors Inventory, II:12
Adolescent Multiphasic Personality Inventory, V:3
Adult Personal Adjustment and Role Skills, II:23
Affects Balance Scale, II:32
Alcadd Test, V:9
Association Adjustment Inventory, I:70
Beck Depression Inventory, II:83
Bem Sex-Role Inventory, III:51
Bipolar Psychological Inventory, II:95
California Psychological Inventory, I:146
California Q-Sort, III:133
Carlson Psychological Survey, IV:144
Center for Epidemiologic Studies Depression Scale, II:144
Child Abuse Potential Inventory, The, V:55
Claybury Selection Battery, II:169
Clinical Analysis Questionnaire, I:202
Comprehensive Drinker Profile, III:175
Comrey Personality Scales, IV:199
Curtis Completion Form, V:83
Depression Adjective Check Lists, III:215
Edwards Personal Preference Schedule, I:252
Ego-Ideal and Conscience Development Test, V:113
Ego State Inventory, II:255
Eight State Questionnaire, III:251
Emotions Profile Index, IV:274
Eysenck Personality Inventory, II:258
Eysenck Personality Questionnaire, I:279
Forty-Eight Item Counseling Evaluation Test: Revised, III:282
Geriatric Depression Scale, V:168
Gordon Personal Profile-Inventory, II:326
High School Personality Questionnaire, III:319
Hopelessness Scale, V:198
Impact Message Inventory, III:349
Impact of Event Scale, III:358
Incomplete Sentences Task, II:347
IPAT Anxiety Scale, II:357
IPAT Depression Scale, I:377
Jackson Personality Inventory, II:369
Jesness Behavior Checklist, V:226

Life Event Scale-Adolescents, III:383
Mathematics Anxiety Rating Scale, I:436
Maudsley Personality Inventory, IV:387
Michigan Alcoholism Screening Test, III:439
Millon Adolescent Personality Inventory, IV:425
Millon Behavioral Health Inventory, III:454
Millon Clinical Multiaxial Inventory, I:455
Minnesota Multiphasic Personality Inventory, I:466
Miskimins Self-Goal-Other Discrepancy Scale, V:266
Mooney Problem Check List, II:495
Multiple Affect Adjective Check List-Revised, IV:449
Myers-Briggs Type Indicator, I:482
Need for Cognition Scale, III:466
Object Relations Technique, IV:469
Offer Self-Image Questionnaire for Adolescents, V:297
Omnibus Personality Inventory, I:494
Polyfactorial Study of Personality, IV:496
Profile of Adaptation to Life: Clinical and Holistic Forms, II:594
Profile of Mood States, I:522
Projective Assessment of Aging Method, III:539
Proverbs Test, II:603
Psychiatric Diagnostic Interview, IV:501
Psychological Screening Inventory, IV:509
Psychosocial Pain Inventory, III:542
Psychotic Inpatient Profile, II:607
Rotter Incomplete Sentences Blank, II:653
School Motivation Analysis Test, III:567
Schutz Measures, I:559
SCL-90-R, III:583
S-D Proneness Checklist, I:568
Self-Consciousness Scale, The, V:412
Self-Rating Depression Scale, III:595
Senior Apperception Technique, III:604
Shorr Imagery Test, I:593
Sixteen Personality Factor Questionnaire, IV:595
Social Behaviour Assessment Schedule, III:608
Somatic Inkblot Series, V:444
State-Trait Anxiety Inventory, I:626
Suicide Probability Scale, IV:649
Survey of Interpersonal Values, II:759
Taylor-Johnson Temperament Analysis, I:652
Thematic Apperception Test, II:799
Ways of Coping Scale, III:686
Western Personality Inventory, II:826
Whitaker Index of Schizophrenic Thinking, III:717

Personality: Child

Burks' Behavior Rating Scales, II:108
California Child Q-Set, The, III:125
Child Anxiety Scale, III:139
Child Behavior Checklist, III:168
Children's Apperception Test, I:185
Children's Hypnotic Susceptibility Scale, IV:162
Children's Personality Questionnaire, I:195
Early School Personality Questionnaire, III:246
Michigan Picture Test-Revised, III:447
Missouri Children's Picture Series, I:473

602 *Subject Index*

Personality Inventory for Children,   II:570
Preschool Behavior Questionnaire,   V:341
Psychological Evaluation of Children's Human Figure Drawings,   I:189
Roberts Apperception Test for Children,   I:543
School Apperception Method,   III:564
State-Trait Anxiety Inventory for Children,   I:633

Personality: Multi-level

Adolescent Separation Anxiety Test,   III:30
Autism Screening Instrument for Educational Planning,   I:75
Balthazar Scales of Adaptive Behavior II: Scales of Social Adaptation,   II:56
Barron-Welsh Art Scale,   IV:58
Behavioral Deviancy Profile,   IV:103
Blacky Pictures, The,   I:99
Children's Depression Inventory, The,   V:65
Coopersmith Self-Esteem Inventories,   I:226
Culture-Free Self-Esteem Inventories for Children and Adults,   II:216
Forer Structured Sentence Completion Test,   IV:300
Four Picture Test,   III:288
Fundamental Interpersonal Relations Orientation—Behavior (B) and Feelings (F),   I:284
Group Embedded Figures Test,   V:189
Hand Test, The,   I:315
Holtzman Inkblot Technique,   I:328
House-Tree-Person Technique,   I:338
Jesness Inventory, The,   I:380
Loevinger's Washington University Sentence Completion Test,   III:395
Louisville Behavior Checklist,   II:430
Make A Picture Story,   II:436
Neuroticism Scale Questionnaire,   V:283
Personality Research Form,   III:499
Rogers Personal Adjustment Inventory,   II:642
Rokeach Value Survey,   I:549
Rorschach Inkblot Test,   IV:523
Rosenzweig Picture-Frustration Study,   V:388
Schedule of Recent Experience,   II:661
Self-Esteem Questionnaire,   II:707
Stroop Color and Word Test,   II:751
Tennessee Self Concept Scale,   I:663
Welsh Figure Preference Test,   V:556
Wide Range Intelligence-Personality Test,   I:762
Word Association Test,   III:736

Research

Attributional Style Questionnaire,   IV:20
Embedded Figures Test,   I:259
Home Observation for Measurement of the Environment,   II:337
Maslach Burnout Inventory,   III:419
Piers-Harris Children's Self Concept Scale,   I:511
Stanford Hypnotic Clinical Scale for Children,   V:447
Stanford Hypnotic Susceptibility Scale,   II:729
Stanford Profile Scales of Hypnotic Susceptibility, Revised Edition,   I:623
Test Anxiety Inventory,   I:673
Three Minute Reasoning Test,   V:513

EDUCATION

Academic Subjects: English and Related—Multi-level
Test of Written Language, I:688
Test of Written Spelling, V:485

Academic Subjects: Fine Arts
Instrument Timbre Preference Test, V:216
Primary Measures of Music Audiation, V:351

Academic Subjects: Foreign Language & English as a Second Language
Modern Language Aptitude Test, V:271
Test of English as a Foreign Language, III:655

Academic Subjects: Mathematics—Basic Math Skills
Sequential Assessment of Mathematics Inventories: Standardized Inventories, IV:590

Achievement and Aptitude: Academic
Academic Instruction Measurement System, IV:3
ACT Assessment, The, I:11
Assessment of Basic Competencies, II:45
Basic Achievement Skills Individual Screener, II:63
Basic Educational Skills Test, V:26
Basic School Skills Inventory—Diagnostic, IV:68
Basic School Skills Inventory—Screen, IV:76
Basic Skills Assessment Program, 1978 Edition, IV:79
Brigance Diagnostic Comprehensive Inventory of Basic Skills, The, III:79
Brigance Diagnostic Inventory of Basic Skills, The, III:84
Brigance Diagnostic Inventory of Essential Skills, The, III:90
California Achievement Tests, Forms C & D, III:111
Canadian Cognitive Abilities Test, V:48
Canadian Tests of Basic Skills, IV:127
Clarke Reading Self-Assessment Survey, IV:172
Comprehensive Assessment Program: Achievement Series, III:164
Comprehensive Tests of Basic Skills, Forms U and V, III:186
Cooper-McGuire Diagnostic Word Analysis Test, III:198
Criterion Test of Basic Skills, IV:213
Detroit Tests of Learning Aptitude-Primary, V:94
Detroit Tests of Learning Aptitude-2, II:223
Diagnostic Achievement Battery, II:235
Diagnostic Skills Battery, IV:245
Differential Aptitude Tests, III:226
Educational Development Series, IV:264
Iowa Tests of Educational Development, I:364
Kaufman Test of Educational Achievement, IV:368
Life Skills: Forms 1 & 2, II:416
Lorge-Thorndike Intelligence Tests, The/Cognitive Abilities Test, I:421
Martinez Assessment of the Basic Skills, II:441
Metropolitan Achievement Test: 5th Edition, III:427
Metropolitan Language Instructional Tests, III:434
Miller Analogies Test, IV:414
Otis-Lennon School Ability Test, I:499
Peabody Individual Achievement Test, III:480
Scales of Independent Behavior, III:551
School and College Ability Tests II & III, V:406
Sequential Tests of Educational Progress, I:578
Stanford Diagnostic Mathematics, I:608

604 *Subject Index*

Stanford Early School Achievement Test: 2nd Edition, I:614
Test of Cognitive Skills, II:780
Tests of Adult Basic Education, V:494
3-R's Test, The, V:517
Wide Range Achievement Test-Revised, I:758
Woodcock-Johnson Psycho-Educational Battery, IV:683
Woodcock Language Proficiency Battery, English Form, III:726

Educational Development and School Readiness

Analysis of Readiness Skills, IV:11
Battelle Developmental Inventory, II:72
Boehm Test of Basic Concepts, I:106
Bracken Basic Concept Scale, I:125
Brief Index of Adaptive Behavior, III:75
Brigance Diagnostic Inventory of Early Development, The, III:87
Brigance K & 1 Screen, III:96
Clymer-Barrett Readiness Test, IV:183
Daberon Screening for School Readiness, V:86
Developmental Activities Screening Inventory-II, V:100
Developmental Indicators for the Assessment of Learning-Revised, IV:220
Early Screening Inventory, II:244
Edinburgh Picture Test, IV:256
Five P's: Parent Professional Preschool Performance Profile, The, III:261
Frostig Developmental Test of Visual Perception, II:293
Gesell Preschool Test, II:310
Gesell School Readiness Test, II:314
Goodman Lock Box, III:310
Howell Prekindergarten Screening Test, V:209
Kaufman Developmental Scale, IV:357
Lollipop Test, The: A Diagnostic Screening Test of School Readiness, II:426
McCarthy Screening Test, I:446
Metropolitan Readiness Tests, II:463
Mullen Scales of Early Learning, IV:444
Peabody Developmental Motor Scales and Activity Cards, V:310
School Readiness Screening Test, II:681
School Readiness Survey, IV:570
School Social Skills Rating Scale, IV:578
Wachs Analysis of Cognitive Structures, V:549

Intelligence and Related

AH5 Group Test of High Grade Intelligence, IV:7
AH6 Group Tests of High Level Intelligence, I:51
Arlin Test of Formal Reasoning, II:40
British Ability Scales, I:130
Expressive One-Word Picture Vocabulary Test: Upper Extension, IV:278
Harding W87 Test, IV:334
Kohs Block Design Test, II:392
Ross Test of Higher Cognitive Processes, V:396
Structure of Intellect Learning Abilities Test-Form P (Primary), V:458
System of Multicultural Pluralistic Assessment, I:648

Reading: Elementary

Botel Reading Inventory, V:37
Diagnostic Reading Scales: Revised 1981 Edition, IV:238
Florida Kindergarten Screening Battery, II:288
Gilmore Oral Reading Test, IV:320
Individual Phonics Criterion Test, V:212

Individualized Criterion Referenced Test—Reading,   III:367
Nelson Reading Skills Test, The,   IV:453
New Sucher-Allred Reading Placement Inventory, The,   IV:458
O'Brien Vocabulary Placement Test, The,   V:290
Roswell-Chall Auditory Blending Test,   IV:553
Roswell-Chall Diagnostic Reading Test of Word Analysis Skills: Revised and Extended,   II:646
Test of Early Reading Ability,   V:470
Visual-Aural Digit Span Test, The,   V:537

Reading: High School and Above

California Phonics Survey,   II:113
Gates-McKillop-Horowitz Reading Diagnostic Tests,   II:303
Nelson-Denny Reading Test: Forms E and F,   III:475

Reading: Multi-level

Gates-MacGinitie Reading Tests, The, Second Edition,   IV:310
Gray Oral Reading Tests—Revised,   V:179
Informal Reading Inventory,   II:350
Spadafore Diagnostic Reading Test,   IV:627
Woodcock Reading Mastery Tests,   IV:704

Sensory-Motor Skills

Bruininks-Oseretsky Test of Motor Proficiency,   III:99

Special Education: Gifted

Creativity Assessment Packet,   II:211
Creativity Attitude Survey,   III:206
Eby Elementary Identification Instrument,   IV:251
Gifted and Talented Screening Form,   III:302
Group Inventory for Finding Creative Talent,   II:332
Thinking Creatively in Action and Movement,   V:505
Watson-Glaser Critical Thinking Appraisal,   III:682

Special Education: Learning Disabled

Dyslexia Determination Test,   V:109
Joseph Pre-School and Primary Self-Concept Screening Test,   V:230
Learning Disability Rating Procedure,   V:237
Learning Efficiency Test,   V:244
SEARCH: A Scanning Instrument for the Identification of Potential Learning Disability,   II:689
Slingerland Screening Tests for Identifying Children with Specific Language Disability,   IV:611
Thinking Creatively with Sounds and Words,   IV:666

Special Education: Mentally Handicapped

AAMD Adaptive Behavior Scale, School Edition,   I:3
Balthazar Scales of Adaptive Behavior I: Scales of Functional Independence,   IV:42
Comprehensive Test of Adaptive Behavior,   V:73
Devereux Child Behavior Rating Scale, The,   II:231
Kaufman Assessment Battery for Children,   I:393

Special Education: Physically Handicapped

Blind Learning Aptitude Test,   V:32
Central Institute for the Deaf Preschool Performance Scale,   IV:157
Hiskey-Nebraska Test of Learning Aptitude,   III:331

606 Subject Index

Special Education: Special Education

Basic Screening and Referral Form for Children with Suspected Learning and Behavioral Disabilities, II:68
Pyramid Scales, The, V:358

Speech, Hearing, and Visual: Auditory

Auditory Discrimination Test, IV:33
Auditory Memory Span Test/Auditory Sequential Memory Test, IV:39
Communication Screen, The: A Pre-school Speech-Language Screening Tool, II:191
Flowers Auditory Test of Selective Attention, III:276
Flowers-Costello Tests of Central Auditory Abilities, V:137
Goldman-Fristoe-Woodcock Auditory Skills Test Battery, IV:327
Goldman-Fristoe-Woodcock Test of Auditory Discrimination, III:304
Lindamood Auditory Conceptualization Test, IV:376
Picture Spondee Threshold Test, IV:493
Peabody Picture Vocabulary Test—Revised, III:488
Test of Auditory Comprehension, III:647
Test of Listening Accuracy in Children, III:669

Speech, Hearing, and Visual: Speech and Language

Arizona Articulation Proficiency Scale: Revised, IV:15
Clinical Evaluation of Language Functions, IV:176
Communicative Abilities in Daily Living, IV:189
Evaluating Communicative Competence: A Functional Pragmatic Procedure, V:118
Frenchay Dysarthria Assessment, III:293
Fullerton Language Test for Adolescents (Experimental Edition), V:141
Goldman-Fristoe Test of Articulation, V:172
Illinois Test of Psycholinguistic Abilities-Revised, I:354
Interpersonal Language Skills Assessment: Final Edition, V:221
Patterned Elicitation Syntax Test, II:562
Phonemic Synthesis, III:521
Preschool Language Assessment Instrument, III:526
Quick Word Test, IV:516
Riley Articulation and Language Test: Revised, V:378
Sequenced Inventory of Communication Development-Revised, II:714
Sklar Aphasia Scales: Revised 1983, IV:606
Test of Early Language Development, V:464
Test of Language Development, IV:659
Utah Test of Language Development-Revised, I:707
Verbal Language Development Scale, I:712
Word Test, The, II:831

Student Evaluation and Counseling: Behavior Problems and Counseling Tools

Analysis of Coping Style, II:35
Behavior Evaluation Scale, IV:87
Behavior Rating Profile, IV:92
Bristol Social Adjustment Guides, II:104
Decision-Making Organizer, V:90
Devereux Adolescent Behavior Rating Scale, III:221
Devereux Elementary School Behavior Rating Scale II, V:104
Education Apperception Test, IV:259
Inferred Self-Concept Scale, IV:351
Learning Styles Inventory, II:402
Normative Adaptive Behavior Checklist, V:287
Politte Sentence Completion Test, V:323
Process for the Assessment of Effective Student Functioning, A, II:584

Revised Behavior Problem Checklist, V:371
School Environment Preference Survey, I:555
Study of Values, I:641

Student Evaluation and Counseling: Student Attitudes

Attitude to School Questionnaire, V:21
Classroom Environment Index, III:158
School Interest Inventory, II:674
Survey of School Attitudes, III:633

Student Evaluation and Counseling: Student Personality Factors

Behavioral Academic Self-Esteem, III:35
Child Behavior Rating Scale, III:145
Children's Adaptive Behavior Scale-Revised, II:161
Test Anxiety Profile, I:682

Vocational

Armed Services Vocational Aptitude Battery, I:61
Career Assessment Inventory, II:128
Career Development Inventory, IV:132
Career Maturity Inventory, I:164
Hall Occupational Orientation Inventory, I:300
Harrington-O'Shea Career Decision-Making System, I:322
Kuder General Interest Survey, Form E, II:395
Ohio Vocational Interest Survey: Second Edition, IV:478
Reading-Free Vocational Interest Inventory-Revised, II:627
Rothwell-Miller Interest Blank, IV:560
Wide Range Interest-Opinion Test, IV:673
Work Values Inventory, II:835

BUSINESS AND INDUSTRY

Aptitude and Skills Screening

Adult Basic Learning Examination, II:16
Basic Occupational Literacy Test, I:83
Comprehensive Ability Battery, I:214
COPSystem Interest Inventory, V:76
Employee Aptitude Survey Tests, I:266
Flanagan Aptitude Classification Tests, II:275
Flanagan Industrial Tests, II:282
General Aptitude Test Battery, V:150
I.P.I. Aptitude-Intelligence Test Series, II:363
Kuder Occupational Interest Survey, Form DD, I:406
SRA Verbal Form, IV:642
Wesman Personnel Classification Test, III:711
Wonderlic Personnel Test, The, I:769

Clerical

General Clerical Test, III:296
SRA Nonverbal Form, IV:635

Computer

Computer Operator Aptitude Battery, II:198
Computer Programmer Aptitude Battery, II:204

Intelligence and Related

Adaptability Test, I:29
Human Information Processing Survey, III:344
Non-Verbal Reasoning, IV:463
Performance Efficiency Test, III:496
Schubert General Ability Battery, III:579
Scott Mental Alertness Test, IV:585
SRA Pictorial Reasoning Test, III:621
Time Perception Inventory, V:522
Western Personnel Tests, III:714

Interests

Career Decision Scale, II:138
Minnesota Importance Questionnaire, II:481
Self-Directed Search, The, II:697
Self-Directed Search, (1985 Revision), The, V:419
Strong-Campbell Interest Inventory, II:737
United States Employment Service Interest Inventory, III:673
Vocational Preference Inventory, V:545
Work Interest Index, V:565

Interpersonal Skills and Attitudes

Culture Shock Inventory, III:209
Famous Sayings, V:128
Inventory of Individually Perceived Group Cohesiveness, IV:354
Minnesota Satisfaction Questionnaire, V:255
Minnesota Satisfactoriness Scale, IV:434
My Vocational Situation, II:509
Occupational Environment Scales, Form E-2, II:535
Organizational Climate Index, The, II:551
Personal Skills Map, The, V:318
Personnel Selection Inventory, III:510
Position Analysis Questionnaire, V:326
Reid Report/Reid Survey, II:631
Stanton Survey, V:451
Survey of Organizations, II:765
Survey of Personal Values, II:773
Temperament and Values Inventory, I:660
Thurstone Temperament Schedule, II:815
Time Problems Inventory, V:524
Trait Evaluation Index, V:529

ABOUT THE EDITORS

Daniel J. Keyser, Ph.D. Since completing postgraduate work at the University of Kansas in 1974, Dr. Keyser has worked in drug and alcohol rehabilitation and psychiatric settings. In addition, he has taught undergraduate psychology at Rockhurst College for 15 years. Dr. Keyser specializes in behavioral medicine—biofeedback, pain control, stress management, terminal care support, habit management, and wellness maintenance—and maintains a private clinical practice in the Kansas City area. Dr. Keyser co-edited *Tests: First Edition, Tests: Supplement,* and *Tests: Second Edition* and has made significant contributions to computerized psychological testing.

Richard C. Sweetland, Ph.D. After completing his doctorate at Utah State University in 1968, Dr. Sweetland completed postdoctoral training in psychoanalytically oriented clinical psychology at the Topeka State Hospital in conjunction with the training program of the Menninger Foundation. Following appointments in child psychology at the University of Kansas Medical Center and in neuropsychology at the Kansas City Veterans Administration Hospital, he entered the practice of psychotherapy in Kansas City. In addition to his clinical work in neuropsychology and psychoanalytic psychotherapy, Dr. Sweetland has been involved extensively in the development of computerized psychological testing. Dr. Sweetland co-edited *Tests: First Edition, Tests: Supplement,* and *Tests: Second Edition.*

REFERENCE

ELIHU BURRITT LIBRARY
CENTRAL CONNECTICUT STATE UNIVERSITY
NEW BRITAIN, CONNECTICUT 06050

Withdrawn from CCSU